Java XML Programmer's Reference

Mohammad Akif
Steven Brodhead
Andrei Cioroianu
James Hart
Eric Jung
Dave Writz

Wrox Press Ltd. ®

Java XML Programmer's Reference

First published July 2001

Published by Wrox Press Ltd,
Arden House, 1102 Warwick Road, Acocks Green,
Birmingham, B27 6BH, UK
Printed in the United States
ISBN 1861005202

In memory of Jim Molony

1965-2001

without whom this book would not have been possible.

Your intelligence, kindness and doughnuts will be missed.

Trademark Acknowledgements

Wrox has endeavored to provide trademark information about all the companies and products mentioned in this book by the appropriate use of capitals. However, Wrox cannot guarantee the accuracy of this information.

Credits

Authors
Mohammad Akif
Stephen Brodhead
Andrei Cioroianu
James Hart
Eric Jung
Dave Writz

Technical Reviewers
Terry Allen
Kapil Apshanker
Steve Barker
Ren Bitonio
Richard Bonneau
Carl Burnham
Robert Chang
Jeremy Crosbie
Justin Foley
Pascal van Geest
Phil Powers de George
Matthew Heimbruch
Brian Hickey
Brian Higdon
Sachin Khanna
Jim Macintosh
James Maidment
Vinay Menon
Ramesh Nagapan
Stephane Osmont
Gary L. Peskin
Eric Rajkovic
Gareth Reakes
Ian Roberts
David Schultz
Keyur Shah
Paul Wilt

Category Manager
Emma Batch

Technical Editors
Helen Callaghan
John R. Chapman
Benjamin Hickman
Robert FE. Shaw

Technical Architect
Jim Molony

Author Agent
Nicola Phillips

Project Administrator
Laura Hall

Production Manager
Simon Hardware

Production Coordinator
Tom Bartlett
Emma Eato

Figures
Paul Grove

Cover Design
Dawn Chellingworth

Proofreader
Agnes Wiggers

Index
Adrian Axinte

About the Authors

Mohammad Akif

Mohammad works for Sun Microsystems as a Java Architect. Living in four countries in the last five years and working on large projects for Hitachi Malaysia, Fujitsu Singapore, Sprint USA and other Fortune 500 companies has exposed him to all facets of Java and its related technologies. His strength lies in establishing the 'best practices' for using these technologies.

There are many who have shaped my life, I would start by thanking the One who created me and blessed me with so many things which I did not deserve to have. Nasim Naqvi, my grandfather who taught me the distinction between right and wrong. Rehana and Akif my parents who deserve all the credit for whatever I am today. Irum and Sultan my very supportive and awesome siblings. Saima, my wife who is also my best friend and companion in everything I do and our lovely daughter Sakina who is the cutest baby in the world!

Mohammad contributed Chapters 8 and 10.

Steven Brodhead

Steven is President of Centcom Inc., a maker of XML database integration tools. and has been innovating and building software products for over 15 years. Some of the more recent products he has built are iConduit, an XML data integration platform and Tibco's Java CORBA ORB. Besides product development, he also does large-scale enterprise integration using J2EE, middleware, and XML.

Steven has served in multiple capacities from entrepreneur, to architecting new products, to technical leadership. But after writing over 350,000 lines of codes in his life, he is still a programmer at heart. Early in his career, Steven received an award that stated: "For inventing so much, it is hard to keep up with it all".

Steven lives in Colorado Springs, Colorado and loves outdoor activities like fly fishing, backcountry skiing, and hiking. Steve's educational background includes a BS in Chemical Engineering from Louisiana State University and an MBA from the University of Chicago.

Steven contributed Chapters 7 and 13.

Andrei Cioroianu

Andrei is the founder of Devsphere.com, where he builds Java development tools and offers consulting services. His projects range from applets and desktop applications to servlets and server side frameworks. He contributed to "*Professional Java XML*" published by Wrox Press and writes articles for the Java Developer's Journal.

Andrei invites you to send comments about Chapters 2-6 to andreic@ziplip.com.

James Hart

James has been developing with Java and open source technologies for two years, and is an editor of Web Services Architect (http://www.webservicesarchitect.com). In his spare time he's an Apple Mac evangelist and a terrible guitarist.

Thanks to Jim, John, Emma and Helen for their help in getting me involved with this book and making my chapter as good as it is, and also to Chris, for her support through late nights and bughunts.

James contributed Chapter 9.

Eric Jung

Eric has a Bachelors degree in Computer Science from Ithaca College, Ithaca, New York. He has ten years of professional experience in software architecture and engineering, in industries such as banking, medical, legal, telecommunications, dot-com startups, television, advertising, marketing, real estate, and education. During this time, he has worked primarily as a consultant with Fortune 500 companies.

Eric lives with his wife, Leah, and their dog, Lulu, in Englewood, Colorado. In his spare time, he enjoys skiing, hiking, and reading.

Thanks, JM, for motivating me and always pushing me for my best.
You will be missed.

Eric contributed Chapter 11.

Dave Writz

Dave is a principal and co-founder of Cornerstone Consulting, a Milwaukee, Wisconsin, based service organization specializing in building distributed applications.

Throughout his career, Dave has concentrated building software solutions using object-oriented analysis, design, and programming techniques. He has lead teams responsible for defining Internet and Intranet strategies, then evaluating, selecting, and introducing new technologies including Java, XML, SOAP, EJB, and other advanced technologies. While serving as a mentor, architect, and developer Dave has been able to help Fortune 1000 as well as emerging companies utilize information technology as a competitive advantage.

Dave would like to thank "Daddy's girls" – Katie, Rachel, and Julie – whose love and support inspire and motivate everything he does.

Dave contributed Chapters 12, 14, 15, and 16.

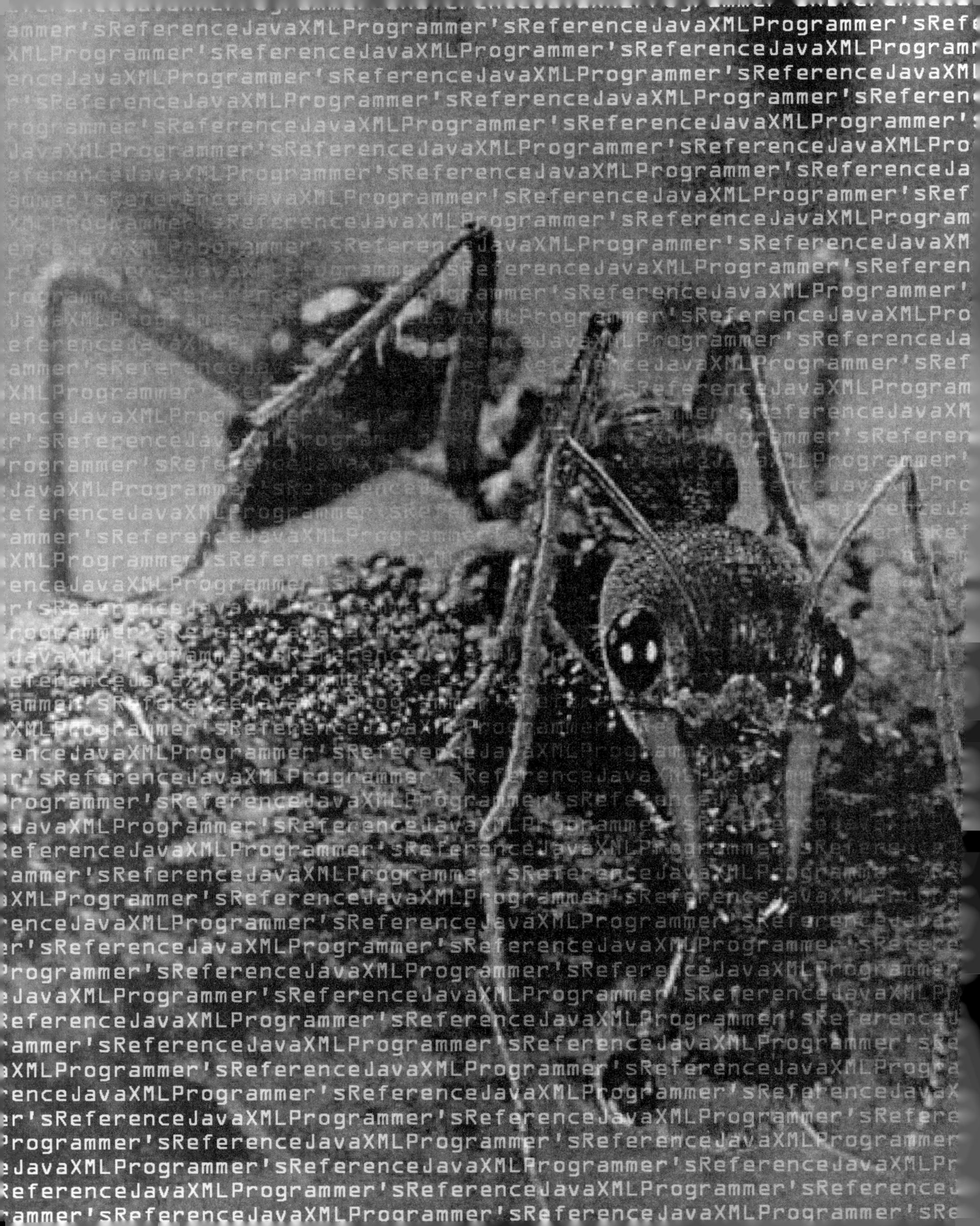
JavaXMLProgrammer'sReference

Table of Contents

Table of Contents

Table of Contents

Table of Contents

Table of Contents

Table of Contents

xiii

Table of Contents

Table of Contents

Table of Contents

Table of Contents

XX

Table of Contents

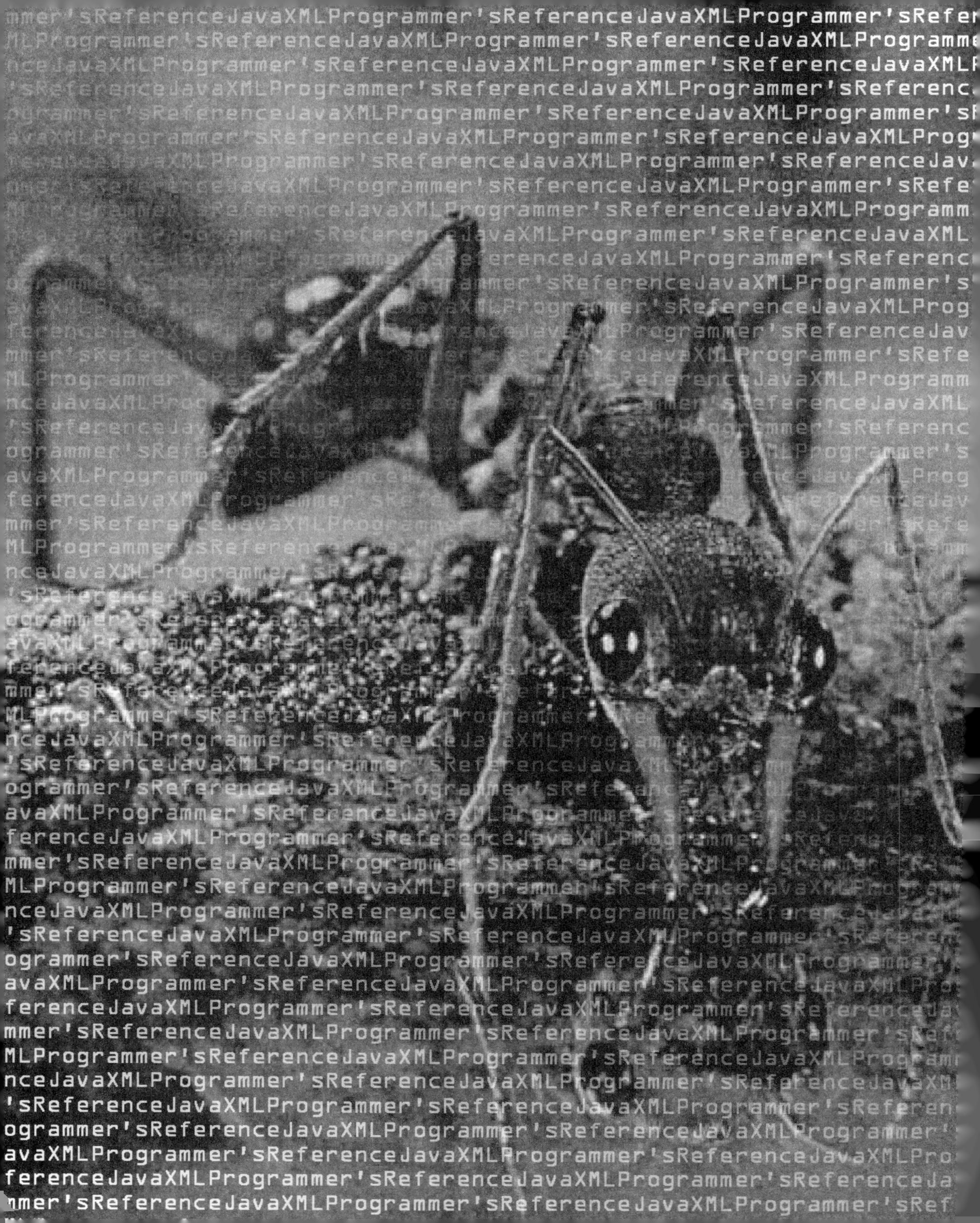

Introduction

The aim of this book is to provide a quick reference source for Java programmers working with XML to the programming interfaces, tools, and techniques they need to use in the course of writing XML-aware applications. As well as the standard reference material, it also aims to provide concise technical chapters covering the main tools, practical themes, and tasks that Java XML programmers face.

Who is This Book for?

This book is aimed primarily at programmers who know Java, XML (and XSLT) and who want to quickly get up to date with a comprehensive range of Java/XML APIs, implementations, and tools.

The book is meant to serve as a desk-side companion to the Java XML programmer, and as well as providing sufficiently detailed reference material, it demonstrates the use of this material in a series of straightforward examples.

What does the Book Cover?

The book is designed to cover the programming interfaces and abstractions that are available to a Java programmer for manipulating XML data. These include:

- ❑ W3C Document Object Model (DOM Levels 1, 2 and 3)
- ❑ Simple API for XML (SAX) 2.0
- ❑ The Java API for XML Processing (JAXP) 1.1 parsing and transforming interfaces (including TrAX)
- ❑ JDOM (Beta 6 at the moment) API for representing XML

In addition, this book will also cover some current commercial and open source implementations, from the viewpoint of how they relate to the above standards. We will also see what additional features are available for working with Java and XML.

❑ Apache XML Project

❑ Oracle XDK

❑ IBM Alphaworks

❑ Java XML @ Sun

❑ XML Tools for Information Appliances

This book will also feature concise technical guides to five advanced Java/XML programming techniques. These short chapters will form a logical sequence or 'story' covering the primary tasks faced by developers in creating an application (in this case an auction service) based around XML and programmed in Java.

How is the Book Structured?

The book is comprised of four distinct parts:

The first part, which is made up of Chapter 1, deals with the basics and preliminaries of working with Java and XML, and the intersection between these two technologies. It provides an overview of the foundations of working with XML using the Java programming language.

The second part (Chapters 2 through 6), concerns itself wholly with the major Java XML APIs, such as SAX, DOM (Core and Extensions), JAXP and JDOM. Full documentation on these APIs is provided, as well as examples scattered throughout to demonstrate how they work.

The third part of the book concerns itself with tools, and Chapters 7 through 11 deal largely with commercial and open source Java XML implementations, such as the Oracle XDK, the Apache XML project, IBM Alphaworks (focussing on WSDL and UDDI), Sun Java Tools and an array of some of the tools available for lightweight information appliances. Again, this part is liberally supplied with working example code that the reader can run on their own machine.

The fourth part, which includes Chapters 12 through 16, demonstrates a series of techniques that one can use these technologies for. This takes the form of an ongoing case study which aims to set up an auction service. Various aspects of manipulating XML through Java are examined and by the end, it should be possible to build a working model of this application.

The Appendix deals with the set-up and build of the Ant installation tool. This tool will enable the reader to set Ant targets for most of the tools and JAR files in this book, and also to test the book code.

The Appendix also outlines which technologies we will be using, where to download them from, and how to prepare them for use with the book code.

At the end of the book is a useful glossary of terms and an index.

What do I Need To Use This Book?

Most of the code examples can be run on Ant, an XML-based build tool.

Full download and deployment details (or clear pointers to existing documentation) are given for all of the tools used in this book, and the details of these tools are available in the Appendix.

Conventions

To help you get the most from the text and keep track of what's happening, a number of conventions have been used throughout the book.

Worked examples – those which you can download and try out for yourself – are generally in a box like this:

Example: Specimen

Source

This section gives the Java source file that will be compiled to run the example. If the file name is given as `example.java`, you will find that file in the archive that you can download from the Wrox web site at http://www.wrox.com/, generally in a subdirectory holding all the examples for one chapter.

```
public class Example {
    ...
}
```

Sample

This section describes the XML files, Schemas, DTDs and stylesheets used to input, validate and manipulate XML data. Again there will usually be a filename such as `sample.xml` so that you can find the file in the Wrox download archive.

```
<?xml version="1.0">
...
```

Output

This section shows the output when you run the source files, and normally will take the form of XML output. Output can also take the form of actual XML files in some instances, which will be written to your directory. The prompt necessary to run the source files appears in bold at the start of the output.

```
>java Example sample.xml
<Output></Output>
```

Any freestanding sections of code are generally shown in a shaded box, like this:

```
import xml.parser.validator;

public class Example{
...
```

As for styles in the text:

- Filenames and code within the text appear as: `courrier.xml`.
- Text in user interfaces, and URLs, are shown as: File/Save As…
- XML element names, function names and attribute names are written as: **`<xsl:value-of>`**, **`concat()`**, **`href`**.

In addition:

> **These boxes hold important, not-to-be forgotten information, which is directly relevant to the surrounding text.**

While the background style is used for asides to the current discussion.

Customer Support

Wrox has three ways to support books. You can:

- Check for book errata at www.wrox.com
- Enroll at the peer-to-peer forums at p2p.wrox.com
- E-mail technical support a query or feedback on our books in general

Errata

You can check for errata for the book at our web site www.wrox.com, simply navigate to the page for this book where you will find a link to the list of errata.

P2P Lists

You can enroll in our peer-to-peer discussion forums at p2p.wrox.com where we provide you with a forum where you can put your questions to the author, reviewers and fellow industry professionals. The java_xml list is available in the 'Java' section. You can choose to join the mailing lists or you can receive them as a weekly digest. If you don't have the time or facility to receive the mailing list, then you can search our online archives. You'll find the ability to search on specific subject areas or keywords. As these lists are moderated, you can be confident of finding good, accurate information quickly. Mails can be edited or moved by the moderator into the correct place, making this a most efficient resource. Junk and spam mail are deleted, and your own e-mail address is protected by the unique Lyris system from web-bots that can automatically collect newsgroup mailing list addresses.

E-mail Support

If you wish to point out an errata to put up on the web site or directly query a problem in the book with an expert who knows the book in detail, then e-mail support@wrox.com. A typical e-mail should include the following things:

❑   The name of the book, the last four digits of the book's ISBN, and the page number of the problem in the Subject field

❑   Your name, contact info and description of the problem in the body of the message

Tell Us What You Think

The authors and the Wrox team have worked hard to make this book a pleasure to read as well as being useful and educational, so we'd like to know what you think. Wrox are always keen to hear what you liked best and what improvements you think are possible. We appreciate feedback on our efforts and take both criticism and praise on board in our future editorial efforts. When necessary, we'll forward comments and queries to the author. If you've anything to say, let us know by sending an e-mail to:

feedback@wrox.com

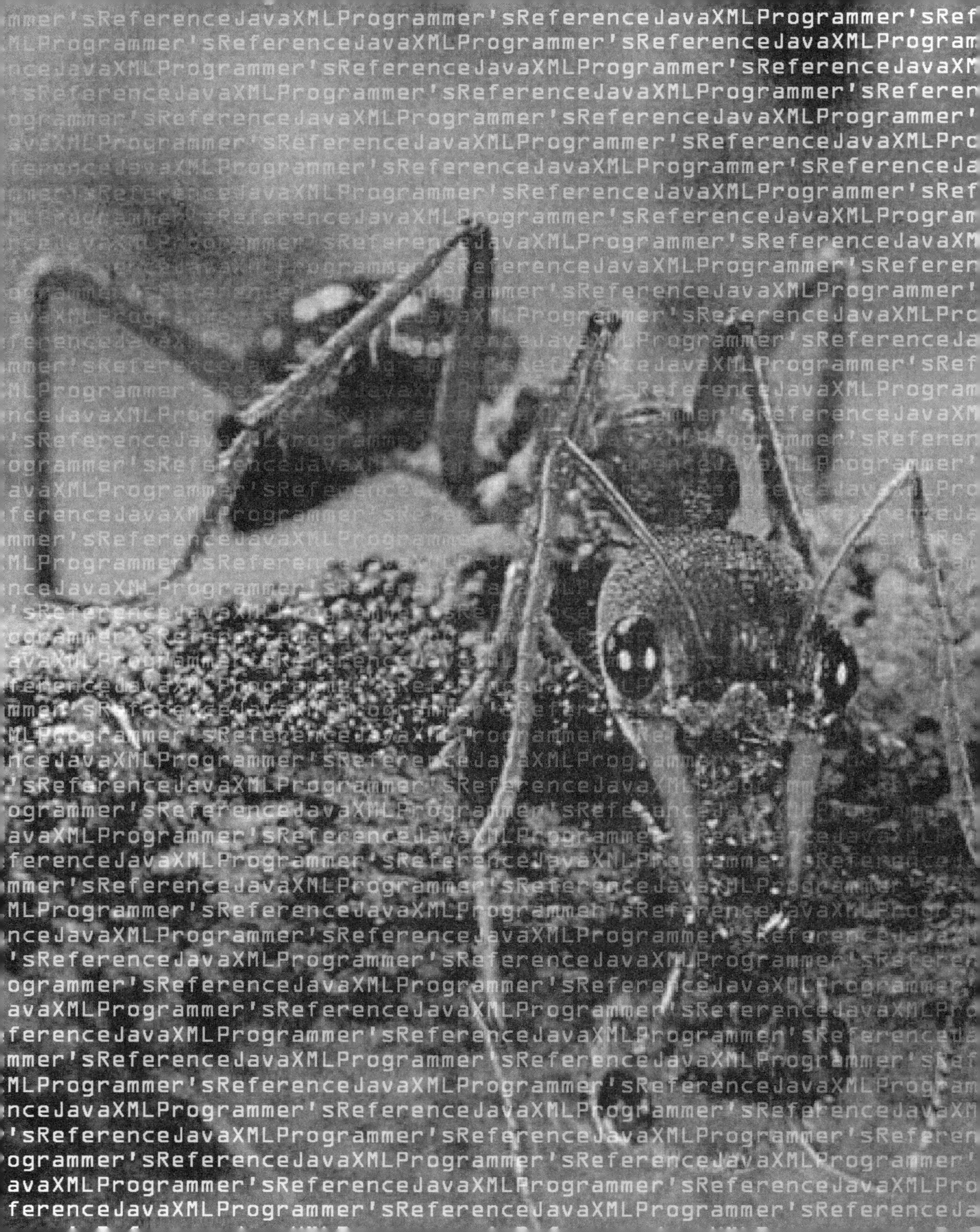

XML by Example

This chapter provides an overview of Java and XML working together through examples and discussion. Effective use of XML requires a sound understanding of its strengths and weaknesses, but to cover this, in all the detail required for working with Java, would need at least whole book. Therefore, while some aspects of the XML language and its associated specifications are covered, we have not attempted to be comprehensive or formal. This chapter assumes the basic notions of XML markup, elements, attributes, and the well-formed syntax of these.

For a close look at XML, a good place to turn to is the actual specification (see the next section for an explanation of XML specifications), the **W3C XML 1.0 Recommendation** at http://www.w3c.org/TR/REC-xml. A good way of absorbing its content is to consult the following version of the document with additional annotations and commentary by one of the original authors, Tim Bray: http://www.xml.com/axml/testaxml.htm.

Further pointers and resources are given at the end of this chapter. We will get to grips with some of the important features of the language through a sequence of Java examples that cover:

- ❑ Parsing
- ❑ Namespaces
- ❑ Stylesheet Transformation
- ❑ Character Encoding
- ❑ Processing Instructions
- ❑ Document Type Definition (DTD) and Entities
- ❑ XML Schema

The aim of this chapter is to introduce the main elements of XML processing with Java, focusing on the individual topics above and providing a set of general examples to refer to.

Some good introductory books on XML include *Learning XML*, Eric T. Ray, 2001, O'Reilly, ISBN 0-596000-46-4, and *Beginning XML*, Curt Cagle et al., Wrox Press, 2000, ISBN 1-861003-41-2. For more advanced material see *Java and XML*, Brett McLaughlin, O'Reilly, 2000, ISBN 0-596000-16-2, and *Professional Java XML*, Kal Ahmed et al., Wrox Press, 2001, ISBN 1-861004-01-X.

XML Organizations

The **World Wide Web Consortium** (http://www.w3.org) presents technical reports moderated and written by a community of respected theorists and enthusiasts. Because of its reputation and role in the building of the Internet, these documents are generally accepted by the programming community as the best hope for a truly universal solution. Furthermore, the support and collaboration of individuals from all the major IT corporations helps to disseminate and solidify the acceptance of the standards. The W3C releases its reports (which normally start out in life as public "Notes") in the following hierarchy:

W3C Report	Description
Working Draft	This is a document that represents commitment by W3C to support continued work in some area, along with external partners, but does not represent a specification.
Last Call Working Draft	A report may be in this stage for about three weeks while an intensive assessment of reviews and comments are made. The Director may then allow the draft to move up to Candidate or Proposed status.
Candidate Recommendation	This is a report that has achieved a level of consensus and which invites provisional implementation by the wider community
Proposed Recommendation	At this stage the specialist group involved has reached consensus and the Director has proposed a report to the Advisory Committee. A working prototype must have been demostrated.
Recommendation	This stage represents a set of standards that has been deemed by the review process of W3C to be of adequate quality to be widely disseminated and to enter the mainstream of commercial and academic development. The W3C should maintain a commitment to supporting the standard.

Links at the end of the chapter provide pointers to specifications on-line at the W3C.

The **Organization for the Advancement of Structured Information Standards (OASIS)** is also an important XML organization. It hosts the "XML Industry Portal" and the seminal mailing list xml-dev – links are provided at the end of the chapter.

XML Parsing

Parsing is the process of converting the unstructured sequence of characters representing an XML document into the structured components of XML syntax: declarations, comments, elements, attributes, processing instructions, and characters. What happens then is dependent upon the chosen pattern for actually processing the data in the XML source. There are two basic models:

- ❑ Use the sequence of syntactic **events** generated by the parser, such as the "start of a <table> element", directly to feed into a consumer process.

- ❑ Read the nested element, or "node", structure of the XML source into a **tree**-like representation within your program, and then manipulate that through the API associated with the tree data type.

These two models have given rise to two different standards in XML parsing:

- ❑ Event-based parsing using a parser which implements the Simple API for XML (SAX)
- ❑ Tree-based parsing using the W3C Document Object Model (DOM), JDOM, and other document models

SAX is an API consisting of a well-defined set of "call-back methods" that may be invoked by an actual XML parser or driver. A separate process, unspecified by SAX, controls the reading in of the raw characters and the invoking of the high-level events (including parsing errors) to the registered "handler" classes.

We will look below at how the basic parsing mechanisms work in the SAX model. The SAX API is covered fully in Chapter 2.

The DOM (W3C Level 1 Recommendation October 1998, Level 2 Recommendation November 2000) specifies a hierarchy of node types and the actions you can perform on them. The DOM "Java Bindings" (implementations are not restricted to Java) are defined entirely using interfaces, so that the code that actually uses the model is non-specific to the concrete tree objects generated by the parser. Using the DOM, for instance, it is impossible to create node types explicitly with the new operator. Instead, you have to use factory methods like createElement() that are implemented by the Document type.

This has the advantage that your program is unaware of the concrete objects that implement the DOM interfaces and these could be switched to another vendor without affecting the code.

The DOM is covered in Chapters 3 and 4.

Simple API for XML (SAX)

SAX is currently in version 2.0. The original 1.0 release now has several deprecated interfaces, although SAX 1.0 is still very much an industry standard. The diagrams on the following pages present the relationship between the various structures in the SAX parsing process.

The home for SAX on the web is http://www.megginson.com/SAX/index.html.

We will look first at SAX 1.0, because it is important to see the correspondence between SAX 1.0 and SAX 2.0, as well as the differences.

SAX 1.0

A parsing routine starts by obtaining an implementation (in this case a parser from Sun Microsystems) of the org.xml.sax.Parser interface:

```
org.xml.sax.Parser parser = new com.sun.xml.parser.Parser();
```

This Parser interface provides methods for reading XML data directly from a file, or accepts a variety of possible input formats (streams, readers, URLs) each wrapped as an org.xml.sax.InputSource (to which an expected character encoding for the input can be assigned):

```
InputSource is = new InputSource();
is.setCharacterStream(new FileReader("xmlfile.xml"));
```

Using an input source provides a wrapper to a variety of possible sources of data, which all, however, appear essentially the same to the parser.

The process is summarized in the diagram below. The black dots represent 'hooks', to which you programmatically register custom handlers and modifiers on top of the default functionality (if any):

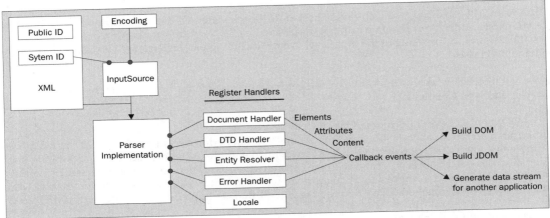

Now we have our parser ready to read in the data and start producing events from the syntactic events generated from the character XML input. Attach, or 'register', an object implementing `org.xml.sax.DocumentHandler`:

```
parser.setDocumentHandler(handler);
```

Similarly, you could attach implementations of `DTDHandler`, `ErrorHandler`, and `EntityResolver`, to handle DTD events, parsing errors and requests for custom resolving of internal and external entities (all these are explained in the SAX chapter through many examples). Finally, you could attach a `java.util.Locale` to allow locale-specific error output and other messages. Now call:

```
parser.parse(is);
```

This will call methods in the registered objects. For example, `startElement()` is called on your implementation of `DocumentHandler` when an element is encountered during the parse.

Note that SAX is very often used as a feeder for creating in-memory representations of XML structures, for instance DOM, or JDOM trees. Many parsers that return a DOM tree build it using the SAX callbacks to drive the process of adding elements and other nodes to the DOM tree.

Note also that rather than implementing all the handlers, one often uses a helper class, for instance the (deprecated) SAX 1.0 `org.xml.sax.HandlerBase` class. The `HandlerBase` class implements all the required handler interfaces, and you can simply extend this class and override just the methods for the events you want to handle.

SAX 2.0

SAX 1.0 was upgraded to SAX 2.0 to provide support for namespaces in XML documents – a way of protecting the content of independently developed XML documents from naming collisions. At the same time, the underlying model was somewhat simplified and improved to give more support for pluggablility of the underlying driver, and for obtaining SAX parsers through JAXP. This was achieved through support for setting and testing of standard, as well as vendor-specific, **features** and **properties** through a fixed interface.

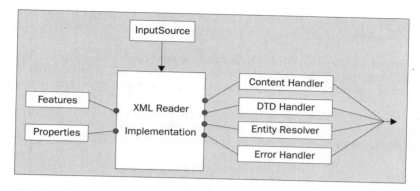

The `Parser` interface has been deprecated (you should now use `XMLReader`) and the `DocumentHandler` interface has been deprecated and replaced with `ContentHandler` in the package `org.xml.sax`. Otherwise, the components of the SAX 2.0 process are schematically the same as in the previous diagram and have not been fully shown in the above diagram. Now we obtain an implementation of `org.xml.sax.XMLReader` as follows (using the Xerces SAX parser):

```
org.xml.sax.XMLReader reader =
    new org.apache.xerces.parsers.SAXParser();
reader.setContentHandler(handler);
reader.parse(is);
```

However, the standard mechanism for creating a SAX 2.0 parser is now to use the **JAXP** (covered in the *JAXP* section below) abstract factory pattern:

- ❑ Call the `newInstance()` method of the abstract class `javax.xml.parsers.SAXParserFactory` to obtain a reference to a concrete parser factory that extends this class

- ❑ Use the factory to get a new `javax.xml.parsers.SAXParser`

- ❑ Obtain an `org.xml.sax.XMLReader` from the SAX parser

```
SAXParserFactory spf = SAXParserFactory.newInstance();
XMLReader reader = spf.newSAXParser().getXMLReader();
```

We can now set specific features on the reader (in this case the instruction to handle namespace declarations as content):

```
reader.setFeature(
    "http://xml.org/sax/features/namespace-prefixes",true);
```

Note the use of a Uniform Resource Identifier (URI) as the name of the feature. We'll have a closer look at JAXP later. SAX is covered in Chapter 2.

DOM

The DOM is a set of interfaces for manipulating and querying XML document structures. It's up to vendors to implement the interfaces with concrete classes representing the various XML structures.

For instance, an implementation of an `org.w3c.dom.Document` interface is part of the Xerces parser package: `org.apache.xerces.dom.DocumentImpl`

However, you would probably never refer to this class in your code. You would obtain a reference to an `org.w3c.dom.Document` and manipulate this according to the W3C specifications. You should not need to know the underlying type that your reference is pointing to in order to use the DOM.

A DOM parser is a parser that returns an implementation of `org.w3c.dom.Document` representing the XML source as a tree of `org.w3c.dom.Node` structures. The top-level Node is both a Node and a Document, as Document is a specialized case (subinterface) of Node. (See Chapter 3.)

Error Handling

XML 1.0 defines three categories of errors:

❑ **Fatal Errors**: non-recoverable errors, such as incorrect syntax

❑ **Errors**: recoverable errors, such as invalidity of a document structure relative to the document type definition

❑ **Warnings**: any other recoverable errors

When you create a parser instance, the default error handler does not usually do anything, which means that your program may be silent when it encounters a non-fatal error. In order to catch the errors you must normally attach an error handler to the parser by registering a class that implements the `org.xml.sax.ErrorHandler` interface. This is true for both DOM- and-SAX based parsers. Most parsers, whether they be SAX- or DOM-based tend to return SAX exceptions for problems encountered during parsing.

There is an `org.w3c.dom.DOMException` class, but it is reserved for severe cases where the internal tree representation has become inconsistent and parsing cannot continue.

SAX or DOM?

One frequently occurring question is whether you should you use SAX or DOM in order to handle the XML. Do you handle events as the document is read in, and then discard the information, or do you build a complete in-memory representation of the XML document and use DOM methods to navigate the node tree?

There are advantages and disadvantages to each approach; they are complementary rather than close rivals. DOM representations are memory intensive. Sometimes you don't need to store the whole document, just a small part of it, or possibly just one element. It would be expensive to read the whole document in to memory just to access a particular fragment.

"Lazy" DOM parsers, such as Apache Xerces, can help with this. Lazy parsers aim to create in-memory structures for just the parts of the XML that you attempt to access. On the other hand, your code performance should not be critically dependent upon particular features offered by some parsers, and not others.

SAX is good when you need to process a document in a single pass and you want to map it directly into another process or data type. Where SAX is less useful is when you need to access a part of the document more than once, or manipulate the document structure in some nontrivial way before passing it on to another application.

JAXP

The Java API for XML Parsing is not a parser or a transformer, but it provides a "pluggability layer" (as frequently referred to in the JAXP specification although some people don't like the term) for these. Before JAXP, programmers would implement wrappers for parsers so that they could present a number of different parser implementations to the rest of their code through a single API. This is what JAXP – now officially – does for the Java platform (it is a key new feature of the Java SDK v1.4 due out late in 2001, see http://java.sun.com/j2se).

JAXP provides ways of obtaining parser and transformer implementations through abstract factory classes. Like working with the DOM, the programmer never has to see or use the actual implementation classes (they just have to be in the classpath).

Having said that it makes the life of the programmer easier, it's worth having a close look at how you obtain a parser through JAXP because it's not a flawless mechanism yet, and can be tricky to work with at first. The procedure for obtaining a transformer is very similar and will be covered by an example later.

The use of factories to create objects is an emerging standard in object-oriented programming languages. A specific factory constructs objects with specific features. By switching to a different factory class, you can create objects with other properties, but without otherwise changing your code. An example is the `java.io.Socket` class. You can implement a custom `java.io.SocketImplFactory` and then attach it to the `Socket` class using the static `setSocketFactory()` method. Sockets created using `new Socket()` will now be your custom sockets.

With JAXP the idea is not to allow programmatic access to the particular factory implementation. Instead, the factory class is specified using one or more of the following methods:

❏ A system property accessed using `System.getProperty()`. This can include properties set at the command-line when running Java, so it's possible to specify at run time which factory class you would like to use. Note that there can be security implications in accessing system properties from within a program, so it is not advisable to write code that depends on it in a production environment.

❏ A dedicated JAXP properties file (a file consisting of `key=value` lines) located in a platform-specific place that the factory class knows how to find.

❏ Using the JAR Services mechanism. JARs may contain special files in the `META-INF/services` directory that act like `key=value` pairs. The filename is the `key` and the first line of the file is the `value`. In this way, a JAR file can indicate to the Java runtime that it contains a suitable extension of an abstract factory class.

❏ A default factory name hard-coded into the abstract factory class. That is, on failure of the previous mechanisms, the factory attempts to create a specific instance of a specific class, which may or may not be available in the classpath.

The difficulties arise because of the multiple ways a factory class can be specified, and the priority order that is used to determine which one to use. The following diagram illustrates how the decision is made when you run the following standard pattern for obtaining a DOM parser, or "document builder":

```
DocumentBuilderFactory dbf = DocumentBuilderFactory.newInstance();
DocumentBuilder db = dbf.newDocumentBuilder();
org.w3c.dom.Document dom = db.parse("myxml.xml");
```

Note that `DocumentBuilderFactory` and `DocumentBuilder` are in the `javax.xml.parsers` package of the JAXP distribution.

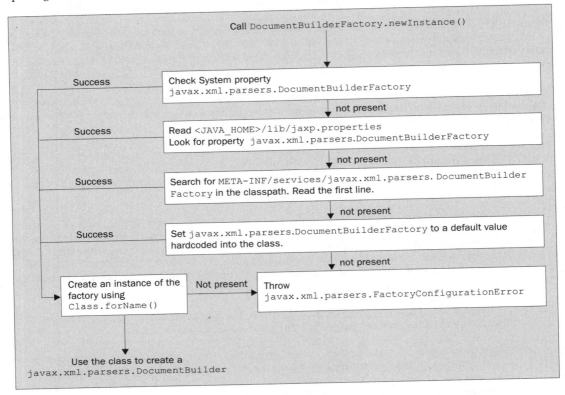

The system property `jaxp.debug=true` may be set at the command line using `-D` or in a program using `System.putProperty()`. It is currently effective in the JAXP 1.1 reference implementation and the `javax.xml.parsers` implementation that comes with the Xerces parser. However, it is not part of the specification, and may be removed. The debug option will print to `System.out` a trace of which method has been used to access the class, and the actual name of the factory class it attempts to instantiate. We will use it in the examples in this chapter.

Problems mostly occur when the JAR services method is used in the case that there is no system property set and no JAXP properties file. Java searches for suitable JAR service file in the same way that it looks for classes in JAR files.

> **Service files are located in the JAR file containing the parser implementation. Having more than one parser in the classpath offering the same services is therefore liable to lead to conflicts.**

The `jar` utility can be used to interrogate these files. This command tabulates the specified directory within the Xerces archive:

```
> jar -tf xerces.jar META-INF/services
META-INF/services/
META-INF/services/javax.xml.parsers.DocumentBuilderFactory
META-INF/services/javax.xml.parsers.SAXParserFactory
```

If you extract the `DocumentBuilderFactory` file (use `-xf` instead of `-tf`) and look at the contents, you'll see:

```
org.apache.xerces.jaxp.DocumentBuilderFactoryImpl
```

This is the concrete class extending `DocumentBuilderFactory` that is returned when you call `newInstance()` on the `DocumentBuilderFactory` object.

If you have more than one JAR file with a `javax.xml.parsers.DocumentBuilderFactory` service file in it, then the runtime will use the first one it comes to. Note the following:

❑ Java looks in JAR files in `<JAVA_HOME>/jre/lib/ext` before it looks in the system or environment classpath. For this reason, parser packages should generally not be installed in `lib/ext`.

❑ In a Java web or EJB container, the effective classpath for a user application is likely to include user JARs **after** the server JARs.

❑ In Jakarta Tomcat 4.0, the J2EE reference web server, this problem has been alleviated by providing all web applications with a 'clean' classloading environment. Previous versions exposed the XML parser used by the server to all web applications.

TrAX

The Transformation API for XML (TrAX) was originally separate from the parsing component of JAXP, but it is now an integrated part of the JAXP 1.1 release. The API provides a way of obtaining a stylesheet processor, or `Transformer`, through the abstract factory pattern in the same way as we obtained parsers above. We cover it in full in Chapter 5, and in an introductory example below on page 21. Using TrAX is similar to JAXP in some respects: it hides the details of the underlying implementation from the programmer, and makes the code more portable.

JDOM

JDOM is an alternative to DOM that is designed to be more accessible to Java programmers, and to be more in tune with the Java environment in general. JDOM continues to be developed by its founders Jason Hunter and Brett McLaughlin and a wide community of contributors, and is rapidly growing in popularity. There is a possibility that JDOM may become the official Java document object model since it is currently a Java Specification Request (JSR) in Sun Microsystems' Java Community Process (JCP). Expect a decision by the community in the next year or so.

See http://jcp.org/jsr/detail/102.jsp for the current status of the JSR.

JDOM is looked at in Chapter 6, and features are used or discussed throughout the book.

Other Parsing Approaches

In Chapter 11 we cover some parsing techniques that don't use the standard APIs because they are not suitable, or available, within the constraints of lightweight devices, which are the subject of that chapter.

In the next section we take a quick tour of using namespaces and show how a parser deals with them.

Namespaces

If you've been writing Java for a while, then you know the value of using packages. One of their advantages is that they provide a way of protecting the names of the classes from collisions with other names.

A good way to understand how namespaces work in an XML document is to write a namespace aware parser utility, and use it to parse a document with namespaces in it. The important thing is not what namespaces look like in a document, but what they come out as – how they are interpreted by parsers. We will do this in an example below.

There are a number of key features of namespaces that we'll look at in the next section.

Namespaces are defined by the W3C Recommendation: http://www.w3.org/TR/REC-xml-names.

The Namespace Prefix

Instead of simply using an element name like <book> we can use the following form:

```
<wrox:book>
```

This indicates that the element <book> belongs to a namespace that we have called wrox locally. The book part is called the **local** name and the combination of prefix and local name is called the **qualified** name. To actually use the prefix though, we need to declare it relative to an "absolute" name using the reserved namespace xmlns (XML Namespace). It is declared as an attribute of an element, and the prefix can then be used in all elements and attributes nested inside that element, including the element itself.

```
xmlns:wrox="http://www.wrox.com/books"
```

By convention, the name is a Uniform Resource Identifier (URI), which should ensure, as with Java package names, that the namespace is unique to the author of the document. This declaration can occur inside the element itself:

```
<wrox:book xmlns:wrox="http://www.wrox.com/books">
   Java XML Programmer's Reference
</wrox:book>
```

or it can occur inside an element higher in the tree. Most often, it is declared in the top-level element of the document:

```
<?xml version="1.0"?>
<library xmlns:wrox="http://www.wrox.com/books">
  <wrox:book>
     Java XML Programmer's Reference
  </wrox:book>
</library>
```

The Default Namespace

Elements with no prefix are in the **default** namespace. If there are no namespace declarations at all, then all elements and attributes are in the default namespace. When a namespace needs to be applied to a document, or part of a document, it is often convenient to change the default namespace of the part of a document in lieu of adding prefixes to all the elements and attributes:

```
xmlns="http://www.wrox.com/book"
```

This is somewhat like declaring a package name in a Java class file: you can only declare one, and all defined classes within that file inherit that fully qualified package name.

```
<book xmlns="http://www.wrox.com/book">
  <title>Java XML Programmer's Reference</title>
</book>
```

Now both `<book>` and `<title>` are interpreted by the parser as having being in the namespace given by the declared default namespace. The next example shows this in action.

Example

This shows by example how a parser interprets the scope of namespace declarations in an XML document. The Java program parses an XML file and reports the local name, qualified name, and actual namespace URI associated with each element or attribute.

Namespace.java

```
import org.xml.sax.XMLReader;
import org.xml.sax.Attributes;
import org.xml.sax.SAXException;
import org.xml.sax.helpers.DefaultHandler;
import javax.xml.parsers.SAXParserFactory;
import javax.xml.parsers.SAXParser;
```

We need a content handler to process the content of the document. The `DefaultHandler` class is a SAX 2.0 helper class that implements `org.xml.sax.ContentHandler`:

```
public class Namespace extends DefaultHandler {
```

We override the default implementation of `startElement()` in `DefaultHandler`. This method is called by the parser whenever it encounters a new XML element in the source document. Overriding just this method is sufficient for our purpose of analysing how the parser processes namespaces.

The callback method supplies four pieces of information about an element: the URI of the namespace the element is in; the unprefixed name; the name with prefix if any; and an `org.xml.sax.Attributes` structure representing the collection of attributes of the element:

```java
public void startElement(String uri, String localName,
    String qName, Attributes atts) throws SAXException {
  print("Elem: " +
        qName, uri, localName);
  for (int i = 0;i < atts.getLength(); ++i) {
    print("Attr: " +
        atts.getQName(i) + "=" + atts.getValue(i),
        atts.getURI(i),
        atts.getLocalName(i));
  }
}
```

This is a utility for pretty-printing the element events:

```java
private void print(String t, String u, String l) {
  System.out.println(t);
  System.out.println("   URI: " + u);
  System.out.println("   Local Name: " + l);
}
```

The `main()` method of the class creates a parser, attaches an instance of the class to it as content handler, and parses the input document shown below:

```java
public static void main(String[] args) throws Exception {
  SAXParserFactory spf = SAXParserFactory.newInstance();
```

We ensure that the SAX parser factory produces instances of namespace-aware parsers:

```java
spf.setNamespaceAware(true);
```

Next we obtain an `XMLReader` from the factory:

```java
XMLReader reader = spf.newSAXParser().getXMLReader();
```

Then we instruct the reader to report namespace attribute declarations as content:

```java
reader.setFeature(
    "http://xml.org/sax/features/namespace-prefixes",true);
```

Now attach an instance of this class to the `XMLReader` to handle content:

```java
reader.setContentHandler(new Namespace());
```

Then finally parse the document:

```
            reader.parse("namespace.xml");
        }
    }
```

namespace.xml

This is the sample document that we will parse. It contains a variety of different namespace declarations:

```xml
<?xml version="1.0" encoding="UTF-8"?>
<mixedbooks xmlns="http://www.defaultnamespace.com/namespace"
    xmlns:isbn="http://www.acmeisbn.com/official/uri"
    xmlns:wrox="http://www.wrox.com/books">

  <book wrox:isbn="5202">
    <title>
      Java XML Programmers Reference
    </title>
  </book>

  <book isbn:isbn="1861005-20-2">
    <title xmlns="http://www.wrox.com/progrefs">
      Java XML Programmers Reference
    </title>
  </book>

</mixedbooks>
```

Output

You will need Crimson, Xerces or another JAXP 1.1. parser in the classpath for this. It is a good idea to use the debug switch that is currently coded into the reference release of JAXP 1.1 (and also in the implementation bundled with the Xerces parser). This will help us build up an instinct for how a parser (or transformer) is obtained through JAXP:

```
> javac Namespace.java
> java -Djaxp.debug=true Namespace
```

The output is shown below. The debug statements in JAXP report how the parser is obtained, in this case through the service file in `xerces.jar`:

```
JAXP: found:
  META-INF/services/javax.xml.parsers.SAXParserFactory
JAXP: loaded from services:
  org.apache.xerces.jaxp.SAXParserFactoryImpl
```

The program then loads an instance of this class, creates an instance of the Xerces `SAXParser`, and proceeds to parse the document:

```
Elem: mixedbooks
    URI: http://www.defaultnamespace.com/namespace
    Local Name: mixedbooks
 Attr: xmlns=http://www.defaultnamespace.com/namespace
    URI:
    Local Name: xmlns
```

```
Attr: xmlns:isbn=http://www.acmeisbn.com/official/uri
    URI:
    Local Name: isbn
Attr: xmlns:wrox=http://www.wrox.com/books
    URI:
    Local Name: wrox
Elem: book
    URI: http://www.defaultnamespace.com/namespace
    Local Name: book
Attr: wrox:isbn=5202
    URI: http://www.wrox.com/books
    Local Name: isbn
Elem: title
    URI: http://www.defaultnamespace.com/namespace
    Local Name: title
Elem: book
    URI: http://www.defaultnamespace.com/namespace
    Local Name: book
Attr: isbn:isbn=1861005-20-2
    URI: http://www.acmeisbn.com/official/uri
    Local Name: isbn
Elem: title
    URI: http://www.wrox.com/progrefs
    Local Name: title
Attr: xmlns=http://www.wrox.com/progrefs
    URI:
    Local Name: xmlns
```

Note that the prefix xmlns is not reported as having an associated URI. It is a reserved prefix and therefore its uniqueness is implicit.

Transformation

Transformation is specified in XML using the eXtensible Stylesheet Language (XSL). This is another standard maintained by the W3C. It is of course XML itself and can be transformed and validated like ordinary XML. We start with an input XML document, and apply the stylesheet. This generates an output document which can be in any form: HTML, WML, XML, or just plain text.

Fundamental to the future of transformation on the Java platform is the Transformation API for XML (TrAX), which is an integral part of the JAXP specification, covered in Chapter 5. This API uses the same principles for obtaining and configuring a transformer as the equivalent system for parsing that was described in the *JAXP* section.

For a definitive guide to the subject of stylesheet transformation, we refer you to *XSLT Programmer's Reference 2nd Edition*, Michael Kay 2001, Wrox Press, ISBN 1-861005-06-7.

In the supportticket.xsl example below, we use the following fundamental elements of XSL, which are identified to the processor by the xsl: prefix.

The standard enclosing element for all stylesheets is an element of the following form. It occurs directly after the XML prolog, and includes a namespace declaration for elements that are reserved for the XSL processor:

```
<xsl:stylesheet
    version="1.0"
    xmlns:xsl="http://www.w3.org/1999/XSL/Transform">

</xsl:stylesheet>
```

A stylesheet transformer processes the input XML document by performing "template matching". A template is an instruction for what to do with part of the document's structure, most often specified by a match with the top-level element of that structure:

```
<xsl:template match="pattern">

</xsl:template>
```

In its simplest form, a pattern is the (namespace qualified) name of an element. When the processor starts to process the contents of the template after finding a matching node, then it may encounter other directives that are specified relative to the understood "context node".

Templates themselves are not nested, but the processor continues to apply templates to elements nested inside the context node when it encounters the `<xsl:apply-templates>` directive:

```
<xsl:apply-templates/>
```

On encountering this instruction, the processor will look for templates that match each child element of the context node and process them in turn.

One of the most frequent operations inside a template is to insert into the output document the value of some part of the input document relative to the context node:

```
<xsl:value-of select="expression"/>
```

For example `select="@att"` is a selection expression that will insert the value of the attibrute `att` of the context node into the output document. See Chapter 16 for more coverage of these expressions.

Example

In this example, we look at a sample "support ticket" XML document, and a stylesheet to translate it into to HTML. Next, we will use the TrAX API in reading an XML file and an XSL file and outputting the result of the transformation.

TrAXUtil.java

```java
import javax.xml.transform.TransformerFactory;
import javax.xml.transform.Transformer;
import javax.xml.transform.stream.StreamSource;
import javax.xml.transform.stream.StreamResult;
import java.io.FileReader;
import java.io.FileWriter;

public class TrAXUtil {
```

Note that the TrAX specification requires that `TransformerFactory` be threadsafe, so it is a normal procedure to create just one during program initialization and to reuse it:

```
private static TransformerFactory tf = null;

public static void main(String[] args) throws Exception {
  if (args.length != 3) {
    System.out.println("Usage: java TrAXUtil XML XSL OUT");
    return;
  }
```

The following shows some of the elegance of the TrAX API, which is covered in Chapter 5.

```
  tf = TransformerFactory.newInstance();

  StreamSource xml =
    new StreamSource(new FileReader(args[0]));
  StreamSource xsl =
    new StreamSource(new FileReader(args[1]));
  StreamResult htm =
    new StreamResult(new FileWriter(args[2]));

  Transformer t = tf.newTransformer(xsl);
  t.transform(xml,htm);
  }

}
```

supportticket.xml

The following is the source file that we will use:

```
<?xml version="1.0"?>
<supportticket
```

In a later example, we will develop a schema and show what to add here to cause schema validation to be performed on this document.

We specifiy the default namespace of the document along with other top-level attributes:

```
xmlns="http://www.wrox.com/support"
id="PP20010621-118"
status="open"
agent="Phil">

<customer
  name ="Herbert Jefferson"
  email="jeff@brixtpot.com"/>
```

A support ticket consists of a customer (above) and a support event (below), which refers to a single book, and has an arbitrary number of `<mail>` subelements. Each of the mail elements contains a summary of the correspondence, and a storage key pointing to the location of the message in a database):

```
  <supportevent>
    <book isbn="6781" chapter="12"/>
    <mail type="in" date="21/06/2001 08:35 GMT"
       length="4201" agent="hjefferson@brixtpot.com"
       storekey="132488832">
     Request for clarification of
     <software>Jakarta Tomcat</software>
     version to be used.
    </mail>
    <mail type="out" date="21/06/2001 11:04 10:45 GMT"
       length="6621" agent="benw@wrox.com"
       storekey="132488879">
     Advised reader of tested combinations. Awaiting
     confirmation of success.
    </mail>
  </supportevent>

</supportticket>
```

supportticket.xsl

This XSL stylesheet will transform the above support ticket sample to an HTML version for browser display:

```
<?xml version="1.0" encoding="UTF-8"?>
<xsl:stylesheet version="1.0"
  xmlns:xsl="http://www.w3.org/1999/XSL/Transform"
```

To be able to match with elements of the target document, we need to refer to them by their qualified name (recall that the source document has a default namespace associated with it):

```
    xmlns:st="http://www.wrox.com/support">
```

Note the necessity to use the qualified name of the target element in `match` expressions:

```
    <xsl:output method="html"/>
    <xsl:template match="st:supportticket">
      <html>
        <head><title>Support Event</title></head>
        <body>
          <h2><i>
            Support Event <xsl:value-of select="@id"/><br/>
            Status: <xsl:value-of select="@status"/><br/>
            Agent: <xsl:value-of select="@agent"/>
          </i></h2>
          <xsl:apply-templates/>
        </body>
      </html>
    </xsl:template>
```

The rest of these templates simply match the support ticket element types in a logical way. As a rule of thumb, define what you want a template to output with a particular element, then put <xsl:apply-templates/> in those places within the instructions where you want the transformation to "recurse" into the subnodes and apply the appropriate templates to those too:

```
<xsl:template match="st:customer">
  <b>Customer:</b>
  <xsl:value-of select="@name"/><br/>
  <b>Email:</b>
  <code><xsl:value-of select="@email"/></code><br/>
</xsl:template>

<xsl:template match="st:supportevent">
  <p/>
  <b>ISBN:</b>
  186100<xsl:value-of select="st:book/@isbn"/><br/>
  <b>Chapter:</b><xsl:value-of select="st:book/@chapter"/>
  <xsl:apply-templates/>
</xsl:template>

<xsl:template match="st:mail">
  <p/>
  <table width="400" bgcolor="#005000" cellpadding="4">
    <tr><td bgcolor="white">
      <b>From:</b>
      <code><xsl:value-of select="@agent"/></code><br/>
      <b>Date:</b>
      <xsl:value-of select="@date"/><br/>
      <b>Length:</b>
      <xsl:value-of select="@length"/>bytes<br/>
      <b>Storekey:</b>
      <xsl:value-of select="@storekey"/><br/>
```

The mail element is a mixed content element – it contains a mixture of text and mark up. This is how we cause the processor to continue processing into the content of the mail element so that it will apply the last template shown below:

```
      <hr/>
      <i><xsl:apply-templates/></i>
      <p/>
    </td></tr>
  </table>
  <p/>
</xsl:template>
```

And this is what we do with the `<software>` elements that we may find inside the mail content:

```
<xsl:template match="st:software">
  <font color="red"><b>
  <xsl:value-of select="text()"/>
  </b></font>
</xsl:template>

</xsl:stylesheet>
```

Output

To generate the transform, you'll need JAXP 1.1 and a JAXP compliant XSLT processor, such as Xalan-J from the Apache XML Project (http://xml.apache.org/xalan-j), in your classpath:

```
> java -Djaxp.debug=true TrAXUtil supportticket.xml
  supportticket.xsl supportticket.html
JAXP: found
  META-INF/services/javax.xml.transform.TransformerFactory
JAXP: loaded from services:
  org.apache.xalan.processor.TransformerFactoryImpl
JAXP: found
  META-INF/services/javax.xml.parsers.SAXParserFactory
JAXP: loaded from services:
  org.apache.xerces.jaxp.SAXParserFactoryImpl
```

Note that the SAXParser is loaded internally by the transformer code in order to parse in the StreamSource as a SAX input to the transformation process. Here is the HTML output:

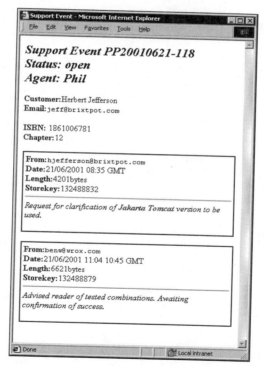

We next have a look at processing instructions.

Processing Instructions

These are nodes within the DOM reserved for instructing the processing application to do something external to the document itself. A processing instruction looks like:

```
<?target data="somedata" more data ?>
```

The form of the data content is loosely specified in XML, but by convention, should consist of attribute-like structures. These have to be manually parsed, as the data content is returned as a single text string.

Example

This shows by example how a parser can read processing instructions from an XML document and execute actions depending upon the content of the 'target' and 'data' components. In this case, we e-mail the 'target' with the message contained in the 'data'. To add to the illustration, we will look at a quite different way of obtaining a DOM tree from the input file mailpi.xml.

MailPI.java

```java
import org.jdom.adapters.OracleV2DOMAdapter;
import org.w3c.dom.Document;
import org.w3c.dom.ProcessingInstruction;
import org.w3c.dom.Node;
import org.w3c.dom.NodeList;
import java.io.FileInputStream;
import org.apache.tools.mail.MailMessage;


public class MailPI {
```

This method recursively searches an org.w3c.dom.Node tree for processing instructions. It calls the process() method when it finds one:

```java
private void search(Node n) {
    if (n instanceof ProcessingInstruction) {
        process((ProcessingInstruction) n);
    }
    if (n.hasChildNodes()) {
        NodeList nl = n.getChildNodes();
        for (int i = 0;i < nl.getLength();++i) {
            search(nl.item(i));
        }
    }
}
```

We use the MailMessage utility that is available in the Jakarta Ant distribution (see Appendix A for installing and using Ant):

```java
private void process(ProcessingInstruction pi) {
    try {
```

Extract the target and the data from the instruction:

```java
String to = pi.getTarget() + "@wrox.com";
String msg = pi.getData();
System.out.println("Sending email to " + to + "...");
```

Open a mail message to an SMTP host and send it:

```
        MailMessage m = new MailMessage("192.168.40.234");
        m.from("mailpi@wrox.com");m.to(to);
        m.setSubject("Processing data enclosed");
        m.getPrintStream().print(msg);
        m.sendAndClose();
      }
      catch (java.io.IOException e) {
        e.printStackTrace();
      }
    }
```

The `main()` method illustrates obtaining an Oracle XML Parser `Document` implementation via JDOM. The document is then passed to the `search()` method:

```
    public static void main(String[] args) throws Exception {
        OracleV2DOMAdapter ora = new OracleV2DOMAdapter();
        Document doc = ora.getDocument(
          new FileInputStream("mailpi.xml"),false);
        new MailPI().search(doc);
    }

  }
```

mailpi.xml

```
    <?xml version="1.0" encoding="UTF-8"?>
    <mailpi>
      <?jim msg="Beginning to parse books"?>
      <book isbn="5202">
        <?ben msg="Entered 5202"?>
        <title >
          Java XML Programmer's Reference
        </title>
        <?helen msg="Left 5202"?>
      </book>
    </mailpi>
```

Note: one of the rules of processing instructions is that a user-defined target cannot begin with `xml` – like the `<?xml ?>` declaration at the beginning of an XML document. This is also interpreted as a processing instruction, as shown by the output below.

Output

You'll need to check that you've got the classpath set with:

❑ `ant.jar` – (for the `org.apache.tools.mail.MailMessage` class)

❑ `jdom.jar` – the JDOM implementation

❑ `xmlparserv2.jar` – Oracle XML Parser v2 (see Chapter 7)

```
> javac MailPI.java
> java MailPI

Sending email to xml@wrox.com...
Sending email to jim@wrox.com...
Sending email to ben@wrox.com...
Sending email to helen@wrox.com...
```

In the next section, we will look briefly at the issue of character encodings used when reading and writing XML data.

Character Encoding

Character encoding is huge area, which could fill several volumes of dedicated material. The basic issue for the Java programmer amounts to the difference between character streams and byte streams. Whereas all byte streams contain sequences of bytes, character streams are all potentially different depending on what encodings have been used to generate them. The XML prolog contains a well-known optional parameter to specify encoding to be used in a document (it is UTF-8 by default):

```
<?xml version="1.0" encoding="UTF-8"?>
```

UTF stands for Unicode Transmission Format.

The issue of encoding is an important concern to the Java XML programmer, particularly when working with multiple locales and languages. The example below illustrates the fundamental principles at work and what can go wrong. Detailed coverage of this facet of XML is beyond the scope of this book; further information can be found at the following links:

❑ The Unicode Standard: http://www.unicode.org/unicode/standard/standard.html

❑ Character Model for the WWW: http://www.w3.org/TR/charmod

Example

This experiment illustrates sending and receiving XML character data as byte streams. Piped streams simulate the transmission of XML bytes from one program to another, and highlight the character encoding issues that arise when we try to read and write the streams assuming different encodings.

Source Encoding.java

```java
import org.xml.sax.InputSource;
import javax.xml.parsers.DocumentBuilderFactory;
import javax.xml.parsers.DocumentBuilder;
import org.w3c.dom.*;
import java.io.*;

public class Encoding {

  private static DocumentBuilderFactory dbf =
    DocumentBuilderFactory.newInstance();
```

The `doencoding()` method sends an XML **byte stream** to itself, and parses it back into an `org.w3c.dom.Document`. It encodes the output using the `outenc` **character** encoding parameter and receives it assuming the `inenc` encoding. The transmitted XML data is of the form `<char>ch</char>` where `ch` is a char passed in as an argument:

```
public static void doencoding(String outenc,
    String inenc, char ch)
    throws Exception {
  System.out.print("" + (int)ch + " " + outenc + " -> ");
  Character c = new Character(ch);
```

A `java.io.PipedInputStream` is connected to a `PipedOutputStream`:

```
PipedOutputStream po = new PipedOutputStream();
PipedInputStream pi = new PipedInputStream(po);
```

We then write bytes to the output stream. The way the bytes are constructed from the `String` objects is determined by the `outenc` parameter (see below for the `encodings` list):

```
po.write("<char>".getBytes(outenc));
po.write(c.toString().getBytes(outenc));
po.write("</char>".getBytes(outenc));
po.flush();
po.close();
```

An `org.xml.sax.InputSource` is created from the input stream:

```
InputSource is = new InputSource(pi);
```

We set the expected encoding on the `InputStream`:

```
is.setEncoding(inenc);
```

We then parse the `InputSource` into a `Document` and extract the character data at the transmitted position:

```
DocumentBuilder db = dbf.newDocumentBuilder();
Document d = db.parse(is);
Element e = d.getDocumentElement();
String r = e.getFirstChild().getNodeValue();
char rt = r.charAt(0);
System.out.println("" + (int)rt + " " + inenc);
}
```

These are the encodings that should be supported on all Java platforms:

```
public static final String encodings[] = {"US-ASCII",
  "ISO-8859-1","UTF-8","UTF-16","UTF-16LE","UTF-16BE"};

public static void main(String[] args) throws Exception {
```

We'll use the trademark character ™ (Unicode 0x2122) to test the transmission using the same encoding at each end:

```
char c = (char)0x2122; // the trademark
for (int i = 0;i < encodings.length; ++i) {
   doencoding(encodings[i],encodings[i],c);
}
```

We'll also check to see what happens if we send using UTF-16 Little Endian, and receive using UTF-16 Big Endian:

```
   doencoding(encodings[4],encodings[5],c);
  }
}
```

Output

To run the program, you'll need Xerces, Crimson, or another JAXP parser in the classpath:

```
> javac Encoding.java
> java Encoding
8482 US-ASCII -> 63 US-ASCII
8482 ISO-8859-1 -> 63 ISO-8859-1
8482 UTF-8 -> 8482 UTF-8
8482 UTF-16 -> 65279 UTF-16
8482 UTF-16LE -> 8482 UTF-16LE
8482 UTF-16BE -> 8482 UTF-16BE
```

Note how the character is misread in the first two cases, and in UTF-16.

When we try to send and recieve using different orderings of UTF-16, then an exception occurs, because the parser rejects the incoming characters in the XML prolog:

```
8482 UTF-16LE -> Exception in thread "main" org.xml.sax.SAXParseException: The markup in the
document preceding the root element must be well-formed.
```

In the next section we take a quick look at validation with DTD, and the often more confusing issue of "entities" that can occur in the DTD.

The DTD and Entities

XML documents can be validated using a Document Type Definition (DTD), and, increasingly, using an XML schema. There are some powerful reasons for combining the universality and extensibility of XML with automated constraint checking of the documents against a formal type definition:

❑ **Validation provides a common interface**
Producers and consumers of XML documents use shared document type definitions (specified using DTD or XML Schema) in the same way that software vendors and programmers use shared API definitions: for example the W3C DOM Java bindings (in this case the validation of the code is performed by the Java compiler).

❑ **Validation saves implementation effort**
The automated checking of document integrity while parsing saves tedious reprogramming to implement validity checks.

❑ **Validation can be used in editing tools**
Type definitions can be used for auto-completion of document components when constructing a document in an editor. The tool knows what you can and cannot insert by checking with the DTD or schema.

A DTD is a set of constraints that can be applied to the components of XML documents, in addition to the syntactic constraint of well-formedness specified by the XML 1.0 Recommendation. Documents that satisfy the constraints of a DTD are "valid" with respect to the DTD.

An XML document declares its DTD definition in the **Document Type Declaration**. This can either refer to an internal subset, an external DTD document, or both. In the following example, `mixedbooks.xml` has an **internal** subset within the [ ] brackets:

```
<!DOCTYPE mixedbooks SYSTEM "mixedbooks.dtd" [
  <!ELEMENT mixedbooks (book*)>
  <!ENTITY ltd "Ltd.">
]>
```

The file `mixedbooks.xml` also has an **external** subset in the file `mixedbooks.dtd`. Definitions of the internal DTD `DOCTYPE` subset of an XML document always override any external definitions if there is any conflict.

Most of the DTD consists of two kinds of definition: **element definitions**, which define the content of elements; and **attribute definitions,** which constrain the attributes of an element. There are also **entities**, which do not constrain the document, but provide a substitution mechanism to assist in writing both DTDs and XML documents. Entities are declared inside the DTD, but may be referenced either from within the XML document or from elsewhere in the DTD (but the declaration must be found before the reference).

This external DTD refers to internal and external parameter entities:

```
<!ENTITY % pubs "(wrox | notwrox)">
<!ENTITY % anotherdtd SYSTEM "anotherdtd.dtd">
```

These respectively represent an enumerated type for the publisher attribute definition, and a system file containing another fragment of DTD. This is inserted into the external DTD using the reference:

```
%anotherdtd;
```

Several external parsed entities are also inserted into the `mixedbooks.xml` file, from the files `comments.xml` and `anotherbook.xml`. In the example below, we will parse the file and output the result, showing the correct substitution of these entities into the final document.

The W3C XML 1.0 Recommendation at http://www.w3c.org/TR/REC-xml provides the definition of the relationship between XML and DTDs.

Example

This example illustrates the key features of the DTD and its associated entities. We will look at a DTD-entity puzzle and then generate the final document using a stylesheet processor.

mixedbooks.xml

This is the source file. It contains an internal DTD, and refers to an external subset in the `mixedbooks.dtd` file:

```
<?xml version="1.0" encoding="UTF-16"?>
<!DOCTYPE mixedbooks SYSTEM "mixedbooks.dtd" [
  <!ELEMENT mixedbooks (book*)>
  <!ENTITY ltd "Ltd.">
]>
<mixedbooks>

  <book isbn="isbn-401X">
    <title>
      Professional Java XML
    </title>
    <publisher pub="wrox" name="&wrox;&space;&ltd;"/>
  </book>

  <!-- External general entity references -->
  &anotherbook;

  &comment;

</mixedbooks>
```

mixedbooks.dtd

This is the main DTD. It imports an additional DTD fragment from `anotherdtd.dtd`:

```
<!ELEMENT book (title,publisher?)>
<!ATTLIST book isbn CDATA #REQUIRED>

<!ELEMENT publisher EMPTY>
<!ENTITY % pubs "(wrox | notwrox)">
<!ATTLIST publisher
   pub %pubs; #REQUIRED
   name CDATA #IMPLIED>

<!ENTITY comment PUBLIC
   "-//Comments Dot Com//Text//EN"
   "file:///C:/comment.xml">

<!ENTITY wrox "Wrox Press">
<!ENTITY space "&#32;">

<!ENTITY % anotherdtd SYSTEM "anotherdtd.dtd">
%anotherdtd;

<!ENTITY anotherbook SYSTEM "anotherbook.xml">
```

anotherdtd.dtd

This is a small DTD fragment constraing the `<title>` of a `<book>`:

```
<!ELEMENT title (#PCDATA)>
<!ATTLIST title xml:lang NMTOKEN "en-US">
```

anotherbook.xml

For illustration, this is an external entity that is referenced by the source document. It is read in by the parser, validated, and incorporated into the document:

```
<book isbn="isbn-0091">
  <title xml:lang="pt">
      Java XML Referência Para o Programador
  </title>
</book>
```

comment.xml

This is another external entity, which also has a PUBLIC ID as defined in the DTD. A public ID may be used by an `org.xml.sax.EntityResolver` to intercept requests for entities and return some appropriate data according to a local lookup of the public or system ID:

```
<!--
    This is a comment that can be inserted
    into documents
-->
```

Output

To see the `mixedbooks.xml` file with substitutions in place, we need to process it through a parser and serialize it back to XML. One way to do this is to transform it with an "identity" transformation:

```
<?xml version="1.0"?>
<xsl:stylesheet version="1.0"
    xmlns:xsl="http://www.w3.org/1999/XSL/Transform">

<xsl:template match="@*|node()">
  <xsl:copy>
    <xsl:apply-templates select="@*|node()"/>
  </xsl:copy>
</xsl:template>

</xsl:stylesheet>
```

We will use a command-line application such as the one available with the Saxon stylesheet processor:

```
> java com.icl.saxon.StyleSheet mixedbooks.xml identity.xsl
<?xml version="1.0" encoding="utf-8"?><mixedbooks>

 <book isbn="isbn-401X">
   <title xml:lang="en-US">
```

```
     Professional Java XML
   </title>
   <publisher pub="wrox" name="Wrox Press Ltd."/>
 </book>

 <!-- External general entity reference -->
 <book isbn="isbn-0091">
 <title xml:lang="pt">
     Java XML Refer•¬ncia Para o Programador
 </title>
</book>

 <!-- Insert a comment -->
 <!--
  This is a comment that can be inserted
  into documents
 -->

</mixedbooks>
```

This shows all the correct substitutions were made when the file was parsed.

Chapter 2 contains a number of examples showing how you can intercept the referencing, resolving, and substitution of entities within the parsing process.

Namespaces and DTD

The xmlns attribute, by definition, belongs to no namespace. However, some older, non-namespace-aware parsers may require an additional attribute definition in the DTD for compatibility:

```
xmlns CDATA #FIXED "http://www.wrox.com/javaxmlref"
```

Note the necessity to declare the xml:lang attribute in the file anotherdtd.dtd in the above example. The xml namespace doesn't itself have to be declared – it is a reserved and recognized namespace, but namespace declarations other than the default namespace have to be declared in a DTD.

Next we take a look at the technology for defining document content that is emerging to replace the role of DTD.

XML Schema

XML schemas provide a more powerful and flexible grammar mechanism for XML than DTDs do. The primary advantage that schemas have over DTDs is that schemas themselves are XML, and share with other XML documents the features of portability, and the ability to apply processes like XSL transformation to them using standard tools. But they are also more expressive and more flexible than DTDs in the types of XML structures they can constrain.

Another essential advantage is their ability to deal adequately with XML namespaces: DTDs have no support for them.

XML Schema has been evolving over quite a long period and finally reached W3C Recommendation status in May 2001. The specification comes in three stages:

❑ **Part 0: Primer**
This is an introduction and guide to using XML Schema.

❑ **Part 1: Structures**
This part contains the XML Schema Definition Language (XSDL), which is a set of special XML elements and the rules for using them to build XML schemas.

❑ **Part 2: Datatypes**
This part documents the built-in data types that schemas can use. Schemas have a much more complex data type base than DTDs.

Although schemas are supposed to validate other documents, their structures are themselves specified by a schema called `XMLSchema.xsd`. This schema is itself validated by an internal XML 1.0 DTD. This schema for XML Schema, Part 1 – Structures, can be read at:

http://www.w3.org/2000/10/XMLSchema.xsd or
http://www.w3.org/2001/XMLSchema.xsd

These are the two most likely versions that you will come across. The first is based on the Candidate Recommendation of October 2000, and has been used as the basis for on-going development work of such parsers as Apache Xerces. The 1.4.0 version of Xerces now provides support for the final Recommendation.

Schemas are relatively complex structures and cannot be covered in detail in this book. The best starting place for learning more about schemas is the W3C Recommendation Primer, which is "Part 0" of the May 2001 XML Schema recommendation: http://www.w3.org/TR/xmlschema-0. See also, *Professional XML Schemas*, Wrox Press, 2001, ISBN 1-861005-47-4.

We use schemas in the specification of web services using WSDL (Chapter 9). We also look at schema validation support with Xerces in the example just below, and with the Oracle parser in Chapter 7, and develop a schema for a "service configuration" file in Chapter 12.

We continue below with the `supportticket` example by developing a schema to specify the document type, and then validating it with Xerces.

Note that "XML Schema" is the W3C specification, whereas "XML schemas" generally means the actual type definitions, or schema documents. It is often better to refer to the specification itself (or more accurately, Part 1 – *Structures*) as XML Schema Definition Language or XSDL.

The following extends the support ticket transformation example on page 21 by looking at how to specify the document type of a support ticket using XSDL.

The example uses the following schema element types, which we very briefly summarize next.

```
<element> <attribute> <attributeGroup>
<sequence> <restriction>
<simpleType> <complexType>
```

The first three correspond in principle to elements and attributes in DTDs. An `<attributeGroup>` is rather like a parameter entity defining a set of attribute definitions that can be referenced from one or more `<!ATTLIST>` definitions.

A `<sequence>` defines an ordered list of further types, like the enumerated element content of an `<!ELEMENT elems (elem1,elem2,...)>` declaration. A `<restriction>` restricts the types of the structures defined within it.

Complex (and simple) types, along with the built-in datatypes of Part 2 of the Recommendation, are the really powerful feature of schemas compared with DTDs. We show here how the types can be nested within elements, and be specific to those elements, and also how they can be non-specific, and referred to by name from other structures that wish to use those types (this is a bit like anonymous inner classes compared to normal classes in Java).

Example

This example refers to the `supportticket.xml` instance on page 21. In this example, we'll step through the schema structures, which illustrate various methods of defining **types** for the document components. Then we'll validate the instance against the schema using Xerces. First, we look at the top-level element of the instance document, to see how to specify the version and location of the schema:

```
<supportticket
  xmlns:xsi=
    "http://www.w3.org/2001/XMLSchema-instance"
  xsi:schemaLocation=
    "http://www.wrox.com/support supportticket.xsd"
  xmlns="http://www.wrox.com/support"
  id="PP20010621-118"
  status="open"
  agent="Phil">
```

Note the final version of XML Schema. If you are using an old parser that supports schemas, then you'll need to write:

```
"http://www.w3.org/2000/10/XMLSchema-instance"
```

in place of the above `xsi` schema instance declaration. (Your parser should report an error if an inappropriate one is used, and tell you what the highest supported version is.)

Sample supportticket.xsd

This is the schema file:

```
<?xml version="1.0" encoding="UTF-8"?>
<schema
```

This is the namespace that elements of the **target document** have to be in, in order to validate against this schema. In this case, it is the default namespace of the target document:

```
targetNamespace="http://www.wrox.com/support"
```

This is our prefix definition for the target namespace within this schema document:

```
xmlns:st="http://www.wrox.com/support"
```

The following is the default namespace for the document. We could have chosen our target namespace as default, and then declared a prefix for the XML Schema namespace, such as the standard `xsd` (note that it's just a namespace prefix like any other and wouldn't have to be `xsd`).

```
xmlns="http://www.w3.org/2001/XMLSchema"
```

Note that for an older validator, you may need to use:

```
<!-- xmlns="http://www.w3.org/2000/10/XMLSchema" -->
```

Finally in the namespace declarations, recall that the `targetNamespace` specifies the namespace URI that the schema's top-level definitions belong to. To make local definitions (for example elements declared inside other elements) **also** belong to this namespace, we specify `elementFormDefault` as follows:

```
elementFormDefault ="qualified">
```

Now we define the top-level document type. The type is defined in this case using a **nested** `complexType` – the type is essentially specific to this element. The type specifies a sequence consisting of a `<customer>` element and a `<supportevent>` element. These two are themselves defined using two different reference mechanisms (for illustration). The first uses `ref` to refer to a defined element elsewhere in the schema. The second refers to a named **type** that is defined elsewhere in the schema. Lastly, we show the group of attributes used by the support ticket as one `<attributeGroup>` construct that is defined afterwards:

```
<element name="supportticket">
  <complexType>
    <sequence>
      <element ref="st:customer"/>
      <element name="supportevent"
          type="st:supporteventType"/>
    </sequence>
    <attributeGroup ref="st:ticketAttributes"/>
  </complexType>
</element>
```

The attribute group defines a set (remember attributes are unordered) of attributes of type `string`, except for `status`, which is an enumeration of three possible values. The `<restriction>` declaration constrains the types of its subelements. Note that unlike an `<!ATTLIST>`, an `attributeGroup` does not refer to the element it is specific to, it is free-standing, which means that it could be imported by reference into other elements:

```
<attributeGroup name="ticketAttributes">
  <attribute name="agent" type="string" use="required"/>
  <attribute name="id" type="string" use="required"/>
  <attribute name="status">
    <simpleType>
      <restriction base="NMTOKEN">
        <enumeration value="open"/>
        <enumeration value="suspended"/>
        <enumeration value="closed"/>
      </restriction>
    </simpleType>
  </attribute>
</attributeGroup>
```

The `<customer>` element is simple. It defines an empty element with two attributes. It was referred to by the `supportticket` type:

```
<element name="customer">
  <complexType>
    <attribute name="name" type="string" use="required"/>
    <attribute name="email" type="string" use="required"/>
  </complexType>
</element>
```

This is the type for support events. Other elements may declare that they have this type by using `type="st:supportEventType"` in their `<element>` definition.

```
<complexType name="supporteventType">
  <sequence>
    <element name="book">
      <complexType>
        <attribute name="isbn"
            type="string" use="required"/>
        <attribute name="chapter"
            type="string" use="required"/>
      </complexType>
    </element>
    <element ref="st:mail"
      minOccurs="1" maxOccurs="unbounded"/>
  </sequence>
</complexType>
```

Here is the `<mail>` element type. It has **mixed** content together with a number of attributes stored in an `attributeGroup`. Recall that the content of `<mail>` may contain `<software>` element markup. Note the use of the `<documentation>` schema element to add comments to the type definitions:

```
<element name="mail">
  <complexType mixed="true">
    <annotation>
      <documentation xml:lang="en">
        This defines the type of of a mail summary that
        occurs in a support transaction. The summary points
        to a database store for the original message
        by means of the required storekey attribute
      </documentation>
    </annotation>
```

The way we allow the content of `<mail>` to be sprinkled with `<software>` elements is to define the `software` type as occuring an arbitrary number of times (the default is precisely 1). However this would only validate *mixed* `<software>` and character data if we specified `mixed="true"` in the definition of the type, as above:

```
<sequence>
  <element name="software" minOccurs="0"
    maxOccurs="unbounded"/>
</sequence>
<attributeGroup ref="st:mailAttributes"/>
```

```
        </complexType>
      </element>

    <attributeGroup name="mailAttributes">
      <attribute name="date" type="string" use="required"/>
      <attribute name="type" use="required">
        <simpleType>
          <restriction base="NMTOKEN">
            <enumeration value="in"/>
            <enumeration value="out"/>
          </restriction>
        </simpleType>
      </attribute>
      <attribute name="length" type="string" use="optional"/>
      <attribute name="agent" type="string" use="required"/>
      <attribute name="storekey" type="string" use="required"/>
    </attributeGroup>
  </schema>
```

Note that the use of the `<software>` element was to illustrate the idea of adding markup to the text of support events, in order to facilitate intelligent searching. We could add more such element definitions.

The following example shows how to build a schema-validating Xerces parser, and to check the `supportticket.xml` file against its schema.

Source SchemaParserXerces.java

This small utility will validate `supportticket.xml` against the schema `supportticket.xsd` declared in the `schemaLocation` attribute of the `supportticket.xml` file. Note the addition of an error handler to the parser so that we can catch warnings and errors as exceptions. This handler throws all errors as exceptions:

```java
import org.apache.xerces.parsers.DOMParser;
import org.xml.sax.ErrorHandler;
import org.xml.sax.SAXException;
import org.xml.sax.SAXParseException;

public class SchemaParserXerces implements ErrorHandler {

  public void warning(SAXParseException e)
    throws SAXException {throw e;}
  public void error(SAXParseException e)
    throws SAXException {throw e;}
  public void fatalError(SAXParseException e)
    throws SAXException {throw e;}

  public static void main(String[] args) throws Exception {
    DOMParser d = new DOMParser();
    d.setFeature(
      "http://xml.org/sax/features/validation", true);
    d.setFeature(
      "http://apache.org/xml/features/validation/schema",true);
    d.setFeature(
      "http://apache.org/xml/features/validation/schema-full-
        checking", true);
```

```
        d.setErrorHandler(new SchemaParserXerces());
        d.parse(args[0]);
        System.out.println("Parsed successfully");
    }

}
```

Output

Ensure that you have Xerces in your classpath, then compile `SchemaParserXerces.java`, and run the following:

```
> java SchemaParserXerces supportticket.xml
Parsed successfully
```

To be certain that it is validating correctly, introduce an error; for instance, change the `type` attribute of a `<mail>` element to `outt`:

```
Error:  org.xml.sax.SAXParseException: Datatype error: Value 'outt' must be one of [in, out].
```

Summary

This completes our brief tour of Java XML by example. In the next chapters, you will find the APIs of the major XML interfaces and abstractions, and many more examples to quickly get you working with them.

W3C Technical Reports

XML 1.0 Recommendation (Includes DTD)	http://www.w3.org/TR/REC-xml
XML Namespaces	http://www.w3.org/TR/REC-xml-names
XML Schema Recommendation (Parts 0, 1, 2)	http://www.w3.org/TR/xmlschema-[0,1,2]
XSLT Recommendation	http://www.w3.org/TR/xslt

Resources on the Web

Annotated XML 1.0 Recommendation	http://www.xml.com/axml/axml.html
OASIS – Organization for the Advancement of Structured Information Standards	http://www.oasis-open.org
SAX	http://www.megginson.com/SAX/index.html

Saxon	http://users.iclway.co.uk/mhkay/saxon/
The DOM	http://www.w3.org/DOM/
The Internet Engineering Task Force	http://www.ietf.org
The Unicode Specification	http://www.unicode.org
The XSL home page	http://www.w3.org/Style/XSL/
Tutorial for JAXP 1.1	http://java.sun.com/xml/tutorial_intro.html
XML 1.0 FAQ	http://www.ucc.ie/xml
XML Industry Portal	http://www.xml.org

Lists

Dev-XML home page	http://groups.yahoo.com/group/dev-xml
JDOM	http://www.jdom.org/involved/lists.html
Xerces/Xalan/Apache XML	http://xml.apache.org/mail.html
XML DEV	http://www.xml.org/xml-dev/index.shtml
XML USENET Newsgroup	news:comp.text.xml
XML-INTEREST	http://java.sun.com/xml
XSL-List	http://www.biglist.com/lists/xsl-list/

JavaXMLProgrammer'sReferenceJavaXMLPr
eferenceJavaXMLProgrammer'sReferenceJ

2

SAX 2.0

The **Simple API for XML (SAX)** is an event-driven programming interface for XML parsing. It was developed by the members of the `xml-dev` mailing list currently hosted by the **Organization for the Advancement of Structured Information Standards (OASIS)** http://www.oasis-open.org. SAX is not an XML parser, but a set of interfaces implemented by many XML parsers. David Megginson, who maintains the http://www.megginson.com site, coordinated this project. The first version of SAX was very successful, but it lacked namespace support. The second version corrected this, by deprecating some of the interfaces and defining new ones. The old interfaces are still available for legacy applications. A SAX 1.0-based program can run using a SAX 2.0 parser, but it must be modified in order to take advantage of the new features.

This chapter contains the same information as the SAX 2.0 API specification (http://www.megginson.com/SAX). In addition, we develop small utility classes and examples that use the SAX API. We will show how to:

- ❏ Configure a SAX parser and parse an XML document
- ❏ Handle elements, attribute lists, character data and processing instructions
- ❏ Build an "XML element-Java method" mapping mechanism using reflection
- ❏ Get all declarations of a DTD: elements, attribute lists, entities and notations
- ❏ Look for input sources in the CLASSPATH and read their content
- ❏ Build simple entity resolvers, error handlers, DTD handlers and lexical handlers

SAX 2.0 contains the following packages:

Package	Description	Page
`org.xml.sax`	Defines handler interfaces. Handler implementations of these interfaces are registered with parsers, which call the handler methods in order to report parsing events and errors	49
`org.xml.sax.ext`	Contains two additional, non-mandatory handlers for dealing with DTD declarations and lexical information	109
`org.xml.sax.helpers`	Provides default implementations for some of the core interfaces defined in `org.xml.sax`.	121

The following section contains a very simple example that uses the SAX API to parse an XML file. The rest of the chapter contains the API documentation of the SAX packages with examples.

Example	Description and Used SAX APIs	Page
`FirstSample`	Starter SAX example that uses the `DefaultHandler` helper class	46
`InputSourceUtils`	Contains static methods for finding input sources in the classpath and getting the content of an InputSource	56
`PrintErrorHandler`	Implements `ErrorHandler` and prints the parsing errors, which are reported as instances of `SAXParseException`	64
`AttributesUtils`	Provides utilities for collecting and converting the values stored in `Attributes`	68
`SmartContentHandler`	Implements `ContentHandler` and builds a mechanism that maps SAX events to Java method calls	75
`TableDTDHandler`	Implements the `DTDHandler` interface for collecting the DTD information on the unparsed entities and notations	84
`XMLReaderSample`	Shows how to use `XMLReader` and the mapping mechanism implemented by our `SmartContentHandler`	94
`ClasspathEntity Resolver`	Implements `EntityResolver` and looks for entities in the classpath	105
`DeclHandlerSample`	Implements the `DeclHandler` and `DTDHandler` interfaces	112

Example	Description and Used SAX APIs	Page
LexicalHandlerSample	Implements LexicalHandler	118
DefaultHandlerCode	Contains code snippets that show two methods for starting the parsing process	134
DefaultHandlerProxy	Proxy handler that dispatches the parsing events to four different specialized handlers	136

Using Sax

SAX is seen as a low-level parsing method: it is faster and uses less memory than other parsing methods such as the Document Object Model (DOM), but it requires more programming effort. In fact, many DOM parsers are built on top of SAX. DOM will be presented in chapter 3.

SAX is a fast and simple way of getting the information contained by an XML document. Unfortunately, no contextual information is provided. For example, when we get the data contained by an element via characters(), we don't get anything about that element such as its name and attributes. This information was provided earlier via a startElement() call. If we need it during the processing of the character data then we have to store it somehow, maybe on a stack. Things get a lot more complex if we use ID and IDREF attributes. DOM is an easier, but more expensive alternative, since it stores all the information in a tree before we get any chance to process it in any way. With SAX, we process the information on the fly disposing of anything we don't need.

SAX Starter Example

In order to parse an input source, such as an XML file, we must obtain an implementation of a SAX parser. The SAX API provides factories for such objects, like XMLReaderFactory, but we prefer the Java API for XML Parsing (JAXP) because it allows us to create a SAX parser object in an implementation-independent manner. With XMLReaderFactory, we would have to set the org.xml.sax.driver system property to something like org.apache.xerces.parsers.SAXParser. In addition, JAXP allows us to configure the parser easily. The JAXP API is presented in Chapter 5.

When we call the parse() method of the SAX parser obtained via JAXP, we have to pass the input source and an event handler. The parser will read the XML content and generate parsing events, which translate to calls to the methods of our handler. For example, the SAX parser calls the startDocument() and endDocument() methods to report the beginning and the ending of the document. It calls startElement() and endElement() to report the start and end tags of an element. It calls the characters() method for each data section contained by an element and processingInstruction() for each processing instruction. The application receives notifications of a parsing error via the warning(), error() and fatalError() methods.

All methods mentioned above are assumed to be synchronous: the parse() method must not return until parsing is complete, and the SAX parser must wait for an event-handler callback, such as characters(), to return before reporting the next event. For more information about the event-handler methods that our example class overrides, see interface ContentHandler (page 71) and interface ErrorHandler (page 62), which describe these methods.

Example: First SAX Example

Our example class extends `org.xml.sax.helpers.DefaultHandler` that provides default implementations for all of the callbacks in the core SAX 2.0 handler interfaces (presented in later sections). We override some of the methods in order to get the information contained by the XML file: elements, attributes, character data and processing instructions.

Source FirstSample.java

```java
import org.xml.sax.Attributes;
import org.xml.sax.InputSource;
import org.xml.sax.SAXException;
import org.xml.sax.SAXParseException;
import org.xml.sax.helpers.DefaultHandler;

import javax.xml.parsers.SAXParser;
import javax.xml.parsers.SAXParserFactory;

public class FirstSample extends DefaultHandler {

  public static String FILENAME = "first.xml";
```

The `main()` method parses the file. It uses the JAXP API to get a SAX parser and then invokes its `parse()` method. An instance of this class is passed as the event handler. Therefore the SAX parser will invoke the `startDocument()`, `endDocument()`, `startElement()`, `endElement()`, `characters()` and `processingInstruction()` methods of this class in order to report the parsing events.

```java
public static void main(String[] args) {
  if (args.length > 0) {
    FILENAME = args[0];
  }
  try {

    // Create an instance of this class
    DefaultHandler handler = new FirstSample();

    // Create the JAXP factory for SAX parsers
    SAXParserFactory saxFactory =
                    SAXParserFactory.newInstance();

    // Create the JAXP SAX parser
    SAXParser saxParser = saxFactory.newSAXParser();

    // Parse the file
    saxParser.parse(new InputSource(FILENAME), handler);

  } catch (SAXParseException e) {

    // Already printed
    System.exit(1);
```

```
    } catch (Exception e) {
      e.printStackTrace();
      System.exit(1);
    }
  }
```

The `println()` method prints a string to the standard output stream.

```
protected void println(String s) {
  System.out.println(s);
}
```

The `startDocument()` method receives notification of the beginning of a document.

```
public void startDocument() throws SAXException {
  println("startDocument");
}
```

The `endDocument()` method receives notification of the end of a document.

```
public void endDocument() throws SAXException {
  println("endDocument");
}
```

The `startElement()` method receives notification of the beginning of an element.

```
public void startElement(String uri, String localName,
      String qName, Attributes atts) throws SAXException {
  println("startElement: "
        + (uri != null && uri.length() > 0 ? uri + ":" :"")
        + localName);
  int n = atts.getLength();
  for (int i = 0; i < n; i++) {
    println("  attribute: " + atts.getLocalName(i) + "=\""
        + atts.getValue(i) + "\"");
  }
}
```

The `endElement()` method receives notification of the end of an element.

```
public void endElement(String uri, String localName,
      String qName) throws SAXException {
  println("endElement");
}
```

47

The `characters()` method receives notification of each piece of character data.

```
public void characters(char ch[], int start,
        int length) throws SAXException {
  String data = new String(ch, start, length).trim();
  if (data.length() > 0) {
    println("characters: " + data);
  }
}
```

The `processingInstruction()` method receives notification of a processing instruction.

```
public void processingInstruction(String target,
        String data) throws SAXException {
  println("processingInstruction: " + target);
  if (data != null && data.length() > 0) {
    println("  data: " + data);
  }
}
```

The `warning()` method prints a warning message.

```
public void warning(SAXParseException e)
        throws SAXException {
  println("WARNING: " + e);
}
```

The `error()` method prints information about a parsing error.

```
public void error(SAXParseException e)
        throws SAXException {
  println("ERROR: " + e);
}
```

The `fatalError()` method prints information about a fatal parsing error and throws the exception.

```
public void fatalError(SAXParseException e)
        throws SAXException {
  println("FATAL ERROR: " + e);
  throw e;
}

}
```

Sample first.xml

```
<?xml version="1.0" encoding='UTF-8'?>
<sample>
```

```
    data before element
      <element attr1="value1" attr2="value2">
        <data1 a="v">some data &amp; one attribute</data1>
        <data2>CDATA follows <![CDATA[more data]]></data2>
      </element>
      data after element
      <?proc data for processing?>
  </sample>
```

Output

```
> java FirstSample first.xml

startDocument
startElement:
characters: data before element
startElement:
  attribute: ="value1"
  attribute: ="value2"
startElement:
  attribute: ="v"
characters: some data
characters: &
characters: one attribute
endElement
startElement:
characters: CDATA follows
characters: more data
endElement
endElement
characters: data after element
processingInstruction: proc
  data: data for processing
endElement
endDocument
```

Package org.xml.sax

This package groups the core interfaces and classes of the SAX API. It provides everything a typical application needs in order to extract the information from an XML file: tag names, element attributes, namespace URI-prefix mappings, character data, ignorable whitespace, processing instructions, notations, unparsed entities' IDs and also the location within the document of the cause of any fatal or non-fatal parsing errors. Lexical information, comments and DTD declarations can be obtained using the SAX extensions described after this package.

Attribute Handling

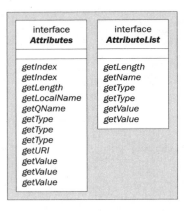

Interface	Since	Description	Page
Attributes	2.0	Interface for a list of XML attributes	65
AttributeList (Deprecated)	1.0	Interface for an element's attribute specifications. Now replaced by `Attributes`.	69

Event Handling

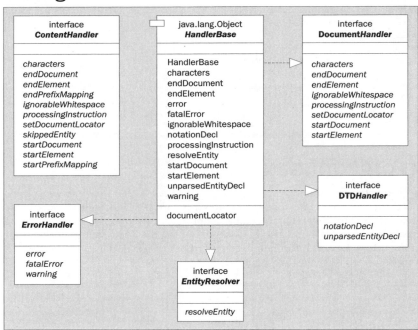

Interface	Since	Description	Page
`ErrorHandler`	1.0	Basic interface for SAX error handlers	62
`ContentHandler`	2.0	Receives notification of the logical content of a document	71
`DocumentHandler` (Deprecated)	1.0	Receives notification of general document events	80
`DTDHandler`	1.0	Receives notification of basic DTD-related events	83
`EntityResolver`	1.0	Basic interface for resolving entities	104
`HandlerBase` (Deprecated)	1.0	Default base class for handlers	107

Parsing

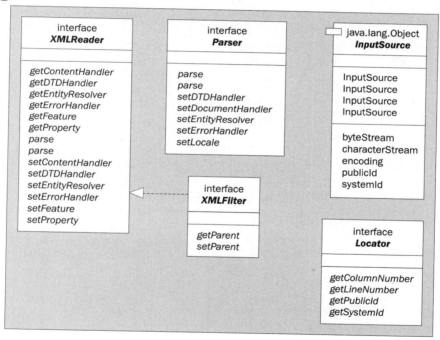

Interface	Since	Description	Page
`InputSource`	1.0	A single input source for an XML entity	53
`Locator`	1.0	Interface for associating a SAX event with a document location	58
`XMLReader`	2.0	Interface for reading an XML document using callbacks	86
`XMLFilter`	2.0	Interface for an XML filter	100
`Parser` (Deprecated)	1.0	Basic interface for SAX parsers. Now replaced by `XMLReader`	101

Exceptions

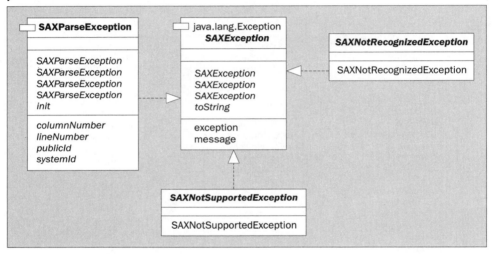

Exception	Since	Page
`SAXException`	1.0	59
`SAXParseException`	1.0	61
`SAXNotRecognizedException`	2.0	85
`SAXNotSupportedException`	2.0	86

Class InputSource

org.xml.sax

> **public class** InputSource

This class allows a SAX application to encapsulate information about an input source in a single object, which may include any of the following:

- ❑ A public identifier
- ❑ A system identifier
- ❑ A character stream
- ❑ A byte stream
- ❑ A character encoding

There are two places where the application will deliver an input source to the parser: as the argument to the XMLReader.parse() method or as the return value of the EntityResolver.resolveEntity() method.

The SAX parser will use the InputSource object to determine how to read XML input. If there is a character stream available, the parser will read that stream directly. If not, the parser will use a byte stream, if available. If neither a character stream nor a byte stream is available, the parser will attempt to open a URI connection to the resource identified by the system identifier.

An InputSource object belongs to the application: the SAX parser never modifies it in any way, but it may modify a copy if required.

Constructors

The InputSource() constructors can take as parameters a system ID, a byte stream or a character stream. Applications may use setPublicId() to include a public identifier, setSystemId() to provide a base for resolving relative URIs or setEncoding() to specify the character encoding, if known.

```
public InputSource()
public InputSource(java.lang.String systemId)
public InputSource(java.io.InputStream byteStream)
public InputSource(java.io.Reader characterStream)
```

Parameters

Parameter	Type	Description
systemId	String	The system identifier (URI)
byteStream	java.io.InputStream	The raw byte stream containing the document
characterStream	java.io.Reader	The character stream containing the document

Methods

The methods allow the getting and setting of five different properties:

- ❑ A public identifier
- ❑ A system identifier
- ❑ A character stream
- ❑ A byte stream
- ❑ A character encoding

The public identifier is always optional: if the application writer includes one, it will be provided as part of the location information.

The system identifier is optional if there is a byte stream or a character stream, but it is still useful to provide one, since the application can use it to resolve relative URIs and can include it in error messages and warnings. The parser will attempt to open a connection to the URI only if there is no byte stream or character stream specified.

If there is a character stream specified, the SAX parser will ignore any byte stream and will not attempt to open a URI connection to the system identifier.

If a character stream wasn't provided, the SAX parser will use the byte stream in preference to opening a URI connection to the system identifier.

If the application knows the character encoding of the object pointed to by the system identifier, it can register the encoding using the setEncoding() method. This method has no effect when the application provides a character stream. The encoding must be a string acceptable for an XML encoding declaration.

```
public void setPublicId(String publicId)
public String getPublicId()
public void setSystemId(String systemId)
public String getSystemId()
public void setByteStream(java.io.InputStream byteStream)
public java.io.InputStream getByteStream()
public void setEncoding(String encoding)
public String getEncoding()
public void setCharacterStream(java.io.Reader characterStream)
public java.io.Reader getCharacterStream()
```

Parameters

Parameter	Type	Description
`publicId`	`String`	The public identifier as a string
`systemId`	`String`	The system identifier as a string
`byteStream`	`java.io.InputStream`	A byte stream containing an XML document or other entity
`encoding`	`String`	A string describing the character encoding
`characterStream`	`java.io.Reader`	The character stream containing the XML document or other entity

Returned Values

Method	Return	Description
`getPublicId()`	`String`	The public identifier, or `null` if none was supplied
`getSystemId()`	`String`	The system identifier, or `null` if none was supplied
`getByteStream()`	`java.io.InputStream`	The byte stream, or `null` if none was supplied
`getEncoding()`	`String`	The encoding, or `null` if none was supplied
`getCharacterStream()`	`java.io.Reader`	The character stream, or `null` if none was supplied

Example: Using org.xml.sax.InputSource

This class provides utilities (static methods) that create or use an `org.xml.sax.InputSource`. The `getResource()` method is used by our `ClasspathEntityResolver` and the `getContent()` utility method is used by `XMLReaderSample`.

Source InputSourceUtils.java

```java
import org.xml.sax.InputSource;

import java.io.BufferedReader;
import java.io.File;
import java.io.FileInputStream;
import java.io.InputStream;
import java.io.InputStreamReader;
```

This class provides utilities (static methods) that create or use an
`org.xml.sax.InputSource`. The `getResource()` method is used by our
`ClasspathEntityResolver` and the `getContent()` utility method is used by
`XMLReaderSample`.

Source InputSourceUtils.java

```java
import org.xml.sax.InputSource;

import java.io.BufferedReader;
import java.io.File;
import java.io.FileInputStream;
import java.io.InputStream;
import java.io.InputStreamReader;
import java.io.IOException;
import java.io.Reader;
import java.net.URL;
import java.net.MalformedURLException;

public class InputSourceUtils {
```

The `getResource()` method creates an input source from a CLASSPATH resource. It uses the
`getResourceAsStream()` method of `java.lang.Class` to get the input stream of the
resource whose name is given as parameter. It returns `null` if the resource isn't found. The
resource's name is expected to follow the conventions used for class names, but it should end
with a file extension such as `.xml` or `.dtd`. (This is a possible example:
`com.company.app.config_file.xml`). We replace all dots with slashes, except the last
one. This format is required by the `getResourceAsStream()` method. We also add a slash at
the beginning of the resource's name so that it can be interpreted as an absolute name. Without
this first slash, the name would be relative to the directory of our `InputSourceUtils` class. A
solution to this issue would be to pass to our `getResource()` method a `java.lang.Class`
instance that should be used instead of `InputSourceUtils.class` when we call
`getResourceAsStream()`. The use of absolute names is less error prone, however.

```java
public static InputSource getResource(String name) {
    int dotIndex = name.lastIndexOf(".");
    name = name.replace('.', '/');
    if (dotIndex != -1) {
        name = name.substring(0, dotIndex) + '.'
                + name.substring(dotIndex + 1);
    }
    name = "/" + name;
    InputStream stream
        = InputSourceUtils.class.getResourceAsStream(name);
    if (stream != null) {
        return new InputSource(stream);
    } else {
        return null;
    }
}
```

The getContent() method returns the content of an input source. It implements the loading strategy used by SAX parsers. It first tries to use the character stream of the input source. If this is not available, it attempts to use the byte stream. If both streams are null, the method will try to open a URL connection using the system identifier of the input source, or to open this resource as a file.

If a character encoding is available, this method uses it to wrap the byte stream with a character stream. Before that, however, the encoding's standard name is replaced with a Java-specific name, that is, ASCII / UTF8 / Unicode / ISO8859_* instead of US-ASCII / UTF-8 / UTF-16 / ISO-8859-*. The default character encoding is UTF8.

The input source's content is read in a loop, collected in a string buffer and returned as a string. This method returns null if it cannot get the stream. It may also throw an IOException if an input error occurs.

```java
public static String getContent(InputSource source) throws
        IOException {
    Reader reader = source.getCharacterStream();
    if (reader == null) {
        InputStream stream = source.getByteStream();
        if (stream == null) {
            String systemId = source.getSystemId();
            if (systemId != null) {
                try {
                    stream = new URL(systemId).openStream();
                } catch (MalformedURLException e) {
                    File file = new File(systemId);
                    if (file.exists()) {
                        stream = new FileInputStream(file);
                    } else {
                        throw new IOException(e.toString());
                    }
                }
            }
        }
        if (stream != null) {
            String encoding = source.getEncoding();
            if (encoding == null) {
                encoding = "UTF8";
            } else {
                if (encoding.equalsIgnoreCase("US-ASCII")) {
                    encoding = "ASCII";
                } else if (encoding.equalsIgnoreCase("UTF-8")) {
                    encoding = "UTF8";
                } else if (encoding.equalsIgnoreCase("UTF-16")) {
                    encoding = "Unicode";
                } else if (encoding.startsWith("ISO-8859-")) {
                    encoding = "ISO8859_"
                        + encoding.substring("ISO-8859-".length());
                }
```

```
        }
        reader = new InputStreamReader(stream, encoding);
      }
    }
    if (reader != null) {
      StringBuffer buf = new StringBuffer();
      try {
        if (!(reader instanceof BufferedReader)) {
          reader = new BufferedReader(reader);
        }
        int ch;
        while ((ch = reader.read()) != -1) {
          buf.append((char) ch);
        }
      }
      finally {
        reader.close();
      }
      return buf.toString();
    }
    return null;
  }
}
```

Interface Locator

org.xml.sax

public interface Locator

If a SAX parser provides location information to the SAX application, it does so by implementing this interface and then passing an instance to the application using the content handler's setDocumentLocator() method. The application can use the object to obtain the location of any other content handler event in the XML source document.

Note that the results returned by the object will be valid only during the scope of each content handler method. The application will receive unpredictable results if it attempts to use the locator at any other time.

SAX parsers are not required to supply a locator, but they are very strongly encouraged to do so. If the parser supplies a locator, it does so before reporting any other document events. If no locator has been set by the time the application receives the startDocument() event, the application should assume that a locator is not available.

Methods

The methods allow the getting of four different properties

- ❏ A public identifier
- ❏ A system identifier
- ❏ A line number
- ❏ A column number

The public and system identifiers tell us the document entity or the external parsed entity in which the markup triggering the event appears.

The line and column numbers are intended only as an approximation for the sake of error reporting. They are not intended to provide sufficient information to edit the character content of the original XML document.

If possible, the SAX parser provides the position of the first character after the text associated with the document event. The first line in the document is line 1 and the first column in each line is column 1.

```
public String getPublicId()
public String getSystemId()
public int getLineNumber()
public int getColumnNumber()
```

Returned Values

Method	Return	Description
getPublicId()	String	A string containing the public identifier, or null if none is available
getSystemId()	String	A string containing the system identifier, or null if none is available
getLineNumber()	int	The line number, or -1 if none is available
getColumnNumber()	int	The column number, or -1 if none is available

Exception SAXException
org.xml.sax

```
public class SAXException
        extends java.lang.Exception
```

This class can contain basic error or warning information from either the XML parser or the application. Application writers can subclass it to provide additional functionality. SAX handlers may throw this exception or any exception subclassed from it.

If the application needs to pass through other types of exceptions, it must wrap those exceptions in a SAXException or an exception derived from a SAXException.

If the application needs to include information about a specific location in an XML document, it should use the SAXParseException subclass.

Constructors

The SAXException instances have a message like any other exception, but they can also wrap an existing exception.

```
public SAXException(String message)
public SAXException(Exception e)
public SAXException(String message, Exception e)
```

Parameters

Parameter	Type	Description
message	String	The error or warning message
e	Exception	The exception to be wrapped in a SAXException

Methods

If there is an embedded exception, and if the SAXException has no detail message of its own, the getMessage() method will return the detail message from the embedded exception. The getException() method returns the embedded exception, if any.

```
public String getMessage()
public Exception getException()
public String toString()
```

Returned Values

Method	Return	Description
getMessage()	String	The error or warning message
getException()	Exception	The embedded exception, or null if there is none
toString()	String	A string representation of this exception

Exception SAXParseException

org.xml.sax

```
public class SAXParseException

        extends SAXException
```

This exception will include information for locating the error in the original XML document. Note that, although the application will receive a SAXParseException as the argument to the handlers in the ErrorHandler interface, the application is not actually required to throw the exception. Instead, it can simply read the information in it and take a different action.

Constructors

The SAXParseException instances have a message like any other exception, they can wrap an existing exception like SAXException, but they can also contain information about the location where the parsing error occurred. This information (public ID, system ID, line and column) can be passed as String and int parameters or it can be grouped by a Locator instance.

```
public SAXParseException(String message, Locator locator)
public SAXParseException(String message, Locator locator, Exception e)
public SAXParseException(String message, String publicId,
                        String systemId, int lineNumber,
                        int columnNumber)
public SAXParseException(String message, String publicId,
                        String systemId, int lineNumber,
                        int columnNumber, Exception e)
```

Parameters

Parameter	Type	Description
message	String	The error or warning message
locator	Locator	The locator object for the error or warning (may be null)
e	Exception	Another exception to embed in this one
publicId	String	The public identifier of the entity that generated the error or warning

Parameter	Type	Description
systemId	String	The system identifier of the entity that generated the error or warning
lineNumber	int	The line number of the end of the text that caused the error or warning
columnNumber	int	The column number of the end of the text that caused the error or warning

Methods

The information describing the location where the parsing error occurred can be obtained with the get methods.

```
public String getPublicId()
public String getSystemId()
public int getLineNumber()
public int getColumnNumber()
```

Returned Values

Method	Return	Description
getPublicId()	String	A string containing the public identifier, or null if none is available
getSystemId()	String	A string containing the system identifier, or null if none is available
getLineNumber()	int	An integer representing the line number, or -1 if none is available
getColumnNumber()	int	An integer representing the column number, or -1 if none is available

Interface ErrorHandler
org.xml.sax

```
public interface ErrorHandler
```

If a SAX application needs to implement customized error handling, it must implement this interface and then register an instance with the XMLReader using the setErrorHandler() method. The SAX parser will then report all errors and warnings through this interface.

If an application does not register an `ErrorHandler`, XML parsing errors will go unreported and bizarre behavior may result.

For XML processing errors, a SAX parser must use this interface instead of throwing an exception. It is up to the application to decide whether to throw an exception for different types of errors and warnings. Note, however, that there is no requirement that the parser continue to provide useful information after a call to `fatalError()` (in other words, a SAX parser class could catch an exception and report a `fatalError()`).

Methods

The `warning()` method receives notification of a warning. SAX parsers will use this method to report conditions that are not errors or fatal errors as defined by the XML 1.0 Recommendation. The default behavior is to take no action. The SAX parser will continue to provide normal parsing events after invoking this method, therefore it will still be possible for the application to process the document through to the end.

The `error()` method receives notification of a recoverable error. This corresponds to the definition of "error" of the W3C XML 1.0 Recommendation. For example, a validating parser would use this callback to report the violation of a validity constraint. The default behavior is to take no action. The SAX parser will continue to provide normal parsing events after invoking this method and it will still be possible for the application to process the document through to the end.

The `fatalError()` method receives notification of a non-recoverable error. This corresponds to the definition of "fatal error" of the W3C XML 1.0 Recommendation. For example, a parser would use this callback to report the violation of a well-formedness constraint. The application must assume that the document is unusable after the parser has invoked this method, and should continue (if at all) only for the sake of collecting additional error messages. SAX parsers are free to stop reporting any other events once this method has been invoked.

```
public void warning(SAXParseException exception)
       throws SAXException
public void error(SAXParseException exception)
       throws SAXException
public void fatalError(SAXParseException exception)
       throws SAXException
```

Parameters

Parameter	Type	Description
exception	SAXParseException	The error or warning information encapsulated in a SAX parse exception

Example: Implementing org.xml.sax.ErrorHandler

This error handler prints the messages to the standard error stream. It is used by several examples of this chapter: `DeclHandlerSample`, `LexicalHandlerSample`, and `XMLReaderSample` (see pages **112**, **118**, and **94**).

Source PrintErrorHandler.java

```java
import org.xml.sax.ErrorHandler;
import org.xml.sax.SAXException;
import org.xml.sax.SAXParseException;

public class PrintErrorHandler implements ErrorHandler {
```

The `warning()` method prints a warning message.

```java
public void warning(SAXParseException e)
        throws SAXException {
  System.err.print("WARNING: ");
  printLocation(e);
  printMessage(e);
}
```

The `error()` method prints information about a parsing error.

```java
public void error(SAXParseException e)
        throws SAXException {
  System.err.print("ERROR: ");
  printLocation(e);
  printStackTrace(e);
}
```

The `fatalError()` method prints information about a fatal parsing error and throws the exception.

```java
public void fatalError(SAXParseException e)
        throws SAXException {
  System.err.print("FATAL ERROR: ");
  printLocation(e);
  printStackTrace(e);
  throw e;
}
```

The `printLocation()` method prints the location of the error.

```java
private void printLocation(SAXParseException e) {
    if (e.getPublicId() != null) {
```

```
        System.err.print(e.getPublicId() + " ");
      }
      if (e.getSystemId() != null) {
        System.err.print(e.getSystemId() + " ");
      }
      if (e.getLineNumber() != -1) {
        System.err.print("line " + e.getLineNumber() + " ");
      }
      if (e.getColumnNumber() != -1) {
        System.err.print("column " + e.getColumnNumber() + " ");
      }
      System.err.println();
    }
```

The printMessage() method prints the message of the given exception.

```
    private void printMessage(SAXException e) {
      if (e.getMessage() != null) {
        System.err.println(e.getMessage());
      }
    }
```

The printStackTrace() method prints the stack trace of the given exception and its nested exceptions.

```
    private void printStackTrace(SAXException e) {
      Exception ex = e;
      while (ex != null) {
        ex.printStackTrace();
        if (ex instanceof SAXException) {
          ex = ((SAXException) ex).getException();
        }
      }
    }
  }
```

Interface Attributes

org.xml.sax

public interface Attributes

This interface allows access to a list of attributes by

- Attribute index
- Namespace URI plus local name
- Qualified (prefixed) name

Access by namespace URI plus local name may not be available if the `http://xml.org/sax/features/namespaces` feature is `false`. The default value of this feature is `true`.

If the `http://xml.org/sax/features/namespace-prefixes` feature is `false` then access by qualified name may not be available. The default value of this feature is `false`.

The list will not contain attributes that were declared `#IMPLIED` but not specified in the start tag. It will also not contain attributes used as namespace declarations (`xmlns*`) unless the `namespace-prefixes` feature is set to `true`.

The order of attributes in the list is unspecified, and will vary from implementation to implementation. So, don't rely on indices to get the value of a particular attribute. Use the name of the attribute instead.

This interface replaces the (now deprecated) SAX 1.0 `AttributeList` interface, which does not contain namespace support.

Methods

Attribute information can be accessed by name or by index. Each attribute can have

- ❏ Namespace URI
- ❏ Local name
- ❏ Qualified name
- ❏ Value
- ❏ Type

The attribute type is one of the strings `CDATA_ID_IDREF_IDREFS_NMTOKEN_NMTOKENS_ENTITY_ENTITIEs_ NOTATION` (always in upper case). If the parser has not read a declaration for the attribute, or if the parser does not report attribute types, then it will return `CDATA`. For an enumerated attribute that is not a notation, the parser will report the type as `NMTOKEN`.

The attribute value is always a string. If the attribute value is a list of tokens (`IDREFS`, `ENTITIES`, or `NMTOKENS`), the tokens will be concatenated into a single string separated by whitespace.

```
public int getLength()
public String getURI(int index)
public String getLocalName(int index)
public String getQName(int index)
public String getType(int index)
public String getType(String uri, String localName)
public String getType(String qName)
public String getValue(int index)
```

```
public String getValue(String uri, String localName)
public String getValue(String qName)
public int getIndex(String uri, String localName)
public int getIndex(String qName)
```

Parameters

Parameter	Type	Description
index	int	The attribute index (zero-based)
uri	String	The namespace URI, or the empty string if the name has no namespace URI
localName	String	The local name of the attribute
qName	String	The qualified (prefixed) name

Returned Values

Method	Return	Description
getLength()	int	The number of attributes in the list
getURI()	String	The namespace URI, or the empty string if none is available, or null if the index is out of range
getLocalName()	String	The local name, or the empty string if namespace processing is not being performed, or null if the index is out of range
getQName()	String	The XML 1.0 qualified name, or the empty string if none is available, or null if the index is out of range
getType()	String	The attribute's type as a string, or null if the index is out of range or if the named attribute is not in the list
getValue()	String	The attribute's value as a string, or null if the index is out of range or if the named attribute is not in the list
getIndex()	int	The index of the attribute, or -1 if it does not appear in the list

Example: Using org.xml.sax.Attributes

This class provides utilities (static methods) for SAX attribute lists. It is used by
`SmartContentHandler`.

Source AttributesUtils.java

```
import org.xml.sax.Attributes;

public class AttributesUtils {
```

The `getValues()` method returns the values of the attributes whose names are specified. It accepts both local and qualified names. It first tries to get the value of an attribute by passing its name to the `getValue()` method of the `Attributes` instance, which accepts a qualified name according to the SAX specification. This will also work if you don't use namespace prefixes for attributes.

If the `getValue(names[i])` call returns `null` and the attribute name doesn't contain the `':'` character, the method iterates over the attributes and compares `names[i]` with the local name of each attribute until they match or the list of attributes ends.

This method returns the obtained attribute values as a string array. Note that some of the elements may be `null`.

```
public static String[] getValues(Attributes attrs,
        String names[]) {
    if (attrs == null || names == null) {
        return null;
    }
    String values[] = new String[names.length];
    for (int i = 0; i < values.length; i++) {
        values[i] = attrs.getValue(names[i]);
        if (values[i] == null && names[i].indexOf(':') == -1) {
            int n = attrs.getLength();
            for (int j = 0; j < n; j++) {
                if (attrs.getLocalName(j).equals(names[i])) {
                    values[i] = attrs.getValue(j);
                    break;
                }
            }
        }
    }
    return values;
}
```

The `convertValues()` method converts an array of strings to an array of primitive wrapper objects (such as `Byte`, `Short`, `Integer`). The types are specified as a list of `Class` objects. `NumberFormatException` may occur and it isn't caught.

```
    public static Object[] convertValues(String values[],
            Class types[]) throws NumberFormatException {
        if (values == null || types == null) {
            return null;
        }
        int n = values.length;
        Object wrappers[] = new Object[n];
        for (int i = 0; i < n; i++) {
            if (values[i] == null) {
                continue;
            }
            if (types[i] == String.class) {
                wrappers[i] = values[i];
            } else if (types[i] == byte.class) {
                wrappers[i] = new Byte(values[i]);
            } else if (types[i] == short.class) {
                wrappers[i] = new Short(values[i]);
            } else if (types[i] == int.class) {
                wrappers[i] = new Integer(values[i]);
            } else if (types[i] == long.class) {
                wrappers[i] = new Long(values[i]);
            } else if (types[i] == float.class) {
                wrappers[i] = new Float(values[i]);
            } else if (types[i] == double.class) {
                wrappers[i] = new Double(values[i]);
            } else if (types[i] == boolean.class) {
                wrappers[i] = new Boolean(values[i]);
            } else if (types[i] == char.class
                    && values.length > 0) {
                wrappers[i] = new Character(values[i].charAt(0));
            }
        }
        return wrappers;
    }
}
```

Interface AttributeList

org.xml.sax

public interface AttributeList

This is the original SAX 1.0 interface for reporting an element's attributes. Unlike the new Attributes interface, it does not support namespace-related information.

When an attribute list is supplied as part of a startElement() event, the list will return valid results only during the scope of the event. Once the event handler returns the control to the parser, the attribute list is invalid. To save a persistent copy of the attribute list, we can use the SAX 1.0 AttributeListImpl helper class.

An attribute list includes only attributes that have been specified or defaulted, that is, #IMPLIED attributes will not be included.

The SAX parser may provide attributes in any arbitrary order, regardless of the order in which they were declared or specified. So, don't rely on indices to get the value of a particular attribute, use the name of the attribute instead.

Methods

The attribute information can be accessed by name or by index. Each attribute has a value and a type.

The attribute type is one of the strings CDATA, ID, IDREF, IDREFS, NMTOKEN, NMTOKENS, ENTITY, ENTITIES, or NOTATION (always in upper case). If the parser has not read a declaration for the attribute, or if the parser does not report attribute types, then it will return CDATA. For an enumerated attribute that is not a notation, the parser will report the type as NMTOKEN.

The attribute value is always a string. If the attribute value is a list of tokens (IDREFS, ENTITIES, or NMTOKENS), the tokens will be concatenated into a single string separated by whitespace.

```
public int getLength()
public String getName(int i)
public String getType(int i)
public String getType(String name)
public String getValue(int i)
public String getValue(String name)
```

Parameters

Parameter	Type	Description
i	int	The index of the attribute in the list (starting at zero)
name	String	The name of the attribute

Returned Values

Method	Return	Description
getLength()	int	The number of attributes in the list
getName()	String	The name of the indexed attribute, or null if the index is out of range
getType()	String	The attribute type as a string, or null if the index is out of range or if the attribute is not in the list
getValue()	String	The attribute value as a string, or null if the index is out of range or if the attribute is not in the list

Interface ContentHandler
org.xml.sax

public interface ContentHandler

If the application needs to be informed of basic parsing events, it implements this interface and registers an instance with the SAX parser using the setContentHandler() method. The parser uses the instance to report basic document-related events like the start and end of elements and character data.

The order of events in this interface mirrors the order of information in the document itself. For example, all of an element's content (character data, processing instructions, and/or sub-elements) will appear, in order, between the startElement() event and the corresponding endElement() event.

This interface is similar to the deprecated SAX 1.0 DocumentHandler interface, but it now has support for namespaces and for reporting skipped entities (in non-validating XML processors).

Method setDocumentLocator()

The setDocumentLocator() method receives an object that can be used to obtain location information about the SAX events that will occur during the parsing of the document.

SAX parsers are strongly encouraged (though not absolutely required) to supply a locator. If it does so, the parser supplies the locator to the application by invoking this method before invoking any of the other methods in the ContentHandler interface.

The locator allows the application to determine the end position within the document of any parsing event. Typically, the application will use this information for reporting its own errors (such as character content that does not match an application's business rules). The information returned by the locator is probably not sufficient for use with a search engine.

Note that the locator will return correct information only during the invocation of the events in this interface. The application should not attempt to use it at any other time.

public void **setDocumentLocator**(Locator locator)

Parameters

Parameter	Type	Description
locator	Locator	An object that can return the location of any SAX document event

Methods startDocument() and endDocument()

The startDocument() method receives notification of the beginning of a document. The SAX parser will invoke this method only once, before any other methods in this interface or in DTDHandler (except for setDocumentLocator()).

The endDocument() method receives notification of the end of a document. The SAX parser will invoke this method only once, and it will be the last method invoked during the parse. The parser shall not invoke this method until it has either abandoned parsing (because of an unrecoverable error) or reached the end of input.

```
public void startDocument()
        throws SAXException
```
```
public void endDocument()
        throws SAXException
```

Methods startPrefixMapping() and endPrefixMapping()

The startPrefixMapping() method begins the scope of a prefix- namespace URI mapping. The endPrefixMapping() method ends the scope of a prefix- namespace URI mapping.

The information from this event is not necessary for normal namespace processing. There are cases, however, when applications need to use prefixes in character data or in attribute values, where they cannot safely be expanded automatically. The startPrefixMapping() and endPrefixMapping() events supply the information for expanding prefixes in those contexts themselves, if necessary.

Note that startPrefixMapping() and endPrefixMapping() events are not guaranteed to be properly nested relative to each other. All startPrefixMapping() events will occur before the corresponding startElement() event, and all endPrefixMapping() events will occur after the corresponding endElement() event, but their order is not otherwise guaranteed.

```
public void startPrefixMapping(String prefix, String uri)
        throws SAXException
```
```
public void endPrefixMapping(String prefix)
        throws SAXException
```

Parameters

Parameter	Type	Description
prefix	String	The namespace prefix
uri	String	The namespace URI the prefix is mapped to

Methods startElement() and endElement()

The startElement() method receives notification of the beginning of an element. The parser will invoke this method at the beginning of every element in the XML document. There will be a corresponding endElement() event for every startElement() event (even when the element is empty). All of the element's content will be reported, in order, before the endElement() event.

This event allows up to three name components for each element

- ❑ Namespace URI
- ❑ Local name
- ❑ Qualified (prefixed) name

Any or all of these may be provided, depending on the values of the
`http://xml.org/sax/features/namespaces` and the
`http://xml.org/sax/features/namespace-prefixes` properties:

❑ The namespace URI and local name are required when the `namespaces` property is `true` (the default), and are optional when the `namespaces` property is `false` (if one is specified, both must be)

❑ The qualified name is required when the `namespace-prefixes` property is `true`, and is optional when the `namespace-prefixes` property is `false` (the default)

Note that the attribute list provided will contain only attributes with explicit values (specified or defaulted). Implied attributes will be omitted. The attribute list will contain attributes used for namespace declarations (`xmlns*` attributes) only if the
`http://xml.org/sax/features/namespace-prefixes` property is `true` (it is `false` by default, and support for a `true` value is optional).

```
public void startElement(String uri, String localName,
                         String qName, Attributes atts)
       throws SAXException
public void endElement(String uri, String localName, String qName)
       throws SAXException
```

Parameters

Parameter	Type	Description
uri	String	The namespace URI, or the empty string if the element has no namespace URI or if namespace processing is not being performed
localName	String	The local name (without prefix), or the empty string if namespace processing is not being performed
qName	String	The qualified name (with prefix), or the empty string if qualified names are not available
atts	Attributes	The attributes attached to the element. If there are no attributes, it shall be an empty `Attributes` object

Methods characters() and ignorableWhitespace()

The `characters()` method receives notification of character data. The parser will call this method to report each chunk of character data. SAX parsers may return all contiguous character data in a single chunk, or they may split it into several chunks. However, all of the characters in any single event come from the same external entity so that the `Locator` provides useful information.

Note that some parsers will report whitespace in element content using the `ignorableWhitespace()` method rather than this one (validating parsers do so).

The `ignorableWhitespace()` method receives notification of ignorable whitespace in element content. Validating parsers use this method to report each chunk of whitespace in element content. Non-validating parsers may also use this method if they are capable of parsing and using content models.

```
public void characters(char[] ch, int start, int length)
        throws SAXException
public void ignorableWhitespace(char[] ch, int start, int length)
        throws SAXException
```

Parameters

Parameter	Type	Description
ch	char[]	The characters from the XML document
start	int	The start position in the array
length	int	The number of characters to read from the array

Method processingInstruction()

The `processingInstruction()` method receives notification of a processing instruction (see Chapter 1). The parser will invoke this method once for each processing instruction found. Note that processing instructions may occur before or after the main document element.

```
public void processingInstruction(String target, String data)
        throws SAXException
```

Parameters

Parameter	Type	Description
target	String	The processing instruction target
data	String	The processing instruction data, or null if none was supplied. The data does not include any whitespace separating it from the target.

Method skippedEntity()

The `skippedEntity()` method receives notification of a skipped entity. The parser will invoke this method once for each entity skipped. Non-validating processors may skip entities if they have not seen the declarations (because, for example, the entity was declared in an external DTD subset). All processors may skip external entities, depending on the values of the `http://xml.org/sax/features/external-general-entities` and the `http://xml.org/sax/features/external-parameter-entities` properties.

```
public void skippedEntity(String name)
        throws SAXException
```

Parameters

Parameter	Type	Description
name	String	The name of the skipped entity. If it is a parameter entity, the name will begin with %, and if it is the external DTD subset, it will be the string "[dtd]".

Example: Implementing org.xml.sax.ContentHandler

This class implements the `org.xml.sax.ContentHandler` interface and dispatches the parsing events to methods that must be implemented by subclasses. This is an "XML element to Java method" mapping mechanism.

For each element type, there must be a method named as the element and suffixed by `Element`, which accepts the values of the attributes as parameters. If the element contains data, there must also be a method suffixed by `Data` that takes the character data of the element as a string parameter. An optional method suffixed by `ElementEnd` would be called when the parser meets the end tag of an element.

For example, an element like this:

```
<invoice number="1234567" month="2" day="20" year="2000">
```

could be mapped to the following method:

```
public void invoiceElement(int number,byte month,
                        byte day, short year) {
...
}
```

The data of a processing instruction is passed to a method whose name starts with the target string and is suffixed by `Proc`.

For example, a processing instruction like this:

```
<?total some data?>
```

could be mapped to the following method:

```
public void totalProc(String data) {
...
}
```

All these methods must be public. XMLReaderSample uses this class and implements the methods for handling element attributes, character data and a processing instruction.

Source SmartContentHandler.java

```
import org.xml.sax.Attributes;
import org.xml.sax.ContentHandler;
import org.xml.sax.Locator;
import org.xml.sax.SAXException;

import java.lang.reflect.InvocationTargetException;
import java.lang.reflect.Method;
import java.util.Hashtable;
import java.util.Stack;

public abstract class SmartContentHandler implements
        ContentHandler {

    protected Locator documentLocator;
    protected Hashtable prefixMappings;
    protected Stack namespaceURIStack;
    protected Stack localNameStack;
    protected Stack qualifiedNameStack;
```

Subclasses must override the getAttributeNames() method to return the list of attribute names of the element type associated with the given method. This information could have been collected using the optional org.xml.sax.ext.DeclHandler interface. This solution wouldn't work, however, with XML formats that don't define a DTD containing ATTLIST declarations, because the DTD contains the declarations of the attribute lists, therefore, no DTD means no ATTLIST declarations.

```
    protected abstract String[] getAttributeNames(
            String methodName);
```

The getParameterTypes() method returns the types of the parameters of a given method. It gets an array of all public methods of this class using getClass().getMethods(), then it iterates over the elements of this array and returns the first method whose name matches the value of the parameter. Subclasses could override this method to make this process more efficient.

```
    protected Class[] getParameterTypes(String methodName) {
        Method methods[] = getClass().getMethods();
        for (int i = 0; i < methods.length; i++) {
            if (methods[i].getName().equals(methodName)) {
                return methods[i].getParameterTypes();
            }
        }
        return null;
    }
```

The invokeMethod() method invokes a given method whose name is given as first parameter. The second parameter can be a string or an org.xml.sax.Attributes instance; it can also be null.

If param is an Attributes instance, invokeMethod() calls getParameterTypes() to get the types of the parameters of the method that will be invoked. It then calls getAttributeNames() to get the names of the attributes of the element associated with that method. The values of the attributes are obtained with AttributesUtils.getValues() and AttributesUtils.convertValues() is used to convert the parameter types.

The method that must be invoked is obtained with getClass().getMethod(name, parameterTypes). This is actually a java.lang.reflect.Method object. We use it to invoke the method with the given name on this object. The call:

```
method.invoke(this, parameterValues)
```

is the equivalent of:

```
"name".(parameterValues[0], parameterValues[1], ...)
```

We use this mechanism for two reasons. First, the name of the invoked method and its list of parameters aren't known by this class. Second, this is a general mechanism for mapping parsing events to method calls.

For more information, see the Reflection Specification included within the JDK documentation, java.lang.Class and the java.lang.reflect package.

```java
protected Object invokeMethod(String name,
            Object param) throws SAXException {
  Class parameterTypes[] = null;
  Object parameterValues[] = null;
  if (param instanceof String) {
    parameterTypes = new Class[] {
      String.class
    };
    parameterValues = new Object[] {
      (String) param
    };
  } else if (param instanceof Attributes) {
    parameterTypes = getParameterTypes(name);
    String attributeNames[] = getAttributeNames(name);
    String stringValues[] = AttributesUtils.getValues
            ((Attributes) param, attributeNames);
    parameterValues = AttributesUtils.convertValues
            (stringValues, parameterTypes);
  } else if (param == null) {
    parameterTypes = new Class[0];
    parameterValues = new Object[0];
  }

  if (parameterTypes == null || parameterValues == null) {
    System.err.println("Method not supported: " + name);
    return null;
```

```
    }

        try {
          Method method = getClass().getMethod(name,
                parameterTypes);
          return method.invoke(this, parameterValues);
        } catch (InvocationTargetException e) {
          Throwable t = e.getTargetException();
          if (t instanceof Exception) {
            throw new SAXException((Exception) t);
          } else {
            throw new SAXException(t.toString());
          }
        } catch (NoSuchMethodException e) {
          if (param != null) {
            System.err.println("Method not found or not public: "
                + name);
          }
          return null;
        } catch (Exception e) {
          throw new SAXException(e);
        }
    }
```

The setDocumentLocator() method receives the document's locator and saves its reference to an instance variable.

```
    public void setDocumentLocator(Locator locator) {
      documentLocator = locator;
    }
```

The startDocument() method receives notification of the beginning of a document. The collection objects of this class are created.

```
    public void startDocument() throws SAXException {
      prefixMappings = new Hashtable();
      namespaceURIStack = new Stack();
      localNameStack = new Stack();
      qualifiedNameStack = new Stack();
    }
```

The endDocument() method receives notification of the end of a document. The collection objects of this class are freed so that the garbage collector can dispose them. We actually call System.gc() in order to request this.

```
    public void endDocument() throws SAXException {
      prefixMappings = null;
      namespaceURIStack = null;
      localNameStack = null;
      qualifiedNameStack = null;
```

```
System.gc();
  }
```

The `startPrefixMapping()` method begins the scope of a prefix-URI namespace mapping. The mapping is saved to a hashtable.

```
public void startPrefixMapping(String prefix,
      String uri) throws SAXException {
  prefixMappings.put(prefix, uri);
}
```

The `endPrefixMapping()` method ends the scope of a prefix-URI mapping. The mapping is removed from the hashtable.

```
public void endPrefixMapping(String prefix) throws
      SAXException {
  prefixMappings.remove(prefix);
}
```

The `startElement()` method receives notification of the beginning of an element. The namespace URI, local name and qualified name are pushed to their stacks. The method associated with this element is invoked.

```
public void startElement(String uri, String localName,
      String qName, Attributes atts) throws SAXException {
  namespaceURIStack.push(uri);
  localNameStack.push(localName);
  qualifiedNameStack.push(qName);
  invokeMethod(localName + "Element", atts);
}
```

The `endElement()` method receives notification of the end of an element. The namespace URI, local name and qualified name are removed from their stacks. The method associated with this element's end, if any, is invoked.

```
public void endElement(String uri, String localName,
      String qName) throws SAXException {
  invokeMethod(localName + "ElementEnd", null);
  namespaceURIStack.pop();
  localNameStack.pop();
  qualifiedNameStack.pop();
}
```

The `characters()` method receives notification of character data. The method associated with this element's data is invoked.

```
public void characters(char ch[], int start,
      int length) throws SAXException {
  String localName = (String) localNameStack.peek();
```

```
        String data = new String(ch, start, length);
            invokeMethod(localName + "Data", data);
        }
```

The `ignorableWhitespace()` method receives notification of ignorable whitespace.

```
        public void ignorableWhitespace(char ch[], int start,
                int length) throws SAXException {}
```

The `processingInstruction()` method receives notification of a processing instruction. The method associated with this processing instruction is invoked.

```
        public void processingInstruction(String target,
                String data) throws SAXException {
            invokeMethod(target + "Proc", data);
        }
```

The `skippedEntity()` method receives notification of a skipped entity. A warning message is printed.

```
        public void skippedEntity(String name) throws SAXException {
            System.err.println("Skipped Entity: " + name);
        }
    }
```

Deprecated Interface DocumentHandler

org.xml.sax

`public interface` `DocumentHandler`

This was the main event-handling interface for SAX 1.0. In SAX 2.0, it has been replaced by `ContentHandler`, which provides namespace support and reporting of skipped entities. This interface is included in SAX 2.0 only to support legacy SAX 1.0 applications.

The order of events in this interface mirrors the order of information in the document itself. For example, all of an element's content (character data, processing instructions, and/or sub-elements) will appear, in order, between the `startElement()` event and the corresponding `endElement()` event.

Application writers who do not want to implement the entire interface can derive a class from `HandlerBase`, which implements the default functionality.

Method setDocumentLocator()

The `setDocumentLocator()` method receives an object for locating the origin of SAX events. SAX parsers are strongly encouraged (though not absolutely required) to supply a locator. If it does so, the parser supplies the locator to the application by invoking this method before invoking any of the other methods in the `DocumentHandler` interface.

The locator allows the application to determine the end position of any document-related event, even if the parser is not reporting an error. Typically, the application will use this information for reporting its own errors (such as character content that does not match an application's business rules). The information returned by the locator is probably not sufficient for use with a search engine.

Note that the locator will return correct information only during the invocation of the events in this interface. The application should not attempt to use it at any other time.

```
public void setDocumentLocator(Locator locator)
```

Parameters

Parameter	Type	Description
locator	Locator	An object that can return the location of any SAX document event

Methods startDocument() and endDocument()

The startDocument() method receives notification of the beginning of a document. The SAX parser will invoke this method only once, before any other methods in this interface or in DTDHandler (except for setDocumentLocator()).

The endDocument() method receives notification of the end of a document. The SAX parser will invoke this method only once, and it will be the last method invoked during the parse. The parser shall not invoke this method until it has either abandoned parsing (because of an unrecoverable error) or reached the end of input.

```
public void startDocument()
        throws SAXException
public void endDocument()
        throws SAXException
```

Methods startElement() and endElement()

The startElement() method receives notification of the beginning of an element. The parser will invoke this method at the beginning of every element in the XML document. There will be a corresponding endElement() event for every startElement() event (even when the element is empty). All of the element's content will be reported, in order, before the corresponding endElement() event.

If the element name has a namespace prefix, the prefix will still be attached. Note that the attribute list provided will contain only attributes with explicit values (specified or defaulted). Implied attributes will be omitted.

```
public void startElement(String name, AttributeList atts)
        throws SAXException
public void endElement(String name)
        throws SAXException
```

Parameters

Parameter	Type	Description
Name	String	The name of the element type
Atts	AttributeList	The attributes attached to the element, if any

Receiving Character Data

The characters() method receives notification of character data. The parser will call this method to report each chunk of character data. SAX parsers may return all contiguous character data in a single chunk, or they may split it into several chunks. However, all of the characters in any single event come from the same external entity, so that the Locator provides useful information.

Note that some parsers will report whitespace using the ignorableWhitespace() method rather than this one (validating parsers do so).

The ignorableWhitespace() method receives notification of ignorable whitespace in element content. Validating parsers use this method to report each chunk of ignorable whitespace. Non-validating parsers may also use this method if they are capable of parsing and using content models.

```
public void characters(char[] ch, int start, int length)
        throws SAXException
public void ignorableWhitespace(char[] ch, int start, int length)
        throws SAXException
```

Parameters

Parameter	Type	Description
ch	char[]	The characters from the XML document
start	int	The start position in the array
length	int	The number of characters to read from the array

Method processingInstruction()

The processingInstruction() method receives notification of a processing instruction. The parser will invoke this method once for each processing instruction found. Note that processing instructions may occur before or after the main document element.

```
public void processingInstruction(String target, String data)
        throws SAXException
```

Parameters

Parameter	Type	Description
target	String	The processing instruction's target
data	String	The processing instruction's data, or null if none was supplied

Interface DTDHandler
org.xml.sax

```
public interface DTDHandler
```

If a SAX application needs information about notations and unparsed entities, then the application implements this interface and registers an instance with the SAX parser using the parser's setDTDHandler() method. The parser uses the instance to report notation and unparsed entity declarations to the application.

Note that this interface includes only those DTD events that the XML recommendation requires processors to report: notation and unparsed entity declarations.

The SAX parser may report these events in any order, regardless of the order in which the notations and unparsed entities were declared. However, all DTD events are reported after the document handler's startDocument() event, and before the first startElement() event.

It is up to the application to store the information for future use (perhaps in a hashtable or object tree). If the application encounters attributes of type NOTATION, ENTITY, or ENTITIES, it can use the information that it obtained through this interface to find the entity and/or notation corresponding with the attribute value.

Methods

The notationDecl() method receives notification of a notation declaration event. At least one of publicId and systemId must be non-null. If a system identifier is present, and it is a URL, the SAX parser resolves it fully before passing it to the application through this event. There is no guarantee that the notation declaration will be reported before any unparsed entities that use it.

The unparsedEntityDecl() method receives notification of an unparsed entity declaration event. Note that the notation name corresponds to a notation reported by the notationDecl() event. If the system identifier is a URL, the parser must resolve it fully before passing it to the application.

```
public void notationDecl(String notationName, String publicId,
                         String systemId)
        throws SAXException
```

```
public void unparsedEntityDecl(String entityName, String publicId,
                               String systemId, String notationName)
        throws SAXException
```

Parameters

Parameter	Type	Description
notationName	String	The notation's name
entityName	String	The unparsed entity's name
publicId	String	The public identifier of the notation/entity, or null if none was given
systemId	String	The system identifier of the notation/entity, or null if none was given

Example: Implementing org.xml.sax.DTDHandler

This class collects the DTD information on the unparsed entities and notations into two hashtables. It implements the org.xml.sax.DTDHandler interface and is used by XMLReaderSample.

Source TableDTDHandler.java

```java
import org.xml.sax.DTDHandler;
import org.xml.sax.SAXException;

import java.util.Hashtable;

public class TableDTDHandler implements DTDHandler {

    private Hashtable notationTable;
    private Hashtable entityTable;
```

The TableDTDHandler() constructor creates the hashtables.

```java
    public TableDTDHandler() {
        notationTable = new Hashtable();
        entityTable = new Hashtable();
    }
```

The notationDecl() method receives notification of a notation declaration event. The information is saved into a hashtable.

```
public void notationDecl(String name, String publicId,
        String systemId) throws SAXException {
    notationTable.put(name, new String[] {
        publicId, systemId
    });
}
```

The `unparsedEntityDecl()` method receives notification of an unparsed entity declaration event. The information is saved into a hashtable.

```
public void unparsedEntityDecl(String name, String publicId,
        String systemId, String notationName)
        throws SAXException {
    entityTable.put(name, new String[] {
        publicId, systemId, notationName
    });
}
```

The `getNotation()` method returns the information on a notation.

```
public String[] getNotation(String name) {
    return (String[]) notationTable.get(name);
}
```

The `getUnparsedEntity()` method returns the information on an unparsed entity.

```
public String[] getUnparsedEntity(String name) {
    return (String[]) entityTable.get(name);
}
}
```

Exception SAXNotRecognizedException
org.xml.sax

```
public class SAXNotRecognizedException
        extends SAXException
```

An `XMLReader` will throw this exception when it finds an unrecognized feature or property identifier. SAX applications and extensions may use this class for other, similar purposes.

Constructor

The constructor creates a new exception with the given message.

```
public SAXNotRecognizedException(String message)
```

Parameters

Parameter	Type	Description
message	String	The text message of the exception

Exception SAXNotSupportedException

org.xml.sax

```
public class SAXNotSupportedException
        extends SAXException
```

The methods of the XMLReader interface will throw this exception when they recognize a feature or property identifier, but cannot perform the requested operation. Other SAX 2.0 applications and extensions may use this class for similar purposes.

Constructor

The constructor creates a new exception with the given message.

```
public SAXNotSupportedException(String message)
```

Parameters

Parameter	Type	Description
message	String	The text message of the exception

Interface XMLReader

org.xml.sax

```
public interface XMLReader
```

Despite its name, this interface does not extend the standard Java java.io.Reader interface, because reading XML is a fundamentally different activity than reading character data.

XMLReader is the interface that an XML parser's SAX 2.0 parser must implement. This interface allows an application to set and query features and properties in the parser, to register event handlers for document processing, and to initiate a document parse.

All SAX interfaces are assumed to be synchronous: the `parse()` methods must not return until parsing is complete, and readers must wait for an event-handler callback to return before reporting the next event.

This interface replaces the (now deprecated) SAX 1.0 `Parser` interface. The `XMLReader` interface contains two important enhancements over the old `Parser` interface: it adds a standard way to query and set features and properties and it adds namespace support, which is required for many higher-level XML standards.

Methods for Getting and Setting Features and Properties

The name of a feature or property can be any fully qualified URI. It is possible for an `XMLReader` to recognize a feature/property name but to be unable to return its value. This is especially true in the case of an adapter for a SAX 1.0 `Parser`, which has no way of knowing whether the underlying parser is performing validation or expanding external entities.

All XML readers are required to recognize the following feature names:

```
http://xml.org/sax/features/namespaces
http://xml.org/sax/features/namespace-prefixes
```

XML readers are not required to recognize any specific property names, though an initial core set is documented for SAX 2.0.

Some feature/property values may be available only in specific contexts, such as before, during, or after a parse.

This `setProperty()` method is also the standard mechanism for setting extended handlers, such as `org.xml.sax.ext.DeclHandler` or `org.xml.sax.ext.LexicalHandler`.

SAX 2.0 defines the following core features:

Feature	Name
namespaces	http://xml.org/sax/features/namespaces
namespace-prefixes	http://xml.org/sax/features/namespace-prefixes
string-interning	http://xml.org/sax/features/string-interning
validation	http://xml.org/sax/features/validation
external-general-entities	http://xml.org/sax/features/external-general-entities
external-parameter-entities	http://xml.org/sax/features/external-parameter-entities

All these features are read-only during the parsing and read-write while not parsing. The following table contains the meaning of the `true` and `false` states:

Feature	True	False
`namespaces`	Perform namespace processing	Optionally do not perform namespace processing (implies `namespace-prefixes`)
`namespace-prefixes`	Report the original prefixed names and attributes used for namespace declarations	Do not report attributes used for namespace declarations, and optionally do not report original prefixed names
`string-interning`	All element names, prefixes, attribute names, namespace URIs, and local names are internalized using the `intern()` method of `java.lang.String`	Names are not necessarily internalized
`validation`	Report all validation errors (implies `external-general-entities` and `external-parameter-entities`)	Do not report validation errors
`external-general-entities`	Include all external general (text) entities	Do not include `external-general-entities`
`external-parameter-entities`	Include all external parameter entities, including the external DTD subset	Do not include any `external-parameter-entities`, even the external DTD subset

SAX 2.0 defines the following core properties:

Property	Name
`dom-node`	`http://xml.org/sax/properties/dom-node`
`xml-string`	`http://xml.org/sax/properties/xml-string`

The following table contains information about the values of the properties:

Property	Data type	Description	Access
dom-node	org.w3c.dom.Node	When parsing, the current DOM node being visited if this is a DOM iterator; when not parsing, the root DOM node for iteration	(parsing) read-only; (not parsing) read/write
xml-string	java.lang.String	The literal string of characters that was the source for the current event	read-only

```
public boolean getFeature(String name)
       throws SAXNotRecognizedException,
              SAXNotSupportedException
public void setFeature(String name, boolean state)
       throws SAXNotRecognizedException,
              SAXNotSupportedException
public Object getProperty(String name)
       throws SAXNotRecognizedException,
              SAXNotSupportedException
public void setProperty(String name, Object value)
       throws SAXNotRecognizedException,
              SAXNotSupportedException
```

Parameters

Parameter	Type	Description
name	String	The feature/property name, which is a fully-qualified URI
state	boolean	The requested state of the feature (true or false)
value	Object	The requested value for the property

Returned Values

Method	Return	Description
`getFeature()`	`boolean`	The current state of the feature (`true` or `false`)
`getProperty()`	`Object`	The current value of the property

Methods setEntityResolver() and getEntityResolver()

The `setEntityResolver()` method allows an application to register an entity resolver. If the application does not register an entity resolver, the `XMLReader` will perform its own default resolution. Applications may register a new or different resolver in the middle of a parse, and the SAX parser must begin using the new resolver immediately.

The `getEntityResolver()` method returns the current entity resolver.

The entity resolvers are described later in interface `EntityResolver` on page 104.

```
public void setEntityResolver(EntityResolver resolver)
public EntityResolver getEntityResolver()
```

Parameters

Parameter	Type	Description
`resolver`	`EntityResolver`	The entity resolver

Returned Values

Method	Return	Description
`getEntity Resolver()`	`EntityResolver`	The current entity resolver, or `null` if none has been registered

Methods setDTDHandler() and getDTDHandler()

The `setDTDHandler()` method allows an application to register a DTD event handler. If the application does not register a DTD handler, all DTD events reported by the SAX parser will be silently ignored. Applications may register a new or different handler in the middle of a parse, and the SAX parser must begin using the new handler immediately.

The `getDTDHandler()` method returns the current DTD handler.

```
public void setDTDHandler(DTDHandler handler)
public DTDHandler getDTDHandler()
```

Parameters

Parameter	Type	Description
handler	DTDHandler	The DTD handler

Returned Values

Method	Return	Description
getDTDHandler()	DTDHandler	The current DTD handler, or null if none has been registered

Methods setContentHandler() and getContentHandler()

The setContentHandler() method allows an application to register a content event handler. If the application does not register a content handler, all content events reported by the SAX parser will be silently ignored. Applications may register a new or different handler in the middle of a parse, and the SAX parser must begin using the new handler immediately.

The getContentHandler() method returns the current content handler.

```
public void setContentHandler(ContentHandler handler)
public ContentHandler getContentHandler()
```

Parameters

Parameter	Type	Description
handler	Content Handler	The content handler

Returned Values

Method	Return	Description
getContent Handler()	Content Handler	The current content handler, or null if none has been registered

Methods setErrorHandler() and getErrorHandler()

The setErrorHandler() method allows an application to register an error event handler. If the application does not register an error handler, all error events reported by the SAX parser will be silently ignored. However, normal processing may not continue. It is highly recommended that all SAX applications implement an error handler to avoid unexpected bugs. Applications may register a new or different handler in the middle of a parse, and the SAX parser must begin using the new handler immediately.

The getErrorHandler() method returns the current error handler.

```
public void setErrorHandler(ErrorHandler handler)
public ErrorHandler getErrorHandler()
```

Parameters

Parameter	Type	Description
handler	ErrorHandler	The error handler

Returned Values

Method	Return	Description
getErrorHandler()	ErrorHandler	The current error handler, or null if none has been registered

Methods parse()

The application can use parse() methods to instruct the XML reader to begin parsing an XML document from any valid input source (a character stream, a byte stream, or a URI). Applications may not invoke this method while a parse is in progress (they should create a new XMLReader instead for each nested XML document). If this method is invoked then a good parser should throw a java.lang.IllegalStateException, a poorly designed parser could lead to unpredictable results. Once a parse is complete, an application may reuse the same XMLReader object, possibly with a different input source.

During the parse, the XMLReader will provide information about the XML document through the registered event handlers.

This method is synchronous: it will not return until parsing has ended. If a client application wants to terminate parsing early, it should throw an exception within a callback method of one of the event handlers.

```
public void parse(InputSource source)
        throws java.io.IOException, SAXException
public void parse(String systemId)
        throws java.io.IOException, SAXException
```

Parameters

Parameter	Type	Description
source	InputSource	The input source for the top-level of the XML document
systemId	String	The system identifier (URI)

Example: External Entities used by invoice.dtd and invoice_ns.dtd

This is a parameter entity used by the DTD file on page 93. This file declares unparsed entities.

Sample invoice.ent

```xml
<?xml version="1.0" encoding="UTF-8"?>

<!-- Unparsed entities -->

<!NOTATION txt PUBLIC "text/plain">
<!ENTITY server_info SYSTEM "server.txt"   NDATA txt>
<!ENTITY computer_info SYSTEM "computer.txt" NDATA txt>
<!ENTITY scanner_info SYSTEM "scanner.txt"  NDATA txt>
<!ENTITY printer_info SYSTEM "printer.txt"  NDATA txt>
```

Unparsed entities

The content of the unparsed entities is included below.

```
server.txt: 4x1000 Mhz, 2G RAM, 2x100G HDD
computer.txt: 800 Mhz, 256M RAM, 40G HDD
scanner.txt: 600 x 1200 dpi, ocr software
printer.txt: 600x600 dpi, 20 ppm
```

Example: DTD file used by invoice.xml

This is the DTD of the XML file on page 94. It declares the elements and the attribute lists. It also declares a general entity (dollar) and an external parameter entity (items_info).

Sample invoice.dtd

```xml
<?xml version="1.0" encoding="UTF-8"?>
<!-- External DTD -->
<!ELEMENT invoice (supplier, buyer, currency, item*)>
<!ATTLIST invoice
        number CDATA #REQUIRED
        month CDATA #REQUIRED
        day CDATA #REQUIRED
        year CDATA #REQUIRED>
<!ELEMENT supplier (email, address)>
<!ATTLIST supplier
        name CDATA #REQUIRED>
<!ELEMENT buyer (email, address)>
<!ATTLIST buyer
        name CDATA #REQUIRED>
<!ELEMENT email (#PCDATA)>
<!ELEMENT address (#PCDATA)>
<!ELEMENT currency (#PCDATA)>
<!ELEMENT item EMPTY>
<!ATTLIST item
        name CDATA #REQUIRED
        quantity CDATA #REQUIRED
```

```
        price CDATA #REQUIRED
        info ENTITY #REQUIRED>
<!ENTITY dollar "$">
<!ENTITY % items_info SYSTEM "invoice.ent">
%items_info;
```

Example: XML file used by XMLReaderSample.java, DeclHandlerSample.java and LexicalHandlerSample.java

This XML file contains the information of an invoice: number, date, supplier, buyer, currency and items. The `<?total?>` processing instruction will activate a routine for computing the total of the invoice.

Sample invoice.xml

```
<?xml version="1.0" encoding="utf-8"?>
<!-- Example XML file -->
<!DOCTYPE invoice SYSTEM "invoice.dtd">
<invoice number="1234567" month="2" day="20" year="2000">
  <supplier name="Sup Company">
    <email>info@supcompany.com</email>
    <address><![CDATA[London, UK]]></address>
  </supplier>
  <buyer name="Buy Company">
    <email>info@buycompany.com</email>
    <address><![CDATA[Paris, France]]></address>
  </buyer>
  <currency>US&dollar;</currency>
  <item name="Computer" quantity="10"
        price="1000" info="computer_info"/>
  <item name="Printer" quantity="5"
        price="200" info="printer_info"/>
  <item name="Server" quantity="1"
        price="5000" info="server_info"/>
  <?total?>
</invoice>
```

Example: Using org.xml.sax.XMLReader

This is an example for `org.xml.sax.XMLReader` based on `SmartContentHandler`.

Source XMLReaderSample.java

```
import org.xml.sax.InputSource;
import org.xml.sax.SAXParseException;
import org.xml.sax.XMLReader;
```

```
import javax.xml.parsers.SAXParser;
import javax.xml.parsers.SAXParserFactory;

import java.io.IOException;
import java.util.Vector;

public class XMLReaderSample extends SmartContentHandler {

  public static String FILENAME = "invoice.xml";

  private TableDTDHandler dtdHandler;
  private PrintErrorHandler errorHandler;
  private boolean supplierFlag;
  private boolean buyerFlag;
  private String currency;
  private Vector itemVector;
```

The XMLReaderSample() method initializes the fields of the new instance.

```
public XMLReaderSample() {
  dtdHandler = new TableDTDHandler();
  errorHandler = new PrintErrorHandler();
  supplierFlag = false;
  buyerFlag = false;
  currency = "";
  itemVector = new Vector();
}
```

The println() method prints a string to the standard output stream.

```
protected void println(String s) {
  System.out.println(s);
}
```

The getAttributeNames() method returns the list of attribute names of the element type associated with the given method. This method is used by the "XML element-Java method" mapping mechanism implemented by SmartContentHandler.

```
protected String[] getAttributeNames(String methodName) {
  if (methodName.equals("invoiceElement")) {
    return new String[] {
      "number", "day", "month", "year"
    };
  } else if (methodName.equals("supplierElement")) {
    return new String[] {
      "name"
    };
  } else if (methodName.equals("buyerElement")) {
    return new String[] {
      "name"
    };
  } else if (methodName.equals("emailElement")) {
    return new String[0];
```

```
    } else if (methodName.equals("addressElement")) {
        return new String[0];
    } else if (methodName.equals("currencyElement")) {
        return new String[0];
    } else if (methodName.equals("itemElement")) {
        return new String[] {
            "name", "quantity", "price", "info"
        };
    }
    return null;
}
```

The `invoiceElement()` method is called for `<invoice>` elements. It prints the invoice's number and date.

```
public void invoiceElement(int number, byte month,
        byte day, short year) {
    println("Invoice " + number);
    println("Date: " + month + "/" + day + "/" + year);
    println("");
}
```

The `supplierElement()` method is called for `<supplier>` elements. It prints the supplier's name and sets the `supplierFlag` to `true`.

```
public void supplierElement(String name) {
    supplierFlag = true;
    println("Supplier: " + name);
}
```

The `supplierElementEnd()` method is called when a `<supplier>` element ends. It sets the `supplierFlag` to `false`.

```
public void supplierElementEnd() {
    supplierFlag = false;
    println("");
}
```

The `buyerElement()` method is called for `<buyer>` elements. It prints the buyer's name and sets the `buyerFlag` to `true`.

```
public void buyerElement(String name) {
    buyerFlag = true;
    println("Buyer: " + name);
}
```

The `buyerElementEnd()` method is called when a `<buyer>` element ends. It sets the `buyerFlag` to `false`.

```
public void buyerElementEnd() {
    buyerFlag = false;
```

```
    println("");
  }
```

The `emailElement()` method is called for `<email>` elements.

```
  public void emailElement() {}
```

The `emailData()` method is called for the data of the `<email>` elements. It determines the name corresponding to the e-mail address and prints this information:

```
  public void emailData(String data) {
    String context = "";
    if (supplierFlag) {
      context = "supplier";
    } else if (buyerFlag) {
      context = "buyer";
    }
    println("Email of " + context + ": " + data);
  }
```

The `addressElement()` method is called for `<address>` elements. It doesn't do anything, but is required by the mapping mechanism implemented by our `SmartContentHandler`.

```
  public void addressElement() {}
```

The `addressData()` method is called for the data of the `<address>` elements. It determines whether the character data is the supplier's address or the buyer's address and prints this information.

```
  public void addressData(String data) {
    String context = "";
    if (supplierFlag) {
      context = "supplier";
    } else if (buyerFlag) {
      context = "buyer";
    }
    println("Address of " + context + ": " + data);
  }
```

The `currencyElement()` method is called for `<currency>` elements. It doesn't do anything, but is required by the mapping mechanism implemented by our `SmartContentHandler`.

```
  public void currencyElement() {}
```

The `currencyData()` method is called for the data of the `<currency>` element. It appends the data to the currency string.

Data methods like this can be invoked multiple times within an element since the data can be split by sub-elements (not this case) or entity references (this case). Multiple CDATA and regular character data sections can generate multiple calls of this method within the same element too. Even a single data section can be split if the XML file is large enough and a read operation ends in the middle of the data section.

If an application needs the entire data contained by an element (most cases), it should collect it in a buffer or a concatenated string and use it only after the end of the element.

```java
public void currencyData(String data) {
   currency += data;
}
```

The itemElement() method is called for <item> elements. It prints item name, quantity, price and information.

The item information is obtained from an unparsed entity. We get first the system ID of the entity from our TableDTDHandler instance that collects the declarations of the unparsed entities. Then we get the content of the entity using the getContent() method of our InputSourceUtils.

```java
public void itemElement(String name, int quantity,
        int price, String info) {
   println("Item: " + name);
   println("Quantity: " + quantity);
   println("Unit Price: " + currency + " " + price);
   String systemId = dtdHandler.getUnparsedEntity(info)[1];
   InputSource source = new InputSource(systemId);
   try {
      String content = InputSourceUtils.getContent(source);
      println("Info: " + content);
   } catch (IOException e) {
      e.printStackTrace();
   }
   println("");
   itemVector.add(new int[] {
      quantity, price
   });
}
```

The totalProc() method is called for the total processing instruction. It computes the total of the invoice using the information collected in a vector by itemElement().

```java
public void totalProc(String data) {
   int total = 0;
   for (int i = 0; i < itemVector.size(); i++) {
      int item[] = (int[]) itemVector.get(i);
      int quantity = item[0];
      int price = item[1];
      total += quantity * price;
   }
```

```
      println("Total: " + currency + " " + total);
      println("");
   }
```

The main() method:

- ❑ Creates an instance of this class
- ❑ Creates a JAXP factory for SAX parsers
- ❑ Configures this factory to do XML validation and be aware of namespaces
- ❑ Gets a new instance of SAXParser, which is a JAXP abstract class
- ❑ Gets the SAX XML Reader of the parser
- ❑ Sets the content, DTD and error handlers of the XML reader
- ❑ Calls the parse() method of the XML reader

```
public static void main(String[] args) {
  .if (args.length > 0) {
    FILENAME = args[0];
  }
  try {

    // Create an instance of this class
    XMLReaderSample sample = new XMLReaderSample();

    // Create the JAXP factory for SAX parsers
    SAXParserFactory
            saxFactory = SAXParserFactory.newInstance();
    saxFactory.setValidating(true);
    saxFactory.setNamespaceAware(true);

    // Create the JAXP SAX parser
    SAXParser saxParser = saxFactory.newSAXParser();

    // Get the SAX XMLReader of the parser
    XMLReader xmlReader = saxParser.getXMLReader();

    // Configure the XMLReader
    xmlReader.setContentHandler(sample);
    xmlReader.setDTDHandler(sample.dtdHandler);
    xmlReader.setErrorHandler(sample.errorHandler);

    // Parse the file
    xmlReader.parse(new InputSource(FILENAME));
  } catch (SAXParseException e) {

    // Already printed by PrintErrorHandler
    System.exit(1);
  } catch (Exception e) {
```

```
    e.printStackTrace();
        System.exit(1);
      }
    }
  }
```

Output

> **java XMLReaderSample**

Invoice 1234567
Date: 20/2/2000

Supplier: Sup Company
Email of supplier: info@supcompany.com
Address of supplier: London, UK

Buyer: Buy Company
Email of buyer: info@buycompany.com
Address of buyer: Paris, France

Item: Computer
Quantity: 10
Unit Price: US$ 1000
Info: 800 Mhz, 256M RAM, 40G HDD

Item: Printer
Quantity: 5
Unit Price: US$ 200
Info: 600x600 dpi, 20 ppm

Item: Server
Quantity: 1
Unit Price: US$ 5000
Info: 4x1000 Mhz, 2G RAM, 2x100G HDD

Total: US$ 16000

Interface XMLFilter

org.xml.sax

```
public interface XMLFilter extends XMLReader
```

An XML filter is like an XML reader, except that it obtains its events from another XML reader rather than a primary source like an XML document. Filters can modify a stream of events as they pass on to the final application.

The XMLFilterImpl helper class provides a convenient base for creating SAX 2.0 filters, by passing on all EntityResolver, DTDHandler, ContentHandler and ErrorHandler events automatically.

Methods

The `setParent()` method sets the parent reader. This method allows the application to link the filter to a parent reader (which may be another filter). The argument may not be `null`.

The `getParent()` method allows the application to query the parent reader (which may be another filter). It is generally a bad idea to perform any operations on the parent reader directly. They should all pass through this filter.

```
public void setParent(XMLReader parent)
public XMLReader getParent()
```

Parameters

Parameter	Type	Description
parent	XMLReader	The parent reader

Returned Values

Method	Return	Description
getParent()	XMLReader	The parent filter, or null if none has been set

Deprecated Interface Parser

org.xml.sax

```
public interface Parser
```

This was the main event supplier interface for SAX 1.0. It has been replaced in SAX 2.0 by `XMLReader`, which includes namespace support and sophisticated configurability and extensibility.

All SAX 1.0 parsers implement this basic interface. It allows applications to register handlers for different types of events and to initiate a parse from a URI, or a character stream.

SAX 1.0 parsers are reusable but not re-entrant, that is, the application may reuse a parser object (possibly with a different input source) once the first parse has completed successfully, but it may not invoke the `parse()` methods recursively within a parse.

Method setLocale()

The `setLocale()` method allows an application to request a locale for errors and warnings. SAX parsers are not required to provide localization for errors and warnings. If they cannot support the requested locale, however, they must throw a SAX exception. Applications may not request a locale change in the middle of a parse.

```
public void setLocale(java.util.Locale locale)
        throws SAXException
```

Parameters

Parameter	Type	Description
locale	java.util. Locale	A Java Locale object

Method setEntityResolver()

The setEntityResolver() method allows an application to register a custom entity resolver. If the application does not register an entity resolver, the SAX parser will resolve system identifiers and open connections to entities itself (this is the default behavior implemented in HandlerBase). Applications may register a new or different entity resolver in the middle of a parse, and the SAX parser must begin using the new resolver immediately.

```
public void setEntityResolver(EntityResolver resolver)
```

Parameters

Parameter	Type	Description
resolver	EntityResolver	The object for resolving entities

Method setDTDHandler()

The setDTDHandler() method allows an application to register a DTD event handler. If the application does not register a DTD handler, all DTD events reported by the SAX parser will be silently ignored (this is the default behavior implemented by HandlerBase). Applications may register a new or different handler in the middle of a parse, and the SAX parser must begin using the new handler immediately.

```
public void setDTDHandler(DTDHandler handler)
```

Parameters

Parameter	Type	Description
handler	DTDHandler	The DTD handler

Method setDocumentHandler()

The setDocumentHandler() method allows an application to register a document event handler. If the application does not register a document handler, all document events reported by the SAX parser will be silently ignored (this is the default behavior implemented by HandlerBase). Applications may register a new or different handler in the middle of a parse, and the SAX parser must begin using the new handler immediately.

```
public void setDocumentHandler(DocumentHandler handler)
```

Parameters

Parameter	Type	Description
handler	DocumentHandler	The document handler

Method setErrorHandler()

The setErrorHandler() method allows an application to register an error event handler. If the application does not register an error event handler, all error events reported by the SAX parser will be silently ignored, except for fatalError(), which will throw a SAXException (this is the default behavior implemented by HandlerBase). Applications may register a new or different handler in the middle of a parse, and the SAX parser must begin using the new handler immediately.

```
public void setErrorHandler(ErrorHandler handler)
```

Parameters

Parameter	Type	Description
handler	ErrorHandler	The error handler

Methods parse()

The application can use the parse() methods to instruct the SAX parser to begin parsing an XML document from any valid input source (a character stream, a byte stream, or a URI).

Applications may not invoke this method while a parse is in progress (they should create a new Parser instead for each additional XML document). Once a parse is complete, an application may reuse the same Parser object, possibly with a different input source.

```
public void parse(InputSource source)
        throws SAXException, java.io.IOException
public void parse(String systemId)
        throws SAXException, java.io.IOException
```

Parameters

Parameter	Type	Description
source	InputSource	The input source for the XML document
systemId	String	The system identifier (URI)

Interface EntityResolver
org.xml.sax

public interface EntityResolver

If a SAX application needs to implement customized handling for external entities, it must implement this interface and register an instance with the SAX parser using the setEntityResolver() method.

The XML reader will then allow the application to intercept any external entities (including the external DTD subset and external parameter entities, if any) before including them.

Many SAX applications will not need to implement this interface, but it will be especially useful for applications that build XML documents from databases or other specialized input sources, or for applications that use URI types other than URLs.

Application writers can use this interface to redirect external system identifiers to secure and/or local URIs, to look up public identifiers in a catalogue, or to read an entity from a database or other input source (including, for example, a dialog box).

Methods

The resolveEntity() method allows the application to resolve external entities. The parser will call this method before opening any external entity except the top-level document entity (including the external DTD subset, external entities referenced within the DTD, and external entities referenced within the document element). The application may request that the parser resolve the entity itself, that it use an alternative URI, or that it use an entirely different input source.

If the system identifier is a URL, the SAX parser must resolve it fully before reporting it to the application.

```
public InputSource resolveEntity(String publicId, String systemId)
        throws SAXException, java.io.IOException
```

Parameters

Parameter	Type	Description
publicId	String	The public identifier of the external entity being referenced, or null if none was supplied
systemId	String	The system identifier of the external entity being referenced

Returned Values

Method	Return	Description
resolveEntity()	InputSource	An InputSource object describing the new input source, or null to request that the parser open a regular URI connection to the system identifier

Example: Implementing org.xml.sax.EntityResolver

The ClasspathEntityResolver class looks for entities in the CLASSPATH environment variable. It implements the org.xml.sax.EntityResolver interface.

Note that the CLASSPATH may contain multiple files with the same name within different directories or jar files. The class loading mechanism, which is used to locate the resource will probably return the first resource (file or jar entry) whose name matches the name of the system ID. Also the input source returned by the resolveEntity() method won't have a system ID since we can't get it from the class loader. Some parsers (such as Apache Crimson) may refuse to resolve a relative entity if the system ID of the document that declares the relative entity is not known.

Source ClasspathEntityResolver.java

```
import org.xml.sax.EntityResolver;
import org.xml.sax.InputSource;

public class ClasspathEntityResolver implements
    EntityResolver {
```

The resolveEntity() method tries to find an entity in CLASSPATH. The name of the CLASSPATH resource is obtained from the systemID parameter, after eliminating all characters before the last slash or backslash including that character. The method returns a SAX InputSource created by the getResource() method of our InputSourceUtils class.

```
public InputSource resolveEntity(String publicID,
        String systemID) {
  if (systemID != null) {
    String name = systemID;
    int slashIndex = name.lastIndexOf('/');
    if (slashIndex != -1) {
      name = name.substring(slashIndex + 1);
    }
    slashIndex = name.lastIndexOf('\\');
    if (slashIndex != -1) {
      name = name.substring(slashIndex + 1);
    }
    if (name.length() > 0) {
      InputSource source
        = InputSourceUtils.getResource(name);
      if (source != null) {
        source.setPublicId(publicID);
      }
      return source;
    }
  }
  return null;
}
}
```

If we want to use this entity resolver with our `XMLReaderSample`, presented in a previous section, we would have to add a line like this in the `main()` method, where we configure the XMLReader:

```
xmlReader.setEntityResolver(new ClasspathEntityResolver());
```

After such a change, Apache Xerces-J would use our resolver to find the `invoice.dtd` and `invoice.ent` files. Apache Crimson would refuse, however, to get the latter file, which is referred by the former. Crimson signals a fatal error:

```
org.xml.sax.SAXParseException: Relative URI "invoice.ent"; can not be
resolved without a document URI.
```

Observe that neither Xerces nor Crimson uses our resolver to find the main XML document (`invoice.xml`). This is correct because the `resolveEntity()` method isn't called for the top-level document entity. You may use the `getResource()` method of our `InputSourceUtils` class to make sure that the main document is searched in CLASSPATH. Just pass the name of the resource as parameter.

You could use the `ClasspathEntityResolver` when XML resources are packaged within the JAR file together with the class files:

Suppose that a `config_file.xml` file with an external DTD `config_file.dtd` are placed in a jar file within a `/com/company/app` directory. The use of `ClasspathEntityResolver` will allow the parser to find the DTD in the jar file as long as this archive is placed in CLASSPATH and the system ID of the DTD is `"com.company.app.config_file.dtd"`

```
...
xmlReader.setEntityResolver(new ClasspathEntityResolver());
String name = "com.company.app.config_file.xml";
xmlReader.parse(InputSourceUtils.getResource(name));
```

You must choose the parser carefully in case you use relative URIs for the external DTD and other external parsed entities. You could also use URLs (absolute URIs) as system identifiers for the DTD and external parsed entities. The parser won't try to load their content over the network as long as the `resolveEntity()` method of the entity resolver returns a non-null local input source.

With parsers like Crimson, that don't allow the use of relative URIs if the base URI isn't known, it is necessary to use http://company.com/com.company.app.config_file.dtd as a system ID for the external DTD instead of just `com.company.app.config_file.dtd`. The http URL doesn't have to point to an existent document because `ClasspathEntityResolver` ignores everything until the last slash. Note that our entity resolver is able to find resources pointed by relative URIs in CLASSPATH and doesn't need an absolute base URI.

Class HandlerBase

org.xml.sax

```
public class HandlerBase
         implements EntityResolver, DTDHandler,
                    DocumentHandler, ErrorHandler
```

This class implements the default behavior for four SAX 1.0 interfaces:

❑   EntityResolver

❑   DTDHandler

❑   DocumentHandler

❑   ErrorHandler

The HandlerBase class is now deprecated, but is included in SAX 2.0 to support legacy SAX 1.0 applications. SAX 2.0 applications should use the org.xml.sax.helpers.DefaultHandler class instead.

Application writers can extend this class when they need to implement only part of an interface. Note that the use of this class is optional.

Constructor

This class has a zero-argument constructor.

```
public HandlerBase()
```

Methods Defined by org.xml.sax.EntityResolver

```
public InputSource resolveEntity(String publicId, String systemId)
        throws SAXException
```

Methods Defined by org.xml.sax.DTDHandler

```
public void notationDecl(String name, String publicId, String systemId)
public void unparsedEntityDecl(String name, String publicId,
                               String systemId, String notationName)
```

Methods Defined by org.xml.sax.DocumentHandler

```
public void setDocumentLocator(Locator locator)
```

```
public void startDocument()
        throws SAXException
```

```
public void endDocument()
        throws SAXException
```

```
public void startElement(String name, AttributeList attributes)
        throws SAXException
```

```
public void endElement(String name)
        throws SAXException
```

```
public void characters(char[] ch, int start, int length)
        throws SAXException
```

```
public void ignorableWhitespace(char[] ch, int start, int length)
        throws SAXException
```

```
public void processingInstruction(String target, String data)
        throws SAXException
```

Methods Defined by org.xml.sax.ErrorHandler

```
public void warning(SAXParseException e)
        throws SAXException
```

```
public void error(SAXParseException e)
        throws SAXException
```

```
public void fatalError(SAXParseException e)
        throws SAXException
```

Package org.xml.sax.ext

This package groups the optional interfaces of the SAX API, which can be used to obtain lexical information and DTD declarations. Typical applications that use SAX to parse XML documents don't need these extensions.

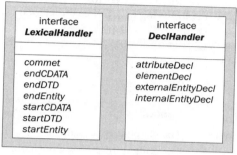

These interfaces were introduced in DOM Level 2:

Interface	Description	Page
DeclHandler	SAX 2.0 extension handler for DTD declaration events	109
LexicalHandler	SAX 2.0 extension handler for lexical events	115

Interface DeclHandler

org.xml.sax.ext

public interface DeclHandler

This is an optional extension handler for SAX 2.0 to provide information about DTD declarations in an XML document. XML readers are not required to support this handler, and this handler is not included in the core SAX 2.0 distribution.

Note that data-related DTD declarations (unparsed entities and notations) are already reported through the DTDHandler interface on page 83.

If you are using the declaration handler together with a lexical handler, all of the events will occur between the startDTD() and the endDTD() events.

To set the DeclHandler for an XML reader, use the setProperty() method with the propertyId set to http://xml.org/sax/properties/declaration-handler. If the reader does not support declaration events, it will throw a SAXNotRecognizedException or a SAXNotSupportedException when you attempt to register the handler.

Method elementDecl()

The `elementDecl()` method reports an element type declaration. The content model will consist of the string EMPTY, the string ANY, or a parenthesized group, optionally followed by an occurrence indicator. The model will be normalized by the parser so that all parameter entities are fully resolved and all whitespace is removed, and will include the enclosing parentheses. Other normalization (such as removing redundant parentheses or simplifying occurrence indicators) is at the discretion of the parser.

```
public void elementDecl(String name, String model)
        throws SAXException
```

Parameters

Parameter	Type	Description
name	String	The element type name
model	String	The content model as a normalized string

Method attributeDecl()

The `attributeDecl()` method reports an attribute type declaration. The type will be one of the strings CDATA_ID_IDREF_IDREFS_NMTOKEN_NMTOKENS_ENTITY_ENTITIES, a parenthesized token group with the separator " | " and all whitespace removed, or the word NOTATION followed by a space followed by a parenthesized token group with all whitespace removed. Any parameter entities in the attribute value will be expanded, but general entities will not.

```
public void attributeDecl(String eName, String aName, String type,
                          String valueDefault, String value)
        throws SAXException
```

Parameters

Parameter	Type	Description
eName	String	The name of the associated element
aName	String	The name of the attribute
type	String	A string representing the attribute type
valueDefault	String	A string representing the attribute default (#IMPLIED, #REQUIRED, or #FIXED) or null if none of these applies
value	String	A string representing the attribute's default value, or null if there is none

Method internalEntityDecl()

The `internalEntityDecl()` method reports an internal entity declaration. All parameter entities in the value will be expanded, but general entities will not, an example is shown on page 112.

```
public void internalEntityDecl(String name, String value)
        throws SAXException
```

Parameters

Parameter	Type	Description
name	String	The name of the entity. If it is a parameter entity, the name will begin with %
value	String	The replacement text of the entity

Method externalEntityDecl()

The `externalEntityDecl()` method reports a parsed external entity declaration.

```
public void externalEntityDecl(String name, String publicId,
                               String systemId)
        throws SAXException
```

Parameters

Parameter	Type	Description
name	String	The name of the entity. If it is a parameter entity, the name will begin with '%'
publicId	String	The declared public identifier of the entity, or null if none was declared
systemId	String	The declared system identifier of the entity

Example: Implementing org.xml.sax.ext.DeclHandler and org.xml.sax.DTDHandler

This example outputs the DTD declarations of an XML file. It implements the `org.xml.sax.ext.DeclHandler` and `org.xml.sax.DTDHandler` interfaces. The former is used to report element, attribute, internal entity and parsed external entity declarations. The latter is used to get information about unparsed entities and notations.

Source DeclHandlerSample.java

```java
import org.xml.sax.DTDHandler;
import org.xml.sax.InputSource;
import org.xml.sax.SAXException;
import org.xml.sax.SAXParseException;
import org.xml.sax.XMLReader;
import org.xml.sax.ext.DeclHandler;

import javax.xml.parsers.SAXParser;
import javax.xml.parsers.SAXParserFactory;

public class DeclHandlerSample implements DeclHandler, DTDHandler {

    public static final String DECL_HANDLER_PROP =
        "http://xml.org/sax/properties/declaration-handler";
    public static String FILENAME = "invoice.xml";
```

The `println()` method prints a string to the standard output stream.

```java
protected void println(String s) {
    System.out.println(s);
}
```

The `elementDecl()` method reports an element type declaration.

```java
public void elementDecl(String name, String model)
        throws SAXException {
    println("<!ELEMENT " + name + " " + model + ">");
}
```

The `attributeDecl()` method reports an attribute type declaration.

```java
public void attributeDecl(String eName, String aName,
        String type, String valueDefault, String value)
        throws SAXException {
    println("<!ATTLIST " + eName + " " + aName + " " + type
        + (valueDefault != null ? " " + valueDefault : "")
        + (value != null ? " \"" + value + "\"" : "")
        + ">");
}
```

The `internalEntityDecl()` method reports an internal entity declaration.

```java
public void internalEntityDecl(String name,
                               String value)
        throws SAXException {
    if (name.startsWith("%")) {
```

```
// Add a space after %
    name = "% " + name.substring(1);
  }
  println("<!ENTITY " + name + " \"" + value + "\">");
}
```

The `externalEntityDecl()` method reports a parsed external entity declaration.

```
public void externalEntityDecl(String name,
        String publicId, String systemId)
        throws SAXException {
  String param = "";
  if (name.startsWith("%")) {
    param = "% ";
    name = name.substring(1);
  }
  println("<!ENTITY " + param + name + " "
          + (publicId != null ? "PUBLIC"
                              : "SYSTEM")
          + (publicId != null ? " \"" + publicId + "\""
                              : "")
          + (systemId != null ? " \"" + systemId + "\""
                              : "")
          + ">");
}
```

The `unparsedEntityDecl()` method reports an unparsed entity declaration.

```
public void unparsedEntityDecl(String name, String publicId,
        String systemId, String notationName)
        throws SAXException {
  println("<!ENTITY " + name + " "
          + (publicId != null ? "PUBLIC"
                              : "SYSTEM")
          + (publicId != null ? " \"" + publicId + "\""
                              : "")
          + (systemId != null ? " \"" + systemId + "\""
                              : "") + " NDATA "
          + notationName + ">");
}
```

The `notationDecl()` method reports a notation declaration.

```
public void notationDecl(String name, String publicId,
        String systemId) throws SAXException {
  println("<!NOTATION " + name + " "
          + (publicId != null ? "PUBLIC"
                              : "SYSTEM")
          + (publicId != null ? " \"" + publicId + "\""
                              : "")
          + (systemId != null ? " \"" + systemId + "\""
```

```
:  "")
            + ">");
  }
```

The XML reader is created using the JAXP API like in the XMLReaderSample class. Once the XML reader is obtained, an instance of this class is registered as DeclHandler and DTDHandler using the setProperty() and setDTDHandler() methods.

```java
public static void main(String[] args) {
  if (args.length > 0) {
    FILENAME = args[0];
  }
  try {

    // Create an instance of this class
    DeclHandlerSample sample = new DeclHandlerSample();

    // Create the JAXP factory for SAX parsers
    SAXParserFactory saxFactory =
              SAXParserFactory.newInstance();
    saxFactory.setValidating(true);
    saxFactory.setNamespaceAware(true);

    // Create the JAXP SAX parser
    SAXParser saxParser = saxFactory.newSAXParser();

    // Get the SAX XMLReader of the parser
    XMLReader xmlReader = saxParser.getXMLReader();

    // Configure the XMLReader
    xmlReader.setProperty(DECL_HANDLER_PROP, sample);
    xmlReader.setDTDHandler(sample);
    xmlReader.setErrorHandler(new PrintErrorHandler());

    // Parse the file
    xmlReader.parse(new InputSource(FILENAME));
  } catch (SAXParseException e) {

    // Already printed by PrintErrorHandler
    System.exit(1);
  } catch (Exception e) {
    e.printStackTrace();
    System.exit(1);
  }
}
```

Output

```
> java DeclHandlerSample

<!ELEMENT invoice (supplier,buyer,currency,item*)>
```

```
<!ATTLIST invoice number CDATA #REQUIRED>
<!ATTLIST invoice month CDATA #REQUIRED>
<!ATTLIST invoice day CDATA #REQUIRED>
<!ATTLIST invoice year CDATA #REQUIRED>
<!ELEMENT supplier (email,address)>
<!ATTLIST supplier name CDATA #REQUIRED>
<!ELEMENT buyer (email,address)>
<!ATTLIST buyer name CDATA #REQUIRED>
<!ELEMENT email (#PCDATA)>
<!ELEMENT address (#PCDATA)>
<!ELEMENT currency (#PCDATA)>
<!ELEMENT item EMPTY>
<!ATTLIST item name CDATA #REQUIRED>
<!ATTLIST item quantity CDATA #REQUIRED>
<!ATTLIST item price CDATA #REQUIRED>
<!ATTLIST item info ENTITY #REQUIRED>
<!ENTITY dollar "$">
<!ENTITY % items_info SYSTEM "invoice.ent">
<!NOTATION txt PUBLIC "text/plain">
<!ENTITY server_info SYSTEM "server.txt" NDATA txt>
<!ENTITY computer_info SYSTEM "computer.txt" NDATA txt>
<!ENTITY scanner_info SYSTEM "scanner.txt" NDATA txt>
<!ENTITY printer_info SYSTEM "printer.txt" NDATA txt>
```

Interface LexicalHandler

org.xml.sax.ext

```
public interface LexicalHandler
```

This is an optional extension handler for SAX 2.0 to provide lexical information about an XML document, such as comments and CDATA section boundaries. XML readers are not required to support this handler, and it is not part of the core SAX 2.0 distribution.

The events in the lexical handler apply to the entire document, not just to the document element, and all lexical handler events must appear between the content handler's startDocument() and endDocument() events.

To set the LexicalHandler for an XML reader, use the setProperty() method with the propertyId set to http://xml.org/sax/properties/lexical-handler. If the reader does not support lexical events, it will throw a SAXNotRecognizedException or a SAXNotSupportedException when you attempt to register the handler.

Methods startDTD() and endDTD()

The start/endDTD() methods report the start/end of DTD declarations, if any. The startDTD() method is intended to report the beginning of the DOCTYPE declaration. If the document has no DOCTYPE declaration, the start/endDTD() methods will not be invoked.

All declarations reported through DTDHandler or DeclHandler events will appear between the startDTD() and endDTD() events. Declarations are assumed to belong to the internal DTD subset unless they appear between startEntity() and endEntity() events. Comments and processing instructions from the DTD are also reported between the startDTD() and endDTD() events, in their original order of (logical) occurrence. They are not required to appear in their correct locations relative to DTDHandler or DeclHandler events, however.

Note that the start/endDTD() events will appear within the start/endDocument() events from ContentHandler and before the first startElement() event.

```
public void startDTD(String name, String publicId, String systemId)
        throws SAXException
```
```
public void endDTD()
        throws SAXException
```

Parameters

Parameter	Type	Description
name	String	The document type name
publicId	String	The declared public identifier for the external DTD subset, or null if none was declared
systemId	String	The declared system identifier for the external DTD subset, or null if none was declared

Methods startEntity() and endEntity()

The start/endEntity() methods report the beginning/end of some internal and external XML entities.

The reporting of parameter entities (including the external DTD subset) is optional, and SAX 2.0 parsers that support LexicalHandler may not support it. You can use the http://xml.org/sax/features/lexical-handler/parameter-entities feature to query or control the reporting of parameter entities.

General entities are reported with their regular names, parameter entities have '%' prepended to their names, and the external DTD subset has the pseudo-entity name [dtd].

When a SAX 2.0 parser is providing these events, all other events must be properly nested within start/endEntity() events. There is no additional requirement that events from DeclHandler or DTDHandler be properly ordered.

Note that skipped entities will be reported through the skippedEntity() event, which is part of the ContentHandler interface.

Because of the streaming event model that SAX uses, some entity boundaries cannot be reported under any circumstances: general entities within attribute values and parameter entities within declarations. These will be silently expanded, with no indication of where the original entity boundaries were.

Note also that the boundaries of character references (which are not really entities anyway) are not reported.

All start/endEntity() events are properly nested.

```
public void startEntity(String name)
        throws SAXException
public void endEntity(String name)
        throws SAXException
```

Parameters

Parameter	Type	Description
name	String	The name of the entity. If it is a parameter entity, the name will begin with '%', and if it is the external DTD subset, it will be [dtd]

Methods startCDATA() and endCDATA()

The start/endCDATA() methods report the start/end of a CDATA section. The contents of the CDATA section will be reported through the regular characters() event. The start/endCDATA() events are intended only to report the boundary of the CDATA section.

```
public void startCDATA()
        throws SAXException
public void endCDATA()
        throws SAXException
```

Method comment()

The comment() method reports an XML comment anywhere in the document. This callback will be used for comments inside or outside the document element, including comments in the external DTD subset (if read). Comments in the DTD must be properly nested inside start/endDTD() and start/endEntity() events (if used).

```
public void comment(char[] ch, int start, int length)
        throws SAXException
```

Parameters

Parameter	Type	Description
ch	char[]	An array holding the characters in the comment
start	int	The starting position in the array
length	int	The number of characters to use from the array

Example: Implementing org.xml.sax.ext.LexicalHandler

This example outputs lexical information about an XML file. It implements the `org.xml.sax.ext.LexicalHandler` interface in order to get data that most applications don't need such as comments, the public and system identifiers of the external DTD and lexical details. The `characters()` method knows whether it gets regular data, a CDATA section or an entity reference.

Source LexicalHandlerSample.java

```
import org.xml.sax.InputSource;
import org.xml.sax.SAXException;
import org.xml.sax.SAXParseException;
import org.xml.sax.XMLReader;
import org.xml.sax.ext.LexicalHandler;
import org.xml.sax.helpers.DefaultHandler;

import javax.xml.parsers.SAXParser;
import javax.xml.parsers.SAXParserFactory;

public class LexicalHandlerSample extends DefaultHandler
   implements LexicalHandler {

   public static final String LEXICAL_HANDLER_PROP =
      "http://xml.org/sax/properties/lexical-handler";
   public static String FILENAME = "invoice.xml";

   private boolean entityFlag;
   private boolean cdataFlag;
```

The `LexicalHandlerSample()` constructor initializes the boolean flags.

```
   public LexicalHandlerSample() {
      entityFlag = false;
      cdataFlag = false;
   }
```

The `println()` method prints a string to the standard output stream:

```
protected void println(String s) {
   System.out.println(s);
 }
```

The startDTD() method reports the start of the DTD declarations, if any.

```
public void startDTD(String name, String publicId,
      String systemId) throws SAXException {
   println("<!DOCTYPE " + name + " "
         + (publicId != null ? "PUBLIC"
                             : "SYSTEM")
         + (publicId != null ? " \"" + publicId + "\""
                             : "")
         + (systemId != null ? " \"" + systemId + "\""
                             : "")
         + ">");
}
```

The endDTD() method could report the end of the DTD declarations.

```
public void endDTD() throws SAXException {}
```

The startEntity() method reports the beginning of some internal or external XML entity. The external DTD, named [dtd] by SAX, is not reported as an entity reference. This method also sets entityFlag to true. The same flag will be set to false by endEntity(). The startCDATA() and endCDATA() methods switch the cdataFlag.

```
public void startEntity(String name) throws SAXException {
   if (!name.equals("[dtd]")) {
     println("Entity reference: " + name);
   }
   entityFlag = true;
}

public void endEntity(String name) throws SAXException {
   entityFlag = false;
}

public void startCDATA() throws SAXException {
   cdataFlag = true;
}

public void endCDATA() throws SAXException {
   cdataFlag = false;
}
```

The comment() method reports an XML comment.

```
public void comment(char ch[], int start,
      int length) throws SAXException {
```

```
   String data = new String(ch, start, length);
      println("Comment: " + data);
   }
```

The `characters()` method receives notification of character data and uses the two flags to find out whether it gets regular data, a `CDATA` section or an entity reference.

```
   public void characters(char ch[], int start,
         int length) throws SAXException {
      String data = new String(ch, start, length);
      if (entityFlag) {
         println("Entity value: " + data);
      } else if (cdataFlag) {
         println("CDATA section: " + data);
      } else {
         println("Data: " + data);
      }
   }
```

The XML reader is created using the JAXP API like in the `XMLReaderSample`. Once the XML reader is obtained, an instance of this class is registered as `LexicalHandler` and `ContentHandler` using the `setProperty()` and `setContentHandler()` methods.

```
   public static void main(String[] args) {
      if (args.length > 0) {
         FILENAME = args[0];
      }
      try {

         // Create an instance of this class
         LexicalHandlerSample sample =
                new LexicalHandlerSample();

         // Create the JAXP factory for SAX parsers
         SAXParserFactory saxFactory =
                  SAXParserFactory.newInstance();
         saxFactory.setValidating(true);
         saxFactory.setNamespaceAware(true);

         // Create the JAXP SAX parser
         SAXParser saxParser = saxFactory.newSAXParser();

         // Get the SAX XMLReader of the parser
         XMLReader xmlReader = saxParser.getXMLReader();

         // Configure the XMLReader
         xmlReader.setProperty(LEXICAL_HANDLER_PROP, sample);
         xmlReader.setContentHandler(sample);
         xmlReader.setErrorHandler(new PrintErrorHandler());

         // Parse the file
         xmlReader.parse(new InputSource(FILENAME));
```

```
        } catch (SAXParseException e) {

            // Already printed by PrintErrorHandler
            System.exit(1);
        } catch (Exception e) {
            e.printStackTrace();
            System.exit(1);
        }
    }
}
```

Output

```
> java LexicalHandlerSample

Comment:  Example XML file
<!DOCTYPE invoice SYSTEM "invoice.dtd">
Comment:  External DTD
Entity reference: %items_info
Comment:  Unparsed entities
Data: info@supcompany.com
CDATA section: London, UK
Data: info@buycompany.com
CDATA section: Paris, France
Data: US
Entity reference: dollar
Entity value: $
```

Package org.xml.sax.helpers

This package groups the helper classes of the SAX API. Many of these classes implement interfaces defined by the SAX core package. The SAX parsers don't have to use these classes, that is, they may have their own implementations, but application developers can use the helper classes for purposes suggested within their descriptions.

The `org.xml.sax.helpers` package contains the following classes:

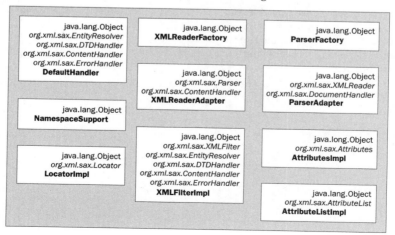

Class	Since	Description	Page
NamespaceSupport	2.0	Encapsulates namespace logic for use by SAX parsers	122
LocatorImpl	1.0	Provides an optional convenience implementation of `Locator`	127
AttributesImpl	2.0	Default implementation of the `Attributes` interface	129
AttributeListImpl (Deprecated)	1.0	Default implementation for `AttributeList`	131
DefaultHandler	2.0	Default base class for SAX 2.0 event handlers	132
ParserFactory (Deprecated)	1.0	Java-specific class for dynamically loading SAX parsers	140
ParserAdapter	2.0	Adapts a SAX 1.0 Parser as a SAX 2.0 `XMLReader`	141
XMLReaderFactory	2.0	Factory for creating an XML reader	143
XMLReaderAdapter	2.0	Adapts a SAX 2.0 `XMLReader` as a SAX 1.0 `Parser`	144
XMLFilterImpl	2.0	Base class for deriving an XML filter	146

Class NamespaceSupport

org.xml.sax.helpers

public class NamespaceSupport

This class encapsulates the logic of namespace processing. It tracks the declarations currently in force for each context and automatically processes qualified XML names into their namespace parts. It can also be used in reverse for generating XML from namespaces.

NamespaceSupport objects are reusable, but the reset() method must be invoked between sessions.

Note that this class is optimized for the use case where most elements do not contain namespace declarations. If the same prefix/URI mapping is repeated for each context (for example), this class will be somewhat less efficient.

Fields

The value of the XMLNS final static String field is the namespace URI that is automatically mapped to the xml prefix:

```
"http://www.w3.org/XML/1998/namespace"
```

Constructor

This class has a zero-argument constructor.

```
public NamespaceSupport()
```

Methods

The reset() method resets the NamespaceSupport object for reuse.

The pushContext() method starts a new namespace context. Normally, you should push a new context at the beginning of each XML element. The new context will automatically inherit the declarations of its parent context, but it will also keep track of which declarations were made within this context. The NamespaceSupport object always starts with a base context already in force. In this context, only the xml prefix is declared.

The popContext() method reverts to the previous namespace context. Normally, you should pop the context at the end of each XML element. After popping the context, all namespace prefix mappings that were previously in force are restored. You must not attempt to declare additional namespace prefixes after popping a context, unless you push another context first.

The declarePrefix() method declares a namespace prefix. This method declares a prefix in the current namespace context. The prefix will remain in force until this context is popped, unless it is shadowed in a descendant context. To declare a default namespace, use the empty string. The prefix must not be xml or xmlns and you must not declare a prefix after you've pushed and popped another namespace.

Note that there is an asymmetry in this library. The getPrefix() method will not return the default " " prefix, even if you have declared one. To check for a default prefix, you have to look it up explicitly using getURI(). This asymmetry exists to make it easier to look up prefixes for attribute names, where the default prefix is not allowed.

The processName() method processes a raw XML 1.0 name in the current context by removing the prefix and looking it up among the prefixes currently declared. The return value will be the array supplied by the caller, filled in as follows:

- ❑ The namespace URI, or an empty string if none is in use
- ❑ The local name (without prefix)
- ❑ The original raw name

All of the strings in the array will be internalized. If the raw name has a prefix that has not been declared, then the return value will be null.

Note that attribute names are processed differently than element names: an unprefixed element name will receive the default namespace (if any), while an unprefixed attribute name will not.

The getURI() method looks up a prefix and gets the currently-mapped namespace URI. This method looks up the prefix in the current context. Use the empty string " " for the default namespace.

The getPrefixes() method returns an enumeration of all prefixes currently declared. If there is a default prefix, it will not be returned in this enumeration. Check for the default prefix using the getURI() with an argument of " ". It is also possible to get an enumeration of all prefixes currently declared for a URI.

The getPrefix() method returns one of the prefixes mapped to a namespace URI. If more than one prefix is currently mapped to the same URI, this method will make an arbitrary selection. If you want all of the prefixes, use the getPrefixes() method instead.

The getDeclaredPrefixes() method returns an enumeration of all prefixes declared in this context. The empty (default) prefix will be included in this enumeration. Note that this behavior differs from that of getPrefix() and getPrefixes().

```
public void reset()
public void pushContext()
public void popContext()
public boolean declarePrefix(String prefix, String uri)
public String[] processName(String qName, String[] parts,
                            boolean isAttribute)
public String getURI(String prefix)
public java.util.Enumeration getPrefixes()
public java.util.Enumeration getPrefixes(String uri)
public String getPrefix(String uri)
public java.util.Enumeration getDeclaredPrefixes()
```

Parameters

Parameter	Type	Description
prefix	String	The namespace prefix
uri	String	The namespace URI
qName	String	The qualified name to be processed
parts	String[]	An array supplied by the caller, capable of holding at least three members
isAttribute	boolean	A flag indicating whether this is an attribute name (true) or an element name (false)

Returned Values

Method	Return	Description
declarePrefix()	boolean	true if the prefix was legal, false otherwise
processName()	String[]	The supplied array holding three internalized strings representing the namespace URI (or empty string), the local name, and the raw XML 1.0 name; or null if there is an undeclared prefix
getURI()	String	The associated namespace URI, or null if the prefix is undeclared in this context
getPrefixes()	java.util. Enumeration	An enumeration of all prefixes declared in the current context except for the empty (default) prefix
getPrefix()	String	One of the prefixes currently mapped to the URI supplied, or null if none is mapped or if the URI is assigned to the default namespace
getDeclared Prefixes()	java.util. Enumeration	An enumeration of all prefixes declared in this context

DTD file used by invoice_ns.xml

This is the DTD of the XML file included within the next section. It is the namespace version of invoice.dtd. We've prefixed the attributes only to test the capabilities of our utility classes. Most applications don't prefix the attributes. We defined an internal parameter entity (xmlns_invoice) that is used to declare the xmlns:invoice attribute of invoice:invoice.

Sample invoice_ns.dtd

```
<?xml version="1.0" encoding="UTF-8"?>
<!-- External DTD -->
<!ENTITY % xmlns_invoice "xmlns:invoice CDATA #FIXED
'http://supcompany.com/invoice'">
<!ELEMENT invoice:invoice (invoice:supplier, invoice:buyer,
invoice:currency, invoice:item*)>
<!ATTLIST invoice:invoice
    %xmlns_invoice;
    invoice:number CDATA #REQUIRED
    invoice:month CDATA #REQUIRED
    invoice:day CDATA #REQUIRED
    invoice:year CDATA #REQUIRED>
<!ELEMENT invoice:supplier (invoice:email, invoice:address)>
```

```
<!ATTLIST invoice:supplier
    invoice:name CDATA #REQUIRED>
<!ELEMENT invoice:buyer (invoice:email, invoice:address)>
<!ATTLIST invoice:buyer
    invoice:name CDATA #REQUIRED>
<!ELEMENT invoice:email (#PCDATA)>
<!ELEMENT invoice:address (#PCDATA)>
<!ELEMENT invoice:currency (#PCDATA)>
<!ELEMENT invoice:item EMPTY>
<!ATTLIST invoice:item
    invoice:name CDATA #REQUIRED
    invoice:quantity CDATA #REQUIRED
    invoice:price CDATA #REQUIRED
    invoice:info ENTITY #REQUIRED>
<!ENTITY dollar "$">
<!ENTITY % items_info SYSTEM "invoice.ent">
%items_info;
```

Example: The Namespace Version of invoice.xml

This is the namespace version of invoice.xml. All elements and attributes are prefixed by invoice.

Sample invoice_ns.xml

```
<?xml version="1.0" encoding="utf-8"?>
<!-- Example XML file -->
<!DOCTYPE invoice:invoice SYSTEM "invoice_ns.dtd">
<invoice:invoice xmlns:invoice="http://supcompany.com/invoice"
    invoice:number="1234567" invoice:month="2"
    invoice:day="20" invoice:year="2000">
  <invoice:supplier invoice:name="Sup Company">
    <invoice:email>info@supcompany.com</invoice:email>
    <invoice:address><![CDATA[London, UK]]></invoice:address>
  </invoice:supplier>
  <invoice:buyer invoice:name="Buy Company">
    <invoice:email>info@buycompany.com</invoice:email>
    <invoice:address><![CDATA[Paris, France]]>
    </invoice:address>
  </invoice:buyer>
  <invoice:currency>US&dollar;</invoice:currency>
  <invoice:item invoice:name="Computer"
      invoice:quantity="10" invoice:price="1000"
      invoice:info="computer_info"/>
  <invoice:item invoice:name="Printer" invoice:quantity="5"
      invoice:price="200" invoice:info="printer_info"/>
  <invoice:item invoice:name="Server" invoice:quantity="1"
      invoice:price="5000" invoice:info="server_info"/>
  <?total?>
</invoice:invoice>
```

```
> java DeclHandlerSample invoice_ns.xml

<!ENTITY % xmlns_invoice
"xmlns:invoice CDATA #FIXED 'http://supcompany.com/invoice'">
<!ELEMENT invoice:invoice
(invoice:supplier,invoice:buyer,invoice:currency,invoice:item*)>
<!ATTLIST invoice:invoice xmlns:invoice CDATA #FIXED
"http://supcompany.com/invoice">
<!ATTLIST invoice:invoice invoice:number CDATA #REQUIRED>
<!ATTLIST invoice:invoice invoice:month CDATA #REQUIRED>
<!ATTLIST invoice:invoice invoice:day CDATA #REQUIRED>
<!ATTLIST invoice:invoice invoice:year CDATA #REQUIRED>
<!ELEMENT invoice:supplier (invoice:email,invoice:address)>
<!ATTLIST invoice:supplier invoice:name CDATA #REQUIRED>
<!ELEMENT invoice:buyer (invoice:email,invoice:address)>
<!ATTLIST invoice:buyer invoice:name CDATA #REQUIRED>
<!ELEMENT invoice:email (#PCDATA)>
<!ELEMENT invoice:address (#PCDATA)>
<!ELEMENT invoice:currency (#PCDATA)>
<!ELEMENT invoice:item EMPTY>
<!ATTLIST invoice:item invoice:name CDATA #REQUIRED>
<!ATTLIST invoice:item invoice:quantity CDATA #REQUIRED>
<!ATTLIST invoice:item invoice:price CDATA #REQUIRED>
<!ATTLIST invoice:item invoice:info ENTITY #REQUIRED>
<!ENTITY dollar "$">
<!ENTITY % items_info SYSTEM "invoice.ent">
<!NOTATION txt PUBLIC "text/plain">
<!ENTITY server_info SYSTEM "server.txt" NDATA txt>
<!ENTITY computer_info SYSTEM "computer.txt" NDATA txt>
<!ENTITY scanner_info SYSTEM "scanner.txt" NDATA txt>
<!ENTITY printer_info SYSTEM "printer.txt" NDATA txt>
```

Class LocatorImpl
org.xml.sax.helpers

```
public class LocatorImpl
        implements org.xml.sax.Locator
```

This class is available mainly for application writers, who can use it to make a persistent snapshot of a locator at any point during a document parse.

SAX parsers aren't required to use this class. They may provide their own more efficient implementation.

Constructors

The LocatorImpl() constructors create an uninitialized locator or a copy of an existing locator.

```
public LocatorImpl()
public LocatorImpl(Locator locator)
```

Parameters

Parameter	Type	Description
locator	Locator	The locator to copy

Methods

This class allows the setting of its properties.

```
public void setPublicId(String publicId)
public void setSystemId(String systemId)
public void setLineNumber(int lineNumber)
public void setColumnNumber(int columnNumber)
```

Parameters

Parameter	Type	Description
publicId	String	The new public identifier, or null if none is available
systemId	String	The new system identifier, or null if none is available
lineNumber	int	The line number, or -1 if none is available
columnNumber	int	The column number, or -1 if none is available

Methods Defined by org.xml.sax.Locator

```
public String getPublicId()
public String getSystemId()
public int getLineNumber()
public int getColumnNumber()
```

Class AttributesImpl

org.xml.sax.helpers

```
public class AttributesImpl
          implements org.xml.sax.Attributes
```

This class provides a default implementation of the SAX 2.0 `Attributes` interface, with the addition of mutators so that the list can be modified or reused.

There are two typical uses of this class: to take a persistent snapshot of an `Attributes` object in a `startElement()` event or to construct or modify an `Attributes` object in a SAX 2.0 parser or filter.

This class replaces the (now deprecated) SAX 1.0 `AttributeListImpl` class. In addition to supporting the updated `Attributes` interface rather than the deprecated `AttributeList` interface, it also provides a more efficient implementation.

Constructors

The `AttributesImpl()` constructors create an empty attribute list or a copy of an existing list.

```
public AttributesImpl()
public AttributesImpl(Attributes atts)
```

Parameters

Parameter	Type	Description
atts	Attributes	The existing Attributes object

Methods

This class provides methods for adding, changing and removing attributes.

```
public void clear()
public void setAttributes(Attributes atts)
public void addAttribute(String uri, String localName, String qName,
                         String type, String value)
public void setAttribute(int index, String uri, String localName,
                         String qName, String type, String value)
public void removeAttribute(int index)
public void setURI(int index, String uri)
```

```
public void setLocalName(int index, String localName)
public void setQName(int index, String qName)
public void setType(int index, String type)
public void setValue(int index, String value)
```

Parameters

Parameter	Type	Description
atts	Attributes	The attributes to copy
uri	String	The attribute's namespace URI, or the empty string if none is available
localName	String	The attribute's local name
qName	String	The qualified name
type	String	The attribute's type
value	String	The attribute's value
index	int	The index of the attribute (zero-based)

Methods Defined by org.xml.sax.Attributes

```
public int getLength()
public String getURI(int index)
public String getLocalName(int index)
public String getQName(int index)
public String getType(int index)
public String getType(String uri, String localName)
public String getType(String qName)
public String getValue(int index)
public String getValue(String uri, String localName)
public String getValue(String qName)
public int getIndex(String uri, String localName)
public int getIndex(String qName)
```

Deprecated Class AttributeListImpl

org.xml.sax.helpers

```
public class AttributeListImpl
        implements org.xml.sax.AttributeList
```

This class implements the deprecated SAX 1.0 AttributeList interface, and has been replaced by the new SAX 2.0 AttributesImpl.

Note that SAX parsers are not required to use this class to provide an implementation of AttributeList. It is supplied only as an optional convenience.

Constructors

The AttributeListImpl() constructors create an empty attribute list or a copy of an existing list.

```
public AttributeListImpl()
public AttributeListImpl(AttributeList atts)
```

Parameters

Parameter	Type	Description
atts	AttributeList	The attribute list to copy

Methods

This class provides methods for adding and removing attributes.

```
public void setAttributeList(AttributeList atts)
public void addAttribute(String name, String type, String value)
public void removeAttribute(String name)
public void clear()
```

Parameters

Parameter	Type	Description
atts	AttributeList	The attribute list to copy
name	String	The attribute name
type	String	The attribute type ("NMTOKEN" for an enumeration)
value	String	The attribute value (must not be null)

Methods Defined by org.xml.sax.AttributeList

```
public int getLength()
public String getName(int i)
public String getType(int i)
public String getType(String name)
public String getValue(int i)
public String getValue(String name)
```

Class DefaultHandler

org.xml.sax.helpers

```
public class DefaultHandler
        implements org.xml.sax.EntityResolver,
                   org.xml.sax.DTDHandler,
                   org.xml.sax.ContentHandler,
                   org.xml.sax.ErrorHandler
```

This class is available as a convenience base class for SAX 2.0 applications. It provides default implementations for all of the callbacks in the four core SAX 2.0 handler classes:

- ❑ EntityResolver
- ❑ DTDHandler
- ❑ ContentHandler
- ❑ ErrorHandler

Application writers can extend this class when they need to implement only part of an interface.

This class replaces the deprecated SAX 1.0 HandlerBase class.

Constructor

This class has a zero-argument constructor.

```
public DefaultHandler()
```

Methods Defined by org.xml.sax.EntityResolver

```
public InputSource resolveEntity(String publicId, String systemId)
        throws SAXException
```

Methods Defined by org.xml.sax.DTDHandler

```
public void notationDecl(String name, String publicId, String systemId)
      throws SAXException
public void unparsedEntityDecl(String name, String publicId,
                             String systemId, String notationName)
      throws SAXException
```

Methods Defined by org.xml.sax.ContentHandler

```
public void setDocumentLocator(Locator locator)
public void startDocument()
      throws SAXException
public void endDocument()
      throws SAXException
public void startPrefixMapping(String prefix, String uri)
      throws SAXException
public void endPrefixMapping(String prefix)
      throws SAXException
public void startElement(String uri, String localName,
                       String qName, Attributes attributes)
      throws SAXException
public void endElement(String uri, String localName, String qName)
      throws SAXException
public void characters(char[] ch, int start, int length)
      throws SAXException
public void ignorableWhitespace(char[] ch, int start, int length)
      throws SAXException
public void processingInstruction(String target, String data)
      throws SAXException
public void skippedEntity(String name)
      throws SAXException
```

133

Methods Defined by org.xml.sax.ErrorHandler

```
public void warning(SAXParseException e)
     throws SAXException
```

```
public void error(SAXParseException e)
     throws SAXException
```

```
public void fatalError(SAXParseException e)
     throws SAXException
```

Example: Parsing an XML File

This class contains code snippets that show two methods for starting the parsing process. One of them uses the DefaultHandlerProxy class to reduce the lines of code.

Source DefaultHandlerCode.java

```java
import org.xml.sax.DTDHandler;
import org.xml.sax.EntityResolver;
import org.xml.sax.ErrorHandler;
import org.xml.sax.InputSource;
import org.xml.sax.SAXException;
import org.xml.sax.XMLReader;
import org.xml.sax.helpers.DefaultHandler;

import javax.xml.parsers.ParserConfigurationException;
import javax.xml.parsers.SAXParser;
import javax.xml.parsers.SAXParserFactory;

import java.io.File;
import java.io.IOException;

public class DefaultHandlerCode {
```

The parse_1() method parses a file using the parse() method of org.xml.sax.XMLReader. The XMLReader instance is obtained from a JAXP javax.xml.parsers.SAXParser and then the event handlers are registered. The java.io.File object must be converted first to a java.net.URL and then to an org.xml.sax.InputSource since the parse() method of XMLReader doesn't accept a File as parameter.

```
    public void parse_1(File file, EntityResolver er,
            DTDHandler dh, ContentHandler ch, ErrorHandler eh)
            throws IOException, SAXException,
            ParserConfigurationException {
        SAXParserFactory saxFactory =
            SAXParserFactory.newInstance();
        SAXParser saxParser = saxFactory.newSAXParser();
        XMLReader xmlReader = saxParser.getXMLReader();

        xmlReader.setEntityResolver(er);
        xmlReader.setDTDHandler(dh);
        xmlReader.setContentHandler(ch);
        xmlReader.setErrorHandler(eh);

        String url = null;
        try {
          file.toURL().toString();
        } catch (java.net.MalformedURLException e) {
          throw new SAXException(e);
        }
        InputSource source = new InputSource(url);
        xmlReader.parse(source);
    }
```

The parse_2() method parses a file using the parse() method of
javax.xml.parsers.SAXParser, which accepts a java.io.File object as parameter.
Since the JAXP API cannot take the four specialized handlers, we use our
DefaultHandlerProxy class (presented in the next section) to group them. This method uses
less lines of code than the previous one.

```
    public void parse_2(File file, EntityResolver er,
            DTDHandler dh, ContentHandler ch,
            ErrorHandler eh) throws IOException, SAXException,
            ParserConfigurationException {
        SAXParserFactory saxFactory =
            SAXParserFactory.newInstance();
        SAXParser saxParser = saxFactory.newSAXParser();
        DefaultHandler handler = new DefaultHandlerProxy(er,
            dh, ch, eh);
        saxParser.parse(file, handler);
    }
}
```

Example: Dispatcher for Parsing Events

This proxy handler dispatches the parsing events to four different specialized handlers. `DefaultHandlerCode` contains code that shows how to use this class.

Source DefaultHandlerProxy.java

```
import org.xml.sax.Attributes;
import org.xml.sax.ContentHandler;
import org.xml.sax.DTDHandler;
import org.xml.sax.EntityResolver;
import org.xml.sax.ErrorHandler;
import org.xml.sax.InputSource;
import org.xml.sax.Locator;
import org.xml.sax.SAXException;
import org.xml.sax.SAXParseException;
import org.xml.sax.helpers.DefaultHandler;

public class DefaultHandlerProxy extends DefaultHandler {

    protected EntityResolver entityResolver;
    protected DTDHandler dtdHandler;
    protected ContentHandler contentHandler;
    protected ErrorHandler errorHandler;
```

The `DefaultHandlerProxy()` method saves the references of the objects passed as parameters to the instance variables so that these objects can be used by the methods of this class.

```
public DefaultHandlerProxy(EntityResolver er, DTDHandler dh,
        ContentHandler ch, ErrorHandler eh) {
    entityResolver = er;
    dtdHandler = dh;
    contentHandler = ch;
    errorHandler = eh;
}
```

The `resolveEntity()` method delegates the resolving of an external entity to the `EntityResolver` instance, if any.

```
public InputSource resolveEntity(String publicId,
        String systemId) throws SAXException {
    if (entityResolver != null) {
      try {
        return entityResolver.resolveEntity(publicId,
                systemId);
      } catch (java.io.IOException e) {
        throw new SAXException(e);
      }
    }
    return null;
}
```

The notationDecl() method dispatches the notification of a notation declaration to the DTDHandler instance, if any.

```
public void notationDecl(String name, String publicId,
      String systemId) throws SAXException {
   if (dtdHandler != null) {
         dtdHandler.notationDecl(name, publicId, systemId);
   }
}
```

The unparsedEntityDecl() method dispatches the notification of an unparsed entity declaration to the DTDHandler instance, if any.

```
public void unparsedEntityDecl(String name, String publicId,
      String systemId, String notationName)
      throws SAXException {
   if (dtdHandler != null) {
     dtdHandler.unparsedEntityDecl(name, publicId,
       systemId, notationName);
   }
}
```

The setDocumentLocator() method passes the org.xml.sax.Locator object to the method with the same name of the ContentHandler instance, if any.

```
public void setDocumentLocator(Locator locator) {
   if (contentHandler != null) {
     contentHandler.setDocumentLocator(locator);
   }
}
```

The startDocument() method dispatches the notification of the beginning of the document to the ContentHandler instance, if any.

```
public void startDocument() throws SAXException {
   if (contentHandler != null) {
     contentHandler.startDocument();
   }
}
```

The endDocument() method dispatches the notification of the end of the document to the ContentHandler instance, if any.

```
public void endDocument() throws SAXException {
   if (contentHandler != null) {
     contentHandler.endDocument();
   }
}
```

The startPrefixMapping() method dispatches the notification of the start of a namespace mapping to the ContentHandler instance, if any.

```
public void startPrefixMapping(String prefix,
        String uri) throws SAXException {
    if (contentHandler != null) {
        contentHandler.startPrefixMapping(prefix, uri);
    }
}
```

The endPrefixMapping() method dispatches the notification of the end of a namespace mapping to the ContentHandler instance, if any.

```
public void endPrefixMapping(String prefix)
        throws SAXException {
    if (contentHandler != null) {
        contentHandler.endPrefixMapping(prefix);
    }
}
```

The startElement() method dispatches the notification of the start of an element to the ContentHandler instance, if any.

```
public void startElement(String uri, String localName,
        String qName, Attributes attributes)
        throws SAXException {
    if (contentHandler != null) {
        contentHandler.startElement(uri, localName, qName,
        attributes);
    }
}
```

The endElement() method dispatches the notification of the end of an element to the ContentHandler instance, if any.

```
public void endElement(String uri, String localName,
        String qName) throws SAXException {
    if (contentHandler != null) {
        contentHandler.endElement(uri, localName, qName);
    }
}
```

The characters() method dispatches the notification of character data inside an element to the ContentHandler instance, if any.

```
public void characters(char ch[], int start,
        int length) throws SAXException {
    if (contentHandler != null) {
```

```
            contentHandler.characters(ch, start, length);
        }
    }
```

The `ignorableWhitespace()` method dispatches the notification of ignorable whitespace to the `ContentHandler` instance, if any.

```
    public void ignorableWhitespace(char ch[], int start,
            int length) throws SAXException {
        if (contentHandler != null) {
            contentHandler.ignorableWhitespace(ch, start, length);
        }
    }
```

The `processingInstruction()` method dispatches the notification of a processing instruction to the `ContentHandler` instance, if any.

```
    public void processingInstruction(String target,
            String data) throws SAXException {
        if (contentHandler != null) {
            contentHandler.processingInstruction(target, data);
        }
    }
```

The `skippedEntity()` method dispatches the notification of a skipped entity to the `ContentHandler` instance, if any.

```
    public void skippedEntity(String name) throws SAXException {
        if (contentHandler != null) {
          contentHandler.skippedEntity(name);
        }
    }
```

The `warning()` method dispatches the notification of a parser warning to the `ErrorHandler` instance, if any.

```
    public void warning(SAXParseException e)
            throws SAXException {
        if (errorHandler != null) {
          errorHandler.warning(e);
        }
    }
```

The `error()` method dispatches the notification of a recoverable parser error to the `ErrorHandler` instance, if any.

```
    public void error(SAXParseException e) throws SAXException {
        if (errorHandler != null) {
          errorHandler.error(e);
        }
    }
```

The `fatalError()` method dispatches the notification of a fatal XML parsing error to the `ErrorHandler` instance, if any.

```
public void fatalError(SAXParseException e)
        throws SAXException {
    if (errorHandler != null) {
        errorHandler.fatalError(e);
    }
    throw e;
    }
}
```

Deprecated Class ParserFactory

org.xml.sax.helpers

```
public class ParserFactory
```

This is a Java-specific class for dynamically loading SAX parsers.

This class is designed to work with the (now deprecated) SAX 1.0 `Parser` class. SAX 2.0 applications should use `XMLReaderFactory` instead.

`ParserFactory` is not part of the platform-independent definition of SAX. It is an additional convenience class designed specifically for Java XML application writers. SAX applications can use the static methods in this class to allocate a SAX parser dynamically at run-time based either on the value of the `org.xml.sax.parser` system property or on a string containing the class name.

Methods

The `makeParser()` method creates a new SAX parser using the `org.xml.sax.parser` system property or a provided class name. The class must implement the `Parser` interface.

```
public static Parser makeParser()
        throws ClassNotFoundException,
               IllegalAccessException,
               InstantiationException,
               NullPointerException,
               ClassCastException
```

```
public static Parser makeParser(String className)
       throws ClassNotFoundException,
              IllegalAccessException,
              InstantiationException,
              ClassCastException
```

Parameters

Parameter	Type	Description
className	String	A string containing the name of the SAX parser class

Returned Values

Method	Return	Description
makeParser()	Parser	A new parser object

Class ParserAdapter

org.xml.sax.helpers

```
public class ParserAdapter
       implements org.xml.sax.XMLReader,
                  org.xml.sax.DocumentHandler
```

This class wraps a SAX 1.0 Parser and makes it act as a SAX 2.0 XMLReader, with feature, property, and namespace support. Note that it is not possible to report skippedEntity() events, since SAX 1.0 does not make that information available. This adapter does not test for duplicate qualified attribute names.

Constructors

The ParserAdapter() constructors create an adapter object that wraps a SAX 1.0 Parser and makes it act as a SAX 2.0 XMLReader. The zero-argument constructor uses the org.xml.sax.parser property to locate the embedded SAX 1.0 parser.

Note that the embedded parser cannot be changed once the adapter is created. To embed a different parser, allocate a new ParserAdapter.

```
public ParserAdapter()
       throws SAXException
public ParserAdapter(Parser parser)
```

Parameters

Parameter	Type	Description
parser	Parser	The SAX 1.0 parser to embed

Methods Defined by org.xml.sax.XMLReader

```
public void setFeature(String name, boolean state)
        throws SAXNotRecognizedException,
            SAXNotSupportedException
```

```
public boolean getFeature(String name)
        throws SAXNotRecognizedException,
            SAXNotSupportedException
```

```
public void setProperty(String name, Object value)
        throws SAXNotRecognizedException,
            SAXNotSupportedException
```

```
public Object getProperty(String name)
        throws SAXNotRecognizedException,
            SAXNotSupportedException
```

```
public void setEntityResolver(EntityResolver resolver)
```

```
public EntityResolver getEntityResolver()
```

```
public void setDTDHandler(DTDHandler handler)
```

```
public DTDHandler getDTDHandler()
```

```
public void setContentHandler(ContentHandler handler)
```

```
public ContentHandler getContentHandler()
```

```
public void setErrorHandler(ErrorHandler handler)
```

```
public ErrorHandler getErrorHandler()
```

```
public void parse(String systemId)
        throws java.io.IOException, SAXException
```

```
public void parse(InputSource input)
        throws java.io.IOException, SAXException
```

Methods Defined by org.xml.sax.DocumentHandler

```
public void setDocumentLocator(Locator locator)
public void startDocument()
       throws SAXException
public void endDocument()
       throws SAXException
public void startElement(String qName, AttributeList qAtts)
       throws SAXException
public void endElement(String qName)
       throws SAXException
public void characters(char[] ch, int start, int length)
       throws SAXException
public void ignorableWhitespace(char[] ch, int start, int length)
       throws SAXException
public void processingInstruction(String target, String data)
       throws SAXException
```

Class XMLReaderFactory

org.xml.sax.helpers

```
public final class XMLReaderFactory
```

This class contains static methods for creating an XML reader from an explicit class name, or for creating an XML reader based on the value of the `org.xml.sax.driver` system property.

Note that these methods will not be usable in environments where system properties are not accessible or where the application or applet is not permitted to load classes dynamically.

Methods

The `createXMLReader()` method attempts to create an XML reader from a system property. This method uses the value of the system property `org.xml.sax.driver` as the full name of a Java class and tries to instantiate that class as a SAX 2.0 `XMLReader`. Note that many Java interpreters allow system properties to be specified on the command line. It is also possible to pass a class name as parameter to the `createXMLReader()` method.

```
public static XMLReader createXMLReader()
       throws SAXException
public static XMLReader createXMLReader(String className)
       throws SAXException
```

Parameters

Parameter	Type	Description
className	String	A string containing the name of the XML reader class

Returned Values

Method	Return	Description
createXMLReader()	XMLReader	A new XMLReader

Class XMLReaderAdapter
org.xml.sax.helpers

```
public class XMLReaderAdapter
       implements org.xml.sax.Parser,
                  org.xml.sax.ContentHandler
```

This class wraps a SAX 2.0 XMLReader and makes it act as a SAX 1.0 Parser. The XMLReader must support a true value for the http://xml.org/sax/features/namespace-prefixes property or parsing will fail with a SAXException. If the XMLReader supports a false value for the http://xml.org/sax/features/namespaces property, that will also be used to improve efficiency.

Constructors

The XMLReaderAdapter() constructors create an adapter object that wraps SAX 2.0 XMLReader and makes it to act like a SAX 1.0 Parser. The zero-argument constructor uses the org.xml.sax.driver property to locate the SAX 2.0 parser to embed.

```
public XMLReaderAdapter()
       throws SAXException
public XMLReaderAdapter(XMLReader xmlReader)
```

Parameters

Parameter	Type	Description
xmlReader	XMLReader	The SAX 2.0 XML Reader to wrap

Methods Defined by org.xml.sax.Parser

```
public void setLocale(java.util.Locale locale)
      throws SAXException
public void setEntityResolver(EntityResolver resolver)
public void setDTDHandler(DTDHandler handler)
public void setDocumentHandler(DocumentHandler handler)
public void setErrorHandler(ErrorHandler handler)
public void parse(String systemId)
      throws java.io.IOException, SAXException
public void parse(InputSource input)
      throws java.io.IOException, SAXException
```

Methods Defined by org.xml.sax.ContentHandler

```
public void setDocumentLocator(Locator locator)
public void startDocument()
      throws SAXException
public void endDocument()
      throws SAXException
public void startPrefixMapping(String prefix, String uri)
public void endPrefixMapping(String prefix)
public void startElement(String uri, String localName,
                         String qName, Attributes atts)
      throws SAXException
public void endElement(String uri, String localName, String qName)
      throws SAXException
```

```
public void characters(char[] ch, int start, int length)
      throws SAXException
public void ignorableWhitespace(char[] ch, int start, int length)
      throws SAXException
public void processingInstruction(String target, String data)
      throws SAXException
public void skippedEntity(String name)
      throws SAXException
```

Class XMLFilterImpl

org.xml.sax.helpers

```
public class XMLFilterImpl
      implements org.xml.sax.XMLFilter,
                 org.xml.sax.EntityResolver,
                 org.xml.sax.DTDHandler,
                 org.xml.sax.ContentHandler,
                 org.xml.sax.ErrorHandler
```

This class is designed to sit between an XMLReader and the client application's event handlers. By default, it does nothing but pass requests up to the reader and events on to the handlers unmodified, but subclasses can override specific methods to modify the event stream or the configuration requests as they pass through.

Constructors

The XMLFilterImpl() constructors create XML filters with or without a parent. If there is no initial parent you must assign a parent before you start a parse or do any configuration with setFeature() or setProperty().

```
public XMLFilterImpl()
public XMLFilterImpl(XMLReader parent)
```

Parameters

Parameter	Type	Description
parent	XMLReader	The parent XML reader

Methods for Setting and Getting Features and Properties

These methods allow the setting and getting of the features and properties.

```
public void setFeature(String name, boolean state)
        throws SAXNotRecognizedException,
            SAXNotSupportedException
public boolean getFeature(String name)
        throws SAXNotRecognizedException,
            SAXNotSupportedException
public void setProperty(String name, Object value)
        throws SAXNotRecognizedException,
            SAXNotSupportedException
public Object getProperty(String name)
        throws SAXNotRecognizedException,
            SAXNotSupportedException
```

Parameters

Parameter	Type	Description
name	String	The name of the feature/property
state	boolean	The feature's state
value	Object	The property's value

Returned Values

Method	Return	Description
getFeature()	boolean	The current state of the feature
getProperty()	Object	The current value of the property

Methods setEntityResolver() and getEntityResolver()

These methods allow the setting and getting of the entity resolver.

```
public void setEntityResolver(EntityResolver resolver)
public EntityResolver getEntityResolver()
```

Parameters

Parameter	Type	Description
resolver	EntityResolver	The new entity resolver

Returned Values

Method	Return	Description
getEntityResolver()	EntityResolver	The current entity resolver, or null if none was set

Methods setDTDHandler() and getDTDHandler()

These methods allow the setting and getting of the DTD event handler.

```
public void setDTDHandler(DTDHandler handler)
public DTDHandler getDTDHandler()
```

Parameters

Parameter	Type	Description
handler	DTDHandler	The new DTD handler

Returned Values

Method	Return	Description
getDTDHandler()	DTDHandler	The current DTD handler, or null if none was set

Methods setContentHandler() and getContentHandler()

These methods allow the setting and getting of the content event handler.

```
public void setContentHandler(ContentHandler handler)
public ContentHandler getContentHandler()
```

Parameters

Parameter	Type	Description
handler	ContentHandler	The new content handler

Returned Values

Method	Return	Description
getContentHandler()	ContentHandler	The current content handler, or null if none was set

Methods setErrorHandler() and getErrorHandler()

These methods allow the setting and getting of the current error handler.

```
public void setErrorHandler(ErrorHandler handler)
public ErrorHandler getErrorHandler()
```

Parameters

Parameter	Type	Description
handler	ErrorHandler	The new error handler

Returned Values

Method	Return	Description
getErrorHandler()	ErrorHandler	The current error handler, or null if none was set

Methods parse()

These methods parse a document.

```
public void parse(InputSource source)
        throws SAXException, java.io.IOException
public void parse(String systemId)
        throws SAXException, java.io.IOException
```

Parameters

Parameter	Type	Description
source	InputSource	The input source for the document entity
systemId	String	The system identifier as a fully-qualified URI.

Methods Defined by org.xml.sax.XMLFilter

```
public void setParent(XMLReader parent)
```
```
public XMLReader getParent()
```

Methods Defined by org.xml.sax.EntityResolver

```
public InputSource resolveEntity(String publicId, String systemId)
        throws SAXException, java.io.IOException
```

Methods Defined by org.xml.sax.DTDHandler

```
public void notationDecl(String name, String publicId, String systemId)
        throws SAXException
```
```
public void unparsedEntityDecl(String name, String publicId,
                               String systemId, String notationName)

        throws SAXException
```

Methods Defined by org.xml.sax.ContentHandler

```
public void setDocumentLocator(Locator locator)
```
```
public void startDocument()
        throws SAXException
```
```
public void endDocument()
        throws SAXException
```
```
public void startPrefixMapping(String prefix, String uri)
        throws SAXException
```
```
public void endPrefixMapping(String prefix)
        throws SAXException
```
```
public void startElement(String uri, String localName,
                         String qName, Attributes atts)
        throws SAXException
```

```
public void endElement(String uri, String localName, String qName)
        throws SAXException
public void characters(char[] ch, int start, int length)
        throws SAXException
public void ignorableWhitespace(char[] ch, int start, int length)
        throws SAXException
public void processingInstruction(String target, String data)
        throws SAXException
public void skippedEntity(String name)
        throws SAXException
```

Methods Defined by org.xml.sax.ErrorHandler

```
public void warning(SAXParseException e)
        throws SAXException
public void error(SAXParseException e)
        throws SAXException
public void fatalError(SAXParseException e)
        throws SAXException
```

Summary

In this chapter, we looked at the SAX API in some depth, and we also built some example utility classes in order to demonstrate SAX functionality:

In particular, we:

❑   Configured a SAX parser and parsed an XML document

❑   Discussed how to handle elements, attribute lists, character data and processing instructions

❑   Built an "XML element-Java method" mapping mechanism

❑   Printed out the various declarations of a DTD: elements, attribute lists, entities and notations

❑   Learned how to examine input sources in the CLASSPATH and read their content

❑   Built some simple entity resolvers, error handlers, DTD handlers and lexical handlers

In the next chapter, we will go on to look at the DOM API, and see how the Document Object Model can be used to traverse and manipulate XML documents.

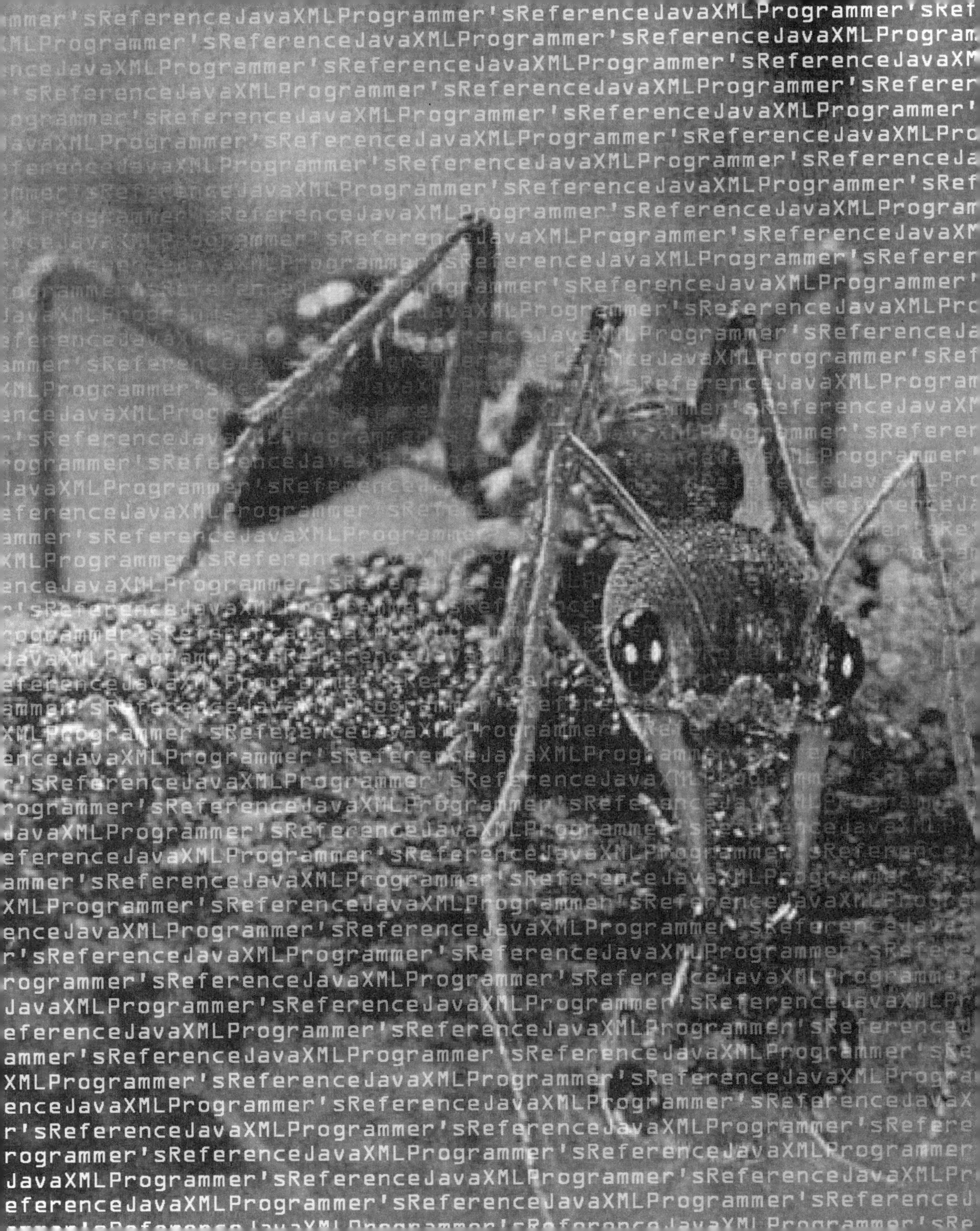
JavaXMLProgrammer'sReference

3

DOM Core

The Document Object Model (DOM) is an API endorsed by W3C (World Wide Web Consortium – www.w3.org) for creating and manipulating the structure and contents of XML and HTML documents. When an XML file is parsed, it is natural to map each XML construct such as an element, text, or comment to an object. These objects are called nodes; they form a tree in memory as XML documents have a hierarchical structure. For example, a node object that represents an element will contain the nodes that represent its sub-elements, character data comments, etc. The nodes that represent the sub-elements will have their own contained nodes (called children), and so on.

The DOM Core API defines a set of interfaces that are implemented by the classes of the node objects. The `org.w3c.dom.Document` interface contains methods for creating new node objects and getting the root element of a document. Most interfaces of the DOM Core API extend `org.w3c.dom.Node`, which defines methods for getting the parent, children and siblings of a node, inserting, replacing or removing a child node, or getting node properties, such as type, name or value. Specialized interfaces represent the various XML constructs. For example, `org.w3c.dom.Element` extends `Node` and defines the operations specific to elements, for example the getting, setting, and removing of the attributes.

Package	Description	Page
`org.w3c.dom`	Contains the interfaces whose instances represent the logical constructs of an XML document, such as elements, attributes, character data, comments, processing instructions, entity references, entities and notations. It also defines interfaces for documents, document fragments, node lists and node maps.	160

This chapter contains the same information as the DOM Level 2 Core API specification (http://www.w3.org/TR/DOM-Level-2-Core/), but in a more compact format. In addition, we will develop small utility classes and examples that use the DOM API. We also present a few details about the next version of DOM (Level 3), which was a work in progress when this book was written. Chapter 4 will describe the DOM API extensions.

In this chapter, we'll look at how to:

- ❑ Configure a DOM parser and parse an XML document
- ❑ Print information about the nodes of a DOM tree
- ❑ Extract the data contained by a node
- ❑ Find the elements of a DOM tree that satisfy some criteria
- ❑ Rename the attributes of an element
- ❑ Create a document tree from scratch

The next section contains a DOM example that parses an XML file and outputs information about its nodes. The rest of the chapter contains the API documentation of the DOM core package with examples.

Example	Description and Used DOM APIs	Page
`DOMPrinter`	Uses `Document`, `Node`, `NodeList`, and `NamedNodeMap` for printing a DOM tree	155
`DoctypeSample`	Demonstrates the use of `Notation`, `Entity`, and `DocumentType` in order to output the name, IDs, internal subset, notations, and entities of a document's DTD	181
`DataUtils`	Uses `CharacterData`, `Text`, `CDATASection`, `EntityReference` and `Comment` for extracting the data contained by a node	185
`DataSample`	Shows how to use our `DataUtils`	187
`ElementUtils`	Provides utilities for finding the `Element` instances of a DOM tree that satisfy some criteria	195
`ElementSample`	Shows how to use our `ElementUtils`	198
`AttrUtils`	Provides utilities for "renaming" `Attr` nodes	203
`AttrSample`	Shows how to use our `AttrUtils`	205
`DocumentSample`	Creates a `Document` instance, which is populated with `Element`, `Comment`, `CDATASection`, `Text`, and `ProcessingInstruction` nodes	217

Using DOM

A DOM-compliant parser will read an XML document and create objects whose classes implement the DOM interfaces. All these objects are linked in a tree as we explained in the introduction of this chapter.

The root node of the DOM tree is a `Document` instance, whose list of child nodes may contain a `DocumentType` representing the `DOCTYPE` declaration, a single `Element` representing the root element of the document, `ProcessingInstruction` nodes and `Comments`.

An `Element` node may contain other `Element` nodes representing its "sub-elements", `Text` and `CDATASection` nodes representing the character data, `ProcessingInstructions`, `Comments` and `EntityReferences`.

The attributes of an element are represented by `Attr` nodes, but they are not considered part of the DOM tree. An `Attr` node may contain `Text` and `EntityReference` nodes.

DOM trees can also be created from scratch. After getting an empty `Document`, we can use its methods to create nodes representing the various XML constructs and link these nodes in a tree using the methods defined by the base `Node` interface.

Having the representation of a whole document in memory can be an important advantage, especially when multiple queries must be performed. (For example, the Apache implementation of XPath is based on DOM and is used by the Xalan XSLT processor.) Unfortunately, the heavy usage of memory is also the DOM's main disadvantage. The SAX API presented in Chapter 2 can be a necessary alternative when we have to parse large documents.

DOM Starter Example

The following example contains methods for parsing a document and creating a new empty document. It can work as a standalone application, but it is also used by other examples in this chapter: `AttrSample`, `DataSample`, `DoctypeSample`, `DocumentSample`, and `ElementSample`. The next two chapters also use our `DOMPrinter`.

The output will contain the type, name and value of all nodes from the DOM tree and also the properties of the `Attr` nodes. Note that the attributes of the elements aren't part of the DOM tree, but we treat them as any other nodes. The only difference is that we get the child nodes of a parent node as an ordered `NodeList` object, while the attributes are obtained as an unordered `NamedNodeMap` instance.

Example: Printing a DOM tree

The `DOMPrinter` class parses an XML file using the JAXP API (which is described in Chapter 5) and prints the DOM tree in an indented manner.

Source DOMPrinter.java

```java
import org.w3c.dom.Document;
import org.w3c.dom.NamedNodeMap;
import org.w3c.dom.Node;
```

```
import org.w3c.dom.NodeList;

import org.xml.sax.SAXException;
import org.xml.sax.SAXParseException;

import javax.xml.parsers.DocumentBuilder;
import javax.xml.parsers.DocumentBuilderFactory;
import javax.xml.parsers.ParserConfigurationException;

import java.io.File;
import java.io.IOException;

public class DOMPrinter {
```

The NODE_TYPES array contains the names of the various DOM node types. Each element of the array corresponds to a constant defined by the org.w3c.dom.Node interface.

```
private static String NODE_TYPES[] = new String[] {
    "",
    "ELEMENT",
    "ATTRIBUTE",
    "TEXT",
    "CDATA_SECTION",
    "ENTITY_REFERENCE",
    "ENTITY",
    "PROCESSING_INSTRUCTION",
    "COMMENT",
    "DOCUMENT",
    "DOCUMENT_TYPE",
    "DOCUMENT_FRAGMENT",
    "NOTATION"
};
```

The two-argument println() method prints a given number of double-spaces followed by a string to the standard output stream.

```
public static void println(String s, int indent) {
    for (int i = 0; i < indent; i++) {
        System.out.print("  ");
    }
    System.out.println(s);
}
```

The single argument println() method prints a string to the standard output stream.

```
public static void println(String s) {
    println(s, 0);
}
```

The print() method prints the DOM tree whose root is given as parameter. We use the printImpl() method described below.

```java
public static void print(Node node) {
  printImpl(node, 0);
}
```

The following is the implementation of the above print() method. It first prints several node properties: nodeType, nodeName, and nodeValue. Empty Text nodes are ignored. Then it prints the attributes and the children of the given node using recursive calls. The attributes are obtained as an org.w3c.dom.NamedNodeMap instance and the children as an org.w3c.dom.NodeList object.

```java
private static void printImpl(Node node, int indent) {
  if (node == null) {
    return;
  }
  String nodeType = NODE_TYPES[node.getNodeType()];
  String nodeName = node.getNodeName();
  String nodeValue = node.getNodeValue();
  if (nodeValue != null) {
    nodeValue = nodeValue.trim();
  }
  if (nodeType.equals("TEXT") && nodeValue.equals("")) {
    ;    // Ignore the empty text node
  } else {
    println(nodeType + " - " + nodeName + " - "
        + nodeValue, indent);
  }

  NamedNodeMap attributes = node.getAttributes();
  if (attributes != null) {
    for (int i = 0; i < attributes.getLength(); i++) {
      printImpl(attributes.item(i), indent + 1);
    }
  }
  NodeList children = node.getChildNodes();
  if (children != null) {
    for (int i = 0; i < children.getLength(); i++) {
      printImpl(children.item(i), indent + 1);
    }
  }
}
```

The newBuilder() method creates a javax.xml.parsers.DocumentBuilder instance, which is then used to obtain empty org.w3c.dom.Document instances or parse XML documents. The javax.xml.parsers.DocumentBuilderFactory object may be configured to produce validating JAXP document builders, which are also namespace aware. Each builder has a SAX error handler. We use the PrintErrorHandler class described in Chapter 2. The JAXP API is presented in Chapter 5 (JAXP 1.1).

```
public static DocumentBuilder newBuilder(boolean validation)
        throws ParserConfigurationException {

   // Create JAXP factory for document builders
   DocumentBuilderFactory domFactory =
      DocumentBuilderFactory.newInstance();

   // Configure the factory
   domFactory.setValidating(validation);
   domFactory.setNamespaceAware(true);

   // Create a document builder
   DocumentBuilder domBuilder =
        domFactory.newDocumentBuilder();

   // Set the error handler
   domBuilder.setErrorHandler(new PrintErrorHandler());

   // Return the builder
   return domBuilder;
}
```

The newDocument() method creates an empty Document.

```
public static Document newDocument()
        throws ParserConfigurationException {

   // Create the builder
   DocumentBuilder domBuilder = newBuilder(false);

   // Create a new empty document
   Document document = domBuilder.newDocument();
   ;

   // Return the document
   return document;
}
```

The following method parses an XML file using a validating or non-validating DOM parser. The newBuilder() call returns a JAXP document builder whose parse() method is invoked.

```
public static Document parse(String path,
     boolean validation) throws ParserConfigurationException,
     IOException, SAXException {

   // Create the builder
   DocumentBuilder domBuilder = newBuilder(validation);

   // Parse the file
   Document document = domBuilder.parse(new File(path));
```

```
            // Return the parsed document
            return document;
        }
```

The `main()` method parses the document whose path is given in the command line and prints the obtained DOM tree. If the command line is empty, it uses `nodes.xml`.

```java
    public static void main(String args[]) {
        try {
            String path = args.length > 0 ? args[0] : "nodes.xml";
            print(parse(path, false));
        } catch (SAXParseException e) {

            // Already printed by PrintErrorHandler
            System.exit(1);
        } catch (Exception e) {
            e.printStackTrace();
            System.exit(1);
        }
    }
}
```

Sample nodes.xml

```xml
<?xml version='1.0' encoding='utf-8'?>
<!DOCTYPE sample [
<!ENTITY dollar "$">
]>
<!-- Some comment -->
<sample>
  data before element
  <element attr1="value1" attr2="value2">
    <data1 a="v">some data &amp; one attribute</data1>
    <data2>CDATA follows <![CDATA[more data]]></data2>
    <data3>&dollar;123 + &dollar;456</data3>
  </element>
  data after element
  <?proc data for processing?>
</sample>
```

Output

```
> java DOMPrinter

DOCUMENT - #document - null
  DOCUMENT_TYPE - sample - null
  COMMENT - #comment - Some comment
  ELEMENT - sample - null
    TEXT - #text - data before element
    ELEMENT - element - null
```

```
ATTRIBUTE - attr1 - value1
  TEXT - #text - value1
ATTRIBUTE - attr2 - value2
  TEXT - #text - value2
ELEMENT - data1 - null
  ATTRIBUTE - a - v
    TEXT - #text - v
  TEXT - #text - some data & one attribute
ELEMENT - data2 - null
  TEXT - #text - CDATA follows
  CDATA_SECTION - #cdata-section - more data
ELEMENT - data3 - null
  ENTITY_REFERENCE - dollar - null
    TEXT - #text - $
  TEXT - #text - 123 +
  ENTITY_REFERENCE - dollar - null
    TEXT - #text - $
  TEXT - #text - 456
TEXT - #text - data after element
PROCESSING_INSTRUCTION - proc - data for processing
```

Package org.w3c.dom

This package groups the interfaces whose instances represent the logical constructs of an XML document, such as elements, attributes, character data, comments, processing instructions, entity references, entities and notations. It also defines interfaces for documents, document fragments, node lists and node maps.

Interface Node

```
              interface                              interface
          org.w3c.dom.Node                      org.w3c.dom.NodeList


        ATTRIBUTE_NODE                         getLength
        CDATA_SECTION_NODE                     item
        COMMENT_NODE
        DOCUMENT_FRAGMENT_NODE
        DOCUMENT_NODE
        DOCUMENT_TYPE_NODE
        ELEMENT_NODE                                 interface
        ENTITY_NODE                        org.w3c.dom.NamedNodeMap
        ENTITY_REFERENCE_NODE
        NOTATION_NODE
        PROCESSING_INSTRUCTION_NODE            getLength
        TEXT_NODE                              getNamedItem
                                               getNamedItemNS
                                               item
        appendChild                            removeNamedItem
        cloneNode                              removeNamedItemNS
        getAttributes                          setNamedItem
        getChildNodes                          setNamedItemNS
        getFirstChild
        getLastChild
        getLocalName
        getNamespaceURI
        getNextSibling
        getNodeName
        getNodeType
        getNodeValue
        getOwnerDocument
        getParentNode
        getPrefix
        getPreviousSibling
        hasAttributes
        hasChildNodes
        insertBefore
        isSupported
        normalize
        removeChild
        replaceChild
        setNodeValue
        setPrefix
```

Interface	Description	Page
Node	The Node interface is the "mother" datatype for the entire Document Object Model	166
NamedNodeMap	Objects implementing the NamedNodeMap interface are used to represent collections of nodes that can be accessed by name	175
NodeList	The NodeList interface provides the abstraction of an ordered collection of nodes, without defining or constraining how this collection is implemented	173

Node Subinterfaces

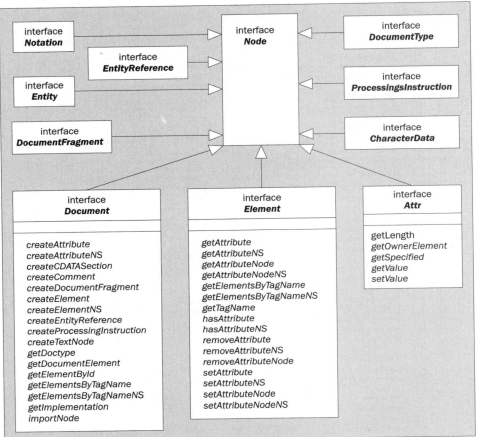

Interface	Description	Page
Node	The Node interface is the "mother" datatype for the entire Document Object Model	166
Notation	This interface represents a notation declared in the DTD	177
Entity	This interface represents an entity (see Chapter 1_XX), either parsed or unparsed, in an XML document	178
EntityReference	EntityReference objects may be inserted into the DOM tree when an entity reference is in the source document, or when the user wishes to insert an entity reference	179
DocumentType	Each Document has a doctype attribute whose value is either null or a DocumentType object	180

Interface	Description	Page
CharacterData	The CharacterData interface extends Node with a set of properties and methods for accessing character data in the DOM	184
Element	The Element interface represents an element in an XML document	191
Attr	The Attr interface represents an attribute in an Element object	201
Processing Instruction	The ProcessingInstruction interface represents a "processing instruction", used in XML as a way to keep processor-specific information in the text of the document	207
DocumentFragment	DocumentFragment is a "lightweight" or "minimal" Document object	208
Document	The Document interface represents the entire XML document	208

CharacterData

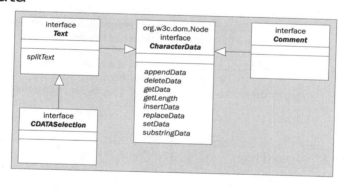

Note that CharacterData extends Node, and is shown in the previous diagram.

Interface	Description	Page
Text	The Text interface inherits from CharacterData and represents the textual content (termed character data in XML) of an Element or Attr	189
CDATASection	CDATA sections are used to escape blocks of text containing characters that would otherwise be regarded as markup	190
Comment	This interface inherits from CharacterData and represents the content of a comment, that is all the characters between the starting ' <!--' and ending '-->'	190

Miscellaneous

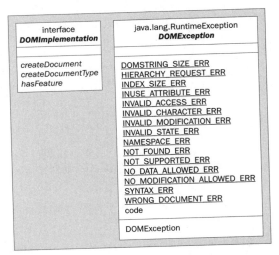

Class	Description	Page
`DOMException`	DOM operations only raise exceptions in "exceptional" circumstances, that is, when an operation is impossible to perform (either for logical reasons, because data is lost, or because the implementation has become unstable)	164
`DOMImplementation`	The `DOMImplementation` interface provides a number of methods for performing operations that are independent of any particular `Document` instance	219

Exception DOMException

org.w3c.dom

```
public class DOMException
        extends java.lang.RuntimeException
```

DOM operations raise exceptions when an operation is impossible to perform.

Fields

This class has a public field for storing the exception's code and also defines the valid values of this field.

Field	Type	Description
code	short	The exception's code
INDEX_SIZE_ERR	short	If index or size is negative, or greater than the allowed value
DOMSTRING_SIZE_ERR	short	If the specified range of text does not fit into a String
HIERARCHY_REQUEST_ERR	short	If any node is inserted somewhere it doesn't belong
WRONG_DOCUMENT_ERR	short	If a node is used in a different document than the one that created it (that doesn't support it)
INVALID_CHARACTER_ERR	short	If an invalid or illegal character is specified, such as in a name
NO_DATA_ALLOWED_ERR	short	If data is specified for a node which does not support data
NO_MODIFICATION_ALLOWED_ERR	short	If an attempt is made to modify an object where modifications are not allowed
NOT_FOUND_ERR	short	If an attempt is made to reference a node in a context where it does not exist
NOT_SUPPORTED_ERR	short	If the implementation does not support the requested type of object or operation
INUSE_ATTRIBUTE_ERR	short	If an attempt is made to add an attribute that is already in use elsewhere
INVALID_STATE_ERR	short	If an attempt is made to use an object that is not, or is no longer, usable
SYNTAX_ERR	short	If an invalid or illegal string is specified
INVALID_MODIFICATION_ERR	short	If an attempt is made to modify the type of the underlying object
NAMESPACE_ERR	short	If an attempt is made to create or change an object in a way which is incorrect with regard to namespaces
INVALID_ACCESS_ERR	short	If a parameter or an operation is not supported by the underlying object

Constructor

The DOMException() constructor creates a new exception object.

```
public DOMException(short code, String message)
```

Parameters

Parameter	Type	Description
code	short	The exception's code
message	String	The exception's message

Interface Node
org.w3c.dom

```
public interface Node
```

The Node interface is the primary data type for the entire Document Object Model. It represents a single node in the document tree. While all objects implementing the Node interface expose methods for dealing with children, not all objects implementing the Node interface may have children. For example, Text nodes may not have children, and adding children to such nodes results in a DOMException being raised.

The properties nodeName, nodeValue, and attributes are included as a mechanism to access node information. In cases where there is no obvious mapping of these properties for a specific nodeType (for example, nodeValue for an Element or attributes for a Comment), this returns null. Note that the specialized interfaces may contain additional and more convenient mechanisms to get and set the relevant information.

Fields

A numeric constant is defined for each node type.

Field	Type	Description
ELEMENT_NODE	short	The node is an Element
ATTRIBUTE_NODE	short	The node is an Attr
TEXT_NODE	short	The node is a Text node

Field	Type	Description
CDATA_SECTION_NODE	short	The node is a CDATASection
ENTITY_REFERENCE_NODE	short	The node is an EntityReference
ENTITY_NODE	short	The node is an Entity
PROCESSING_INSTRUCTION_NODE	short	The node is a ProcessingInstruction
COMMENT_NODE	short	The node is a Comment
DOCUMENT_NODE	short	The node is a Document
DOCUMENT_TYPE_NODE	short	The node is a DocumentType
DOCUMENT_FRAGMENT_NODE	short	The node is a DocumentFragment
NOTATION_NODE	short	The node is a Notation

Methods for Getting Node Properties

A node has the following properties:

- Name
- Namespace URI
- Prefix
- Local name
- Type
- Value

The getNodeName() method returns the name of this node, which depends on its type.

The getNamespaceURI() method returns the namespace URI of this node, or null if it is unspecified. This is not a computed value that is the result of a namespace lookup, based on an examination of the namespace declarations in scope. It is merely the namespace URI given at creation time.

The setPrefix() method sets the namespace prefix of this node. Note that setting this property, when permitted, changes the nodeName property, which holds the qualified name, as well as the tagName and name properties of the Element and Attr interfaces, when applicable. Note also that changing the prefix of an attribute that is known to have a default value, does not make a new attribute with the default value and the original prefix appear, since the namespaceURI and localName do not change.

The getPrefix() method returns the namespace prefix of this node, or null if it is unspecified.

The getLocalName() method returns the local part of the qualified name of this node.

For nodes of any type other than ELEMENT_NODE and ATTRIBUTE_NODE and nodes created with DOM Level 1 methods, such as createElement() from the Document interface, the namespaceURI, prefix and localName properties are always null.

167

The getNodeType() method returns a numeric code representing the type of the underlying object. The setNodeValue() method sets the value of this node. For a node that can't have a value, such as an Element, setting it has no effect.

The getNodeValue() method returns the value of this node. It may return null for some node types.

```
public String getNodeName()

public String getNamespaceURI() (Since DOM Level 2)

public void setPrefix(String prefix)
        throws DOMException (Since DOM Level 2)

public String getPrefix() (Since DOM Level 2)

public String getLocalName() (Since DOM Level 2)

public short getNodeType()

public void setNodeValue(String nodeValue)
        throws DOMException

public String getNodeValue()
        throws DOMException
```

Parameters

Parameter	Type	Description
prefix	String	The new namespace prefix of this node
nodeValue	String	The new value of the node

Returned Values

Method	Return	Description
getNodeName()	String	The name of this node, depending on its type
getNamespaceURI()	String	The namespace URI of this node, or null if it is unspecified
getPrefix()	String	The namespace prefix of this node, or null if it is unspecified
getLocalName()	String	The local part of the qualified name of this node
getNodeType()	short	A numeric code representing the type of the underlying object
getNodeValue()	String	The value of this node, depending on its type

Methods for Getting Owner Document, Parent, Siblings, Children and Attributes

A node is linked to the following objects:

- ❑ Owner document
- ❑ Parent node
- ❑ Sibling nodes
- ❑ Child nodes

The attributes of an element are not considered to be part of the DOM tree.

The `getOwnerDocument()` method returns the `Document` object associated with this node. This is also the `Document` object used to create new nodes. When this node is a `Document` or a `DocumentType` that is not used with any `Document` yet, this is `null`.

The `getParentNode()` method returns the parent of this node or `null` if there is no such node. All nodes, except `Attr`, `Document`, `DocumentFragment`, `Entity`, and `Notation` may have a parent. However, if a node has just been created and not yet added to the tree, or if it has been removed from the tree, this is `null`.

The `getPreviousSibling()` method returns the node immediately preceding this node, or `null` if there is no such node.

The `getNextSibling()` method returns the node immediately following this node, or `null` if there is no such node.

The `hasChildNodes()` method returns whether or not this node has any children.

The `getChildNodes()` method returns a `NodeList` that contains all children of this node. If there are no children, this is a `NodeList` containing no nodes.

The `getFirstChild()` method returns the first child of this node, or `null` if there is no such node.

The `getLastChild()` method returns the last child of this node, or `null` if there is no such node.

The `hasAttributes()` method returns whether or not this node (if it is an element) has any attributes.

The `getAttributes()` method returns a `NamedNodeMap` containing the attributes of this node if it is an `Element`, or `null` otherwise.

```
public Document getOwnerDocument() (Since DOM Level 2)
public Node getParentNode()
public Node getPreviousSibling()
public Node getNextSibling()
public boolean hasChildNodes()
```

```
public NodeList getChildNodes()
```

```
public Node getFirstChild()
```

```
public Node getLastChild()
```

```
public boolean hasAttributes()  (Since DOM Level 2)
```

```
public NamedNodeMap getAttributes()
```

Returned Values

Method	Return	Description
getOwnerDocument()	Document	The Document object associated with this node
getParentNode()	Node	The parent of this node, or null if there is no such node
getPreviousSibling()	Node	The node immediately preceding this node, or null if there is no such node
getNextSibling()	Node	The node immediately following this node, or null if there is no such node
hasChildNodes()	boolean	true if this node has any children, false otherwise
getChildNodes()	NodeList	A NodeList that contains all children of this node
getFirstChild()	Node	The first child of this node, or null if there is no such node
getLastChild()	Node	The last child of this node, or null if there is no such node
hasAttributes()	boolean	true if this node has any attributes, false otherwise
getAttributes()	NamedNode Map	A NamedNodeMap containing the attributes of this node if it is an Element, or null otherwise

Inserting, Adding, Replacing, and Removing Child Node Methods

The insertBefore() method inserts a new child node before an existing reference child. If the reference child is null, the new child is inserted at the end of the list of children. If the new child is a DocumentFragment object, all of its children are inserted, in the same order, before the reference child. If the new child is already in the tree, it is first removed.

The appendChild() method adds a new child node to the end of the list of children of this node. If the new child is already in the tree, it is first removed.

The `replaceChild()` method replaces an old child node with a new child in the list of children, and returns the old child. If the new child is a `DocumentFragment` object, the old child is replaced by all of the `DocumentFragment` children, which are inserted in the same order. If the new child is already in the tree, it is first removed.

The `removeChild()` method removes a child node from the list of children, and returns it.

```
public Node insertBefore(Node newChild, Node refChild)
      throws DOMException
public Node appendChild(Node newChild)
      throws DOMException
public Node replaceChild(Node newChild, Node oldChild)
      throws DOMException
public Node removeChild(Node oldChild)
      throws DOMException
```

Parameters

Parameter	Type	Description
newChild	Node	The node to insert/add/use as replacement
refChild	Node	The reference node – in other words, the node before which the new node must be inserted
oldChild	Node	The node being replaced/removed in the list

Returned Values

Method	Return	Description
insertBefore()	Node	The node being inserted
appendChild()	Node	The node being added
replaceChild()	Node	The node being replaced
removeChild()	Node	The node being removed

Cloning Nodes

The `cloneNode()` method returns a duplicate of this node. It serves as a generic copy constructor for nodes. The duplicate node has no parent (`parentNode` is `null`). If the `deep` parameter is `true` the new copy will contain clones of the children of the original node. Otherwise, the new copy will have no children even if the original node has.

Cloning an `Element` copies all attributes and their values, including those generated by the XML processor to represent defaulted attributes. Cloning an `Attribute` directly, as opposed to being cloned as part of an `Element` cloning operation, returns a specified attribute (its `specified` property is `true`). Cloning any other type of node simply returns a copy of this node.

Note that cloning an **immutable subtree** results in a mutable copy, but the children of an `EntityReference` clone are read-only. A node is immutable or read-only when its list of children, attributes and properties cannot be changed.

Cloning `Document`, `DocumentType`, `Entity`, and `Notation` nodes is implementation dependent.

```
public Node cloneNode (boolean deep)
```

Parameters

Parameter	Type	Description
deep	boolean	If `true`, recursively clone the subtree under the specified node; if `false`, clone only the node itself (and its attributes, if it is an `Element`)

Returned Values

Method	Return	Description
cloneNode()	Node	The duplicate node

The normalize() Method

The `normalize()` method puts all `Text` nodes in the full depth of the subtree underneath this `Node` (including attribute nodes) into a "normal" form where only structure (for example, elements, comments, processing instructions, CDATA sections, and entity references) separates `Text` nodes. This means that there are neither adjacent `Text` nodes nor empty `Text` nodes in a list of child nodes.

This can be used to ensure that the DOM view of a document is the same as if it were saved and re-loaded, and is useful when operations (such as XPointer lookups) depend on a particular document tree structure. In cases where the document contains `CDATASections` the normalize operation alone may not be sufficient, since XPointers do not differentiate between `Text` nodes and `CDATASection` nodes. Our `DataUtils` example shows how extract the data of a node and merge the text and CDATA sections.

```
public void normalize() (Since DOM Level 2)
```

The isSupported()Method

The isSupported() method tests whether the DOM implementation implements a specific feature and that feature is supported by this node.

```
public boolean isSupported(String feature, String version)
```

(Since DOM Level 2)

Parameters

Parameter	Type	Description
feature	String	The name of the feature to test. This same name can be passed to the method hasFeature() on DOMImplementation.
version	String	This is the version number of the feature to test. In Level 2, this is the string "2.0". If the version is not specified, supporting any version of the feature will cause the method to return true.

Returned Values

Method	Return	Description
isSupported()	boolean	Returns true if the specified feature is supported on this node, false otherwise

Note: the org.w3c.dom.Node interface is used by our DOMPrinter class. Since most of the DOM interfaces inherit from Node, many other examples of this chapter use methods defined by this interface. These include DataUtils and ElementUtils that iterate over the children of a node using getFirstChild() and getNextSibling(), AttrUtils uses getOwnerDocument(), and DocumentSample that uses insertBefore(), appendChild() and replaceChild().

Interface NodeList
org.w3c.dom

```
public interface NodeList
```

The NodeList interface provides the abstraction of an ordered collection of nodes, without defining or constraining how this collection is implemented.

The items in the NodeList are accessible via an index, starting from 0.

NodeList objects in the DOM are live. Suppose you get the child nodes of an element using the getChildNodes() method. Any addition, replacement or removal of a node using the insertBefore(), appendChild(), replaceChild(), or removeChild methods will affect the NodeList object. In other words, the getLength() and item() methods might return different values. In the case of Apache Xerces, the class that implements Node also implements NodeList and its getChildNodes() method returns this.

These, however, are implementation-specific details – the DOM specification just says that node lists are "live". It is important to understand what this means, especially when you iterate over a node list containing the children of a parent node in order to insert or remove nodes.

Methods

The getLength() method returns the number of nodes in the list. The range of valid child node indices is 0 to length-1 inclusive.

The item() method returns the item at position index item in the collection. If index is greater than or equal to the number of nodes in the list, this returns null.

```
public int getLength()
```
```
public Node item(int index)
```

Parameters

Parameter	Type	Description
index	int	Index into the collection

Returned Values

Method	Return	Description
getLength()	int	The number of nodes in the list
item()	Node	The node at the index position in the NodeList, or null if that is not a valid index

Note: The org.w3c.dom.NodeList interface is used by our DOMPrinter example on page 155.

Interface NamedNodeMap

org.w3c.dom

> **public interface** NamedNodeMap

Objects implementing the NamedNodeMap interface are used to represent collections of nodes that can be accessed by name. Note that NamedNodeMap does not inherit from NodeList and that NamedNodeMaps are not maintained in any particular order. Objects contained in an object implementing NamedNodeMap may also be accessed by an ordinal index, but this is simply to allow convenient enumeration of the contents of a NamedNodeMap, and does not imply that the DOM specifies an order to these nodes.

NamedNodeMap instances in the DOM are live. Suppose you get the attributes of an element using the getAttributes() method inherited by Element from Node. Any addition or removal of an attribute using the setAttribute() and removeAttribute() methods of Element will affect the NamedNodeMap object. In addition, any call of the setNamedItem() and removeNamedItem() methods on the attributes node map will change the element's attribute list. In many DOM implementations, including Apache Xerces, the attribute-related methods defined by the Element interface actually operate on a NamedNodeMap instance using its methods. For example Element.getAttributeNode() uses NamedNodeMap.getNamedItem(). The getAttributes() method inherited by Element from Node returns that internal attribute node map, not a copy or a clone. These are implementation-specific details; the DOM specification just says that node maps are "live". It is important to understand what this means, especially when you iterate over a node map containing the attributes of an element in order to change the element's attribute list.

Methods

The getLength() method returns the number of nodes in this map. The range of valid child node indices is 0 to length-1 inclusive.

The item() method returns the item at position index in the map. If index is greater than or equal to the number of nodes in this map, this returns null.

The setNamedItem() method adds a node using its nodeName property. If a node with that name is already present in this map, it is replaced by the new one. As the nodeName property is used to derive the name that the node must be stored under, multiple nodes of certain types (those that have a "special" string value) cannot be stored as the names would clash. This is seen as preferable to allowing nodes to be aliased.

The setNamedItemNS() method adds a node using its namespaceURI and localName. If a node with that namespace URI (and that local name) is already present in the map, it is replaced by the new one.

The getNamedItem() method retrieves a node specified by name.

The getNamedItemNS() method retrieves a node specified by local name and namespace URI.

The `removeNamedItem()` and `removeNamedItemNS()` methods remove a node. When this map contains the attributes attached to an element, if the removed attribute is known to have a default value, an attribute immediately appears containing the default value as well as the corresponding namespace URI, local name, and prefix when applicable.

```
public int getLength()
```
```
public Node item(int index)
```
```
public Node setNamedItem(Node arg)
        throws DOMException
```
```
public Node setNamedItemNS(Node arg)
        throws DOMException (Since DOM Level 2)
```
```
public Node getNamedItem(String name)
```
```
public Node getNamedItemNS(String namespaceURI,
                           String localName) (Since DOM Level 2)
```
```
public Node removeNamedItem(String name)
        throws DOMException
```
```
public Node removeNamedItemNS(String namespaceURI, String localName)
        throws DOMException (Since DOM Level 2)
```

Parameters

Parameter	Type	Description
index	int	Index into this map
arg	Node	A node to store in this map
name	String	The nodeName of a node to retrieve/remove
namespaceURI	String	The namespace URI of the node to retrieve/remove
localName	String	The local name of the node to retrieve/remove

Returned Values

Method	Return	Description
getLength()	int	The number of nodes in this map
item()	Node	The node at the index position in the map, or null if that is not a valid index

176

Method	Return	Description
setNamedItem()	Node	If the new Node replaces an existing node the replaced Node is returned, otherwise null is returned
setNamedItemNS()	Node	If the new Node replaces an existing node the replaced Node is returned, otherwise null is returned
getNamedItem()	Node	A Node (of any type) with the specified nodeName, or null if it does not identify any node in this map
getNamedItemNS()	Node	A Node (of any type) with the specified local name and namespace URI, or null if they do not identify any node in this map
removeNamedItem()	Node	The node removed from this map if a node with such a name exists
removeNamedItemNS()	Node	The node removed from this map if a node with such a local name and namespace URI exists

Note: The org.w3c.dom.NamedNodeMap interface is used by our DOMPrinter example on page 155.

Interface Notation

org.w3c.dom

public interface Notation

extends Node

This interface represents a notation declared in the DTD. A notation can declare, by name, the format of an unparsed entity or it may be used for formal declaration of processing instruction targets. The nodeName property inherited from Node is set to the declared name of the notation.

The DOM does not support editing Notation nodes; they are therefore read-only.

A Notation node does not have any parent.

Methods

The getPublicId() method returns the public identifier of this notation or null if the public identifier was not specified.

The getSystemId() method returns the system identifier of this notation or null if the system identifier was not specified.

```
public String getPublicId()
public String getSystemId()
```

Returned Values

Method	Return	Description
getPublicId()	String	The public identifier of this notation, or null if the public identifier was not specified
getSystemId()	String	The system identifier of this notation, or null if the system identifier was not specified

> Note: The `org.w3c.dom.Notation` interface is used by our `DoctypeSample` on page 181.

Interface Entity

org.w3c.dom

```
public interface Entity

extends Node
```

This interface represents an entity, either parsed or unparsed, in an XML document. Note that this models the entity itself not the entity declaration. Entity declaration modeling has been left for a later Level of the DOM specification.

The nodeName property that is inherited from Node contains the name of the entity.

An XML processor may choose to completely expand entities before the structure model is passed to the DOM. In this case there will be no EntityReference nodes in the document tree. Sometimes you don't want to deal with the entity references. Other times you want to be aware of them. The JAXP API lets you control this. A full list of configuration options will be given in Chapter 5.

XML does not mandate that a non-validating XML processor read and process entity declarations made in the external subset or declared in external parameter entities. This means that parsed entities declared in the external subset need not be expanded by some classes of applications, and that the replacement value of the entity may not be available. When the replacement value is available, the corresponding Entity node's child list represents the structure of that replacement text. Otherwise, the child list is empty.

The DOM Level 2 does not support editing Entity nodes. If a user wants to make changes to the contents of an Entity, every related EntityReference node has to be replaced in the structure model by a clone of the Entity's contents, and then the desired changes must be made to each of those clones instead. Entity nodes and all their descendants are read-only.

An `Entity` node does not have any parent. If the entity contains an unbound namespace prefix, the `namespaceURI` of the corresponding node in the `Entity` node subtree is `null`. The same is true for `EntityReference` nodes that refer to this entity, when they are created using the `createEntityReference` method of the `Document` interface. The DOM Level 2 does not support any mechanism to resolve namespace prefixes.

Methods

The `getPublicId()` method returns the public identifier associated with the entity, if specified. If the public identifier was not specified, this is `null`.

The `getSystemId()` method returns the system identifier associated with the entity, if specified. If the system identifier was not specified, this is `null`.

The `getNotationName()` method returns the name of the notation for an unparsed entity. For parsed entities, this is `null`.

```
public String getPublicId()

public String getSystemId()

public String getNotationName()
```

Returned Values

Method	Return	Description
getPublicId()	String	The public identifier associated with the entity, or null if this was not specified
getSystemId()	String	The system identifier associated with the entity, or null if this was not specified
getNotationName()	String	The name of the notation for the unparsed entity, or null if this is a parsed entity

Note: The `org.w3c.dom.Entity` interface is used by our `DoctypeSample` on page 181.

Interface EntityReference
org.w3c.dom

```
public interface EntityReference
extends Node
```

`EntityReference` objects may be inserted into the structure model when an entity reference is in the source document, or when the user wishes to insert an entity reference. Note that character references and references to predefined entities are considered to be expanded by the XML processor, so that characters are represented by their Unicode equivalent rather than by an entity reference. Moreover, the XML processor may completely expand references to entities while building the structure model, instead of providing `EntityReference` objects. If it does provide such objects, then for a given `EntityReference` node, it may be that there is no `Entity` node representing the referenced entity. If such an `Entity` exists, then the subtree of the `EntityReference` node is in general a copy of the `Entity` node subtree. However, this may not be true when an entity contains an unbound namespace prefix. In such a case, because the namespace prefix resolution depends on where the entity reference is, the descendants of the `EntityReference` node may be bound to different namespace URIs.

As for `Entity` nodes, `EntityReference` nodes and all their descendants are read-only.

> Note: The `org.w3c.dom.EntityReference` interface is used by our `DataUtils` example on page 185.

Interface DocumentType
org.w3c.dom

`public interface` DocumentType

`extends` Node

Each `Document` has a `doctype` property whose value is either `null` or a `DocumentType` instance. The `DocumentType` interface in the DOM Core provides an interface to the list of entities and notations that are defined for the document.

The DOM Level 2 doesn't support editing `DocumentType` nodes. The DOM Level 3 will add support for content models such as DTDs and XML Schemas.

Methods

The `getName()` method returns the element type of the root element, that is, the name immediately following the `DOCTYPE` keyword.

The `getPublicId()` method returns the public identifier of the external subset of the DTD.

The `getSystemId()` method returns the system identifier of the external subset of the DTD.

The `getInternalSubset()` method returns the internal subset of the DTD as a string. The actual content returned depends on how much information is available to the implementation. This may vary depending on various parameters, including the XML processor used to build the document.

The `getNotations()` method returns a `NamedNodeMap` containing the notations declared in the DTD. Duplicates are discarded. Every node in this map also implements the `Notation` interface. The DOM Level 2 does not support editing notations.

The getEntities() method also returns a NamedNodeMap containing the general entities, both external and internal, declared in the DTD. Parameter entities are not contained. Duplicates are discarded. Every node in this map also implements the Entity interface. The DOM Level 2 does not support editing entities.

```
public String getName()

public String getPublicId() (Since DOM Level 2)

public String getSystemId() (Since DOM Level 2)

public String getInternalSubset() (Since DOM Level 2)

public NamedNodeMap getNotations()

public NamedNodeMap getEntities()
```

Returned Values

Method	Return	Description
getName()	String	The name immediately following the DOCTYPE keyword, which must match the element type of the root element
getPublicId()	String	The public identifier of the external subset of the DTD
getSystemId()	String	The system identifier of the external subset of the DTD
getInternalSubset()	String	The internal subset of the DTD as a string
getNotations()	NamedNodeMap	A NamedNodeMap containing the notations declared in the DTD
getEntities()	NamedNodeMap	A NamedNodeMap containing the general entities, both external and internal, declared in the DTD

Example: Obtaining DTD information

This example parses the doctype.xml file using the parse() method inherited from DOMPrinter and obtains the DocumentType instance using the getDoctype() method defined by org.w3c.dom.Document. Then it uses the println() method inherited from DOMPrinter to output the name, IDs, internal subset, notations and entities of the DTD, which are obtained using the methods of the interfaces described above.

Source DoctypeSample.java

```java
import org.w3c.dom.Document;
import org.w3c.dom.DocumentType;
import org.w3c.dom.Entity;
import org.w3c.dom.NamedNodeMap;
import org.w3c.dom.Notation;

public class DoctypeSample extends DOMPrinter {
  public static void main(String args[]) {
    try {
      Document doc = parse("doctype.xml", true);
      DocumentType doctype = doc.getDoctype();
      if (doctype != null) {
        println("Name: " + doctype.getName());
        println("Public ID: " + doctype.getPublicId());
        println("System ID: " + doctype.getSystemId());
        println("Internal subset: "
            + doctype.getInternalSubset());
        NamedNodeMap notations = doctype.getNotations();
        if (notations != null) {
          for (int i = 0; i < notations.getLength(); i++) {
            Notation notation = (Notation) notations.item(i);
            println("Notation: " + notation.getNodeName()
                + " - "
                + notation.getPublicId() + " - "
                + notation.getSystemId());
          }
        }
        NamedNodeMap entities = doctype.getEntities();
        if (entities != null) {
          for (int i = 0; i < entities.getLength(); i++) {
            Entity entity = (Entity) entities.item(i);
            println("Entity: " + entity.getNodeName() + " - "
                    + entity.getPublicId() + " - "
                    + entity.getSystemId()
                    + " - " + entity.getNotationName());
          }
        }
      }
    } catch (org.xml.sax.SAXParseException e) {

      // Already printed by PrintErrorHandler
      System.exit(1);
    } catch (Exception e) {
      e.printStackTrace();
      System.exit(1);
    }
  }
}
```

Sample doctype.ent

```
<?xml version="1.0" encoding="UTF-8"?>

<!-- Unparsed entities -->

<!NOTATION txt PUBLIC "text/plain">

<!ENTITY server_info   SYSTEM "server.txt"   NDATA txt>
<!ENTITY computer_info SYSTEM "computer.txt" NDATA txt>
<!ENTITY scanner_info  SYSTEM "scanner.txt"  NDATA txt>
<!ENTITY printer_info  SYSTEM "printer.txt"  NDATA txt>
```

Sample doctype.dtd

```
<?xml version="1.0" encoding="UTF-8"?>

<!-- External DTD -->

<!ELEMENT sample (#PCDATA)>

<!ENTITY % parameterEntity SYSTEM "doctype.ent">

%parameterEntity;
```

Sample doctype.xml

```
<?xml version='1.0' encoding='utf-8'?>

<!-- XML document -->

<!DOCTYPE sample PUBLIC "DTD for DoctypeSample" "doctype.dtd"
[ <!ENTITY generalEntity "General Entity"> ]>

<sample>&generalEntity;</sample>
```

Output

```
> java DoctypeSample

Name: sample
Public ID: DTD for DoctypeSample
System ID: doctype.dtd
Internal subset:  <!ENTITY generalEntity "General Entity">
Notation: txt - text/plain - null
Entity: computer_info - null - computer.txt - txt
Entity: generalEntity - null - null - null
Entity: printer_info - null - printer.txt - txt
Entity: scanner_info - null - scanner.txt - txt
Entity: server_info - null - server.txt - txt
```

Interface CharacterData
org.w3c.dom

```
public interface CharacterData

extends Node
```

The `CharacterData` interface extends `Node` with a set of properties and methods for accessing character data in the DOM. No DOM objects correspond directly to `CharacterData`, though `Text` and others do inherit this interface. All offsets in this interface start from 0.

Text strings in the DOM API are represented in UTF-16; in other words, as a sequence of characters, using the `java.lang.String` class.

Methods

The `getLength()` method returns the number of characters that are available through the `getData()` method. This may have the value zero, that is, `CharacterData` nodes may be empty.

The `setData()` and `getData()` methods set and return the character data of the node that implements this interface. The DOM implementation may not put arbitrary limits on the amount of data that may be stored in a `CharacterData` node.

The `substringData()` method extracts a range of data from the node.

The `appendData()` method appends the string to the end of the character data of the node.

The `insertData()` method inserts a string at the specified character offset.

The `replaceData()` method replaces the characters starting at the specified character offset with the specified string.

The `deleteData()` method removes a range of characters from the node.

```
public int getLength()

public void setData(String data)
        throws DOMException

public String getData()
        throws DOMException

public String substringData(int offset, int count)
        throws DOMException

public void appendData(String arg)
        throws DOMException

public void insertData(int offset, String arg)
        throws DOMException
```

```
public void replaceData(int offset, int count, String arg)
        throws DOMException
public void deleteData(int offset, int count)
        throws DOMException
```

Parameters

Parameter	Type	Description
data	String	The new character data of this node
offset	int	The start offset from which to start extracting/inserting/replacing/deleting
count	int	The number of characters to extract/replace/delete
arg	String	The String to append/insert/use as replacement

Returned Values

Method	Return	Description
getLength()	int	The number of characters contained by the node that implements this interface
getData()	String	The character data of the node that implements this interface
substringData()	String	The specified substring. If the sum of offset and count exceeds the length, then all characters to the end of the data are returned.

Example: Collecting character data

This class contains a method for extracting the data contained by a node. If the node is an Element or EntityReference instance, the data might be split in adjacent Text and CDATASection nodes. Comments may also act as splitters. Logically, however, only sub-elements and processing instructions split the data. An application might not want to be bothered by a CDATA section, an entity reference or a comment separating two Text nodes.

Source DataUtils.java

```java
import org.w3c.dom.CDATASection;
import org.w3c.dom.CharacterData;
import org.w3c.dom.Comment;
import org.w3c.dom.EntityReference;
import org.w3c.dom.Node;
import org.w3c.dom.Text;
```

```
import java.util.Vector;

public class DataUtils {
```

The `getData()` method extracts the character data contained by a node. If the node is a `Text` or a `CDATASection`, this will return the node's data. Otherwise, it iterates over its children and collects the character data in a string array. Each component of this array is the concatenation of the data contained by adjacent `Text` and `CDATASection` nodes after the entity references were replaced with their values. Therefore, the array has multiple components only if sub-elements or processing instructions separate the character data. Note that the data contained by sub-elements is not included. If the node contains no data a string array containing an empty string is returned.

```
public static String[] getData(Node node) {
  Vector vector = new Vector();
  StringBuffer buf = new StringBuffer();
  getDataImpl(node, buf, vector);
  if (buf.length() > 0) {
    vector.add(buf.toString());
  }
  String array[] = new String[vector.size()];
  for (int i = 0; i < array.length; i++) {
    array[i] = (String) vector.get(i);
  }
  if (array.length == 0) {
    array = new String[] {
      ""
    };
  }
  return array;
}
```

The `getDataImpl()` method implements the data extraction mechanism. The `getData()` method calls `getDataImpl()` passing as parameters an empty `StringBuffer` and an empty `Vector`. This method iterates over the children of the given node and appends the data of the `Text` and `CDATASection` nodes to the given string buffer. The method is called recursively for each `EntityReference` so that their data can be collected. Comments are ignored. When this method finds a child node that acts as data separator (sub-element or processing instruction), the content of the string buffer (if any) is added to the vector and the buffer is emptied. The `getData()` method will convert the vector to a string array.

```
private static void getDataImpl(Node node, StringBuffer buf,
                                Vector vector) {
  if (node instanceof Text || node instanceof CDATASection){
    buf.append(((CharacterData) node).getData());
    return;
  }
  Node child = node.getFirstChild();
```

```
      while (child != null) {
        if (child instanceof Text || child instanceof
            CDATASection) {
          buf.append(((CharacterData) child).getData());
        } else if (child instanceof EntityReference) {
          getDataImpl(child, buf, vector);
        } else if (!(child instanceof Comment)) {
          if (buf.length() > 0) {
            vector.add(buf.toString());
            buf.setLength(0);
          }
        }
        child = child.getNextSibling();
      }
    }
  }
```

Source DataSample.java

This example uses the `DataUtils` class to collect the data contained by an element. After parsing the `data.xml` file using the `parse()` method inherited from `DOMPrinter`, the `main()` method gets the root element of the document using the `getDocumentElement()` method defined by the `org.w3c.dom.Document` interface. The `getData()` method of `DataUtils` extracts the entire data of the element. The document is printed using the `print()` method inherited from `DOMPrinter`.

```java
import org.w3c.dom.Document;
import org.w3c.dom.Element;

public class DataSample extends DOMPrinter {

  public static void main(String args[]) {
    try {
      Document doc = parse("data.xml", false);
      Element root = doc.getDocumentElement();
      String data[] = DataUtils.getData(root);
      print(doc);
      println("\r\n*** Data of the root element:");
      for (int i = 0; i < data.length; i++) {
        println("" + i + ": \"" + data[i] + "\"");
      }
    } catch (org.xml.sax.SAXParseException e) {

      // Already printed by PrintErrorHandler
      System.exit(1);
    } catch (Exception e) {
      e.printStackTrace();
      System.exit(1);
    }
  }
}
```

Sample data.xml

```xml
<?xml version='1.0' encoding='utf-8'?>
<!DOCTYPE sample [
<!ENTITY thirdRowEntity "rd ro">
<!ENTITY entityWithElement "fifth<break/>row">
]>
<sample>
  first row <element>data within element</element>
  second row <!-- ignored comment -->
  thi&thirdRowEntity;w
  <![CDATA[fourth row]]>
  &entityWithElement;
  sixth row <?proc?>
  seventh row
</sample>
```

Output

```
> java DataSample

DOCUMENT - #document - null
  DOCUMENT_TYPE - sample - null
  ELEMENT - sample - null
    TEXT - #text - first row
    ELEMENT - element - null
      TEXT - #text - data within element
    TEXT - #text - second row
    COMMENT - #comment - ignored comment
    TEXT - #text - thi
    ENTITY_REFERENCE - thirdRowEntity - null
      TEXT - #text - rd ro
    TEXT - #text - w
    CDATA_SECTION - #cdata-section - fourth row
    ENTITY_REFERENCE - entityWithElement - null
      TEXT - #text - fifth
      ELEMENT - break - null
      TEXT - #text - row
    TEXT - #text - sixth row
    PROCESSING_INSTRUCTION - proc -
    TEXT - #text - seventh row

*** Data of the root element:
0: "
  first row "
1: "
  second row

  third row
  fourth row
  fifth"
2: "row
  sixth row "
3: "
  seventh row
  "
```

Interface Text

org.w3c.dom

```
public interface Text
extends CharacterData
```

The Text interface inherits from CharacterData and represents the textual content (termed character data in XML) of an Element or Attr. If there is no markup inside an element's content, the text is contained in a single object implementing the Text interface that is the only child of the element. If there is markup, it is parsed into the information items (elements, comments, and so on) and Text nodes that form the list of children of the element.

When a document is first made available via the DOM, there is only one Text node for each block of text. Users may create adjacent Text nodes that represent the contents of a given element without any intervening markup, but we should be aware that there is no way to represent the separations between these nodes in XML, so they will not (in general) persist between DOM editing sessions. The normalize() method on Node merges any such adjacent Text objects into a single node for each block of text.

Methods

The splitText() method breaks this node into two nodes at the specified offset, keeping both in the tree as siblings. After being split, this node will contain all the content up to the offset point. A new node of the same type, which contains all the content both at and after the offset point, is returned. If the original node had a parent node, the new node is inserted as the next sibling of the original node. When the offset is equal to the length of this node, the new node has no data.

```
public Text splitText(int offset)
       throws DOMException
```

Parameters

Parameter	Type	Description
offset	int	The character offset at which to split, starting from 0

Returned Values

Method	Return	Description
splitText()	Text	The new node, of the same type as this node

Note: The org.w3c.dom.Text interface is used by our DataUtils example on page 185

Interface CDATASection

org.w3c.dom

```
public interface CDATASection
        extends Text
```

CDATA sections are used to escape blocks of text containing characters that would otherwise be regarded as markup. The only delimiter that is recognized in a CDATA section is the "]]>" string that ends the CDATA section. CDATA sections cannot be nested. Their primary purpose is for including material such as XML fragments, without needing to escape all the delimiters.

The `data` property inherited from `CharacterData` holds the text that is contained by the CDATA section. Note that this may contain characters that need to be escaped outside of CDATA sections and that, depending on the character encoding (`charset`) chosen for serialization, it may be impossible to write out some characters as part of a CDATA section.

The `CDATASection` interface inherits from the `CharacterData` interface through the `Text` interface. Adjacent `CDATASection` nodes are not merged by use of the `Element.normalize()` method of the `Node` interface. Because no markup is recognized within a `CDATASection`, character numeric references cannot be used as an escape mechanism when serializing. Therefore, action needs to be taken when serializing a `CDATASection` with a character encoding where some of the contained characters cannot be represented. Failure to do so would not produce well-formed XML. One potential solution in the serialization process is to end the CDATA section before the character, output the character using a character reference or entity reference, and open a new CDATA section for any further characters in the text node. Note, however, that some code conversion libraries do not return an error or exception when a character is missing from the encoding, making the task of ensuring that data is not corrupted on serialization more difficult.

> Note: The `org.w3c.dom.CDATASection` interface is used by our `DataUtils` example on page 185.

Interface Comment

org.w3c.dom

```
public interface Comment
        extends CharacterData
```

This interface inherits from `CharacterData` and represents the content of a comment, that is, all the characters between the starting '`<!--`' and ending '`-->`'. Note that this is the definition of a comment in XML.

> Note: The `org.w3c.dom.Comment` interface is used by our `DataUtils` example on page 185.

Interface Element
org.w3c.dom

> **public interface** Element
>   **extends** Node

The Element interface represents an element in an XML document. Elements may have attributes associated with them. The Element interface inherits from Node the generic Node interface method getAttributes(). This may be used to retrieve the attributes property, which may be used to retrieve the set of all attributes for an element. There are methods on the Element interface to retrieve either an Attr object by name or an attribute value by name. In XML, an attribute value may contain entity references. Attr objects can be retrieved to examine the possibly complex sub-tree representing the attribute value. In DOM Level 2, the method normalize() is inherited from the Node interface where it was moved. (In DOM Level 1, the normalize() method was defined in the Element interface.)

The methods inherited from Node can be used to retrieve and modify the list of children, which in the case of an Element may include Text, CDATASection, ProcessingInstruction, Comment, EntityReference and Element nodes.

Method getTagName()

The getTagName() method returns the type of the element. Note that this is case-preserving in XML, as are all of the operations of the DOM.

> public String **getTagName**()

Returned Values

Method	Return	Description
getTagName()	String	The name of the element type

Methods for Setting, Getting, and Removing Attributes

The setAttribute() method adds a new attribute. If an attribute with that name is already present in the element, its value is changed to be that of the value parameter.

The setAttributeNS() method adds a new attribute with namespace information. If an attribute with the same local name and namespace URI is already present on the element, its prefix is changed to be the prefix part of the qualifiedName parameter, and its value is changed to be the value parameter.

The value passed to the above two methods is a simple string. It is not parsed as it is being set. So any markup (such as syntax to be recognized as an entity reference) is treated as literal text, and needs to be appropriately escaped by the implementation when it is written out.

In order to assign an attribute value that contains entity references, the user must create an Attr node plus any Text and EntityReference nodes, build the appropriate subtree, and use setAttributeNodeNS() or setAttributeNode().

The getAttribute() and getAttributeNS() methods retrieve an attribute's value.

The getAttributeNode() and getAttributeNodeNS() methods retrieve an attribute node.

The hasAttribute() and hasAttributeNS() methods return true when an attribute with a given name (or local name – namespace URI pair) is specified on this element or has a default value.

The removeAttribute(), removeAttributeNS() and removeAttributeNode() methods remove an attribute. If the removed attribute is known to have a default value, an attribute immediately appears containing the default value as well as the corresponding namespace URI, local name and prefix when applicable.

```
public void setAttribute(String name, String value)
        throws DOMException
```

```
public void setAttributeNS(String namespaceURI, String qualifiedName,
                           String value)
        throws DOMException (Since DOM Level 2)
```

```
public Attr setAttributeNode(Attr newAttr)
        throws DOMException
```

```
public Attr setAttributeNodeNS(Attr newAttr)
        throws DOMException (Since DOM Level 2)
```

```
public String getAttribute(String name)
```

```
public String getAttributeNS(String namespaceURI, String localName)
```
(Since DOM Level 2)

```
public Attr getAttributeNode(String name)
```

```
public Attr getAttributeNodeNS(String namespaceURI, String localName)
```
(Since DOM Level 2)

```
public boolean hasAttribute(String name) (Since DOM Level 2)
```

```
public boolean hasAttributeNS(String namespaceURI, String localName)
```
(Since DOM Level 2)

```
public void removeAttribute(String name)
        throws DOMException
```

```
public void removeAttributeNS(String namespaceURI, String localName)
        throws DOMException (Since DOM Level 2)
```

```
public Attr removeAttributeNode(Attr oldAttr)
        throws DOMException
```

Parameters

Parameter	Type	Description
name	String	The name of the attribute to set retrieve/look for/remove
value	String	The value to set in string form
namespaceURI	String	The namespace URI of the attribute to set/retrieve/look for/remove
qualifiedName	String	The qualified name of the attribute to set
newAttr	Attr	The Attr node to add to the attribute list
localName	String	The local name of the attribute to set/retrieve/look for/remove
oldAttr	Attr	The Attr node to remove from the attribute list

Returned Values

Method	Return	Description
setAttributeNode()	Attr	If the newAttr attribute replaces an existing attribute, the replaced Attr node is returned, otherwise null is returned
setAttributeNodeNS()	Attr	If the newAttr attribute replaces an existing attribute with the same local name and namespace URI, the replaced Attr node is returned, otherwise null is returned
getAttribute()	String	The Attr value as a string, or the empty string if that attribute does not have a specified or default value
getAttributeNS()	String	The Attr value as a string, or the empty string if that attribute does not have a specified or default value
getAttributeNode()	Attr	The Attr node with the specified name (nodeName) or null if there is no such attribute
getAttributeNodeNS()	Attr	The Attr node with the specified attribute local name and namespace URI or null if there is no such attribute
hasAttribute()	boolean	true if an attribute with the given name is specified on this element or has a default value, false otherwise
hasAttributeNS()	boolean	true if an attribute with the given local name and namespace URI is specified or has a default value on this element, false otherwise
removeAttributeNode()	Attr	The Attr node that was removed

Getting Elements By Tag Name

The getElementsByTagName() method returns a NodeList of all descendant Elements with a given tag name, in the order in which they are encountered in a preorder traversal of this Element tree. The preorder is the order in which the start tags occur in the text representation of the document.

The getElementsByTagNameNS() method returns a NodeList of all the descendant Elements with a given local name and namespace URI in the order in which they are encountered in a preorder traversal of this Element tree.

```
public NodeList getElementsByTagName(String name)
public NodeList getElementsByTagNameNS(String namespaceURI,
                                       String localName)
```
(Since DOM Level 2)

Parameters

Parameter	Type	Description
name	String	The name of the tag to match on. The special value "*" matches all tags.
namespaceURI	String	The namespace URI of the elements to match on. The special value "*" matches all namespaces.
localName	String	The local name of the elements to match on. The special value "*" matches all local names.

Returned Values

Method	Return	Description
getElementsByTagName()	NodeList	A list of matching Element nodes
getElementsByTagNameNS()	NodeList	A new NodeList object containing all the matched Elements

Example: Searching elements in a DOM tree

This class contains methods for finding the elements of a DOM tree that satisfy some criteria. We can specify the tag name, local name and namespace URI, character data that must be contained by the elements and a list of attributes with the wanted values. We use the getData() method of our DataUtils to extract the data of an element.

Source ElementUtils.java

```java
import org.w3c.dom.Element;
import org.w3c.dom.Node;

import java.util.Vector;

public class ElementUtils {#
```

The findElements() method traverses a DOM tree in preorder and collects the Element instances whose tag names match tagName (if not null), contain the strings of the data array (if not null) and have the given attributes set to the given values (if the arrays aren't null). The root element can be any Element instance; it doesn't have to be the root of a document.

```
public static Element[] findElements(Element root,
    String tagName, String data[], String attrNames[],
    String attrValues[]) {
  return findElementsImpl(root, null, tagName, data,
      attrNames, attrValues);
}
```

The following is the namespace-aware version of the previous method:

```
public static Element[] findElements(Element root,
    String namespaceURI, String localName, String data[],
    String attrNames[], String attrValues[]) {
  return findElementsImpl(root, namespaceURI, localName,
      data, attrNames, attrValues);
}
```

The findElementsImpl() method creates a vector and passes it to the method with the same name that follows this one. Then, it converts the vector to an array of Elements, which is returned:

```
private static Element[] findElementsImpl(Element root,
    String namespaceURI, String name, String data[],
    String attrNames[], String attrValues[]) {
  Vector vector = new Vector();
  findElementsImpl(root, namespaceURI, name, data,
      attrNames, attrValues, vector);
  Element array[] = new Element[vector.size()];
  for (int i = 0; i < array.length; i++) {
    array[i] = (Element) vector.get(i);
  }
  return array;
}
```

The findElementsImpl() method implements the finding of the elements within the DOM tree. If the given element satisfies the finding criteria, it is added to the vector. Then, the method iterates over the children of the given node and a recursive call is made for each Element instance.

If the name isn't null, it must match the tag name (if the namespace URI is null) or the local name in order to be considered for further checking. The element's character data must contain all the strings of the data array (if any). All the attributes specified by attrNames must have the values contained by attrValues. If all these conditions are met the element is added to the vector.

Whether the element satisfies the criteria or not, its sub-elements are passed to recursive calls of this method so that they can be verified too:

```java
private static void findElementsImpl(Element root, String
    namespaceURI, String name, String data[],
    String attrNames[], String attrValues[], Vector vector){
  boolean flag = false;
  if (name == null
        || (namespaceURI == null &&
        name.equals(root.getTagName()))
        || (namespaceURI != null
        && namespaceURI.equals(root.getNamespaceURI())
        && name.equals(root.getLocalName())))) {
    flag = true;
    if (data != null) {
      String rootData[] = DataUtils.getData(root);
      for (int i = 0; i < data.length; i++) {
        flag = false;
        for (int j = 0; j < rootData.length; j++) {
          if (rootData[j].indexOf(data[i]) != -1) {
            flag = true;
            break;
          }
        }
        if (flag == false) {
          break;
        }
      }
    }
    if (flag && attrNames != null && attrValues != null) {
      for (int i = 0; i < attrNames.length; i++) {
        String value = root.getAttribute(attrNames[i]);
        if (value == null ||!value.equals(attrValues[i])) {
          flag = false;
          break;
        }
      }
    }
  }

  if (flag) {
    vector.add(root);

  }
  Node child = root.getFirstChild();
  while (child != null) {
    if (child instanceof Element) {
      findElementsImpl((Element) child, namespaceURI, name,
          data, attrNames, attrValues, vector);
```

```
      }
      child = child.getNextSibling();
    }
  }
}
```

Source ElementSample.java

This example uses the `ElementUtils` class to find elements within a document. After parsing the `element.xml` file using the `parse()` method inherited from `DOMPrinter`, the `main()` method gets the root element of the document using the `getDocumentElement()` method defined by the `org.w3c.dom.Document` interface. The `findElements()` method of `ElementUtils` traverses a DOM tree in preorder and collects the `Element` instances that satisfy some criteria. It is possible to specify the tag name, namespace URI and local name of the elements, strings that must be contained by them and attributes.

```java
import org.w3c.dom.Document;
import org.w3c.dom.Element;

public class ElementSample extends DOMPrinter {
```

The `print()` method prints the values of the `id` attribute of the elements contained by the given array:

```java
private static void print(int test, Element elemArray[]) {
  StringBuffer buf = new StringBuffer();
  buf.append("*** " + test + " ***");
  for (int i = 0; i < elemArray.length; i++) {
    buf.append(" ");
    buf.append(elemArray[i].getAttribute("id"));
  }
  println(buf.toString());
}
```

The `main()` method parses the XML document and calls `ElementUtils.findElements()` using various combinations of parameters:

```java
public static void main(String args[]) {
  try {
    Document doc = parse("element.xml", false);
    Element root = doc.getDocumentElement();
    String uri = "http://company.com/sample";
    Element elemArray[];
    String data[], attr[], val[];
    elemArray = ElementUtils.findElements(root, uri, "elem",
        null, null, null);
    print(1, elemArray);
```

```
    elemArray = ElementUtils.findElements(root,
        "sample:elem", null, null, null);
    print(2, elemArray);

    elemArray = ElementUtils.findElements(root, "elem",
        null, null, null);
    print(3, elemArray);

    data = new String[] {
      "1", "2"
    };
    elemArray = ElementUtils.findElements(root, null, data,
        null, null);
    print(4, elemArray);

    elemArray = ElementUtils.findElements(root, "array",
        null, null, null);
    print(5, elemArray);

    Element array = elemArray[0];

    elemArray = ElementUtils.findElements(array, null, null,
        null, null);
    print(6, elemArray);

    attr = new String[] {
      "attr"
    };
    val = new String[] {
      "b"
    };
    elemArray = ElementUtils.findElements(array, null, null,
        attr, val);
    print(7, elemArray);

    attr = new String[] {
      "attr"
    };
    val = new String[] {
      "a"
    };
    data = new String[] {
      "4"
    };
    elemArray = ElementUtils.findElements(array, null, data,
        attr, val);
    print(8, elemArray);

    attr = new String[] {
      "attr", "id"
    };
    val = new String[] {
```

```
            "a", "e5"
        };
        elemArray = ElementUtils.findElements(array, null, null,
            attr, val);
        print(9, elemArray);
    } catch (org.xml.sax.SAXParseException e) {

        // Already printed by PrintErrorHandler
        System.exit(1);
    } catch (Exception e) {
        e.printStackTrace();
        System.exit(1);
    }
  }
}

}
```

Sample element.xml

```xml
<?xml version='1.0' encoding='utf-8'?>
<sample:sample xmlns:sample="http://company.com/sample">
  <sample:elem attr="a" id="e1"> 1
    <sample:elem attr="b" id="e2"> 1 2
      <sample:elem attr="c" id="e3"> 1 2 3
      </sample:elem>
    </sample:elem>
  </sample:elem>
  <array id="e4">
    <elem attr="a" id="e5"> 1 </elem>
    <elem attr="b" id="e6"> 2 </elem>
    <elem attr="c" id="e7"> 3 </elem>
    <elem attr="a" id="e8"> 4 </elem>
    <elem attr="b" id="e9"> 5 </elem>
  </array>
</sample:sample>
```

Sample Output

```
> java ElementSample

*** 1 *** e1 e2 e3
*** 2 *** e1 e2 e3
*** 3 *** e5 e6 e7 e8 e9
*** 4 *** e2 e3
*** 5 *** e4
*** 6 *** e4 e5 e6 e7 e8 e9
*** 7 *** e6 e9
*** 8 *** e8
*** 9 *** e5
```

Interface Attr

org.w3c.dom

> **public interface** Attr
>
> **extends** Node

The Attr interface represents an attribute in an Element object.

Attr objects inherit the Node interface, but since they are not actually child nodes of the element they describe, the DOM does not consider them part of the document tree. Thus, the Node properties parentNode, previousSibling, and nextSibling have a null value for Attr objects. The DOM takes the view that attributes are properties of elements rather than having a separate identity from the elements with which they are associated. Furthermore, Attr nodes may not be immediate children of a DocumentFragment. However, they can be associated with Element nodes contained within a DocumentFragment. In short, users of the DOM API need to be aware that Attr nodes have some things in common with other objects inheriting the Node interface, but they also are quite distinct.

The attribute's effective value is determined as follows:

❑ If the attribute has been explicitly assigned any value, that value is the attribute's effective value

❑ Otherwise, if there is a declaration for this attribute in the DTD, and that declaration includes a default value, then that default value is the attribute's effective value

❑ Otherwise, the attribute does not exist on this element in the structure model until it has been explicitly added

Note that the nodeValue property on the Attr instance can also be used to retrieve the string version of the attribute's value.

In XML, where the value of an attribute can contain entity references, the child nodes of the Attr node may be either Text or EntityReference nodes (when these are in use; see the description of EntityReference for discussion). Because the DOM Level 2 Core is not aware of attribute types, it treats all attribute values as simple strings, even if the DTD or schema declares them as having tokenized types.

Methods

The getName() and getValue() methods allow the getting of the attribute's properties (name and value). When the value of the attribute is returned as a string by getValue(), character and general entity references are replaced with their values. Note that you may also use the getNamespaceURI(), getPrefix(), and getLocalName() methods defined by Node.

The setValue() method creates a Text node with the unparsed contents of the string parameter. This node is attached as a child to the Attr node.

The getSpecified() method returns true if the attribute was explicitly given a value in the original document. Note that the implementation is in charge of the attribute, not the user. If the user changes the value of the attribute then the specified flag is automatically flipped to true. To re-specify the attribute as the default value from the DTD, the user must delete the attribute. The implementation will then make a new attribute available with specified set to false and the default value (if one exists). In summary, if the attribute has an assigned value in the document then specified is true, and the value is the assigned value. If the attribute has no assigned value in the document and has a default value in the DTD, then specified is false, and the value is the default value in the DTD. If the attribute has no assigned value in the document and has a value of #IMPLIED in the DTD, then the attribute does not appear in the structure model of the document. If the ownerElement property is null (that is, because it was just created or was set to null by the various removal and cloning operations) specified is true.

The getOwnerElement() method allows the getting of the Element node the attribute is attached to.

```
public String getName()

public void setValue(String value)
        throws DOMException

public String getValue()

public boolean getSpecified()

public Element getOwnerElement() (Since DOM Level 2)
```

Parameters

Parameter	Type	Description
value	String	The new value of the attribute

Returned Values

Method	Return	Description
getName()	String	The name of this attribute
getValue()	String	The value of this attribute
getSpecified()	boolean	true if this attribute was explicitly given a value in the original document
getOwnerElement()	Element	The Element node this attribute is attached to, or null if this attribute is not in use

Example: Renaming attributes

This example contains methods for renaming attributes. We normally don't have to rename an attribute and the DOM API doesn't define such an operation. If the elements and attributes of a document become obsolete, we can apply an XSLT transformation, which allows us to change the whole structure of the document.

Source AttrUtils.java

In case we just have to rename some attributes, we could use this class.

```
import org.w3c.dom.Attr;
import org.w3c.dom.Document;
import org.w3c.dom.Element;

public class AttrUtils {
```

The `renameAttr()` method renames an attribute of an element. The DOM API actually doesn't allow the renaming of the nodes. Therefore, this method creates a copy of the given `Attr` node with the new name and returns that object:

```
public static Attr renameAttr(Attr attr, String newName) {
    return renameAttrImpl(attr, null, newName);
}
```

The following is the namespace-aware version of the previous method:

```
public static Attr renameAttr(Attr attr,
    String newNamespaceURI, String newQualifiedName) {
  return renameAttrImpl(attr, newNamespaceURI,
      newQualifiedName);
}
```

The `renameAttrImpl()` method implements the "renaming" of the attributes. It uses the owner document of the original `Attr` node to create a new `Attr` instance with the new name and namespace URI (if not `null`). The value of the attribute is preserved. If the old attribute is owned by an element, this method removes it from the element's attribute list and adds the new attribute to that list.

```
private static Attr renameAttrImpl(Attr attr,
    String newNamespaceURI, String newName) {
  Document document = attr.getOwnerDocument();
  Attr newAttr = null;
  if (document != null) {

    // Any Attr should have an owner Document
```

```
      // Using Crimson 1.1, however, we got null
      if (newNamespaceURI != null) {
        newAttr = document.createAttributeNS
            (newNamespaceURI, newName);
      } else {
        newAttr = document.createAttribute(newName);
      }
      newAttr.setValue(attr.getValue());
    }
    Element element = attr.getOwnerElement();
    if (element != null) {
      element.removeAttributeNode(attr);
      if (newAttr != null) {
        if (newNamespaceURI != null) {
          element.setAttributeNodeNS(newAttr);
        } else {
          element.setAttributeNode(newAttr);
        }
      } else {

        // We weren't able to create the new Attr node
        // because the owner Document of the given
        // attribute node was null. Parser bug!
        // But we have an owner element so we actually
        // are able to set the attribute
        if (newNamespaceURI != null) {
          element.setAttributeNS(newNamespaceURI, newName,
              attr.getValue());
          String newLocalName = newName;
          int k = newLocalName.indexOf(':');
          if (k >= 0) {
            newLocalName = newLocalName.substring(k + 1);
          }
          newAttr = element.getAttributeNodeNS
              (newNamespaceURI, newLocalName);
        } else {
          element.setAttribute(newName, attr.getValue());
          newAttr = element.getAttributeNode(newName);
        }
      }
    }
    return newAttr;
  }
}
```

Source AttrSample.java

This example uses the `AttrUtils` class to rename an attribute. After parsing the `attr.xml` file using the `parse()` method inherited from `DOMPrinter`, the `main()` method gets a specific element of the document using the `getElementById()` method defined by the `org.w3c.dom.Document` interface. This element must have an ID attribute with `"abc"` as value and another attribute named `oldAttr`. The `renameAttr()` method of `AttrUtils` "renames" `oldAttr` to `newAttr` by removing the old attribute and adding a new one.

The element is printed using the `print()` method inherited from `DOMPrinter`:

```java
import org.w3c.dom.Attr;
import org.w3c.dom.Document;
import org.w3c.dom.Element;

public class AttrSample extends DOMPrinter {
  public static void main(String args[]) {
    try {
      Document doc = parse("attr.xml", true);
      Element elem = doc.getElementById("abc");
      if (elem != null) {
        println("\r\n*** Before renaming");
        print(elem);
        Attr oldAttr = elem.getAttributeNode("oldAttr");
        if (oldAttr != null) {
          Attr newAttr = AttrUtils.renameAttr(oldAttr,
              "newAttr");
          println("\r\n*** After renaming");
          print(elem);
          newAttr.setValue("new value");
          println("\r\n*** After changing the value");
          print(elem);
        }
      }
    } catch (org.xml.sax.SAXParseException e) {

      // Already printed by PrintErrorHandler
      System.exit(1);
    } catch (Exception e) {
      e.printStackTrace();
      System.exit(1);
    }
  }
}
```

Sample attr.xml

```xml
<?xml version="1.0" encoding="utf-8"?>
<!DOCTYPE sample [
  <!ELEMENT sample (elemWithID)>
  <!ELEMENT elemWithID EMPTY>
  <!ATTLIST elemWithID
  elemID ID #REQUIRED
    oldAttr CDATA #IMPLIED
    newAttr CDATA #IMPLIED
>
]>
<sample>
  <elemWithID elemID="abc" oldAttr="old value"/>
</sample>
```

Output

```
> java AttrSample

*** Before renaming
ELEMENT - elemWithID - null
  ATTRIBUTE - elemID - abc
    TEXT - #text - abc
  ATTRIBUTE - oldAttr - old value
    TEXT - #text - old value

*** After renaming
ELEMENT - elemWithID - null
  ATTRIBUTE - elemID - abc
    TEXT - #text - abc
  ATTRIBUTE - newAttr - old value
    TEXT - #text - old value

*** After changing the value
ELEMENT - elemWithID - null
  ATTRIBUTE - elemID - abc
    TEXT - #text - abc
  ATTRIBUTE - newAttr - new value
    TEXT - #text - new value
```

Note: This example was affected by a parser bug when we tested it with Apache Crimson 1.1, but we were able to find a workaround. At some point we weren't able to create a new **Attr** node because the `getOwnerDocument()` method of the given attribute node returned **null**. We were able, however, to get the **Element** instance with `getOwnerElement()` and set the new attribute.

Also, when you run the example with Crimson 1.1, you'll see that none of the attribute nodes contains a text node as specified by the DOM API documentation. This is another parser bug.

Interface ProcessingInstruction
org.w3c.dom

```
public interface ProcessingInstruction
        extends Node
```

The `ProcessingInstruction` interface represents a "processing instruction", used in XML as a way to keep processor-specific information in the text of the document.

Methods

The `getTarget()` method returns the target of this processing instruction. XML defines this as being the first token following the markup that begins the processing instruction.

The `setData()` method sets the data of this processing instruction.

The `getData()` method returns the data of this processing instruction. This is from the first non-whitespace character after the target to the character immediately preceding the ?>.

```
public String getTarget()
public void setData(String data)
        throws DOMException
public String getData()
```

Parameters

Parameter	Type	Description
data	String	The data of this processing instruction

Returned Values

Method	Return	Description
getTarget()	String	The target of this processing instruction
getData()	String	The data of this processing instruction

Note: The `org.w3c.dom.ProcessingInstruction` interface is used by our `DocumentSample` example on page 217.

Interface DocumentFragment

org.w3c.dom

```
public interface DocumentFragment

        extends Node
```

`DocumentFragment` is a "lightweight" or "minimal" `Document` object. It is very common to want to extract a portion of a document's tree or to create a new fragment of a document. Imagine implementing a user command like cut or rearranging a document by moving fragments around. It is desirable to have an object that can hold such fragments and it is quite natural to use a `Node` for this purpose. While it is true that a `Document` object could fulfill this role, a `Document` object can potentially be a heavyweight object, depending on the underlying implementation. What is really needed for this is a very lightweight object. `DocumentFragment` is such an object.

Furthermore, various operations (such as inserting nodes as children of another `Node`) may take `DocumentFragment` objects as arguments; this results in all the child nodes of the `DocumentFragment` being moved to the child list of this node.

The children of a `DocumentFragment` node are zero or more nodes representing the tops of any subtrees defining the structure of the document. `DocumentFragment` nodes do not need to be well-formed XML documents (although they do need to follow the rules imposed upon well-formed XML parsed entities, which can have multiple top nodes). For example, a `DocumentFragment` might have only one child and that child node could be a `Text` node. Such a structure model doesn't represent a well-formed XML document.

> When a **DocumentFragment** is inserted into a **Document** (or indeed any other **Node** that may take children) the children of the **DocumentFragment** and not the **DocumentFragment** itself are inserted into the **Node**.

This makes the `DocumentFragment` very useful when the user wishes to create nodes that are siblings. The `DocumentFragment` acts as the parent of these nodes so that the user can use the standard methods from the `Node` interface, such as `insertBefore()` and `appendChild()`.

Interface Document

org.w3c.dom

```
public interface Document

        extends Node
```

The `Document` interface represents the entire XML document. Conceptually, it is the root of the document tree, and provides the primary access to the document's data.

Since elements, text nodes, comments and processing instructions cannot exist outside the context of a Document instance, the Document interface also contains the factory methods needed to create these node objects. The ownerDocument property defined by Node associates the objects with the Document within whose context they were created.

Getting the DocumentType

The getDoctype() method returns the DocumentType instance associated with this document or null if there is no DTD. The DOM Level 2 does not support editing the Document Type Declaration. The DocumentType instance cannot be altered in any way, including through the use of methods inherited from the Node interface, such as insertBefore(), replaceChild(), removeChild or appendChild().

```
public DocumentType getDoctype()
```

Returned Values

Method	Return	Description
getDoctype()	DocumentType	The DocumentType instance associated with this document, or null if there is no DTD

Getting the Document Element

The getDocumentElement() method returns the child node that is the root element of the document.

```
public Element getDocumentElement()
```

Returned Values

Method	Return	Description
getDocument Element()	Element	The root element of the document

Getting Elements by Tag Name

These methods return a NodeList of all the Elements with a given tag name, in the order in which they are encountered in a preorder traversal of the Document tree.

```
public NodeList getElementsByTagName(String tagName)
```

```
public NodeList getElementsByTagNameNS(String namespaceURI,
                                       String localName)
```

(Since DOM Level 2)

Parameters

Parameter	Type	Description
tagName	String	The name of the tag to match on. The special value "*" matches all tags.
namespaceURI	String	The namespace URI of the elements to match on. The special value "*" matches all namespaces.
localName	String	The local name of the elements to match on. The special value "*" matches all local names.

Returned Values

Method	Return	Description
getElements ByTagName()	NodeList	A new NodeList object containing all matched Elements
getElements ByTagNameNS()	NodeList	A new NodeList object containing all matched Elements for the namespace specified

Getting the Element by Id

The getElementById() method returns the Element whose ID is given by elementId. If no such element exists, it returns null. Behavior is not defined if more than one element has the same ID. The DOM implementation must have information that says which attributes are of type ID. Attributes with the name "ID" are not of type ID unless so defined. Implementations that do not know whether attributes are of type ID or not are expected to return null.

```
public Element getElementById(String elementId) (Since DOM Level 2)
```

Parameters

Parameter	Type	Description
elementId	String	The unique id value for an element

Returned Values

Method	Return	Description
getElement ById()	Element	The matching element

Creating Elements

The createElement() method creates an element of the type specified. Note that the instance returned implements the Element interface, so attributes can be specified directly on the returned object. In addition, if there are known attributes with default values, Attr nodes representing them are automatically created and attached to the element. To create an element with a qualified name and namespace URI, use the createElementNS() method.

```
public Element createElement(String tagName)
        throws DOMException
public Element createElementNS(String namespaceURI,
                              String qualifiedName)
        throws DOMException (Since DOM Level 2)
```

Parameters

Parameter	Type	Description
tagName	String	The name of the element type to instantiate
namespaceURI	String	The namespace URI of the element to create
qualifiedName	String	The qualified name of the element type to instantiate

Returned Values

Method	Return	Description
create Element()	Element	A new Element object with the nodeName property set to tagName. The localName, prefix and namespaceURI properties are set to null.
create ElementNS()	Element	A new Element object with the following properties: Node.nodeName and Element.tagNameset to qualifiedName, Node.namespaceURI set to namespaceURI, Node.prefix extracted from qualifiedName or null if there is no prefix, Node.localName extracted from qualifiedName.

Creating Attributes

The createAttribute() method creates an Attr node with the given name. Note that the Attr instance can then be set on an Element using the setAttributeNode method. To create an attribute with a qualified name and namespace URI, use the createAttributeNS() method.

```
public Attr createAttribute(String name)
        throws DOMException
public Attr createAttributeNS(String namespaceURI,
                              String qualifiedName)
        throws DOMException (Since DOM Level 2)
```

Parameters

Parameter	Type	Description
name	String	The name of the attribute
namespaceURI	String	The namespace URI of the attribute to create
qualifiedName	String	The qualified name of the attribute to instantiate

Returned Values

Method	Return	Description
create Attribute()	Attr	A new Attr object with the nodeName property set to name. The localName, prefix and namespaceURI properties are set to null. The value of the attribute is the empty string.
create AttributeNS()	Attr	A new Attr object with the following attributes: Node.nodeName and Attr.name set to qualifiedName, Node.namespaceURI set to namespaceURI, Node.prefix extracted from qualifiedName or null if there is no prefix, Node.localName extracted from qualifiedName, Node.nodeValue and Attr.value set to the empty string

Creating TextNodes, CDATASections, and Comments

These methods create Text, CDATASection and Comment nodes. The data contained by such a node is specified as a parameter.

```
public Text createTextNode(String data)
```

```
public CDATASection createCDATASection(String data)
        throws DOMException
```

```
public Comment createComment(String data)
```

Parameters

Parameter	Type	Description
data	String	The data for the node

Returned Values

Method	Return	Description
createTextNode()	Text	The new Text object
createCDATASection()	CDATASection	The new CDATASection object
createComment()	Comment	The new Comment object

Method createEntityReference()

The createEntityReference() method creates an EntityReference object. In addition, if the referenced entity is known, the child list of the EntityReference node is made the same as that of the corresponding Entity node. If any descendant of the Entity node has an unbound namespace prefix, the corresponding descendant of the created EntityReference node is also unbound (its namespaceURI is null). The DOM Level 2 does not support any mechanism to resolve namespace prefixes.

```
public EntityReference createEntityReference(String name)
        throws DOMException
```

Parameters

Parameter	Type	Description
name	String	The name of the entity to reference

Returned Values

Method	Return	Description
`createEntityReference()`	`EntityReference`	The new `EntityReference` object

Creating a Processing Instruction

The `createProcessingInstruction()` method creates a `ProcessingInstruction` node with the given target and data strings.

```
public ProcessingInstruction createProcessingInstruction(
                       String target, String data)
       throws DOMException
```

Parameters

Parameter	Type	Description
`target`	`String`	The target part of the processing instruction
`data`	`String`	The data for the node

Returned Values

Method	Return	Description
`createProcessing Instruction()`	`Processing Instruction`	The new `Processing Instruction` object

Creating a Document Fragment

The `createDocumentFragment()` method creates an empty `DocumentFragment` object.

```
public DocumentFragment createDocumentFragment()
```

Returned Values

Method	Return	Description
`createDocument Fragment()`	`Document Fragment`	A new `DocumentFragment`

Importing a Node

The `importNode()` method imports a node from another document to this document. The node that is imported has no parent. The source node is not altered or removed from the original document. This method creates a new copy of the source node. For all nodes, importing a node creates a node object owned by the importing document, with property values identical to the source node's `nodeName` and `nodeType`, plus the properties related to namespaces (`prefix`, `localName`, and `namespaceURI`). Additional information is copied as appropriate, attempting to mirror the behavior expected if a fragment of XML source was copied from one document to another, recognizing that the two documents may have different DTDs.

```
public Node importNode(Node importedNode, boolean deep)
       throws DOMException (Since DOM Level 2)
```

The following table describes the specifics for each type of node:

Node Type	Action
ATTRIBUTE_NODE	The `ownerElement` property is set to `null` and the `specified` flag is set to `true` on the generated `Attr`. The descendants of the source `Attr` are recursively imported and the resulting nodes reassembled to form the corresponding subtree. Note that the `deep` parameter has no effect on `Attr` nodes; they always carry their children with them when imported.
DOCUMENT_FRAGMENT_NODE	If the `deep` option was set to `true`, the descendants of the source element are recursively imported and the resulting nodes reassembled to form the corresponding subtree. Otherwise, this simply generates an empty `DocumentFragment`.
DOCUMENT_NODE	`Document` nodes cannot be imported
DOCUMENT_TYPE_NODE	`DocumentType` nodes cannot be imported
ELEMENT_NODE	Specified attribute nodes of the source element are imported, and the generated `Attr` nodes are attached to the generated `Element`. Default attributes are not copied, though if the document being imported into defines default attributes for this element name, those are assigned. If the `deep` parameter is `true`, the descendants of the source element are recursively imported and the resulting nodes reassembled to form the corresponding subtree.

Table continued on following page

Node Type	Action
ENTITY_NODE	Entity nodes can be imported, though in DOM Level 2 the DocumentType is read-only. Ability to add these imported nodes to a DocumentType will be considered for addition to a future release of the DOM. On import, the publicId, systemId, and notationName properties are copied. If a deep import is requested, the descendants of the source Entity are recursively imported and the resulting nodes reassembled to form the corresponding subtree.
ENTITY_REFERENCE_NODE	Only the EntityReference itself is copied, even if a deep import is requested, since the source and destination documents might have defined the entity differently. If the document being imported into provides a definition for this entity name, its value is assigned.
NOTATION_NODE	Notation nodes can be imported, though in the DOM Level 2 the DocumentType is read-only. (The ability to add these imported nodes to a DocumentType will be considered for addition to a future release of the DOM.) On import, the publicId and systemId properties are copied. Note that the deep parameter has no effect on Notation nodes since they never have any children.
PROCESSING_INSTRUCTION _NODE	The imported node copies its target and data values from those of the source node
TEXT_NODE CDATA_SECTION_NODE COMMENT_NODE	These three types of nodes, inheriting from CharacterData, copy their data and length properties from those of the source node

Parameters

Parameter	Type	Description
importedNode	Node	The node to import
deep	boolean	If true, recursively imports the subtree under the specified node, if false, imports only the node itself, as explained above. This has no effect on Attr, EntityReference, and Notation nodes.

Returned Values

Method	Return	Description
`importNode()`	`Node`	The imported node that belongs to this `Document`

Method getImplementation()

The `getImplementation()` method returns the `DOMImplementation` object that handles this document. A DOM application may use objects from multiple implementations.

```
public DOMImplementation getImplementation()
```

Returned Values

Method	Return	Description
`getImplementation()`	`DOMImplementation`	The `DOMImplementation` object that handles this document

Example: Creating a DOM Tree

This example creates a `Document` using the `newDocument()` method inherited from `DOMPrinter`. Then it uses the methods defined by the `org.w3c.dom.Document` interface to create `Element`, `Comment`, `CDATASection`, `Text`, and `ProcessingInstruction` nodes, which are included within the DOM tree using `appendChild()` and `insertBefore()`. At some point, a comment is replaced with an element using `replaceChild()`. One of the elements will also have an attribute. The populated document is printed using the `print()` method inherited from `DOMPrinter`.

Source DocumentSample.java

```java
import org.w3c.dom.CDATASection;
import org.w3c.dom.Comment;
import org.w3c.dom.Document;
import org.w3c.dom.Element;
import org.w3c.dom.ProcessingInstruction;
import org.w3c.dom.Text;

public class DocumentSample extends DOMPrinter {
  public static void main(String args[]) {
    try {
      Document doc = newDocument();

      Element root = doc.createElement("root");
      doc.appendChild(root);
```

```
            Comment comment = doc.createComment("a comment");
            root.appendChild(comment);

            Comment removable = doc.createComment("removable");
            root.appendChild(removable);

            Element elem = doc.createElement("elem");
            root.replaceChild(elem, removable);
            elem.setAttribute("attr", "value");
            elem.appendChild(doc.createTextNode("data"));

            CDATASection cdata = doc.createCDATASection(">data<");
            root.appendChild(cdata);

            Text text = doc.createTextNode("some text");
            root.insertBefore(text, cdata);

            ProcessingInstruction proc =
                doc.createProcessingInstruction("target",
                "1 2 3");
            root.appendChild(proc);

            print(doc);
        } catch (Exception e) {
            e.printStackTrace();
            System.exit(1);
        }
    }
}
```

Output

```
> java DocumentSample

DOCUMENT - #document - null
  ELEMENT - root - null
    COMMENT - #comment - a comment
    ELEMENT - elem - null
      ATTRIBUTE - attr - value
        TEXT - #text - value
      TEXT - #text - data
    TEXT - #text - some text
    CDATA_SECTION - #cdata-section - >data<
    PROCESSING_INSTRUCTION - target - 1 2 3
```

Note: All executable examples of this chapter use some of the methods of the
org.w3c.dom.Document interface. For example, AttrSample uses
getElementById(), DataSample and ElementSample use
getDocumentElement().

Interface DOMImplementation
org.w3c.dom

```
public interface DOMImplementation
```

The DOMImplementation interface provides a number of methods for performing operations that are independent of any particular instance of the document object model.

Method hasFeature()

The hasFeature() method tests if the DOM implementation supports a specific feature.

```
public boolean hasFeature(String feature, String version)
```

Parameters

Parameter	Type	Description
feature	String	The name of the feature to test (case-insensitive). The name must be an XML name. To avoid possible conflicts, as a convention, names referring to features defined outside the DOM specification should be made unique by reversing the name of the Internet domain name of the person (or the organization that the person belongs to) who defines the feature, component by component, and using this as a prefix. For instance, the W3C SVG Working Group defines the feature "org.w3c.dom.svg".
version	String	This is the version number of the feature to test. In Level 2, the string can be either "2.0" or "1.0". If the version is not specified, supporting any version of the feature causes the method to return true.

Returned Values

Method	Return	Description
hasFeature()	boolean	true if the feature is implemented in the specified version, false otherwise

Creating DocumentTypes

The createDocumentType() method creates an empty DocumentType node. Entity declarations and notations are not made available. Entity reference expansions and default attribute additions do not occur. It is expected that a future version of the DOM will provide a way for populating a DocumentType.

```
public DocumentType createDocumentType(String qualifiedName,
                 String publicId, String systemId)
       throws DOMException (Since DOM Level 2)
```

Parameters

Parameter	Type	Description
qualifiedName	String	The qualified name of the document type to be created
publicId	String	The external DTD's public identifier
systemId	String	The external DTD's system identifier

Returned Values

Method	Return	Description
create DocumentType()	DocumentType	A new DocumentType node with Node.ownerDocument set to null

Creating XML Document Objects

The createDocument() method creates an XML Document object of the specified type with its document element.

```
public Document createDocument(String namespaceURI,
             String qualifiedName, DocumentType doctype)
       throws DOMException (Since DOM Level 2)
```

Parameters

Parameter	Type	Description
namespaceURI	String	The namespace URI of the document element to create
qualifiedName	String	The qualified name of the document element to be created
doctype	DocumentType	The type of document to be created or null. When doctype is not null, its Node.ownerDocument property is set to the document being created.

Returned Values

Method	Return	Description
createDocument()	Document	A new Document object

DOM Level 3 Core

When this book was written, DOM3 was just a working draft. The following table includes some of the features that were proposed for this third version of the DOM Core.

Interface	Description
Node	The getBaseURI() method returns the absolute base URI of this node
	The compareDocumentOrder() and compareTreePosition() methods compare two nodes with regard to their position in the document or tree
	The new textContent property is used for the text content of a node and its descendants.
	The isSameNode() method tests whether two nodes are the same object, while equalsNode() tests the equality of two nodes
	The lookupNamespacePrefix() and lookupNamespaceURI() methods look up the prefix associated to the given namespace URI and vice-versa
	The normalizeNS() method walks down the tree, starting from a node, and adds namespace declarations where needed so that every namespace being used is properly declared. It also changes or assigns prefixes when needed. This effectively makes sure that this node subtree is namespace well-formed.

Interface	Description
Document	The version, encoding and standalone properties specify the attributes of the XML declaration. The actual encoding of the document can be modified using a different property: actualEncoding. The strictErrorChecking property specifies whether errors checking is enforced or not. When set to false, the implementation is free to not test every possible error case normally defined on DOM operations, and not raise any DOMException. The adoptNode() method changes the ownerDocument of a node, its children, as well as the attached attribute nodes if there were any. This effectively allows moving a subtree from one document to another.
Entity	The version and encoding properties specify the attributes of the XML declaration. The actual encoding of the external parsed entity can be modified using a different property: actualEncoding.
Text	The getIsWhitespaceInElementContent() method returns whether this text node contains whitespace in element content, often abusively called "ignorable whitespace". An implementation can only return true if, one way or another, it has access to the relevant information (for example, the DTD or schema).

Summary

In this chapter, we have looked at the DOM Core API. Additionally we have implemented some example classes, in order to:

- Configure a DOM parser and parse an XML document
- Print information about the nodes of a DOM tree
- Extract the data contained by a node
- Find the elements of a DOM tree that satisfy some criteria
- Rename the attributes of an element
- Create a document tree from scratch

In the next chapter we will look at the extensions to DOM.

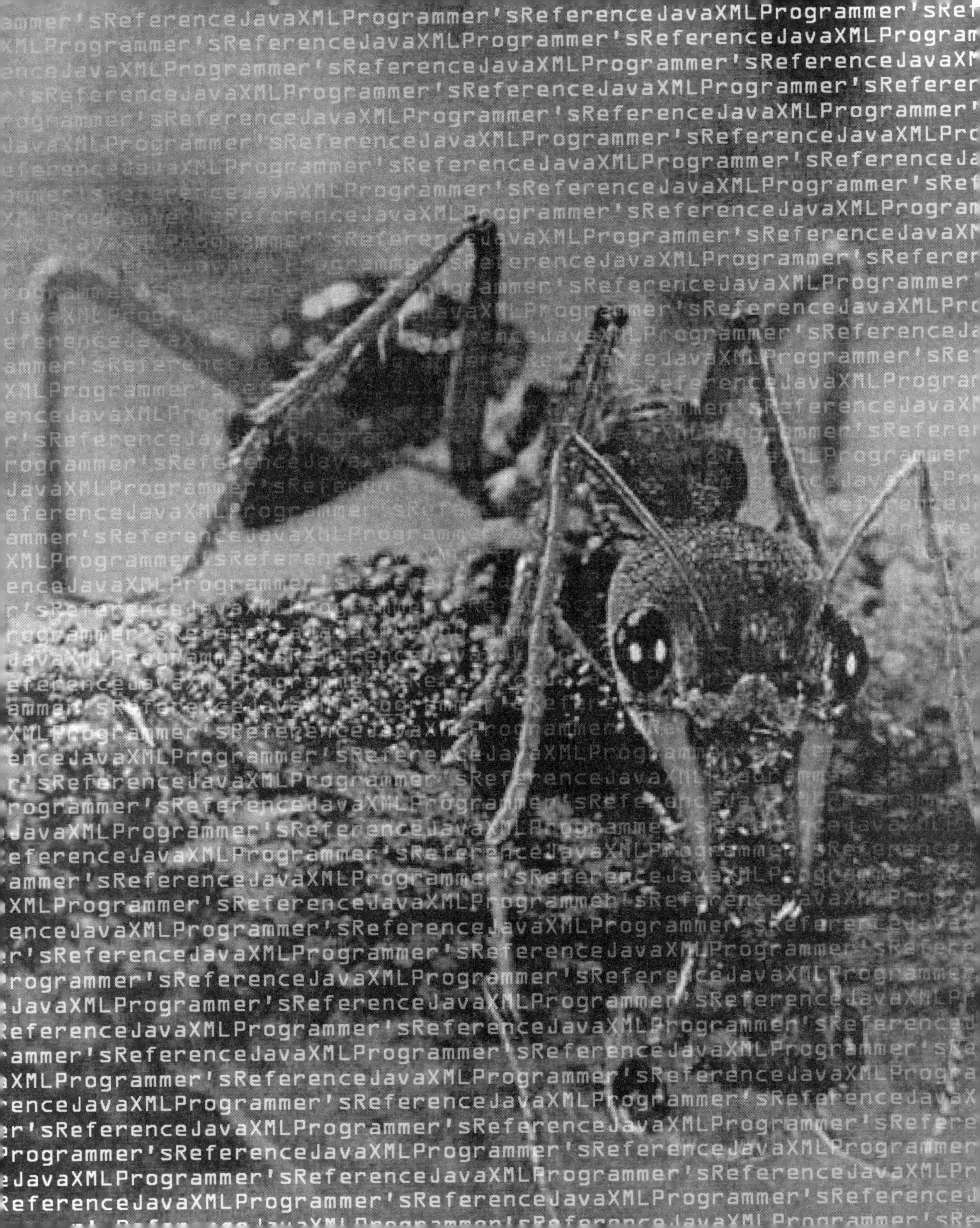
JavaXMLProgrammer'sReference

DOM Extensions

In addition to the DOM Core API presented in the chapter 3, the World Wide Web Consortium (W3C) defines extensions to DOM Level 2: **Views**, **Events**, **Traversal** and **Ranges**. However, it is worth remembering that not every DOM parser supports these extensions. Apache Xerces 1.4.0, which we used to test our examples, supports DOM Events, Traversal and Ranges, however Apache Crimson 1.1 supports none of the DOM extensions. The specifications for all DOM extensions can be found at http://www.w3.org/DOM/DOMTR.

The examples included in this chapter show how to:

❑ Create and register event listeners to the nodes of a DOM tree

❑ Iterate over the nodes of a document using filters

❑ Use ranges to perform different operations, such as content cloning, extraction, deletion and insertion

This chapter covers the following packages:

Package	Description	Page
`org.w3c.dom.views`	Is useful to browsers and other GUI applications, but it normally isn't supported by XML parsers	226
`org.w3c.dom.events`	Allows an application to be notified by the DOM implementation when something related to the DOM tree happens	227
`org.w3c.dom.traversal`	Provides access to the nodes of a document as flattened list and tree navigation. Node filters can be used to restrict the traversal domain.	257
`org.w3c.dom.ranges`	Specifies how one can identify chunks of a document using a pair of boundary points	273

Throughout the chapter, there are a number of examples of using these DOM extensions, which are listed in the table below:

Examples	Used APIs	Page
`PrintEventListener`	`Event`, `EventListener`, `MutationEvent`	242
`EventsSample`	`EventListener`, `EventTarget`	246
`FilterFactory`	`NodeFilter`	260
`NodeIteratorSample`	`DocumentTraversal`, `NodeFilter`, `NodeIterator`	265
`TreeWalkerSample`	`DocumentTraversal`, `NodeFilter`, `TreeWalker`	270
`RangesSample`	`DocumentRange`, `Range`, `DocumentTraversal`, `NodeFilter`, `NodeIterator`	283

Package org.w3c.dom.views

This DOM extension isn't supported by many XML parsers yet. We include it within this chapter for completeness and because the UI events presented later use its interfaces. Apache Xerces supports neither the DOM views nor the UI events.

> **At the time of writing, W3C has released a public Working Draft of the Views and Formatting model. This will be the next version of the DOM Views extension, but due to lack of progress, it is no longer included in DOM Level 3.**

The `org.w3c.dom.views` package contains the following interfaces.

Interfaces

These interfaces below were introduced in DOM Level 2.

Interface	Description	Page
`AbstractView`	A base interface that all views shall derive from	226
`DocumentView`	The `DocumentView` interface is implemented by the same class that implements `Document` (in DOM implementations supporting Views)	227

Interface AbstractView
org.w3c.dom.views

```
public interface AbstractView
```

All views shall derive from this base interface.

Method getDocument()

The getDocument() method returns the source DocumentView of which this is an AbstractView.

```
public DocumentView getDocument()
```

Returned Values

Return	Description
DocumentView	The source DocumentView of which this is an AbstractView

Interface DocumentView
org.w3c.dom.views

```
public interface DocumentView
```

The DocumentView interface is implemented by Document objects in DOM implementations supporting DOM Views. It provides a property to retrieve the default view of a document.

Note that this interface does not extend AbstractView. When you read DocumentView, you should think "viewable document."

Method getDefaultView()

The getDefaultView() method returns the default AbstractView for this Document.

```
public AbstractView getDefaultView()
```

Returned Values

Return	Description
AbstractView	The default AbstractView for this Document, or null if none is available

Package org.w3c.dom.events

This extension allows an application to be notified by the DOM implementation when something related to the DOM tree happens, such as:

❑ A node is inserted into or removed from the DOM tree

❑ An attribute is added to or removed from an element

❑ The value of an attribute is changed

❑ The character data of a text node is changed

As noted before not every XML parser that implements the DOM core interfaces also supports this extension.

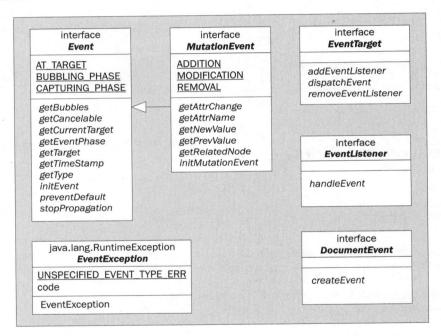

DOM Event Model

The DOM specification defines an event model that is superficially similar to the JavaBeans' delegation event model, though there are many differences.

The JavaBeans event model is used by AWT (Abstract Windowing Toolkit) and Swing. For example, when the user moves the mouse or clicks a mouse button, the AWT creates an event object, in which it wraps the mouse coordinates, the identifier of the pressed/released/clicked mouse button, etc. If the application wants to know when the user clicks on a GUI component, an event listener for mouse clicks will be registered to that component. The user's action (mouse clicking) causes the GUI framework to fire an event to the JavaBean, which acts as a target. The targeted JavaBean, which is a GUI component in this example, is responsible for dispatching the events to the registered listeners.

Events aren't just for GUIs. For example, an event might be fired if a property value of a non-GUI bean is changed. In this case, the application itself triggers the event. Obviously, the application knows that it changed the value of a property. So, why would the application want to be notified of something it already knows? The answer is simple: for greater modularity. Let's say that our application consists of three modules (or packages): A, B and C. Suppose that module A does something that modules B and C need to know. One possible solution is to let A call methods of the classes defined by B and C. In this case, A must know about B and C. If we add a D module, we'll have to change the code of A to notify D too.

The use of events is a much more elegant solution. Module A from the above example could define an event class for wrapping all information associated with a particular event type. Module A would also define an event listener interface containing one method that accepts an event object as parameter. Modules B and C (and later D) would just have to implement the event listener interface and register its instances to A. When A fires an event, it will call the methods of all registered listeners without having to know anything about the other modules or their classes since the event listener interface was defined by module A.

Let's compare the above examples with the event model defined by DOM.

The DOM specification defines two types of events: user interface events and mutation events. The UI events aren't normally interesting for an XML developer, but we'll present them because they are defined by the DOM standard. Apache Xerces up to version 1.4.0 supports only the mutation events. Future versions of Xerces will probably not support UI events either.

A mutation event is fired by the DOM implementation when the DOM tree is modified by the application. Each class that implements an interface derived from `org.w3c.dom.Node` also implements `org.w3c.dom.events.EventTarget`. The latter defines methods for adding and removing event listeners. We'll use these methods to register and unregister the instances of our classes that implement `org.w3c.dom.events.EventListener`. The `org.w3c.dom.events.EventListener` interface defines a `handleEvent()` method that takes an `org.w3c.dom.events.Event` (or an instance of a subclass) as parameter. We know, of course, when our application modifies the properties or the children of a node. However, if we want to be notified via events, we have to do the following:

- ❑ Cast the `Node` object to `EventTarget`
- ❑ Create an instance of a class that implements `EventListener`
- ❑ Register the listener to the node using the `addEventListener()` method defined by `EventTarget`
- ❑ Modify the properties or the children of the node
- ❑ Process DOM events through the listener's `handleEvent()` method, which is called as required by the DOM implementation
- ❑ Unregister the listener when we no longer wish to receive events

This will be demonstrated in the *example EventsSample.java, on page 246.*

Before reaching its target, a DOM event can be captured by an ancestor of the target node. If a listener wants to capture the events targeted to all nodes of a DOM sub-tree, except the root, the application has to register the listener only to the root of the sub-tree. If the listener also wants to get the events targeted to the root of the sub-tree, the application must register the listener for the second time as non-capturing listener to the root node. The type of the listener (capturing or non-capturing) is given by a `boolean` parameter of the `addEventListener()` method defined by `EventTarget`.

If a node has multiple ancestors that capture the events, the remotest ancestor (the nearest to the document's root) will capture the events first.

After reaching its target, an event may "bubble," that is, the event is propagated to its ancestors starting with its parent, and the listeners of these ancestors are triggered (their `handleEvent()` method is called). The DOM standard specifies which events bubble and which don't. The ancestors that have already captured the event are skipped during the bubbling. In addition, if the document's structure is changed during the bubbling (possibly by the event listeners), any new ancestor doesn't get the already fired event for its listeners.

The event flow described above can be stopped using the `stopPropagation()` method of `org.w3c.dom.events.Event`. The stopping can occur in any phase of the event flow: capture, at target or bubbling.

As we noted above, the DOM events are fired by an operation. Sometimes it is possible to cancel that operation before it is performed. The DOM standard specifies which events are cancelable. Some of the UI events are, but none of the mutation events are cancelable.

The event model is not just for improving the modularity of the applications. For example, we can capture all events for logging and debugging. Note however, that the usage of events may slow down the execution of the application. In a deep DOM tree, the bubbling of the events may consume a lot more processing resources than the execution of the operations that fired the events.

The `org.w3c.dom.events` package contains the following interfaces and exceptions.

Interfaces

These interfaces were introduced in DOM level 2:

Interface	Description	Page
`Event`	Used to provide contextual information about an event to the handler processing the event	231
`MutationEvent`	Provides specific contextual information associated with Mutation events	234
`UIEvent`	Provides specific contextual information associated with user interface events	237
`MouseEvent`	Provides specific contextual information associated with mouse events	239
`EventListener`	Defines a callback method for handling events that must be implemented by application classes and is invoked by the DOM implementation	242
`EventTarget`	Defines methods for registering and unregistering `EventListeners` and also for dispatching events to event targets	244
`DocumentEvent`	Provides a mechanism by which the application can create an `Event` of a type supported by the implementation	255

Exceptions

This exception was introduced in DOM level 2:

Exception	Description	Page
EventException	Event operations may throw an EventException	231

Exception EventException

org.w3c.dom.events

```
public class EventException
        extends java.lang.RuntimeException
```

Event operations may throw an EventException.

Fields

The EventException class has the following fields:

Field	Type	Description
code	short	The code of this exception
UNSPECIFIED_EVENT_TYPE_ERR	short	This constant is assigned to the code field if the Event's type was not specified. Specification of the Event's type as null or an empty string will also trigger this exception.

Constructor

This constructor creates an exception with the given code and message.

```
public EventException (short code, String message)
```

Parameters

Parameter	Type	Description
code	short	The exception's code
message	String	The exception's message

Interface Event
org.w3c.dom.events

```
public interface Event
```

The Event interface is used to provide contextual information about an event to the handler processing the event. An object which implements the Event interface is generally passed as parameter to a handleEvent() method of an EventListener instance. More specific context information is passed to event handlers by deriving additional interfaces from Event, which contain information directly relating to the type of event they accompany.

Fields

The Event interface defines the following constant fields:

Field	Type	Description
CAPTURING_PHASE	short	The current event phase is the capturing phase
AT_TARGET	short	The event is currently being evaluated at its EventTarget
BUBBLING_PHASE	short	The current event phase is the bubbling phase

Methods for Getting Event's Properties

```
public String getType()
public EventTarget getTarget()
public EventTarget getCurrentTarget()
public short getEventPhase()
public boolean getBubbles()
public boolean getCancelable()
public long getTimeStamp()
```

Returned Values

Method	Return	Description
getType()	String	The type of the event (case-insensitive). The type must be an XML name.
getTarget()	EventTarget	The EventTarget to which the event was originally dispatched
getCurrentTarget()	EventTarget	The EventTarget whose EventListeners are currently being processed. This is particularly useful during capturing and bubbling.

Method	Return	Description
getEventPhase()	short	The phase of event flow that is currently being evaluated
getBubbles()	boolean	true if the event is a bubbling event
getCancelable()	boolean	true if the event can have its default action prevented
getTimeStamp()	long	The time (in milliseconds) at which the event was created. Because some systems may not provide this information, the value of timeStamp may be not available for all events. When not available, a value of 0 will be returned.

Method stopPropagation()

The stopPropagation() method is used to prevent further propagation of an event during the event flow. If this method is called by any EventListener object, the event will cease propagating through the tree. The event will be dispatched to all listeners on the current EventTarget before the event flow stops. This method may be used during any stage of the event flow.

```
public void stopPropagation()
```

Method preventDefault()

If an event is cancelable, the preventDefault() method is used to signify that the event is to be canceled. Any default action normally taken by the implementation because of the event, will not occur. If, during any stage of the event flow, the preventDefault() method is called, the event is canceled. Calling this method for a non-cancelable event has no effect. Once the preventDefault() method has been called, it remains in effect throughout the remainder of that event's propagation. This method may be used during any stage of event flow.

```
public void preventDefault()
```

Method initEvent()

The initEvent() method is used to initialize the value of an Event created through the DocumentEvent interface. This method may only be called before the Event has been dispatched via the dispatchEvent() method, though it may be called multiple times during that phase if necessary. If called multiple times the final invocation takes precedence. If called from a subclass of Event only the values specified in the initEvent() method are modified, all other attributes are left unchanged.

The eventTypeArg parameter may be any event type defined in the DOM specification or an XML name. Any new event type must not begin with any upper, lower, or mixedcase version of the string "DOM". This prefix is reserved for future DOM event sets. It is also strongly recommended that third parties adding their own events use their own prefix to avoid confusion and lessen the probability of conflicts with other new events.

```
public void initEvent(String eventTypeArg, boolean
                      canBubbleArg, boolean cancelableArg)
```

Parameters

Parameter	Type	Description
eventTypeArg	String	Specifies the event type
canBubbleArg	boolean	Specifies whether the event can bubble
cancelableArg	boolean	Specifies whether the event's default action can be prevented

Note: The `org.w3c.dom.events.Event` interface is used by our `PrintEventListener` and you can watch the event flow with the `EventsSample` example, see page 246.

Interface MutationEvent
org.w3c.dom.events

```
public interface MutationEvent
extends Event
```

The `MutationEvent` interface provides specific contextual information associated with mutation events.

The DOM Events specification defines the following types of mutation events. None of the following mutation events are cancelable:

Type	Target	Bubbles	Context info
DOMSubtreeModified	The lowest common parent of the changed nodes	true	None
DOMNodeInserted	The node being inserted	true	relatedNode holds the parent node
DOMNodeRemoved	The node being removed	true	relatedNode holds the parent node
DOMNodeInsertedInto Document	The node being inserted	false	None

Type	Target	Bubbles	Context info
DOMNodeRemovedFrom Document	The node being removed	false	None
DOMAttrModified	The element whose attribute list is modified	true	attrName, attrChange, prevValue, newValue, relatedNode
DOMCharacterData Modified	The node whose data is modified	true	prevValue, newValue

In order to get the properties of an event whose possible values are listed in the above table, use the getType(), getBubbles() and getCancelable() methods defined by org.w3c.dom.events.Event.

Note that the event types are Strings.

The DOMSubtreeModified event is a general event for notifying that some changes were made to the document.

The DOMNodeInserted and DOMNodeRemoved events are fired after a child node is inserted into or removed from a parent node. The target of this event is the node being inserted or removed.

The DOMNodeInsertedIntoDocument and DOMNodeRemovedFromDocument events are fired when a node is being inserted into or removed from a document. The insertion and removal may be direct or indirect via a sub-tree that contains the node.

A DOMAttrModified event is fired when the value of an attribute is changed (or the attribute list of an element is modified) by adding or removing an attribute.

A DOMCharacterDataModified event is fired when the character data of a Text, CDATASection or Comment node is changed. It is also used when the data of a processing instruction is modified.

Fields

The MutationEvent interface has the following constants, which define the valid values of the attrChange property:

Field	Type	Description
MODIFICATION	short	The Attr was modified in place
ADDITION	short	The Attr was added
REMOVAL	short	The Attr was removed

Methods for Getting MutationEvent Properties

These methods return the following information about an event:

- ❑ The related node (if any)
- ❑ The previous value (if any)
- ❑ The new value (if any)
- ❑ The attribute name (if any)
- ❑ The type of the attribute change (if any)

Additional information can be obtained using the methods inherited from Event.

```
public Node getRelatedNode()
```

```
public String getPrevValue()
```

```
public String getNewValue()
```

```
public String getAttrName()
```

```
public short getAttrChange()
```

Returned Values

Method	Return	Description
getRelatedNode()	Node	A secondary node related to a mutation event. For example, if a mutation event is dispatched to a node indicating that its parent has changed, the relatedNode is the changed parent. If an event is instead dispatched to a sub-tree indicating a node was changed within it, the relatedNode is the changed node. In the case of the DOMAttrModified event it indicates the Attr node that was modified, added, or removed.
getPrevValue()	String	The previous value of the Attr node in DOMAttrModified events, and of the CharacterData node in DOMCharDataModified events
getNewValue()	String	The new value of the Attr node in DOMAttrModified events, and of the CharacterData node in DOMCharDataModified events
getAttrName()	String	The name of the changed Attr node in a DOMAttrModified event
getAttrChange()	short	The type of change that triggered the DOMAttrModified event. The values can be MODIFICATION, ADDITION, or REMOVAL.

Method initMutationEvent()

The `initMutationEvent()` method is used to initialize the value of a `MutationEvent` created through the `DocumentEvent` interface. This method may only be called before the `MutationEvent` has been dispatched via the `dispatchEvent()` method, though it may be called multiple times during that phase if necessary. If called multiple times, the final invocation takes precedence.

```
public void initMutationEvent(String typeArg, boolean
          canBubbleArg, boolean cancelableArg, Node
          relatedNodeArg, String prevValueArg, String
          newValueArg, String attrNameArg, short
          attrChangeArg)
```

Parameters

Parameter	Type	Description
typeArg	String	Specifies the event type
canBubbleArg	boolean	Specifies whether the event can bubble
cancelableArg	boolean	Specifies whether the event's default action can be prevented
relatedNodeArg	Node	Specifies the Event's related Node
prevValueArg	String	Specifies the Event's prevValue property. This value may be null.
newValueArg	String	Specifies the Event's newValue property. This value may be null.
attrNameArg	String	Specifies the Event's attrName property. This value may be null.
attrChangeArg	short	Specifies the Event's attrChange property

Note: The `org.w3c.dom.events.MutationEvent` interface is used by our `PrintEventListener` example and you can watch the event flow with the `EventsSample` example, see page 246.

Interface UIEvent

org.w3c.dom.events

```
public interface UIEvent
extends Event
```

The `UIEvent` interface provides specific contextual information associated with user interface events.

Methods for Getting UIEvent's Properties

These methods return the following information about an event:

- ❏ The view from which the event was generated
- ❏ Some detail information

Additional information can be obtained using the methods inherited from `Event`.

```
public org.w3c.dom.views.AbstractView getView()
public int getDetail ()
```

Returned Values

Method	Return	Description
getView()	org.w3c.dom.views. AbstractView	The AbstractView from which the event was generated
getDetail()	int	Some detail information about the Event, depending on its type

Method initUIEvent()

The `initUIEvent()` method is used to initialize the value of a `UIEvent` created through the `DocumentEvent` interface. This method may only be called before the `UIEvent` has been dispatched via the `dispatchEvent()` method, though it may be called multiple times during that phase if necessary. If called multiple times, the final invocation takes precedence.

```
public void initUIEvent(String typeArg,
         boolean canBubbleArg, boolean cancelableArg,
         org.w3c.dom.views.AbstractView viewArg,
         int detailArg)
```

Parameters

Parameter	Type	Description
typeArg	String	Specifies the event type
canBubbleArg	boolean	Specifies whether the event can bubble
cancelableArg	boolean	Specifies whether the event's default action can be prevented
viewArg	org.w3c.dom.views. AbstractView	Specifies the Event's AbstractView
detailArg	int	Specifies the Event's detail

Note: XML parsers normally don't support the UI events. The DOM specification defines them for GUI applications, such as Web browsers.

Interface MouseEvent
org.w3c.dom.events

```
public interface MouseEvent
extends UIEvent
```

The `MouseEvent` interface provides specific contextual information associated with mouse events.

The `detail` property inherited from `UIEvent` indicates the number of times a mouse button has been pressed and released over the same screen location during a user action.

In the case of nested elements, mouse events are always targeted at the most deeply nested element. Ancestors of the targeted element may use bubbling to obtain notification of mouse events, which occur within its descendant elements.

Methods for Getting MouseEvent's Properties

These methods return the following information about an event:

- ❑ The X and Y screen coordinates
- ❑ The X and Y client area coordinates
- ❑ The number of the mouse button
- ❑ The state of the *Ctrl, Shift, Alt* and *Meta* keys
- ❑ A related target (if any)

Additional information can be obtained using the methods inherited from `Event` and `UIEvent`.

```
public int getScreenX()
```
```
public int getScreenY()
```
```
public int getClientX()
```
```
public int getClientY()
```
```
public boolean getCtrlKey()
```
```
public boolean getShiftKey()
```
```
public boolean getAltKey()
```
```
public boolean getMetaKey()
```
```
public short getButton()
```
```
public EventTarget getRelatedTarget()
```

Returned Values

Method	Return	Description
getScreenX()	int	The horizontal coordinate at which the event occurred, relative to the origin of the screen coordinate system
getScreenY()	int	The vertical coordinate at which the event occurred, relative to the origin of the screen coordinate system
getClientX()	int	The horizontal coordinate at which the event occurred, relative to the DOM implementation's client area
getClientY()	int	The vertical coordinate at which the event occurred, relative to the DOM implementation's client area
getCtrlKey()	boolean	true if the *Ctrl* key was down during the firing of the event
getShiftKey()	boolean	true if the *Shift* key was down during the firing of the event
getAltKey()	boolean	true if the *Alt* key was down during the firing of the event. On some platforms this key may map to an alternative key name.
getMetaKey()	boolean	true if the *Meta* key was down during the firing of the event. On some platforms this key may map to an alternative key name.
getButton()	short	The number of the mouse button that changed its state. 0 indicates the left button of the mouse, 1 indicates the middle button if present, and 2 indicates the right button. The state change occurs when the user presses or releases a mouse button.
getRelatedTarget()	EventTarget	A secondary EventTarget related to a UI event.

Method initMouseEvent()

The initMouseEvent() method is used to initialize the value of a MouseEvent created through the DocumentEvent interface. This method may only be called before the MouseEvent has been dispatched via the dispatchEvent() method, though it may be called multiple times during that phase if necessary. If called multiple times, the final invocation takes precedence.

```
public void initMouseEvent(String typeArg,
        boolean canBubbleArg, boolean cancelableArg,
        org.w3c.dom.views.AbstractView viewArg,
        int detailArg, int screenXArg, int screenYArg,
        int clientXArg, int clientYArg,
        boolean ctrlKeyArg, boolean altKeyArg,
        boolean shiftKeyArg, boolean metaKeyArg,
        short buttonArg, EventTarget relatedTargetArg)
```

Parameters

Parameter	Type	Description
typeArg	String	Specifies the event type
canBubbleArg	boolean	Specifies whether the event can bubble
cancelableArg	boolean	Specifies whether the event's default action can be prevented
viewArg	org.w3c.dom. views.AbstractView	Specifies the Event's AbstractView
detailArg	int	Specifies the Event's mouse click count
screenXArg	int	Specifies the Event's screen x coordinate
screenYArg	int	Specifies the Event's screen y coordinate
clientXArg	int	Specifies the Event's client x coordinate
clientYArg	int	Specifies the Event's client y coordinate
ctrlKeyArg	boolean	Specifies whether the *Control* key was down during the Event
altKeyArg	boolean	Specifies whether the *Alt* key was down during the Event
shiftKeyArg	boolean	Specifies whether the *Shift* key was down during the Event
metaKeyArg	boolean	Specifies whether *Meta* key was down during the Event
buttonArg	short	Specifies the Event's mouse button
relatedTargetArg	EventTarget	Specifies the Event's related EventTarget

> **Note: XML parsers normally don't support the mouse events. The DOM specification defines them for GUI applications, such as Web browsers.**

Interface EventListener
org.w3c.dom.events

> **public interface** EventListener

The EventListener interface defines a callback method for handling events. Applications implement the EventListener interface and register their listener on an EventTarget using the addEventListener() method. The applications should also remove their EventListener from its EventTarget after they have finished using the listener.

When a Node is copied using the cloneNode() method, the EventListener/s attached to the source Node are not attached to the created Node. If the application wishes the same EventListeners to be added to the newly created copy, the application must add them manually.

Method handleEvent()

The handleEvent() method is called whenever an event occurs of the type for which the EventListener interface was registered.

> public void **handleEvent**(Event evt)

Parameters

Parameter	Type	Description
evt	Event	The Event contains contextual information about the event. It also contains the stopPropagation() and preventDefault() methods.

Example: Building a Listener for Events

This class implements the org.w3c.dom.events.EventListener interface. The following example handles events, which consists of printing their properties. Our EventsSample on page 246 uses this PrintEventListener class.

Source PrintEventListener.java

```
import org.w3c.dom.events.Event;
import org.w3c.dom.events.EventListener;
```

```
import org.w3c.dom.events.MutationEvent;

import org.w3c.dom.Node;

public class PrintEventListener implements EventListener {
  private boolean stopPropagationFlag;
```

The `PrintEventListener()` constructor creates a new event listener that doesn't stop the propagation of events.

```
public PrintEventListener() {
  stopPropagationFlag = false;
}
```

The second `PrintEventListener()` constructor creates a new event listener that can stop the propagation of the events.

```
public PrintEventListener(boolean stopPropagationFlag) {
  this.stopPropagationFlag = stopPropagationFlag;
}
```

The `handleEvent()` method is called when an event is fired to a target with which the listener was registered. If `stopPropagationFlag` was set to `true`, the propagation of the event is stopped. The properties of the event are printed using the next method.

```
public void handleEvent(Event evt) {
  if (stopPropagationFlag)
    evt.stopPropagation();
  print(evt);
}
```

The `print()` method prints the properties of the event object. If the parameter is an instance of the `MutationEvent` interface, there is additional output information.

```
public static void print(Event evt) {
  StringBuffer buf = new StringBuffer();
  int phase = evt.getEventPhase();
  switch (phase) {
    case Event.CAPTURING_PHASE:
      buf.append("Captured Event");
      break;
    case Event.AT_TARGET:
      buf.append("Targeted Event");
      break;
    case Event.BUBBLING_PHASE:
      buf.append("Bubbled Event");
      break;
  }
  buf.append(": ");
  buf.append(evt.getType());
```

```
System.out.println(buf.toString());
    if (evt.getTarget() instanceof Node) {
      System.out.println("  Target: "
        + ((Node) evt.getTarget()).getNodeName());
    }
    if (evt.getCurrentTarget() instanceof Node) {
      System.out.println("  Current Target: "
        + ((Node) evt.getCurrentTarget()).getNodeName());
    }
    if (evt instanceof MutationEvent) {
      MutationEvent mevt = (MutationEvent) evt;
      if (mevt.getRelatedNode() != null)
        System.out.println("  Related node: "
          + mevt.getRelatedNode().getNodeName());
      switch (mevt.getAttrChange()) {
        case MutationEvent.MODIFICATION:
          System.out.println("  Modification");
          break;
        case MutationEvent.ADDITION:
          System.out.println("  Addition");
          break;
        case MutationEvent.REMOVAL:
          System.out.println("  Removal");
          break;
      }
      if (mevt.getAttrName() != null)
        System.out.println("  Attribute name: "
          + mevt.getAttrName());
      if (mevt.getPrevValue() != null)
        System.out.println("  Old value: "
          + mevt.getPrevValue());
      if (mevt.getNewValue() != null)
        System.out.println("  New Value: "
          + mevt.getNewValue());
    }
    System.out.println();
  }
}
```

Interface EventTarget
org.w3c.dom.events

```
public interface EventTarget
```

This interface defines methods for registering, unregistering, and dispatching EventListeners events to event targets. The EventTarget interface is implemented by all classes that implement an interface derived from Node in a DOM parser that supports the DOM Event Model.

Methods for Adding and Removing Listeners

The addEventListener() method allows the registration of event listeners on the event target. The listener parameter is an instance of a class that must implement EventListener. This interface declares a handleEvent() method to be called when an event occurs.

The removeEventListener() method allows the removal of event listeners from the event target. After removing an EventListener, its handleEvent() method is not called again. Calling removeEventListener() with arguments, which do not identify any currently registered EventListener on the EventTarget, has no effect.

If an EventListener is added to an EventTarget while it is processing an event, it will not be triggered by the current actions but could be triggered during a later stage of event flow, such as the bubbling phase.

If an EventListener is removed from an EventTarget while the target is processing an event, the listener will not be triggered by the current actions.

If multiple identical EventListeners are registered on the same EventTarget with the same parameters, the duplicate instances are discarded. They do not cause the EventListener to be called twice and since they are discarded, they do not need to be removed with the removeEventListener() method.

If true, the useCapture parameter indicates that the application wishes to initiate capture. After initiating capture, all events of the specified type will be dispatched to the registered EventListener before being dispatched to any EventTargets beneath them in the tree.

Events that are bubbling upward through the tree will not trigger an EventListener designated to use capture. If a listener is registered twice, one with capture and one without, the removal can only be done separately. Removal of a capturing listener does not affect a non-capturing version of the same listener, and vice versa.

```
public void addEventListener(String type,
        EventListener listener, boolean useCapture)
public void removeEventListener(String type,
        EventListener listener, boolean useCapture)
```

Parameters

Parameter	Type	Description
type	String	Specifies the event type of the EventListener being added or removed
listener	EventListener	Indicates the EventListener to be added or removed
useCapture	boolean	Specifies whether the EventListener is a capturing listener or not

Method dispatchEvent()

The dispatchEvent() method allows the dispatch of events into the implementation's event model. Events dispatched in this manner will have the same capturing and bubbling behavior as events dispatched directly by the implementation. The target of the event is the EventTarget on which dispatchEvent() is called.

```
public boolean dispatchEvent(Event evt)
                throws EventException
```

Parameters

Parameter	Type	Description
evt	Event	Specifies the event type, behavior, and contextual information to be used in processing the event

Returned Values

Method	Return	Description
dispatchEvent()	boolean	The return value of dispatchEvent() indicates whether any of the listeners, which handled the event, called preventDefault(). If preventDefault() was called the value is false, else the value is true.

Example: Watching the Event Flow

This example registers event listeners to the nodes of a document and shows what events are fired when the DOM tree is modified. The event flow can also be studied since we capture events, let them bubble, and stop their propagation in different phases.

Source EventsSample.java

```java
import org.w3c.dom.events.EventListener;
import org.w3c.dom.events.EventTarget;

import org.w3c.dom.Document;
import org.w3c.dom.Element;
import org.w3c.dom.Node;
import org.w3c.dom.Text;

public class EventsSample extends DOMPrinter {

    // Define the mutation event types as String constants
    public static final String DOMSubtreeModified
        = "DOMSubtreeModified";
    public static final String DOMNodeInserted
        = "DOMNodeInserted";
```

```
public static final String DOMNodeRemoved
    = "DOMNodeRemoved";
public static final String DOMNodeInsertedIntoDocument
    = "DOMNodeInsertedIntoDocument";
public static final String DOMNodeRemovedFromDocument
    = "DOMNodeRemovedFromDocument";
public static final String DOMAttrModified
    = "DOMAttrModified";
public static final String DOMCharacterDataModified
    = "DOMCharacterDataModified";
```

If `captureFlag` is `false`, the `registerPrintListener()` method registers an event listener that will print information about all mutation events (except `DOMSubtreeModified`) that are fired to the given node (target). If `captureFlag` is `true`, the listener will get all events fired to any of the descendants of the given node, but not the events targeted to the given node itself.

It is possible to request the stopping of the event propagation using the second flag.

The method returns the listener, which is created and registered.

```
private static EventListener registerPrintListener(
    Node node, boolean captureFlag,
    boolean stopPropagationFlag) {
  // Cast the Node instance to EventTarget
  EventTarget nodeAsTarget = (EventTarget) node;

  // Create the listener for capturing all events
  EventListener listener
    = new PrintEventListener(stopPropagationFlag);

  // Register the event listener
  nodeAsTarget.addEventListener(
    DOMNodeInserted, listener, captureFlag);
  nodeAsTarget.addEventListener(
    DOMNodeRemoved, listener, captureFlag);
  nodeAsTarget.addEventListener(
    DOMNodeInsertedIntoDocument, listener, captureFlag);
  nodeAsTarget.addEventListener(
    DOMNodeRemovedFromDocument, listener, captureFlag);
  nodeAsTarget.addEventListener(
    DOMAttrModified, listener, captureFlag);
  nodeAsTarget.addEventListener(
    DOMCharacterDataModified, listener, captureFlag);

  // Return the event listener
  return listener;
}
```

The `unregisterPrintListener()` method unregisters a listener that was registered by `registerPrintListener()`. The `captureFlag` must have the same value as the one used at registration.

```
private static void unregisterPrintListener(Node node,
       EventListener listener, boolean captureFlag) {
    // Cast the Node instance to EventTarget
    EventTarget nodeAsTarget = (EventTarget) node;

    // Unregister the event listener
    nodeAsTarget.removeEventListener(
      DOMNodeInserted, listener, captureFlag);
    nodeAsTarget.removeEventListener(
      DOMNodeRemoved, listener, captureFlag);
    nodeAsTarget.removeEventListener(
      DOMNodeInsertedIntoDocument, listener, captureFlag);
    nodeAsTarget.removeEventListener(
      DOMNodeRemovedFromDocument, listener, captureFlag);
    nodeAsTarget.removeEventListener(
      DOMAttrModified, listener, captureFlag);
    nodeAsTarget.removeEventListener(
      DOMCharacterDataModified, listener, captureFlag);
}
```

The main() method creates a document and registers listeners that print the events fired when the DOM tree is modified. In a first phase, we register a single listener to the Document instance that captures all events. Then, we register various listeners that allow us to study the event flow.

```
public static void main(String args[]) {
  try {
    // Create the document using the newDocument()
    // method inherited from DOMPrinter
    println("*** Create doc \r\n");
    Document doc = newDocument();

    // Register a listener that will capture all
    // events targeted to any node contained
    // by the document.
    println("*** Register doc listener \r\n");
    EventListener docListener
      = registerPrintListener(doc, true, false);

    // Create the root element of the document
    println("*** Create root \r\n");
    Element root = doc.createElement("root");
    println("*** Append root \r\n");
    doc.appendChild(root);
    print(doc);
    println("");

    // Add some character data
    println("*** Add character data \r\n");
    Text text = doc.createTextNode("some data");
    root.appendChild(text);
```

```
// Modify character data
    println("*** Modify character data \r\n");
    text.setData("new data");

    // Create a sub-three
    println("*** Create sub-tree \r\n");
    Element level_1 = doc.createElement("level_1");
    Element level_2 = doc.createElement("level_2");
    Element level_3 = doc.createElement("level_3");
    level_1.appendChild(level_2);
    level_2.appendChild(level_3);

    // Append the sub-tree
    println("*** Append sub-tree \r\n");
    root.appendChild(level_1);
    println("*** DOM Tree");
    print(doc);
    println("");

    // Remove the sub-tree
    println("*** Remove sub-tree \r\n");
    root.removeChild(level_1);
    println("*** DOM Tree");
    print(doc);
    println("");

    // Replace the root with the sub-tree
    println("*** Replace root with sub-tree \r\n");
    doc.replaceChild(level_1, root);
    println("*** DOM Tree");
    print(doc);
    println("");

    // Remove the document's listener
    println("*** Unregister doc listener \r\n");
    unregisterPrintListener(doc, docListener, true);

    // Register listeners to all nodes
    // These listeners will not capture the events
    // and will not stop the bubbling
    println("*** Register listeners to all nodes \r\n");
    EventListener listener_1
      = registerPrintListener(level_1, false, false);
    EventListener listener_2
      = registerPrintListener(level_2, false, false);
    EventListener listener_3
      = registerPrintListener(level_3, false, false);

    // Add an attribute and see how the event bubbles
    println("*** Add attribute \r\n");
    level_3.setAttribute("attr", "a");

    // Stop propagation at level_2
```

```
// The bubbling events won't reach level_1 anymore
      println("*** Stop propagation at level_2 \r\n");
      unregisterPrintListener(level_2, listener_2, false);
      listener_2
        = registerPrintListener(level_2, false, true);

      // Add an attribute to the node that stops
      // the propagation of the events
      println("*** Add attribute \r\n");
      level_2.setAttribute("u2", "v2");

      // Change the attribute's value
      println("*** Change attribute value \r\n");
      level_3.setAttribute("attr", "b");

      // Capture events at level_1,
      // but don't stop the event flow
      println("*** Capture events at level_1 \r\n");
      unregisterPrintListener(level_1, listener_1, false);
      listener_1
        = registerPrintListener(level_1, true, false);

      // Change the attribute's value
      println("*** Change attribute value \r\n");
      level_3.setAttribute("attr", "c");

      // Capture events at level_1 and stop propagation
      // The captured events will not reach their target
      println("*** Capture events at level_1"
        + " and stop propagation \r\n");
      unregisterPrintListener(level_1, listener_1, true);
      listener_1
        = registerPrintListener(level_1, true, true);

      // Add an attribute to the node that captures
      // the events and stops their propagation (level_1).
      // The event isn't printed because the listener
      // that captures the events of the descendants
      // doesn't get the events fired directly to level_1.
      // A second listener that doesn't capture
      // the events would get the missed event.
      // Uncomment the following line to see this.
      // registerPrintListener(level_1, false, false);
      println("*** Add attribute \r\n");
      level_1.setAttribute("u1", "v1");

      // Remove the attribute
      println("*** Remove attribute \r\n");
      level_3.removeAttribute("attr");
    } catch (Exception e) {
      e.printStackTrace();
```

```
System.exit(1);
        }
    }
}
```

Output

> **java EventsSample**

*** Create doc

*** Register doc listener

*** Create root

*** Append root

Captured Event: DOMNodeInserted
  Target: root
  Current Target: #document
  Related node: #document

Captured Event: DOMNodeInsertedIntoDocument
  Target: root
  Current Target: #document

DOCUMENT - #document - null
  ELEMENT - root - null

*** Add character data

Captured Event: DOMNodeInserted
  Target: #text
  Current Target: #document
  Related node: root

*** Modify character data

Captured Event: DOMCharacterDataModified
  Target: #text
  Current Target: #document
  Old value: some data
  New Value: new data

*** Create sub-tree

*** Append sub-tree

Captured Event: DOMNodeInserted
  Target: level_1
  Current Target: #document
  Related node: root

```
*** DOM Tree
DOCUMENT - #document - null
  ELEMENT - root - null
    TEXT - #text - new data
    ELEMENT - level_1 - null
      ELEMENT - level_2 - null
        ELEMENT - level_3 - null

*** Remove sub-tree

Captured Event: DOMNodeRemoved
  Target: level_1
  Current Target: #document
  Related node: root

*** DOM Tree
DOCUMENT - #document - null
  ELEMENT - root - null
    TEXT - #text - new data

*** Replace root with sub-tree

Captured Event: DOMNodeInserted
  Target: level_1
  Current Target: #document
  Related node: #document

Captured Event: DOMNodeInsertedIntoDocument
  Target: level_1
  Current Target: #document

Captured Event: DOMNodeInsertedIntoDocument
  Target: level_2
  Current Target: #document

Captured Event: DOMNodeInsertedIntoDocument
  Target: level_3
  Current Target: #document

Captured Event: DOMNodeInsertedIntoDocument
  Target: root
  Current Target: #document

Captured Event: DOMNodeInsertedIntoDocument
  Target: #text
  Current Target: #document

Captured Event: DOMNodeRemoved
  Target: root
  Current Target: #document
  Related node: #document

Captured Event: DOMNodeRemovedFromDocument
  Target: root
```

```
  Current Target: #document

Captured Event: DOMNodeRemovedFromDocument
  Target: #text
  Current Target: #document

*** DOM Tree
DOCUMENT - #document - null
  ELEMENT - level_1 - null
    ELEMENT - level_2 - null
      ELEMENT - level_3 - null

*** Unregister doc listener

*** Register listeners to all nodes

*** Add attribute

Targeted Event: DOMAttrModified
  Target: level_3
  Current Target: level_3
  Related node: attr
  Addition
  Attribute name: attr
  New Value: a

Bubbled Event: DOMAttrModified
  Target: level_3
  Current Target: level_2
  Related node: attr
  Addition
  Attribute name: attr
  New Value: a

Bubbled Event: DOMAttrModified
  Target: level_3
  Current Target: level_1
  Related node: attr
  Addition
  Attribute name: attr
  New Value: a

*** Stop propagation at level_2

*** Add attribute

Targeted Event: DOMAttrModified
  Target: level_2
  Current Target: level_2
  Related node: u2
  Addition
  Attribute name: u2
  New Value: v2
```

```
*** Change attribute value

Targeted Event: DOMAttrModified
  Target: level_3
  Current Target: level_3
  Related node: attr
  Modification
  Attribute name: attr
  Old value: a
  New Value: b

Bubbled Event: DOMAttrModified
  Target: level_3
  Current Target: level_2
  Related node: attr
  Modification
  Attribute name: attr
  Old value: a
  New Value: b

*** Capture events at level_1

*** Change attribute value

Captured Event: DOMAttrModified
  Target: level_3
  Current Target: level_1
  Related node: attr
  Modification
  Attribute name: attr
  Old value: b
  New Value: c

Targeted Event: DOMAttrModified
  Target: level_3
  Current Target: level_3
  Related node: attr
  Modification
  Attribute name: attr
  Old value: b
  New Value: c

Bubbled Event: DOMAttrModified
  Target: level_3
  Current Target: level_2
  Related node: attr
  Modification
  Attribute name: attr
  Old value: b
  New Value: c
```

```
*** Capture events at level_1 and stop propagation

*** Add attribute

*** Remove attribute

Captured Event: DOMAttrModified
  Target: level_3
  Current Target: level_1
  Removal
  Attribute name: attr
  Old value: c
```

When we appended a sub-tree within the root element, the Apache Xerces-J 1.4.0 implementation fired only a DOMNodeInserted event. When we removed the sub-tree, a DOMNodeRemoved event was fired. When we replaced the root element with the sub-tree, Xerces also fired DOMNodeInsertedIntoDocument and DOMNodeRemovedFromDocument events, which is correct.

The DOM specification says that the DOMNodeInsertedIntoDocument and DOMNodeRemovedFromDocument events should be fired when a node is inserted into or removed from a document directly or indirectly via a sub-tree. The parent node where the sub-tree is inserted or removed can be any node of the DOM tree, but the version of Xerces used fires these events only if the parent node is a Document instance.

Interface DocumentEvent
org.w3c.dom.events

public interface DocumentEvent

The DocumentEvent interface provides a mechanism by which the application can create an Event of a type supported by the implementation. In an implementation supporting the event model, the class implementing the Document interface also implements the DocumentEvent interface.

Note that this interface does not extend Event. When you read DocumentEvent, you should actually think of "event factory."

Method createEvent()

This method creates an event of the given type. If the Event interface specified by the eventType parameter is supported by the implementation, this method will return a new Event of the interface type requested. If an Event is to be dispatched via the dispatchEvent() method, the appropriate event initialization method must be called after creation in order to set the Event's properties.

As an example, an application wishing to synthesize some kind of UIEvent would call createEvent() with the parameter "UIEvents". The initUIEvent() method could then be called on the newly created UIEvent to set the specific type of UIEvent to be dispatched and set its context information. The createEvent() method is used in creating Events when it is either inconvenient or unnecessary for the application to create an Event itself. In cases where the implementation provided Event is insufficient, applications may supply their own Event implementations for use with the dispatchEvent() method.

```
public Event createEvent(String eventType)
        throws DOMException
```

Parameters

Parameter	Type	Description
eventType	String	The eventType parameter specifies the type of Event interface to be created

Returned Values

Return	Description
Event	The newly created Event

Events in DOM Level 3

For the next version of the DOM Events extension, W3C intends to add the following interfaces to the org.w3c.dom.events package. The material of this section is based on a work in progress. When this book was written, the DOM Level 3 Events specification was at the working draft stage.

Interfaces

All these are new in DOM Level 3:

Interface	Description
DocumentEvent Group	The DocumentEventGroup interface provides a mechanism by which the application can create an EventGroup of a type supported by the implementation. The DocumentEventGroup interface will be implemented by the same class that implements Document.
EventGroup	The EventGroup interface functions primarily as a placeholder for separating the event flows when there are multiple groups of listeners for a DOM tree. EventListeners can be registered without an EventGroup by using the existing EventTarget interface, or with an associated EventGroup using the new EventTargetGroup interface. When an event is dispatched, it is dispatched independently to each EventGroup. In particular, the stopPropagation() method of the Event interface only stops propagation within an EventListener's associated EventGroup.

Interface	Description
EventTarget Group	The `EventTargetGroup` interface is implemented by the same set of objects that implement the `EventTarget` interface, namely all `EventTargets` in an implementation that supports the event model and the event group extension
KeyEvent	The `KeyEvent` interface provides specific contextual information associated with key events

Package org.w3c.dom.traversal

The interfaces defined by this DOM extension provide an easy-to-use solution for traversing a DOM tree. It is possible to delimit a sub-tree of a document and filter the nodes by type. We can also build our own custom filters.

The `org.w3c.dom.traversal` package contains the following interfaces:

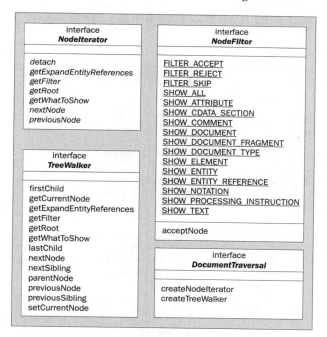

Interfaces

These interfaces are new in DOM level 3:

Interface	Description	Page
`NodeFilter`	Filters are objects that know how to "filter out" nodes	258
`NodeIterator`	`Iterators` are used to step through a set of nodes	263
`TreeWalker`	`TreeWalker` objects are used to navigate a document tree or sub-tree	266
`Document Traversal`	`DocumentTraversal` contains methods that create iterators and tree-walkers to traverse a node and its children in document order. This is equivalent to the order in which the start tags occur in the text representation of the document.	271

Interface NodeFilter
org.w3c.dom.traversal

```
public interface NodeFilter
```

Filters are objects that know how to "filter out" nodes. If a `NodeIterator` or `TreeWalker` is given a `NodeFilter`, it applies the filter before it returns the next node. If the filter says to accept the node, the traversal logic returns it. Otherwise, traversal looks for the next node and pretends that the rejected node was not there.

The DOM does not provide any filters. `NodeFilter` is just an interface that applications can implement to provide their own filters.

`NodeFilters` do not need to know how to traverse from node to node, nor do they need to know anything about the data structure that is being traversed. This makes it very easy to write filters, since the only thing they have to know how to do is evaluate a single node. One filter may be used with a number of different kinds of traversals, encouraging code reuse.

Fields

The `FILTER_*` constants define the valid values that may be returned by the `acceptNode()` method of this interface. The `SHOW_*` flags can be combined with a bitwise-OR and the obtained values are used for the `whatToShow` property of `NodeIterator` or `TreeWalker`.

Field	Type	Description
`FILTER_ACCEPT`	`short`	Accept the node. Navigation methods defined for `NodeIterator` or `TreeWalker` will return this node.
`FILTER_REJECT`	`short`	Reject the node. Navigation methods defined for `NodeIterator` or `TreeWalker` will not return this node. For `TreeWalker`, the children of this node will also be rejected. `NodeIterators` treat this as a synonym for `FILTER_SKIP`.

Field	Type	Description
FILTER_SKIP	short	Skip this single node. Navigation methods defined for NodeIterator or TreeWalker will not return this node. For both NodeIterator and TreeWalker, the children of this node will still be considered.
SHOW_ALL	int	Show all Nodes
SHOW_ELEMENT	int	Show Element nodes
SHOW_ATTRIBUTE	int	Show Attr nodes. This is meaningful only when creating an iterator or tree-walker with an attribute node as its root; in this case, it means that the attribute node will appear in the first position of the iteration or traversal. Since attributes are never children of other nodes, they do not appear when traversing over the document tree.
SHOW_TEXT	int	Show Text nodes
SHOW_CDATA_SECTION	int	Show CDATASection nodes
SHOW_ENTITY_ REFERENCE	int	Show EntityReference nodes
SHOW_ENTITY	int	Show Entity nodes. This is meaningful only when creating an iterator or tree-walker with an Entity node as its root; in this case, it means that the Entity node will appear in the first position of the traversal. Since entities are not part of the document tree, they do not appear when traversing over the document tree.
SHOW_PROCESSING_ INSTRUCTION	int	Show ProcessingInstruction nodes
SHOW_COMMENT	int	Show Comment nodes
SHOW_DOCUMENT	int	Show Document nodes
SHOW_DOCUMENT_TYPE	int	Show DocumentType nodes
SHOW_DOCUMENT_ FRAGMENT	int	Show DocumentFragment nodes
SHOW_NOTATION	int	Show Notation nodes. This is meaningful only when creating an iterator or tree-walker with a Notation node as its root; in this case, it means that the Notation node will appear in the first position of the traversal. Since notations are not part of the document tree, they do not appear when traversing over the document tree.

Method acceptNode()

The `acceptNode()` method tests whether a specified node is visible in the logical view of a `TreeWalker` or `NodeIterator`. This function will be called by the implementation of `TreeWalker` and `NodeIterator` for each node that could be included in the logical view. It is not normally called directly from application code, although you could do so if you wanted to use the same filter to guide your own application logic.

```
public short acceptNode(Node n)
```

Parameters

Parameter	Type	Description
n	Node	The node to be checked to see if it passes the filter or not

Returned Values

Method	Return	Description
acceptNode()	short	A constant to determine whether the node is accepted, rejected, or skipped, as defined above

Example: Creating node filters

This class can be used to create filters that accept the elements with a given tag name or attribute. It is also possible to compound two filters into another filter using an "and" or "or" operation.

Source FilterFactory.java

```java
import org.w3c.dom.traversal.NodeFilter;
import org.w3c.dom.Element;
import org.w3c.dom.Node;

public class FilterFactory {
```

The `getElementFilter()` method returns a filter that accepts the elements of a given type, skips the nodes that might contain acceptable elements and rejects any other node. The skipped nodes are instances of `Document`, `DocumentFragment`, `Entity`, `EntityReference` and `Element` nodes whose tag names don't match the value of the parameter. Nodes that aren't accepted, but can contain acceptable elements are skipped. The other nodes are rejected.

```java
    public static NodeFilter getElementFilter(
        final String tagName) {
      return getElementFilterImpl(null, tagName);
    }
```

The following method is the namespace-aware version of the previous method.

```
public static NodeFilter getElementFilter(
    final String namespaceURI, final String localName) {
  return getElementFilterImpl(namespaceURI, localName);
}
```

The `getElementFilterImpl()` method is used by the two public methods above that accept elements of a given type.

```
private static NodeFilter getElementFilterImpl(
    final String namespaceURI, final String name) {
  return new NodeFilter() {
    public short acceptNode(Node node) {
      if (node instanceof Element) {
        Element elem = (Element) node;
        if (namespaceURI == null) {
          if (name.equals(elem.getTagName()))
            return NodeFilter.FILTER_ACCEPT;
        } else {
          if (namespaceURI.equals(elem.getNamespaceURI())
            && name.equals(elem.getLocalName()))
            return NodeFilter.FILTER_ACCEPT;
        }
      }
      switch (node.getNodeType()) {
        case Node.DOCUMENT_NODE:
        case Node.DOCUMENT_FRAGMENT_NODE:
        case Node.ELEMENT_NODE:
        case Node.ENTITY_NODE:
        case Node.ENTITY_REFERENCE_NODE:
          return NodeFilter.FILTER_SKIP;
      }
      return NodeFilter.FILTER_REJECT;
    }
  };
}
```

The `getAttrFilter()` method returns a filter that accepts the elements that have a given attribute set to a given value, skips `Document`, `DocumentFragment`, `Entity`, `EntityReference` and the other `Element` nodes, and rejects the rest of the nodes.

```
public static NodeFilter getAttrFilter(
    final String name, final String value) {
  return getAttrFilterImpl(null, name, value);
}
```

The following method is the namespace-aware version of the previous method.

```
public static NodeFilter getAttrFilter(
    final String namespaceURI, final String localName,
    final String value) {
  return getAttrFilterImpl(
    namespaceURI, localName, value);
}
```

The `getAttrFilterImpl()` method is used by the above two public methods that accept elements with a given attribute set to a given value. Nodes that aren't accepted, but can contain acceptable elements are skipped. The other nodes are rejected.

```
private static NodeFilter getAttrFilterImpl(
    final String namespaceURI, final String name,
    final String value) {
  return new NodeFilter() {
    public short acceptNode(Node node) {
      if (node instanceof Element) {
        String attrValue = null;
        if (namespaceURI == null)
          attrValue = ((Element) node).getAttribute(name);
        else
          attrValue = ((Element) node).getAttributeNS(
            namespaceURI, name);
        if (attrValue != null && attrValue.equals(value))
          return NodeFilter.FILTER_ACCEPT;
      }
      switch (node.getNodeType()) {
        case Node.DOCUMENT_NODE:
        case Node.DOCUMENT_FRAGMENT_NODE:
        case Node.ELEMENT_NODE:
        case Node.ENTITY_NODE:
        case Node.ENTITY_REFERENCE_NODE:
          return NodeFilter.FILTER_SKIP;
      }
      return NodeFilter.FILTER_REJECT;
    }
  };
}
```

The `getAndFilter()` method returns a filter that accepts nodes that are accepted by the two given filters, rejects nodes that are rejected by at least one of the given filters and skips nodes in any other case.

```
public static NodeFilter getAndFilter(
    final NodeFilter filter1, final NodeFilter filter2) {
  return new NodeFilter() {
    public short acceptNode(Node node) {
      short a1 = filter1.acceptNode(node);
      short a2 = filter2.acceptNode(node);
      if (a1 == NodeFilter.FILTER_ACCEPT
        && a2 == NodeFilter.FILTER_ACCEPT)
```

```
        return NodeFilter.FILTER_ACCEPT;
            if (a1 == NodeFilter.FILTER_REJECT
             || a2 == NodeFilter.FILTER_REJECT)
             return NodeFilter.FILTER_REJECT;
            return NodeFilter.FILTER_SKIP;
        }
      };
    }
```

The `getOrFilter()` method returns a filter that accepts nodes that are accepted by at least one of the given filters, rejects nodes that are rejected by the two given filters and skips nodes in any other case.

```
    public static NodeFilter getOrFilter(
        final NodeFilter filter1, final NodeFilter filter2) {
      return new NodeFilter() {
        public short acceptNode(Node node) {
          short a1 = filter1.acceptNode(node);
          short a2 = filter2.acceptNode(node);
          if (a1 == NodeFilter.FILTER_ACCEPT
             || a2 == NodeFilter.FILTER_ACCEPT)
            return NodeFilter.FILTER_ACCEPT;
          if (a1 == NodeFilter.FILTER_REJECT
             && a2 == NodeFilter.FILTER_REJECT)
            return NodeFilter.FILTER_REJECT;
          return NodeFilter.FILTER_SKIP;
        }
      };
    }
}
```

Interface NodeIterator

org.w3c.dom.traversal

public interface NodeIterator

Iterators are used to step through a set of nodes – for instance, the set of nodes in a `NodeList`, the document sub-tree governed by a particular `Node`, the results of a query, or any other set of nodes. The set of nodes to be iterated through is determined by the implementation of the `NodeIterator`. DOM Level 2 specifies a single `NodeIterator` implementation for document-order traversal of a document sub-tree. Instances of these iterators are created by calling the `createNodeIterator()` method, defined by `DocumentTraversal`.

Methods for Getting NodeIterator's Properties

The `getRoot()` method returns the root node of the `NodeIterator`, as specified when it was created.

The getWhatToShow() method determines which node types are presented via the iterator. The SHOW_* constants defined in the NodeFilter interface can be combined with " | " and the obtained values can be returned by this method. Nodes not accepted by whatToShow will be skipped, but their children may still be considered. Note that this skip takes precedence over the filter, if any.

The getFilter() method returns the NodeFilter used to screen nodes.

The getExpandEntityReferences() method determines whether the children of the entity reference nodes are visible to the iterator. If the value returned by this method is false, the children of the entity reference nodes and their descendants will be rejected. Note that this rejection takes precedence over whatToShow and the filter. Also, note that this is currently the only situation where NodeIterators may reject a complete sub-tree rather than skipping individual nodes.

To produce a view of the document that has entity references expanded and does not expose the entity reference node itself, use the whatToShow flags to hide the entity reference node and set expandEntityReferences to true when creating the iterator. To produce a view of the document that has entity reference nodes but no entity expansion, use the whatToShow flags to show the entity reference node and set expandEntityReferences to false.

```
public Node getRoot()
```
```
public int getWhatToShow()
```
```
public NodeFilter getFilter()
```
```
public boolean getExpandEntityReferences()
```

Returned Values

Method	Return	Description
getRoot()	Node	The root node of the NodeIterator, as specified when it was created
getWhatToShow()	int	The node types that are presented via the iterator
getFilter()	NodeFilter	The NodeFilter used to screen nodes
getExpandEntity References()	boolean	true if the children of entity reference nodes are visible to the iterator

Methods nextNode() and previousNode()

The nextNode() method returns the next node in the set and advances the position of the iterator in the set. After a NodeIterator is created, the first call to nextNode() returns the first node in the set.

The previousNode() method returns the previous node in the set and moves the position of the NodeIterator backwards in the set.

```
public Node nextNode() throws DOMException
```
```
public Node previousNode () throws DOMException
```

Returned Values

Method	Return	Description
`nextNode()`	`Node`	The next `Node` in the set being iterated over, or `null` if there are no more members in that set
`previousNode()`	`Node`	The previous `Node` in the set being iterated over, or `null` if there is no such node in that set

Method detach()

The `detach()` method detaches the `NodeIterator` from the set which it iterated over, releasing any computational resources and placing the iterator in an invalid state. After `detach()` has been invoked, calls to `nextNode()` or `previousNode()` will raise a `DOMException` with the error code set to `INVALID_STATE_ERR`.

```
public void detach()
```

Example: Iterating over the Nodes

This example shows how to use the `NodeIterator`. The `main()` method parses an XML document, creates a compound filter using the methods of our `FilterFactory` and then creates an iterator based on the filter.

Source NodeIteratorSample.java

```java
import org.w3c.dom.traversal.DocumentTraversal;
import org.w3c.dom.traversal.NodeFilter;
import org.w3c.dom.traversal.NodeIterator;

import org.w3c.dom.Document;
import org.w3c.dom.Element;

public class NodeIteratorSample extends DOMPrinter {

  public static void main(String args[]) {
    try {
      // Parse the document using DOMPrinter.parse()
      Document doc = parse("iterator.xml", false);
      String uri = "http://company.com/sample";

      // Create a compound filter
      NodeFilter filter = FilterFactory.getOrFilter(
        FilterFactory.getAndFilter(
          FilterFactory.getElementFilter(uri, "elem1"),
          FilterFactory.getAttrFilter("attr", "a")),
        FilterFactory.getAndFilter(
          FilterFactory.getElementFilter("elem2"),
```

```
FilterFactory.getOrFilter(
          FilterFactory.getAttrFilter("attr", "b"),
          FilterFactory.getAttrFilter("attr", "c")))));

    // Create a node iterator that uses the filter
    DocumentTraversal traversal = (DocumentTraversal) doc;
    NodeIterator iterator = traversal.createNodeIterator(
      doc, NodeFilter.SHOW_ALL, filter, true);

    // Print the IDs of the accepted elements
    StringBuffer buf = new StringBuffer("Element IDs:");
    Element elem;
    while ((elem = (Element) iterator.nextNode()) != null) {
      buf.append(" ");
      buf.append(elem.getAttribute("id"));
    }
    println(buf.toString());
  } catch (org.xml.sax.SAXParseException e) {
    // Already printed by PrintErrorHandler
    System.exit(1);
  } catch (Exception e) {
    e.printStackTrace();
    System.exit(1);
  }
}

}
```

Sample iterator.xml

```
<?xml version="1.0" encoding="utf-8"?>
<sample:sample xmlns:sample="http://company.com/sample">
  <sample:elem1 attr="a" id="e1"> skipped text
    <sample:elem1 attr="b" id="e2"> skipped text
      <sample:elem1 attr="c" id="e3"> skipped text
      </sample:elem1> skipped text
    </sample:elem1> skipped text
  </sample:elem1> skipped text
  <array id="e4"> skipped text
    <elem2 attr="a" id="e5"/> skipped text
    <elem2 attr="b" id="e6"/> skipped text
    <elem2 attr="c" id="e7"/> skipped text
    <elem2 attr="a" id="e8"/> skipped text
    <elem2 attr="b" id="e9"/> skipped text
  </array>
</sample:sample>
```

Output

```
> java NodeIteratorSample

Element IDs: e1 e6 e7 e9
```

Interface TreeWalker

org.w3c.dom.traversal

public interface TreeWalker

TreeWalker objects are used to navigate a document tree or sub-tree, using a logical view of the document defined by whatToShow flags and an optional custom filter.

Omitting nodes from the logical view of a sub-tree can result in a structure that is substantially different from the same sub-tree in the complete, unfiltered document. Nodes that are siblings in the TreeWalker view may be children of different, widely separated nodes in the original view.

For instance, consider a NodeFilter that skips all nodes except for Text nodes and the root element of a document. In the logical view that results, all text nodes will be siblings and appear as direct children of the root element, no matter how deeply nested the structure of the original document.

Methods for Getting TreeWalker's Properties

The getRoot() method returns the root node of the TreeWalker, as specified when it was created.

The getWhatToShow() method determines which node types are presented via the TreeWalker. The available set of constants is defined in the NodeFilter interface. Nodes not accepted by whatToShow will be skipped, but their children may still be considered. Note that this skip takes precedence over the filter, if any.

The getFilter() method returns the filter used to screen the nodes.

The getExpandEntityReferences() method determines whether the children of entity reference nodes are visible to the TreeWalker. If false, they and their descendants will be rejected. Note that this rejection takes precedence over whatToShow and the filter, if any. To produce a view of the document that has entity references expanded and does not expose the entity reference node itself, use the whatToShow flags to hide the entity reference node and set expandEntityReferences to true when creating the TreeWalker. To produce a view of the document that has entity reference nodes but no entity expansion, use the whatToShow flag select the entity reference nodes and set expandEntityReferences to false.

```
public Node getRoot()

public int getWhatToShow()

public NodeFilter getFilter()

public boolean getExpandEntityReferences()
```

Returned Values

Method	Return	Description
getRoot()	Node	The root node of the TreeWalker, as specified when it was created

Table continued on following page

Method	Return	Description
getWhatToShow()	int	The node types that are presented via the TreeWalker
getFilter()	NodeFilter	The filter used to screen nodes
getExpandEntity References()	boolean	true if the children of entity reference nodes are visible to the TreeWalker

Methods for Setting and Getting the Current Node

The setCurrentNode() method locates the TreeWalker to a given node, which may or may not be within the sub-tree specified by the root node. Further traversal occurs relative to the new currentNode even if it is not part of the current view, by applying the filters in the requested direction. If no traversal is possible, currentNode is not changed.

The getCurrentNode() method returns the node at which the TreeWalker is currently positioned. Alterations to the DOM tree may cause the current node no longer to be accepted by the TreeWalker's associated filter.

```
public void setCurrentNode(Node currentNode)
        throws DOMException
```
```
public Node getCurrentNode()
```

Parameters

Parameter	Type	Description
currentNode	Node	The node at which the TreeWalker will be positioned, whether or not it is within the sub-tree specified by the root node or would be accepted by the filter and whatToShow flags

Returned Values

Method	Return	Description
getCurrentNode()	Node	The node at which the TreeWalker is currently positioned

Method parentNode()

The parentNode() method moves to and returns the closest visible ancestor node of the current node. If the search for parentNode attempts to step upward from the TreeWalker's root node, or if it fails to find a visible ancestor node, this method retains the current position and returns null.

```
public Node parentNode()
```

Method	Return	Description
`parentNode()`	**Node**	The new parent node, or `null` if the current node has no parent in the `TreeWalker`'s logical view

Methods firstChild() and lastChild()

These methods move the `TreeWalker` to the first or last visible child of the current node and return the new node. If the current node has no visible children, the methods return `null` and retain the current node.

```
public Node firstChild()
public Node lastChild()
```

Returned Values

Method	Return	Description
`firstChild()`	**Node**	The new node, or `null` if the current node has no visible children in the `TreeWalker`'s logical view
`lastChild()`	**Node**	The new node, or `null` if the current node has no children in the `TreeWalker`'s logical view

Methods previousSibling() and nextSibling()

These methods move the `TreeWalker` to the previous or next sibling of the current node and return the new node. If the current node has no visible previous or next sibling respectively, the methods return `null`, and retain the current node.

```
public Node previousSibling()
public Node nextSibling()
```

Returned Values

Method	Return	Description
`previousSibling()`	**Node**	The new node, or `null` if the current node has no previous sibling in the `TreeWalker`'s logical view
`nextSibling()`	**Node**	The new node, or `null` if the current node has no next sibling in the `TreeWalker`'s logical view

Methods previousNode() and nextNode()

These methods move the `TreeWalker` to the previous or next visible node in the document order relative to the current node and return the new node. If the current node has no previous or next node respectively, or if the search for that node attempts to step upward from the `TreeWalker`'s `root` node, the methods return `null` and retain the current node.

```
public Node previousNode()
```

```
public Node nextNode()
```

Returned Values

Method	Return	Description
previousNode()	Node	The new node, or null if the current node has no previous node in the TreeWalker's logical view
nextNode()	Node	The new node, or null if the current node has no next node in the TreeWalker's logical view

Example: Navigating in the document tree

This example shows how to use the TreeWalker. The main() method parses an XML document, creates a tree walker that selects only the elements and the processing instructions, and then navigates through this structure.

Source TreeWalkerSample.java

```java
import org.w3c.dom.traversal.DocumentTraversal;
import org.w3c.dom.traversal.NodeFilter;
import org.w3c.dom.traversal.TreeWalker;

import org.w3c.dom.Document;
import org.w3c.dom.Element;

public class TreeWalkerSample extends DOMPrinter {

  public static void main(String args[]) {
    try {
      // Parse the document using DOMPrinter.parse()
      Document doc = parse("walker.xml", false);
      Element root = doc.getDocumentElement();

      // Create a tree walker
      DocumentTraversal traversal = (DocumentTraversal) doc;
      TreeWalker walker = traversal.createTreeWalker(root,
        NodeFilter.SHOW_ELEMENT |
        NodeFilter.SHOW_PROCESSING_INSTRUCTION, null, true);
      // Navigate using the walker
      println(walker.getCurrentNode().getNodeName());
      println(walker.nextNode().getNodeName());
      println(walker.nextNode().getNodeName());
      println(walker.firstChild().getNodeName());
      println(walker.nextSibling().getNodeName());
      println(walker.parentNode().getNodeName());
      println(walker.lastChild().getNodeName());
```

```
println(walker.nextNode().getNodeName());
    println(walker.previousSibling().getNodeName());
    println(walker.previousNode().getNodeName());
  } catch (org.xml.sax.SAXParseException e) {
    // Already printed by PrintErrorHandler
    System.exit(1);
  } catch (Exception e) {
    e.printStackTrace();
    System.exit(1);
  }
 }
}
```

Sample walker.xml

```xml
<?xml version="1.0" encoding="utf-8"?>
<sample> skipped text
  <elem1> skipped text
    <elem2> skipped text
      <elem3/> skipped text
      <?proc4?> skipped text
      <elem5/> skipped text
    </elem2> skipped text
    <?proc6?> skipped text
  </elem1> skipped text
  <?proc7?> skipped text
</sample>
```

Output

```
> java TreeWalkerSample

sample
elem1
elem2
elem3
proc4
elem2
elem5
proc6
elem2
elem1
```

Interface DocumentTraversal
org.w3c.dom.traversal

```
public interface DocumentTraversal
```

`DocumentTraversal` contains methods that create iterators and tree-walkers to traverse a node and its children in document order. This is equivalent to the order in which the start tags occur in the text representation of the document (this is know in algorithmic terms as depth first, pre-order traversal). In DOM implementations that support the traversal feature, `DocumentTraversal` will be implemented by the same objects that implement the `Document` interface.

Method createNodeIterator()

The `createNodeIterator()` method creates a new `NodeIterator` over the sub-tree rooted at the specified node.

```
public NodeIterator createNodeIterator (Node root,
                     int whatToShow, NodeFilter filter,
                     boolean entityReferenceExpansion)
     throws DOMException
```

Parameters

Parameter	Type	Description
root	Node	The node that will be iterated together with its children. The iterator is initially positioned just before this node. The `whatToShow` flags and the filter, if any, are not considered when setting this position. The root must not be `null`.
whatToShow	int	This flag specifies which node types may appear in the logical view of the tree presented by the iterator. See the description of `NodeFilter` for the set of possible `SHOW_` values. These flags can be combined using a " `|` " (bitwise-OR).
filter	NodeFilter	The `NodeFilter` to be used with this `TreeWalker`, or `null` to indicate no filter
entityReference Expansion	boolean	The value of this flag determines whether entity reference nodes are expanded

Returned Values

Method	Return	Description
createNode Iterator()	NodeIterator	The newly created `NodeIterator`

Method createTreeWalker()

The createTreeWalker() method creates a new TreeWalker over the sub-tree rooted at the specified node.

```
public TreeWalker createTreeWalker(Node root,
                   int whatToShow, NodeFilter filter,
                   boolean entityReferenceExpansion)
        throws DOMException
```

Parameters

Parameter	Type	Description
root	Node	The node that will serve as the root for the TreeWalker. The whatToShow flags and the NodeFilter are not considered when setting this value; any node type will be accepted as the root. The currentNode of the TreeWalker is initialized to this node, whether or not it is visible. The root functions as a stopping point for traversal methods that look upward in the document structure, such as parentNode() and nextNode(). The root must not be null.
whatToShow	int	This flag specifies which node types may appear in the logical view of the tree presented by the tree-walker. See the description of NodeFilter for the set of possible SHOW_ values. These flags can be combined using " | " (bitwise-OR).
filter	NodeFilter	The NodeFilter to be used with this TreeWalker, or null to indicate no filter
entityReference Expansion	boolean	If this flag is false, the contents of EntityReference nodes are not presented in the logical view

Returned Values

Method	Return	Description
createTreeWalker()	TreeWalker	The newly created TreeWalker

The org.w3c.dom.traversal.DocumentTraversal interface is used by NodeIteratorSample (page 265) and TreeWalkerSample (page 270).

Package org.w3c.dom.range

A Range instance identifies the contiguous content between two boundary points of a DOM document, document fragment, or attribute node. Imagine you open an XML file in a text editor and use the mouse to select some of the content. You may start the selection within a character data section (or comment) and end it within another or the same character data section (or comment). It doesn't matter whether we are dealing with Text, CDATASection or Comment nodes. You may also start the selection within the value of an attribute, but in this case, you must end it within the same attribute value. The selection you've done can be identified by a Range. Note that you may not start or end a Range within the middle of a tag or entity reference. You can start it, however, right before or after such an XML construct.

Therefore, a start point and an end point delimit a range, and such a boundary point is characterized by a container node and an offset. The offset gives the position of the boundary point within the container node.

The units used for offsets are Unicode characters if the container node is a Text, CDATASection, Comment or ProcessingInstruction node, which means that a boundary point can be placed anywhere within a character data section or within the data of a processing instruction.

If the container is a Document, DocumentFragment, Element, Attr or EntityReference node, the offset is between its child nodes; in other words, a boundary point can be placed right before or after a child node (or between two child nodes).

The container node and its ancestor nodes are called the **ancestor containers** of the boundary point. The start and end boundary points of a Range must have a common ancestor container that is either a Document, DocumentFragment or Attr node. Therefore, you may not start a range between two elements of a document and end it within the value of an attribute. As you may recall from Chapter 3, attribute nodes can contain Text and EntityReference nodes and these attribute trees are not considered part of the document tree.

A DocumentType, Notation, or Entity node cannot be the ancestor container of a boundary point. In other words, nodes whose classes implement one of these three interfaces cannot be container nodes for boundary points and their direct and indirect descendants cannot be container nodes either.

The org.w3c.dom.ranges package contains the following interfaces and exceptions.

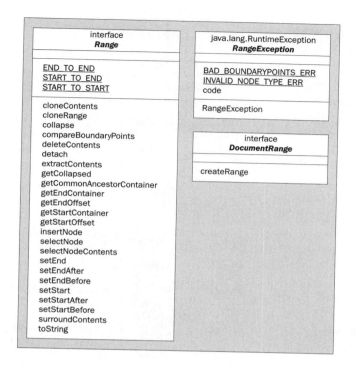

Interfaces

These interfaces were introduced in DOM level 2:

Interface	Description	Page
Range	A Range instance identifies the contiguous content between two boundary points of a DOM document, document fragment or attribute node	276
DocumentRange	This interface is implemented by the same class that implements Document.	288

Exceptions

This exception was introduced in DOM level 2:

Exception	Description	Page
RangeException	Range operations may throw a RangeException	275

Exception RangeException

org.w3c.dom.ranges

```
public class RangeException
        extends java.lang.RuntimeException
```

Range operations may throw a `RangeException`.

Fields

The `RangeException` class has the following fields:

Field	Type	Description
code	short	The code of this exception
BAD_BOUNDARYPOINTS_ERR	short	If the boundary points of a Range do not meet specific requirements
INVALID_NODE_TYPE_ERR	short	If the container of a boundary point of a Range is being set to either a node of an invalid type or a node with an ancestor of an invalid type

Constructor

The constructor creates an exception with the given code and message.

```
public RangeException(short code, String message)
```

Parameters

Parameter	Type	Description
code	short	The exception's code
message	String	The exception's message

Interface Range

org.w3c.dom.ranges

```
public interface Range
```

A `Range` instance identifies the contiguous content between two boundary points of a DOM document, document fragment, or attribute node.

A boundary point is characterized by a container node and an offset. The offset gives the position of the boundary point within the container node.

The units used for offsets are Unicode characters if the container node is a Text, CDATASection, or Comment or ProcessingInstruction node – for instance, a boundary point can be placed anywhere within a character data section or within the data of a processing instruction.

If the container is a Document, DocumentFragment, Element, Attr or EntityReference node, the offset is between its child nodes, which means that a boundary point can be placed before or after a child node (or between two child nodes). A DocumentType, Notation, or Entity node cannot contain a boundary point directly or indirectly.

Fields

The Range interface defines the following constant fields:

Field	Type	Description
START_TO_START	short	Compare start boundary point of sourceRange to start boundary point of Range on which compareBoundaryPoints() is invoked
START_TO_END	short	Compare start boundary point of sourceRange to end boundary point of Range on which compareBoundaryPoints() is invoked
END_TO_END	short	Compare end boundary point of sourceRange to end boundary point of Range on which compareBoundaryPoints() is invoked
END_TO_START	short	Compare end boundary point of sourceRange to start boundary point of Range on which compareBoundaryPoints() is invoked

Methods setStart() and setEnd()

These methods set the properties describing the start and end of a Range.

```
public void setStart(Node refNode, int offset)
        throws RangeException, DOMException
public void setEnd(Node refNode, int offset)
        throws RangeException, DOMException
```

Parameters

Parameter	Type	Description
refNode	Node	The container node
offset	int	The offset value expressed in characters or nodes depending on the type of the container node

Methods setStartBefore() and setEndBefore()

These methods set the start and end positions to be before a node.

```
public void setStartBefore(Node refNode)
        throws RangeException, DOMException
public void setEndBefore(Node refNode)
        throws RangeException, DOMException
```

Parameters

Parameter	Type	Description
refNode	Node	The reference node. The container node of the boundary point will be the parent of this node.

Methods setStartAfter() and setEndAfter()

These methods set the start and end positions to be after a node.

```
public void setStartAfter(Node refNode)
        throws RangeException, DOMException
public void setEndAfter(Node refNode)
        throws RangeException, DOMException
```

Parameters

Parameter	Type	Description
refNode	Node	The reference node. The container node of the boundary point will be the parent of this node.

Methods getStartContainer() and getEndContainer()

These methods return the nodes within which the Range begins and ends:

```
public Node getStartContainer() throws DOMException
public Node getEndContainer() throws DOMException
```

Returned Values

Method	Return	Description
getStartContainer()	Node	The node within which the Range begins
getEndContainer()	Node	The node within which the Range ends

Methods getStartOffset() and getEndOffset()

These methods return the offsets within the starting and ending node of the Range.

```
public int getStartOffset() throws DOMException
public int getEndOffset() throws DOMException
```

Returned Values

Method	Return	Description
getStartOffset()	int	The offset within the starting node of the Range
getEndOffset()	int	The offset within the ending node of the Range

Method getCommonAncestorContainer()

The getCommonAncestorContainer() method returns the deepest common ancestor container of the Range's two boundary points.

```
public Node getCommonAncestorContainer() throws DOMException
```

Returned Values

Method	Return	Description
getCommonAncestor Container()	Node	The deepest common ancestor container of the Range's two boundary points

Method compareBoundaryPoints()

The compareBoundaryPoints() method compares the boundary points of two Ranges in a document:

```
public short compareBoundaryPoints(short how, Range
        sourceRange)
    throws DOMException
```

Parameters

Parameter	Type	Description
how	short	A code representing the type of comparison, as defined in the table of constant fields above
sourceRange	Range	The Range with which this current Range is compared

Returned Values

Method	Return	Description
compareBoundary Points()	short	-1, 0 or 1 depending on whether the corresponding boundary point of the Range is respectively before, equal to, or after the corresponding boundary point of sourceRange

Methods collapse() and getCollapsed()

A `Range` is said to be collapsed if its two boundary points are equal – in other words, they have the same container node and the same offset.

The `collapse()` method collapses a `Range` onto one of its boundary points. If the parameter's value is `true`, the start boundary point also becomes the end boundary point. Otherwise, the range will start and end at the current end boundary point.

The `getCollapsed()` method returns `true` if the `Range` is collapsed.

```
public void collapse(boolean toStart) throws DOMException

public boolean getCollapsed() throws DOMException
```

Parameters

Parameter	Type	Description
toStart	boolean	If true, collapses the Range onto its start – if false, collapses it onto its end

Returned Values

Method	Return	Description
getCollapsed()	boolean	true if the Range is collapsed

Methods selectNode() and selectNodeContents()

The `selectNode()` method selects a node and its contents, which means that the start boundary point is placed before the node and the end boundary point is placed after the node.

The `selectNodeContents()` method selects the contents within a node, which means that the start boundary point is placed before the first child or character of the node and the end boundary point is placed after the last child or character of the given node.

```
public void selectNode(Node refNode)
        throws RangeException, DOMException

public void selectNodeContents(Node refNode)
        throws RangeException, DOMException
```

Parameters

Parameter	Type	Description
refNode	Node	The reference node

Method insertNode()

The `insertNode()` method inserts a node into the `Document` or `DocumentFragment` at the start of the `Range`. If the container is a `Text` node, this will be split at the start of the `Range` (as if the `Text` node's `splitText()` method was performed at the insertion point) and the insertion will occur between the two resulting `Text` nodes. Adjacent `Text` nodes will not be automatically merged. If the node to be inserted is a `DocumentFragment` node, the children will be inserted rather than the `DocumentFragment` node itself.

```
public void insertNode(Node newNode)
        throws DOMException, RangeException
```

Parameters

Parameter	Type	Description
newNode	Node	The node to insert at the start of the `Range`

Method surroundContents()

The `surroundContents()` method moves the contents of the `Range` into the given node and inserts the new parent node at the position of the start of the `Range`. After this operation the boundary points of the range will be set before and after the given node.

```
public void surroundContents(Node newParent)
        throws DOMException, RangeException
```

Parameters

Parameter	Type	Description
newParent	Node	The node with which to surround the contents

Method extractContents()

The `extractContents()` method moves the contents of a `Range` from the containing document or document fragment to a new `DocumentFragment`.

```
public DocumentFragment extractContents()
        throws DOMException
```

Returned Values

Return	Description
DocumentFragment	A `DocumentFragment` containing the extracted contents

Method deleteContents()

The `deleteContents()` method removes the contents of a `Range` from the containing document or document fragment without returning a reference to the removed content.

```
public void deleteContents() throws DOMException
```

Method cloneContents()

The cloneContents() method duplicates the contents of a Range.

```
public DocumentFragment cloneContents() throws DOMException
```

Returned Values

Return	Description
DocumentFragment	A DocumentFragment that contains content equivalent to this Range

Method cloneRange()

The cloneRange() method produces a new Range whose boundary points are equal to the boundary points of this Range.

```
public Range cloneRange() throws DOMException
```

Returned Values

Return	Description
Range	The duplicated Range

Method detach()

The detach() method is called to indicate that the Range is no longer in use and that the implementation may relinquish any resources associated with this Range. Subsequent calls to any methods on this Range will result in a DOMException being thrown with an error code of INVALID_STATE_ERR.

```
public void detach() throws DOMException
```

Method toString()

The toString() method returns the contents of a Range as a string. This string contains only the data characters, not any markup.

```
public String toString() throws DOMException
```

Returned Values

Return	Description
String	The contents of the Range

Example: Working with document ranges

This example shows how to use DOM ranges. We will parse an XML document, create `Range` objects, and perform different operations. These operations includes, contents cloning, extraction, deletion, and node insertion.

Source RangesSample.java

```java
import org.w3c.dom.ranges.DocumentRange;
import org.w3c.dom.ranges.Range;

import org.w3c.dom.traversal.DocumentTraversal;
import org.w3c.dom.traversal.NodeFilter;
import org.w3c.dom.traversal.NodeIterator;

import org.w3c.dom.Document;
import org.w3c.dom.DocumentFragment;
import org.w3c.dom.Element;
import org.w3c.dom.Node;
import org.w3c.dom.NodeList;
import org.w3c.dom.Text;
import org.w3c.dom.ProcessingInstruction;

public class RangesSample extends DOMPrinter {
  public static final int BEFORE = -2;
  public static final int AFTER = -1;
```

The `createRange()` method creates a `Range` instance and sets its boundary points. The `id` is just for output.

```java
    private static Range createRange(int id, Document doc,
        Node startContainer, int startOffset,
        Node endContainer, int endOffset) {
      // Create the Range instance
      DocumentRange rangeFactory = (DocumentRange) doc;
      Range range = rangeFactory.createRange();
      println("Creating Range " + id);

      // Set the starting boundary-point
      if (startOffset >= 0)
        range.setStart(startContainer, startOffset);
      else if (startOffset == BEFORE)
        range.setStartBefore(startContainer);
      else if (startOffset == AFTER)
        range.setStartAfter(startContainer);
      println("  Start: "
        + range.getStartContainer().getNodeName() + " - "
        + range.getStartOffset());

      // Set the ending boundary-point
      if (endOffset >= 0)
```

```
    range.setEnd(endContainer, endOffset);
      else if (endOffset == BEFORE)
        range.setEndBefore(endContainer);
      else if (endOffset == AFTER)
        range.setEndAfter(endContainer);
      println("  End: "
        + range.getEndContainer().getNodeName() + " - "
        + range.getEndOffset());

      // Return the created Range
      println("");
      return range;
    }
```

The `findElement()` method finds the first element with the given tag name in a document:

```
    private static Element findElement(
        Document doc, String tagName) {
      NodeList list = doc.getElementsByTagName(tagName);
      if (list.getLength() > 0)
        return (Element) list.item(0);
      else
        return null;
    }
```

The `trimTextNodes()` method trims the data of the text nodes and removes the empty text nodes. We use a node iterator to get all `Text` nodes contained by the DOM tree.

```
    private static void trimTextNodes(Document doc) {
      DocumentTraversal iteratorFactory
        = (DocumentTraversal) doc;
      NodeIterator iterator
        = iteratorFactory.createNodeIterator(
          doc, NodeFilter.SHOW_TEXT, null, true);
      Text text = (Text) iterator.nextNode();
      while (text != null) {
        String data = text.getData();
        String tdata = data.trim();
        if (tdata.length() == 0)
          text.getParentNode().removeChild(text);
        else if (tdata.length() < data.length())
          text.setData(tdata);
        text = (Text) iterator.nextNode();
      }
    }
```

The `main()` method parses an XML document, gets its nodes, and performs different operations using ranges, such as contents cloning, extraction, deletion, and node insertion.

```
    public static void main(String args[]) {
      try {
```

```
// Parse the document using DOMPrinter.parse()
    Document doc = parse("ranges.xml", true);
    trimTextNodes(doc);
    println("*** Parsed document");
    print(doc);
    println("");

    // Get the document's nodes
    Element root = doc.getDocumentElement();
    Element elem = findElement(doc, "elem");
    Text textBeforeElem = (Text) elem.getPreviousSibling();
    Text textAfterElem = (Text) elem.getNextSibling();
    Element data1 = findElement(doc, "data1");
    Text textOfData1 = (Text) data1.getFirstChild();
    Element data2 = findElement(doc, "data2");
    Text textOfData2 = (Text) data2.getFirstChild();

    // Clone the contents of a range
    Range range1 = createRange(1, doc,
      textBeforeElem,
      textBeforeElem.getData().indexOf("before"),
      textAfterElem,
      textAfterElem.getData().indexOf("after") + 5);
    DocumentFragment clone = range1.cloneContents();
    println("*** Cloned contents");
    print(clone);
    println("");
    println("*** Unchanged document after cloning");
    print(doc);
    println("");

    // Extract the contents of a range
    Range range2 = createRange(2, doc,
      textOfData1, 6, textOfData2, 6);
    DocumentFragment contents = range2.extractContents();
    println("*** Extracted contents");
    print(contents);
    println("");
    println("*** Document after content extraction");
    print(doc);
    println("");

    // Delete the contents of a range
    Range range3 = createRange(3, doc,
      data1, BEFORE, data2, AFTER);
    range3.deleteContents();
    println("*** Document after content deletion");
    print(doc);
    println("");

    // Insert a node into an empty range
    Range range4 = createRange(4, doc,
      elem, 0, elem, 0);
```

```
ProcessingInstruction proc =
        doc.createProcessingInstruction("proc", "data");
    range4.insertNode(proc);
    println("*** Document after proc insertion");
    print(doc);
    println("");
} catch (org.xml.sax.SAXParseException e) {
    // Already printed by PrintErrorHandler
    System.exit(1);
} catch (Exception e) {
    e.printStackTrace();
    System.exit(1);
}
}
}
```

Sample ranges.xml

```
<?xml version='1.0' encoding='utf-8'?>
<!DOCTYPE sample [
  <!ELEMENT sample ANY>
  <!ELEMENT elem (data1, data2)>
  <!ELEMENT data1 (#PCDATA)>
  <!ELEMENT data2 (#PCDATA)>
]>
<sample>
  data before elem
  <elem>
    <data1>text of data1</data1>
    <data2>text of data2</data2>
  </elem>
  data after elem
</sample>
```

Output

```
> java RangesSample

*** Parsed document
DOCUMENT - #document - null
  DOCUMENT_TYPE - sample - null
  ELEMENT - sample - null
    TEXT - #text - data before elem
    ELEMENT - elem - null
      ELEMENT - data1 - null
        TEXT - #text - text of data1
      ELEMENT - data2 - null
        TEXT - #text - text of data2
    TEXT - #text - data after elem

Creating Range 1
  Start: #text - 5
  End: #text - 10
```

```
*** Cloned contents
DOCUMENT_FRAGMENT - #document-fragment - null
  TEXT - #text - before elem
  ELEMENT - elem - null
    ELEMENT - data1 - null
      TEXT - #text - text of data1
    ELEMENT - data2 - null
      TEXT - #text - text of data2
  TEXT - #text - data after

*** Unchanged document after cloning
DOCUMENT - #document - null
  DOCUMENT_TYPE - sample - null
  ELEMENT - sample - null
    TEXT - #text - data before elem
    ELEMENT - elem - null
      ELEMENT - data1 - null
        TEXT - #text - text of data1
      ELEMENT - data2 - null
        TEXT - #text - text of data2
    TEXT - #text - data after elem

Creating Range 2
  Start: #text - 6
  End: #text - 6

*** Extracted contents
DOCUMENT_FRAGMENT - #document-fragment - null
  ELEMENT - data1 - null
    TEXT - #text - f data1
  ELEMENT - data2 - null
    TEXT - #text - text o

*** Document after content extraction
DOCUMENT - #document - null
  DOCUMENT_TYPE - sample - null
  ELEMENT - sample - null
    TEXT - #text - data before elem
    ELEMENT - elem - null
      ELEMENT - data1 - null
        TEXT - #text - text o
      ELEMENT - data2 - null
        TEXT - #text - f data2
    TEXT - #text - data after elem

Creating Range 3
  Start: elem - 0
  End: elem - 2

*** Document after content deletion
DOCUMENT - #document - null
  DOCUMENT_TYPE - sample - null
  ELEMENT - sample - null
    TEXT - #text - data before elem
    ELEMENT - elem - null
    TEXT - #text - data after elem
```

```
Creating Range 4
  Start: elem - 0
  End: elem - 0

*** Document after proc insertion
DOCUMENT - #document - null
  DOCUMENT_TYPE - sample - null
  ELEMENT - sample - null
    TEXT - #text - data before elem
    ELEMENT - elem - null
      PROCESSING_INSTRUCTION - proc - data
    TEXT - #text - data after elem
```

Apache Xerces 1.4.0 appears to ignore the offset within CDATASection, Comment, *and* ProcessingInstruction *nodes. However, it does handle the offsets well within* Text *nodes as you can see in the above example.*

Interface DocumentRange
org.w3c.dom.ranges

public interface DocumentRange

The DocumentRange interface provides a mechanism by which the application can create Range instances. It is expected that the DocumentRange interface will be implemented on the same class that implements the Document interface in any DOM implementation, which supports this extension.

Note that this interface does not extend Range. When you read DocumentRange, you should actually think of "range factory".

Method createRange()

This method creates a Range instance. The initial state of the Range returned from this method is such that both of its boundary points are positioned at the beginning of the corresponding Document, before any content. The Range returned could only be used to select content associated with this Document, or with DocumentFragments and Attrs for which this Document is the ownerDocument.

```
public Range createRange()
```

Returned Values

Return	Description
Range	A new Range instance

org.w3c.dom.ranges.DocumentRange interface is used by our example RangesSample on page 283.

Summary

In this chapter we have looked at the extensions to the DOM API, and in particular, the four main packages:

- Views
- Events
- Traversal
- Range

In addition, we used these extensions with some examples of our own, where we created and registered event listeners to the nodes of a DOM tree, iterated over the nodes of a document using filters, and used ranges to perform different operations, such as content cloning, extraction, deletion and insertion.

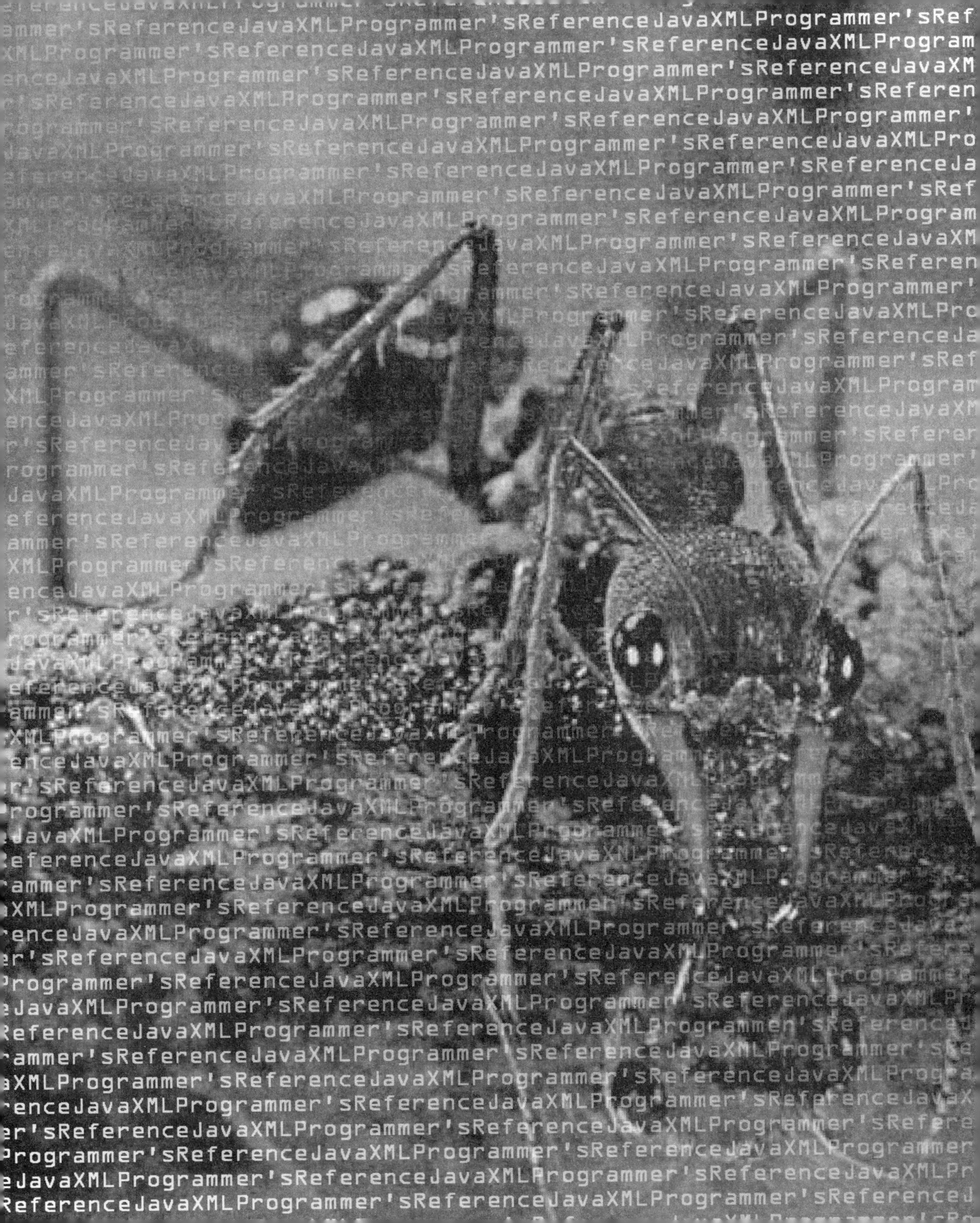

JAXP 1.1

The Java API for XML Parsing (JAXP) allows us to build Java-XML applications that are based on the SAX, DOM, and XSLT standards but are not bound to a particular implementation. JAXP was developed through the Java Community Process (http://jcp.org/jsr/detail/063.jsp). The first version, JAXP 1.0, allowed applications to do SAX and DOM parsing in an implementation-independent manner. The second version, JAXP 1.1, added support for doing transformations in a way that doesn't make code dependent on a particular XSLT processor. This addition is also known as Transformation API for XML (TrAX).

This chapter contains the same information as the JAXP API specification, but in a more compact format. We will use the code and documentation that is distributed as part of Xalan under the Apache license as source for this chapter. This XSLT processor implements the TrAX API. Apache Xerces and Crimson implement the parsing functionality, which is exposed with the JAXP API.

In this chapter, we'll present small examples that use JAXP (including TrAX). To get these examples to work, you will need to download the JAXP 1.1 reference implementation from http://java.sun.com/xml/xml_jaxp.html and add `jaxp.jar`, `crimson.jar` and `xalan.jar` to the `CLASSPATH` environment variable. Alternatively, you can use Xalan, available from http://xml.apache.org/xalan-j/index.html and add `xerces.jar` and `xalan.jar` to your `CLASSPATH`.

We'll show how to:

- ❏ Start SAX parsing with JAXP and validate XML files
- ❏ Parse a file with DOM and create new documents with JAXP
- ❏ Save a DOM tree to an XML file with TrAX
- ❏ Apply XSLT transformations to an XML document using TrAX
- ❏ Chain together transformations
- ❏ Use TrAX templates

JAXP 1.1 contains the following packages:

Package	Description	Page
`javax.xml.parsers`	This package contains factory classes for retrieving parsers. The use of factories allows substitution of implementations according to performance, cost, or other considerations	293
`javax.xml.transform`	The `java.xml.transform` package defines APIs for applying transformations	312
`javax.xml.transform.stream`	Defines classes for expressing transformation sources and results as streams	346
`javax.xml.transform.sax`	The classes in this package implement APIs for SAX 2.0 transformation	351
`javax.xml.transform.dom`	The classes in this this package implement APIs for DOM transformations	360

The following gives a guide to the main classes and interfaces used in the examples:

Example	Used APIs	Page
`SAXValidator`	`SAXParser,` `SAXParserFactory`	301
`DOMPrinter`	`DocumentBuilder,` `DocumentBuilderFactory`	310
`PrintErrorListener`	`ErrorListener, SourceLocator,` `TransformerException`	324

`SerializationSample`	`OutputKeys, Result, Source,`
	`Templates, Transformer,`
	`TransformerFactory,`
	`DOMSource, SAXResult, StreamResult`
		331

`TransformationSample`	`OutputKeys, Transformer,`
	`TransformerFactory, StreamResult`
	`StreamSource`
		338

`ChainedTransformation`
`Sample`
	`OutputKeys, Templates,`
	`Transformer, TransformerFactory,`
	`DOMResult, DOMSource, SAXSource,`
	`StreamResult, StreamSource`
		343

Package javax.xml.parsers

This package provides parser classes supporting SAX (Simple API for XML) and DOM (Document Object Model). The SAXParser class creates instances of the SAX XMLReader interface, while DocumentBuilder creates instances of the DOM Document interface. Factory classes allow the creation of parser instances in an implementation-independent manner.

These classes have all been introduced since JAXP 1.0.

java.lang.Object **SAXParserFactory**	java.lang.Object **SAXParser**	java.lang.Object **DocumentBuilderFactory**	java.lang.Object **DocumentBuilder**
getFeature *isNamespaceAware* *isValidating* <u>*newInstance*</u> *newSAXParser* *setFeature* *setNamespaceAware* *setValidating*	*getParser* *getProperty* *getXMLReader* *isNamespaceAware* *IsValidating* *parse* (10 Variants) *setProperty*	*getAttribute* *isCoalescing* *isExpandEntityReferences* *isIgnoringComments* *isIgnoringElementContentWhitespace* *isNamespaceAware* *isValidating* *newDocumentBuilder* <u>*newInstance*</u> *setAttribute* *setCoalescing* *setExpandEntityReferences* *setIgnoringComments* *setIgnoringElementContentWhitespace* *setNamespaceAware* *setValidating*	*getDOMImplementation* *isNamespaceAware* *isValidating* *newDocument* *parse* *parse* (4 Variants) *setEntityResolver* *setErrorHandler*

Note: these classes are public abstract.

Class	Description	Page
`SAXParserFactory`	SAXParserFactory is used to obtain a SAX parser. This class also has various methods for setting configuration parameters such as whether the parser returned should be a validating one, etc	295
`SAXParser`	This class is used to parse a document and assign a handler to the events that it will generate	298
`DocumentBuilder Factory`	This class is used to retrieve a DocumentBuilder instance. This class has various methods for setting properties of the returned parser. Examples include whether the parser ignores comments, is namespace aware, and is validating, among others	303
`DocumentBuilder`	DocumentBuilder produces a DOM object tree form an XML document	307

Exceptions and Errors

Class	Description	Page
`FactoryConfiguration Error`	Thrown if the parser factory is misconfigured	294
`ParserConfiguration Exception`	This exception is thrown for misconfigured parsers	295

Error FactoryConfigurationError

javax.xml.parsers

```
public class FactoryConfigurationError
        extends java.lang.Error
```

Usually thrown if the system-configured parser factory can not be found or instantiated, but indicates any parser factory configuration error.

Constructors

These constructors create `FactoryConfigurationErrors`, which can wrap an exception and a message.

```
public FactoryConfigurationError()
```

```
public FactoryConfigurationError(String msg)
```

```
public FactoryConfigurationError(Exception e)
```

```
public FactoryConfigurationError(Exception e, String msg)
```

Parameters

Parameter	Type	Description
`msg`	`String`	Any error message to be passed on
`e`	`Exception`	The exception that occurred to cause this error to be thrown can be encapsulated by the `FactoryConfigurationError`

Methods

The `getMessage()` method returns the value of the `msg` parameter if it exists. Otherwise, if there is an encapsulated exception, the message for the encapsulated exception is returned.

If there is an encapsulated exception, it can be retrieved using the `getException()` method.

```
public String getMessage()
```

```
public Exception getException()
```

Returned Values

Method	Return	Description
getMessage()	String	The error message, or otherwise the encapsulated exception's message
getException()	Exception	The encapsulated exception. If there is no encapsulated message this method will return null

Exception ParserConfigurationException
javax.xml.parsers

```
public class ParserConfigurationException
        extends java.lang.Exception
```

This exception is thrown by a factory if it cannot create the specified parser with the given configuration. Two methods can throw this exception, SAXParserFactory's newSAXParser() method and DocumentBuilderFactory's newDocumentBuilder() method.

Constructors

These constructors create ParserConfigurationException instances.

```
public ParserConfigurationException()
```

```
public ParserConfigurationException(String msg)
```

Parameters

Parameter	Type	Description
msg	String	A message for the exception can be specified with this parameter

Class SAXParserFactory
javax.xml.parsers

```
public abstract class SAXParserFactory
```

`SAXParserFactory` is used to configure and instantiate SAX parsers.

Constructor

The constructor for this class is protected. Applications use the static `newInstance()` method of this class to create factory objects.

```
protected SAXParserFactory()
```

Method newInstance()

The `newInstance()` method is used to create new instances of parser factories. This method first checks if the `javax.xml.parsers.SAXParserFactory` system property has been set and if so dynamically loads the class specified there. If this property has not been set it check for a file named `jaxp.properties` in `%JAVA_HOME%/lib/` for a name-value pair corresponding to the system property above and a valid factory implementation. Here, `%JAVA_HOME%` represents the installation directory for the JDK.

If no factory can be found, the `newInstance()` method will check if the class has been specified in the `INF/services/javax.xml.parsers.SAXParserFactory` in the JARs available to the runtime using the services API. Finally, if none of the previous steps has been successful the default `SAXParserFactory` will be returned.

```
public static SAXParserFactory newInstance()
```

Returned Values

Method	Return	Description
`newInstance()`	`SAXParserFactory`	Returns a new instance of a `SAXParserFactory`. Note that `SAXParserFactory` is not thread safe. This method throws a `FactoryConfigurationException` if an implementation is not available or cannot be instantiated.

Methods for Setting and Getting Properties

The following methods set and retrieve the configuration parameters for the `SAXParsers` this factory creates.

```
public void setNamespaceAware(boolean awareness)
```
```
public boolean isNamespaceAware()
```
```
public void setValidating(boolean validating)
```
```
public boolean isValidating()
```

```
public abstract void setFeature(String name, boolean value)
        throws ParserConfigurationException,

            org.xml.sax.SAXNotRecognizedException,

            org.xml.sax.SAXNotSupportedException
```

```
public abstract boolean getFeature(String name)
     throws ParserConfigurationException,

            org.xml.sax.SAXNotRecognizedException,

            org.xml.sax.SAXNotSupportedException
```

Parameters

Parameter	Type	Description
awareness	boolean	If this is set to true the parser returned will be namespace aware. The default is false.
validating	boolean	If set to true the parser returned will validate parsed documents. The default value is false.
name	String	The name of the feature to be set or retrieved
value	boolean	The value of the feature to be set in the underlying implementation of org.xml.sax.XMLReader. See Chapter 2 for details.

Returned Values

Method	Return	Description
isNamespaceAware()	boolean	Indicates whether the factory will return namespace aware parsers
isValidating()	boolean	Indicates whether the factory will return validating parsers
getFeature()	boolean	Returns the value of the specified property in the underlying org.xml.sax.XMLReader

Method newSAXParser()

Applications use this method to instantiate an implementation of a SAXParser.

```
public abstract SAXParser newSAXParser()
     throws ParserConfigurationException,

            org.xml.sax.SAXException
```

Returned Values

Method	Return	Description
newSAXParser()	SAXParser	The method returns a new instance of a SAXParser. Note that SAXParserFactory is not thread safe.

Note: The `javax.xml.parsers.SAXParserFactory` class is used by our SAXValidator example on page 301.

Class SAXParser
javax.xml.parsers

```
public abstract class SAXParser
```

This class wraps an org.xml.sax.XMLReader implementation to provide a SAX parser. For ease of transition to the new specifications this class implements all of the methods defined in JAXP 1.0 together with new functionality.

A SAXParser accepts a File, URL, and InputStream as input as well as a SAX InputSource through overloaded parse() methods. As the underlying parser parses the content, methods of the given SAX 2.0 DefaultHandler or SAX 1.0 HandlerBase are called. See Chapter 2 for details about the SAX parsing mechanisms.

Constructor

This is a protected constructor. Applications use SAXParserFactory to create instances of this class.

```
protected SAXParser()
```

Methods getXMLReader() and getParser()

These methods return the encapsulated implementation of the SAX parsing interfaces. Note that the parser interface of SAX 1.0 was deprecated by SAX 2.0 and replaced by XMLReader.

```
public abstract org.xml.sax.XMLReader getXMLReader()
        throws org.xml.sax.SAXException

public abstract org.xml.sax.Parser getParser()
        throws org.xml.sax.SAXException
```

Returned Values

Method	Return	Description
`getXMLReader()`	`org.xml.sax.XMLReader`	The `XMLReader` that is encapsulated by the implementation class
`getParser()`	`org.xml.sax.Parser`	The SAX parser that is encapsulated by the implementation class

Methods for Setting and Getting Properties

The following methods return the configuration parameters of this object.

The `namespaceAware` and `validating` properties are set by the `SAXParserFactory` when it creates the `SAXParser` object. Changing the configuration of the factory at a later time doesn't affect the objects already created.

The `setProperty()` method can be used to set the SAX `LexicalHandler` and `DeclHandler` to be used by the `XMLReader`. A list of the core features and properties can be found at http://www.megginson.com/SAX/Java/features.html.

```
public abstract boolean isNamespaceAware()
```

```
public abstract boolean isValidating()
```

```
public abstract void setProperty(String name, Object value)
        throws org.xml.sax.SAXNotRecognizedException,
            org.xml.sax.SAXNotSupportedException
```

```
public abstract Object getProperty(String name)
        throws org.xml.sax.SAXNotRecognizedException,
            org.xml.sax.SAXNotSupportedException
```

Parameters

Parameter	Type	Description
`name`	`String`	The name of the property to be set or retrieved
`value`	`Object`	The value of the property to be set in the underlying implementation of `org.xml.sax.XMLReader`. See Chapter 2 for details.

Returned Values

Method	Return	Description
`isNamespaceAware()`	`boolean`	Indicates whether this parser is namespaces aware
`isValidating()`	`boolean`	Indicates whether this is a validating parser
`getProperty()`	`Object`	The value of a property in the underlying implementation of `org.xml.sax.XMLReader`

Methods for Parsing

These methods parse the content of a given input source as XML using the specified handler. It should be noted that the methods using `DefaultHandler` are recommended over the ones using `HandlerBase` since the latter is deprecated in SAX 2.0 and doesn't support namespaces.

```
public void parse(java.io.InputStream is,
                  org.xml.sax.HandlerBase hb)
    throws org.xml.sax.SAXException, java.io.IOException
```

```
public void parse(java.io.InputStream is,
                  org.xml.sax.HandlerBase hb, String
                  systemId)
    throws org.xml.sax.SAXException, java.io.IOException
```

```
public void parse(java.io.InputStream is,
                  org.xml.sax.helpers.DefaultHandler dh)
    throws org.xml.sax.SAXException, java.io.IOException
```

```
public void parse(java.io.InputStream is,
                  org.xml.sax.helpers.DefaultHandler dh,
                  String systemId)
    throws org.xml.sax.SAXException, java.io.IOException
```

```
public void parse(String uri, org.xml.sax.HandlerBase hb)
    throws org.xml.sax.SAXException, java.io.IOException
```

```
public void parse(String uri,
                  org.xml.sax.helpers.DefaultHandler dh)
    throws org.xml.sax.SAXException, java.io.IOException
```

```
public void parse(java.io.File f hb), org.xml.sax.HandlerBase
    throws org.xml.sax.SAXException, java.io.IOException
```

```
public void parse(java.io.File f,
                  org.xml.sax.helpers.DefaultHandler dh)
    throws org.xml.sax.SAXException, java.io.IOException
```

```
public void parse(org.xml.sax.InputSource src,
                  org.xml.sax.HandlerBase hb)
     throws org.xml.sax.SAXException, java.io.IOException
```

```
public void parse(org.xml.sax.InputSource src,
                  org.xml.sax.helpers.DefaultHandler dh)
     throws org.xml.sax.SAXException, java.io.IOException
```

Parameters

Parameter	Type	Description
is	java.io.InputStream	The document to parse as an InputStream
hb	org.xml.sax.HandlerBase	The SAX HandlerBase to use. Note that this class is deprecated in SAX 2.0.
systemId	String	systemId is used to resolve relative URIs
dh	org.xml.sax.helpers. DefaultHandler	The DefaultHandler of events
uri	String	The location of the content to be parsed asa URI
f	java.io.File	The file containing the content to parse
src	org.xml.sax.InputSource	An InputSource containing the content to be parsed

Example: JAXP Support for SAX

This is a utility that can be used to validate an XML file, whose path is provided in the command line. If the command line is empty, it parses invalid.xml, which is an XML document with a few errors. These are printed to the standard output stream.

This example uses a slightly modified version of the PrintErrorHandler class presented in Chapter 2. We just don't print the stack traces anymore and send the messages to System.out instead of System.err so that the output can be redirected to a file.

Source SAXValidator.java

```
import org.xml.sax.SAXParseException;
import org.xml.sax.XMLReader;
```

```
import javax.xml.parsers.SAXParser;
import javax.xml.parsers.SAXParserFactory;

public class SAXValidator {
```

This method:

❑ Creates a JAXP factory for SAX parsers

❑ Configures this factory to do XML validation and be aware of namespaces

❑ Gets a new instance of SAXParser, which is a JAXP abstract class

❑ Gets the SAX XMLReader of the parser

❑ Sets the error handler of the XML reader

❑ Calls the parse() method of the XML reader

```
public static void main(String[] args) {
  if (args.length == 0) {
    System.err.println("java SAXValidator filename");
    System.exit(1);
  }
  try {

    // Create the JAXP factory for SAX parsers
    SAXParserFactory saxFactory =
      SAXParserFactory.newInstance();
    saxFactory.setValidating(true);
    saxFactory.setNamespaceAware(true);

    // Create the JAXP SAX parser
    SAXParser saxParser = saxFactory.newSAXParser();

    // Get the SAX XMLReader of the parser
    XMLReader xmlReader = saxParser.getXMLReader();

    // Configure the XMLReader
    xmlReader.setErrorHandler(new PrintErrorHandler());

    // Parse the file
    xmlReader.parse(args[0]);

  } catch (SAXParseException e) {

    // Already printed by PrintErrorHandler
    System.exit(1);
  } catch (Exception e) {
    e.printStackTrace();
    System.exit(1);
  }
}
}
```

Sample invalid.xml

```xml
<?xml version='1.0' encoding='utf-8'?>
<!DOCTYPE sample [
  <!ELEMENT sample ANY>
  <!ELEMENT elem (data1, data2)>
  <!ELEMENT data1 (#PCDATA)>
  <!ATTLIST data1 present CDATA #REQUIRED>
  <!ELEMENT data2 (#PCDATA)>
  <!ATTLIST data2 missing CDATA #REQUIRED>
]>
<sample attr="value">
  data before elem
  <elem>
    <data1 present="abc">text of data1</data1>
    <data2>text of data2</data2>
    <data3/>
  </elem>
  data after elem
  &unknown;
</sample>
```

Output

```
> java SAXValidator invalid.xml

ERROR: invalid.xml line 10 column 22
Attribute "attr" must be declared for element type "sample".

ERROR: invalid.xml line 14 column 12
Attribute "missing" is required and must be specified for element type
"data2".

ERROR: invalid.xml line 15 column 10
Element type "data3" must be declared.

ERROR: invalid.xml line 16 column 11
The content of element type "elem" must match "(data1,data2)".

FATAL ERROR: invalid.xml line 18 column 12
The entity "unknown" was referenced, but not declared.
```

Class DocumentBuilderFactory

javax.xml.parsers

```
public abstract class DocumentBuilderFactory
```

The `DocumentBuilderFactory` class is used to obtain `DocumentBuilder` objects, which produce DOM object trees from XML documents.

Constructor

This is a protected constructor. Applications use the static `newInstance()` method of this class to create factory objects.

```
protected DocumentBuilderFactory()
```

Method newInstance()

This static method creates a new factory instance. It looks up the implementation class to load by checking the `javax.xml.parsers.DocumentBuilderFactory` system property. If the class has not been specified, this method checks the `%JAVA_HOME%/lib/` directory (`%JAVA_HOME%` represents the JDK installation directory) for a property file named `jaxp.properties` that contains the name of the implementation class with a name/value pair corresponding to the system property above.

Otherwise, the method checks for `META-INF/services/javax.xml.parsers.DocumentBuilderFactory` in JARs available to the runtime using the Services API, and finally returns the default factory should the previous lookups fail.

An application uses the factory to configure and obtain parser instances.

```
public static DocumentBuilderFactory newInstance()
```

Returned Values

Method	Return	Description
`newInstance()`	`DocumentBuilder Factory`	The method returns a new instance of a `DocumentBuilderFactory`. Note that `DocumentBuilderFactory` is not thread safe.

Methods for Setting and Getting Properties

The following methods set and retrieve the configuration parameters for the `DocumentBuilders` this factory creates.

```
public void setNamespaceAware(boolean awareness)
```

```
public boolean isNamespaceAware()
```

```
public void setValidating(boolean validating)
```

```
public boolean isValidating()
```

```
public void setIgnoringElementContentWhitespace(boolean whitespace)
```

```
public boolean isIgnoringElementContentWhitespace()
```

```
public void setExpandEntityReferences(boolean expandEntityRef)

public boolean isExpandEntityReferences()

public void setIgnoringComments(boolean ignoreComments)

public boolean isIgnoringComments()

public void setCoalescing(boolean coalescing)

public boolean isCoalescing()

public abstract void setAttribute(String name, Object value)
        throws IllegalArgumentException

public abstract Object getAttribute(String name)
        throws IllegalArgumentException
```

Parameters

Parameter	Type	Description
awareness	boolean	Specifies that the parser produced by this code will provide support for XML namespaces. By default the value of this property is set to `false`.
validating	boolean	Specifies that parsers returned should validate documents as they are parsed. By default the value of this property is set to `false`.
whitespace	boolean	Specifies that the parsers created by this factory must eliminate whitespace in element content (sometimes known as "ignorable whitespace") when parsing XML documents.
		Note that only whitespace that is directly contained within element content that has an element-only content model will be eliminated.
		Due to reliance on the content model this setting requires the parser to be in validating mode.
		By default the value of this property is set to `false`.
expandEntityRef	boolean	Specifies that the parser produced by this code will expand entity reference nodes.
		By default the value of this property is set to `true`.
ignoreComments	boolean	Specifies that the parser produced by this code will ignore comments. By default the value of this property is set to `false`.

Table continued on following page

Parameter	Type	Description
coalescing	boolean	Specifies that the parser produced by this code will convert CDATA nodes to Text nodes and append them to the adjacent (if any) text node. By default the value of this property is set to false.
name	String	The name of a specific attribute on the underlying implementation
value	Object	The value of a specific attribute on the underlying implementation

Returned Values

Method	Return	Description
isNamespaceAware()	boolean	Indicates whether the factory will instantiate namespace aware parsers
isValidating()	boolean	Indicates whether the factory will instantiate validating parsers
IsIgnoringElement ContentWhitespace()	boolean	Indicates whether the factory will produce parsers that ignore whitespace in element content
isExpandEntity References()	boolean	Indicates whether instantiated parsers will expand entity reference nodes
isIgnoringComments()	boolean	Indicates whether the factory produces parsers that ignore comments
isCoalescing()	boolean	Indicates whether parser instances will convert CDATA nodes to Text nodes. Converted nodes will be appended to adjacent Text node, if any
getAttribute()	Object	Returns the value of the specified attribute in the underlying implementation

Method newDocumentBuilder()

This method creates a new instance of a DocumentBuilder with the current configuration parameters.

```
public abstract DocumentBuilder newDocumentBuilder()
        throws ParserConfigurationException
```

Returned Values

Method	Return	Description
`newDocumentBuilder()`	`DocumentBuilder`	Returns a new instance of `DocumentBuilder`.

Note: The javax.xml.parsers.DocumentBuilderFactory class is used in the DOMPrinter example on page 310.

Class DocumentBuilder
javax.xml.parsers

```
public abstract class DocumentBuilder
```

The `DocumentBuilder` accepts an XML document, from which it creates a `org.w3c.dom.Document`. An application uses `DocumentBuilderFactory` to retrieve an instance of `DocumentBuilder`. `DocumentBuilder` accepts input as an `InputStream`, `File`, `URL`, as well as a SAX `InputSource`.

Note that this class reuses several classes from the SAX API, which was presented in Chapter 2. This does not require that the underlying DOM implementation use a SAX parser to parse XML document into a `Document`. It merely requires that the implementation communicate with the application using these existing APIs.

Constructor

This is a protected constructor. Applications use `DocumentBuilderFactory` to create instances of this class.

```
protected DocumentBuilder()
```

Methods for Setting and Getting Properties

The following methods return the configuration parameters of this object set by the `DocumentBuilderFactory` when it created the `DocumentBuilder` object. Therefore, the factory object must be configured before creating document builders. Changing the configuration of the factory at a later time doesn't affect the created objects.

```
public abstract boolean isNamespaceAware()
```
```
public abstract boolean isValidating()
```

Returned Values

Method	Return	Description
`isNamespaceAware()`	`boolean`	Indicates whether the parser is namespaces aware
`isValidating()`	`boolean`	Indicates whether the parser validates input documents

Method setEntityResolver()

The `setEntityResolver()` method allows the application to specify a SAX `EntityResolver` to be used by the underlying DOM implementation to resolve entities. The `EntityResolver` interface was presented in Chapter 2.

```
public abstract void setEntityResolver(org.xml.sax.EntityResolver er)
```

Parameters

Parameter	Type	Description
`er`	`org.xml.sax.EntityResolver`	Specifies the `EntityResolver` to be used to resolve entities present in the XML document to be parsed. To set the underlying implementation to use its own default implementation and behavior, pass `null` as the parameter.

Method setErrorHandler()

The `setErrorHandler()` method allows the application to specify a SAX `ErrorHandler` to be used by the underlying DOM implementation to report all parsing errors and warnings. The `ErrorHandler` interface was presented in Chapter 2.

```
public abstract void setErrorHandler(org.xml.sax.ErrorHandler eh)
```

Parameters

Parameter	Type	Description
`eh`	`org.xml.sax.ErrorHandler`	Specifies the `ErrorHandler` to be used to report all parsing errors and warnings. As with the `setEntityResolver()` method above, if you wish to set the implementation to use its own default implementation and behavior, pass `null` as the parameter.

Method getDOMImplementation()

This method returns the underlying DOM implementation. The returned object provides methods for creating empty documents, but this can also be done with the JAXP DocumentBuilder. See Chapter 3 for details about the DOMImplementation interface.

```
public abstract org.w3c.dom.DOMImplementation
        getDOMImplementation()
```

Returned Values

Method	Return	Description
getDOMImplementation()	org.w3c.dom. DOMImplementation	Returns an instance of DOMImplementation

Method newDocument()

The newDocument() method creates a new empty org.w3c.dom.Document instance. This can be further used to create a whole DOM tree. See Chapter 3 for an example that does this.

```
public abstract org.w3c.dom.Document newDocument()
```

Returned Values

Method	Return	Description
newDocument()	org.w3c.dom. Document	A new instance of the DOM Document interface to build a DOM tree with

Methods for Parsing

The following methods parse the content of a given input source as an XML document and return the org.w3c.dom.Document object containing the resulting DOM tree.

```
public org.w3c.dom.Document parse(java.io.InputStream is)
        throws org.xml.sax.SAXException, java.io.IOException
public org.w3c.dom.Document parse(java.io.InputStream is,
                                  String systemId)
        throws org.xml.sax.SAXException, java.io.IOException
public org.w3c.dom.Document parse(String uri)
        throws org.xml.sax.SAXException, java.io.IOException
public org.w3c.dom.Document parse(java.io.File f)
        throws org.xml.sax.SAXException, java.io.IOException
public abstract org.w3c.dom.Document parse(
                                 org.xml.sax.InputSource src)
        throws org.xml.sax.SAXException, java.io.IOException
```

Parameters

Parameter	Type	Description
is	java.io. InputStream	The content to be parsed as an InputStream
systemId	String	Used to resolve relative URIs
uri	String	The location of the content to be parsed as a URI
f	java.io.File	The name of the file containing the XML to parse
src	org.xml.sax. InputSource	InputSource containing the content to be parsed

Returned Values

Method	Return	Description
parse()	org.w3c.dom. Document	The resulting DOM Document object is returned as Document.
		This method will throw an IllegalArgumentException if the parameter given is null, IOException for an IO error, and a SAXException if any parse errors occur.

Example: JAXP Support for DOM

This example was already presented in Chapter 3. We include here only the code that uses JAXP to create an empty document and parse an XML file.

Source DOMPrinter.java

```java
import org.w3c.dom.Document;
import org.w3c.dom.NamedNodeMap;
import org.w3c.dom.Node;
import org.w3c.dom.NodeList;

import org.xml.sax.SAXException;
import org.xml.sax.SAXParseException;

import javax.xml.parsers.DocumentBuilder;
import javax.xml.parsers.DocumentBuilderFactory;
import javax.xml.parsers.ParserConfigurationException;

import java.io.File;
import java.io.IOException;
```

```
public class DOMPrinter {

...
```

The `newBuilder()` method creates a `DocumentBuilder` instance, which is then used to obtain empty `org.w3c.dom.Document` instances or parse XML documents. The `DocumentBuilderFactory` object may be configured to produce validating JAXP document builders, which are also namespace aware. Each builder has a SAX error handler.

```
public static DocumentBuilder newBuilder(boolean validation)
        throws ParserConfigurationException {
  // Create JAXP factory for document builders
  DocumentBuilderFactory domFactory =
          DocumentBuilderFactory.newInstance();

  // Configure the factory
  domFactory.setValidating(validation);
  domFactory.setNamespaceAware(true);

  // Create a document builder
  DocumentBuilder domBuilder =
          domFactory.newDocumentBuilder();

  // Set the error handler
  domBuilder.setErrorHandler(new PrintErrorHandler());

  // Return the builder
  return domBuilder;
}
```

The `newDocument()` method creates an empty `Document`. It uses the previous method to get a `DocumentBuilder` instance and calls its `newDocument()` method.

```
public static Document newDocument()
        throws ParserConfigurationException {
  // Create the builder
  DocumentBuilder domBuilder = newBuilder(false);

  // Create a new empty document
  Document document = domBuilder.newDocument();;

  // Return the parsed document
  return document;
}
```

The `parse()` method parses an XML document using a validating or non-validating DOM parser. After getting the `DocumentBuilder`, the `parse()` method of this object is called. This will create a DOM tree from the XML file whose path is provided as parameter. The validation of the parsing is done only if the value of the second parameter is `true`.

```
public static Document parse(String path,
                                  boolean validation)
             throws ParserConfigurationException, IOException,
                 SAXException {
    // Create the builder
    DocumentBuilder domBuilder = newBuilder(validation);

    // Parse the file
    Document document = domBuilder.parse(new File(path));

    // Return the parsed document
    return document;
}
```

Package javax.xml.transform

This package defines implementation-independent APIs for performing transformations. The interfaces maintain independence from SAX or DOM by defining the Source and Result interfaces, which contain the information required to act as source and result. The factory class for this package provides the getFeature() method to ascertain if the type of source or result is supported.

In order to create Source and Result instances, the transformation API defines three concrete representations for each of these objects:

❑ StreamSource and StreamResult in javax.xml.transform.stream

❑ SAXSource and SAXResult in javax.xml.transform.sax

❑ DOMSource and DOMResult in javax.xml.transform.dom

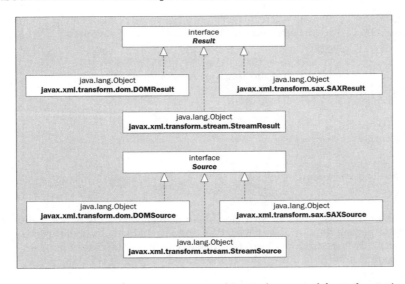

The API allows a concrete TransformerFactory object to be created from the static method newInstance().

The no argument method `newTransformer()` creates a transformer that copies the source to the result, in order to create a DOM tree from SAX events, or create an XML stream from a DOM tree or SAX events using the transformer's `transform()` method.

An overloaded method takes as its parameter a `Source` holding the transformation instructions. Note that, conceptually, this isn't the same kind of source as those passed to the `transform()` method of `Transformer`. In both cases the source can be a stream, a sequence of SAX events or a DOM tree, so it makes sense to use the same `Source` interface. The logical difference, however, is very important. The source passed to `transform()` represents the document that must be transformed, while the source passed to `newTransformer()` describes the transformation and it usually represents an XSL document.

In many cases, we have to apply the same transformation to many documents. As we explained in the above paragraph, the `TransformerFactory` class lets us create `Transformer` instances based on an XSL source. The `TransformerFactory` class also has a `newTemplates()` method that takes an XSL source as parameter too, but returns a `Templates` instance. This acts as a specialized factory of templates, that is, all transformers created with the `newTransformer()` method of `Templates` will be based on the same XSL transformation, allowing the implementation to do optimization. For example, the XSL document will be parsed only once and the resulting objects might be shared by all `Transformers` created with the same `Templates` instance. It may be helpful to think of a `Templates` object as a "compiled" version of an XSLT stylesheet while the `Transformer` is the run-time environment needed to "execute" the `Templates` object.

The `Transformer` class isn't thread safe, but its instances are reusable – you may not use the same `Transformer` instance in multiple threads at the same time, but you can use it to perform multiple transformations one at a time. The `newTransformer()` methods of `TransformerFactory` and `Templates` can be called from concurrent threads, but you should not configure a `TransformerFactory` in one thread and use it to create `Transformers` in a concurrent thread.

Transformation

java.lang.Object *TransformerFactory*	java.lang.Object *Transformer*	java.lang.Object *Templates*
getAssociatedStylesheet *getAttribute* *getErrorListener* *getFeature* *getURIResolver* <u>newInstance</u> *newTemplates* *newTransformer* *newTransformer* *setAttribute* *setErrorListener* *setURIResolver*	*clearParameters* *getErrorListener* *getOutputProperties* *getOutputProperty* *getParameter* *getURIResolver* *setErrorListener* *setOutputProperties* *setOutputProperty* *setParameter* *setURIResolver* *transform*	*getOutputProperties* *newTransformer*

Interface/Abstract Class	Description	Page
Source	Source implementations contain the information required to act as the input of a transformation	315
Result	Result implementations contain the information required to act as a result of the transformation	316
TransformerFactory	TransformerFactory is used to create Transformer and Templates objects	327
Transformer	Class that extend the Transformer abstract class to carry out transformations on Source objects.	334
Templates	An object that implements this interface is the run-time representation of processed transformation instructions	342

Utilities

Class	Description	Page
SourceLocator	This interface defines methods for locating the column and line numbers where an error has occurred in the XML source or transformation instructions	317
URIResolver	URIResolver contains just one method, resolve(), which returns a Source object of the document given by the absolute or relative URI passed as its paramter. A second parameter, base, is a String representing the base URI for resolving relative references.	322
OutputKeys	Defines constants that are used to set and retrieve the output properties of Transformer and Templates	334

Exceptions and Errors

Class	Description	Page
TransformerFactory ConfigurationError	This error is thrown when a configuration problem with the TransformerFactory exists, usually if the implementation class can not be found or instantiated	318
Transformer Exception	This class is thrown as a result of an exception in the transformation process	319
Transformer Configuration Exception	This class is thrown as a result of a configuration error	321

Class	Description	Page
`ErrorListener`	The `ErrorListener` defines three methods that are called if error, warning, or fatal error conditions occur. Application developers implement this interface to handle application errors reported by the `Transformer`.	323

Interface Source
javax.xml.transform

```
public interface Source
```

`Source` implementations contain the information required to act as the input of a transformation

Methods

`setSystemId()` sets the system identifier for this `Source` as a `String` representing the URL of the source. The application can use a system identifier to resolve relative URLs and may also include it in error messages and warnings.

The `getSystemId()` method returns the system identifier. This methods returns `null` if no system ID exists. Although no system ID is necessary if the source cannot be represented by a URL, it may help to identify the source in errors and warnings.

```
public void setSystemId(String systemId)
public String getSystemId()
```

Parameters

Parameter	Type	Description
`systemId`	`String`	The system ID as a string URL

Returned Values

Method	Return	Description
`getSystemId()`	`String`	This method returns the system identifier, or `null` if no system ID was provided

Note: The javax.xml.transform.Source interface is used in the SerializationSample example on page 331.

315

Interface Result

javax.xml.transform

```
public interface Result
```

Result implementations contain the information required to act as a result of the transformation.

Fields

This class defines the following String constants:

Field	Type	Description
PI_DISABLE_ OUTPUT_ESCAPING	String	The processing instruction inserted in the DOM tree if output escaping is to be disabled. This means that reserved characters (such as <, >, and &) are passed without escaping and the resultant document will not be well formed XML. This may be useful if the output does not need to be well formed or a later process will correct the ill-formed output.
PI_ENABLE_ OUTPUT_ESCAPING	String	The name of the processing instruction sent if the result tree enables output escaping. This value is only sent if a PI_DISABLE_OUTPUT_ESCAPING has previously been sent

Methods

setSystemId() sets the system identifier for this Result. Although this the system ID is optional for results that are not to be saved to file, it may be provided to provide information for errors and warnings.

getSystemId() gets the system identifier, or null if none is available.

```
public void setSystemId(String systemId)
public String getSystemId()
```

Parameters

Parameter	Type	Description
systemId	String	The system ID as a string URI

Returned Values

Method	Return	Description
getSystemId()	String	The system identifier or null if no system ID has been set

Note: The javax.xml.transform.Result interface is used by the SerializationSample example on page 331.

Interface SourceLocator

javax.xml.transform

public interface SourceLocator

SourceLocator provides methods for identifying the column and line number of the document or transformation instructions where the error has been identified.

Remember that this may not be the actual location of the problem; for example, a missing closing tag will be noticed at the next tag after the missing tag was expected.

Methods

These methods return the following information about the current document event:

❑   The public identifier

❑   The system identifier

❑   The line number where the error was detected

❑   The column number where the error was detected

public String **getPublicId**()

public String **getSystemId**()

public int **getLineNumber**()

public int **getColumnNumber**()

Returned Values

Method	Return	Description
getPublicId()	String	This method returns the public ID of the entity in which the event occurred. Returns null if not available.
getSystemId()	String	The system ID of the entity where the event occurred. Returns null if not available.
getLineNumber()	int	The line number where the markup that triggered the event appears. -1 if the line number isn't available. The location indicates where an error was detected and may not be the location of the error itself.

Table continued on following page

317

Method	Return	Description
`getColumnNumber()`	`int`	The column number where the markup that triggered the event appears. -1 if the column number isn't available. The location represents where the error was detected and may not be the location of the error itself.

> Note: The javax.xml.transform.SourceLocator interface is used by our PrintErrorListener example on page 324.

Error TransformerFactoryConfigurationError

javax.xml.transform

```
public class TransformerFactoryConfigurationError
        extends java.lang.Error
```

This error is thrown if a configuration problem is detected. Typically thrown when the `TransformerFactory` implementation cannot be found or instantiated.

Constructors

The constructors create new error objects that may have a message and a wrapped exception.

```
public TransformerFactoryConfigurationError()
```
```
public TransformerFactoryConfigurationError(String msg)
```
```
public TransformerFactoryConfigurationError(Exception e)
```
```
public TransformerFactoryConfigurationError(Exception e,
                                            String msg)
```

Parameters

Parameter	Type	Description
`msg`	`String`	An error message that more exactly describes the problem can be stored in the thrown exception
`e`	`Exception`	The wrapped exception

Methods

If a message has been set for the `TranformerFactoryConfigurationError`, the `getMessage()` will return it. If there is no message for this error but it wraps an exception, it will return the exception's message.

The getException() method returns the actual exception that caused this error to be raised. If there is no wrapped exception this method returns null.

```
public String getMessage()
```

```
public Exception getException()
```

Returned Values

Method	Return	Description
getMessage()	String	Return the message (if any) for this error. If there is no message for the exception and there is an encapsulated exception, then the message of that exception will be returned. (Exception returns null if no message exists.)
getException()	Exception	The encapsulated exception, or null if there is none

Exception TransformerException
javax.xml.transform

```
public class TransformerException
        extends java.lang.Exception
```

TranformerException is thrown should the transformer encounter a problem, and may contain a SourceLocator that points to the column and line number in the content at which the exception was identified. It also accepts an exception to wrap and a message that details the problem. Remember that the point at which the error was noticed may not be the source of the trouble; for example, a missing closing bracket would be noticed at the element directly after it was expected.

If an ErrorListener is registered, it will receive the event for handling.

Constructors

These constructors create TransformerExceptions. They may wrap another exception and optionally include a SourceLocator and a message.

```
public TransformerException(String message)
```

```
public TransformerException(Throwable e)
```

```
public TransformerException(String message, Throwable e)
```

```
public TransformerException(String message, SourceLocator locator)
```

```
public TransformerException(String message, SourceLocator
                            locator, Throwable e)
```

Parameters

Parameter	Type	Description
`message`	`String`	A detail message about the exception
`e`	`Throwable`	The exception to be wrapped
`locator`	`SourceLocator`	The locator object for the error

Methods

The `setLocator()` and `getLocator()` methods set and retrieve the `SourceLocator` object that specifies where an error occurred.

The `getException()` method returns any exception (of type `Throwable`) that this exception wraps.

The `initCause()` method accepts a `Throwable` that represents the cause of this exception. This method will throw an `IllegalStateException` if called more than once, or if the exception was constructed with a `Throwable` parameter. An `IllegalArgumentException` will be thrown if this method is passed a reference to the `Throwable` on which this method is being called. The `getCause()` method returns the wrapped exception.

The `printStackTrace()` methods print the stack trace to the point the exception occurred. Wrapped exceptions will also be traced. The overloaded methods accept a `PrintStream` or `PrintWriter` to print the trace to.

```
public void setLocator(SourceLocator location)

public SourceLocator getLocator()

public Throwable getException()

public Throwable initCause(Throwable cause)

public Throwable getCause()

public String getMessageAndLocation()

public String getLocationAsString()

public void printStackTrace()

public void printStackTrace(java.io.PrintStream s)

public void printStackTrace(java.io.PrintWriter w)
```

Parameters

Parameter	Type	Description
`location`	`SourceLocator`	A `SourceLocator` object, or `null` to clear the location
`cause`	`Throwable`	This method returns the `Throwable` cause for this exception. A `null` value is permitted, and indicates that the cause is nonexistent or unknown although the value of calling this method to initialize a `null` property with `null` is questionable.

Parameter	Type	Description
s	java.io.PrintStream	The stream to print the stack trace to
w	java.io.PrintWriter	The writer to print the stack trace to

Returned Values

Method	Return	Description
getLocator()	SourceLocator	This method returns the SourceLocator object, or null if none is available
getException()	Throwable	The Throwable that this exception wraps, or null
initCause()	Throwable	A reference to this Throwable instance
getCause()	Throwable	The Throwable cause of this exception or null if the cause is unknown.
getMessageAndLocation()	String	This method returns the error message with the location information appended to it
getLocationAsString()	String	A string representation of the location info. If there is no location information this method will return null

Note: The javax.xml.transform.TransformerException class is used in the PrintErrorListener example on page 324.

Exception TransformerConfigurationException
javax.xml.transform

```
public class TransformerConfigurationException
     extends TransformerException
```

TransformerConfigurationException is thrown in the case of a configuration error. For example, the newTransformer() method of TransformerFactory may throw a TransformerConfigurationException if there is a syntax error in the transformation instructions and the parsing of the XSL file fails.

Constructors

The various constructors accept a error detail message, location information for the error, and a cause exception.

```
public TransformerConfigurationException()

public TransformerConfigurationException(String msg)

public TransformerConfigurationException(Throwable e)

public TransformerConfigurationException(String msg,
                                         Throwable e)

public TransformerConfigurationException(String msg,
                                         SourceLocator locator)

public TransformerConfigurationException(String msg,
                                         SourceLocator locator,
                                         Throwable e)
```

Parameters

Parameter	Type	Description
msg	String	A detailed message about the nature of the error
e	Throwable	The exception to be wrapped by this object
locator	SourceLocator	The location information in the source giving where the error was identified as a SourceLocator object

Interface URIResolver

javax.xml.transform

```
public interface URIResolver
```

URIResolver is used to resolve URIs in the stylesheet or transformation. A class that wishes to provide this service must implement this interface. The class is registered using the setURIResolver() method of the TransformerFactory and Transformer objects.

Method resolve()

This class defines a single method, resolve() that returns a Source object that results from the resolved URI. This method will be called when the processor encounters the xsl:include element, the xsl:import element, or the document() function.

The method accepts string parameters with the URI found in the instruction or function as either a relative or absolute URI and a base URI against which to resolve the URI.

```
public Source resolve(String href, String base)
        throws TransformerException
```

Parameters

Parameter	Type	Description
href	String	A relative or absolute URI to resolve
base	String	The base URI in effect when the instruction was encountered

Returned Values

Method	Return	Description
resolve()	Source	The method returns a Source object representing the resolved source. If the reference cannot be resolved the method will return null indicating that the processor must resolve the URI itself

Interface ErrorListener

javax.xml.transform

```
public interface ErrorListener
```

The ErrorListener is implemented by classes that wish to handle errors and warnings raised by the transformer. The implementation class must be registered using Transformer.setErrorListener().

The transformer will register the event with the class before deciding whether to report the error or warning itself. The application should throw an error if appropriate. If the transformer calls this interface's fatalError() method it may discontinue the transformation process, as this indicates that the operation cannot be completed successfully.

The implementation registers a default listener implementation to make sure that errors and warnings are handled if the application does not register its own listener.

Methods

The warning() is called by the transformer to report conditions that are not errors or fatal errors. The transformer continues processing.

The error() method is called in case of a recoverable error. The transformer will again continue processing.

After calling the fatalError() method, which represents a non-recoverable error, the transformer may choose to discontinue processing as processing will not succeed. If the application throws an exception following any of these conditions, then processing will discontinue of course.

```
public void warning(TransformerException exception)
        throws TransformerException
```

```
public void error(TransformerException exception)
        throws TransformerException
```

```
public void fatalError(TransformerException exception)
        throws TransformerException
```

Parameters

Parameter	Type	Description
exception	Transformer Exception	The transformer exception that occurred

Example: Listening for Transformation Errors

This is an error listener that prints the messages to the standard error stream. It is similar to the PrintErrorHandler example of the Chapter 2, but it implements javax.xml.transform.ErrorListener instead of org.xml.sax.ErrorHandler. As a consequence, it uses TransformerException and SourceLocator instead of SAXParseException, SAXException and Locator.

Source PrintErrorListener.java

```java
import javax.xml.transform.ErrorListener;
import javax.xml.transform.SourceLocator;
import javax.xml.transform.TransformerException;

public class PrintErrorListener implements ErrorListener {
```

The warning() method prints a warning message:

```java
public void warning(TransformerException e)
        throws TransformerException {
  System.err.print("WARNING: ");
  printLocation(e);
  printMessage(e);
}
```

The error() method prints information about a parsing error:

```java
public void error(TransformerException e)
        throws TransformerException {
  System.err.print("ERROR: ");
  printLocation(e);
  printStackTrace(e);
}
```

The `fatalError()` method prints information about a fatal parsing error and throws an exception in order to stop the transformation:

```
public void fatalError(TransformerException e)
        throws TransformerException {
  System.err.print("FATAL ERROR: ");
  printLocation(e);
  printStackTrace(e);
  throw e;
}
```

The `printLocation()` method prints the location of the error:

```
private void printLocation(TransformerException e) {
  SourceLocator locator = e.getLocator();
  if (locator == null) {
    return;
  }
  if (locator.getPublicId() != null) {
    System.err.print(locator.getPublicId() + " ");
  }
  if (locator.getSystemId() != null) {
    System.err.print(locator.getSystemId() + " ");
  }
  if (locator.getLineNumber() != -1) {
    System.err.print("line "
                        + locator.getLineNumber() + " ");
  }
  if (locator.getColumnNumber() != -1) {
    System.err.print("column "
                        + locator.getColumnNumber() + " ");
  }
  System.err.println();
}
```

The `printMessage()` method prints the message of the given exception:

```
private void printMessage(TransformerException e) {
  if (e.getMessage() != null) {
    System.err.println(e.getMessage());
  }
}
```

The `printStackTrace()` method prints the stack trace of the given exception and its nested exceptions:

```
private void printStackTrace(TransformerException e) {
  e.printStackTrace();
}
}
```

Class OutputKeys

javax.xml.transform

```
public class OutputKeys
```

This class provides string constants used to set and retrieve output properties for a transformer, and to retrieve output properties from a `Templates` object.

Fields

The following table contains all standard output properties that must be supported by the XSLT processors that implement TrAX. Processors may also have their own properties, in addition to these:

Field	Type	Value
METHOD	String	The defined values for this are xml, text, and html. Other undefined values are allowed if the implementation accepts them. An IllegalArgumentException is thrown is the output method is not supported and is not namespace qualified.
VERSION	String	The version of the output method as given above. For example, in XML the only possible current value is 1.0
ENCODING	String	The preferred character encoding. The IANA character encoding value or a value beginning with X- for implementation specific encoding. The character encoding specified should be specified using printable ASCII character
OMIT_XML_DECLARATION	String	The value of this should be a boolean specifying whether the XML declaration should be omitted (as it would be for non-XML output)
STANDALONE	String	A boolean value that specifies whether a standalone document declaration should be output
DOCTYPE_PUBLIC	String	The value of the public identifier to be used in the doctype declaration (check the XML specification for an explanation of the DOCTYPE declaration)
DOCTYPE_SYSTEM	String	The value of system ID for the doctype declaration of this document. (check the XML specification for an explanation of the DOCTYPE declaration

Field	Type	Value
CDATA_SECTION_ELEMENTS	String	A list of elements whose child text nodes should be output using CDATA sections separated by whitespace
INDENT	String	A boolean value that specifies whether the transformer should add whitespace for the (human) readability of the document
MEDIA_TYPE	String	The MIME type of the output

> Note: The javax.xml.transform.OutputKeys class is used by our SerializationSample example on page 331, TransformationSample example on page 338 and ChainedTransformationSample example on page 343.

Class TransformerFactory
javax.xml.transform

public abstract class TransformerFactory

An instance of TransformerFactory is necessary in order to create a Transformer or a Template object. These classes were discussed in the section concerning the javax.xml.transform package.

Constructor

TransformerFactory has a protected constructor. The static newInstance() method of this class is used to create factory objects.

protected **TransformerFactory**()

Method newInstance()

A new factory instance is created by using this static method. In order to determine the correct implementation of TransformerFactory to load, the following steps should be taken in the lookup:

❑ javax.xml.transform.TransformerFactory system property is used

❑ Then the JAVA_HOME/lib/jaxp.properties for a property file that contains the name of the implementation class is used, where the name of the implementation class is keyed upon the same value as the system property defined above

❑ The Services API is used to determine the class name, if this is available. This is detailed in the JAR specification of the JDK. The Services API will look in JAR files available during run time for a class name in the file
META-INF/services/javax.xml.transform.TransformerFactory.

❑ Finally, the platform default TransformerFactory instance can be used.

Once a reference to a `TransformerFactory` is obtained, `Transformer` instances can be created and configured by the factory.

```
public static TransformerFactory newInstance()
         throws TransformerFactoryConfigurationError
```

Returned Values

Method	Return	Description
`newInstance()`	`Transformer Factory`	A new `TransformerFactory` instance, which is never `null`

Methods for Setting and Getting Properties

The `getAssociatedStylesheet()` method gets the stylesheet specification(s) associated via the `xml-stylesheet` processing instruction with the document specified in the source parameter. Note that it is possible to return several stylesheets, in which case they are applied as if they were a list of imports or cascades in a single stylesheet.

The `getFeature()` method looks up the value of a feature. The feature name is any absolute URI.

The `setAttribute()` method allows the user to set specific attributes on the underlying implementation. An attribute in this context is defined to be an option that the implementation provides.

The `getAttribute()` method lets the user retrieve particular attributes on the underlying implementation.

```
public abstract Source getAssociatedStylesheet(Source source,
                         String media, String title, String
                         charset)
         throws TransformerConfigurationException
public abstract boolean getFeature(String featureName)
public abstract void setAttribute(String attrName,
                 Object attrValue)
         throws IllegalArgumentException
public abstract Object getAttribute(String attrName)
         throws IllegalArgumentException
```

Parameters

Parameter	Type	Description
`source`	`Source`	The XML source document
`media`	`String`	The media attribute to be matched. This may be `null`, which means that the preferred templates will be used (such as, `alternate = no`).

Parameter	Type	Description
title	String	The value of the title attribute to be matched. This can be null.
charset	String	The value of the charset attribute to be matched. This can be null.
featureName	String	The feature name (an absolute URI)
attrName	String	Attribute name
attrValue	Object	Attribute value

Returned Values

Method	Return	Description
getAssociated Stylesheet()	Source	Source object to be passed to the TransformerFactory
getFeature()	boolean	Current feature state (true or false)
getAttribute()	Object	Attribute value

Methods setURIResolver() and getURIResolver()

These methods set and retrieve the object that is used by default during the creation of the Templates or Transformer objects, to resolve URIs used in xsl:import and xsl:include.

```
public abstract void setURIResolver(URIResolver resolver)
```
```
public abstract URIResolver getURIResolver()
```

Parameters

Parameter	Type	Description
resolver	URIResolver	Object implementing the URIResolver interface. This can be null.

Returned Values

Method	Return	Description
getURI Resolver()	URIResolver	URIResolver set with setURIResolver()

Methods setErrorListener() and getErrorListener()

These methods set and retrieve the ErrorListener for the TransformerFactory. The error listener processes transformation instructions, but does not process the transformation itself.

329

```
public abstract void setErrorListener(ErrorListener listener)
        throws IllegalArgumentException
```

```
public abstract ErrorListener getErrorListener()
```

Parameters

Parameter	Type	Description
listener	ErrorListener	The error listener

Returned Values

Method	Return	Description
getError Listener()	ErrorListener	The current error listener, which is not null

Method newTransformer()

One of the newTransformer() methods takes a Source parameter and processes it into a Transformer object. Usually the parameter represents an XSL transformation though the API specification doesn't state this. The Transformer can be used to transform a source tree into a result tree.

The other newTransformer() method creates a new Transformer object that performs a copy of the source tree to the result tree without any transformation. Such an "identity transformer" can be used, for example, to save a DOM tree to an XML file. In this example the transformer acts as serializer.

Be careful not to use the same Transformer object in multiple threads running concurrently. Different Transformer objects may be used by different threads.

```
public abstract Transformer newTransformer(Source source)
        throws TransformerConfigurationException
```

```
public abstract Transformer newTransformer()
        throws TransformerConfigurationException
```

Parameters

Parameter	Type	Description
source	Source	This object holds a URI or input stream

Returned Values

Method	Return	Description
new Transformer()	Transformer	A Transformer object used to perform a transformation in a single thread. This is never null

Method newTemplates()

The newTemplates() method processes the given Source into a Templates object, which is a compiled representation of the source. A Templates instance can be used across multiple threads concurrently. The creation of a Templates object allows the TransformerFactory to optimize performance of transformation instructions. Runtime transformation will not be penalized, however.

```
public abstract Templates newTemplates(Source source)
        throws TransformerConfigurationException
```

Parameters

Parameter	Type	Description
source	Source	Object holding a URL or input stream

Returned Values

Method	Return	Description
newTemplates()	Templates	A Templates object, which can be used for transformation purposes. This object is never null.

Example: Saving DOM Trees to Files

This example is similar to the DocumentSample of Chapter 3. We get a new Document instance and use its methods to create other nodes that are linked in a DOM tree. However, instead of printing the created DOM tree to the console, the new serialize() method is used to save the DOM tree to a file – saved.xml.

Source SerializationSample.java

```java
import javax.xml.transform.OutputKeys;
import javax.xml.transform.Result;
import javax.xml.transform.Source;
import javax.xml.transform.Templates;
import javax.xml.transform.Transformer;
import javax.xml.transform.TransformerFactory;
import javax.xml.transform.dom.DOMSource;
import javax.xml.transform.sax.SAXResult;
import javax.xml.transform.stream.StreamResult;

import org.w3c.dom.CDATASection;
import org.w3c.dom.Comment;
import org.w3c.dom.Document;
import org.w3c.dom.Element;
import org.w3c.dom.Node;
import org.w3c.dom.ProcessingInstruction;
import org.w3c.dom.Text;
```

```
import org.xml.sax.ContentHandler;

import java.io.File;
import java.io.OutputStream;
import java.io.Writer;
import java.util.Properties;

public class SerializationSample extends DOMPrinter {

  public static final String XALAN_INDENT_AMOUNT =
    "{http://xml.apache.org/xslt}indent-amount";
```

The `serialize()` method serializes a DOM tree to a file, stream, writer, or SAX
`ContentHandler`. It creates a `TransformerFactory` instance using the static
`newInstance()` method. The factory object is used to obtain a `Transformer` instance using
the `newTransformer()` method. This object acts as a `serializer` because no
transformation instructions are provided to the `newTransformer()` method. The transformer
is configured to produce indented XML output. The
`"{http://xml.apache.org/xslt}indent-amount"` property is specific to Apache
Xalan and should be ignored by other XSLT processors. Finally, the effective saving of the DOM
tree is requested by calling the `transform()` method.

```
public static void serialize(Node node, Object out)
        throws Exception {

   // Create the transformer factory
   TransformerFactory factory =
     TransformerFactory.newInstance();

   // Create the transformer object
   Transformer serializer = factory.newTransformer();

   // Configure the transformer
   Properties props = new Properties();
   props.put(OutputKeys.METHOD, "xml");
   props.put(OutputKeys.INDENT, "yes");
   props.put(XALAN_INDENT_AMOUNT, "2");
serializer.setOutputProperties(props);

   // Create the source and result objects
   Source source = new DOMSource(node);
   Result result = null;
   if (out instanceof String) {
     result = new StreamResult((String) out);
   } else if (out instanceof File) {
     result = new StreamResult((File) out);
   } else if (out instanceof OutputStream) {
     result = new StreamResult((OutputStream) out);
   } else if (out instanceof Writer) {
     result = new StreamResult((Writer) out);
   } else if (out instanceof ContentHandler) {
result = new SAXResult((ContentHandler) out);
```

```
    }

        if (result != null) {
          // Ask the serializer to produce the output
          serializer.transform(source, result);
        }
    }
```

The main() method of this example creates a DOM Document using the newDocument()
method inherited from DOMPrinter. Then it uses the methods defined by the
org.w3c.dom.Document interface to create Element, Comment, CDATASection, Text,
and ProcessingInstruction nodes, which are included within the DOM tree using
appendChild() and insertBefore().

The populated document is saved to a file using the above serialize() method.

```
    public static void main(String args[]) {
      try {
        Document doc = newDocument();

        Element root = doc.createElement("root");
        doc.appendChild(root);

        Comment comment = doc.createComment("a comment");
        root.appendChild(comment);

        Comment removable = doc.createComment("removable");
        root.appendChild(removable);

        Element elem = doc.createElement("elem");
        root.replaceChild(elem, removable);
        elem.setAttribute("attr", "value");
        elem.appendChild(doc.createTextNode("data"));

        CDATASection cdata = doc.createCDATASection(">data<");
        root.appendChild(cdata);
Element elem2 = doc.createElement("elem2");
        root.appendChild(elem2);

        Text text = doc.createTextNode("some text");
        root.insertBefore(text, cdata);

        ProcessingInstruction proc =
          doc.createProcessingInstruction("target", "1 2 3");
        root.appendChild(proc);

        serialize(doc, new File("saved.xml"));
      } catch (Exception e) {
        e.printStackTrace();
        System.exit(1);
      }
    }
  }

}
```

Output saved.xml

```
> java SerializationSample

<?xml version="1.0" encoding="UTF-8"?>
<root>
  <!--a comment-->
  <elem attr="value">data</elem>some text<![CDATA[>data<]]><elem2/>
  <?target 1 2 3?>
</root>
```

Class Transformer
javax.xml.transform

public abstract class Transformer

An instance of the Transformer class can be obtained with the newTransformer() methods of TransformerFactory or Templates. Such a Transformer instance can then be used in processing and transforming XML from many different sources.

A Transformer object may not be used in multiple threads running concurrently, but different Transformers may be used concurrently by different threads.

A Transformer object may be used multiple times. Parameters and output properties are preserved across transformations.

Constructor

Transformer has a protected constructor. TransformerFactory or Templates should be used to create instances of this class.

```
protected Transformer()
```

Methods for Setting and Getting Properties

The API defines the following naming convention for parameter and output property names. The namespace URI, if any, must be enclosed in curly braces ({}), followed by the local name. If the name has a null URI, the curly braces are omitted and the name only contains the local name. An application can safely check for a non-null URI by testing to see if the first character of the name is a '{' character. For example, "indent" and "{http://xml.apache.org/xslt}indent-amount" are valid output properties if you use Apache Xalan. The former is actually supported by all XSLT processors since it is required by the XSLT Recommendation.

The setParameter() method adds a top-level parameter for the transformation. The getParameter() method returns a parameter that was explicitly set with setParameter(). The clearParameters() method clears all parameters that were set with setParameter().

334

The setOutputProperties() method sets the output properties for the transformation. These properties will override properties set with xsl:output. If the argument to this function is null, any properties previously set are removed, and the value will revert to the values set with xsl:output.

The getOutputProperties() method returns a copy of the output properties for the transformation. This object contains properties set by both the user and the stylesheet, and some of these properties have default values specified by the XSL Transformations (XSLT) W3C Recommendation.

The properties that were specifically set by the user or the stylesheet are in the base Properties list, while the XSLT default properties are in the defaults Properties list (defaults is a protected field of java.util.Properties). This means that getOutputProperties().getProperty() will fetch the properties that were set by setOutputProperty(), or setOutputProperties(), in either the stylesheet or the default properties. On the other hand, getOutputProperties().get() will only retrieve those properties that were explicitly set by either setOutputProperty(), or setOutputProperties(), or were in the stylesheet.

The setOutputProperty() method sets an output property. This property is the one that will be true throughout the transformation. The getOutputProperty() method returns an output property that is in effect for the transformation. The property specified here may be a property set with setOutputProperty(), or one from the stylesheet.

```
public abstract void setParameter(String paramName, Object paramValue)

public abstract Object getParameter(String paramName)

public abstract void clearParameters()

public abstract void setOutputProperties(java.util.Properties
                                         oformat)
       throws IllegalArgumentException

public abstract java.util.Properties getOutputProperties()

public abstract void setOutputProperty(String propName,
                                       String propValue)
       throws IllegalArgumentException

public abstract String getOutputProperty(String propName)
       throws IllegalArgumentException
```

Parameters

Parameter	Type	Description
paramName	String	The name of the parameter, which may begin with a namespace URI in curly braces ({})
paramValue	Object	Any valid Java object, which is the value object. The processor should provide the proper object or it may pass the object on for use in an extension.
oformat	java.util. Properties	A set of output properties. They can override other properties in place for the duration of the transformation.

Table continued on following page

335

Parameter	Type	Description
propName	String	A non-null String that specifies an output property name. This parameter may be namespace qualified.
propValue	String	Output property's non-null string value

Returned Values

Method	Return	Description
get Parameter()	Object	A parameter that has been set with setParameter(), or null if the named parameter was not found
getOutput Properties()	java.util. Properties	The output properties in effect for the next transformation
getOutput Property()	String	The string value of the output property, or null if no property was found

Methods setURIResolver() and getURIResolver()

The setURIResolver() method sets an object that resolves URIs used in the document() XSLT function. When the resolver argument is null, the default response will be initiated, and the URIResolver property will be cleared.

The getURIResolver() method returns the object that will be used to resolve URIs used in the document() method.

```
public abstract void setURIResolver(URIResolver resolver)
public abstract URIResolver getURIResolver()
```

Parameters

Parameter	Type	Description
resolver	URIResolver	Object implementing the URIResolver interface, or null

Returned Values

Method	Return	Description
getURI Resolver()	URIResolver	Object implementing the URIResolver interface, or null

Methods setErrorListener() and getErrorListener()

These methods set and get the error event listener being used during the transformation.

```
public abstract void setErrorListener(ErrorListener listener)
        throws IllegalArgumentException
```

```
public abstract ErrorListener getErrorListener()
```

Parameters

Parameter	Type	Description
listener	Error Listener	The new error listener

Returned Values

Method	Return	Description
getError Listener()	Error Listener	The current error listener, which should not be null.

Method transform()

The transform() method applies the transformation to the given Source and stores the output in the Result object.

This method throws a TransformerException if an unrecoverable error occurs during the course of the transformation.

```
public abstract void transform(Source xmlSource, Result outputTarget)
        throws TransformerException
```

Parameters

Parameter	Type	Description
xmlSource	Source	The input for the source tree
outputTarget	Result	The output target

Example: Applying a Transformation

This example transforms the invoice.xml file to invoice.html using invoice.xsl. The XML file is taken from Chapter 2, where we parse it with SAX in order to extract information that is printed to the standard output. The use of XSLT is a natural solution for producing the HTML for visualization in a Web browser. However, we also have to compute the total of the invoice. This is possible in XSLT, but it's a lot more complex than the Java equivalent. In XSLT you may initialize a variable, but after that you cannot change its value because XSLT doesn't have an assignment statement like Java. So, we used a recursive template called totalProc that takes the list of items as parameters. Explaining how XSLT works is beyond the scope of this chapter. (We recommend *XSLT Programmer's Reference*, ISBN 1861005067, published by Wrox Press.)

The `main()` method creates a `TransformerFactory` instance using the static `newInstance()` method. The factory object is used to obtain a `Transformer` instance using the `newTransformer()` method. This object is configured to produce indented HTML output. The `"{http://xml.apache.org/xslt}indent-amount"` property is specific to Apache Xalan and should be ignored by other XSLT processors. Finally, the transformation instructions are applied by calling the `transform()` method. The XML document is processed and the result is stored in the HTML file.

Source TransformationSample.java

```java
import javax.xml.transform.OutputKeys;
import javax.xml.transform.Transformer;
import javax.xml.transform.TransformerFactory;
import javax.xml.transform.stream.StreamResult;

import javax.xml.transform.stream.StreamSource;

import java.util.Properties;

public class TransformationSample {
  public static final String XALAN_INDENT_AMOUNT =
    "{http://xml.apache.org/xslt}indent-amount";

  public static void main(String args[]) {
    try {
      String stylesheetID = "invoice.xsl";
      String sourceID = "invoice.xml";
      String resultID = "invoice.html";

      // Create the transformer factory
      TransformerFactory factory =
        TransformerFactory.newInstance();

      // Set the error listener of the factory
      factory.setErrorListener(new PrintErrorListener());

      // Create the transformer object
      Transformer transformer = factory.newTransformer(
        new StreamSource(stylesheetID));

      // Set the error listener of the transformer
      transformer.setErrorListener(new
                                   PrintErrorListener());

      // Configure the transformer
      Properties props = new Properties();
      props.put(OutputKeys.METHOD, "html");
      props.put(OutputKeys.INDENT, "yes");
      props.put(XALAN_INDENT_AMOUNT, "2");
      transformer.setOutputProperties(props);

      // Apply the transformation
```

```
        transformer.transform(new StreamSource(sourceID),
                              new StreamResult(resultID));
      } catch (Exception e) {
        e.printStackTrace();
        System.exit(1);
      }
    }

  }
```

Sample invoice.dtd

```
<?xml version="1.0" encoding="UTF-8"?>

<!-- External DTD -->


<!ELEMENT invoice (supplier, buyer, currency, item*)>
<!ATTLIST invoice number CDATA #REQUIRED>
<!ATTLIST invoice month  CDATA #REQUIRED>
<!ATTLIST invoice day    CDATA #REQUIRED>
<!ATTLIST invoice year   CDATA #REQUIRED>

<!ELEMENT supplier (email, address)>
<!ATTLIST supplier name CDATA #REQUIRED>

<!ELEMENT buyer (email, address)>
<!ATTLIST buyer name CDATA #REQUIRED>

<!ELEMENT email (#PCDATA)>

<!ELEMENT address (#PCDATA)>

<!ELEMENT currency (#PCDATA)>

<!ELEMENT item EMPTY>
<!ATTLIST item name     CDATA   #REQUIRED>
<!ATTLIST item quantity CDATA   #REQUIRED>
<!ATTLIST item price    CDATA   #REQUIRED>
<!ATTLIST item info     CDATA   #REQUIRED>

<!ENTITY dollar "$">
```

Sample invoice.xml

```
<supplier name="Sup Company">
   <email>info@supcompany.com</email>
   <address><![CDATA[London, UK]]></address>
 </supplier>
 <buyer name="Buy Company">
   <email>info@buycompany.com</email>
   <address><![CDATA[Paris, France]]></address>
 </buyer>
 <currency>US&dollar;</currency>
```

```
<item name="Computer" quantity="10" price="1000"
    info="800 Mhz, 256M RAM, 40G HDD"/>
  <item name="Printer" quantity="5" price="200"
    info="600x600 dpi, 20 ppm"/>
  <item name="Server" quantity="1" price="5000"
    info="4x1000 Mhz, 2G RAM, 2x100G HDD"/>
  <?total?>
</invoice><?xml version="1.0" encoding="utf-8"?>
<!DOCTYPE invoice SYSTEM "invoice.dtd">
<invoice number="1234567" month="2" day="20" year="2000">
```

Sample invoice.xsl

```
<?xml version="1.0" encoding="utf-8"?>

<xsl:stylesheet version="1.0"
  xmlns:xsl="http://www.w3.org/1999/XSL/Transform">

  <xsl:template match="invoice">
    <html>
      <head>
        <title>Invoice</title>
      </head>
      <body>
        <h1>Invoice</h1>

        <p>
          Number:
          <xsl:value-of select="@number"/>
          <br />Date:
          <xsl:value-of select="@month"/> /
          <xsl:value-of select="@day"/> /
          <xsl:value-of select="@year"/>
        </p>

        <p>
          Supplier:
          <xsl:value-of select="supplier/@name"/>
          <br />Address:
          <xsl:value-of select="supplier/address"/>
          <br />Email:
          <xsl:value-of select="supplier/email"/>
        </p>

        <p>
          Buyer:
          <xsl:value-of select="buyer/@name"/>
          <br />Address:
          <xsl:value-of select="buyer/address"/>
          <br />Email:
          <xsl:value-of select="buyer/email"/>
        </p>

        <table border="1" cellspacing="5"  cellpadding="5">
          <tr>
```

```
       </xsl:when>
           <xsl:otherwise>0</xsl:otherwise>
         </xsl:choose>

      </xsl:template>

   </xsl:stylesheet>
```

Output invoice.html

```
> java TransformationSample

<html>
  <head>
    <META http-equiv="Content-Type" content="text/html; charset=UTF-8">
    <title>Invoice</title>
  </head>
  <body>
    <h1>Invoice</h1>
    <p>
          Number:
          1234567<br>Date:
          2 /
          20 /
          2000</p>
    <p>
          Supplier:
          Sup Company<br>Address:
          London, UK<br>Email:
          info@supcompany.com</p>
    <p>
          Buyer:
          Buy Company<br>Address:
          Paris, France<br>Email:
          info@buycompany.com</p>
    <table cellpadding="5" cellspacing="5" border="1">
      <tr>
        <th align="left">Item</th><th align="right">Qty</th><th
align="right">Price</th><th align="left">Info</th>
      </tr>
      <tr>
        <td align="left">Computer</td><td align="right">10</td><td
align="right">1000</td><td align="left">800 Mhz, 256M RAM, 40G HDD</td>
      </tr>
      <tr>
        <td align="left">Printer</td><td align="right">5</td><td
align="right">200</td><td align="left">600x600 dpi, 20 ppm</td>
      </tr>
      <tr>
        <td align="left">Server</td><td align="right">1</td><td
align="right">5000</td><td align="left">4x1000 Mhz, 2G RAM, 2x100G HDD</td>
      </tr>
    </table>
<p>
          Total: US$16000</p>
  </body>
</html>
```

Interface Templates

javax.xml.transform

> **public interface** Templates

This interface creates an object that represents the transformation instructions during run time.

Templates may be run over several threads concurrently, and also be reused by different threads.

Method getOutputProperties()

The getOutputProperties() method returns the static properties for xsl:output. The object returned will be a clone of the internal values.

The properties that were specifically set by the stylesheet are in the base Properties list, while the XSLT default properties that were not specifically set are in the defaults Properties list (defaults is a protected field of java.util.Properties). Thus, getOutputProperties().getProperty() will obtain any property that was set by the stylesheet or a default property, while getOutputProperties().get() will only retrieve properties that were explicitly set in the stylesheet.

> public java.util.Properties **getOutputProperties**()

Returned Values

Method	Return	Description
getOutput Properties()	java.util. Properties	A Properties object, which is not null

Method newTransformer()

newTransformer() creates a new transformation context for the Templates object.

> public Transformer **newTransformer**()
>   throws TransformerConfigurationException

Returned Values

Method	Return	Description
newTransformer()	Transformer	A valid instance of a Transformer, which is not null

Example: Chaining Two Transformations

This example is similar to the `TransformationSample` example on page 338, but the items of the invoice are sorted by unit price before producing the HTML file. Therefore, we have two chained transformations, that is, the latter uses as its source the result of the former.

The `main()` method creates a `TransformerFactory` instance using the static `newInstance()` method. The factory object is used for creating a `Templates` instance that is used to create a `Transformer` based on `sorter.xsl`. This is just to show how to use `Templates` and there is no benefit in the case of this simple example. However, if the application needed multiple `Transformers` based on the same XSL file, the `Templates` would allow the TrAX implementation to do optimizations.

The `DOMResult` class is used to obtain the sorted invoice as a DOM tree in memory, which is serialized to `System.out` and also used to create the DOM source for the second transformation.

Next, the factory object is used to obtain a `Transformer` instance based on `invoice.xsl`. This object is configured to produce indented HTML output.

Finally, the sorted DOM tree is processed and the result is stored in the `sorted.html` file.

Source ChainedTransformationSample.java

```java
import javax.xml.transform.OutputKeys;
import javax.xml.transform.Templates;
import javax.xml.transform.Transformer;
import javax.xml.transform.TransformerFactory;
import javax.xml.transform.dom.DOMResult;
import javax.xml.transform.dom.DOMSource;
import javax.xml.transform.sax.SAXSource;
import javax.xml.transform.stream.StreamResult;
import javax.xml.transform.stream.StreamSource;

import org.w3c.dom.Node;

import org.xml.sax.InputSource;

import java.util.Properties;

public class ChainedTransformationSample {
  public static final String XALAN_INDENT_AMOUNT =
    "{http://xml.apache.org/xslt}indent-amount";

  public static void main(String args[]) {
    try {
      String sorterID = "sorter.xsl";
      String stylesheetID = "invoice.xsl";
      String sourceID = "invoice.xml";
      String resultID = "sorted.html";
```

```java
        // Create the transformer factory
        TransformerFactory factory =
          TransformerFactory.newInstance();

        // Create a Templates instance
        Templates sorterTemplates =
          factory.newTemplates(new StreamSource(sorterID));

        // Use the Templates to create a transformer
        Transformer sorter = sorterTemplates.newTransformer();

        // Create the holder for the sorted result
        DOMResult sortedResult = new DOMResult();

        // Sort the XML invoice
        sorter.transform(new StreamSource(sourceID),
                         sortedResult);

        // Get the DOM tree of the sorted document
        Node sortedDoc = sortedResult.getNode();

        // Print the sorted document using the serialize()
        // method of the SerializationSample class
        SerializationSample.serialize(sortedDoc, System.out);

        // Create a DOM source that holds the sorted document
        DOMSource sortedSource = new DOMSource(sortedDoc);

        // Create a transformer object based on invoice.xsl
        Transformer transformer = factory.newTransformer(
          new SAXSource(new InputSource(stylesheetID)));

        // Configure the transformer to produce
        // indented HTML output
        Properties props = new Properties();
        props.put(OutputKeys.METHOD, "html");
        props.put(OutputKeys.INDENT, "yes");
        props.put(XALAN_INDENT_AMOUNT, "2");
        transformer.setOutputProperties(props);

        // Apply the transformation on the sorted DOM tree
        transformer.transform(sortedSource,
                              new StreamResult(resultID));
    } catch (Exception e) {
      e.printStackTrace();
      System.exit(1);
    }
  }
```

Sample sorter.xsl

```xml
<?xml version="1.0" encoding="utf-8"?>

<xsl:stylesheet version="1.0"
  xmlns:xsl="http://www.w3.org/1999/XSL/Transform">

  <xsl:template match="@*|node()">
    <xsl:copy>
      <xsl:apply-templates select="@*"/>
      <xsl:apply-templates select="node()">
        <xsl:sort select="@price"
          data-type="number" order="descending"/>
      </xsl:apply-templates>
    </xsl:copy>
  </xsl:template>

</xsl:stylesheet>
```

Output

```
> java ChainedTransformationSample
<?xml version="1.0" encoding="UTF-8"?>
<invoice day="20" month="2" number="1234567" year="2000">
  <item info="4x1000 Mhz, 2G RAM, 2x100G HDD" name="Server" price="5000"
quantity="1"/>
  <item info="800 Mhz, 256M RAM, 40G HDD" name="Computer" price="1000"
quantity="10"/>
  <item info="600x600 dpi, 20 ppm" name="Printer" price="200"
quantity="5"/>
  <supplier name="Sup Company">
    <email>info@supcompany.com</email>
    <address>London, UK</address>
  </supplier>
  <buyer name="Buy Company">
    <email>info@buycompany.com</email>
    <address>Paris, France</address>
  </buyer>
  <currency>US$</currency>


  <?total?>
</invoice>
```

Output sorted.html

```html
<html>
  <head>
    <META http-equiv="Content-Type" content="text/html; charset=UTF-8">
    <title>Invoice</title>
```

```
    </head>
    <body>
      <h1>Invoice</h1>
      <p>
            Number:
            1234567<br>Date:
            2 /
            20 /
            2000</p>
      <p>
            Supplier:
            Sup Company<br>Address:
            London, UK<br>Email:
            info@supcompany.com</p>
      <p>
            Buyer:
            Buy Company<br>Address:
            Paris, France<br>Email:
            info@buycompany.com</p>
      <table cellpadding="5" cellspacing="5" border="1">
        <tr>
          <th align="left">Item</th><th align="right">Qty</th><th
align="right">Price</th><th align="left">Info</th>
        </tr>
        <tr>
          <td align="left">Server</td><td align="right">1</td><td
align="right">5000</td><td align="left">4x1000 Mhz, 2G RAM, 2x100G HDD</td>
        </tr>
        <tr>
          <td align="left">Computer</td><td align="right">10</td><td
align="right">1000</td><td align="left">800 Mhz, 256M RAM, 40G HDD</td>
        </tr>
        <tr>
          <td align="left">Printer</td><td align="right">5</td><td
align="right">200</td><td align="left">600x600 dpi, 20 ppm</td>
        </tr>
      </table>
      <p>
            Total: US$16000</p>
    </body>
  </html>
```

Package javax.xml.transform.stream

This package implements stream-specific transformation APIs.

The `StreamSource` class provides methods for specifying an input source for transformation, such as a `java.io.File`, `java.io.InputStream`, `java.io.Reader`, or URL.

In order for the transformer to be able to resolve relative URIs, the system identifier should still be provided, even if the source is an input stream or reader. On the other hand, the public identifier is optional, and if one is included it will be along with the rest of the information provided by `javax.xml.transform.SourceLocator`.

The `StreamResult` class provides methods for specifying `java.io.File`, `java.io.Writer`, `java.io.OutputStream`, or a system ID as the output for the result.

It is recommended that streams, rather than readers or writers, should be used for the source and the result, as readers and writers conform to the Unicode format. Byte streams are preferred as this means that data can be parsed according to the character encoding specified by the XML declaration. However, it is sometimes useful to use readers and writers, depending on the task at hand.

Classes

Class	Description	Page
StreamSource	Holds the transformation source as a stream of XML markup	347
StreamResult	Holds a transformation result. This can be text, XML, HTML, or another markup form.	349

Class StreamSource

javax.xml.transform.stream

```
public class StreamSource
        implements javax.xml.transform.Source
```

This class holds a transformation source as a stream of XML markup. This can be referenced to an `InputStream`, a system ID, or a reader.

Fields

This class defines the following `String` constant:

Field	Type	Description
FEATURE	String	String passed to the `getFeature()` static method of `TransformerFactory`. This tests whether the feature is supported by the JAXP implementation being used.

Constructors

These constructors can create `StreamSources` from a byte stream, reader, URL, or file.

```
public StreamSource()
public StreamSource(java.io.InputStream inputStream)
public StreamSource(java.io.InputStream inputStream, String systemId)
public StreamSource(java.io.Reader reader)
```

```
public StreamSource(java.io.Reader reader, String systemId)
public StreamSource(String systemId)
public StreamSource(java.io.File f)
```

Parameters

Parameter	Type	Description
inputStream	java.io.InputStream	InputStream reference to an XML stream
systemId	String	String conforming to the URI syntax
reader	java.io.Reader	Reader reference to an XML character stream
f	java.io.File	A File reference. This cannot be null.

Methods

These methods are used in the setting and getting of the character stream, byte stream, public identifier, and system identifier.

```
public void setInputStream(java.io.InputStream inputStream)
public java.io.InputStream getInputStream()
public void setReader(java.io.Reader reader)
public java.io.Reader getReader()
public void setPublicId(String publicId)
public String getPublicId()
public void setSystemId(java.io.File f)
```

Parameters

Parameter	Type	Description
inputStream	java.io.InputStream	InputStream reference to an XML stream
reader	java.io.Reader	Reader reference to an XML CharacterStream
publicId	String	String representing the public identifier
f	java.io.File	A File reference. This may not be null.

Returned Values

Method	Return	Description
`getInputStream()`	`java.io.InputStream`	The byte stream set with `setByteStream()`, or `null`
`getReader()`	`java.io.Reader`	The character stream set with `setReader()`, or `null`
`getPublicId()`	`String`	The public identifier set with `setPublicId()`, or `null`

Methods Defined by javax.xml.transform.Source

```
public void setSystemId(String systemId)
public String getSystemId()
```

> Note: The `javax.xml.transform.stream.StreamSource` class is used by our `TransformationSample` example on page 338 and `ChainedTransformationSample` example on page 343.

Class StreamResult

javax.xml.transform.stream

```
public class StreamResult
        implements javax.xml.transform.Result
```

This class holds a transformation result in text, XML, HTML, or some other form of markup. A `StreamResult` instance can refer to an `InputStream`, `Reader`, or system ID.

Fields

This class defines the following `String` constant:

Field	Type	Description
`FEATURE`	`String`	This parameter passes a `String` to the `getFeature()` static method of `TransformerFactory`. It tests whether stream results are supported by the current JAXP implementation.

Constructors

These constructors create `StreamResult` objects from a byte stream, character stream, URL, or file.

```
public StreamResult()
public StreamResult(java.io.OutputStream outputStream)
public StreamResult(java.io.Writer writer)
public StreamResult(String systemId)
public StreamResult(java.io.File f)
```

Parameters

Parameter	Type	Description
output Stream	java.io. OutputStream	A valid OutputStream reference
writer	java.io.Writer	A valid Writer reference
system Id	String	A String conforming to URI syntax
f	java.io.File	A File reference that is not null

Methods

These methods set and get the byte stream, character stream and system identifier.

```
public void setOutputStream(java.io.OutputStream
                            outputStream)
public java.io.OutputStream getOutputStream()
public void setWriter(java.io.Writer writer)
public java.io.Writer getWriter()
public void setSystemId(java.io.File f)
```

Parameters

Parameter	Type	Description
outputStream	java.io. OutputStream	An OutputStream reference
writer	java.io.Writer	A Writer reference
f	java.io.File	A File reference that is not null

Returned Values

Method	Return	Description
`getOutputStream()`	`java.io.` `OutputStream`	The byte stream set with `setOutputStream()` or `null`
`getWriter()`	`java.io.` `Writer`	The character stream set with `setWriter()` or `null`

Methods Defined by javax.xml.transform.Result

```
public void setSystemId(String systemId)
```

```
public String getSystemId()
```

> Note: The `javax.xml.transform.stream.StreamResult` class is used by our
> `SerializationSample` example on page 331, `TransformationSample` example on
> page 338 and `ChainedTransformationSample` example on page 343.

Package javax.xml.transform.sax

This package implements SAX 2.0-specific transformation APIs. It takes input from SAX-parsing events and classes that produce SAX-parsing events. It can also create transformers to be used as `org.xml.sax.XMLFilters`.

Interfaces

Interfaces	Description	Page
`Templates Handler`	A SAX `ContentHandler` that processes SAX parse events (parsing transformation instructions) into a `Templates` object	356
`Transformer Handler`	A `TransformerHandler` that listens for SAX `ContentHandler` parse events and transforms them to a `Result`	357

Classes

Class	Description	Page
`SAXSource`	Holds a SAX-style source	352
`SAXResult`	Holds a transformation result	354
`SAXTransformer Factory`	Extends `TransformerFactory` to provide SAX-specific factory methods	358

Class SAXSource

javax.xml.transform.sax

```
public class SAXSource
          implements javax.xml.transform.Source
```

The SAXSource class holds an org.xml.sax.InputSource. In this way the instance maintains a reference to an InputSource.

Fields

This class defines the following String constant:

Field	Type	Description
FEATURE	String	This String can be passed as a parameter to the getFeature() static method of TransformerFactory. This will test whether the current JAXP implementation supports SAX sources.

Constructors

These constructors are used to make a SAXSource object, using a SAX XMLReader (which is created automatically is none is provided) and a SAX InputSource. When the source's content is needed, the implementation provides its own ContentHandler to the XMLReader and then calls the reader's parse() method passing the InputSource as a parameter.

```
public SAXSource()
```
```
public SAXSource(org.xml.sax.XMLReader reader,
                 org.xml.sax.InputSource inputSource)
```
```
public SAXSource(org.xml.sax.InputSource inputSource)
```

Parameters

Parameter	Type	Description
reader	org.xml.sax.XMLReader	The XMLReader that will do the parsing
input Source	org.xml.sax.InputSource	A (non-null) SAX input source reference that is passed to the parse() method of the reader

Methods for Setting and Getting Properties

These methods get and set XMLReader and InputSource SAX objects.

```
public void setXMLReader(org.xml.sax.XMLReader reader)
public org.xml.sax.XMLReader getXMLReader()
public void setInputSource(org.xml.sax.InputSource
                                inputSource)
public org.xml.sax.InputSource getInputSource()
```

Parameters

Parameter	Type	Description
reader	org.xml.sax. XMLReader	An XMLReader or XMLFilter reference
input Source	org.xml.sax. InputSource	A (non-null) SAX input source reference to be passed to the parse() method of the reader

Returned Values

Method	Return	Description
getXML Reader()	org.xml.sax. XMLReader	An XMLReader or XMLFilter reference. This can be null.
getInput Source()	org.xml.sax. InputSource	An InputSource reference. This can be null.

Methods

The static sourceToInputSource() method attempts to obtain a SAX InputSource object from a TrAX Source object.

```
public static org.xml.sax.InputSource sourceToInputSource(
                                Source source)
```

Parameters

Parameter	Type	Description
source	Source	A Source reference, that is not null

Returned Values

Method	Return	Description
sourceTo InputSource()	org.xml.sax. InputSource	An InputSource, or null

Methods Defined by javax.xml.transform.Source

```
public void setSystemId(String systemId)
```

```
public String getSystemId()
```

> Note: The `javax.xml.transform.sax.SAXSource` class is used by our
> `ChainedTransformationSample` example on page 343.

Class SAXResult

javax.xml.transform.sax

```
public class SAXResult
        implements javax.xml.transform.Result
```

The SAXResult class allows the setting of an `org.xml.sax.ContentHandler` to be the receiver of SAX events from the transformation.

Fields

This class defines the following `String` constant:

Field	Type	Description
FEATURE	String	This `String` can be passed as a parameter to the `getFeature()` static method of `TransformerFactory`. This will test whether the current JAXP implementation supports SAX sources.

Constructors

These constructors create SAXResult objects that target SAX `ContentHandlers`.

```
public SAXResult()
```

```
public SAXResult(org.xml.sax.ContentHandler ch)
```

Parameters

Parameter	Type	Description
ch	org.xml.sax. ContentHandler	A `ContentHandler` reference that is not `null`

Methods

The setHandler() method sets the target to be a SAX ContentHandler. The result of the transformation will be passed as SAX events to the methods of this handler.

The getHandler() method returns the ContentHandler.

The setLexicalHandler() method set the SAX LexicalHandler for the output. This is needed to handle XML comments and the like. If the lexical handler is not set, an attempt is made by the transformer to cast the ContentHandler to a LexicalHandler.

The getLexicalHandler() method gets a SAX LexicalHandler for the output.

```
public void setHandler(org.xml.sax.ContentHandler ch)
```
```
public org.xml.sax.ContentHandler getHandler()
```
```
public void setLexicalHandler(org.xml.sax.ext.LexicalHandler lh)
```
```
public org.xml.sax.ext.LexicalHandler getLexicalHandler()
```

Parameters

Parameter	Type	Description
ch	org.xml.sax.ContentHandler	A ContentHandler reference that is not null
lh	org.xml.sax.ext.LexicalHandler	A LexicalHandler for handling lexical parse events that is not null

Returned Values

Method	Return	Description
getHandler()	org.xml.sax.ContentHandler	The ContentHandler that is to be transformation output
getLexicalHandler()	org.xml.sax.ext.LexicalHandler	A LexicalHandler. This can also be null

Methods Defined by javax.xml.transform.Result

```
public void setSystemId(String systemId)
```
```
public String getSystemId()
```

Note: The javax.xml.transform.sax.SAXResult class is used by our SerializationSample example on page 331.

Interface TemplatesHandler

javax.xml.transform.sax

```
public interface TemplatesHandler
         extends org.xml.sax.ContentHandler
```

The `TemplatesHandler` interface allows the creation of `javax.xml.transform.Templates` objects from SAX parse events. The `Templates` object may be obtained from `TemplatesHandler.getTemplates()`. Note that `TemplatesHandler.setSystemId()` should be called in order to establish a base system ID from which relative URLs may be resolved.

Normally, an application doesn't use this interface because it can create a `Templates` instance from a SAX input source by using the `TransformerFactory` class and passing a `SAXSource` to the `newTemplates()` method. This will use a SAX `XMLReader` to parse the input source. An application uses this interface when the transformation instructions are generated by itself, as opposed to being read in from an external source. For example, an application might store transformation instructions in a relational database and retrieve that information, generating SAX events to be handled by a `Templates` handler.

Methods

If a `TemplatesHandler` object is used as a SAX `ContentHandler` in order to parse transformation instructions, a `Templates` object is created which the user can access using `getTemplates()`.

The `setSystemId()` method sets the base ID for the `Templates` object, which can be either a URI or system ID. To resolve relative URIs in the stylesheet, however, this must be set before the `startDocument()` event.

The `getSystemId()` method gets the base ID from where relative URLs will be resolved. This can be a URI or a system ID.

```
public Templates getTemplates()

public void setSystemId(String systemID)

public String getSystemId()
```

Parameters

Parameter	Type	Description
systemID	String	Stylesheet URI

Returned Values

Method	Return	Description
get Templates()	Templates	The `Templates` object that was created during the SAX event process. If no `Templates` object has been created, this value is `null`.
getSystemId()	String	The system ID set with `setSystemId()`

Interface TransformerHandler

javax.xml.transform.sax

```
public interface TransformerHandler
        extends org.xml.sax.ContentHandler,
                org.xml.sax.ext.LexicalHandler,
                org.xml.sax.DTDHandler
```

A TransformerHandler listens for SAX parsing events and transforms them to a result. The TransformerHandler interface extends the ContentHandler, LexicalHandler, and DTDHandler interfaces of the SAX API. Normal parse events are received through the ContentHandler interface, lexical events are received through the LexicalHandler interface, and events that signal the enabling and disabling of the output escaping are received via ContentHandler.processingInstruction(), with the target parameter being Result.PI_DISABLE_OUTPUT_ESCAPING or Result.PI_ENABLE_OUTPUT_ESCAPING.

Normally, an application doesn't use this interface because it can create a Transformer instance from a SAX input source by using the TransformerFactory class and passing a SAXSource to the newTransformer() method. Once a Transformer instance is obtained the application can invoke its transform() method for applying the transformation instructions. This would be used when SAX events are generated from an application program rather than an XMLReader or XMLFilter.

Methods

The setResult() method enables the user of the TransformerHandler to set the Result, and the setSystemId() and getSystemId() methods set and retrieve the base ID. Relative URLs will be resolved from the base ID.

The getTransformer() method gets the Transformer associated with this handler. This is necessary to set the correct output properties and parameters.

```
public void setResult(Result result)
        throws IllegalArgumentException
public void setSystemId(String systemID)
public String getSystemId()
public Transformer getTransformer()
```

Parameters

Parameter	Type	Description
result	Result	A Result instance. This should not be null
systemID	String	Source tree base URI

Returned Values

Method	Return	Description
get SystemId()	String	The systemID set with setSystemId()
get Transformer()	Transformer	The Transformer associated with this handler, required to set parameters and output properties

Class SAXTransformerFactory
javax.xml.transform.sax

```
public abstract class SAXTransformerFactory
       extends javax.xml.transform.TransformerFactory
```

The SAXTransformerFactory extends javax.xml.transform.TransformerFactory to provide factory methods for creating TemplatesHandler, TransformerHandler, and org.xml.sax.XMLFilter instances.

Fields
This class defines the following String constants:

Field	Type	Description
FEATURE	String	This String is passed as a parameter to the getFeature() static method of the TransformerFactory class. This tests that the TransformerFactory objects returned from the newInstance() method can be properly cast to a SAXTransformerFactory.
FEATURE_ XMLFILTER	String	This String can be passed to the getFeature() static method of the TransformerFactory class to test if the newXMLFilter() methods are supported

Constructor
This is a protected constructor.

To obtain a SAXTransformerFactory, the caller must cast the TransformerFactory instance returned from the newInstance() method of javax.xml.transform.TransformerFactory.

```
protected SAXTransformerFactory()
```

Methods newTransformerHandler()

The newTransformerHandler() method returns a TransformerHandler object that processes SAX ContentHandler events and returns a Result. This result is based on any transformation instructions specified by the argument.

Where an argument is not specified, the transformation is defined as an identity (or copy) transformation.

```
public abstract TransformerHandler newTransformerHandler(
                                     Source src)
        throws TransformerConfigurationException
public abstract TransformerHandler newTransformerHandler(
                                     Templates templates)
        throws TransformerConfigurationException
public abstract TransformerHandler newTransformerHandler()
        throws TransformerConfigurationException
```

Parameters

Parameter	Type	Description
src	Source	Transformation instructions contained in Source
templates	Templates	Transformation instructions (compiled)

Returned Values

Method	Return	Description
newTransformer Handler()	Transformer Handler	TransformerHandler to transform SAX events

Method newTemplatesHandler()

The newTemplatesHandler() method returns a TemplatesHandler object. This object then processes SAX ContentHandler events into a Templates object.

```
public abstract TemplatesHandler newTemplatesHandler()
        throws TransformerConfigurationException
```

Returned Values

Method	Return	Description
newTemplates Handler()	Templates Handler	A TemplatesHandler object that processes SAX ContentHandler events into a Templates object

Methods newXMLFilter()

The newXMLFilter() methods can create an XMLFilter that uses the given Source as the transformation instructions or an XMLFilter that is based on the Templates argument.

This filter will have no parent: you must assign a parent before you start a parse or do any configuration with setFeature() or setProperty().

```
public abstract org.xml.sax.XMLFilter newXMLFilter(Source src)
        throws TransformerConfigurationException

public abstract org.xml.sax.XMLFilter newXMLFilter(Templates
                                                        templates)

        throws TransformerConfigurationException
```

Parameters

Parameter	Type	Description
src	Source	Transformation instructions Source
templates	Templates	Transformation instructions (compiled)

Returned Values

Method	Return	Description
newXML Filter()	org.xml.sax. XMLFilter	An XMLFilter object. If this is not supported, this is null.

Package javax.xml.transform.dom

javax.xml.transform.dom implements DOM-specific transformation APIs.

This class allows a DOM org.w3c.dom.Node to be specified as the source of the input tree by the client of the implementation. The nodes derived the Node are all considered valid input.

The DOMResult class specifies an org.w3c.dom.Node that DOM nodes can be appended to. If an output node is not specified the newDocument() method javax.xml.parsers.DocumentBuilder is used to create an output org.w3c.dom.Document node. However, if a node is actually specified, it has to be one of these three:

❏ org.w3c.dom.Document

❏ org.w3c.dom.Element

❏ org.w3c.dom.DocumentFragment

Any other node is implementation-dependent and beyond the scope of this API. If the result is cast into an org.w3c.dom.Document, the output needs to have a single root element.

The DOMLocator node can be passed to javax.xml.transform.TransformerException objects. The result of TransformerException.getLocator() should be tested with an instanceof, as there is nothing to make the system use a DOMLocator instead of a javax.xml.transform.SourceLocator.

Interfaces

Interfaces	Description	Page
DOMLocator	Gives the position of a node in a source DOM. This is used to report errors.	364

Classes

Class	Description	Page
DOMSource	Holds a transformation source tree as a Document Object Model (DOM) tree	361
DOMResult	Holds a transformation result tree, as a Document Object Model (DOM) tree	363

Class DOMSource

javax.xml.transform.dom

```
public class DOMSource
        implements javax.xml.transform.Source
```

This class object holds a transformation source tree in the form of a Document Object Model (DOM) tree. It maintains reference to a DOM Node.

Fields

This class defines the following String constant:

Field	Type	Description
FEATURE	String	This String can be passed as parameter to the getFeature() static method of TransformerFactory. This will test whether the current JAXP implementation supports it.

Constructors

These constructors create new input sources that contain a DOM node.

```
public DOMSource()
public DOMSource(org.w3c.dom.Node node)
public DOMSource(org.w3c.dom.Node node, String systemID)
```

Parameters

Parameter	Type	Description
n	org.w3c.dom.Node	The DOM node containing the Source tree
systemID	String	Base URI the node is associated with

Methods

These methods set and retrieve the node representing a source DOM tree.

```
public void setNode(org.w3c.dom.Node node)
public org.w3c.dom.Node getNode()
```

Parameters

Parameter	Type	Description
node	org.w3c.dom.Node	Node to be transformed

Returned Values

Method	Return	Description
getNode()	org.w3c.dom.Node	Node to be transformed

Methods Defined by javax.xml.transform.Source

```
public void setSystemId(String baseID)
public String getSystemId()
```

Note: The javax.xml.transform.dom.DOMSource class is used by our SerializationSample example on page 331 and ChainedTransformationSample example on page 343.

Class DOMResult

javax.xml.transform.dom

```
public class DOMResult
        implements javax.xml.transform.Result
```

This object holds a transformation result tree, in the form of a Document Object Model (DOM) tree. In the absence of an output node being set, the transformation creates an `org.w3c.dom.Document` node to hold the transformation result.

Fields

This class defines the following `String` constant:

Field	Type	Description
FEATURE	String	This `String` can be passed as parameter to the `getFeature()` static method of `TransformerFactory`. This will test whether the current JAXP implementation supports `DOMResults`.

Constructors

A new output target is created with these constructors, comprising a DOM node. Such a node should be one of the following:

- ❏ `org.w3c.dom.Document` node
- ❏ `org.w3c.dom.DocumentFragment`
- ❏ `org.w3c.dom.Element` node

```
public DOMResult()
public DOMResult(org.w3c.dom.Node node)
public DOMResult(org.w3c.dom.Node node, String systemID)
```

Parameters

Parameter	Type	Description
node	org.w3c. dom.Node	DOM node to contain the result tree
systemID	String	The system identifier to be used in association with the node

Methods

The `setNode()` method sets the node that will contain the result DOM tree. Such a node should be one of the following:

- org.w3c.dom.Document node

- org.w3c.dom.DocumentFragment node

- org.w3c.dom.Element node

The getNode() method returns the node that will contain the result DOM tree. If a node wasn't set using setNode(), it will be set by the transformation instead. It can be obtained from the method when the transformation is complete.

```
public void setNode(org.w3c.dom.Node node)
```

```
public org.w3c.dom.Node getNode()
```

Parameters

Parameter	Type	Description
node	org.w3c.dom.Node	The DOM node containing the result tree

Returned Values

Method	Return	Description
getNode()	org.w3c.dom.Node	The node to which the transformation will be appended

Methods Defined by javax.xml.transform.Result

```
public void setSystemId(String systemId)
```

```
public String getSystemId()
```

> Note: The javax.xml.transform.dom.DOMResult class is used by our ChainedTransformationSample example on page 343.

Interface DOMLocator

javax.xml.transform.dom

```
public interface DOMLocator
        extends javax.xml.transform.SourceLocator
```

This indicates the position of a node in a source DOM. Its purpose is mainly for error reporting. However, a Transformer could also use this interface to show the source node that a result node originated from.

Method getOriginatingNode()

This method returns the node where the event originated.

```
public org.w3c.dom.Node getOriginatingNode()
```

Returned Values

Method	Return	Description
getOriginatingNode()	org.w3c.dom.Node	The location of an event, as a node

Summary

In this chapter we have looked at the JAXP 1.1 API. In addition, we provided examples that:

- ❑ Start SAX parsing with JAXP and validate XML files
- ❑ Parse a file with DOM and create new documents with JAXP
- ❑ Save a DOM tree to an XML file with TrAX
- ❑ Apply XSLT transformations on an XML document using TrAX
- ❑ Chain together transformations
- ❑ Use TrAX template

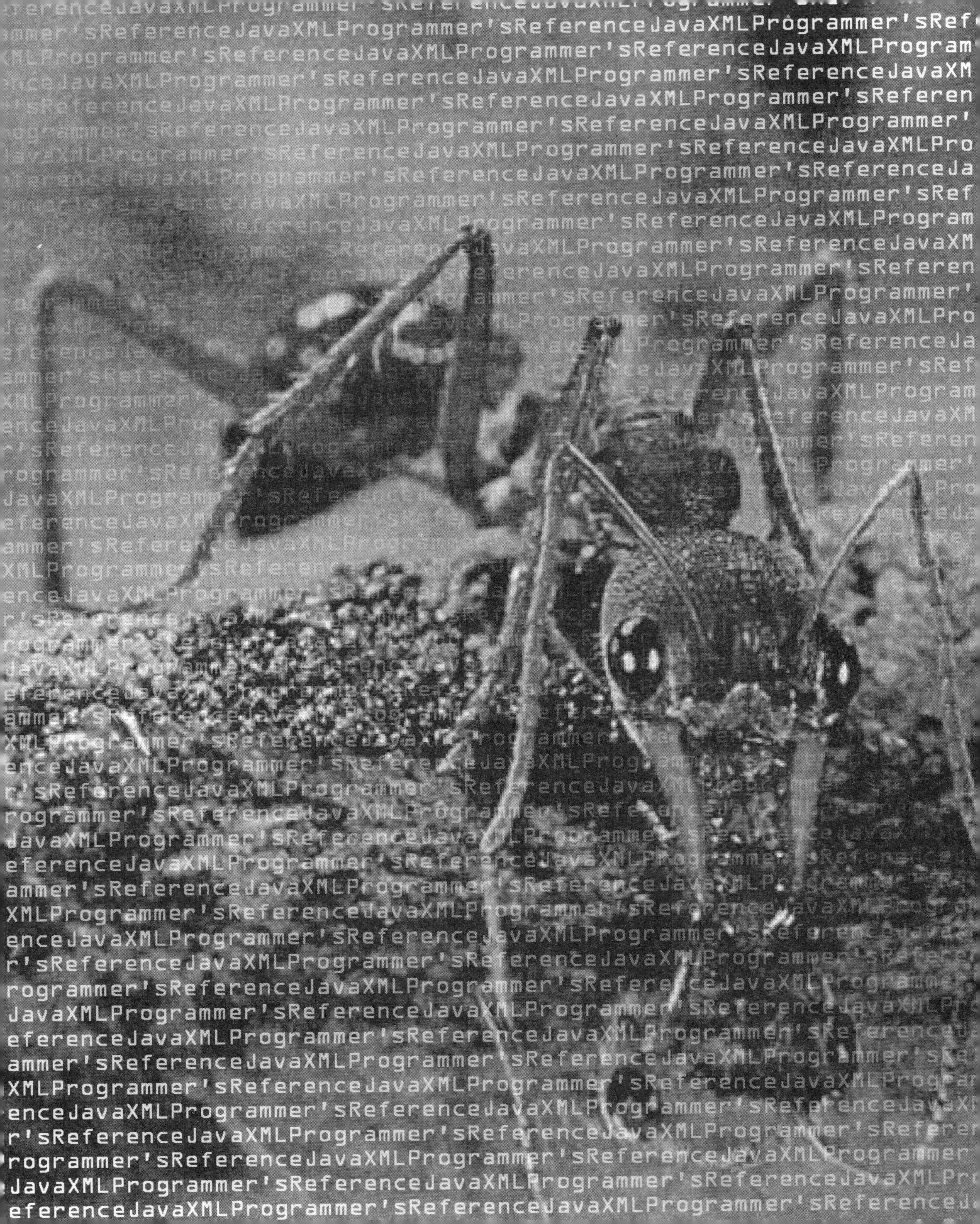

6

JDOM Examples

The Document Object Model (DOM) API presented in Chapter 3 is a language-neutral solution for creating and manipulating XML document structure and contents. JDOM is a similar API, but it was designed specifically for Java developers.

JDOM consists of voluntary contributions made by many individuals on behalf of the JDOM Project and was originally created by Brett McLaughlin and Jason Hunter. They have submitted the API for standardization to the Sun's Community Process. More information on the JDOM Project and a downloadable package with the complete source code can be found at http://www.jdom.org. The current API for the latest beta of JDOM can be obtained from this site.

We develop small utility classes and examples that use the JDOM API. Most of them are modified versions of the examples from Chapter 3 so that you can compare and contrast the two similar APIs.

In this chapter, we'll show how to:

- ❑ Parse an XML document to obtain a JDOM tree
- ❑ Print information about the nodes of a JDOM tree
- ❑ Extract the data contained by a node
- ❑ Find the elements of a JDOM tree that satisfy some criteria
- ❑ Create a document tree from scratch
- ❑ Filter an XML document using JDOM and SAX

At the time of writing JDOM was in a late beta stage (beta 6). Since the API is still in flux, it is possible you might experience minor compilation or running problems with the examples in due course, as given here. Also some of the APIs presented in this chapter might be deprecated, while new ones are added.

The overall structure of the JDOM API is as follows:

Package	Description
`org.jdom`	Groups the classes whose instances represent the logical constructs of an XML document, such as elements, attributes, CDATA sections, comments, processing instructions, entity references and namespaces
`org.jdom.input`	Contains classes for building a JDOM tree
`org.jdom.output`	Contains classes for outputting a JDOM tree
`org.jdom.adapters`	Contains classes that help JDOM to interact with XML parsers

Examples

In this chapter we will look at the following set of Java examples:

Classes	Description	Page
`JDOMPrinter`	Parses an XML document using JDOM, and prints its structure and contents in an indented manner	369
`ElementUtils`	Contains methods for finding the elements of a JDOM tree that satisfy some criteria	373
`ElementSample`	Uses the `ElementUtils` class to find elements within a JDOM document	375
`DataUtils`	Contains a method for extracting the data contained by a JDOM node	378
`DataSample`	Uses the `DataUtils` class to collect the data contained by an element	380
`CreationSample`	Creates a JDOM tree composed of `Document`, `Element`, `Comment`, `CDATA`, `ProcessingInstruction` and `String` nodes. The populated document is printed using the `print()` method inherited from `JDOMPrinter`	382
`FilteringSample`	Parses and filters a file using JDOM `SAXBuilder` and SAX `XMLFilter`	383

Using JDOM

JDOM is a Java-centric API, so rather than defining interfaces for maintaining the lists and maps of nodes like DOM, JDOM uses the Java Collections API. Instead of defining language neutral mechanisms for cloning and testing the equality for two nodes like DOM, JDOM classes have Java-specific `clone()` and `equals()` methods, as well as `toString()` for debugging.

The JDOM API also supports the Java object serialization mechanism, which means that many of its classes implement `java.io.Serializable`, though JDOM trees are normally saved to XML documents.

JDOM uses an XML parser (such as Xerces) that supports SAX and DOM in order to:

❑ Parse an XML document using SAX and produce the JDOM tree

❑ Serialize a JDOM tree as a sequence of SAX events

❑ Convert an existing DOM tree to a JDOM tree and vice-versa

JDOM also has its own serialization mechanism for saving JDOM trees to XML documents.

JDOM Starter Example

This example parses an XML file and prints the JDOM tree. It can work as a standalone application, but it is also used by other examples of this chapter: `CreationSample`, `DataSample` and `ElementSample`.

The `JDOMPrinter` class parses an XML document using JDOM, and prints its structure and contents in an indented manner.

Source JDOMPrinter.java

```java
import org.jdom.Attribute;
import org.jdom.CDATA;
import org.jdom.Comment;
import org.jdom.DocType;
import org.jdom.Document;
import org.jdom.Element;
import org.jdom.Entity;
import org.jdom.JDOMException;
import org.jdom.ProcessingInstruction;
import org.jdom.input.SAXBuilder;

import java.io.File;
import java.io.IOException;
import java.util.Iterator;
import java.util.List;

public class JDOMPrinter {
```

The `println()` method prints a given number of double spaces followed by a string to the standard output stream.

```java
public static void println(String s, int indent) {
    for (int i = 0; i < indent; i++) {
        System.out.print("  ");
    }
    System.out.println(s);
}
```

The `println()` method prints a string to the standard output stream.

```
public static void println(String s) {
    println(s, 0);
}
```

The `print()` method prints the JDOM tree whose root is given as parameter.

```
public static void print(Object node) {
    printImpl(node, 0);
}
```

The `printImpl()` method implements the above `print()` method. It first prints several node properties: type, name and value. Empty text nodes are ignored. Then it prints the attributes and the children of the given node using recursive calls.

```
private static void printImpl(Object node, int indent) {
    if (node == null) {
        return;
    }
    if (node instanceof Document) {

        Document doc = (Document) node;
        println("Document", indent);
        printImpl(doc.getMixedContent(), indent + 1);

    } else if (node instanceof DocType) {

        DocType dtd = (DocType) node;
        println("DocType - " + dtd.getElementName() + " - "
                + dtd.getPublicID() + " - "
                + dtd.getSystemID(), indent);

    } else if (node instanceof Element) {

        Element elem = (Element) node;
        println("Element - " + elem.getName(), indent);
        printImpl(elem.getAttributes(), indent + 1);
        printImpl(elem.getMixedContent(), indent + 1);

    } else if (node instanceof Attribute) {

        Attribute attr = (Attribute) node;
        println("Attribute - " + attr.getName() + " - "
                + attr.getValue(),
                indent);

    } else if (node instanceof String) {

        String str = ((String) node).trim();
        if (str.length() > 0) {
            println("String - " + str, indent);
        }

    } else if (node instanceof CDATA) {
```

```
            CDATA cdata = (CDATA) node;
            String str = cdata.getText().trim();
            if (str.length() > 0) {
              println("CDATA - " + str, indent);
            }

        } else if (node instanceof Comment) {

            Comment comm = (Comment) node;
            String str = comm.getText().trim();
            if (str.length() > 0) {
              println("Comment - " + str, indent);
            }

        } else if (node instanceof ProcessingInstruction) {

            ProcessingInstruction proc = (ProcessingInstruction)
                  node;
            println("ProcessingInstruction - " + proc.getTarget()
                  + " - "
                  + proc.getData(), indent);

        } else if (node instanceof Entity) {

            Entity entity = (Entity) node;
            println("Entity - " + entity.getName(), indent);
            printImpl(entity.getMixedContent(), indent + 1);

        } else if (node instanceof List) {

            List list = (List) node;
            Iterator iterator = list.iterator();
            while (iterator.hasNext()) {
              printImpl(iterator.next(), indent);
            }
        }
    }
}
```

The parse() method parses an XML document and returns the resulting JDOM tree.

```
public static Document parse(String path,
      boolean validation) throws JDOMException {

  // Create the JDOM SAXBuilder
  SAXBuilder saxBuilder = new SAXBuilder(validation);

  // Return the JDOM tree
  return saxBuilder.build(new File(path));
}
```

The main() method parses the document whose path is given in the command line and prints the obtained JDOM tree. If the command line is empty, it uses nodes.xml which is supplied in the code download:

```java
    public static void main(String args[]) {
        try {
            String path = args.length > 0 ? args[0] : "nodes.xml";
            print(parse(path, false));
        } catch (Exception e) {
            e.printStackTrace();
            System.exit(1);
        }
    }
}
```

Sample nodes.xml

```xml
<?xml version="1.0" encoding="utf-8"?>
<!DOCTYPE sample [
  <!ENTITY dollar "$">
]>
<!-- Some comment -->
<sample>
  data before element
  <element attr1="value1" attr2="value2">
    <data1 a="v">some data &amp; one attribute</data1>
    <data2>CDATA follows <![CDATA[more data]]></data2>
    <data3>&dollar;123 + &dollar;456</data3>
    </element>
  data after element
  <?proc data for processing?>
</sample>
```

Output

```
> java JDOMPrinter
Document
  Comment - Some comment
  Element - sample
    String - data before element
    Element - element
      Attribute - attr1 - value1
      Attribute - attr2 - value2
      Element - data1
        Attribute - a - v
        String - some data & one attribute
      Element - data2
        String - CDATA follows
        CDATA - more data
      Element - data3
        Entity - dollar
          String - $
        String - 123 +
        Entity - dollar
```

```
         String - $
         String - 456
     String - data after element
     ProcessingInstruction - proc - data for processing
```

Searching Elements in a DOM Tree

This class contains methods for finding the elements of a JDOM tree that satisfy some criteria. We can specify the tag name, local name, namespace URI, and character data that must be contained by the elements and a list of attributes with the wanted values.

Source ElementUtils.java

We use the getData() method of our DataUtils to extract the data of an element.

```
import org.jdom.Element;

import java.util.Iterator;
import java.util.Vector;

public class ElementUtils {
```

The findElements() method traverses a DOM tree in preorder and collects the Element instances whose tag name matches tagName (if not null), contains the strings of the data array (if not null) and has the given attributes set to the given values (if the arrays aren't null). The root element can be any Element instance; it doesn't have to be the root of a document.

```
public static Element[] findElements(Element root,
        String tagName, String data[], String attrNames[],
        String attrValues[]) {
    return findElementsImpl(root, null,
        tagName, data,
        attrNames, attrValues);
}
```

This is the namespace-aware version of the previous method:

```
public static Element[] findElements(Element root,
        String namespaceURI, String localName, String data[],
        String attrNames[], String attrValues[]) {
    return findElementsImpl(root, namespaceURI, localName,
        data, attrNames, attrValues);
}
```

The findElementsImpl() method creates a vector and passes it to the method with the same name that follows this one. Then, it converts the vector to an array of Elements, which is returned.

```
 private static Element[] findElementsImpl(Element root,
         String namespaceURI, String name, String data[],
         String attrNames[], String attrValues[]) {
  Vector vector = new Vector();
  findElementsImpl(root, namespaceURI, name, data,
         attrNames, attrValues, vector);
  Element array[] = new Element[vector.size()];
  for (int i = 0; i < array.length; i++) {
    array[i] = (Element) vector.get(i);
  }
  return array;
 }
```

The findElementsImpl() method implements the finding of the elements within the JDOM tree. If the given element satisfies the criteria, it is added to the vector. Then, the method iterates over the children of the given node and a recursive call is made for each Element instance.

If the name isn't null, it must match the tag name (if the namespace URI is null) or the local name in order to be considered for further checking. The element's character data must contain all strings of the data array (if any). All attributes specified by attrNames must have the values contained by attrValues. If all these conditions are met, the element is added to the vector.

Whether the element satisfies the criteria or not, its sub-elements are passed to recursive calls of this method so that they can be verified too.

```
    private static void findElementsImpl(Element root,
           String namespaceURI, String name, String data[],
           String attrNames[], String attrValues[],
           Vector vector) {
     boolean flag = false;
     if (name == null || (namespaceURI == null && name
         .equals(root
           .getQualifiedName())) || (namespaceURI != null
             && namespaceURI
           .equals(root.getNamespaceURI()) && name
             .equals(root.getName()))) {
       flag = true;
       if (data != null) {
         String rootData[] = DataUtils.getData(root);
         for (int i = 0; i < data.length; i++) {
           flag = false;
           for (int j = 0; j < rootData.length; j++) {
             if (rootData[j].indexOf(data[i]) != -1) {
               flag = true;
               break;
             }
           }
           if (flag == false) {
             break;
           }
         }
       }
     }
```

```
        if (flag && attrNames != null && attrValues != null) {
            for (int i = 0; i < attrNames.length; i++) {
                String value = root.getAttributeValue(attrNames[i]);
                if (value == null ||!value.equals(attrValues[i])) {
                    flag = false;
                    break;
                }
            }
        }
    }

    if (flag) {
      vector.add(root);
    }

    Iterator iterator = root.getChildren().iterator();
    while (iterator.hasNext()) {
      Object child = iterator.next();
      findElementsImpl((Element) child, namespaceURI, name,
          data, attrNames, attrValues, vector);
    }
  }
}
```

Finding Elements in a JDOM Document

This example uses the `ElementUtils` class to find elements within a JDOM document. After parsing the `element.xml` file using the `parse()` method inherited from `JDOMPrinter`, the `main()` method gets the root element of the document using the `getRootElement()` method defined by the `org.jdom.Document` class. The `findElements()` method of `ElementUtils` traverses a JDOM tree in preorder and collects the `Element` instances that satisfy some criteria. It is possible to specify the tag name, namespace URI, local name of the elements, strings that must be contained by them,
and attributes.

Source ElementsSample.java

```
import org.jdom.Document;
import org.jdom.Element;

public class ElementSample extends JDOMPrinter {
```

The `print()` method prints the values of the `id` attribute of the elements contained by the given array.

```
private static void print(int test, Element elemArray[]) {
  StringBuffer buf = new StringBuffer();
  buf.append("*** " + test + " ***");
  for (int i = 0; i < elemArray.length; i++) {
    buf.append(" ");
    buf.append(elemArray[i].getAttributeValue("id"));
  }
```

```
        println(buf.toString());
    }
```

The `main()` method parses the XML document and calls `ElementUtils.findElements()` using various combinations of parameters.

```
public static void main(String args[]) {
    try {
        Document doc = parse("element.xml", false);
        Element root = doc.getRootElement();
        String uri = "http://company.com/sample";
        Element elemArray[];
        String data[], attr[], val[];

        elemArray = ElementUtils.findElements(root, uri, "elem",
                null, null, null);
        print(1, elemArray);

        elemArray = ElementUtils.findElements(root,
                "sample:elem", null, null, null);
        print(2, elemArray);

        elemArray = ElementUtils.findElements(root, "elem",
                null, null, null);
        print(3, elemArray);

        data = new String[] {
          "1", "2"
        };
        elemArray = ElementUtils.findElements(root, null, data,
                null, null);
        print(4, elemArray);

        elemArray = ElementUtils.findElements(root, "array",
                null, null, null);
        print(5, elemArray);

        Element array = elemArray[0];

        elemArray = ElementUtils.findElements(array, null, null,
                null, null);
        print(6, elemArray);

        attr = new String[] {
          "attr"
        };
        val = new String[] {
          "b"
        };
        elemArray = ElementUtils.findElements(array, null, null,
                attr, val);
        print(7, elemArray);

        attr = new String[] {
```

```
              "attr"
            };
            val = new String[] {
              "a"
            };
            data = new String[] {
              "4"
            };
            elemArray = ElementUtils.findElements(array, null, data,
                attr, val);
            print(8, elemArray);

            attr = new String[] {
              "attr", "id"
            };
            val = new String[] {
              "a", "e5"
            };
            elemArray = ElementUtils.findElements(array, null, null,
                attr, val);
            print(9, elemArray);

        } catch (Exception e) {
          e.printStackTrace();
          System.exit(1);
        }
      }
    }
```

Sample element.xml

```
<?xml version="1.0" encoding="utf-8"?>
<sample:sample xmlns:sample="http://company.com/sample">
  <sample:elem attr="a" id="e1"> 1
    <sample:elem attr="b" id="e2"> 1 2
      <sample:elem attr="c" id="e3"> 1 2 3
      </sample:elem>
    </sample:elem>
  </sample:elem>
  <array id="e4">
    <elem attr="a" id="e5"> 1 </elem>
    <elem attr="b" id="e6"> 2 </elem>
    <elem attr="c" id="e7"> 3 </elem>
    <elem attr="a" id="e8"> 4 </elem>
    <elem attr="b" id="e9"> 5 </elem>
  </array>
</sample:sample>
```

Output

```
> java ElementSample

*** 1 *** e1 e2 e3
*** 2 *** e1 e2 e3
*** 3 *** e5 e6 e7 e8 e9
*** 4 *** e2 e3
*** 5 *** e4
*** 6 *** e4 e5 e6 e7 e8 e9
*** 7 *** e6 e9
*** 8 *** e8
*** 9 *** e5
```

Collecting Character Data

This class contains a method for extracting the data contained by a JDOM node. If the node is an Element or Entity instance, the data might be split in adjacent String and CDATA nodes. Comments may also act as splitters. Logically, however, only sub-elements and processing instructions split the data. An application might not want to be bothered by a CDATA section, an entity reference or a comment separating the text maintained in two String objects.

Source DataUtils.java

```java
import org.jdom.CDATA;
import org.jdom.Comment;
import org.jdom.Element;
import org.jdom.Entity;

import java.util.Iterator;
import java.util.List;
import java.util.Vector;

public class DataUtils {
```

The getData() method extracts the character data contained by a node. If the node is a String or a CDATA section, this will return the node's data. Otherwise, it iterates over its children and collects the character data in a string array. Each component of this array is the concatenation of the data contained by adjacent String and CDATA nodes after the entity references were replaced with their values. Therefore, the array has multiple components only if sub-elements or processing instructions separate the character data. Note that the data contained by sub-elements is not included. If the node contains no data, a string array containing an empty string is returned.

```java
    public static String[] getData(Object node) {
        Vector vector = new Vector();
        StringBuffer buf = new StringBuffer();
        getDataImpl(node, buf, vector);
        if (buf.length() > 0) {
```

```
      vector.add(buf.toString());
    }
    String array[] = new String[vector.size()];
    for (int i = 0; i < array.length; i++) {
      array[i] = (String) vector.get(i);
    }
    if (array.length == 0) {
      array = new String[] {
        ""
      };
    }
    return array;
  }
```

The `getDataImpl()` method implements the data extraction mechanism. The `getData()` method calls `getDataImpl()` passing as parameters an empty string buffer and an empty vector. This method iterates over the children of the given node and appends the data of the `String` and `CDATA` nodes to the given string buffer. The method is called recursively for each `Entity` so that their data can be collected, `comments` are ignored.

When this method finds a child node that acts as data separator (a sub-element or processing instruction), the content of the string buffer (if any) is added to the vector and the buffer is emptied. The `getData()` method will convert the vector to a `String` array.

```
private static void getDataImpl(Object node, StringBuffer
        buf, Vector vector) {
  if (node instanceof String) {
    buf.append((String) node);
    return;
  }
  if (node instanceof CDATA) {
    buf.append(((CDATA) node).getText());
    return;
  }

  List content = null;
  if (node instanceof Element) {
    content = ((Element) node).getMixedContent();
  } else if (node instanceof Entity) {
    content = ((Entity) node).getMixedContent();
  }
  if (content == null) {
    return;

  }
  Iterator iterator = content.iterator();
  while (iterator.hasNext()) {
    Object child = iterator.next();
    if (child instanceof String) {
```

```
                buf.append((String) child);
            } else if (child instanceof CDATA) {
                buf.append(((CDATA) child).getText());
            } else if (child instanceof Entity) {
                getDataImpl(child, buf, vector);
            } else if (!(child instanceof Comment)) {
                if (buf.length() > 0) {
                    vector.add(buf.toString());
                    buf.setLength(0);
                }
            }
        }
    }
}
```

Data Collection

This example uses the DataUtils class to collect the data contained by an element. After parsing the data.xml file using the parse() method inherited from JDOMPrinter, the main() method gets the root element of the document using the getRootElement() method defined by the org.jdom.Document class. The getData() method of DataUtils extracts all of the data of the element. The document is printed using the print() method inherited from JDOMPrinter.

Scource Data.java

```java
import org.jdom.Document;
import org.jdom.Element;

public class DataSample extends JDOMPrinter {

    public static void main(String args[]) {
        try {
            Document doc = parse("data.xml", false);
            Element root = doc.getRootElement();
            String data[] = DataUtils.getData(root);
            print(doc);
            println("\r\n*** Data of the root element:");

            for (int i = 0; i < data.length; i++) {
                println("" + i + ": \"" + data[i] + "\"");
            }
        } catch (Exception e) {
            e.printStackTrace();
            System.exit(1);
        }
    }
}
```

Sample data.xml

```
<?xml version="1.0" encoding="utf-8"?>
<!DOCTYPE sample [
  <!ENTITY thirdRowEntity "rd ro">
]>
<sample>
  first row <element>data within element</element>
  second row <!-- ignored comment -->
  thi&thirdRowEntity;w
  <![CDATA[fourth row]]>
  fifth row <?proc?>
  sixth row
</sample>
```

Output

```
> java DataSample
Document
  Element - sample
    String - first row
    Element - element
      String - data within element
    String - second row
    Comment - ignored comment
    String - thi
    Entity - thirdRowEntity
      String - rd ro
    String - w
    CDATA - fourth row
    String - fifth row
    ProcessingInstruction - proc -
    String - sixth row

*** Data of the root element:
0: "
  first row "
1: "
  second row
  third row
  fourth row
  fifth row "
2: "
  sixth row
  "
```

Creating a JDOM Tree

This example creates a JDOM tree composed of Document, Element, Comment, CDATA, ProcessingInstruction and String nodes. The populated document is printed using the print() method inherited from JDOMPrinter.

CreationSample.java

```java
import org.jdom.CDATA;
import org.jdom.Comment;
import org.jdom.Document;
import org.jdom.Element;
import org.jdom.ProcessingInstruction;

import org.jdom.output.XMLOutputter;

import java.io.FileOutputStream;

public class CreationSample extends JDOMPrinter {

  public static void main(String args[]) {
    try {
      Element root = new Element("root");

      Document doc = new Document(root);

      Element elem = new Element("elem");
      elem.addAttribute("attr", "value");
      elem.addContent("data");
      root.addContent(elem);

      CDATA cdata = new CDATA(">data<");
      root.addContent(cdata);

      Comment comment = new Comment("a comment");
      root.getMixedContent().add(0, comment);

      ProcessingInstruction proc = new
          ProcessingInstruction("target", "1 2 3");
      root.addContent(proc);

      print(doc);

      FileOutputStream out = new
          FileOutputStream("created.xml");
      try {
        XMLOutputter outputter = new XMLOutputter();
        outputter.setNewlines(true);
        outputter.setIndent(true);
        outputter.output(doc, out);
```

```
      }
      finally {
        out.close();
      }
    } catch (Exception e) {
      e.printStackTrace();
      System.exit(1);
    }
  }
}
```

Output

```
> java CreationSample
Document
  Element - root
    Comment - a comment
    Element - elem
      Attribute - attr - value
      String - data
    CDATA - >data<
    ProcessingInstruction - target - 1 2 3
```

Output created.xml

```
<?xml version="1.0" encoding="UTF-8"?>
<root>
  <!--a comment-->
  <elem attr="value">data</elem>
  <![CDATA[>data<]]>
  <?target 1 2 3?>
</root>
```

Filtering Based On JDOM and SAX

This example parses and filters a file using SAXBuilder of JDOM and XMLFilter of SAX. The
filter strips all attributes, character data and processing instructions, allowing only elements to
pass through. The FilteringSample class extends
org.xml.sax.helpers.XMLFilterImpl.

Source FilteringSample.java

```
import org.jdom.Document;
import org.jdom.JDOMException;
import org.jdom.input.SAXBuilder;
import org.jdom.output.XMLOutputter;

import org.xml.sax.Attributes;
```

```
import org.xml.sax.SAXException;
import org.xml.sax.helpers.AttributesImpl;
import org.xml.sax.helpers.XMLFilterImpl;

import java.io.File;

public class FilteringSample extends XMLFilterImpl {
```

The startElement() method calls the default implementation provided by XMLFilterImpl, but passes an empty attribute list.

```
public void startElement(String uri, String localName,
    String qName, Attributes attributes) throws
    SAXException {
  super.startElement(uri, localName, qName, new
    AttributesImpl());
}
```

The endElement() method calls the default implementation provided by XMLFilterImpl.

```
public void endElement(String uri, String localName,
    String qName) throws SAXException {
  super.endElement(uri, localName, qName);
}
```

The characters() method overrides the default implementation so that the character data can be ignored.

```
public void characters(char ch[], int start,
                       int length) throws SAXException {

  // Ignore character data
}
```

The ignorableWhitespace() method overrides the default implementation so that the indentation whitespace can be ignored.

```
public void ignorableWhitespace(char ch[], int start,
    int length) throws SAXException {

  // Ignore indentation whitespace
}
```

The processingInstruction() method overrides the default implementation so that any processing instruction can be ignored.

```
        public void processingInstruction(String target,
            String data) throws SAXException {

        // Ignore processing instruction
        }
```

The `parseAndFilter()` method parses and filters an XML document and returns a JDOM tree containing only elements.

```
        public static Document parseAndFilter(String path)
            throws JDOMException {

        // Create the JDOM SAXBuilder
        SAXBuilder saxBuilder = new SAXBuilder();

        // Set the filter
        saxBuilder.setXMLFilter(new FilteringSample());

        // Build the JDOM tree
        return saxBuilder.build(new File(path));
        }
```

The `main()` method parses the `filtering.xml` file using `parseAndFilter()` and the resulting JDOM tree is printed as XML.

```
        public static void main(String args[]) {
          try {

            // Parse and filter the file
            Document doc = parseAndFilter("filtering.xml");

            // Output the resulted document
            XMLOutputter outputter = new XMLOutputter();
            outputter.setNewlines(true);
            outputter.setIndent(true);
            outputter.output(doc, System.out);
          } catch (Exception e) {
            e.printStackTrace();
            System.exit(1);
          }
        }
      }
```

Sample filtering.xml

```
    <?xml version="1.0" encoding="utf-8"?>
    <sample first="1" second="2">
      <elem1 a1="v1"> text 1
```

```
      <elem2 a2="v2"> text 2
        <elem3 a3="v3"/> text 3
        <?proc4?> text 4
        <elem5 a5="v5"/> text 5
      </elem2> text
      <?proc6?> text 6
    </elem1> text
    <?proc7?> text 7
  </sample>
```

Output

```
> java FilteringSample
<?xml version="1.0" encoding="UTF-8"?>
<sample>
  <elem1>
    <elem2>
      <elem3 />
      <elem5 />
    </elem2>
  </elem1>
</sample>
```

Summary

In this chapter, we looked at examples using JDOM that compare and contrast with the DOM versions in Chapter 3. JDOM looks to be a more intuitive and natural approach for integrating XML-aware code into the Java platform, and we keenly await a stable release and acceptance into the Java API through the Community Process.

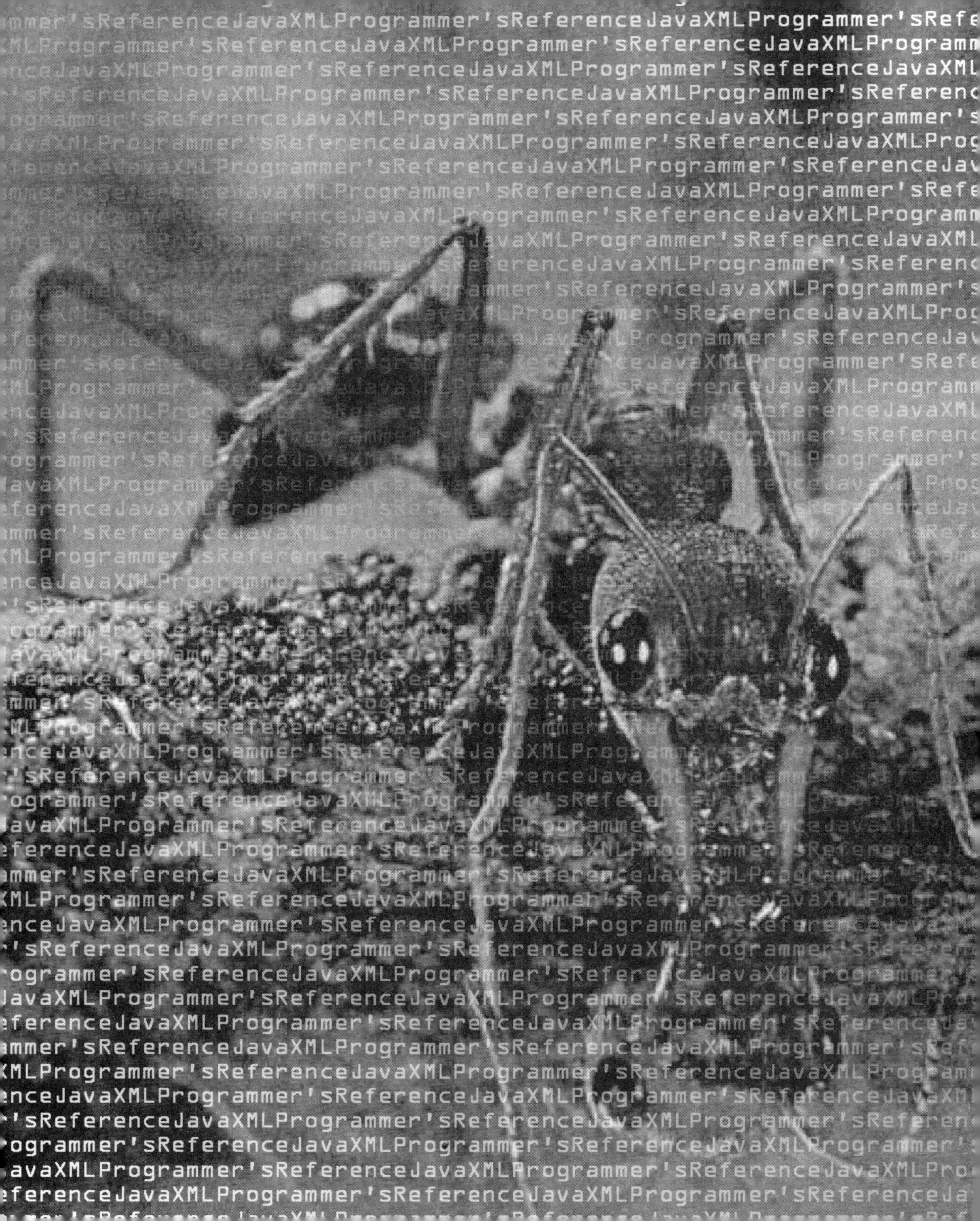

Oracle XDK

The Oracle XML Developers Kit (XDK) is Oracle's collection of XML-based tools, and is available for Java, C++, and PL/SQL. At one level, the Java XDK competes with the Apache XML toolset. At another level, the XDK has some exciting database related tools that make it easy to interact with an Oracle database.

This chapter is not meant to be a tutorial or complete reference on Oracle or XDK as a whole (that is the subject for a whole book), but to introduce those parts of the XDK most relevant to the working Java programmer. It provides a framework and reference point for programmers intending to, or considering, using Oracle XML tools along with other Java XML tools covered in this book.

The Oracle XDK is commercial software, not open source; nor is it GNU Public Licensed software. You can purchase XDK Support Services from Oracle if you have a commercial license. In fact, Oracle XDK is the only commercial XML development kit. This could be important as many companies will not even consider using open source software, simply because no official support arrangement is available.

Many would argue that the converse is more appropriate, that for all practical purposes, open-source software is more stable because you can fix the code yourself or get help from the thousands of enthusiasts on the web. Open-source projects like the Apache HTTP Server can rival, in features and stability, its commercial brethren (and in fact Apache is the HTTP server embedded in Oracle iAS). At the other extreme, since anything can be GNU Public Licensed, the software might simply be of very poor quality. In reality, the decision depends on your application requirements and the business environment in which you will use XDK.

What is certain is that, commercial or not, the official documentation for the XDK is somewhat sparse. However, there are a couple of good books that cover working with Oracle XML tools in detail: *Building Oracle XML Applications*, Steve Meunch, O'Reilly, 2000, ISBN 1565926-91-9, and *Oracle 8i Application Programming with Java, XML, and PL/SQL*, Wrox Press, 2000, ISBN 1861004-84-2. There are also Oracle staff-monitored forums for Oracle XML programmers at http://technet.oracle.com/.

Obtaining Oracle XDK

You can currently download the versions of the Oracle XDK for Java described in this chapter from http://technet.oracle.com/tech/xml/xdk_java/. You may need a username and password to access the material, which you can get by registering (for free) at the Oracle Technology Network site.

As of Spring 2001, Oracle grants a **development license only** (which allows you to use the software only for development purposes). Any commercial or production usage, classroom teaching, or internal data processing operations, requires purchase of the appropriate licenses.

The Components of the XDK

The XDK is comprised of four major subcomponents described briefly in the following sections.

XML Parser Related Tools

Component	Description	Page
XML Parser	The parser classes support SAX, DOM, and and incorporates **XSL processing** within the same JAR, `xmlparserv2.jar`	393
XPath Extensions	Extensions to the DOM implementation are available for evaluating XPath expressions	397
XML Schema Processor	The Beta Release includes an XML Schema processor JAR file called `xschema.jar`. Schema validation is invoked directly by the parser, and this JAR just needs to be in the classpath.	401

XSU – XML SQL Utility

The XML SQL Utility is a JAR file `xsu12.jar` that provides powerful utilities which can take in an SQL query and a database connection and then convert the query's output to an XML document. The XSU supports all four primary SQL operations – INSERT, UPDATE, SELECT, and DELETE.

The key Java classes in `xsu12.jar` are `OracleXMLQuery` for querying the database and `OracleXMLSave` for inserting into, updating to, and deleting the database. The XSU can be used from within a Java program as well as from the command line.

XSQL Pages & Servlet

XSQL Pages are a special XML document format that embeds SQL statements into an XML script. The XSQL Page evaluator evaluates the SQL query and creates XML output. Depending on processing flags embedded in the XSQL file, the XML output can be manipulated in many ways. Most typically, it is used to transform the XML output into HTML using a standard reference to an XSL stylesheet.

Oracle wanted a utility that had the simplicity of JSP combined with the power of the XML SQL Utility. XSQL Pages are both more powerful and easier to use than the straight XSU. (In fact, structurally the XSQL Java classes are built on top of the XSU classes.) The download comes with a web application framework that enables relatively straightforward installation into a Java web container.

Component	Description	Page
XSQL Pages	XSQL Pages are a special XML document type that describe database operations to be performed (most typically a query). The database connections over which it may operate are stored in a configuration file called `XSQLConfig.xml` file. The output of these operations is always an XML document. When coupled with XSLT, complete web pages can be readily created from one (or more) database query(s).	418
XSQL Servlet	This is a Java servlet, which processes requests for XSQL pages. The `XSQLRequest` class processes the XSQL pages and creates any XML output from the database queries. The special file extension `.xsql` for XSQL pages is redirected to the servlet by means of server configuration, or the provided `web.xml` file.	423

Oracle XML Class Generator for Java

This toolkit has been under continuous development since 1999 and provides a mechanism for the generation of object templates in Java directly from DTDs or XML schemas. This is powerful stuff, and worthy of a book in its own right along with more recent initiatives such as the early access release of the Java Architecture for XML Binding (JAXB). We do not cover it here, but refer the reader to either of the two books mentioned in the opening section of this chapter.

XDK Versions and Feature Differences

Right now, Oracle has three different versions of the XDK that can be downloaded. XDK version 8.1.7.1.0A, identified by Oracle as the XDK 8i Production Release, was released in February 2001. The 9i Production Release 9.0.1.0.0 came out at the beginning of June 2001. A 9i Beta version 9.0.0.0.0A, identified by Oracle as the XDK Beta Release, was released in March 2001 and is still available from the Oracle Technology Network at the time of writing.

Surprisingly, Oracle does not yet provide support for newer standards like JAXP 1.1 and JDOM, but it is rumored that the next significant release of the XDK, with JAXP compatibility, will be associated with a further release of Oracle 9i database.

In fact, what the XML Parser/XDK does or does not support is confusing and very scantily documented. It can be summarized approximately as follows, using Oracle's own references to W3C Recommendations (or Candidate Recommendations) where appropriate:

Features	8i Production	9i Production
XML	XML 1.0	XML 1.0
SAX	SAX 1.0	SAX 2.0
DOM	DOM Level 1	DOM Level 2 Core Dom Level 2 Traversal

Table continued on following page

Features	8i Production	9i Production
Namespace Support	`http://www.w3.org/TR/1999/REC-xml-names-19990114`	`http://www.w3.org/TR/1999/REC-xml-names-19990114`
XSLT	1.0	1.0
DTD Validation	Yes	Yes
XML schema validation	No	`http://www.w3.org/TR/2000/CR-xmlschema-1-20001024`

To confuse matters futher, the XDK Beta Release is numbered prior to the 9i Production Release, but supports some enhancements, notably XSLT 1.1 and SAX events as output from XSL processing, that are not in the 9i Production Release.

Bear in mind that Production Releases seem to contain more advanced features than they claim to, but that the features actually claimed may be fairly well relied upon.

JDOM Support (Beta 6)

JDOM has support for both v1 and v2 Oracle parsers in the sense that its `adapters` package provides utility classes that can use the Oracle parsers as drivers to create a `www.w3c.dom.Document` from XML input.

By providing all necessary SAX 2.0 classes (some of which are not found in the Oracle parser package) it is possible for JDOM to use the Oracle v2 parser to instantiate an `org.jdom.SAXBuilder` and return an `org.jdom.Document`. See the example later on page 403.

Classpath Issues

You can install both versions of the XDK on the same machine. You can similarly install other Java XML parsers too. However, a single global classpath environment variable setting becomes a liability in this case.

Java's class loader uses a sequential search algorithm. It searches for class files (which can be embedded in JAR files), from left to right, as they are encountered on the classpath. The situation, where multiple XML parser JAR files are specified in the classpath, is atypical. The generic SAX API classes will then be found in multiple JAR files. The class loader will arbitrarily load a class file from the first JAR in the classpath, which contains the sought-after class. So if both Xalan and the XDK JAR files are in the classpath, it is extremely important that the intended JAR file be found first. If an implementation class is loaded from one JAR and the SAX classes (an incompatible version) are loaded from another JAR, then your programs will crash.

Signs of Classpath Problems

If the application gets a `java.lang.ClassNotFoundException`, then it can be assumed that either a necessary JAR file is missing from the classpath or the implementation parser classes are being loaded from the wrong JAR.

Occurrence of a `java.lang.NoSuchMethodError` indicates that one parser implementation has called methods in a different implementation. The conflict arises from two different implementations providing the interfaces (`org.xml.sax` or `org.w3c.dom`) for different versions of SAX or DOM.

Summarizing, when working with multiple Java XML parsers on one machine, unique classpath settings on the command line are mandatory. Do not use the global `CLASSPATH` environment variable.

The Core XML Parser

At the heart of the XDK are Oracle's XML Parser and XSLT Processor. The classes for these are contained in a single large JAR file, `xmlparserv2.jar`.

We will look at the API for the three main parser classes in the `oracle.xml.parser.v2` package: `XMLParser`, `SAXParser`, and `DOMParser`. The former is a base class which itself cannot be instantiated. The SAX and DOM parsers extend this class to provide a proprietary (with respect to JAXP) SAX 2.0 and DOM parsing API. We will look at XSLT processing later in the chapter.

The `SAXParser` class implements `org.xml.sax.XMLReader`, and it is in fact theoretically possible to implement a JAXP compatible `SAXParserFactory` that could return instances of the Oracle SAX parser. However, this has not yet been officially released by Oracle.

Confusingly, there is a class called `oracle.xml.parser.v2.DocumentBuilder`, however this does not extend `javax.xml.parsers.DocumentBuilder`, and support for DOM parser pluggability with JAXP also remains to be integrated.

Class XMLParser

oracle.xml.parser.v2

```
public class XMLParser

        implements oracle.xml.parser.v2.XMLConstants
```

This forms a base class for the two main parser implementations, `SAXParser` and `DOMParser`, that extend it. It cannot be instantiated itself as it has no public constructor and no static new instance methods.

It corresponds to the Xerces 1 base class `org.apache.xerces.framework.XMLParser`.

Parsing Methods

The standard input types are supported via the overloaded `parse()` methods: `org.xml.sax.InputSource`, `java.io.InputStream`, `java.io.Reader`, `java.lang.String` (representing a URL), and `java.net.URL`.

All the methods return `void`. The mechanism for registering content handlers or obtaining generated DOM documents is implemented in the two superclasses respectively.

There is a `reset()` method for resetting the parser ready for further processing.

Validation

Validation is activated by one of `setValidationMode(boolean)` or `setValidationMode(int)`. The former is the older method which just switches the validation on or off. The arguments taken by the latter are integer constants specified in `oracle.xml.parser.v2.XMLConstants` (see the example below). There are corresponding `getValidationMode()` methods to access the current validation status.

You can manually attach a DTD (represented by `oracle.xml.parser.v2.DTD`) to the parser, without having to rely on a `DOCTYPE` declaration in the instance document, using `setDocType()`. There is support in version 2.1.0 for also registering a schema instance on the parser with `setXMLSchema()`. Schemas are represented internally using the `oracle.xml.parser schema XMLSchema` object (this is in `xschema.jar`).

SAX Methods

A subset of the SAX registration methods is implemented in `XMLParser`: `get/setEntity Resolver()`, `get/setErrorHandler()`, and `setLocale()`. The others required for `org.xml.sax.XMLReader` are implemented in the superclass `SAXParser`. Methods for get/setting features on the underlying driver are supplied as `get/setAttribute()`.

Class SAXParser
oracle.xml.parser.v2

```
public class SAXParser
        extends oracle.xml.parser.v2.XMLParser
        implements
        org.xml.sax.XMLReader,
        org.xml.sax.Parser,
        oracle.xml.parser.v2.XMLConstants
```

SAX Methods

This class adds methods to the base class to make up implementations for both SAX 2.0 `XMLReader` and the deprecated SAX 1.0 `Parser`. The remaining handler registration methods are provided: `get/setContentHandler()`, `get/setDTDHandler()`, and for `Parser`, the deprecated `get/setDocumentHandler()`. Finally, `get/setFeature()` and `get/setProperty()` complete the `XMLReader` and `Parser` implementations.

Using SAX with the XDK

The traditional SAX method instantiates an implementation-specific SAX parser object. This parser object then implements the generic SAX object interfaces.

Example: XDK SAX Example

The following program implements a simple validating command-line SAX parser.

Source XdkSAX.java

```
import org.xml.sax.*;
import oracle.xml.parser.v2.*;

public class XdkSAX implements ErrorHandler {
```

A validating parser should always register an error handler. This class implements one:

```
public void warning(SAXParseException e)
    throws SAXException { throw e; }
public void error(SAXParseException e)
    throws SAXException { throw e; }
public void fatalError(SAXParseException e)
    throws SAXException { throw e; }

static public void main(String[] args) {
  if (args.length != 1) {
    System.err.println("Usage: XdkSAX URL");
    System.exit(1);
  }
```

Create an instance of Oracle's SAX parser:

```
SAXParser parser = new SAXParser();
```

In the latest release (XML Parser v2.1.0), you set the validation mode of the parser to one of the four types: NONVALIDATING, PARTIAL_VALIDATION, DTD_VALIDATION or SCHEMA_VALIDATION:

```
parser.setValidationMode(SAXParser.DTD_VALIDATION);
```

The older version, setValidationMode(boolean) only takes a boolean value rather than the integer value associated with the above constants. Note the constants are actually defined in oracle.xml.parser.v2.XMLContants, which is implemented by SAXParser. There is very little documentation on the large number of constants in this interface. Here we set a new instance of this object as the error handler for our parser:

```
parser.setErrorHandler(new XdkSAX());

try {
  parser.parse(args[0]);
  System.out.println("Parse successful: " + args[0]);
```

```
        }
        catch (java.io.IOException i) {
            System.out.println(i.toString());
        }
        catch (SAXException e) {
          System.out.println(e.toString());
        }
    }

    }
```

You can find out about using the Jakarta Ant to build and run the complete example code of this chapter in Appendix A along with further detail about configuring your system and obtaining the packages.

Class DOMParser
oracle.xml.parser.v2

```
public class DOMParser

       extends oracle.xml.parser.v2.XMLParser

       implements oracle.xml.parser.v2.XMLConstants
```

Note this class should eventually be superceded by an extension of the abstract `javax.xml.parsers.DocumentBuilder` to make the implementation compatible with JAXP. In the meantime it packs a number of `parseDTD()` operations for DTD parsing, and adds a number of proprietary utilities for reporting on and configuring a DOM parse operation.

The hard parsing work is already implemented in the underlying `XMLParser` class. Note the basic pattern for returning an `org.w3c.dom.Document` is to parse with one of the methods defined in the subclass `XMLParser` (above) and then to call `getDocument()` on the parser, as seen in the example below.

Example: XDK DOM Example

The following changes to the SAX example above implement a simple command-line validating DOM parser:

Source XdkDOM.java

```java
import org.w3c.dom.*;
import org.xml.sax.*;
import oracle.xml.parser.v2.*;

public class XdkDOM {

  static public void main(String[] args) {
    if (args.length != 1) {
      System.err.println("Usage: java XdkDOM filename");
      System.exit(1);
    }

    DOMParser parser = new DOMParser();
    parser.setValidationMode(XMLParser.DTD_VALIDATION);
    parser.showWarnings(true);
    parser.setDebugMode(true);
```

Note we can reuse our XdkSAX class as an error handler:

```java
    parser.setErrorHandler(new XdkSAX());

    try {
      parser.parse(args[0]);
      Document doc = parser.getDocument();
      System.out.println("Parse successful: " + args[0]);
    } catch (java.io.IOException i) {
      System.out.println(i.toString());
    } catch (SAXException e) {
      System.out.println(e.toString());
    }
  }
}
```

XDK XPath Extensions for DOM

Oracle's XDK provides some very useful XPath query methods. They are part of the XMLNode implementation class (of the DOM Node interface). An XPath query can return either a collection of Nodes (as a NodeList) or a single Node.

XPath expressions (or patterns) are commonly used in XSL template definitions as the value of the match attribute in an <xsl:template> command.

XPath-Related Methods in Class XMLNode

XMLNode is Oracle's implementation of the DOM Node interface. It has several XPath query methods that you can use from an XDK DOM program.

With relative XPath locator expressions, the context node is the same as the XMLNode upon which the XPath-related methods are called.

Class XMLNode
oracle.xml.parser.v2

```
public class XMLNode
        implements org.wc3.dom.Node
```

XPath Related Methods

```
public NodeList selectNodes(String pattern)
        throws XSLException
```

```
public Node selectSingleNode(String pattern)
        throws XSLException
```

```
public String valueOf(String pattern) throws XSLException
```

XPath Extension Methods

selectNodes() returns a NodeList containing all of the nodes that match the XPath pattern.

Using the NodeList Methods

selectSingleNode() returns a single Node which is the first node that matches the XPath pattern.

valueOf() similarly returns the self::text() value for that first matching node.

ClassifiedAds.xml is a sample XML file. It is queried by the following demonstration program using XPath. The Classified Ads file is a simplified extract of fictional advertisements from a newspaper's Classified Ads section.

Example: Using Oracle XPath Methods

This program has an XPath expression, which is the search pattern on the input XML document. The resulting NodeList is then iterated over to print out the matching elements' names and their type attributes. In the sub-examples following, we will change the XPath match expression several times and show how that affects the program's output:

Source XpathDemo.java

```java
import java.io.*;
import java.net.*;
import org.w3c.dom.*;
import oracle.xml.parser.v2.*;
```

```java
public class XpathDemo {
  static public void main(String[] argv) {
    try {
      if (argv.length != 1) {
        System.err.println(
          "Usage: java XpathDemo filename");
        System.exit(1);
      }

      DOMParser parser = new DOMParser();

      // Generate a URL from the filename.
      URL url = URLutil.makeURL(argv[0]);

      // Parse the document.
      parser.parse(url);
      Document doc = parser.getDocument();

      String match =
        "/ClassifiedAds/category[@type='Rentals']";

      // String match = "/ClassifiedAds//category";
      // String match = "/ClassifiedAds/category";
      NodeList list = ((XMLNode) doc).selectNodes(match);

      // Print out the resultant Category names and types
      Node node = null;
      for (int i = 0; (node = list.item(i)) != null; i++) {
        switch (node.getNodeType()) {
        case Node.ELEMENT_NODE: {
          Element ele = (Element) node;
          String tag = ele.getTagName();
          String type = ele.getAttribute("type");

          System.out.println(tag + ": " + type);
        }
        }
      }
      System.out.println("Successful XPATH evaluation");
    } catch (Exception e) {
      System.out.println(e.getMessage());
    }
  }
}
```

Sample classifiedAds.xml

```xml
<?xml version="1.0"?>
<ClassifiedAds>
  <category type="Rentals">
    <ad>The Old Vicarage - Grantchester</ad>
    <ad>30 Almond Avenue - Ealing</ad>
  </category>
  <category type="HelpWanted">
    <category type="Computer Science">
      <category type="XML">
        <ad>One year's experience required</ad>
      </category>
      <category type="Java">
        <ad>Wrox Enterprises</ad>
      </category>
    </category>
  </category>
  <category type="For Sale">
    <category type="Furniture">
      <ad>Love Seat - in good condition</ad>
    </category>
    <category type="Musical Instruments">
      <ad>Grand Piano - Steinway</ad>
      <ad>Clarinet - only one owner</ad>
    </category>
  </category>
</ClassifiedAds>
```

Example Expression: /ClassifiedAds//category

The XPath expression /ClassifiedAds//category finds all the <category> elements that are descendants (children, grandchildren, etc.) of the root <ClassifiedAds> element.

The // is a shortcut for the more formal notation /descendants-or-self::node()/ (called in XPath lingo, a "descendant-or-self axis"). A single slash selects the children of the node to the left of the slash. A double slash finds all descendants, which can be nested to any depth (as children, grandchildren, great grandchildren, etc.).

This is the resultant output from using this pattern on ClassifiedAds.xml. Note that it matches all <category> elements occurring inside the root <ClassifiedAds> element.

This is the command line invocation:

```
> java XpathDemo file:src/oracle/classifiedAds.xml


category: Rentals
category: HelpWanted
```

```
category: Computer Science
category: XML
category: Java
category: For Sale
category: Furniture
category: Musical Instruments
Successful XPATH evaluation
```

Example Expression: /ClassifiedAds/category

Let's further restrict the selection to just the direct children category elements – not all descendant category elements. This is the correct XPath expression: "/ClassifiedAds/category". The only change was to change the double slash to a single slash. Now only the direct children nodes should be selected.

```
> java XpathDemo file:src/oracle/classifiedAds.xml

category: Rentals
category: HelpWanted
category: For Sale
Successful XPATH evaluation
```

Example Expression: /ClassifiedAds/category [@type='Rentals']

Finally, let's restrict the category elements to those having a type attribute that equals Rentals. The XPath expression /ClassifiedAds/category[@type='Rentals'] finds the children <category> elements that satisfy the predicate [@type='Rentals']. An XPath predicate applies a conditional test to the nodes initially selected by the locator portion of the expression. If the predicate evaluates to false, then the selected Node is removed from the resultant NodeList.

```
> java XpathDemo file:src/oracle/classifiedAds.xml

category: Rentals
Successful XPATH evaluation
```

XML Schema Validation and the XDK

The Oracle XML Schema Processor is one of the rare viable tools out there for the working Java XML programmer. One of the few alternatives is Xerces-J from the Apache XML Project. Support for schemas has been incorporated into the XDK since early 2000. The Java classes that perform XML schema validation are contained within a separate JAR file called, appropriately enough, xschema.jar. Make sure it is in your classpath setting.

This example uses serviceconfigurationXSD.xml and its associated XML schema file serviceconfiguration.xsd (see Chapter 12).

The `xsi:schemaLocation` attribute of the root `<ServiceConfiguration>` element states that the file `serviceconfiguration.xsd` contains type definitions in the specified namespace `http://www.wrox.com/javaxmlref`. For example:

```
<ServiceConfiguration
    xmlns:xsi="http://www.w3.org/2000/10/XMLSchema-instance"
    xsi:schemaLocation="http://www.wrox.com/javaxmlref
      serviceconfiguration.xsd"
    xmlns="http://www.wrox.com/javaxmlref">
```

Example: Schema Validation

This example code is only slightly different from the earlier example using the traditional SAX XDK parsing approach. The only change needed (from that earlier example) is to explicitly enable XML schema validation.

Source XdkXSchema.java

```java
import java.io.*;
import java.net.*;
import org.w3c.dom.*;
import oracle.xml.parser.v2.*;

public class XdkXSchema {
  static public void main(String[] args) {
    try {
      if (args.length != 1) {
        System.err.println("Usage: java XdkXSchema file");
        System.exit(1);
      }

      DOMParser parser = new DOMParser();
      parser.showWarnings(true);
      parser.setErrorHandler(new XdkSAX());
```

This is the old method of setting schema validation:

```java
      //parser.setValidationMode(false);
      //parser.setSchemaValidationMode(true);
```

And this is the new method:

```java
      parser.setValidationMode(DOMParser.SCHEMA_VALIDATION);

      parser.parse(args[0]);
      Document doc = parser.getDocument();

      System.out.println("Successful XSchema validation");
    } catch (Exception e) {
```

```
        System.out.println(e.getMessage());
    }
  }
}
```

This is how we invoke this on the command line:

```
> java XdkXSchema serviceconfigurationXSD.xml
```

```
Successful XSchema validation
```

It almost looks like no validation is being performed. To see what happens when validation fails, we will introduce some errors and re-run the test.

In `serviceconfigurationXSD.xml`, add an invalid attribute to `<user>`, `name="bob"`:

```
<User name="bob">test</User>
<Password>test</Password>
<ResultSetType>4</ResultSetType>
```

And run the command again:

```
> java XdkXSchema serviceconfigurationXSD.xml
```

```
Attribute 'name' not expected.
```

If you try setting `<ResultSetType>` content to an incorrect value (it must be between 1 and 4 according to the schema), you will get a result like this:

```
Invalid text '12' in element: 'ResultSetType'
```

Using JDOM (Beta 6) with the XDK

JDOM is an exciting replacement for the more cumbersome DOM API, and it is only for Java. However, it has not yet stabilized into a standard. The current version is beta 6, and as time goes on, other beta versions may become available and eventually a true JDOM standard should be available. At the same time it could become a Java platform standard through the Java Specification Request Process – see http://jcp.org/jsr/detail/102.jsp.

Out of the box, the XDK does not currently support JDOM. If you try and use it with just the XDK JAR files, you will get a `java.lang.ClassNotFoundException` related to the absence of the classes `org.xml.sax.ext.LexicalHandler` and `org.xml.sax.ext.DeclHandler`. The XDK does not provide a couple of classes that JDOM expects.

There is a simple workaround. The trick here is to include the Xerces JAR file, `xerces.jar` in the classpath. It is extremely important that it follow is the XDK's `xmlparserv2.jar` in the classpath – otherwise, the Xerces parser will be loaded first and not the XDK's.

Example: First SAX Example

Here JDOM is to parse an input file into an in-memory JDOM tree. Using an instance of the JDOM XMLOutputter class, the JDOM tree is then printed back out to System.out.

Source XdkJDOM.java

```
import java.io.*;
import org.jdom.*;
import org.jdom.input.*;
import org.jdom.output.*;

public class XdkJDOM {
  static public void main(String[] argv) {
    try {
      if (argv.length != 1) {
        System.err.println("Usage: java XdkJDOM filename");
        System.exit(1);
      }

      SAXBuilder builder = new
        SAXBuilder("oracle.xml.parser.v2.SAXParser");

      // Create the document by parsing an XML file
      Document doc = builder.build(new File(argv[0]));

      // Spit out the document, showing same as input
      XMLOutputter fmt = new XMLOutputter();
      fmt.output(doc, System.out);

      System.out.println("Successful JDOM parse");
    } catch (Exception e) {
      System.out.println(e.getMessage());
    }
  }
}
```

This is the Java command line invocation. Note the use of the -verbose option. We want to be certain that JDOMs internal mechanisms are not picking up another parser driver from somewhere. This option streams out class names as the Java runtime loads them in:

```
> java -verbose XdkJDOM troubleticket.xml

<!-- Unformatted XML output not shown -->
Successful JDOM parse
```

Traditional XSL Translation

Oracle XDK (in both the Production and Beta releases) supports the XSL 1.0 and 1.1 standards respectively. Some calls to proprietary XDK methods are needed to create an application that does XSL transformation. This example source code takes an XML URL and a XSL stylesheet URL and transforms the XML URL to the standard output.

```java
import java.io.*;
import java.net.*;
import org.w3c.dom.*;
import oracle.xml.parser.v2.*;

public class XdkXSL {
  static public void main(String[] argv) {
    try {
      if (argv.length != 2) {
        System.err.println(
          "Usage: java XdkXSL xmlFile(orUrl) xslFile(orURL)");
        System.exit(1);
      }

      DOMParser parser = new DOMParser();

      // Generate a URL from the filename.
      URL xmlUrl = URLutil.makeURL(argv[0]);
      URL xslUrl = URLutil.makeURL(argv[1]);

      parser.showWarnings(true);    // Show warnings

      parser.parse(xmlUrl);
      XMLDocument doc = parser.getDocument();

      XSLProcessor processor = new XSLProcessor();
      XSLStylesheet sheet = new
      XSLStylesheet(xslUrl.openStream(), null);

      processor.processXSL(sheet, doc, System.out);

      System.out.println("\nSuccessful XSL transformation");
    } catch (Exception e) {
      System.out.println(e);
      e.printStackTrace();
    }
  }
}
```

The oracle class `XSLProcessor` performs XSL transformations. It provides multiple `processXSL()` variant methods. In this chapter, only the most general will be thrown. Here is its prototype declaration:

```java
public void processXSL(XSLStylesheet xsl, XMLDocument
                       xml, java.io.OutputStream os)
       throws XSLException, java.io.IOException
```

Parameters

Parameter	Description
xml	Oracle DOM object created from parsing in the input XML file
xsl	Oracle stylesheet object created by parsing in the XSL stylesheet file
os	Output stream to write the output XML document to

An XSL Example

One example of using XSL is filtering out all of the classified ads that do not fall under the category type of HelpWanted from the input file classifiedAds.xml.

The goal of this example is to create an output XML file that has all of the ads that fall under a specific category type. Category types can be nested to any level. For instance, the HelpWanted category might have sub-categories called Programming, Cooking, Carpentry, etc.

This example ignores the intermediate sub-categories – instead all HelpWanted-related ads are output.

Example: Using the XDK StyleSheet Processor

Here is a test harness for the XSL processor.

Sample findAds.xsl

```
<?xml version="1.0" ?>
<xsl:stylesheet version="1.0"
  xmlns:xsl="http://www.w3.org/1999/XSL/Transform">
<xsl:output method="xml" indent="yes"/>

<xsl:template match="ClassifiedAds">
  <xsl:apply-templates select="descendant::category[@type='HelpWanted']"/>
</xsl:template>

<xsl:template match="category">
    <adsUnderCategory>
       <xsl:attribute name="type">
          <xsl:value-of select="@type"/>
       </xsl:attribute>
       <xsl:apply-templates select="descendant::ad"/>
    </adsUnderCategory>
</xsl:template>

<xsl:template match="ad">
  <xsl:copy-of select="."/>
</xsl:template>

</xsl:stylesheet>
```

Testing the XDK XSL Example

This is the command line invocation:

```
> java XdkXSL src/oracle/classifiedAds.xml
    src/oracle/findAds.xsl
```

which produces this output:

```
<?xml version = '1.0' encoding = 'UTF-8'?>
<adsUnderCategory type="HelpWanted">
    <ad>One year's experience required</ad>
    <ad>Wrox Enterprises</ad>
</adsUnderCategory>
Successful XSL transformation
```

XML SQL Utility (XSU)

The Oracle XML SQL Utility is the base level for converting SQL queries into XML and conversely converting XML and storing it into the database. The more advanced (and simpler to use) XSQL Pages are implemented on top of the lower-level XSU Java implementation classes.

The XSU depends on the mapping from SQL resultsets into a corresponding XML document. Oracle has a well-defined methodology whereby an SQL query resultset is converted into XML, which has an analogous element hierarchy to the underlying database schema.

The XSU supports the 4 basic SQL operations from the Java programming level: SELECT, INSERT, UPDATE, and DELETE. The command line XSU Java program OracleXML only supports either SELECT or INSERT. (This restriction might be dropped in future versions.)

Installation

The XML SQL Utility is comprised of a single JAR file, xsu12.jar. For JDK 1.1.x, there is a different JAR file, xsu111.jar. The first, xsu12.jar, depends on a minimum of JDK 1.2. Both xsu12.jar and xmlparserv2.jar must be in the classpath.

The Oracle JDBC drivers, installed with Oracle's Client database are required. The appropriate JDBC ZIP file (for some reason, Oracle does not provide a JAR version) must be in the classpath.

JDBC Connections

In practice, three things are needed to establish a JDBC connection:

❑ **JDBC driver URL**
(such as: jdbc:oracle:thin:@dbserver:1521:database)
Typically the server hostname, server port, and database SID may need to be modified. See Oracle's JDBC documentation for details.

❑ **User name**
    This is the user name for the given database schema.

❑ **Password**
    This is the given database login's password.

Command Line Usage

The XSU provides two different Java programs – one supports just SELECT queries, while the other also supports INSERTs. (Note: The current XDK versions do not support UPDATEs and DELETEs from the command line.

OracleXML getXML

This program just performs select queries on the database and formats its output using the standard XSU SQL-XML mapping.

This is the usage for OracleXML getXML:

```
> java OracleXML getXML [options] SQLString
```

These are the most useful options to the getXML variant:

Option	Description
-user user/password	Authenticates the user, for example: −user scott/tiger
-conn jdbcConnectString	Identifies the JDBC database connection to use (for example: -conn jdbc:oracle:thin:@myServer:1521:ORCL)
-fileName file | SQLString	Takes either the SQL Query or a file containing it (for example: "SELECT * FROM emp")

OracleXML putXML

This program just performs SQL INSERTs to put the data into the specific table. The XSU XML-SQL mapping rules are used to convert the XML input to its SQL equivalents.

The usage for OracleXML putXML is as follows:

```
> java OraclXML putXML [options] SQLString
```

These are the most important options to the putXML version (in addition to the user and connection strings identical to getXML):

Option	Description
`-fileName file | -URL documentURL -xmlDoc "xml..."`	XML document filename or URL of XML document, or the actual XML document string
`tablename`	The table to insert the records into in the database

Oracle Example Database

All of the following demonstrations use the standard Oracle demonstration database `scott/tiger`. If this is not present, it can be installed using the file `<ORACLE_HOME>/rdbms/adim/scott.sql` and the default tables created using `<ORACLE_HOME>/sqlplus/demo/demobld.sql`. (This may require the assistance of your database administrator.)

All of the examples make queries on the `emp` table. To see the table schema definition, simple type this SQL command:

```
SQL> describe emp;

Name              Null?     Type
-----------       --------  ------------
EMPNO             NOT NULL  NUMBER(4)
ENAME                       VARCHAR2(10)
JOB                         VARCHAR2(9)
MGR                         NUMBER(4)
HIREDATE                    DATE
SAL                         NUMBER(7,2)
COMM                        NUMBER(7,2)
DEPTNO                      NUMBER(2)
```

The `Name` column is the attribute name. The `Null?` column states whether that column can have a `NULL` value (be undefined) or not. Finally, the `Type` column gives the Oracle datatype for that attribute.

Each of the examples in this chapter will use a single SQL select query. The intent of the examples is to show the many different ways the XSU and XSQL Pages can be used. The `SELECT` query below gets the employee ID, employee name, and the employee's job title. The output is ordered by employee name. From SQL*Plus the following command does the selection:

```
SQL> SELECT empno, ename, job FROM emp ORDER BY ename;

    EMPNO ENAME        JOB
--------- ----------   ---------
     7876 ADAMS        CLERK
     7499 ALLEN        SALESMAN
     7698 BLAKE        MANAGER
     7782 CLARK        MANAGER
     7902 FORD         ANALYST
     7900 JAMES        CLERK
     7566 JONES        MANAGER
     7839 KING         PRESIDENT
     7654 MARTIN       SALESMAN
     7934 MILLER       CLERK
     7788 SCOTT        ANALYST
```

```
7369  SMITH     CLERK
7844  TURNER    SALESMAN
7521  WARD      SALESMAN
```

14 rows selected.

XSU Command Line Example

This example queries the database and uses the default SQL-XML mapping to format the output XML document.

Here is the command line invocation (obviously varying according to your own Oracle connection address):

```
> java OracleXML getXML -user scott/tiger -conn
    jdbc:oracle:thin:@dbserver:1521:database "SELECT empno,
    ename, job FROM emp ORDER BY ename"
```

Here is an excerpt of the actual XML output.

Note that the root XML element, <ROWSET>, contains a sequence of <ROW> elements. Each <ROW> element corresponds to a single record chosen by the SELECT statement. Inside a <ROW> there are three different elements, <EMPNO>, <ENAME>, and <JOB>. These correspond to the EMPNO, ENAME, and JOB columns in the table emp. (Remember that SQL is case-insensitive – unlike XML – so emp and EMP refer to the same table).

```xml
<?xml version = '1.0'?>
<ROWSET>
    <ROW num="1">
        <EMPNO>7876</EMPNO>
        <ENAME>ADAMS</ENAME>
        <JOB>CLERK</JOB>
    </ROW>
    <ROW num="2">
        <EMPNO>7499</EMPNO>
        <ENAME>ALLEN</ENAME>
        <JOB>SALESMAN</JOB>
    </ROW>

...<!-- Further rows omitted for brevity.-->

    <ROW num="14">
        <EMPNO>7521</EMPNO>
        <ENAME>WARD</ENAME>
        <JOB>SALESMAN</JOB>
    </ROW>
</ROWSET>
```

Java Program Usage

The key class for processing SQL selection queries is `OracleXMLQuery`. The most important constructor takes a JDBC Connection and a SQL query string. The query is evaluated and its output can be requested as either a DOM document or as an XML document (returned as a `String`).

Class OracleXMLQuery

oracle.xml.sql.query

```
public class OracleXMLQuery
```

Constructors

```
public OracleXMLQuery(java.sql.Connection conn, java.sql.ResultSet rs)
public OracleXMLQuery(java.sql.Connection conn, String sql)
```

`OracleXMLQuery(Connection conn, ResultSet rs)` takes a JDBC connection and a JDBC `ResultSet` object as a source of SQL data.

`OracleXMLQuery(Connection conn, String sql)` takes a JDBC connection and a SQL statement, and evaluates the statement as source of SQL data.

Selected Retrieval Methods

`OracleXMLQuery` has 51 different methods, to keep this chapter from exploding in size; we have only mentioned a couple of the most interesting here.

```
public Document getXMLDOM()
public String getXMLString()
```

`getXMLDOM()` returns an `org.w3c.dom.Document` containing the resultant XSU-generated XML.

`getXMLString()` returns the XSU-generated XML document as a `String`.

Another way of using the XSU is to call its Java methods directly from a program that you write. This example program does exactly the same thing as the preceding `OracleXMLQuery getXML` example:

Example: Listing Employees

This file should test the XSU on the table of employees.

Source ListEmployeesXML.java

```java
import java.sql.*;
import oracle.xml.sql.query.OracleXMLQuery;

public class ListEmployeesXML {
  static public void main(String[] argv) {
    try {
      if (argv.length != 3) {
        System.err.println("Usage: java ListEmployeesXML
          JdbcConnectString user password");
        System.exit(1);
      }
      String sql = "SELECT empno, ename, job FROM emp ORDER
        BY ename";

      DriverManager.registerDriver(new
        oracle.jdbc.driver.OracleDriver());

      Connection conn = DriverManager.getConnection(argv[0],
        argv[1], argv[2]);

      OracleXMLQuery query = new OracleXMLQuery(conn, sql);

      System.out.println(query.getXMLString());
      conn.close();

    } catch (Exception e) {
      e.printStackTrace();
    }
  }
}
```

Though using the XSU to generate XML is interesting, it is typically not the desired final output report format. This program uses the XSLT processor to style the XML output using the XSL stylesheet that is specified.

```java
import java.sql.*;
import oracle.xml.parser.v2.*;
import oracle.xml.sql.query.OracleXMLQuery;

public class ListEmployeesXSL {
  static public void main(String[] argv) {
    try {
      if (argv.length != 4) {
        System.err.println("Usage: java ListEmployeesXSL
```

```
            XSLurl JdbcConnectString user password");
        System.exit(1);
    }
    String sql = "SELECT empno, ename, job " +
        "FROM emp ORDER BY ename";

    DriverManager.registerDriver(new
        oracle.jdbc.driver.OracleDriver());

    Connection conn = DriverManager.getConnection(argv[1],
        argv[2], argv[3]);

    OracleXMLQuery query = new OracleXMLQuery(conn, sql);

    XMLDocument doc = (XMLDocument) query.getXMLDOM();
    XSLProcessor processor = new XSLProcessor();
    java.net.URL xslUrl = URLutil.makeURL(argv[0]);

    XSLStylesheet sheet = new
        XSLStylesheet(xslUrl.openStream(), null);

    processor.processXSL(sheet, doc, System.out);

    conn.close();

    } catch (Exception e) {
        e.printStackTrace();
    }
  }
}
```

This example stylesheet, listEmployeesText.xsl, transforms input XML into a regular text file, not in XML or HTML format. Inside the XSL stylesheet is a <xsl:output .../> XSL command element. Its method is set to type "text". (The method can be set to one of XML, HTML, or text. The default is XML.)

The <xsl:template> fragments here have no XML or HTML elements, but are instead XML text nodes. These text nodes are output as is.

There is one exception: chains of whitespace are compressed down to a single blank. The numerous <xsl:text .../> XSLT elements output without modifying the whitespace. They output the whitespace exactly as it is in the input documents.

```
<?xml version="1.0" ?>
<xsl:stylesheet version="1.0"
xmlns:xsl="http://www.w3.org/1999/XSL/Transform">
<xsl:output method="text"/>

<xsl:template match="/page">
```

```
<xsl:text>
== Our Employees ==

</xsl:text>
<xsl:apply-templates select="ROWSET"/>
</xsl:template>

<xsl:template match="ROWSET">
<xsl:text>
 ID      Name         Job
==================================
</xsl:text>
     <xsl:apply-templates select="ROW"/>
</xsl:template>

<xsl:template match="ROW">
<xsl:value-of select="EMPNO"/><xsl:text>     </xsl:text>
<xsl:value-of select="ENAME"/><xsl:text>     </xsl:text>
<xsl:value-of select="JOB"/><xsl:text>
</xsl:text>
</xsl:template>

</xsl:stylesheet>
```

This is the formatted text report produced by this stylesheet:

```
 ID      Name         Job
==================================
7876    ADAMS     CLERK
7499    ALLEN     SALESMAN
7698    BLAKE     MANAGER
7782    CLARK     MANAGER
7902    FORD     ANALYST
7900    JAMES     CLERK
7566    JONES     MANAGER
7839    KING     PRESIDENT
7654    MARTIN     SALESMAN
7934    MILLER     CLERK
7788    SCOTT     ANALYST
7369    SMITH     CLERK
7844    TURNER     SALESMAN
7521    WARD      SALESMAN
```

The jagged third column is caused by the varying number of characters in each row's output for the second column. We will fix this using the XSL **extension mechanism** in a following example.

Formatting the Output – Adding XSL Extensions

To fixed the jagged third column in the previous example, the effective width for every item in a single column has to be the same across all rows. A function to blank pad the output of each column would be nice. But XSL does not support this feature. The next example illustrates usage of a couple XSL extension functions to correctly pad the report output.

Declaring XSL Extensions

The XDK supports the addition of new XSL functions. Any public Java method can be invoked from XPath, as long as the containing Java class has been registered as an XSL extension class. With the XDK's XSL, extension class registration is performed by declaring special namespaces – one per extension class. The namespace URI follows a precise pattern that tells the XSL processor which Java class to load. For an extension Java class named `mypackage.myClass`, the namespace declaration looks like:

```
xmlns:myPrefix=
    "http://www.oracle.com/XSL/Transform/java/myPackage.myClass"
```

The italicized parts of the declaration are the portions that need to be customized for each different extension class.

Let's say that `myClass` has a single method: `void doSomething()`
Then calls to it in an XPath expression look like:

```
<xsl:value-of select="myPrefix:doSomething()" />
```

Java to XPath Datatype Conversion

The basic internal XSL datatypes and their corresponding Java type declarations are:

XPath Datatype	Java Type
Boolean	boolean
Number	int, float, double
String	Java.lang.String
NodeSet	org.w3c.dom.NodeList
ResultTree	oracle.xml.parser.v2.XMLDocumentFragment

Static and Non-Static Java Methods

Both static and non-static Java methods can be invoked from XSL. For non-static methods, the first function argument in the XSL expression call must be a Java object instance. These object instances must be either constructed in an XSL expression or returned by another method call.

Java object instances can be stored in XSL variables. Inside another XSL expression that variable may be referenced by *$variableName*. This sample code fragment invokes the Java method `myPackage.myClass.getSomeObject()`, then stores the object in an XSL variable named *aVar*, and then finally gets that object's string representation by a call to its `toString()` method. Instead of using this Java expression `aVar.toString()`, the correct XSL expression has to be `toString(aVar)`.

```
<xsl:variable name="aVar" select="myPrefix:getSomeObject(): />
<xsl:value-of select="toString($aVar)" />
```

Calling a Java Constructor

Java constructors are mapped to the extension function 'new'. Overloading the new function with different constructor method parameters is supported. The rules on method overloading are more restrictive in XSL than in Java. It is possible to have certain constructor (and methods for that matter) overloading combinations that create ambiguities of which method to call. The types of `Number`, `String`, `Boolean`, and `ResultSet` are implicitly convertible *before* the Java method is selected.

An Extension Class to Pad Strings

This simple extension class provides two extension function methods. The `pad()` method blank pads out its string argument to the specified number of characters.

The `maxLen()` method takes as its input an entire `Node List`. The length of the longest string in the list is returned. (Implementation note: For element nodes, all of the text nodes enclosed by that element are concatenated together).

Finding the largest item in each column is the key to this whole process. XPath location expressions always return node lists, which are a collection of references to nodes in the DOM tree.

```
import org.w3c.dom.*;

public class StrUtil {

  public static String pad(String s, int length) {
    int padLen = Math.max(0, length - s.length());

    if (padLen == 0) {
      return s;

    }
    StringBuffer buf = new StringBuffer(s);
    for (int i = 0; i < padLen; i++) {
      buf.append(' ');
    }

    return buf.toString();
  }
```

Find the longest text node in the `NodeList`:

```
public static int maxLen(NodeList list) {
  int max = 0;
  for (int i = 0, cnt = list.getLength(); i < cnt; i++) {
    max = java.lang.Math.max(max, len(list.item(i)));
  }
  return max;
}
```

Find the length of the concatenated text nodes from this `Node`'s descendants-or-self:

```
static int len(Node item) {
  int _len = 0;

  switch (item.getNodeType()) {
```

```
        case Node.TEXT_NODE:
        case Node.CDATA_SECTION_NODE:
          return item.getNodeValue().length();
      default:
        NodeList list = item.getChildNodes();

        if (list == null) {
          return 0;

        }
        for (int i = 0, cnt = list.getLength(); i < cnt; i++) {
          _len += len(list.item(i));
        }
      }
      return _len;
    }
  }
```

The most difficult change, at least conceptually, is that for each column, the longest string in it must be found. In our jagged output example, it's the Employee Name column, ENAME, that is causing the problem. In the original example, the length of each name string varied from row to row. By padding all the items in that column to a specific size, the jagged edge is removed.

In this example, the XSL global variable, maxENAME, holds the length of the longest name string. It is calculated by the StrUtil.maxLen() method. That method's parameter is a node list. XPath is used to create the input node list. In this case, the correct XPath expression is:

/page/ROWSET/ROW/ENAME

The evaluation of this XPath expression creates the desired result set. It contains every ENAME element node in the document.

This is the modified XSL stylesheet listEmployeesPad.xsl. Note the strUtil namespace declaration. strUtil will be the prefix used to designate function calls to the extension StrUtil class.

```
<?xml version="1.0" ?>
<!-- this stylesheet creates a plain text report -->
<xsl:stylesheet version="1.0"
  xmlns:xsl="http://www.w3.org/1999/XSL/Transform"
  xmlns:strUtil="http://www.oracle.com/XSL/Transform/java/StrUtil"
>
<xsl:output method="text"/>

<!-- global variable holding the longest str in each category -->
<xsl:variable name='maxEMPNO' select="strUtil:maxLen(/page/ROWSET/ROW/EMPNO)"/>
<xsl:variable name='maxENAME' select="strUtil:maxLen(/page/ROWSET/ROW/ENAME)"/>
<xsl:variable name='maxJOB'   select="strUtil:maxLen(/page/ROWSET/ROW/JOB)"/>

<xsl:template match="/page">
<xsl:text>
== Our Employees ==

</xsl:text>
  <xsl:apply-templates select="ROWSET"/>
```

```
</xsl:template>

<xsl:template match="ROWSET">
<xsl:text>
 ID      Name         Job
=================================
</xsl:text>
    <xsl:apply-templates select="ROW"/>
</xsl:template>

<xsl:template match="ROW">
  <xsl:value-of select="strUtil:pad(EMPNO,  $maxEMPNO)"/><xsl:text>    </xsl:text>
  <xsl:value-of select="strUtil:pad(ENAME,  $maxENAME)"/><xsl:text>    </xsl:text>
  <xsl:value-of select="strUtil:pad(JOB,    $maxJOB)"/><xsl:text>
  </xsl:text>
</xsl:template>

</xsl:stylesheet>
```

Here is the formatted text report produced by this stylesheet:

```
ID      Name         Job
=================================
7876    ADAMS        CLERK
7499    ALLEN        SALESMAN
7698    BLAKE        MANAGER
7782    CLARK        MANAGER
7902    FORD         ANALYST
7900    JAMES        CLERK
7566    JONES        MANAGER
7839    KING         PRESIDENT
7654    MARTIN       SALESMAN
7934    MILLER       CLERK
7788    SCOTT        ANALYST
7369    SMITH        CLERK
7844    TURNER       SALESMAN
7521    WARD         SALESMAN
```

Examples of using the XML returned by XSU to display data in HTML or PDF are given in Chapter 16.

XSQL Pages

XSQL Pages makes it easy to do database queries and transform those query results into HTML. Before XSQL, the Java platform made it tough to consolidate data from a database query with HTML output. (More recently, custom JSP tag libraries have eased that integration problem.)

The fact that XML is being used (often under the covers) is irrelevant. XSQL Pages are easy to use. It makes little difference if they are accessed over the Web, by the xsql command-line utility, or through your own custom Java program. It beats any other alternative for a competent XML practitioner. (Some, might say that XSQL's dependence on XSL is a weakness – since XSL can be a tough language to master).

Installation

The XSQL Pages installation is more complex than for the XSU. The XSQL Page Processor and associated XSQL Servlet classes have to be installed on the actual Java servlet engine.

Fortunately, (for Windows users only) as part of XSQL Oracle provides the Web-to-go server, this is pre-configured to use XSQL. This is a limited, single-user server but it's useful for testing XSQL pages.

> *Oracle JDeveloper – since version 3.1 – also comes with the Web-to-go server. JDeveloper recognizes XSQL pages and will run them for you within its development environment.*

Oracle supports a wide variety of servlet engines and the installation steps are so varied between the engines, we will refer you to Oracle's documentation on XSQL Pages for installation details. These instructions can currently be found at:

http://technet.oracle.com/tech/xml/xsql_servlet/htdocs/relnotes.htm

However, Oracle's documentation does not include the reference servlet engine Tomcat 4.0, which we have used for all relevant examples in this book.

Installing XSQL with Tomcat 4.0

In the WEB-INF directory of XSQL (<XSQL_HOME>/WEB-INF) create two new directories, lib and classes. Copy <XSQL_HOME>/lib/XSQLConfig.xml to <XSQL_HOME>/WEB-INF/classes. See the section *JDBC Connections and XSQLConfig.xml* further down for more information on modifying this file for your database configuration.

Copy all these files:

```
<XSQL_HOME>/lib/classes12.zip
<XSQL_HOME>/lib/oraclexsql.jar
<XSQL_HOME>/lib/sax2.jar
<XSQL_HOME>/lib/xmlparserv2.jar
<XSQL_HOME>/lib/xsqlserializers.jar
<XSQL_HOME>/lib/xsu12.jar
```

to <XSQL_HOME>/WEB-INF/lib. Rename classes12.zip to something like oraclejdbc.jar. We do this, as Tomcat does not seem to autoload ZIPs from the web application lib folder (plus it's not a very good name either).

A server.xml file is provided with the code bundle (config/server.xml) for this book. If you are using this, simply copy it to <TOMCAT_HOME>/conf/server.xml. If you wish to modify your own server.xml file, add a new context to the <Host>section as follows, inserting the full path to the XSQL distribution directory (for example C:/xsql):

```
<Context path="/xsql" docBase="<XSQL_HOME>"
         reloadable="true" debug="0"/>
```

Place the example .xsql files from src/oracle somewhere in the <XSQL_HOME> directory, for example <XSQL_HOME>/demo/5202/. Start Tomcat and point your browser at:

http://localhost:5202/xsql/demo/5202/listEmployeesXML.xsql.

You should see a page of unprocessed XML generated from the database by the XSQL servlet.

Some problems were encountered using the XDK Beta Release version of XSU with this installation, but the Production Release worked flawlessly.

Configuration of Utility xsql.bat

The xsql.bat file (or xsql script on Unix/Linux) is the command line utility that allows you to evaluate the SQL query (which is embedded into the .xsql file) directly from the command line. The script needs to be checked and modified to match your own local environment settings.

JDBC Connections and XSQLConfig.xml

JDBC Connection information is stored in a global XSQLConfig.xml configuration file. The directory that holds the file must be added to the classpath.

The JDBC Connections are stored under the XSQLConfig/connectionDefs element. Here is an example connection specification:

Example: JDBC Connection Specification

Having added or modified a suitably named <connection> element, you would refer to this connection from within the <page> declaration below.

```
<connection name="demo">
  <username>scott</username>
  <password>tiger</password>
  <dburl>jdbc:oracle:thin:@dbserver:1521:database</dburl>
  <driver>oracle.jdbc.driver.OracleDriver</driver>
</connection>
```

```
<page connection="demo" xmlns:xsql="urn:oracle-xsql">
  ...
</page>
```

XSQL Pages Browser Usage

Once XSQL Pages has been installed on your Java Servlet engine, you can point your Web browser at an XSQL Page by simply typing in the URL of that page.

Depending on whether the XSQL Page outputs plain text, HTML, or XML, the appropriate display action will be taken by the browser. The type is set in the method attribute of the XSL stylesheet's <xsl:output> declaration. The default is XML output. If no stylesheet is used, then the output will also be the text/xml type by default.

If the servlet engine has not been configured to pass XSQL pages to the XSQL servlet for processing, the browser will simply display the original XSQL Page source code. In the Tomcat installation above, this dispatching is taken care of by the configuration setting in the web.xml file that comes ready bundled with XSQL Servlet.

XSQL Pages Command Line Usage

The usage for XSQL pages on the command line is:

```
> xsql xsqlFileURI [outFileName] [param1=value1 ... paramN=valueN]
```

This utility processes an XSQL page and outputs it to standard output, unless an output file has been specified. XSQL pages can have embedded XSL parameter expansions in them. These parameter name/value pairs may be specified on the command line.

Option	Description
`xsqlfileURI`	URL for the input XSQL file
`outputfile`	Pathname for the output XML file (optional)
`param_n=value_n`	Sets value for each numbered parameter

Note that the command-line script is a very simple interface to the class `oracle.xml.xsql.XSQLCommandLine`.

XSQL Pages Command Line

In the XSU section, an example of transforming the output XML to a text-formatted report was given. This XSQL `listEmployeesTEXT.xsql` file specifies the same SQL query plus the usage of `listEmployeesTEXT.xsl` for the XSL transformation. The processing command `<?xml-stylesheet ...?>` says which XSL file to use as the stylesheet for the transformation.

```xml
<?xml version="1.0"?>
<?xml-stylesheet type="text/xsl" href="listEmployeesText.xsl"?>
<page connection="demo" xmlns:xsql="urn:oracle-xsql">
   <xsql:query null-indicator="yes">
        SELECT empno, ename, job
          FROM emp
         ORDER BY ename
   </xsql:query>
</page>
```

Here, the `xsql.bat` command line utility is invoked on the preceding XSQL file example:

```
> xsql src/oracle/listEmployeesText.xsql
```

```
ID        Name        Job
=================================
7876      ADAMS       CLERK
7499      ALLEN       SALESMAN
7698      BLAKE       MANAGER
7782      CLARK       MANAGER
7902      FORD        ANALYST
7900      JAMES       CLERK
7566      JONES       MANAGER
7839      KING        PRESIDENT
```

```
7654    MARTIN    SALESMAN
7934    MILLER    CLERK
7788    SCOTT     ANALYST
7369    SMITH     CLERK
7844    TURNER    SALESMAN
7521    WARD      SALESMAN
```

This XSQL file (`listEmployeesXML.xsql`) does not transform the XML output at all. Note that there is no `xml-stylesheet` processing instruction.

```xml
<?xml version="1.0"?>
<page connection="demo" xmlns:xsql="urn:oracle-xsql">
  <xsql:query null-indicator="yes">
      SELECT empno, ename, job
        FROM emp
        ORDER BY ename
  </xsql:query>
</page>
```

Finally, this XSQL file (`listEmployees.xsql`) specifies the `listEmployees.xsl` file for the transformation. It generates HTML output.

```xml
<?xml version="1.0"?>
<?xml-stylesheet type="text/xsl" href="listEmployees.xsl"?>
<page connection="demo" xmlns:xsql="urn:oracle-xsql">
  <xsql:query null-indicator="yes">
      SELECT empno, ename, job
        FROM emp
        ORDER BY ename
  </xsql:query>
</page>
```

This template (`listEmployees.xsl`) transforms the output to HTML.

```xml
<?xml version="1.0" ?>
<xsl:stylesheet version="1.0" xmlns:xsl="http://www.w3.org/1999/XSL/Transform">
<xsl:output method="html" indent="yes"/>

<xsl:template match="/page">
  <html>
  <head> <title>Our Employees</title> </head>
  <body>
  <h2>Our Employees</h2>
    <xsl:apply-templates select="ROWSET"/>
  </body>
  </html>
</xsl:template>

<xsl:template match="ROWSET">
  <table cellspacing="2" cellpadding="2" border="1">
  <tr  align="center" bgcolor="#C0C0C0" >
    <th>ID</th>
```

```
      <td>Name</td>
      <td>Job</td>
    </tr>
      <xsl:apply-templates select="ROW"/>
    </table>
  </xsl:template>

  <xsl:template match="ROW">
    <tr>
      <td><xsl:value-of select="EMPNO"/></td>
      <td><xsl:value-of select="ENAME"/></td>
      <td><xsl:value-of select="JOB"/></td>
    </tr>
  </xsl:template>

</xsl:stylesheet>
```

Using XSQL Pages and Servlet from Java Programs

The key class for processing SQL selection queries is XSQLRequest. The most important constructor takes a JDBC connection and a SQL Query string. The query is evaluated and its output can be requested as either a DOM document or as an XML document (returned as a String).

Class XSQLRequest

oracle.xml.xsql

```
public class XSQLRequest
```

Constructors

```
public XSQLRequest(java.net.URL url)
```

```
public XSQLRequest(java.lang.String url)
```

XSQLRequest(URL url) creates an XSQL Request from a java.net.URL that corresponds to a XSQL page.

XSQLRequest(String url) creates an XSQL Request from a String url.

Selected Methods

process() writes the XSU generated XML document either an OutputStream or to a PrintWriter.

```
public void process(OutputStream os, PrintWriter err)
```

```
public void process(PrintWriter out, PrintWriter err)
```

Another way of using the XSU is to call its Java methods directly from a program that you write. This example program does exactly the same thing as the preceding one.

Example: Directly calling XSU

This file directly calls the XSU.

Source JavaXSQL.java

```java
import java.io.PrintWriter;
import oracle.xml.parser.v2.*;
import oracle.xml.xsql.XSQLRequest;

public class JavaXSQL {
  static public void main(String[] argv) {
    try {
      if (argv.length != 1) {
        System.err.println(
          "Usage: java ListEmployeesTextXSQL xsqlFile");
        System.exit(1);
      }

      java.net.URL xsqlUrl = URLutil.makeURL(argv[0]);

      // Create the XSQLRequest object from the inpout URL
      XSQLRequest request = new XSQLRequest(xsqlUrl);

      // Process the XSQL file, Ouput to System.out,
      // errors to System.err
      request.process(null, System.out, new
        PrintWriter(System.err));

    } catch (Exception e) {
      e.printStackTrace();
    }
  }
}
```

Performance and Scalability Issues

Current XML and XSLT solutions are relatively heavy-weight. The processing power needed to handle a single record output from a database is significant. In the real world, many applications sit on top of mountains of data. These applications need to be able to process millions of data records in a batch. XML's flexibility is unmatched. It works well with small batches of data. But will XML adequately scale to millions of data items?

For illustrative purposes, let's use a baseline of 100 database records from a small database table like scott.emp, the demonstration employee table that is pre-installed on all Oracle database instances.

Let's also use a query: SELECT * FROM emp. Here are the attributes in the emp table. There are 8 of them, making this a small-to-medium sized table.

```
EMPNO              NOT NULL  NUMBER(4)
ENAME                        VARCHAR2(10)
JOB                          VARCHAR2(9)
MGR                          NUMBER(4)
HIREDATE                     DATE
SAL                          NUMBER(7,2)
COMM                         NUMBER(7,2)
DEPTNO                       NUMBER(2)
```

This is a single record's worth of data in XML format:

```
<ROW num="1">
  <EMPNO>7876</EMPNO>
  <ENAME>ADAMS</ENAME>
  <JOB>CLERK</JOB>
  <MGR>7788</MGR>
  <HIREDATE>1987-05-23 00:00:00.0</HIREDATE>
  <SAL>1100</SAL>
  <COMM NULL="YES" />
  <DEPTNO>20</DEPTNO>
</ROW>
```

Nineteen DOM nodes will have to be created to store this record in memory. Internally there is more overhead than just 19 nodes. A fair assumption is that a minimum of 2000 objects will have to be allocated to store these 100 items in memory.

Doing a single XSL transformation might triple the memory requirements. XSL transformations are both memory and CPU-intensive.

Batching and Maximum Batch Sizes

The XSU assumes that in real-world usage, maximum query sizes would be enforced. Typically, the application would "page" through the whole collection of records, especially for large tables. So for a batch size of 100 records, 10,000 queries will be needed if the table has 1 million records in it.

How to Approach Scaling Problems

These are some strategies that you may wish to consider when tackling problems of scaling.

Use Adequate Hardware

For large-scale operations, you can increase the capacity by getting better hardware, or more servers. XML requires a lot of physical memory. DOM Processing is a memory hog and virtually every tool mentioned in this chapter is DOM-based.

Use Many Cheap Servers in a Clustered Setting

XML Parsing and Transformation is a very CPU-intensive activity. The Internet search site Google finds that their web-searching engines similarly impose high CPU utilization on their servers. Google discovered that using literally thousands of low-end PCs was a more efficient architecture than having a handful of very powerful boxes. In a single data center, Google typically hosts between 2000 and 5000 servers. To get good performance, Google has found that a single PC can only handle about two active queries at a time!

The lesson here is to distribute the CPU load of XML processing.

Prototyping and Benchmarking

In short:

❑ Expect scaling problems and tackle them early in an implementation project

❑ Be very alert to the trade-offs between richer functionality and better performance

❑ Test your architecture, early and often

❑ Prototype alternative solutions

How to Avoid XSL Transformations

The XML SQL Utility mapping can be modified to some extent when the XML documents are generated. You might be able to generate the final tags upfront, making it unnecessary to use XSL transformation upon large batches of data items.

Don't Ignore Non-XML Legacy Approaches

Evaluate Oracle's SQL Loader against doing the same operation with XML. A hybrid XML/legacy solution may have all the required features with substantially better performance.

Summary

Oracle provides a wide range of supported XML technologies. Each could be a book in its own right and we couldn't cover everything here. This chapter has provided a framework and starting point for working with Oracle XML, particularly for those migrating from other tools, or using Oracle tools in conjunction with other XML tools.

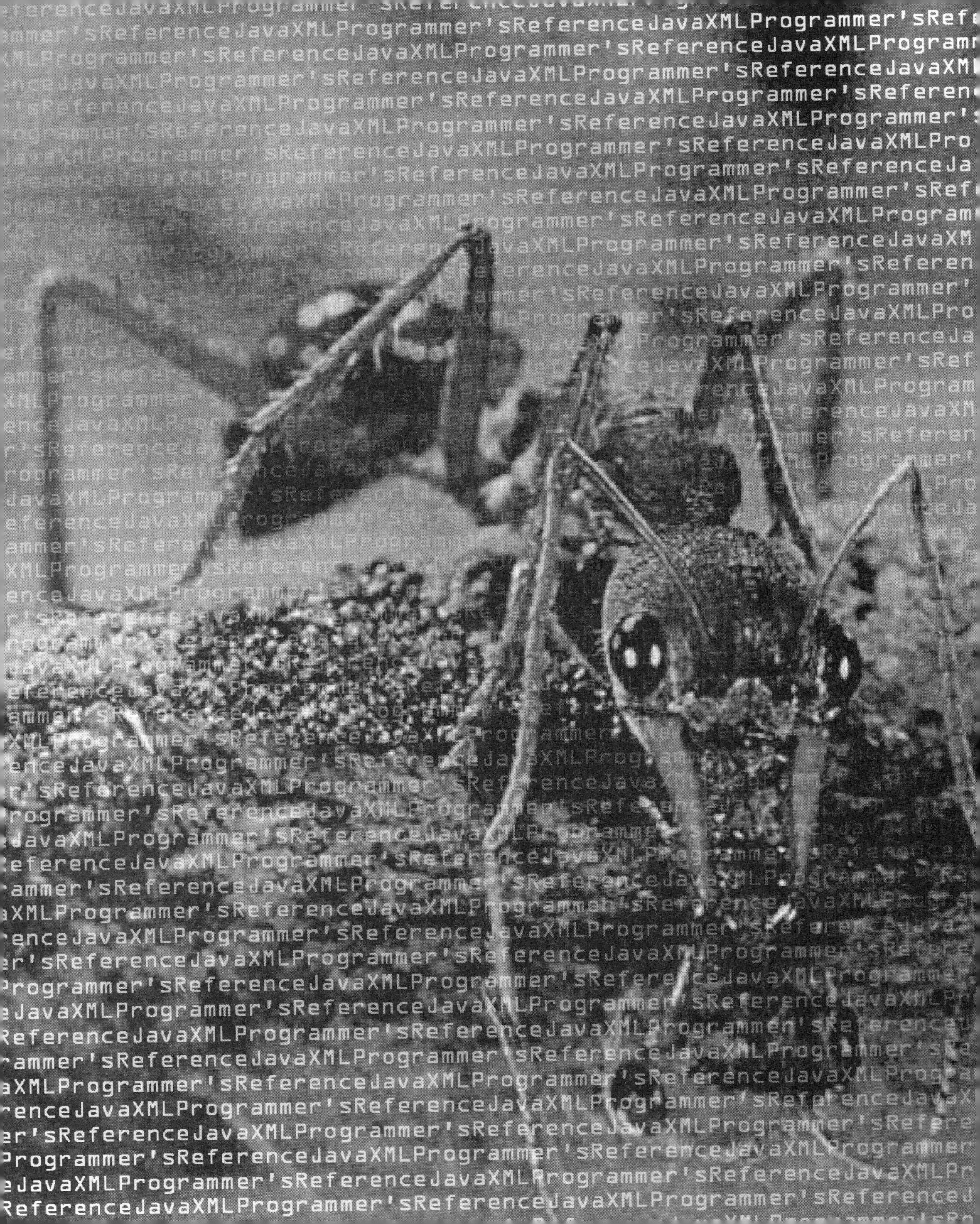
JavaXMLProgrammer'sReference

Apache XML Tools

The Apache Software Foundation has a large following in the XML community and has support from companies like Sun Microsystems, IBM and Lotus. IBM has donated the code for its SOAP4J implementation and the XML4J parser to Apache. Sun Microsystems has donated its XML parser, Project X (now known as Crimson), and more recently, the XSLTC translet compiler project has found a new home with the Apache Xalan stylesheet processor.

This chapter will cover some of the initiatives that are currently under development within Apache – however, we have focused on projects that are widely accepted and used in the industry, and are within the scope of this book.

Project	Description	Page
Xerces	XML parsers in Java	429
SOAP	Simple Object Access Protocol client/server implementation	437
Axis	Redesign of the Apache SOAP project (brief mention)	446
Xalan	XSLT stylesheet processors, in Java, now including the XSLTC stylesheet compiler donated by Sun	446

The chapter will focus primarily on Apache SOAP, Xerces, and Xalan.

An example of using Apache **FOP** is given in Chapter 16. The new Apache/Xalan distribution of Sun's **XSLTC** translet compiler is discussed in Chapter 11.

Xerces

Xerces 1 was originally developed to be the "fastest XML parser on the planet". As the focus was on performance, other considerations like modularity and maintainability of the code were not given the top priority. The result of this effort was a powerful parser whose code was hard to understand, maintain and extend. Currently there is an ongoing effort to develop Xerces 2, a major redesign.

The objective of the Xerces 2 redesign is to make Xerces modular and highly configurable, so that it can be used in a wide variety of environments, from IDEs to small devices. The project is completely open, and can be joined, contributed to, or just browsed at http://xml.apache.org/~andyc/xerces2/.

The Apache XML Project also maintains and develops the Crimson parser, which is now the Java reference XML parser for JAXP and J2EE. Xerces is also fully JAXP compliant (in fact it currently comes with its own implementation of JAXP which will load a Xerces parser by default) and therefore Chapter 5 covers its core parsing and validation features. Xerces accepts feature and property configuration settings that are summarized later in the chapter.

Xerces supports the XML 1.0 Recommendation, XML Schema 1.0 Recommendation, DOM Level 2 version (Views, Events, Traversal and Ranges), and SAX 2.0.

At the time of writing the most recent version is Xerces 1.4.0, which is available from the Apache XML Project at http://xml.apache.org/xerces-j/. This version is the first to provide support for the May 2001 XML Schema Recommendation.

A summary of the code examples used and resources needed for this chapter is given in Appendix A.

Parsing

Chapters 1, 2, and 3 cover the more general details of XML parsing. The following example shows the code for a basic non-validating Xerces SAX parser:

Source SParser.java

```java
import org.apache.xerces.parsers.SAXParser;
import org.xml.sax.Attributes;
import org.xml.sax.helpers.DefaultHandler;
import org.xml.sax.SAXParseException;
import org.xml.sax.SAXException;
import java.io.IOException;

public class SParser extends DefaultHandler {

  public SParser(String xmlFile) {
    SAXParser parser = new SAXParser();

    parser.setContentHandler(this);

    try {
      parser.parse(xmlFile);
    } catch (SAXException e) {
      System.err.println(e);
    } catch (IOException e) {
      System.err.println(e);
    }
  }

  public void startElement(String uri, String local,
      String qName, Attributes atts) {
    System.out.println(local);
  }

  public static void main(String[] args) {
```

```
      SParser sParser = new SParser(args[0]);
   }
}
```

Sample result1.xml

```
<?xml version="1.0" encoding="UTF-8"?>
<!DOCTYPE result SYSTEM "result.dtd">
<result>
  <student name="John">
    <score>78</score>
  </student>
</result>
```

Sample result.dtd

```
<!ELEMENT result (student)+>
<!ELEMENT student (score)>
<!ATTLIST student name CDATA #REQUIRED>
<!ELEMENT score (#PCDATA)>
```

Ensure you have Xerces in your classpath, for example:
`xerces-1_4_0/xerces.jar`

```
> javac SParser.java
> java SParser result1.xml
result
student
score
```

Let's see what happens if we introduce an error into the XML file:

Sample result2.xml

```
<?xml version="1.0" encoding="UTF-8"?>
<!DOCTYPE result SYSTEM "result.dtd">
<result>
  <student>
    <score>78</score>
  </student>
</result>
```

Notice that the `<student>` element has no name attribute, making `result2.xml` invalid according to `result.dtd`.

```
> java SParser result2.xml
result
student
score
```

431

As this is a non-validating parser, no error is reported.

Parser features like validation are manipulated using the SAX 2.0 XMLReader methods get/setFeature(). (See the following sections for feature and property settings.)

Source DParser.java

```
import org.apache.xerces.parsers.DOMParser;
import org.xml.sax.ErrorHandler;
import org.w3c.dom.Document;
import org.w3c.dom.Node;
import org.w3c.dom.Element;
import org.w3c.dom.NodeList;
import org.xml.sax.SAXException;
import org.xml.sax.SAXParseException;
import org.xml.sax.SAXNotRecognizedException;
import org.xml.sax.SAXNotSupportedException;
import java.io.IOException;

public class DParser implements ErrorHandler {

  public DParser(String xmlFile) {

    // Create a Xerces DOM Parser
    DOMParser parser = new DOMParser();
```

Turn validation on:

```
    try {
      parser.setFeature(
        "http://xml.org/sax/features/validation", true);
    } catch (SAXNotRecognizedException e) {
      System.err.println(e);
    } catch (SAXNotSupportedException e) {
      System.err.println(e);
    }

    parser.setErrorHandler(this);

    try {
      parser.parse(xmlFile);
      Document document = parser.getDocument();
      traverse(document);
    } catch (SAXException e) {
      System.err.println(e);
    } catch (IOException e) {
      System.err.println(e);
    }
  }
```

This is a simple recursive traversal through the elements of the tree:

```
  private void traverse(Node node) {
    int type = node.getNodeType();
```

```
    if (type == Node.ELEMENT_NODE) {
      System.out.println(node.getNodeName());
    }
    NodeList children = node.getChildNodes();
    if (children != null) {
      for (int i = 0; i < children.getLength(); i++) {
        traverse(children.item(i));
      }
    }
  }
}
```

These methods print out any errors encountered during the parse. They override the default implementations in `DefaultHandler`, which implements `org.xml.sax.ErrorHandler`:

```
public void warning(SAXParseException e) throws SAXException {
  System.err.println("Warning:  " + e);
}

public void error(SAXParseException e) throws SAXException {
  System.err.println("Error:  " + e);
}

public void fatalError(SAXParseException e) throws SAXException {
  System.err.println("Fatal Error:  " + e);
}

public static void main(String[] args) {
  DParser dParser = new DParser(args[0]);
}
}
```

Now we'll repeat the tests from the previous example on page 431. For `result1.xml` (valid XML file) the output is the same:

```
> java DParser result1.xml
result
student
score
```

```
> java DParser result2.xml
Error:  org.xml.sax.SAXParseException: Attribute "name" is required and must
be specified for element type "student".
result
student
score
```

Now the document is being validated as for `result2.xml` (invalid XML file) an "error" is produced.

Aspects of the parser like whether validation is on or off are manipulated using the SAX 2.0 features and properties mechanism. We will look at those relevant to Xerces next.

Setting Features

To get or set a feature on either `org.apache.xerces.parsers.SAXParser` or `org.apache.xerces.parsers.DOMParser`, we use the SAX 2.0 methods `get/setFeature()`. To get the current `boolean` value of whether the feature is set or not, we use the SAX 2.0 method `getFeature()`.

For example, to turn on **validation**:

```
SAXParser s = new SAXParser();
s.setFeature("http://xml.org/sax/features/validation", true);
```

Setting features may cause an `org.xml.sax.SAXNotRecognizedException` or `SAXNotSupportedException` to be thrown.

Note that features and properties are handled by the class `org.apache.xml.parsers.XMLParser`, whose source you can examine.

Validation Features

Current features and properties supported by Xerces can be found at http://xml.apache.org/xerces-j/features.html and /properties.html. Note that general SAX properties are covered in Chapter 2. Here we give the defaults for Xerces:

http://xml.org/sax/features/...

❑ `validation` – default `false`
Perform validation with a DTD or schema

❑ `namespaces` – default `true`
Perform namespace-aware parsing

❑ `external-parameter-entities` – default `true`
Include external parameter entities and external DTD

❑ `external-general-entities` – default `true`
Include external entities

http://apache.org/xml/features/validation/...

❑ `schema` – default `true`
Enable schema validation

❑ `schema-full-checking` – default `false`
Enable full constraint checking (some time-consuming validation methods may be disabled by default)

❑ `warn-on-duplicate-attdef` – default `true`
`warn-on-undeclared-elemdef` – default `true`
These can be used to disable duplicated attribute checking, and to disable reporting of elements not declared in the DTD or schema

http://apache.org/xml/features/nonvalidating/...

❏ `load-dtd-grammar` – default `true`
Can be used to disable default attribute insertion when the DTD is present but the parser is in non-validating mode

❏ `load-external-dtd` – default `true`
If false, ignore the external DTD subset in non-validating mode

Non-Validating Parsers May Still Read the DTD

Even if Xerces is in non-validating mode, it may (depending upon above settings) read in the DTD if one is available, and perform entity substitution, default attribute value substitution (if no attribute value is specified), and attribute normalization (applying substitution to references in attributes).

Java Encoding

http://apache.org/xml/features/allow-java-encodings

If set to `true`, Xerces will recognize Java values for character encodings used in the XML declaration. The default is `false`.

Error Handling

http://apache.org/xml/features/continue-after-fatal-error

Setting this option to `true` will cause Xerces to continue processing after a fatal error. The default is `false`.

DOM Features

http://apache.org/xml/features/dom/...

❏ `defer-node-expansion` – default `true`
Use lazy parsing, that is, defer expanding nodes until requested during the parse process

❏ `create-entity-ref-nodes` – default `true`
If `false`, then replace an entity with its substitution value. Otherwise, insert an `EntityReference` node

❏ `include-ignorable-whitespace` default `true`
If set to `false`, then exclude whitespace that is ignorable with respect to the DTD

SAX Features

http://xml.org/sax/features/namespace-prefixes

This feature treats namespace declarations as content (normally they are not reported by a namespace-aware parser). The default is `false`. It cannot be changed during parsing.

http://xml.org/sax/features/string-interning

This feature can be used to allow some `java.lang.String` storing optimization with the `String.intern()` method. The `String` class maintains an internal pool of strings and can return pointers to an existing identical string with this method instead of creating a new (immutable) string. The default is `false`. It cannot be changed during parsing.

Setting Properties

To get/set a property on either `org.apache.xerces.parsers.SAXParser` or `org.apache.xerces.parsers.DOMParser`, we use the SAX 2.0 methods `get/setProperty()`.

For example, to get the name of the document class used in the underlying tree implementation:

```
SAXParser s = new SAXParser();
s.getProperty(
  "http://apache.org/xml/properties/dom/document-class-name");
```

Getting or setting properties may cause an `org.xml.sax.SAXNotRecognizedException` or `SAXNotSupportedException` to be thrown.

http://apache.org/xml/properties/schema/...

❑ `external-schemaLocation` – type `java.lang.String`
You can use this to specify the location of the schema to use, as an alternative to declaring a `schemaLocation` in the document root element

❑ `external-noNamespaceSchemaLocation` – type `java.lang.String`
This applies similarly to no-namespace schema validation

DOM Parser Properties

http://apache.org/xml/properties/dom/...

❑ `current-element-node` – type `org.w3c.dom.Node`
The current element node in the parse. It cannot be set!

❑ `document-class-name` – type `java.lang.String`
This property identifies the name of the concrete class implementing `org.w3c.dom.Document` in the parse tree: the default is `org.apache.xerces.dom.DocumentImpl`. It can be set to another implementation, but then other Apache features (such as lazy parsing) may not work.

SAX Parser Properties

http://xml.org/sax/properties/...

❑ `declaration-handler` – type `org.xml.sax.ext.DeclHandler`
Set the handler for DTD declarations (see Chapter 2)

❑ `lexical-handler` – type `org.xml.sax.ext.LexicalHandler`
Set the lexical handler (see Chapter 2)

❑ `dom-node` – type `org.w3c.dom.Node`
Return the node currently being visited, or `null` if not parsing

We now move on to look at the Apache SOAP implementation.

Apache SOAP

Simple Object Access Protocol is generating a lot of interest in the industry. When combined with technologies such as **Universal Discovery, Description, and Integration (UDDI)** and **Web Services Description Language (WSDL)** (discussed in Chapter 9) SOAP is set to radically change the way business applications communicate over the Web.

According to the W3C specification: "SOAP is a lightweight protocol for exchange of information in a decentralized, distributed environment". It is an XML-based protocol that consists of three parts:

❑ An "envelope" for bundling together the message and instructions for processing it

❑ Encoding rules for transmitting custom datatypes

❑ A convention for representing remote procedure calls and responses

See http://www.w3.org/TR/SOAP/ for the May 2000 W3C Note on SOAP 1.1.

Downloading and Installing Apache SOAP

You can download the latest version of Apache SOAP (2.2 a the time of writing) at http://xml.apache.org/soap/.

Apache SOAP ships with:

❑ The JAR file `soap.jar` which contains both client and server library classes

❑ A web application containing the RPC Router Servlet and a JSP-based application for administering the deployment of services

To run Apache SOAP 2.2, you will also need:

❑ Xerces (however with Apache SOAP 2.2, you may get away with another JAXP pluggable parser, since the code now uses JAXP for all parsing)

❑ JavaMail 1.2 (`mail.jar`)

❑ Java Activation Framework 1.0.1 (`activation.jar`)

The last two can be obtained separately from JavaSoft: see Appendix A for details of obtaining packages.

The router servlet is the front end of the HTTP server component. It redirects requests to objects stored in the servlet context of the web application, to EJBs via JNDI, and to other "providers".

The way that the server redirects requests to services is specified by descriptor information which can be sent as an XML file remotely to the server over the network, or configured using forms on the JSP administration panel.

A service has a name, often starting with `urn:` but not necessarily so. A service needs to know how to **create** an object – or access a previously created object – and which method to call on the object.

In Java, it does this by extracting information from the descriptor and using the Reflection API to create and manipulate objects by name.

Note that Apache SOAP can expose non-Java services like CGI scripts and JavaScript.

Setting Up SOAP

A `<Context>` declaration within the `<Host>` element of a `<Service>` in the Tomcat 4.0 `server.xml` configuration file is all that is needed to point the web server at the default web application that comes bundled with SOAP:

```
<Context
  path="/apache-soap"
  docBase="C:/soap-2_2/webapps/soap"
  debug="0" reloadable="true"/>
```

If you use the `server.xml` that comes with the code bundle for the book, then there's an HTTP service set up on port 5202. Otherwise, use whichever port Tomcat is listening on.

Start the server and open http://localhost:5202/apache-soap and you should be able to navigate to the administration panel.

To make a Java service available to the server, put the class files or JARs containing the required code in `webapps/soap/WEB-INF/classes`, or `/WEB-INF/lib` respectively. Also, include any library JARs required by the services.

In addition, you need to make the SOAP JAR and its dependent libraries (see above) available to the application. These can be put in `WEB-INF/lib`.

It is worth running SOAP in a fully compliant Servlets 2.3 environment, as this will prevent problems with exposure to server libraries. A common problem, for instance with Tomcat 3.x.x installations, is that various libraries like JAXP, older DOM versions, and other server libraries could be found by linear search before the library versions that make SOAP work are found (a common problem is related to JAXP conflict with Xerces own dedicated JAXP implementation). There are fixes to this, but they are messy and temporary, and we recommend using the clean classloader environment of a Servlets 2.3 web application to deploy all necessary code.

It's possible to automate the construction of a custom web application that integrates the SOAP server with Java applications and moves the whole package to a new location. We do this in Chapter 15.

Remote Procedure Calls Over HTTP

Before we build a client for this service let's dive inside SOAP to see how it handles Remote Procedure Calls (RPC) over HTTP. The Apache SOAP infrastructure consists of the `rpcrouter` servlet and `soap.jar`. All Apache SOAP services must have a unique service Object ID, within the Apache SOAP server on which the service is deployed. The package that deals with the RPC is `org.apache.soap.rpc`.

In order to invoke the service, a client must set up an `org.apache.soap.rpc.Call` object with the required service Object ID, the name of the method to be invoked, and the corresponding parameters. After setting this `Call` object, the client calls the `invoke()` method which takes two parameters. The first is a URL to the `rpcrouter` servlet; in this case, the URL is http://localhost:8080/apache-soap/servlet/rpcrouter. The second parameter is the `SOAPAction` header.

The diagram below shows the process of creating a `Call` object, and how it is dispatched by the client, processed by the server and then returned to the client as a `Response`. The client pattern is one of registering a set of configured objects on the `Call` object, invoking it, and then performing an inverse process on the `Response` to extract the return value of the method call, and/or any fault descriptions:

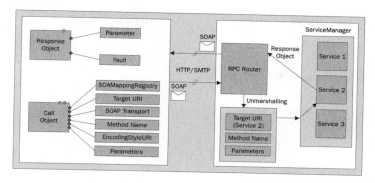

The example below will clarify the steps involved in setting up a call.

The method doing most of the work on the client side is `Call.invoke()`. This method converts the `Call` object into an XML SOAP request and sends that request to the `rpcrouter` servlet, as indicated by the URL. Once the response has been received from the servlet the `invoke()` method returns an `org.apache.soap.rpc.Response` object, which contains the service response or the error. Please note that the HTTP dictates that every request must have a response; so even if the service itself does not return anything, the `rpcrouter` servlet always does.

On the other side, the Apache SOAP server (`rpcrouter` servlet) receives the POSTed SOAP request from the client and constructs the `Call` object. The servlet uses the `Object ID` from the rebuilt `Call` object to locate the object in the service manager. Next the servlet verifies the method name and invokes it on the located object. The servlet also serializes the return value from this call and sends it back in the HTTP response.

Apache SOAP handles the marshaling and unmarshaling of Java data types to and from XML via a type-mapping registry (`org.apache.soap.encoding.SOAPMappingRegistry`), and via serialization (`org.apache.soap.util.xml.Serializer`) and deserialization (`org.apache.soap.util.xml.Deserializer`) interfaces that all marshalers and unmarshalers, respectively, must implement. Apache SOAP provides a number of built-in marshalers and unmarshalers that implement these interfaces (for instance, the `BeanSerializer` that we will use in our example).

If a service method requires a parameter that is a JavaBean, it must manually register the `BeanSerializer` with the type-mapping registry. Serializers and deserializers for the Java primitive types (`int`, `long`, `double`, etc.) and their objectified forms (Integer, Long, Double, etc.) are preregistered in the type-mapping registry. Therefore, using Java primitives and their objectified forms as method parameters is seamless to a client.

Example: Deploying a Service

Applications in SOAP are called services. A service has to be defined and implemented in a programming language, and clients are written to invoke the service.

The following example shows a Distance Converter Service whereby a client can get miles converted to kilometers. We are not going to use many conversions, since our purpose here is to focus on SOAP. We will use a JavaBean to pass the miles parameter, in order to highlight the process.

439

The following provides the code for both the classes:

Source DistanceConverter.java

```
package converter;

public class DistanceConverter {
   private double result;
   private String statement;

   public String convertToKm(ConverterBean bean) {
     double miles = bean.getMiles();
     result = miles * 1.6;
     statement = miles +
       " miles are equal to " + result + " kilometers";
     System.out.println(statement);
     return statement;
   }

}
```

The other file, `ConverterBean.java`, is as follows:

```
package converter;

public class ConverterBean {
   private double miles;

   public double getMiles() {
     return miles;
   }
   public void setMiles(double miles) {
     this.miles = miles;
   }
}
```

Remote Deployment

We use the utility `org.apache.soap.server.ServiceManagerClient`, which comes with Apache SOAP. This class takes two mandatory parameters: a URL to the Apache SOAP's router servlet (`rpcrouter`) and an "action". The action can be one of the following: `deploy`, `undeploy`, `list`, or `query`.

Based on the specified action, an additional parameter may be required. For example, if the action is `deploy`, you must provide the name of the XML deployment descriptor file that contains all the information required by the Apache SOAP server to successfully deploy the service at the command line.

The deployment XML for the `DistanceConverter` service can be specified as follows in the `DC_DeploymentDescriptor.xml`:

```
<isd:service
    xmlns:isd="http://xml.apache.org/xml-soap/deployment"
    id="serv:DistanceConverter">
  <isd:provider
    type="java"
    scope="Application"
    methods="convertToKm">
  <isd:java
      class="converter.DistanceConverter"
      static="false"

  />
  </isd:provider>
  <isd:mappings>
    <isd:map
      encodingStyle="http://schemas.xmlsoap.org/soap/encoding/"
      xmlns:x="serv:DistanceConverter"
      qname="x:converter.ConverterBean"
      javaType=" converter.ConverterBean"
      java2XMLClassName=
        "org.apache.soap.encoding.soapenc.BeanSerializer"
      xml2JavaClassName=
        "org.apache.soap.encoding.soapenc.BeanSerializer"
    />
  </isd:mappings>
</isd:service>
```

Note if this program was not using JavaBeans then the mapping tag (and the code enclosed within it) would not need to be there.

To deploy the `DistanceConverter` descriptor from the command line, you need to check you have the following in your classpath:

- ❑ Xerces, for example `xerces-1_4_0/xerces.jar`
- ❑ SOAP, for example `soap-2_2/lib/soap.jar`
- ❑ JavaMail, for example `javamail-1.2/mail.jar`
- ❑ Java Activation Framework, for example `jaf-1.0.1/activation.jar`

```
> java org.apache.soap.server.ServiceManagerClient
http://localhost:5202/apache-soap/servlet/rpcrouter deploy
DC_DeploymentDescriptor.xml
```

`DC_DepolymentDescriptor.xml` is the name of the file that contains the deployment XML shown above. To verify that the server has been successfully deployed, try the following:

```
> java org.apache.soap.server.ServiceManagerClient
http://localhost:5202/apache-soap/servlet/rpcrouter query
serv:DistanceConverter
```

You should see the same XML file that is contained in DC_DeploymentDescriptor.xml.

The last step necessary on the server side is to copy in the compiled classes to the soap/WEB-INF/classes directory to make them visible to the server when they need to be invoked.

Writing the Distance Converter Client

The following is the complete client program, and we will analyze it step-by-step:

```
package converter;

import java.net.URL;
import java.util.Vector;
import org.apache.soap.SOAPException;
import org.apache.soap.Constants;
import org.apache.soap.Fault;
import org.apache.soap.rpc.Call;
import org.apache.soap.rpc.Parameter;
import org.apache.soap.rpc.Response;
import org.apache.soap.encoding.SOAPMappingRegistry;
import org.apache.soap.encoding.soapenc.BeanSerializer;
import org.apache.soap.util.xml.QName;

public class Client {
  public static void main(String[] args) throws Exception {
    if (args.length == 0) {
      System.err
        .println("Usage: java converter.Client " +
           " <distance in miles>");
      System.exit(1);
    }

    URL url = null;
    double miles;

    try {
```

We point our client directly at the router servlet. Apache SOAP comes with a utility called the tunnel monitor that can be used as a proxy end point routing HTTP traffic between two ports. So we could point our client at 8080, and redirect all traffic through to 5202. At the same time, we'd be able to see all the information in transit both ways. We use this technique in Chapter 15.

```
      url = new URL(
        "http://localhost:5202/apache-soap/servlet/rpcrouter");
      miles = (new Double(args[0])).doubleValue();
```

The major task of the client is to set up the Call object, which requires the following information:

❑ The object ID of the service being invoked, which is set via the `setTargetObjectURI()` method on the `Call` object. Our object ID is `serv:DistanceConverter`.

❑ The name of the method to invoke on the service, which is set via the `setMethodName()` method on the `Call` object. Our method name is `convertTokm()`.

❑ The encoding style used to encode the parameters, which is set via the `setEncodingStyleURI()` method on the `Call` object. We are interested in the standard SOAP encoding style recognized by the URI `http://schemas.xmlsoap org/soap /encoding/`.

```
// Setting up the Call object.
Call call = new Call();
call.setTargetObjectURI("serv:DistanceConverter");
call.setMethodName("convertToKm");
call.setEncodingStyleURI(Constants.NS_URI_SOAP_ENC);
```

Since one of the parameters to the method call is a JavaBean, we need to set up a type-mapping registry. Complete this task by creating a new instance of the class `org.apache.soap encoding SOAPMappingRegistry` and calling the `mapTypes()` method on it.

As the name indicates, that method is used to inform the registry of a previously unknown type, like a custom JavaBean. `mapTypes()` takes the encoding style to be used, the qualified name, the type's fully qualified class name, and the serializer and deserializer to use, which in our case are standard bean serializers.

A qualified name consists of an element's name, including the namespace it belongs to. In our case, the qualified name of the JavaBean is formed by combining the namespace URI (`serv:DistanceConverter`) and the local name (`converter.ConverterBean`).

```
// Type mapping registry
SOAPMappingRegistry smr = new SOAPMappingRegistry();
BeanSerializer beanSer = new BeanSerializer();

// Map the types.
smr.mapTypes(Constants.NS_URI_SOAP_ENC,
  new QName("serv:DistanceConverter",
            "converter.ConverterBean"),
  converter.ConverterBean.class, beanSer, beanSer);

// Set the Call object to use it..
call.setSOAPMappingRegistry(smr);
```

The parameters for the method call are set via the `setParams()` method on the `Call` object. The `setParams()` method takes a Java Vector as its parameter. The vector contains all the parameters, with index 0 being the first parameter in the method signature starting from the left, index 1 being the second parameter starting from the left, and so on.

Each element in the vector is an instance of `org.apache.soap.rpc.Parameter`. The `Parameter()` constructor takes the parameter's name, Java type, and value, as well as an optional encoding styles. If the encoding style is set to `null` (as is done here), then the `Call` object's encoding style will be used. Even though each parameter corresponds to a name, that name can be set to anything and is not used by the Apache SOAP server while invoking the method. Therefore, it is absolutely imperative that you maintain the same order of the parameters in the vector and the method signature.

```
// Set the Parameters
Vector params = new Vector();
ConverterBean bean = new ConverterBean();
bean.setMiles(miles);
params.addElement(
   new Parameter("miles",
      converter.ConverterBean.class, bean, null));
call.setParams(params);
```

Now it's time to actually invoke the method on the remote `DistanceConverter` service. To do so, the client calls the `invoke()` method on the `Call` object. This method returns an `org.apache.soap.rpc.Response` object, as shown on the next page:

```
// Invoke the call.
Response resp = null;
try {
   resp = call.invoke(url, "");
} catch (SOAPException e) {
   System.err.println("Caught SOAPException (" +
      e.getFaultCode()+
      "): " + e.getMessage());
   System.exit(-1);
}
```

Next, the client checks the `Response` object. If the method invocation results in an error, the `generatedFault()` method returns a `true` value, and the actual fault is retrieved and displayed:

```
// Check the response.
if (!resp.generatedFault()) {
   Parameter ret = resp.getReturnValue();
   Object value = ret.getValue();
   System.out.println(value);
} else {
   Fault fault = resp.getFault();
   System.err.println("Generated fault: ");
   System.out.println(" Fault Code = " +
      fault.getFaultCode());
   System.out.println(" Fault String = " +
      fault.getFaultString());
}
} catch (Exception e) {
   e.printStackTrace();
}
}
}
```

Compile and Run the Programs

To compile and run this example all we need in the classpath is the `converter` directory containing the source, `soap.jar`, `mail.jar`, `activation.jar`, and `xerces.jar`.

```
> javac Client.java
> java converter.Client 7
```

You will see the following output on your console:

```
7.0 miles are equal to 11.200000000000001 kilometers
```

In the above discussion, we didn't mention how the actual transport mechanism for dispatching the `Call` object is assigned. This is because the `org.apache.soap.transport.http. SOAPHTTPConnection` mechanism is used by default when you create a `Call` object. You can assign a different transport mechanism using the `setSOAPTransport()` method. The object assigned must implement the `org.apache.soap.transport.SOAPTransport` interface. The following diagram shows the three current implementations available with the current release :

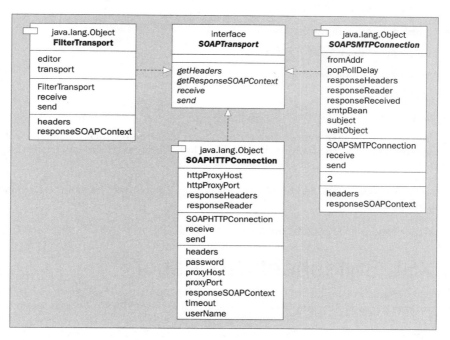

One reason for explicitly assigning a `SOAPTransport` to a `Call` is when you need to specify particular properties of the HTTP connection, such as a proxy host to use, or authentication details. The following is an example of explicitly creating, configuring, and assigning a `SOAPTransport` implementation:

```
SOAPHTTPConnection sht = new SOAPHTTPConnection();
if (tunnelhost != null) {
  sht.setProxyHost("proxy.wrox.com");
  sht.setProxyPort(80);
}
call.setSOAPTransport(sht);
```

RPC Over SMTP

In the example above we used RPC over HTTP, however it's also possible to do "RPC over e-mail". Apache provides a POP3 to HTTP to SMTP proxy server to divert e-mails to an HTTP SOAP service and return the results back to the sender of the original e-mail message via SMTP.

Axis

There is a new project underway at Apache called "Axis" previously known as SOAP 3. This project will supersede the current implementation of SOAP. However, there are plans to release at least one more version of Apache SOAP and the current one will not be discontinued until the release 1.0 of Axis. This project is still at a very early alpha stage; at the time of writing no release builds were available (however nightly builds are available).

The goals for the eventual Axis 1.0 release include:

❑ Full implementation of the SOAP 1.1 specification

❑ It must be faster than Apache SOAP 2.x

❑ Support for streaming parsing

❑ Pluggability

❑ To be "production" quality with full documentation

Axis is also looking at the use of intermediaries, where a SOAP message travels from the initiator to the destination via intermediary applications. This would allow the development of very flexible web applications.

A preview release of Axis is included in IBM's Web Services Toolkit from version 2.3 (see Chapter 9 for more information on WSTK).

You can read more about Axis at http://xml.apache.org/axis/.

Xalan: XSL Stylesheet Processor

Xalan (named after an almost unheard of musical instrument) provides high-performance XSLT stylesheet processing. Xalan fully implements the W3C XSLT 1.0 and XPath 1.0 recommendations.

Perhaps wisely, Xalan has not rushed to fully implement the XSLT 1.1 Working Draft, since this has now been withdrawn (as of May 2001) pending work on version 2.0. Features in the 1.1 draft may not be accepted into the next recommendation.

Xalan-Java

Xalan is a processor for transforming XML documents into HTML, text, or other XML document types.

Xalan can be used from the command line, in an applet or a servlet, or as a module in other programs. By default, it uses the Xerces XML parser, but it can interface to any XML parser that conforms to the DOM level 2 or SAX level 1 specification.

Architecture and Design

The current version of Xalan is 2.1.0. Xalan 2 was a redesign of Xalan 1 with the primary objective being a more modular API that enables a wider community of developers to work on the project. At the time of writing, this philosophy was being put to the test by the migration of the XSLT Compiler project from Sun Microsystems to Xalan at the Apache XML Project. This new part of Xalan is covered in Chapter 11. So far, the integration appears to have gone smoothly, and both Xalan and XSLTC should benefit from pooling resources.

Xalan-Java version 2 reimplemented Xalan version 1 to conform with **TraX (Transformation API for XML)** interfaces, part of JAXP 1.1. We covered TrAX programming in Chapter 11.

The internal architecture of Xalan 2 is divided into four major modules, and various smaller modules. The main modules are:

- ❑ **org.apache.xalan.processor**
  This module contains the TrAX transformer factory class implementation and the core transformation engine.

- ❑ **org.apache.xalan.templates**
  This module defines the in-memory stylesheet structures.

- ❑ **org.apache.xalan.transformer**
  This is the module that applies the source tree to the Templates, and produces a result tree. It contains the TrAX transformer implementation.

- ❑ **org.apache.xpath**
  The module that processes both XPath expressions, and XSLT match patterns.

Below we'll look at some applications of the XPath module.

Student Scores Example

In many cases XPath and XSLT provide simpler, more elegant ways of solving application problems than pure Java/XML. In the following example we will compare a pure Java/XML solution with one that utilizes XPath and/or XSLT.

Using XPath to Locate Nodes in an XML Document

As stated above, the XPath language addresses specific parts of XML documents. In general it is used by an XSLT stylesheet, however we can use it in a Java program to avoid lengthy iteration over a DOM element hierarchy. Using XPath in this way is covered in detail in Chapter 13.

In our example scenario the user gets an XML document and modifies sections of that document. To reduce network traffic, only the updated data is sent back. On receiving the modifications, the application updates the source document with the modified data. For this example, we assume that the application deals with the record in a score record book, the `<ssn>` element is used to uniquely identify a student; it serves as the primary key. A sample score record book document `recordbook.xml` looks like this:

```xml
<?xml version="1.0" encoding="UTF-8"?>
<recordbook>
  <record>
    <student>Bill Philips</student>
    <ssn>334652165</ssn>
    <score>67</score>
  </record>
  <record>
    <student>Jeniffer Roberts</student>
    <ssn>556763212</ssn>
    <score>86</score>
  </record>
  <record>
    <student>Irum Mujtaba</student>
    <ssn>243567854</ssn>
    <score>97</score>
  </record>
  <record>
```

```
         <student>Yoko Griffin</student>
         <ssn>335458765</ssn>
         <score>86</score>
      </record>
   </recordbook>
```

It keeps an instance of the `recordbook` in memory as a DOM `Document` object and when the user changes a record, the application's front-end sends only the updated `<record>` element.

Next, we will write the code to identify the `<record>` element in the source tree that needs to be replaced with the updated element. The `findRecord()` method below shows how that can be accomplished.

Example: Creating the Student Record Locator

We will build `SearchRecords.java` and `XPathHelper.java` to locate a record from `recordbook.xml`. The functionality of `XpathHelper` class can easily be included within the `SearchRecords`. However, the reason for separating it out is that in cases where you have more flexible and complex XPath handling, it's generally a good idea to process that in a separate class. The following provides the code for both the classes. In order to keep the example simple and focused we have not included the error handling code.

Source SearchRecords.java

```java
import java.io.FileInputStream;
import java.io.FileNotFoundException;
import java.util.Properties;
import org.apache.xerces.parsers.DOMParser;
import org.apache.xpath.XPathAPI;
import org.apache.xml.utils.TreeWalker;
import org.apache.xml.utils.DOMBuilder;
import org.w3c.dom.*;
import org.w3c.dom.traversal.NodeIterator;
import org.xml.sax.SAXException;
import org.xml.sax.InputSource;
import javax.xml.parsers.DocumentBuilder;
import javax.xml.parsers.DocumentBuilderFactory;
import javax.xml.parsers.ParserConfigurationException;
import javax.xml.transform.*;
import javax.xml.transform.stream.*;
import javax.xml.transform.dom.*;

public class SearchRecords {
  public String xmlfile;
  public String socialSecurityNumber;

  public Node findRecord(String name, Document source)
      throws Exception {
    XPathHelper xpathHelper = new XPathHelper();
    Node node =
      xpathHelper.processXPath(source.getDocumentElement(),
      "//record[child::ssn[text() = '" +
      socialSecurityNumber + "']]");
    return node;
```

```
    }

public void execute(String args[]) throws Exception {
    socialSecurityNumber = args[0];
    xmlfile = args[1];
    if ((xmlfile != null) && (xmlfile.length() > 0)
        && (socialSecurityNumber != null)
        && (socialSecurityNumber.length() > 0)) {

      //Create a DOM tree
      InputSource inputSource =
        new InputSource(new FileInputStream(xmlfile));
      DocumentBuilderFactory docFactory =
        DocumentBuilderFactory.newInstance();
      Document doc =
        docFactory.newDocumentBuilder().parse(inputSource);

      // Set up an identity transformer to use as serializer.
      Transformer serializer =
        TransformerFactory.newInstance()
          .newTransformer();
      serializer
        .setOutputProperty(
          OutputKeys.OMIT_XML_DECLARATION, "yes");

      // Calling the find record method
      Node n = findRecord(socialSecurityNumber, doc);
      if (n != null) {
        serializer.transform(new DOMSource(n),
          new StreamResult(System.out));
        System.out.println();
      } else {
        System.out.println("There is no student with SSN:" +
          socialSecurityNumber +
          ". Please refer to the XML file");
      }
    } else {
      System.out.println("Incorrect arguments");
    }
}

public static void main(String[] args) throws Exception {
  if (args.length != 2) {
    System.out
      .println("Usage : SearchRecords " +
        "<social security number> <xmlFileName>");
    return;
  }

  SearchRecords searchRecords = new SearchRecords();
  searchRecords.execute(args);
```

```
    }

  }
```

The other file, `XPathHelper.java`, is as follows:

```java
import org.w3c.dom.Node;
import org.xml.sax.SAXException;
import org.apache.xpath.XPathAPI;
import javax.xml.transform.TransformerException;

public class XPathHelper {

  public Node processXPath(Node target, String xpath)
      throws SAXException, TransformerException {
    Node n = XPathAPI.selectSingleNode(target, xpath);
    return n;
  }
}
```

Ensure you have

❑   Xerces, for example `xerces-1_4_0/xerces.jar`

❑   Xalan, for example `xalan-j-2_1_0/bin/xalan.jar`

in your classpath. Note that JAXP parsing and transforming implementations are currently bundled with Xerces and Xalan respectively.

```
> javac SearchRecords.java XPathHelper.java
```

To run the program:

```
> java SearchRecords 243567854 recordbook.xml
```

You should see the following output on screen:

```
<record>
<student>Irum Mujtaba</student>
<ssn>243567854</ssn>
<score>97</score>
</record>
```

The XPath API is an easy to use (though slower) API that encapsulates the more advanced classes in the API; it's a good starting point if you are new to XPath. Once you have compiled and run the program it will be a good exercise to add more advanced XPath functionality to the helper class. You can read the complete XPath specifications at http://www.w3.org/TR/xpath/.

See also Chapter 13 on querying XML techniques, and Chapter 7 for the Oracle XDK XPath tools.

In the example below we will look at a program that takes an XML file, an XSL stylesheet and a stylesheet parameter; it then generates the transformed output. The parameter is a number that will be prefixed to all the social security numbers for the students in `recordbook.xml`.

Example: Creating the Student SSN Transformer

We will build `TransformStudentSSN.java` and `scoreStyleSheet.xsl`.

Source TransformStudentSSN.java

```java
import java.io.*;
import javax.xml.transform.*;
import javax.xml.transform.stream.StreamSource;
import javax.xml.transform.stream.StreamResult;

public class TransformStudentSSN {
  public String xmlfile;
  public String xslStyleSheet;
  public String prefixNumber;

  public void transform(String args[])
      throws TransformerException,
      TransformerConfigurationException,
      FileNotFoundException, IOException {
    xmlfile = args[0];
    xslStyleSheet = args[1];
    prefixNumber = args[2];

    TransformerFactory transformerFactory =
      TransformerFactory.newInstance();
    Transformer transformer =
      transformerFactory
        .newTransformer(new StreamSource(xslStyleSheet));
    transformer.setParameter("param", prefixNumber);
    transformer.transform(new StreamSource(xmlfile),
      new StreamResult(System.out));
  }

  public static void main(String[] args) throws Exception {
    if (args.length != 3) {
      System.err.println("Usage : TransformStudentScores " +
        "<xmlfile> <xslStyleSheet> <prefixNumber> ");
      return;
    }
    TransformStudentSSN transformStduentSSN =
      new TransformStudentSSN();
    transformStduentSSN.transform(args);
  }

}
```

Sample Style Sheet

The style sheet, `scoreStyleSheet.xsl` is as follows:

```xml
<?xml version="1.0"?>
<xsl:stylesheet
    xmlns:xsl="http://www.w3.org/1999/XSL/Transform"
    version="1.0"
    xmlns:xalan="http://xml.apache.org/xslt">
  <xsl:output
    method="xml"
    indent="yes"
    xalan:indent-amount="5"/>
<xsl:param name="param" select="'default value'"/>
<xsl:template match="recordbook">
  <recordbook>
    <xsl:apply-templates select="record"/>
  </recordbook>
</xsl:template>
<xsl:template match="record">
  <record>
    <xsl:apply-templates select="student"/>
    <xsl:apply-templates select="ssn"/>
    <xsl:apply-templates select="score"/>
  </record>
</xsl:template>
<xsl:template match="student">
  <student>
    <xsl:value-of select="."/>
  </student>
</xsl:template>
<xsl:template match="ssn">
  <newSSN>
    <xsl:value-of select="$param"/>
    <xsl:value-of select="."/>
  </newSSN>
</xsl:template>
<xsl:template match="score">
  <score>
    <xsl:value-of select="."/>
  </score>
</xsl:template>
</xsl:stylesheet>
```

In case you are not passing any parameters and simply transforming using a style sheet you will not need to call the `setParameter()` method.

Ensure you have:

❑ Xerces, for example `xerces-1_4_0/xerces.jar`

❑ Xalan, for example `xalan-j-2_1_0/bin/xalan.jar`

in your classpath. Note that JAXP parsing and transforming packages are currently bundled with Xerces and Xalan respectively:

```
> javac TransformStudentSSN.java
```

Once you have compiled the source file successfully run the following command

```
> java TransformStudentSSN recordbook.xml
    scoreStyleSheet.xsl 99
```

Output

You should see the following output. Note the indenting of 5 as specified using the Xalan extension in the `<xsl:output>` directive (see below):

```
<recordbook>
     <record>
          <student>Bill Philips</student>
          <newSSN>99334652165</newSSN>
          <score>67</score>
     </record>
     <record>
          <student>Jeniffer Roberts</student>
          <newSSN>99556763212</newSSN>
          <score>86</score>
     </record>
     <record>
          <student>Irum Mujtaba</student>
          <newSSN>99243567854</newSSN>
          <score>97</score>
     </record>
     <record>
          <student>Yoko Griffin</student>
          <newSSN>99335458765</newSSN>
          <score>86</score>
     </record>
</recordbook>
```

As you can see, the number 99 has been prefixed to all `<ssn>` text and the `<ssn>` tag has been replaced by `<newSSN>`.

See also Chapter 5 for more on JAXP for transformers, and Chapter 7 for the Oracle XDK stylesheet processor.

Setting Properties

Default output properties for XML, HTML, and text transformation output are defined in property files in the `org.apache.xalan.templates` package.

You can change these settings by declaring the Xalan namespace in your stylesheet element:

```
xmlns:xalan="http://xml.apache.org/xslt"
```

and using the namespace prefix we assign to redefine properties of interest in the stylesheet `<xsl:output>` element (for example, `xalan:indent-amount="5"`).

Using the Command-Line Utility

Xalan can be called from the command line. The `java.org.apache.xalan.xslt.Process` class provides a utility for performing transformations from the command line. This utility is useful for trying out XSL stylesheets you have written, to make sure they do what you expect with the XML source files they are designed to transform.

To perform a transformation from the command line, or a script, you need to set the Java classpath to include `xalan.jar` and `xerces.jar` (or another JAXP compliant parser). Then call:

```
> java org.apache.xalan.xslt.Process -IN inputurl [-XSL xslurl] [-OUT outputfile]
```

The command line utility can take the following important flags and arguments (the flags are case-insensitive):

Option	Description
-V	Version info
-XSL xslurl	The input filename or URL of the stylesheet (optional)
-OUT outputfile	The output location (optional)
-IN inputurl	The input filename or URL of the source XML
-XML, -TEXT, -HTML	Use appropriate formatter and add header for output
-PARAM name value	Equivalent to global `<xsl:variable name="name" select="'value'"/>` occurring in the stylesheet

Run the program without any arguments to see a full help listing.

As well as for running batch processes (for example from Ant), another use of command line interface is in providing a simple plug-in for another application. Altova's XML Spy (an XML IDE) provides a feature whereby you can specify a Java command as the default XSL processor for testing out transformations. This enables you to use Xalan, Saxon, or any other Java XSL processor that has a command line interface.

Summary

In this chapter we have looked at the core details of working with the most topical and pervasive components of the Apache XML toolset.

We have not at looked at several important parts of the Apache XML Project, including Cocoon (an XML web framework), FOP (an XSL Formatting Objects to PDF formatter), and Batik (an SVG graphics toolkit), each of which is becoming a topical subject of increasing importance in its own right.

An example of using Apache **FOP** is given in Chapter 16. The new Apache/Xalan distribution of Sun's **XSLTC** stylesheet compiler is covered in Chapter 11.

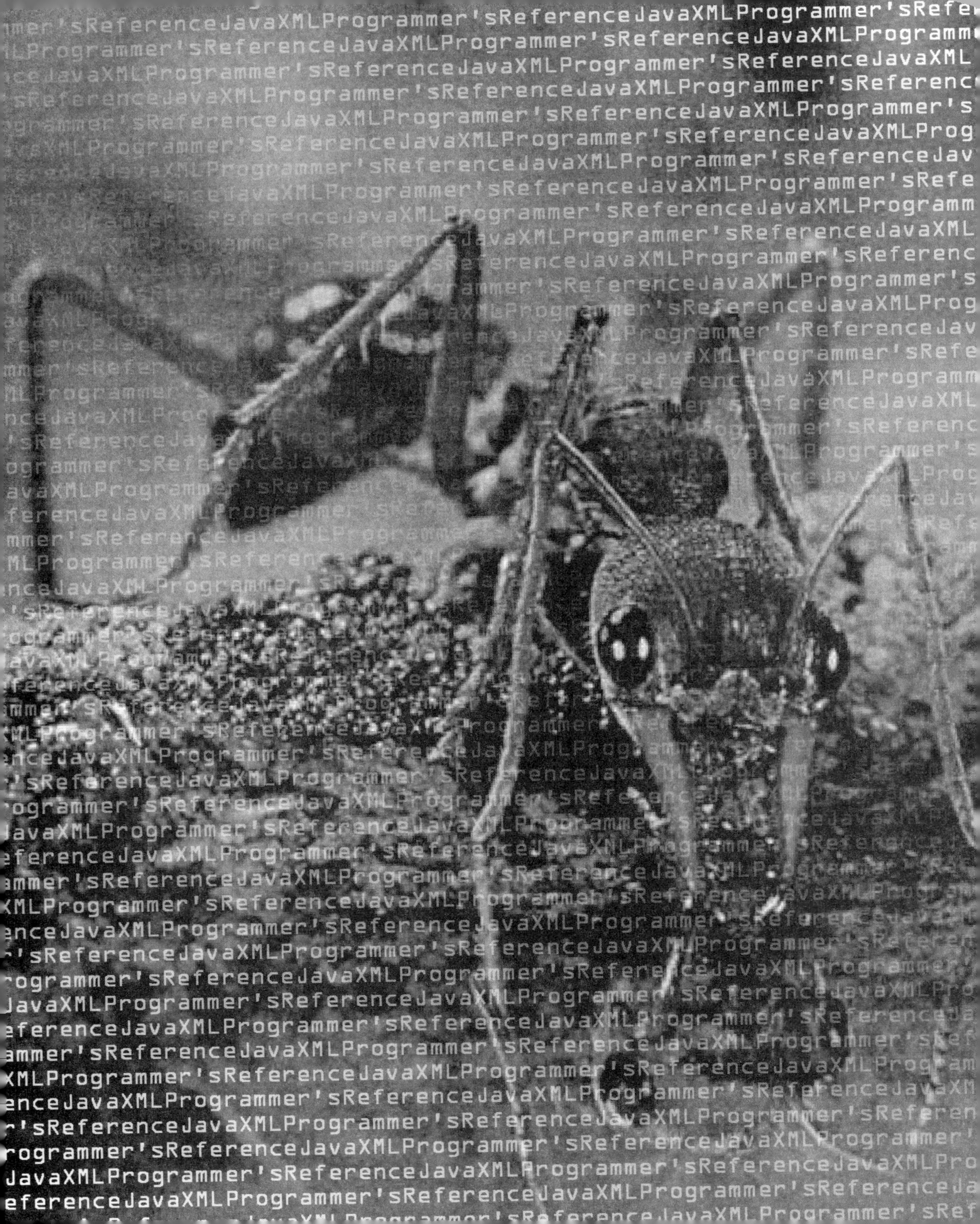

IBM Web Services Tools

During the early part of 2001, hardly a week has gone by without some vendor or another announcing a web services product initiative. Web services are essentially software components, hosted on Internet servers, and accessed over standard protocols such as HTTP and SOAP that provide a service to software clients. A typical example is a stock-ticker service, which provides the latest selling price when sent a stock symbol. This service, perhaps published on a public web server, is then available to any developer wanting to incorporate current stock prices into an application – whether that application is a web site for day-traders, or a stock portfolio tracker on a handheld device.

IBM is, together with Microsoft, probably the most advanced vendor when it comes to building up a complete set of development tools for web services. Both are key players in the development of web services standards – a co-operative relationship which could well ensure that web services become the de facto standard way of accessing software in the not-too-distant future. While Microsoft's tools are intended for use with its .NET platform, IBM's are built in Java, and form a powerful set of APIs, libraries and utilities for building and accessing web services as a Java programmer.

This chapter provides a reference to the tools and APIs included in IBM's web services toolkit (the WSTK), and examples for the most common web services related tasks a programmer is likely to perform.

Web Services Standards

Web services are designed to be interoperable across platforms, operating systems and languages. For this reason, they are based around standards. These standards form a communications stack, from low-level data transmission up to high level services, which looks something like this:

Layer	Protocols/Standards
Transport	HTTP, SMTP over TCP/IP, WAP
Messaging	SOAP, XML-RPC, XML, GET/POST
Definition	WSDL, WSFL
Discovery	UDDI

As you can see, the transport layer contains existing Internet protocols. This enables web services to be activated across all of the existing channels that exist for e-mail and web traffic.

The messaging layer contains the standards that define how messages are communicated between clients and services in ways that both can understand. Messages in web services are typically the parameters passed to a service operation, or the results of that operation.

Just as with Java methods, these parameters and results can be either simple pieces of data, like integers or strings, or they can be complex data structures, in the form of objects. The transport layer has to be able to encode and decode these pieces of data into a format that can be passed across the underlying protocol.

One solution to this problem is SOAP, which we've already met, and which allows for object graphs to be encoded as XML data for transmission to a web service, or from a service to a client. But this layer also contains a range of simpler protocols. Dave Winer's XML-RPC (XML Remote Procedure Call) standard has a following among open source developers, and offers a scaled down, simpler version of the sort of capabilities SOAP offers. It is also possible to use arbitrary XML as a messaging format.

Web services can also be activated over HTTP via the traditional methods HTML forms use to communicate with web sites: GET and POST requests.

The definition layer is important in turning web services from a simple client server communication framework into a service-publishing framework. The **Web Services Definition Language, WSDL**, will be one of the principal focuses of this chapter. It provides a mechanism for a service provider to publish a machine-readable document which details exactly how a particular service can be accessed – what types of message over what protocols it will respond to, and what format those responses will take. The **Web Services Flow Language (WSFL)** is a relatively new announcement, but it provides machine-readable documentation of how a series of web services together can be used to undertake a complete business transaction, such as a purchase.

The discovery layer is used to find web services that provide a particular service. **The Universal Description, Discovery and Integration protocol (UDDI)** is a specification for a machine-accessible directory service that provides these facilities. In fact, UDDI registries are themselves a web service, and are accessed via SOAP.

Vendors and Web Services

IBM's Web Services Toolkit builds upon the IBM SOAP implementation (which we looked at in Chapter 8 since it has been donated to the Apache Software Foundation) and provides a set of libraries for working with WSDL and UDDI. This will be the main focus of this chapter. At the time of publication, IBM's tools were the only Java implementations available that can work with these standards. Sun have announced their intention to develop Java extension APIs for messaging, remote-procedure invocation, and XML repository access, which should provide a standardized API for accessing UDDI, SOAP and WSDL information.

For this reason, this chapter will be focusing on IBM products.

Appendix A contains a summary of the example code for this chapter.

The Web Services Toolkit

The WSTK is available for download from IBM's AlphaWorks site:

http://www.alphaworks.ibm.com/tech/webservicestoolkit

At the time of writing, the latest version was version 2.3. This includes the following elements:

- ❑ Apache SOAP v 2.1
- ❑ IBM UDDI4J, an API for accessing UDDI registries
- ❑ The WSDL toolkit – a set of Java classes for accessing and manipulating WSDL information and a set of tools to help with building web services and clients.

It also includes the WSDL and WSFL specification documents. There are also a number of preview technologies included in the toolkit, as well as a UDDI server that you can install if you have access to IBM DB/2.

The WSTK depends on several libraries and tools, including Xerces 1.2 and Xalan 1, but includes the files for all of these dependencies. Assuming you have already got a JDK installed, you should be able to simply run the installer or unpack the download to install the WSTK files. A configuration tool is supplied, but you do not need to run it to develop with the toolkit.

In addition, in order to host web services developed using the toolkit, you will need a servlet container. The wstk-2.3/soap directory contains a standard Apache SOAP 2.1 distribution, so you can use this. It is recommended that this version is used, as SOAP 2.2 does not include all the required class files (for example XMLParserLiaison.class). An Ant build-target, which will deploy a SOAP server to your servlet engine, is included in the code download for the book (see Appendix A).

> For the purposes of this chapter, we will assume that you have an Apache SOAP web application installed and available at **http://localhost:8080/apache-soap** (or listening on an arbitrary port with a tunnel monitor routing to it from port 8080).

This chapter will focus on the two key elements of the WSTK: the WSDL toolkit, with its tools for interpreting and creating WSDL documents; and UDDI4J, the UDDI client API.

The WSDL Toolkit

IBM's WSDL toolkit is a set of tools that are designed to help developers of web services and web service clients. When developing a web service, you can either develop the service first, by writing Java classes which implement the service logic, and then expose the service's interface later, or you can take an existing or new interface definition, and develop a service that implements it. Both of these functions are assisted by the WSDL toolkit.

Also, if you want to develop an application that uses a web service, you will need to develop a client. Again, the web services toolkit can help.

The WSDL toolkit contains two main tools: one which generates WSDL files and SOAP service deployment descriptors from existing code; and one which generates template code for services and clients from WSDL files. We'll look at how these tools can be used to accomplish several common tasks. But first, we'll look at WSDL itself, in order to construct WSDL files of our own.

WSDL Syntax

WSDL is a language for describing web services. It is an XML vocabulary, and it is used to create WSDL documents that are published alongside a web service on an ordinary web server. The WSDL file can then be downloaded by a developer looking to write a client to the web service, and used to automatically generate code to handle the raw communications, leaving the developer focusing on business logic. We'll look at how to accomplish this later on.

A WSDL document contains definitions of entities. Those entities represent the following:

Entity	Description
Data types	Data types
Messages	Collections of pieces of data
Operations	Collections of messages
Port types	Collections of related operations
Bindings	Mapping of a port type onto a protocol
Services	Collection of ports, specifying port types and bindings

Together, these are used to define the exact characteristics of one or more separate web services. Services can present one or more ports: addresses where requests to the service should be addressed, in a specified protocol. For example, one port might be an HTTP URL, another might be an e-mail address. Each port has a port-type (you can have several ports of the same type, or several ports of different types, or just one port), which defines, in abstract terms, exactly what operations can be performed through that port. If a service defines more than one port of the same type, then accessing the service through the different ports to perform the same operation should produce exactly the same results.

The definition of a port type is in terms of the operations it supports. An operation is a complete message exchange. The most common type of operation is a request-response operation, but all of the following four operations are possible:

Operation Type	Message Exchange
One-way	The service receives a message
Request-response	The service receives a message, and sends a message in return
Solicit-response	The service sends a message, and expects a message in return
N Notification	The service sends a message

It may be hard to imagine how a web service can send a message and demand a response (this isn't how web sites typically behave), but imagine the following scenario:

A web service provides auction management services. The operations making up this service might include an operation which allows you to put an item up for auction (one-way), an operation which allows you to retrieve a list of available items (request-response), an operation which allows you to bid (one-way), which leads to the service sending the seller a message asking if the bid should be accepted (solicit-response), and send the last highest bidder a message telling them they've been outbid (notification). If the seller accepts a bid, then the bidder gets a message telling them they've won the auction (notification).

These operations make up a definition of a port type. A port describes a concrete manner in which these operations can all be carried out via a particular physical interface, or protocol. One port for this service might provide a binding to SMTP, which would allow clients to interact with the service via e-mail. Another port might provide a binding to an instant messaging protocol.

Operations are defined in terms of the messages that have to be exchanged in order to perform them. Each message can consist of one or more data items, each of which is defined in terms of an abstract type. So, a bid in our auction example might consist of two pieces of data: the bid price, as a floating-point number; and the ID of the item being bid upon, as an integer. Another message might need a more complex data type, such as the list of auction items. This would need to be defined as a complex type and then referred to in the message definition.

Whenever we define any of these things, we give them a name, so we can refer to the entity elsewhere in the WSDL file. WSDL is namespace-aware, and when we allocate names, we can give them namespace prefixes to tell the WSDL interpreter that they belong to a particular namespace. Obviously, we need to declare the namespaces we intend to use in the root element of the WSDL file. By convention, we usually declare two namespaces that belong to the WSDL file. WSDL files also make use of a number of elements that belong to specific namespaces. The following namespaces are often used in WSDL files:

Namespace	Description	Typical Prefix	URI
WSDL	Contains all of the elements that make up a WSDL document. Used as the default namespace for a WSDL file	None (default namespace)	http://schemas.xmlsoap.org/wsdl/
W3C XML Schema Definition	Contains the standard XML schema data types and schema elements, which we need to define types	xsd	http://www.w3.org/2000/10/XMLSchema
WSDL SOAP binding	Contains elements needed to define a binding to the SOAP protocol	soap	http://schemas.xmlsoap.org/wsdl/soap/

Table continued on following page

Namespace	Description	Typical Prefix	URI
WSDL HTTP binding	Contains elements needed to define a binding to the HTTP protocol	`http`	`http://schemas.xmlsoap.org/wsdl/http/`
WSDL MIME binding	Contains elements needed to define a binding to a multi-part MIME message	`mime`	`http://schemas.xmlsoap.org/wsdl/mime/`
User-defined types	Contain the data types we create	`xsd1`	User-defined
WSDL entities	Contain the WSDL messages, operations, port types, bindings and services we create	`tns`	User-defined

The namespace prefix is, of course, user-defined, but those shown above are used in most examples you'll find elsewhere (including in the WSDL specification, which is included in the WSTK installation documentation), and will be used in the examples in this book. We'll also refer to namespaces by these prefixes throughout.

The three binding namespaces are extensions to the core WSDL standard, and other bindings are possible (such as the instant messaging binding suggested above), but not defined by the WSDL standard.

WSDL Syntax

The following is a guide to the elements that make up a WSDL service definition.

Element	Description	Page
`<definitions>`	Root element of a WSDL document	464
`<documentation>`	Element allowing insertion of documentation	465
`<import>`	Element allowing the import of entities defined in another file into this one	466
`<types>`	Element used to contain type definitions, if these are needed, and aren't imported from a separate file	468
`<message>`	Element representing an abstract message – a collection of pieces of data that will be sent to or by the web service as part of an operation	469
`<part>`	Element representing a piece of data within an abstract message	470
`<portType>`	Element representing an interface to a service	472

Element	Description	Page
`<operation>` (within `<portType>`)	Element describing one of four operation types	473
`<input>` (within `<portType>`)	'Param' type element. The purpose is to reference a previously defined message entity, and associate it with part of a WSDL operation	474
`<output>` (within `<portType>`)	'Param' type element. The purpose is to reference a previously defined message entity, and associate it with part of a WSDL operation	474
`<fault>` (within `<portType>`)	Element identifying a previously defined message structure that will convey fault details	475
`<binding>`	Element describing how a particular port-type interface is exposed over a particular protocol	477
`<soap:binding>`	Element setting some of the basic settings which apply to the soap binding	478
`<soap:operation>`	SOAP binding operation can contain a `<soap:operation>` element, depending on whether the default SOAP encoding style needs to be overridden, and whether the SOAP transport being used requires a `SOAPAction` to be specified	480
`<operation>` (within `<binding>`)	A binding must contain one `<operation>` element to match each operation defined in its port type	479
`<input>` & `<output>` (within `<binding>`)	Binding extension elements which indicate how exactly the messages they represent, and the parts of those messages, are to be encoded for transmission	481
`<soap:body>`	Element describing how to encode all or part of the message into the body of a SOAP envelope	481
`<service>`	Element describing a collection of ports which together make up a complete web service	484
`<port>`	A port is an address on which a particular binding is available, and is represented by a `<port>` element	484
`<soap:address>`	Element used to specify the physical location to which SOAP messages should be sent	485

<definitions>

```
<definitions [targetNamespace="tns_URI"]
             [name="service_name"]>
    ...
</definitions>
```

`<definitions>` is the root element of a WSDL document. As well as the two optional attributes, `targetNamespace` and `name`, this element will usually contain all the namespace declarations for the document. See the table on Page 461 for a list of namespace URIs and typical prefix assignments.

Attributes

Attribute	Type	Description
`targetNamespace`	URI	Identifies a namespace to which all names defined in this document will belong (optional)
`name`	Name	A name for the service (optional)

One convention is to use a URL at which the WSDL document is available as the `targetNamespace` URI. If you don't specify a target namespace, all the names you define will not belong to any namespace.

Child Elements

Element	Required	Maximum
`<documentation>`	No	Unlimited
`<import>`	No	Unlimited
`<types>`	No	1
`<message>`	No	Unlimited
`<portType>`	No	Unlimited
`<binding>`	No	Unlimited
`<service>`	No	Unlimited
`<*:*>`	No	Unlimited

These elements are all detailed below. Where present, they must occur in the order given. The `<*:*>` element indicates that any element belonging to a namespace other than the WSDL namespace may be included. This is to allow for different bindings to define elements at this level, and is a common feature throughout the WSDL specification.

Example: <definitions>

A typical WSDL document will be contained within a <definitions> element like the following, including namespace declarations for all of the namespaces in the document:

```
<?xml version="1.0"?>
<definitions name="MyWebService"
   targetNamespace="http://example.com/myservice.wsdl"
          xmlns="http://schemas.xmlsoap.org/wsdl/"
       xmlns:xsd="http://www.w3.org/2000/10/XMLSchema"
      xmlns:xsd1="http://example.com/mytypes.xsd"
       xmlns:tns="http://example.com/myservice.wsdl"
      xmlns:soap="http://schemas.xmlsoap.org/wsdl/soap/"
      xmlns:mime="http://schemas.xmlsoap.org/wsdl/mime/"
      xmlns:http="http://schemas.xmlsoap.org/wsdl/http/">

   ...

</definitions>
```

You can omit namespace declarations for any of the binding extensions you do not need to use.

Notice the targetNamespace URI is the same URI as that declared for the tns: namespace prefix. This means that any names declared within this document will be able to be referenced by prefixing them with the tns: namespace identifier. The choice of namespace URI for this purpose is therefore arbitrary. Here is a summary of the three potentially most confusing namespace declarations in the WSDL document:

The xmlns attribute is used to tell the XML parser which namespace any elements in the document which aren't qualified by a namespace prefix belong to, and prevents us from having to prefix every element in the document with a wsdl: prefix.

The targetNamespace attribute tells the WSDL parser that any names you define in this document belong to a certain namespace, the namespace defined by the URI we supply – that namespace is the target namespace into which the things you define should be placed.

We subsequently define a namespace prefix, tns:, for the **same** URI which you can then use to tell the WSDL parser that a name you are referring to is one of the names in that namespace – one of the named entities you define in this document.

<documentation>

```
<documentation>
    ...
</documentation>
```

`<documentation>` is an element which can be used inside many WSDL elements. It can contain mixed content, and any types of element are allowed. This allows the insertion of, for example, XHTML formatted documentation inside elements of a WSDL file.

<import>

```
<import namespace="URI"
        location="URI">
    ...
</import>
```

`<import>` allows you to import entities defined in another file into this one. For example , this can be used to import type definitions, , from an external schema, or to import definitions of WSDL entities defined elsewhere. It functions in a similar manner to the `<import>` element in the W3C schemas specification.

Attributes

Attribute	Type	Description
namespace	URI	Specifies the namespace from which entities defined in the other document should be imported *(Required)*
location	URI	The location of the document *(Required)*

The namespace URI identifies the namespace within the target document that contains the names of the objects you want to import. The imported elements will belong to this namespace within the importing document. In order to refer to them, you will need to have declared a prefix for this namespace in the document root element.

The location may be an absolute or relative URI.

Child Elements

Element	Required	Maximum
`<documentation>`	No	Unlimited

If no documentation is provided, then the `<import>` element can, naturally, be written as an empty element:

```
<import namespace="http://example.com/myTypes"
        location="mytypes.xsd" />
```

Example: <import> Data Types

One common use for `<import>` is to import a set of data types from an external file:

Schema

```
<?xml version="1.0"?>
<schema
    targetNamespace="http://example.com/mytypes.xsd"
            xmlns="http://www.w3.org/2000/10/XMLSchema">

    <element name="bid">
        <complexType>
            <all>
                <element name="bidPrice" type="float"/>
                <element name="itemID" type="int"/>
            </all>
        </complexType>
    </element>
</schema>
```

WSDL file

```
<?xml version="1.0"?>
<definitions name="MyWebService"
    targetNamespace="http://example.com/myservice.wsdl"
            xmlns="http://schemas.xmlsoap.org/wsdl/"
        xmlns:xsd1="http://example.com/mytypes.xsd"
          xmlns:tns="http://example.com/myservice.wsdl"
```

```
        <import namespace="http://example.com/mytypes.xsd"
                 location="mytypes.xsd"/>

    ...

    </definitions>
```

The schema file contains a definition of an element, `bid`, which, because of its `targetNamespace`, is inserted into the http://www.w3.org/2000/10/XMLSchema namespace. The WSDL file associates the `xsd1:` prefix with this namespace, and then imports the schema file into it. It is now possible to refer to the defined element as `xsd1:bid` later in the WSDL document.

<types>

```
<types>
    [<xsd:schema ... >
        ...
    </xsd:schema>]
</types>
```

A `<types>` element is used to contain type definitions, if these are needed, and aren't imported from a separate file. Normally, this means having an `<xsd:schema>` element inside the `<types>` element, although other type definitions are allowed, provided they are understood by the bindings which handle messages containing data of that type.

Note that unlike any other child of the root element, there can only ever be a maximum of one `<types>` element.

Type definitions are considered abstract – that is, they are a definition of what pieces of data make up a certain data type, not a definition of how that data will be written down. Some bindings may choose to use the standard mapping of W3C schema types to XML, but this is defined by the binding, not by the type definition.

Child Elements

Element	Required	Maximum
`<documentation>`	No	Unlimited
`<xsd:schema>`	No	Unlimited
`<*:*>`	No	Unlimited

The schema for WSDL documents does not in fact mandate the use of any particular typing mechanism, simply leaving it open for users to include any element belonging to a namespace other than the WSDL namespace. In practice, WSDL processors expect a W3C schema definition.

Schemas allow you to define data types and elements. A data type is a definition of the attributes and child elements that are permitted for an element of that type. An element is a named element that conforms to a particular type. A schema type is more like a Java interface, and a schema element is more like a Java class. Both types of schema entity can be used by WSDL. See <part> on page 470 to find out how.

Example: Using <types> to Define Data Types

To declare the same type as in the previous example without using a separate document, we can use the <types> element like this:

```xml
<?xml version="1.0"?>
<definitions name="MyWebService"
    targetNamespace="http://example.com/myservice.wsdl"
            xmlns="http://schemas.xmlsoap.org/wsdl/"
        xmlns:xsd1="http://example.com/mytypes.xsd"
          xmlns:tns="http://example.com/myservice.wsdl">

    <types>
        <schema
          targetNamespace="http://example.com/mytypes.xsd"
                  xmlns="http://www.w3.org/2000/10/XMLSchema">

            <element name="bid">
                <complexType>
                    <all>
                        <element name="bidPrice" type="float"/>
                        <element name="itemID" type="int"/>
                    </all>
                </complexType>
            </element>
        </schema>
    </types>

    ...

</definitions>
```

Notice that by declaring the XSD namespace as the default namespace for the <schema> element, we avoid having to prefix every element and name with the xsd: namespace identifier. Again, the schema's target namespace is the namespace we have declared at the root of the document to have the xsd1: prefix, so we can refer to the bid data type later in the document as xsd1:bid.

<message>

```
<message name="message_name">...</message>
```

A `<message>` element represents an abstract message – a collection of pieces of data that will be sent to or by the web service as part of an operation. A message consists of zero or more parts, represented by nested `<part>` elements.

Attributes

Attribute	Type	Description
name	Name	A name by which the message will be known. The name will belong to the document's target namespace. *(Required)*

The name must be unique among messages within this document's target namespace. Although it is possible to have the same name apply to a message and another type of entity within the same namespace, it is recommended, for clarity, that this is avoided.

Child Elements

Element	Required	Maximum
<documentation>	No	Unlimited
<part>	No	Unlimited

A message can contain no parts, in which case it carries no data at all. This does not mean the message won't be sent. A call to a method that takes no arguments, or the return value from a method that returns void, might be perfectly valid uses for an empty message.

<part>

```
<message name="message_name">
      <part [name="part_name"]
            [type="data_type"]
         [element="data_type"] ... />
</message>
```

A `<part>` element represents piece of data within an abstract message. A part has to be associated with a data type, and there are two ways of doing this for W3C schema data types:

❑ By referring to a defined data type by name using the `type` attribute

❑ By referring to a defined element by name using the `element` attribute

If you are using an alternative typing mechanism, the element can contain other attributes that can be used to refer to those types.

The name attribute is used to provide a unique name among the parts within a single message.

A `<part>` is always an empty element.

Attributes

Attribute	Type	Description
name	Name	A name by which the message part will be known. Only meaningful in the context of the message. (Optional)
type	Reference	Identifies a W3C schema data type which describes the data this message part will contain (Optional)
element	Reference	Identifies a W3C schema element definition which describes the data this message part will contain (Optional)
*	Reference	Identifies another data type definition which describes the data this message part will contain (Optional)

The name must be unique among messages within this document's target namespace. Although it is possible to have the same name apply to a message and another type of entity within the same namespace, it is recommended, for clarity, that this is avoided.

Only one data type reference should be provided.

It is possible (and often desirable) to refer directly to the primitive data types defined by the W3C schema specification, as well as to types defined in the `<types>` element or imported via `<import>`. If your WSDL only requires primitive data types, you won't need to have a `<types>` element or schema reference at all.

Example: <message> and <part>

The following example declares a multi-part message, containing one part of the bid data type which we created in the previous examples, and one part which is an XML schema data type: string.

```xml
<?xml version="1.0"?>
<definitions name="MyWebService"
    targetNamespace="http://example.com/myservice.wsdl"
            xmlns="http://schemas.xmlsoap.org/wsdl/"
        xmlns:xsd1="http://example.com/mytypes.xsd"
         xmlns:tns="http://example.com/myservice.wsdl"
         xmlns:xsd="http://www.w3.org/2000/10/XMLSchema">

    <!-- import or types element as before -->

    <message name="bidMessage">
        <part name="itemBid" element="xsd1:bid"/>
        <part name="bidderName" type="xsd:string"/>
    </message>

    ...

</definitions>
```

We have to declare the W3C schema namespace so we can refer to the data types declared in it. The bid message consists of two parts, a bid for an item and the name of the bidder. The bid is described by the data type we created previously. The bidder name is simply a string, as defined by the XML schema data type.

<portType>

```xml
<portType name="portType_name">
        ...
</portType>
```

A <portType> element represents an interface to a service. It does so by defining a set of operations, or message exchanges. Effectively, this element is used to define the method signatures that your service exposes. Much like a Java interface, a port type simply defines the method names, the arguments, and the return types that make up the service's public face.

Attributes

Attribute	Type	Description
name	Name	A name by which the port type will be known. The name will belong to the document's target namespace. *(Required)*

The name must be unique among port types within this document's target namespace.

It's worth noting that when you use some of IBM's WSDL tools, the value of this attribute is used to form the names of classes. For that reason, you might want to stick to Java naming conventions, and give a name that begins with a capital letter.

Child Elements

Element	Required	Maximum
`<documentation>`	No	Unlimited
`<operation>`	No	Unlimited

`<operation>` (within `<portType>`)

```
<portType name="portType_name">
    <operation name="operation_name">
        ...
    </operation>
</portType>
```

`<operation>` elements come in four types, which we discussed earlier in the chapter:

- ❑ Request-response
- ❑ Solicit-response
- ❑ Notification
- ❑ One-way

These types are embodied in the operation's child elements, and their ordering. Three child elements are permitted: `<input>`, `<output>`, and `<fault>`. Each of these associates a message with a phase of the operation.

A notification operation contains a single `<output>` element, identifying the message that defines the form the notification will take.

```
<operation name="notification">
  <output message="data"/>
</operation>
```

A one-way operation, similarly, contains a single `<input>` element.

```
<operation name="one-way">
  <input message="data"/>
</operation>
```

Request-response operations have an `<input>` element, followed by an `<output>` element. These represent the parameters that make up the request and the message containing the response, respectively. If the service is unable to provide the response, due to incorrect input, or some other circumstances, it is possible that the service might send a fault message instead of a return value (much like a Java method throwing an exception). WSDL allows you to insert multiple `<fault>` elements to represent these possibilities.

```
<operation name="request-response">
  <input message="params"/>
  <output message="return"/>
  <fault message="exception"/>
</operation>
```

Solicit-response operations are the same, only in reverse: an `<output>`, then an `<input>`. Similarly, if the client is unable to provide a valid response, it can send a fault report, and again, multiple `<fault>` messages can be added to this type of operation as well.

```
<operation name="solicit-response">
  <output message="solicitation"/>
  <input message="response"/>
  <fault message="exception"/>
</operation>
```

Attributes

Attribute	Type	Description
name	Name	A name by which the operation will be known. The name must be unique within the port type. *(Required)*

Again, it's worth noting that when you use some of IBM's WSDL tools, the value of this attribute is used to form the names of methods.

Child Elements

Element	Required	Maximum
`<documentation>`	No	Unlimited
`<input>`	No	1
`<output>`	No	1
`<fault>`	No	Unlimited (if both `<input>` and `<output>` elements are present)

As we saw above, the exact possible combinations of child elements are quite strictly controlled, and the order is significant.

<input> & <output> (within <portType>)

```
<portType name="portType_name">
    <operation name="operation_name">
        <input message="request" />
        <output message="response" />
    </operation>
</portType>
```

These two elements can be treated together, since they both have exactly the same type in the WSDL schema – it refers to them as 'param' type elements. The purpose of both is to reference a previously defined message entity, and associate it with part of a WSDL operation.

Attributes

Attribute	Type	Description
name	Name	A name for this parameter *(Optional)*
message	Reference	A qualified name for the message that constitutes this part of this operation. Remember to use the tns: namespace prefix when referring to messages created in this document.*(Required)*

Child Elements

Element	Required	Maximum
<documentation>	No	Unlimited

<fault> (within <portType>)

```
<portType name="portType_name">
    <operation name="operation_name">
        ...
        <fault message="response"
               name="fault_name" />
    </operation>
</portType>
```

The difference between a fault and the parameter elements is that faults must specify a name. This is because there can be more than one fault within a single operation (think of the situation where a Java method might throw more than one type of exception – that's why you need to be able to have multiple fault types). Otherwise, this element is very similar, identifying a previously defined message structure that will convey the fault details.

Attributes

Attribute	Type	Description
name	Name	A name for this fault type (*Required*)
message	Reference	A qualified name for the message that constitutes this fault report. Remember to use the tns: namespace prefix when referring to messages created in this document. (*Required*)

Child Elements

Element	Required	Maximum
<documentation>	No	Unlimited

Example: <portType> and <operation>

Here is a port type which declares one request-response operation, based around the bid message we declared above:

```xml
<?xml version="1.0"?>
<definitions name="MyWebService"
    targetNamespace="http://example.com/myservice.wsdl"
            xmlns="http://schemas.xmlsoap.org/wsdl/"
        xmlns:xsd1="http://example.com/mytypes.xsd"
        xmlns:tns="http://example.com/myservice.wsdl"
        xmlns:xsd="http://www.w3.org/2000/10/XMLSchema">

<!-- import or types element as before -->

<!-- message element as before -->

<portType name="AuctionBid">
    <operation name="placeBid">
        <input message="tns:bidMessage"/>
        <output message="tns:emptyMessage"/>
        <fault name="auctionClosed"
            message="tns:bidFailureMessage"/>
```

```
            </operation>
        </portType>

        ...

    </definitions>
```

The port type is named AuctionBid. When naming a port type, imagine it as a Java interface name – would it make sense to have a class 'implement' that port type? The WSDL tools will generate class files for the service and client by appending the word 'Service' and 'Proxy' to this name. This means we will have classes called AuctionBidService and AuctionBidProxy.

Similarly, the name we choose for the operation will form the name of a method in the generated classes. The parameters will take their names from the parts of the input message – parts we named when we created the message before.

<binding>

```
<binding name="binding_name" type="portType">
    ...
</binding>
```

<binding> elements describe how a particular port type interface is exposed over a particular protocol. The binding specifies how the data in the messages is encoded, and how the port type's operations are exposed. There must be at least one binding for each port type that is declared, although it is possible to have more.

Physical addressing is not part of a binding definition – it only declares how the messages should be packaged, not where they should be sent.

<binding> elements need to contain extension elements, from a different namespace, specific to the binding being used. WSDL defines three bindings: HTTP, SOAP and MIME.

SOAP encoding can be used to encode messages into HTTP POST request bodies, and the responses, as well as to encode messages in SMTP mail messages. The HTTP encoding can be used to encode message data within the URL of a GET request, or the body of a POST request. The MIME binding is used typically in association with the other bindings to build multi-part messages, or to describe encodings of data within HTTP requests.

Details of the HTTP and MIME bindings are contained in the WSDL specification, but since these aren't supported by the WSDL toolkit, we will concentrate here on the SOAP binding, and in particular to the SOAP RPC binding to HTTP, which is the format most likely to be used by web services developers.

477

Attributes

Attribute	Type	Description
`name`	Name	A name for this binding (*Required*)
`type`	Reference	A qualified name for the port type which this binding implements (*Required*)

Child Elements

Element	Required	Maximum
`<documentation>`	No	Unlimited
`<soap:binding>`	For SOAP bindings	1
`<operation>`	One for each operation defined in the port type	One for each operation defined in the port type

---

`<soap:binding>`

```
<binding ... >
     <soap:binding [style="soap_style"]
                   transport="soap_transport"/>
          . . .
</binding>
```

A SOAP binding must contain a `<soap:binding>` element, which sets a couple of the basic settings which apply to the binding as a whole. These are the style of SOAP message, which can be either RPC or document, and the SOAP transport, which specifies the underlying protocol over which the SOAP messages will be transferred.

The encoding style specification simply specifies the default encoding for the binding – it can be changed for each operation. RPC style explicitly encodes the messages as requests and responses to methods. Document style encodes the messages as simply a set of objects.

The transport attribute is a URI, most likely to be `http://schemas.xmlsoap.org/soap/http`, the HTTP transport. Others are possible, specifying transport via SMTP, JMS, etc.

The `<soap:binding>` element is always an empty element.

Attributes

Attribute	Type	Description
style	SOAP style: rpc or document	The default style for this binding (*Optional*)
transport	URI	The URI indicating the SOAP transport to be used for this binding (*Required*)

<operation> (within <binding>)

```
<binding ... >
      <operation name="operation_name">
         ...
      </operation>
</binding>
```

A binding must contain one <operation> element to match each operation defined in its port type. The operations are matched up according to the name element. The structure of this operation must also match the operation within the port type – it must have the same ordering of input, output and fault children, although with the addition of extension elements that define how the operation is bound to the protocol.

Attributes

Attribute	Type	Description
name	Name	A name for this binding (*Required*)

Child Elements

Element	Required	Maximum
<documentation>	No	Unlimited
<soap:operation>	For SOAP bindings	1
<input>	As defined in the operation definition within the port type	See under **Required** column

Table continued on following page

Element	Required	Maximum
`<output>`	As defined in the operation definition within the port type	See under **Required** column
`<fault>`	As defined in the operation definition within the port type	See under **Required** column

`<soap:operation>`

```
<binding ... >
        <operation name="operation_name">
            <soap:operation
                [style="soap_style"]
            [soapAction="action_URI"]/>
                ...
        </operation>
</binding>
```

A SOAP binding operation can contain a `<soap:operation>` element, depending on whether the default SOAP encoding style needs to be overridden, and whether the SOAP transport being used requires a `SOAPAction` to be specified.

The SOAP Action is a URI used by the HTTP SOAP transport as the value for the `SOAPAction` HTTP header in the request and responses. It is used in the process of distinguishing what the purpose of a SOAP message is, and we looked at an example in the previous chapter. As such, it is required if you are using the HTTP transport, but is not for other transports.

> Apache SOAP doesn't pay any attention to the **SOAPAction** header, so you can supply an empty string for the value when the service will be hosted on the Apache SOAP servlet. However, you must still supply the attribute, even if the soap action is an empty string.

If no style is specified here or in the `<soap:binding>` element, then document style is assumed.

The `<soap:operation>` element is always an empty element.

Attributes

Attribute	Type	Description
style	SOAP style: rpc or document	The default style for this binding (Optional)
soapAction	URI	The URI indicating the SOAP Action to be used for this operation (Required for HTTP binding)

`<input>` & `<output>` (within `<binding>`)

```
<binding ...>
      <operation ...>
            <input>
                  ...
            </input>
            <output>
                  ...
            </output>
      </operation>
</portType>
```

Again, we can treat these two together since they are identical in behavior. They must each contain binding extension elements which indicate how exactly the messages they represent, and the parts of those messages, are to be encoded for transmission. For SOAP operations, this is accomplished using `<soap:body>` elements to encode data into the body of a SOAP envelope, and `<soap:header>` elements to encode data into the header of a SOAP envelope.

Child Elements

Element	Required	Maximum
`<documentation>`	No	Unlimited
`<soap:body>`	No	1
`<soap:header>`	No	1

There may be no need to have a `<soap:body>` or `<soap:header>` child element if the message the `<input>` or `<output>` represents has no data parts. `<soap:header>` is only required for low-level SOAP engineering (such as accessing security protocols), and does not offer much functionality with current SOAP implementations. Consequently, we will only be looking at `<soap:body>` here.

<soap:body>

```
<binding ...>
      <operation ...>
            <input>
                  <soap:body
                    [parts="parts_list"]
                      use="format"
            [encodingStyle="encoding_URI"]
                  [namespace="namespace_URI"]/>
            </input>
      </operation>
</portType>
```

The input and output messages of a SOAP operation may contain a <soap:body> element. The purpose of this element is to describe how to encode all or part of the message into the body of a SOAP envelope.

The optional parts attribute is a list of named parts belonging to the underlying message, which will be encoded into the SOAP body. The other parts should be encoded using a <soap:header> element, or as part of other sections of a MIME multi-part message. If this attribute is omitted, it is assumed that all the parts making up the message will be encoded in the body.

The way SOAP encodes the parts specified will depend on the style attribute of either the enclosing operation or binding. If RPC style is selected, then the parts are arranged inside a structure that represents a SOAP method-call or method-response, wrapped in elements to indicate this structure. If the style is document, then the parts aren't wrapped up in this way, and simply appear as children of the SOAP body.

The use attribute is used to indicate whether the literal representation of the data is defined precisely by the schema data types we defined, or whether SOAP encoding should be used to create the literal XML for each part. The options for this attribute are either literal (use the exact schema specified), or encoded (SOAP should provide the physical structure).

Literal use of data types works for both element and type definitions. Elements appear exactly as specified in the schema in the encoded document. If a type is used 'literally', the element in the encoded document which will contain the piece of data will be given the specified data type. There is no need to specify an encoding style, since the encoding has effectively been performed manually.

Encoded use only works with type definitions. An encoding style must be supplied (the default SOAP encoding is http://schemas.xmlsoap.org/soap/encoding/) to tell users of the document what format they should use to represent data types.

The namespace attribute specifies what namespace URI should be used for any elements that are created by the encoding process, either in embedding parts in an RPC-style message, or in encoding data.

Again, <soap:body> is always an empty element.

Attributes

Attribute	Type	Description
parts	List of names	The message parts which should be placed in the SOAP body (Optional)
use	SOAP format: literal or encoded	Whether to encode the data using an encoding scheme, or use the schema definitions literally (Required)
encodingStyle	URI	The encoding style to use (required if use="encoded")
namespace	URI	Namespace to use for any elements created in the encoding process (Optional)

Example: <binding>

Here is a SOAP RPC binding for the port type we declared above:

```
<?xml version="1.0"?>
<definitions name="MyWebService"
  targetNamespace="http://example.com/myservice.wsdl"
          xmlns="http://schemas.xmlsoap.org/wsdl/"
      xmlns:xsd1="http://example.com/mytypes.xsd"
       xmlns:tns="http://example.com/myservice.wsdl"
       xmlns:xsd="http://www.w3.org/2000/10/XMLSchema">

  <!-- import or types element as before -->

  <!-- message element as before -->

  <!-- portType element as before -->

<binding name="AuctionBidSOAPrpc">
    <soap:binding style="rpc"
       transport="http://schemas.xmlsoap.org/soap/http"/>
    <operation name="placeBid">
       <soap:operation soapAction="urn:auctionbid"/>
       <input>
          <soap:body use="literal"
             namespace="http://example.com/auctionbid"/>
       </input>
       <output/>
    </operation>
  </binding>
```

```
      ...
   </definitions>
```

The binding is actually very simple: all we have to do is define a SOAP binding extension element at each level – first to identify the transport and document format, then to give a `SOAPAction` value for the HTTP header (we choose to use a URN style URI, because a URL used as a SOAP action can look a lot like an address – it's important to remember that it isn't. You are giving the *name* of the service you want this request to reach, not its physical location. A service with the same name might be reachable at a number of locations, just as a person might have multiple e-mail addresses. Another suitable format for this URI would be to use the `guid:` scheme).

After this, encoding the input message is simple: we use literal encoding, since that will work with both elements and types, and we provide a namespace for any elements that arise.

<service>

```
<service name="service_name">
      ...
</service>
```

`<service>` elements describe a collection of ports which together make up a complete web service. One WSDL document can contain more than one `<service>` element (although most WSDL tools expect there to be just the one).

The names you give to services are significant when it comes to registering them with registries, and we will come back to this issue when we look at UDDI later on.

Attributes

Attribute	Type	Description
name	Name	A name for this service (*Required*)

Child Elements

Element	Required	Maximum
<documentation>	No	Unlimited
<port>	No	Unlimited

<port>

```
<service name="service_name">
   <port name="port_name"
      binding="binding_ref">
      ...
   </port>
</service>
```

A port is an address on which a particular binding is available, and is represented by a `<port>` element. The element will have as a child a binding-specific element that provides the addressing information required to communicate over the bound protocol.

Attributes

Attribute	Type	Description
name	Name	A name for this port *(Required)*
binding	Reference	The binding available via this port *(Required)*

Child Elements

Element	Required	Maximum
<documentation>	No	Unlimited
<soap:address>	For SOAP binding	1

<soap:address>

```
<service ...>
   <port ...>
      <soap:address location="SOAP_URL"/>
   </port>
</service>
```

The `<soap:address>` element is used to specify the physical location to which SOAP messages should be sent. The type of URL used will depend on the soap transport (mailto: scheme for SMTP transport, etc.), but for HTTP transport, it will be the http: scheme URL of the SOAP server. The local URL of a standard Apache-SOAP installation running on Tomcat's default port would be http://localhost:8080/apache-soap/servlet/rpcrouter.

485

Attributes

Attribute	Type	Description
location	URL	The physical network location of the SOAP service *(Required)*

Using WSDL

We've now covered the format of WSDL documents. The WSDL Toolkit includes several tools for manipulating, parsing and creating WSDL, which we'll now take a look at in turn.

First, it's important to note that the IBM tools only work with a subset of WSDL – they don't provide a full implementation. In particular:

❑ They are limited to handling a single service, containing a single port definition.

❑ Only RPC-style SOAP bindings are supported. Other bindings won't be parsed, and selecting 'document' style for a SOAP binding makes no difference to the resulting files.

❑ SOAP Transport settings are ignored (the HTTP transport is assumed). It's possible to change the transport by editing the resulting source code.

❑ Use is always treated as encoded, not literal. Even if you specify literal, you must specify an encoding style, and this will be used to perform the encoding.

❑ A limited subset of schema's is supported. To be safe, you should follow the rules given below. Also, the URI for the schemas namespace should be http://www.w3.org/1999/XMLSchema, which the Apache-SOAP implementation supports.

❑ Namespace support is broken. Although the style given above (using the tns: prefix for all locally defined names) is that given in the WSDL specification, it is not compatible with the IBM WSDL tools. You still need to declare a targetNamespace for the WSDL file, but you do not need to reference it with a prefix on your names. This does not apply to schemas, which do use namespace prefixes to reference definitions of types.

Schemas are mapped to simple Java classes that represent the data types they define. When using simple xsd: types, you should stick to the following:

❑ xsd:string

❑ xsd:int

❑ xsd:float

❑ xsd:boolean

Complex types are supported where they consist only of elements whose type is one of the above simple types, or of another complex type that follows this rule.

These types can all be easily mapped by the WSDL toolkit into Java classes or primitives. Complex types will be turned into classes with one public data member for each element specified, of the appropriate type.

Sample WSDL

For the following examples, we'll be using this IBM-compatible WSDL file for a simple lookup service, which provides book details in exchange for an ISBN:

BookLookup.wsdl

```xml
<?xml version="1.0"?>

<definitions name="BookLookupService"
  targetNamespace="http://wrox.com/javaxmlref/BookLookup.wsdl"
            xmlns="http://schemas.xmlsoap.org/wsdl/"
        xmlns:xsd="http://www.w3.org/1999/XMLSchema"
       xmlns:xsd1="http://wrox.com/javaxmlref/booklookup"
       xmlns:soap="http://schemas.xmlsoap.org/wsdl/soap/">

  <types>
    <xsd:schema
          targetNamespace="http://wrox.com/javaxmlref/booklookup"
                xmlns:xsd="http://www.w3.org/1999/XMLSchema">
        <xsd:complexType name="book">
          <xsd:element name="isbn" type="xsd:string"/>
          <xsd:element name="title" type="xsd:string"/>
          <xsd:element name="author" type="xsd:string"/>
          <xsd:element name="price" type="xsd:float"/>
          <xsd:element name="pubDate" type="xsd1:pubDate"/>
        </xsd:complexType>
        <xsd:complexType name="pubDate">
          <xsd:element name="year" type="xsd:int"/>
          <xsd:element name="month" type="xsd:int"/>
        </xsd:complexType>
    </xsd:schema>
  </types>

  <message name="BookLookupInput">
    <part name="isbn" type="xsd:string"/>
  </message>

  <message name="BookLookupOutput">
    <part name="book" type="xsd1:book"/>
  </message>

  <portType name="BookLookup">
    <operation name="getBook">
      <input message="BookLookupInput"/>
      <output message="BookLookupOutput"/>
    </operation>
  </portType>

  <binding name="BookLookupSoapBinding" type="BookLookup">
    <soap:binding style="rpc"
              transport="http://schemas.xmlsoap.org/soap/http"/>
    <operation name="getBook">
      <soap:operation soapAction=""/>
      <input>
        <soap:body use="encoded"
```

```
              encodingStyle="http://schemas.xmlsoap.org/soap/encoding/"
                  namespace="http://wrox.com/javaxmlref/booklookup"/>
        </input>
      </operation>
    </binding>

    <service name="BookLookupService">
      <port name="BookLookupPort" binding="BookLookupSoapBinding">
        <soap:address
           location=
              "http://localhost:8080/apache-soap/servlet/rpcrouter"/>
      </port>
    </service>

  </definitions>
```

This defines a service with a single getbook() method, to which we pass an ISBN as a String (ISBN numbers can end in the character X, so an int is not a suitable data type), and which returns a complex object containing information about the book.

Note that the sample Tomcat server.xml file provided with the download code listens by default on port 5202 (the short ISBN for this book).

Generating Web Service Classes from WSDL

The WSDL toolkit class com.ibm.wsdl.Main, which is in the wsdl.jar file contained in the WSDL toolkit's lib directory, is a command-line entry point that can be used to generate web service classes. Here is the basic command line syntax used to generate Java code from WSDL with this class:

```
> java com.ibm.wsdl.Main -in wsdl_file [-target target_type]
```

Other arguments are possible. All the arguments have default values, and can therefore be omitted. Here is the full list of possible arguments:

Argument	Possible Values	Default	Description
-in	URL or filename	Standard input is read	Specifies the source to use for WSDL data
-target	client or server	client	Tells the tool whether to generate a client stub or a service skeleton and deployment descriptor
-dir	Any directory path	.	Specifies the directory into which resulting files will be written. Package directory structures, where needed, will also be created under this directory.

Argument	Possible Values	Default	Description
-package	Name of a Java package		Package to put resulting classes in. Wherever a package is implied by the WSDL that will be used instead,
-verbose	on or off	on	Whether to output progress information to the console
-override	on or off	off	Whether to overwrite existing files
-javac	on or off	on	Whether to compile resulting .java files
-nasslOnly	on or off	off	Whether to create NASSL files rather than WSDL files (NASSL is an older description language created by IBM)

The following JAR files need to be on the classpath for this command to work:

From the WSTK

❑ <wstk_home>/wsdl-toolkit/lib/wsdl.jar

❑ <wstk_home>/soap/lib/soap.jar

❑ <wstk_home>/lib/xerces.jar

❑ <wstk_home>/lib/xalan.jar

❑ <wstk_home>/lib/bsf.jar

> **Many of these JAR files are available from other sources, but the specific version requirements of the WSTK mean you should probably stick with the versions provided by IBM.**

From the JDK

❑ <java_home>/lib/tools.jar

Generating the Service Template

Here is the command we need to issue in order to generate the template web service from our example WSDL file:

```
> java com.ibm.wsdl.Main -in BookLookup.wsdl -target server -dir .
    -javac no -override on
```

In our example's case, the following files will be generated:

❑   `BookLookupService.java`

❑   `DeploymentDescriptor.xml`

❑   `com.wrox.javaxmlref.booklookup.Book.java`

❑   `com.wrox.javaxmlref.booklookup.BookSerializer.java`

❑   `com.wrox.javaxmlref.booklookup.PubDate.java`

❑   `com.wrox.javaxmlref.booklookup.PubDateSerializer.java`

Note that these package names are generated automatically from the target namespace URI in the WSDL.

BookLookupService.java

This is the source code for a skeleton web service which implements the interface described in the WSDL. This file takes its name from the `portType` declared in the WSDL source code, with `Service` appended to the name.

Before compiling this file into a class, you should edit it to add the functionality you require for your web service: it is only a skeleton of the service, and all methods will return `null` or `zero` values by default. This is why we turned off the `-javac` argument when running the generator.

The class, `BookLookupService`, simply has one method for each of the operations defined for the port type, with the names defined by the WSDL file `<operation>` elements. Their parameters will be the parts of the message that make up the input, and the return value will be the output message (which must have one single part). For our example, it has one method:

```
public class BookLookupService
{
    public synchronized com.wrox.javaxmlref.booklookup.Book getBook
      (java.lang.String isbn)
    {
        return null;
    }

}
```

Simply replace the return value with your service-logic, and you have a web service class.

DeploymentDescriptor.xml

This is the Apache-SOAP deployment descriptor for the web service, which can be used to make the `BookLookupService` class available as a SOAP service. This is in the format discusses in Chapter 8, and defines the provider class (`BookLookupService`), and the required mapping classes for the complex types.

com.wrox.javaxmlref.booklookup.Book.java and PubDate.java

These two classes are Java representations of the two complex datatypes we declared. Their package name is derived from the namespace the type definitions belong to (`http://wrox.com/javaxmlref/booklookup`). They are each quite simple, having data members for each of the elements their type contains, and a constructor. `Book.java` looks like this:

```
package com.wrox.javaxmlref.booklookup;

public class Book{

  //instance variables
  public java.lang.String  isbn_Elem;
  public java.lang.String  title_Elem;
  public java.lang.String  author_Elem;
  public float  price_Elem;
  public PubDate  pubDate_Elem;


  //constructors
  public Book () { }

  public Book (java.lang.String isbn_Elem, java.lang.String title_Elem,
java.lang.String author_Elem, float price_Elem, PubDate pubDate_Elem) {
    this.isbn_Elem  = isbn_Elem;
    this.title_Elem  = title_Elem;
    this.author_Elem  = author_Elem;
    this.price_Elem  = price_Elem;
    this.pubDate_Elem  = pubDate_Elem;
  }

}
```

The class isn't exactly a masterpiece of standard Java class design – instance variables are simply given public access, rather than being private and using accessor methods for mutation, for example. The variables also have slightly awkward names. But this is probably the simplest piece of code that could be used to build a pure data object to represent the schema types.

You can add methods of your own to this class, although you may find it better to build functionality into these data objects by extension or composition, rather than by editing. That way, if you regenerate this class from the WSDL, you don't lose the modifications you have made.

com.wrox.javaxmlref.booklookup.BookSerializer.java and PubDateSerializer.java

These implement the Apache SOAP Serializer and Deserializer interfaces, and provide a mapping between XML data in SOAP envelopes and the two Java classes defined above. They are used by SOAP to encode Java objects into XML, and vice versa. They are referenced in the deployment descriptor, which allows the SOAP RPC router servlet to perform the mapping.

Example: The BookLookupService Web Service

The following amendment needs to be made to the BookLookupService.java file to create a working service:

Source BookLookupService

```
import com.wrox.javaxmlref.booklookup.*;
import java.util.HashMap;
```

```
public class BookLookupService
{

  private HashMap books = new HashMap();

  public BookLookupService() {
      books.put("1861005202", new Book("1861005202", "Java XML Programmer's
Reference", "Writz et al", 34.99, new PubDate(2001,6)));
      books.put("186100401X", new book("186100401X", "Professional Java XML",
"Ahmed et al", 59.99, new PubDate(2001,4)));
  }

  public synchronized Book getBook
    (java.lang.String isbn)
  {
    return (Book) books.get(isbn);
  }
}
```

Having amended the service skeleton to contain actual service code, we can compile the generated classes before deploying to an Apache SOAP server.

Deploying the Service

For the service to be usable by Apache SOAP, the SOAP RPC router needs to be able to access the .class files for the service itself, the serializers, and the mapping classes. You can accomplish this by bundling together the necessary files into a JAR file. This file then needs to be placed somewhere where Apache SOAP can see it – most likely in the SOAP Webapp's WEB-INF/lib directory. Alternatively, the classes can be added to the WEB-INF/classes directory. Be careful to maintain the package structure.

Then, to deploy the service, we can simply use the Apache SOAP command line deployment utility, passing the deployment descriptor that was generated for us as the argument. Remember, the servlet container must be running before you execute this command.

```
> java org.apache.soap.server.ServiceManagerClient RPC_router_url
    deploy Deployment_Descriptor_Path
```

So, for our example (and most other trivial examples), that would be:

```
> java org.apache.soap.server.ServiceManagerClient
    http://localhost:8080/apache-soap/servlet/rpcrouter deploy
    DeploymentDescriptor.xml
```

To avoid repeated statements of classpath requirements, we encourage the reader to refer to Appendix A, where building the code in the book is described precisely in terms of the Ant scripting language.

Generating the Client Proxy

Again, we use the `com.ibm.wsdl.Main` class, with the simpler syntax of:

```
> java com.ibm.wsdl.Main -in BookLookup.wsdl -dir . -override on
```

This will generate a client proxy stub class, which implements methods with the same signatures as the web service skeleton. The stub is a full implementation, however, and we won't need to make any changes to the generated class. For this reason, we can allow the WSDL tool to compile the classes for us.

Again, the serializers and data object classes will be generated by this process. They will need to be available on the classpath for any class which uses this proxy stub, since they are used as either return types or parameters to the proxy's methods.

Using the Client Proxy

Using the client proxy is a simple case of instantiating it, and calling the methods it exposes. The proxy uses the Apache SOAP library to perform encoding of parameters into a web service RPC call, and then interpret the results and return a Java object. From the perspective of a class using the service, it's a 100% Java operation – no XML in sight.

Example: Accessing a Web Service from a Console App

Here is a client class which makes use of the web service proxy to access the service we created earlier:

Source BookLookupClient.java

```java
import com.wrox.javaxmlref.booklookup.*;

public class BookLookupClient {

  public static void main(String[] args) {

    if(args.length != 1) {
      System.out.println(
        "Usage: java BookLookupClient <isbn>");
    } else {
      String isbn = args[0];

      try {
        BookLookupProxy blp = new BookLookupProxy();
        Book b = blp.getBook(isbn);

        System.out.println(b.title_Elem);
        System.out.println(b.author_Elem);
        System.out.println("$" + b.price_Elem);
```

```
System.out.println(b.isbn_Elem);
        System.out.println("" +
          b.pubDate_Elem.month_Elem + "/" +
          b.pubDate_Elem.year_Elem);
      } catch (Exception e) { }
    }
  }
}
```

To execute it, you'll need the SOAP, JavaBean Activation Framework, JavaMail and Xerces JAR files on your classpath, as well as the directory containing the classes generated by the WSDL tools.

Example: Accessing a Web Service from a Servlet

When creating a servlet to access a web service, the process is very similar to that of creating a console program. The only difference comes in deploying the servlet as part of a web application.

This servlet uses the `BookLookupProxy` class to access the web service we have developed:

Source BookLookupServlet.java

```
import javax.servlet.*;
import javax.servlet.http.*;
import java.io.*;
import com.wrox.javaxmlref.booklookup.*;

public class BookLookupServlet extends HttpServlet {
```

The `doGet()` method produces a form which the user can use to enter an ISBN. The form data is posted back to this servlet.

```
public void doGet(HttpServletRequest req,
    HttpServletResponse res)
  throws IOException, ServletException {

  ServletOutputStream out = res.getOutputStream();
  out.println("<html><head><title>Book Lookup Web " +
    "Service</title></head>");
  out.println("<body>");
  out.println("<h1>Book Lookup Web Service</h1>");
  out.println("<form action='" + req.getContextPath() +
    req.getServletPath() + "' method='post'>");
  out.println("Enter an ISBN: <input type='text'" +
    "size='20' name='isbn' /><br />");
  out.println("<input type='submit' />");
  out.println("</form>");
```

```
   out.println("</body>");
     out.println("</html>");

     out.flush();
     out.close();

   }
```

The doPost() method handles the form input, extracting the ISBN from the request and passing it on to the BookLookupProxy class:

```
   public void doPost(HttpServletRequest req,
     HttpServletResponse res)
     throws IOException, ServletException {

     String isbn = req.getParameter("isbn");
     ServletOutputStream out = res.getOutputStream();

     BookLookupProxy blp = new BookLookupProxy();

     Book book=null;

     try {
       book = blp.getBook(isbn);
     } catch (Exception e) { }

     out.println("<html><head><title>Book Lookup Web
   Service</title></head>");
     out.println("<body>");
     out.println("<h1>Book Lookup Web Service</h1>");

     if (book != null) {

     out.println("<table>");

     out.println("<tr><td>Title:</td><td>" +
       book.title_Elem + "</td></tr>");
     out.println("<tr><td>Author:</td><td>" +
       book.author_Elem + "</td></tr>");
     out.println("<tr><td>ISBN:</td><td>" +
       book.isbn_Elem + "</td></tr>");
     out.println("<tr><td>Price:</td><td>$" +
       book.price_Elem + "</td></tr>");
     out.println("<tr><td>Publication Date:</td><td>" +
       book.pubDate_Elem.month_Elem + "/" +
       book.pubDate_Elem.year_Elem + "</td></tr>");

     out.println("</table>");

     } else {
     out.println("<p>No such book in database</p>");
     }
```

```
out.println("</body>");
    out.println("</html>");

    out.flush();
    out.close();

  }

}
```

Sample web.xml

```xml
<?xml version="1.0" encoding="ISO-8859-1"?>
<!DOCTYPE web-app PUBLIC "-//Sun Microsystems, Inc.//DTD Web Application
2.3//EN" "http://java.sun.com/j2ee/dtds/web-app_2_3.dtd">

<web-app>
    <servlet>
        <servlet-name>
            BookLookupServlet
        </servlet-name>
        <servlet-class>
            BookLookupServlet
        </servlet-class>
    </servlet>

    <servlet-mapping>
        <servlet-name>
            BookLookupServlet
        </servlet-name>
        <url-pattern>
            /booklookup
        </url-pattern>
    </servlet-mapping>
</web-app>
```

As for a command line client, this servlet needs access to soap.jar, activation.jar, mail.jar, and xerces.jar. It also needs the proxy, serializers and data classes. One option is to include these service access classes, and the servlet itself, in the web application's WEB-INF/classes directory, and the JARs in the WEB-INF/lib directory.

```
webapps/
    booklookupaccess/
        WEB-INF/
            classes/
                BookLookupServlet.class
                BookLookupProxy.class
                com/
                    wrox/
                        javaxmlref/
                            booklookup/
```

```
        Book.class

                            PubDate.class
                            BookSerializer.class
                            PubDateSerializer.class
                  lib/
                      soap.jar
                      activation.jar
                      mail.jar
                      xerces.jar
                  web.xml
```

Alternatively, you might compile the service access classes into a JAR file of their own.

Generating WSDL

The WSTK contains a GUI tool that can be used to generate WSDL files automatically from existing Java classes and beans. The GUI tool is activated by running the wsdlgen program in the wstk-2.3/bin directory.

As well as generating WSDL, this tool will also create serializer classes and deployment descriptors. It's also capable of analyzing an EJB JAR file and creating a deployment descriptor for Apache-SOAP that exposes some or all of the EJB's interface as a web service. For an example of an EJB being used in this way, see the example in Chapter 15.

UDDI

Universal Description, Discovery and Integration is a standard for a web service which provides directory services. Essentially, much as search engines provide one of the crucial pieces of infrastructure that make web sites useful, UDDI registries provide the crucial infrastructure to make web services useful. UDDI allows programmers and programs to search for services to use, either at design-time or at run-time.

The idea is that there should be two types of UDDI registry: public and private. Public UDDI registries, such as those currently operated by Microsoft and IBM (see http://www.uddi.org/find.html for a list), function like public search engines – providing a central lookup point for users to find all published services. Arrangements exist so that anything registered with one public UDDI registry is reflected in other registries.

Private registries can be operated by an individual enterprise, perhaps to provide lookup services for internally published services, or by a group of enterprises, to provide a closed environment for services within a particular marketplace. IBM supply a UDDI registry which can be installed on a servlet container, which uses DB/2 as its data store.

A UDDI registry provides three kinds of lookup service:

Lookup Type	Description
White Pages	Discover physical contact details of known business entities by name
Yellow Pages	Discover business entities which provide services of a specific type
Green Pages	Discover technical specifications for accessing specific web services

Essentially, this means we can perform general, high level searches for businesses by name and by service-type, and then drill-down to find out exactly how to access a specific web service – that is, obtain the WSDL document which describes the service implementation.

UDDI4J, which ships as part of the IBM WSTK, is a client API for accessing and manipulating data in UDDI registries.

The UDDI Data Model

UDDI has a fairly simple data model, and a slightly less simple metadata model, and the UDDI specification explains this data model in two ways: in terms of entity-relationship diagrams, and in terms of the XML schema for the data structure.

The main entities that UDDI defines are:

- ❑ **Business Entities**, which represent service providers, and contain information specific to such entities, like contact details, web site URLs, and so on

- ❑ **Business Services**, which represent types of service operated by a Business Entity

- ❑ **Binding Templates**, which represent technical specifications for accessing specific web services that make up a Business Service

In addition, UDDI has a metadata construct, called a **tModel**. The UDDI data model specification (available from http://www.uddi.org/) is very vague about what exactly a tModel is for – the architects of UDDI don't want to limit the possible applications of tModels for adding metadata to UDDI descriptions. Two applications for tModels, which are endorsed by the specification, are:

- ❑ For declaring that a particular web service follows a specific well-known specification – this is termed a service 'fingerprint'.

- ❑ For declaring that a particular piece of data's meaning should be interpreted in accordance with a certain rule – for example, that a number should be interpreted as a US tax code, or as a phone number, etc.

In order to group sets of like-items together, UDDI makes extensive use of 'bags' and 'lists'. A bag is essentially a set – a container of unordered things (strictly speaking, a bag can contain duplicates while a set cannot, but since duplicate entries in UDDI bags have no semantic meaning, we can think of them as sets). A list, on the other hand, is an ordered collection.

We'll look at the data model in detail when we look at the object model provided by the UDDI4J API, which provides a direct mapping of the entities described by the data model specification into Java classes.

UDDI Operations

UDDI registries support a simple set of operations for registering and for querying data. These fall into five main categories:

- Authentication and verification methods
- **Find** methods: these perform a search for a specific entity based on various qualities and return general information about matching entities
- **Get** methods: these fetch detailed information about a named entity
- **Save** methods: these create or amend an entity in the registry
- **Delete** methods: these remove an entity from the registry

These operations are all exposed via methods of the `com.ibm.uddi.client.UDDIProxy` class, provided in the UDDI4J bundle, which can be used to access any UDDI registry.

UDDI4J Reference

UDDI4J contains a large number of classes, particularly to represent entities that are part of the UDDI data model. They all follow the bean pattern, however, with `get` and `set` methods for each of the entity's properties. These bean properties are listed in the following style:

Bean Properties

Property	Type	Description
`property`	`com.wrox.beanproperty.Property`	Represents a property

This means that the class has two methods, with the following signatures:

```
public void setProperty(com.wrox.beanproperty.Property property)
public com.wrox.beanproperty.Property getProperty()
```

Other methods will be listed in the usual style.

Two constructors for the data type classes are always provided:

- A default constructor
- A constructor which takes a DOM `Element` argument, for parsing XML-formatted UDDI data

A third constructor is sometimes provided, which sets all of the required properties of the data entity.

Any class which extends `UDDIElement` inherits a `saveToXML()` method, which is used by UDDI4J's internal classes to write the data into an `org.w3c.dom.Element` object passed in as an argument.

Common UDDI Data Types

The following classes are used throughout the UDDI data model.

Class	Description	Page
Description	A language-tagged String that can be used to describe various other UDDI entities	500
Name	A String that can be used to name various other UDDI entities	501
OverviewDoc	An overview document is a source of information about an UDDI entity, providing descriptive information, and an onward link to an online resource with more information	501
OverviewURL	An overview URL is a pointer to further detailed overview information online	502
CategoryBag	A category bag is a bag data type that contains a set of categories that describe the entity that owns the bag	503
IdentifierBag	An identifier bag is a bag data type that contains a set of identifying statements that describe the entity that owns the bag	503
KeyedReference	A key-value pair, optionally qualified by a reference to a tModel (using the tModel as a sort of namespace qualifier).	504

Class Description

com.ibm.uddi.datatype

```
public class Description
extends UDDIElement
```

A description element is a language-tagged String that can be used to describe various other UDDI entities. A vector of Description objects (in different languages) is often used as a property of a UDDI data type.

Constructors

```
public Description()
```

```
public Description(org.w3c.dom.Element xmlElement)
```

```
public Description(String text)
```

Bean Properties

Property	Type	Description	Get	Set
lang	String	A two-character language code, or two-plus two dialect code, representing the language the description is in	Y	Y
text	String	The text of the description in the specified language	Y	Y

Class Name
com.ibm.uddi.datatype

```
public class Name
extends UDDIElement
```

A name element is a String that can be used to name various other UDDI entities.

Constructors

```
public Name()
```

```
public Name(org.w3c.dom.Element xmlElement)
```

```
public Name(String text)
```

Bean Properties

Property	Type	Description	Get	Set
text	String	The name	Y	Y

Class OverviewDoc
com.ibm.uddi.datatype

```
public class OverviewDoc
extends UDDIElement
```

An overview document is a source of information about an UDDI entity, providing descriptive information, and an onward link to an online resource with more information. One important use for an overview document is in referencing the WSDL specification of a service.

Constructors

```
public OverviewDoc()
```

```
public OverviewDoc(org.w3c.dom.Element xmlElement)
```

Bean Properties

Property	Type	Description	Get	Set
defaultDescription String	String	The default description information	Y	Y
descriptionVector	java.util. Vector	A vector of descriptions in different languages	Y	Y
overviewURL	OverviewURL	A URL to more in depth information	Y	Y

Methods

```
public void setOverviewURL(String s)
```

```
public String getOverviewURLString()
```

These two methods provide a convenient way to sidestep the OverviewURL class which is the type of the overviewURL bean property, and which only stores a simple String.

Class OverviewURL

com.ibm.uddi.datatype

```
public class OverviewURL
extends UDDIElement
```

An overview URL is a pointer to further detailed overview information online.

Constructors

```
public OverviewURL()
```

```
public OverviewURL(org.w3c.dom.Element xmlElement)
```

```
public OverviewURL(String text)
```

Bean Properties

Property	Type	Description	Get	Set
text	String	The URL	Y	Y

Class CategoryBag

com.ibm.uddi.util

```
public class CategoryBag
extends UDDIElement
```

A category bag is a bag data type that contains a set of categories that describe the entity that owns the bag.

Constructors

```
public CategoryBag()
```

```
public CategoryBag(org.w3c.dom.Element xmlElement)
```

Bean Properties

Property	Type	Description	Get	Set
KeyedReference Vector	java.util. Vector	A vector of KeyedReference objects which represent categories	Y	Y

Class IdentifierBag

com.ibm.uddi.util

```
public class IdentifierBag
extends UDDIElement
```

An identifier bag is a bag data type that contains a set of identifying statements that describe the entity that owns the bag.

Constructors

```
public IdentifierBag()
```

```
public IdentifierBag(org.w3c.dom.Element xmlElement)
```

Bean Properties

Property	Type	Purpose	Get	Set
keyed Reference Vector	java.util. Vector	A vector of KeyedReference objects which represent categories	Y	Y

Class KeyedReference
com.ibm.uddi.util

```
public class KeyedReference
extends UDDIElement
```

A key-value pair, optionally qualified by a reference to a tModel (using the tModel as a sort of namespace qualifier).

Constructors

```
public KeyedReference()
```

```
public KeyedReference(org.w3c.dom.Element xmlElement)
```

```
public KeyedReference(String keyName, String keyValue)
```

Bean Properties

Property	Type	Description	Get	Set
keyName	String	The name of the key	Y	Y
keyValue	String	The value	Y	Y
tModelKey	String	The key of a tModel which provides metadata about this key-value pair	Y	Y

One use for keyed references in UDDI is to indicate what sort of services a company provides. UDDI endorses two systems for identifying the type of service offered by a company – the **UNSPSC (Universal Standard Products and Services Classification)** system, and the **NAICS (North American Industry Classification System)**. Both of these systems associate a company type with a numerical code. In UNSPSC, for example, 55101509 signifies a publisher of educational or vocational textbooks. In NAICS, a book publisher is represented by the code 51113.

A browser tool is included in the WSTK which allows you to look up these codes – a command line tool to run it, called `categoryhelper`, is included in the WSTK's `bin` directory. Run either:

```
> categoryhelper naics
```

or

```
> categoryhelper unspsc
```

A keyed reference to represent a UNSPSC or NAICS value will have this code as its key value, a textual indication of the company or service type as its key name, and the key of the UNSPSC or NAICS tModel as its tModel key. These tModel keys are available as constants in the UDDI4J `TModel` class.

```
KeyedReference kr = new KeyedReference();
kr.setKeyName("Book publisher");
kr.setKeyValue("51113");
kr.setTModelKey(TModel.NAICS_TMODEL_KEY);
```

Business Entity Data Types

The following classes are used to represent aspects of a business entity.

Class	Description	Page
BusinessEntity	A business entity represents a provider of services	506
Contacts	A `Contacts` object represents a set of contactable individuals – contacts – at a business	507
Contact	A `Contact` object provides a description of a way of contacting a person at a business entity	507
Address	`Address` objects are provided by a `Contact` object. They represent a way to reach the specified individual via postal mail.	508
AddressLine	`AddressLines` are provided by an `Address` object. They represent a line of an address.	509
Email	`Email` addresses are provided by a `Contact` object, and they represent a line of an address	510
PersonName	A `PersonName` represents the name of a contact	510
Phone	`Phone` objects are provided by a `Contact` object. They represent a line of an address.	511

Class BusinessEntity

com.ibm.uddi.datatype.business

```
public class BusinessEntity
extends UDDIElement
```

A business entity represents a provider of services. It has properties specifying the provider's contact details, and provides a route in to the provider's services.

Constructors

```
public BusinessEntity()
```

```
public BusinessEntity(org.w3c.dom.Element xmlElement)
```

```
public BusinessEntity(String businessKey, String name)
```

Bean Properties

All these properties have both get and set methods:

Property	Type	Description
authorizedName	String	The name of the individual who registered the entity with a UDDI registry
businessKey	String	A unique ID for this business entity
businessServices	com.ibm.uddi.datatype.service.BusinessServices	A list of business services provided by the entity
categoryBag	com.ibm.uddi.util.CategoryBag	A bag containing categories describing the type of business this entity represents
contacts	Contacts	A list of contact details for the business entity
default Description String	String	The default description of the business entity
description Vector	java.util.Vector	A list of description objects, describing the business entity in different languages
discoveryURLs	com.ibm.uddi.util.DiscoveryURLs	A list of URLs which can be used to retrieve service descriptions

Property	Type	Description
`identifierBag`	`com.ibm.uddi.util.IdentifierBag`	A bag containing identifying pieces of information about the business entity this represents
`name`	`com.ibm.uddi.datatype.Name`	An object containing the business entity's name
`operator`	`String`	The operator of the registry which accepted this entry

Methods

```
public void setName(String s)
```

```
public String getNameString()
```

These two methods provide a convenient way to sidestep the Name class which is the type of the name bean property, and which only stores a simple String.

Class Contacts

com.ibm.uddi.datatype.business

```
public class Contacts
extends UDDIElement
```

A Contacts object represents a set of contactable individuals – contacts – at a business.

Constructors

```
public Contacts()
```

```
public Contacts(org.w3c.dom.Element xmlElement)
```

Bean Properties

Property	Type	Description	Get	Set
`contactVector`	`java.util.Vector`	A vector of contact objects	Y	Y

Class Contact

com.ibm.uddi.datatype.business

```
public class Contact
extends UDDIElement
```

A `Contact` object provides a description of a way of contacting a person at a business entity.

Constructors

```
public Contact()
```

```
public Contact(org.w3c.dom.Element xmlElement)
```

```
public Contact(String personName)
```

Bean Properties

All these properties have both `get` and `set` methods:

Property	Type	Description
addressVector	java.util.Vector	A vector of Address objects, representing different postal addresses for the contact
default Description String	String	The default description of the contact
description Vector	java.util.Vector	A list of description strings, describing the contact in different languages
emailVector	java.util.Vector	A vector of Email objects representing different e-mail addresses for the contact
personName	PersonName	An object containing the name of the person this contact represents
phoneVector	java.util.Vector	A vector of Phone objects, representing different telephone numbers for the contact
useType	String	A string specifying what the contact should be contacted in relation to, for example 'sales'

Methods

```
public void setPersonName(String s)
```

```
public String getPersonNameString()
```

These two methods provide a convenient way to sidestep the `PersonName` class which is the type of the `personName` bean property, and which only stores a simple `String`.

Class Address

com.ibm.uddi.datatype.business

```
public class Address
extends UDDIElement
```

Address objects are provided by a Contact object. They represent a way to reach the specified individual via postal mail.

Constructors

```
public Address()
```

```
public Address(org.w3c.dom.Element xmlElement)
```

Bean Properties

All these properties have both get and set methods:

Property	Type	Description
addressLine Strings	java.util. Vector	A vector of strings representing lines of the address
addressLineVector	java.util. Vector	A vector of AddressLine objects, representing lines of the address
sortCode	String	A value which can be used in sorting addresses in order of preference, priority, etc.
useType	String	A string describing what this address should be used for

Class AddressLine

com.ibm.uddi.datatype.business

```
public class AddressLine extends UDDIElement
```

AddressLines are provided by an Address object. They represent a line of an address.

Constructors

```
public Address()
public Address(org.w3c.dom.Element xmlElement)
public Address(String text)
```

Bean Properties

Property	Type	Description	Get	Set
text	String	The line of the address	Y	Y

Class Email

com.ibm.uddi.datatype.business

```
public class Email
extends UDDIElement
```

Email addresses are provided by a Contact object, and they represent a line of an address.

Constructors

```
public Email()
public Email(org.w3c.dom.Element xmlElement)
public Email(String text)
```

Bean Properties

Property	Type	Description	Get	Set
text	String	The e-mail address	Y	Y
useType	String	A string indicating what type of contact this e-mail address should be used for	Y	Y

Class PersonName

com.ibm.uddi.datatype.business

```
public class PersonName
extends UDDIElement
```

A `PersonName` represents the name of a contact.

Constructors

```
public PersonName()
```

```
public PersonName(org.w3c.dom.Element xmlElement)
```

```
public PersonName(String text)
```

Bean Properties

Property	Type	Description	Get	Set
text	String	The contact's name	Y	Y

Class Phone

com.ibm.uddi.datatype.business

```
public class Phone
extends UDDIElement
```

`Phone` objects are provided by a `Contact` object. They represent a line of an address.

Constructors

```
public Phone()
```

```
public Phone(org.w3c.dom.Element xmlElement)
```

```
public Phone(String text)
```

Bean Properties

Property	Type	Description	Get	Set
text	String	The phone number	Y	Y
useType	String	A string indicating what type of contact this phone number should be used for	Y	Y

Example: Building a Contact Object

The style of coding needed to build up a `Contact` object is typical of UDDI4J. Here is a short example which illustrates the process:

Sample ContactsBuilder.java

```java
import java.util.Vector;
import java.io.DataInputStream;
import java.io.IOException;
import com.ibm.uddi.datatype.business.*;
import javax.xml.parsers.*;
import javax.xml.transform.*;
import javax.xml.transform.dom.DOMSource;
import javax.xml.transform.stream.StreamResult;
import org.w3c.dom.*;

public class ContactsBuilder {

  public static void main(String[] args) {
    if (args.length < 3) {
      System.out.println("Usage: java ContactsBuilder " +
         "<name> <e-mail> <phone>");
    } else {
```

First, we instantiate the objects which will make up our contact. Then, we use command line arguments to populate the first three.

```java
Contact theContact = new Contact(args[0]);
Email theEmail = new Email(args[1]);
Phone thePhone = new Phone(args[2]);
Address theAddress = new Address();
```

Next, we set any properties we want to use on the objects.

```java
theContact.setUseType("Sales");
theEmail.setUseType("Work");
thePhone.setUseType("Work");
theAddress.setUseType("Work");
```

This next section reads in an address, line by line. Within the `while` loop we add each line to the `Vector` of address lines that belongs to our `Address` object.

```java
String addressLine;

System.out.print  ("Enter address, line by line - " +
  "enter to finish");

try {
```

```
            DataInputStream in = new DataInputStream(System.in);
            while (!(addressLine = in.readLine()).equals("")) {
              theAddress.getAddressLineVector()
                .add(new AddressLine(addressLine));
            }
          } catch (IOException e) {

            e.printStackTrace();
          }
```

Next, we add each of the contact's child elements to the appropriate vector.

```
          theContact.getPhoneVector().add(thePhone);
          theContact.getEmailVector().add(theEmail);
          theContact.getAddressVector().add(theAddress);
```

This last section is really a quick and dirty hack that outputs the assembled contact as an XML data structure.

```
          try {

            DocumentBuilder db = DocumentBuilderFactory
              .newInstance().newDocumentBuilder();
            Document doc = db.newDocument();
            Element el = doc.createElement("ourContact");
            theContact.saveToXML(el);
            doc.appendChild(el);

            TransformerFactory.newInstance().newTransformer()
                .transform(new DOMSource(doc),
                    new StreamResult(System.out));

          } catch (Exception e) {
            e.printStackTrace();
          }
        }
      }
    }
  }
```

Business Service Data Types

The following classes are used to represent aspects of a business service.

Class	Description	Page
BusinessService	A business service represents a service, which may consist of one or more web services	513
BusinessServices	A BusinessServices object represents a set of services provided by a business	515

Class BusinessService

com.ibm.uddi.datatype.service

```
public class BusinessService
extends UDDIElement
```

A business service represents a service, which may consist of one or more web services. It belongs to a business entity – the services provided by a particular business entity can be obtained via the businessServices property of the BusinessEntity object.

Constructors

```
public BusinessService()
```

```
public BusinessService(org.w3c.dom.Element xmlElement)
```

```
public BusinessService(String serviceKey, String name,
                       com.ibm.uddi.datatype.binding.
                       BindingTemplates bindingTemplates)
```

Bean Properties

All these properties have both get and set methods:

Property	Type	Description
bindingTemplates	com.ibm.uddi. datatype.binding. BindingTemplates	A list of the binding templates that describe the web services which make up this service
businessKey	String	The business key of the business entity to which this service belongs
categoryBag	com.ibm.uddi.util .CategoryBag	A bag containing categories describing the type of service this entity represents
default Description String	String	The default description of the business service
description Vector	java.util.Vector	A list of description objects, describing the business service in different languages
name	com.ibm.uddi. datatype.Name	The name of the service
serviceKey	String	A unique identifier for this service, generated by the registry when the record for the service is created

Methods

```
public void setName(String s)
```

```
public String getNameString()
```

These two methods provide a convenient way to sidestep the `Name` class which is the type of the `name` bean property, and which only stores a simple `String`.

Class BusinessServices

com.ibm.uddi.datatype.service

```
public class BusinessServices
extends UDDIElement
```

A `BusinessServices` object represents a set of services provided by a business.

Constructors

```
public BusinessServices()
```

```
public BusinessServices(org.w3c.dom.Element xmlElement)
```

Bean Properties

Property	Type	Description	Get	Set
business ServiceVector	java.util. Vector	A vector of business service objects	Y	Y

Binding Template Data Types

The following classes are used to represent details about a specific web service.

Class	Description	Page
BindingTemplate	A binding template represents a set of instructions for accessing a web service	516
BindingTemplates	A BindingTemplates object represents a set of binding templates provided by a business service	517
AccessPoint	An AccessPoint is a URL at which initial contact with a service must be directed	518

Table continued on following page

Class	Description	Page
HostingRedirector	A hosting redirector specifies an alternative binding template which should be consulted for access details	519
TModelInstance Details	TModelInstanceDetails is a container that holds tModels that describe the interface exposed by a web service	519
TModelInstanceInfo	TModelInstanceInfo holds a reference to a tModel which describes an interface which a service implements	520
InstanceDetails	A service which implements an interface defined by a particular tModel may make available additional information about how it differs from the standard interface, or how it should be treated in particular, beyond the specification for the interface, by providing instance details	521
InstanceParms	InstanceParms are settings that indicate how to modify a particular web service interface in order to access a specific instance of it	522
TModel	The TModel class represents a piece of tModel metadata	522

Class BindingTemplate

com.ibm.uddi.datatype.binding

```
public class BindingTemplate
extends UDDIElement
```

A binding template represents a set of instructions for accessing a web service. It belongs to a business service – the binding templates provided by a particular business service can be obtained via the bindingTemplates property of the BusinessService object.

Constructors

```
public BindingTemplate()
```

```
public BindingTemplate(org.w3c.dom.Element xmlElement)
```

```
public BindingTemplate(String bindingKey, TModelInstanceDetails
                       tModelInstancedetails)
```

Bean Properties

All these properties have both get and set methods:

Property	Type	Description
accessPoint	AccessPoint	An access point object which represents a location at which the service is accessible A BindingTemplate may have EITHER an access point, or a hosting redirector, but not both
bindingKey	String	A unique key which is allocated to the binding template by the registry when it is registered
default DescriptionString	String	The default description information for the binding
descriptionVector	java.util.Vector	A vector of descriptions of the binding in different languages
hosting Redirector	Hosting Redirector	A hosting redirector object which specifies another binding template which should be consulted to find out the service details A BindingTemplate may have EITHER an access point, or a hosting redirector, but not both
serviceKey	String	The key of the business service to which this binding template belongs
tModelInstance Details	TModelInstance Details	tModelInstanceDetails are how information about the interface presented by a service is presented via UDDI

Class BindingTemplates
com.ibm.uddi.datatype.binding

```
public class BindingTemplates
extends UDDIElement
```

A BindingTemplates object represents a set of binding templates provided by a business service.

Constructors

```
public BindingTemplates()
```

```
public BindingTemplates(org.w3c.dom.Element xmlElement)
```

Bean Properties

Property	Type	Description	Get	Set
binding TemplateVector	java.util. Vector	A vector of binding template objects	Y	Y

Class AccessPoint

com.ibm.uddi.datatype.service

```
public class AccessPoint
extends UDDIElement
```

An `AccessPoint` is a URL at which initial contact with a service must be directed. How contact should be made is defined by the `tModelInstanceDetails`.

Constructors

```
public AccessPoint()
```

```
public AccessPoint(org.w3c.dom.Element xmlElement)
```

```
public AccessPoint(Stringtext, String URLType)
```

Bean Properties

Property	Type	Description	Get	Set
text	String	The URL which should be used to access the service	Y	Y
URLType	String	A string indicating what type of URL this access point relates to, to facilitate searching for an access point of a type a client wants	Y	Y

An access point can be specified as one of the following types of URL:

- ❑ http
- ❑ mailto
- ❑ https
- ❑ ftp
- ❑ fax
- ❑ phone
- ❑ other

Class HostingRedirector
com.ibm.uddi.datatype.service

```
public class HostingRedirector
        extends UDDIElement
```

A hosting redirector specifies an alternative binding template which should be consulted for access details.

Constructors

```
public HostingRedirector()
```
```
public HostingRedirector(org.w3c.dom.Element xmlElement)
```
```
public HostingRedirector(String bindingKey)
```

Bean Properties

Property	Type	Description	Get	Set
bindingKey	String	The key of the binding that this hosting redirector points to	Y	Y

Class TModelInstanceDetails
com.ibm.uddi.datatype.binding

```
public class TModelInstanceDetails
        extends UDDIElement
```

TModelInstanceDetails is a container that holds tModels that describe the interface exposed by a web service.

Constructors

```
public TModelInstanceDetails()
```

```
public TModelInstanceDetails(org.w3c.dom.Element xmlElement)
```

Bean Properties

Property	Type	Description	Get	Set
tModelInstance InfoVector	java.util. Vector	A vector of TModelInstanceInfo objects, representing tModels for interfaces which this service implements	Y	Y

Class TModelInstanceInfo

com.ibm.uddi.datatype.binding

```
public class TModelInstanceInfo
        extends UDDIElement
```

TModelInstanceInfo holds a reference to a tModel which describes an interface which a service implements.

Constructors

```
public TModelInstanceInfo()
```

```
public TModelInstanceInfo (org.w3c.dom.Element xmlElement)
```

```
public TModelInstanceInfo(String tModelKey)
```

Bean Properties

All these properties have both get and set methods:

Property	Type	Description
defaultDescription String	String	The default description of the interface
descriptionVector	java.util. Vector	A list of description objects, describing the interface in different languages
instanceDetails	InstanceDetails	Information which supplements the tModel with data about this specific service instance
tModelKey	String	The key of the tModel which the service implements

Class InstanceDetails

com.ibm.uddi.datatype.binding

```
public class InstanceDetails
extends UDDIElement
```

A service which implements an interface defined by a particular tModel may make available additional information about how it differs from the standard interface, or how it should be treated in particular, beyond the specification for the interface, by providing instance details.

Constructors

```
public InstanceDetails()
```
```
public InstanceDetails(org.w3c.dom.Element xmlElement)
```

Bean Properties

All these properties have both get and set methods:

Property	Type	Description
defaultDescription String	String	The default description of the instance details
descriptionVector	java.util. Vector	A list of description objects, describing the instance details in different languages

Property	Type	Description
`instanceParms`	`InstanceParms`	An object which describes how to find machine-readable information about this instance
`overviewDoc`	`com.ibm.uddi.datatype.OverviewDoc`	An object which explains how to find human readable information about this instance

Class InstanceParms
com.ibm.uddi.datatype.binding

```
public class InstanceParms extends UDDIElement
```

`InstanceParms` are settings that indicate how to modify a particular web service interface in order to access a specific instance of it.

Constructors

```
public InstanceParms()
```

```
public InstanceParms(org.w3c.dom.Element xmlElement)
```

```
public InstanceParms(String text)
```

Bean Properties

Property	Type	Description	Get	Set
`text`	`String`	Either an XML string containing instance-specific settings, or a URL to a file containing such settings	Y	Y

Class TModel
com.ibm.uddi.datatype.tmodel

```
public class TModel
extends UDDIElement
```

The TModel class represents a piece of tModel metadata. This could represent either:

❑ A specification of an interface
❑ A qualification for a piece of data

Two tModel Key values are defined as public static finals by this class:

❑ NAICS_TMODEL_KEY is the key for the tModel representing the NAICS business classification system

❑ UNSPSC_TMODEL_KEY is the key for the tModel representing the UNSPSC business classification system

Constructors

```
public TModel()

public TModel(org.w3c.dom.Element xmlElement)

public TModel(String tModelKey, String name)
```

Bean Properties

All these properties have both get and set methods:

Property	Type	Description
authorizedName	String	The name of the registry user who created this tModel entry
categoryBag	com.ibm.uddi. util.CategoryBag	A bag of categories which provide information about what context the tModel relates to
defaultDescription String	String	The default description of the tModel
descriptionVector	java.util.Vector	A list of description objects, describing the tModel in different languages
identifierBag	com.ibm.uddi. util.IdentifierBag	A bag of name-value pairs which can be used to help narrow down a search for tModels
name	com.ibm.uddi. datatype.Name	A name object representing the name for this tModel
operator	String	The UDDI registry operator which registered this tModel
overviewDoc	com.ibm.uddi. datatype.Overview Doc	A link to human-readable documentation about this tModel
tModelKey	String	A unique key which identifies this tModel

Methods

```
public void setName(String s)
```

```
public String getNameString()
```

These two methods provide a convenient way to sidestep the Name class which is the type of the name bean property, and which only stores a simple String.

Example: Using TModels To Represent WSDL Services

To register a WSDL service description with a UDDI registry, you must split the definition into two parts, publish them both at accessible URLs, and register them separately. The abstract interface should be registered as a tModel, and the concrete binding to a specific address should be registered as a binding template, and associated with the tModel. You can split a WSDL document in half by writing one document which contains all of the abstract definitions (types, messages, operations and port types), and a second which imports the first, and defines the bindings and service ports.

A tModel to represent the interface portion of a WSDL document should be constructed as follows:

Sample WSDLTModel.java

```java
import java.util.Vector;
import com.ibm.uddi.client.UDDIProxy;
import com.ibm.uddi.datatype.tmodel.*;
import com.ibm.uddi.util.*;
import com.ibm.uddi.response.*;
import com.ibm.uddi.datatype.*;

public class WSDLTModel {

  public static final String WSDL_TMODEL_KEY =
    "uuid:C1ACF26D-9672-4404-9D70-39B756E62AB4";
  public static final String WSDL_KEY_NAME =
    "uddi-org:types";
  public static final String WSDL_KEY_VALUE =
    "wsdlSpec";

  public static final String USERNAME="username";
  public static final String PASSWORD="password";

  public static void main(String[] args) {

    if (args.length < 1) {
      System.out.println(
        "Usage: java WSDLTModel <servicename>");
    } else {
```

```
        UDDIProxy proxy = new UDDIProxy();

    try {
      proxy.setInquiryURL("http://www-3.ibm.com/services/" +
        "uddi/testregistry/inquiryapi");
      proxy.setPublishURL("http://www-3.ibm.com/services/" +
        "uddi/testregistry/publishapi");
      TModel tm = new TModel();
      OverviewDoc od = new OverviewDoc();
      CategoryBag cb = new CategoryBag();

KeyedReference kr =
        new KeyedReference(WSDL_KEY_NAME, WSDL_KEY_VALUE);
      kr.setTModelKey(WSDL_TMODEL_KEY);

      od.setDefaultDescriptionString(
        "WSDL Service Interface Definition");
      od.setOverviewURL("http://localhost:8080/"
        + args[0] + ".wsdl");

      tm.setName(args[0]);
      tm.setOverviewDoc(od);
      tm.setDefaultDescriptionString("WSDL Defined " + "
        "Service: " + args[0]);

      cb.getKeyedReferenceVector().add(kr);

      tm.setCategoryBag(cb);

      Vector tmVector = new Vector();
      tmVector.add(tm);

      AuthToken at =
        proxy.get_authToken(USERNAME, PASSWORD);

      tmVector = proxy.save_tModel(
          at.getAuthInfoString(),tmVector)
            .getTModelVector();

      tm = (TModel) tmVector.firstElement();

      System.out.println("Registered TModel as: " +
        tm.getTModelKey());

    } catch (Exception e) {
      e.printStackTrace();
    }
  }
 }
}
```

The TModel has the URL to the WSDL document set as its overview document, and it has a category bag added which contains a single keyed reference, indicating that this is a WSDL specification. This keyed reference is qualified by the UDDI internal 'types' tModel, whose key is given in the constant at the start.

A document explaining best practices in deploying WSDL descriptions to UDDI registries is available at http://www.uddi.org/pubs/wsdlbestpractices-V1.04-Open-20010420.pdf.

UDDI Registry Access Classes

Class	Description	Page
UDDIProxy	Provides a set of methods which, when you call them, cause it to construct SOAP calls to a UDDI registry to perform the operations, then return the result in Java object form	527
FindQualifiers	Used to tell the registry how to arrange results on find operations	531
FindQualifier	Used to tell the registry how to arrange results on find operations	531
AuthToken	An authentication token is returned by the server's get_authToken operation, but all of the operations that require authentication take a String as an argument for their authentication information	533
AuthInfo	Authentication information	534
List Response Classes	These classes all have a single read/write bean property. The name of this property varies for each class, as does the type of object it contains	534
*Infos Classes	These classes all have a single read/write bean property of a java.util.Vector. The name of this property varies for each class, as does the type of object it contains.	535
BusinessInfo	A BusinessInfo object is a small summary of a business entity	535
ServiceInfo	A ServiceInfo object is a small summary of a business service	536
TModelInfo	A TModelInfo object is a small summary of a tModel	537

Class	Description	Page
Detailed Response Classes	These classes all have a single read/write bean property of a `java.util.Vector`. The name of this property varies for each class, as does the type of object it contains	537
DispositionReport	Delete, discard and validate operations produce a disposition report indicating whether the operation succeeded	538

Class UDDIProxy

com.ibm.uddi.client

```
public class UDDIProxy
```

The `UDDIProxy` class behaves just like one of the proxies for a web service which we generated earlier on – it provides a set of methods which, when you call them, cause it to construct SOAP calls to a UDDI registry to perform the operations, then return the result in Java object form to you.

The data type objects above are used as arguments and return values for these methods.

Constructors

```
public UDDIProxy()
```

```
public UDDIProxy(java.net.URL inquiryURL, java.net.URL
                 publishURL, org.apache.soap.transport.
                 SOAPTransport transport)
```

Bean Properties

Property	Type	Description	Get	Set
inquiryURL	java.net.URL	The URL to direct all find and get operations to	N	Y
publishURL	java.net.URL	The URL to direct all save and delete operations to	N	Y
transport	org.apache.soap.transport.SOAPTransport transport	The SOAP transport which should be used to contact the registry	N	Y

Find Methods

The following methods perform high-level searches of the UDDI registry. They all perform UDDI operations, which require the proxy to perform SOAP communication tasks, so all can throw a `com.ibm.uddi.UDDIException` and an `org.apache.soap.SOAPException`.

```
public com.ibm.uddi.response.BindingDetail
find_binding(com.ibm.uddi.util.FindQualifiers
            findQualifiers, String serviceKey,
            com.ibm.uddi.util.TModelBag tmodelbag, int maxRows)
```

```
public com.ibm.uddi.response.BusinessList
find_business(com.ibm.uddi.util.CategoryBag bag,
            com.ibm.uddi.util.FindQualifiers
            findQualifiers, int maxRows)
```

```
public com.ibm.uddi.response.BusinessList find_business(
            com.ibm.uddi.util.DiscoveryURLs bag,
            com.ibm.uddi.util.FindQualifiers
            findQualifiers, int maxRows)
```

```
public com.ibm.uddi.response.BusinessList find_business(String name,
com.ibm.uddi.util.FindQualifiers findQualifiers, int maxRows)
```

```
public com.ibm.uddi.response.BusinessList find_business(
            com.ibm.uddi.util.TModelBag bag,
            com.ibm.uddi.util.FindQualifiers
            findQualifiers, int maxRows)
```

```
public com.ibm.uddi.response.ServiceList find_service(String
            businessKey, String name,
            com.ibm.uddi.util.FindQualifiers
            findQualifiers, int maxRows)
```

```
public com.ibm.uddi.response.ServiceList find_service(String
            businessKey, com.ibm.uddi.util.CategoryBag bag,
            com.ibm.uddi.util.FindQualifiers
            findQualifiers, int maxRows)
```

```
public com.ibm.uddi.response.ServiceList find_service(String
            businessKey, com.ibm.uddi.util.TModelBag
            bag, com.ibm.uddi.util.FindQualifiers
            findQualifiers, int maxRows)
```

```
public com.ibm.uddi.response.TModelList find_tModel(
            com.ibm.uddi.util.CategoryBag bag,
            com.ibm.uddi.util.FindQualifiers findQualifiers,
            int maxRows)
```

```
public com.ibm.uddi.response.TModelList find_tModel(
            com.ibm.uddi.util.IdentifierBag bag,
            com.ibm.uddi.util.FindQualifiers findQualifiers,
            int maxRows)
```

```
public com.ibm.uddi.response.TModelList find_tModel(
            String name, com.ibm.uddi.util.FindQualifiers
            findQualifiers, int maxRows)
```

Get Methods

The following methods perform drill-down searches of the UDDI registry, given a known key (or keys) for entities in the registry. They all perform UDDI operations, which require the proxy to perform SOAP communication tasks, so all can throw a `com.ibm.uddi.UDDIException` and an `org.apache.soap.SOAPException`.

```
public com.ibm.uddi.response.BindingDetail get_bindingDetail(String
                                                          bindingKey)
```

```
public com.ibm.uddi.response.BindingDetail get_bindingDetail(
                              java.util.Vector bindingKeyStrings)
```

```
public com.ibm.uddi.response.BusinessDetail get_businessDetail(String
                                                          businessKey)
```

```
public com.ibm.uddi.response.BusinessDetail get_businessDetail(
                              java.util.Vector businessKeyStrings)
```

```
public com.ibm.uddi.response.ServiceDetail get_serviceDetail(String
                                                          serviceKey)
```

```
public com.ibm.uddi.response.ServiceDetail get_serviceDetail
                              (java.util.Vector serviceKeyStrings)
```

```
public com.ibm.uddi.response.TModelDetail get_tModelDetail(String
                                                          tModelKey)
```

```
public com.ibm.uddi.response.TModelDetail get_tModelDetail
                              (java.util.Vector tModelKeyStrings)
```

Save Methods

The following methods add or update entities in the registry. They typically take incomplete entities as arguments and return the completed entity, with data added by the registry, such as a unique key, and operator or authenticated user information. They all perform UDDI operations, which require the proxy to perform SOAP communication tasks, so all can throw a `com.ibm.uddi.UDDIException` and an `org.apache.soap.SOAPException`.

```
public com.ibm.uddi.response.BindingDetail save_binding(String
                    authInfo, java.util.Vector bindingTemplates)
```

```
public com.ibm.uddi.response.BusinessDetail save_business(String
                    authInfo, java.util.Vector businessEntities)
```

```
public com.ibm.uddi.response.ServiceDetail save_service(String
                    authInfo, java.util.Vector businessServices)
```

```
public com.ibm.uddi.response.TModelDetail save_tModel(String authInfo,
                    java.util.Vector tModels)
```

Delete Methods

The following methods delete entities from the registry. They all perform UDDI operations, which require the proxy to perform SOAP communication tasks, so all can throw a `com.ibm.uddi.UDDIException` and an `org.apache.soap.SOAPException`.

```
public com.ibm.uddi.response.DispositionReport delete_binding(String
                                     authInfo, String bindingKey)
```

```
public com.ibm.uddi.response.DispositionReport delete_binding(String
                        authInfo, java.util.Vector bindingKeystrings)
```

```
public com.ibm.uddi.response.DispositionReport delete_business(String
                                     authInfo, String businessKey)
```

```
public com.ibm.uddi.response.DispositionReport delete_business(String
                        authInfo, java.util.Vector businessKeystrings)
```

```
public com.ibm.uddi.response.DispositionReport delete_service(String
                                     authInfo, String serviceKey)
```

```
public com.ibm.uddi.response.DispositionReport delete_service(String
                        authInfo, java.util.Vector serviceKeystrings)
```

```
public com.ibm.uddi.response.DispositionReport delete_tModel(String
                                     authInfo, String tModelKey)
```

```
public com.ibm.uddi.response.DispositionReport delete_tModel(String
                        authInfo, java.util.Vector tModelKeystrings)
```

Authentication and Validation Methods

The following methods are concerned with interacting with the registry's authentication and validation systems. They all perform UDDI operations, which require the proxy to perform SOAP communication tasks, so all can throw a `com.ibm.uddi.UDDIException` and an `org.apache.soap SOAPException`.

```
com.ibm.uddi.response.AuthToken get_authToken(String userID,
                                     String credentials)
```

```
public com.ibm.uddi.response.DispositionReport discard_authToken(
                                     AuthInfo authInfo)
```

```
public com.ibm.uddi.response.DispositionReport validate_categorization(
String tModelKey, String keyValueString, BusinessEntity businessEntity)
```

```
public com.ibm.uddi.response.DispositionReport validate_categorization(
         String tModelKey, String keyValueString, BusinessService
         businessService)
```

```
public com.ibm.uddi.response.DispositionReport validate_categorization(
         String tModelKey, String keyValueString, TModel tModel)
```

Class FindQualifiers
com.ibm.uddi.util

```
public class FindQualifiers
extends UDDIElement
```

FindQualifiers are used to tell the registry how to arrange results on find operations. If you don't want to use any find qualifiers, submit null to the find methods in place of a FindQualifiers instance.

Constructors

```
public FindQualifiers()
```

```
public FindQualifiers(org.w3c.dom.Element xmlElement)
```

Bean Properties

Property	Type	Description	Get	Set
findQualifier Vector	java.util. Vector	A Vector of FindQualifier Objects	Y	Y

Class FindQualifier
com.ibm.uddi.util

```
public class FindQualifier
extends UDDIElement
```

FindQualifiers are used to tell the registry how to arrange results on find operations. The following static String values are defined by the FindQualifier class, which can be used as values for a FindQualifier object:

- ❑ caseSensitiveMatch
- ❑ exactNameMatch
- ❑ sortByDateAsc
- ❑ sortByDateDesc
- ❑ sortByNameAsc
- ❑ sortByNameDesc

Constructors

```
public FindQualifier()
public FindQualifier(org.w3c.dom.Element xmlElement)
public FindQualifier(String text)
```

Bean Properties

Property	Type	Description	Get	Set
text	String	The find qualifier value	Y	Y

Example: Finding a Service

Finding a service with the UDDI proxy is simple. This program searches the IBM test registry for a business whose name matches the argument supplied on the command line, and displays the details returned for the first match.

Source UDDIFind.java

```java
import com.ibm.uddi.client.UDDIProxy;
import com.ibm.uddi.response.*;

public class UDDIFind {

  public static void main(String[] args) {

    if (args.length < 1) {
      System.out.println("Usage: java UDDIFind " +
      "<businessname>");
    } else {

    UDDIProxy proxy = new UDDIProxy();
    try {
```

```
proxy.setInquiryURL("http://www-3.ibm.com/services/" +
    "uddi/testregistry/inquiryapi");

BusinessList bl = proxy.find_business(args[0], null, 1);

BusinessInfo bi = (BusinessInfo) bl.getBusinessInfos()
  .getBusinessInfoVector().firstElement();

System.out.println("Name: " + bi.getNameString());
System.out.println("Description: " +
  bi.getDefaultDescriptionString());
System.out.println("Key: " + bi.getBusinessKey());

} catch (Exception e) {
e.printStackTrace();
}
}
}
}
```

Class AuthToken
com.ibm.uddi.response

```
public class AuthToken
extends UDDIElement
```

An authentication token is returned by the server's `get_authToken` operation, but all of the operations that require authentication take a `String` as an argument for their authentication information. To get at the string, you have to unwrap the `AuthToken` entity.

Constructors

```
public AuthToken()
```
```
public AuthToken(org.w3c.dom.Element xmlElement)
```
```
public AuthToken(String operator, String authInfo)
```

Bean Properties

Property	Type	Description	Get	Set
operator	String	The registry operator which issued the AuthToken	Y	Y
authInfo	com.ibm.uddi. util.AuthInfo	The authentication information itself	Y	Y

Methods

```
public void setAuthInfo(String s)
```

```
public String getAuthInfoString()
```

These two methods provide a convenient way to sidestep the AuthInfo class which is the type of the AuthInfo bean property, and which only stores a simple String.

Class AuthInfo
com.ibm.uddi.util

```
public class AuthInfo
extends UDDIElement
```

Constructors

```
public AuthInfo()
```

```
public AuthInfo(org.w3c.dom.Element xmlElement)
```

```
public AuthInfo(String text)
```

Bean Properties

Property	Type	Description	Get	Set
text	String	The authentication information	Y	Y

The List Response Classes
com.ibm.uddi.response

```
public class BusinessList
extends UDDIElement
```

```
public class ServiceList
extends UDDIElement
```

```
public class TModelList
extends UDDIElement
```

These classes all have a single read/write bean property. The name of this property varies for each class, as does the type of object it contains. Here is a summary table:

Bean Properties

Class	Property Name	Type
BusinessList	businessInfos	com.ibm.uddi.response.BusinessInfos
ServiceDetail	serviceInfos	com.ibm.uddi.response.ServiceInfos
TModelDetail	tModelInfos	com.ibm.uddi.response.TModelInfos

The *Infos Classes
com.ibm.uddi.response

```
public class BusinessInfos
extends UDDIElement
```

```
public class ServiceInfos
extends UDDIElement
```

```
public class TModelInfos
extends UDDIElement
```

These classes all have a single read/write bean property of a `java.util.Vector`. The name of this property varies for each class, as does the type of object it contains. Here is a summary table:

Bean Properties

Class	Vector Property Name	Type Vector Contains
BusinessInfos	businessInfo Vector	com.ibm.uddi.response.BusinessInfo
ServiceInfos	serviceInfo Vector	com.ibm.uddi.response.ServiceInfo
TModelInfos	tModelInfo Vector	com.ibm.uddi.response.TModelInfo

Class BusinessInfo
com.ibm.uddi.response

```
public class BusinessInfo
extends UDDIElement
```

A business info object is a small summary of a business entity.

Bean Properties

Property	Type	Description
businessKey	String	The business key for the business entity
defaultDescription String	String	The default description of the tModel
descriptionVector	java.util. Vector	A list of description objects, describing the tModel in different languages
name	com.ibm.uddi. datatype.Name	The name of the business entity
serviceInfos	ServiceInfos	An object containing summaries of all the services this entity has registered

Methods

```
public void setName(String s)
```

```
public String getNameString()
```

Class ServiceInfo
com.ibm.uddi.response

```
public class ServiceInfo
extends UDDIElement
```

A service info object is a small summary of a business service.

Bean Properties

The following properties all have both get and set methods:

Property	Type	Description
businessKey	String	The business key for the business entity which owns this service
name	com.ibm.uddi. datatype.Name	The name of the service
serviceKay	String	The service key for the full business service

Methods

```
public void setName(String s)
```

```
public String getNameString()
```

Class TModelInfo
com.ibm.uddi.response

```
public class TModelInfo
extends UDDIElement
```

A TModelInfo object is a small summary of a tModel.

Bean Properties

Property	Type	Description
name	com.ibm.uddi.datatype.Name	The name of the tModel
tModelKey	String	The tModel key for the full tModel

Methods

```
public void setName(String s)
```

```
public String getNameString()
```

The Detailed Response Classes
com.ibm.uddi.response

```
public class BindingDetail
extends UDDIElement
```

```
public class BusinessDetail
extends UDDIElement
```

```
public class ServiceDetail
extends UDDIElement
```

```
public class TModelDetail
extends UDDIElement
```

These classes all have a single read/write bean property of a `java.util.Vector`. The name of this property varies for each class, as does the type of object it contains. Here is a summary table:

Bean Properties

Class	Vector Property Name	Type Vector Contains
`BindingDetail`	`bindingTemplate Vector`	`com.ibm.uddi.datatype.binding. BindingTemplate`
`BusinessDetail`	`businessEntity Vector`	`com.ibm.uddi.datatype.business. BusinessEntity`
`ServiceDetail`	`businessService Vector`	`com.ibm.uddi.datatype.service. BusinessService`
`TModelDetail`	`tModelVector`	`com.ibm.uddi.datatype. tmodel.TModel`

Class DispositionReport

com.ibm.uddi.response

```
public class DispositionReport
        extends UDDIElement
```

Delete, discard and validate operations produce a disposition report indicating whether the operation succeeded.

Error Code Fields

Field	Signature	Error Meaning
`E_accountLimit Exceeded`	`static String E_accountLimit Exceeded`	You have exceeded a user account limit
`E_authToken Expired`	`static String E_authToken Expired`	The auth info token has expired
`E_authToken Required`	`static String E_authToken Required`	Authentication supplied is not valid

Field	Signature	Error Meaning
E_categorization NotAllowed	static String E_categorization NotAllowed	The registry is not allowing you to declare that an entity belongs in a certain category, perhaps because the tModel associated with it implies some form of regulation
E_invalidCategory	static String E_invalidCategory	The key value specified in a category was not one permitted by the tModel applied to that category

Methods

```
public String setErrCode()
```

```
public String getErrInfoText()
```

```
public int getErrNo()
```

```
public String getGeneric()
```

```
public String getOperator()
```

Summary

We've looked briefly at the existing tools that enable developers to build and access web services from Java. The massive cross-vendor support for web services standards means that there will soon be web services APIs available from BEA, Oracle, Sun and so on, but IBM's tools have the advantage of existing and working today.

We've examined WSDL as a language for specifying web service interfaces, and looked at IBM's UDDI4J UDDI client API for accessing UDDI registries programmatically. Together, these tools provide the foundations for deploying and accessing web services.

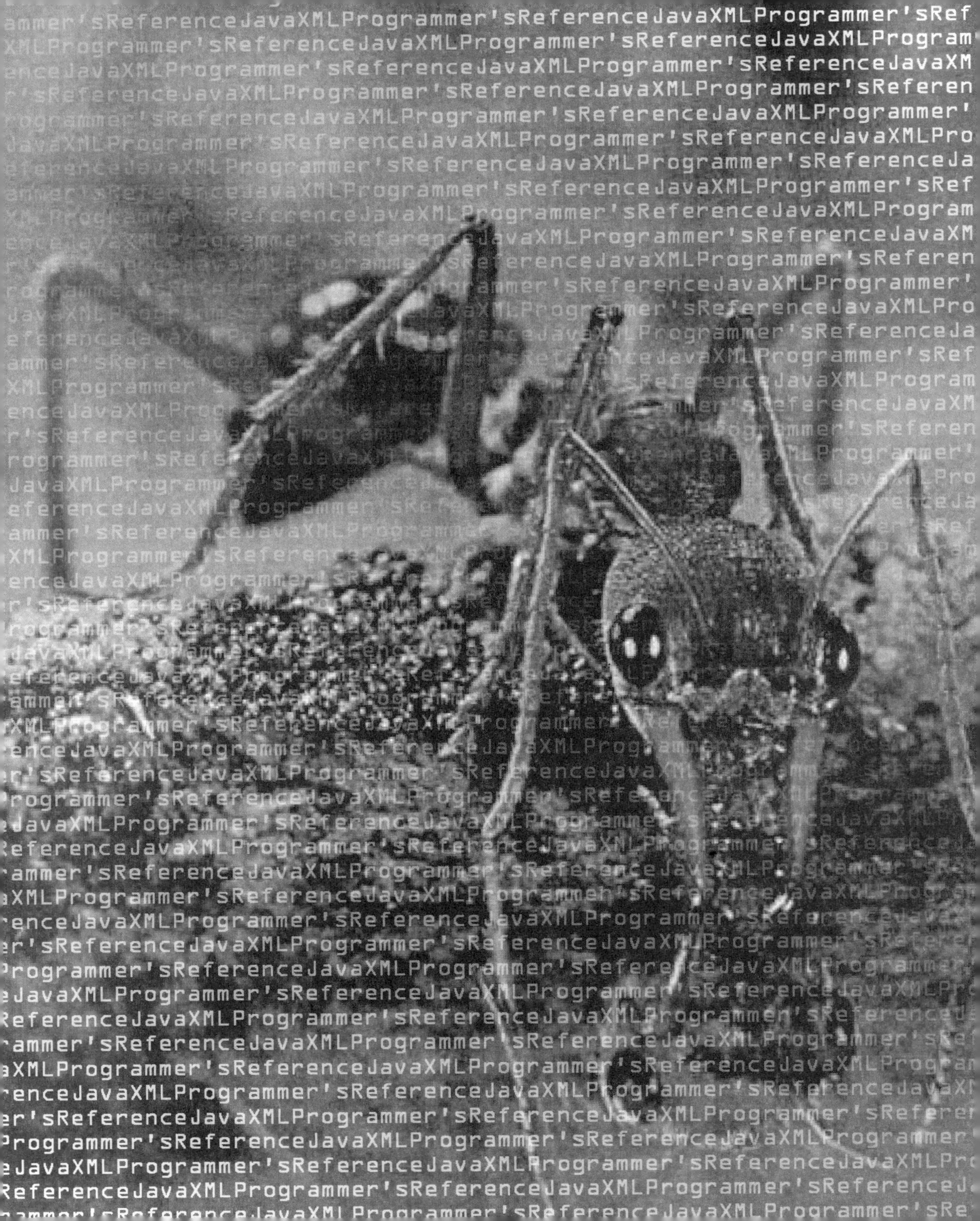

Java APIs for XML

This chapter collects together some examples and resources on a number of Java XML projects that are currently emerging from Sun Microsystems' Java Community Process (JCP). In several cases where an Early Access reference implementation is available, we take a closer look at the API and develop some illustrative examples. For the other projects we will restrict ourselves to providing a short overview.

The following table details some of the XML Java Specification Requests (JSR) in progress:

Project	Description	JSR	Page
JAXB	Java Architecture for XML Java Binding	31	542
JAXM	Java API for XML Messaging	67	554
JAXR	Java XML Registry	93	557
JAX-RPC	Java API for XML RPC	101	558
JAXP	Java API for XML Processing	63	Chapter 5

We also look at the "WebRowSet" on page 547. This is an early access implementation of the `javax.sql.RowSet` interface, which is currently under review as JSR 114, JDBC Rowset Implementations. This is an XML-serializable "container" for the rows of a SQL query.

It is planned to bundle the above Java-XML APIs together into what is being called a JAX Pack. JAX Pack will include all of the publicly available Java APIs and architectures for XML. JAX Pack will also include documentation describing how the components work both individually and together, with scenarios illustrating when and how to utilize the technology, along with detailed code examples.

JSR progress may be accessed through http://jcp.org/.

Java Architecture for XML Java Binding (JAXB)

On May 30, Sun Microsystems released version 0.21 of their working draft for JAXB, which is tentatively slated to be part of the v1.4 J2SE package which is currently well into Beta. It is also to be included in the "JAX Pack", which will include a selection of XML APIs in one download.

JAXB is the Java API for XML Binding. XML binding is an approach to the knotty topic of using XML data as input to Java applications. What JAXB aims to do is map the elements of such XML documents to classes and their attributes to properties of that class. Whilst doing this, it reproduces the hierarchical organization of XML data into a series of classes that mimic it.

In order to do this, the API uses what is described rather vaguely in the Working Draft as a "scheme" for these documents, which could be either the DTD or the XML Schema, though at present it would only support "a simple subset of the W3C XML Schema language". This may or may not be indicative of a certain hesitancy developers feel towards XML Schema, though equally supporting the higher-level functions of XML Schema would be a difficult task. The recommendation of XML Schema 1.0, however, means that developing compatibility with XML Schema should be a lot less hit-or-miss than it was.

The API covers three major areas – deserialization, or unmarshaling (the conversion of the XML data into classes), marshaling, or serialization (the conversion of said classes back into XML), and validation of XML documents and/or classes against their "scheme" (by which it means the DTD or XML Schema the document is being validated by).

In this it stands in contrast to Castor, one of its nearest competitors, in that it requires such a schematic in order to convert the XML document (for more information on Castor, see http://castor.exolab.org/).

Three major components to accomplish this conversion via schematic are identified in the working draft:

❑ The schema compiler – this compiles a source schema to a set of derived classes

❑ The binding framework – this is a set of public classes and interfaces which the derived classes use to implement the various JAXB operations

❑ The binding language – this XML-based language described the binding of a source schema to the classes derived from it. Such a language would be used in the **binding schema** that describes the classes that would be derived from the source schema. Rather confusingly, the binding schema is a different animal altogether from the source schema, and represents a mapping *based* upon the source schema.

Such an API could be profoundly useful – it would enable Java applications to directly implement XML data-centric documents as objects, and hide the messy parsing and validating such documents prior to use from the programmer, as well as sparing them the effort of writing their own such XML-object maps. All of this would greatly facilitate the mapping of XML to databases and database objects.

Example: XML To Object Mapping Using JAXB

This example illustrates the use of JAXB. The object here is to create Java files corresponding to the elements of an XML Library document, which our "books out of stock" printing program will read in and analyze.

The document is still validated and parsed (though this is still quite rudimentary in the Early Access version); however these processes are hidden from the user. This is a very powerful and exciting new technology, and using it makes it much easier to manipulate XML data.

In our example, we will use a DTD (library.dtd) as the basis for an XJS file (library.xjs). An XJS file is the binding schema we discussed above. We will enter both our DTD and our binding schema on the command line, and generate a series of classes based on elements defined within the DTD.

Finally, we will run a small program that will populate the classes so obtained with values from our XML file, library.xml. It then prints out the titles of books that have a quantity attribute of zero.

Sample library.dtd

```
<?xml version="1.0" encoding="UTF-8"?>
<!ELEMENT library (book)+>
<!ELEMENT book (author+,title)>
<!ATTLIST book quantity NMTOKEN "0">
<!ELEMENT author EMPTY>
<!ATTLIST author name CDATA #REQUIRED>
<!ELEMENT title EMPTY>
<!ATTLIST title name CDATA #REQUIRED>
```

This DTD, as we can see, defines an uncomplicated XML file called library.xml. The root element is <library>, which may contain one or more <book> elements. Child elements of <book> are, logically enough, <author> (of which there may be more than one) and <title>. <book> also has one attribute, quantity, which is the number of that particular book in stock at any one time. We can see here that the default value of quantity is "0".

Sample library.xml

```
<?xml version="1.0" encoding="UTF-8"?>
<!DOCTYPE library SYSTEM "library.dtd">
<library>
  <book quantity="3">
    <author name="Charlotte Bronte"/>
    <title name="Villette"/>
  </book>
  <book quantity="6">
    <author name="Charlotte Bronte"/>
    <title name="Jane Eyre"/>
  </book>
  <book>
    <author name="Jane Austen"/>
    <title name="Persuasion"/>
  </book>
  <book quantity="0">
    <author name="Jane Austen"/>
    <title name="Pride and Prejudice"/>
  </book>
</library>
```

Sample library.xjs

```
<xml-java-binding-schema version="1.0-ea">
<element name="library" type="class" root="true"/>
</xml-java-binding-schema>
```

As we saw earlier, JAXB requires a "schema" (which can be either a DTD or a very simple XML Schema) in order to define the classes that it will build.

This is a very simple XJS (it simply declares the library element to be firstly converted into a class, and secondly, to make `root true`. (All JAXB bindings require at least one root class.)

If you are interested in building your own custom XJS as we have done here (though it is expected that there will be a utility that builds XJS files automatically) it is worth looking through the Working Draft (see under *Resources* for the web site address). However, it is also possible to run JAXB's schema compiler without a specific XJS file – the API merely creates the classes from a set of default bindings.

Downloading the Required JAR Files

The next thing to do is to obtain the correct JAR files. You should be able to download the Early Access version on JAXB at http://developer.java.sun.com/developer/earlyAccess/xml/jaxb/. This includes two JAR files, and an `xjc` script that will enable UNIX users to run a series of command line utilities. (Windows users need not worry, however, as we have the alternative command line prompts for these utilities.)

The JAR files are:

- `jaxb-rt-1.0-ea.jar`
- `jaxb-xjc-1.0-ea.jar`

Place both of the JAR files in your classpath, and if you are using UNIX, edit and execute the `xjc` script provided in the `bin` directory of the download.

Now you are ready to generate your classes!

Creating Classes from the DTD

With the JAR files in our classpath, all we need to do is enter the following on the command line (if you are a UNIX user):

```
% xjc library.dtd library.xjs
```

With the `-d` option at the end of this, it is possible to specify a directory you would like the classes to go into.

For Windows, the prompt is as follows:

```
> java com.sun.tools.xjc.Main library.dtd library.xjs
```

This should generate the following files in your directory:

- ❑ `Author.java`
- ❑ `Book.java`
- ❑ `Library.java`
- ❑ `Title.java`

Notice that these classes are capitalized, while the elements they were generated from in our DTD are lowercase.

As we mentioned earlier, however, it is also possible to generate classes from a DTD (and possibly XML Schema in the future) without an XJS file.

Here is the UNIX syntax:

```
% xjc -roots library library.dtd
```

And for Windows, as you can probably guess, the syntax is:

```
> java com.sun.tools.xjc.Main library library.dtd
```

This will generate the same files as the previous command, though obviously with a custom XJS file it is possible to specify the class properties more vigorously. The `-roots` option is necessary here as it will specify the important root class (which is mandatory), creating it from the root element of the DTD. It is not necessary to specify the root with our custom XJS, in fact this is illegal.

Compile all your `.java` files now, as we are about to make use of them.

Running the Example

In order to demonstrate how JAXB works, we are going to write a small program that takes in `library.xml` and copies its values to the object values in our class files.

Our created Java files come complete with a wide variety of methods for accessing these values. We are particularly interested in a couple of these for our purposes, and we will use these in our code.

Source: JAXBPrint.java

```
import java.io.*;
import java.util.*;
import javax.xml.bind.*;
import javax.xml.marshal.*;

public class JAXBPrint {
```

The first thing we need to do is declare our `Library` object. We then run a simple `getLibrary()` utility method, which populates the library object with the XML sample above and then performs a search through the books:

```
public static Library library = new Library();

public static void main(String args[]) throws Exception {
  getLibrary();
}
```

Next, we will write our XML file, `library.xml`, into a `FileInputStream`. We will then write the data contained within it into property values through the use of the `unmarshal()` method.

This will then iterate through our `Book` objects, returning them in a `List` and then checking if there are any in stock. Here is an extract of our generated `Book.java`.

```
public List getBook() {
    return _Book;
}
```

If the quantity (accessed by `getQuantity()`) is 0, then the program will print out the title of the book that is out of stock:

```
public static void getLibrary() throws Exception {

    File f = new File("library.xml");
    FileInputStream in = new FileInputStream(f);
    library = library.unmarshal(in);

    List books = library.getBook();
    for (Iterator it = books.iterator(); it.hasNext() ;) {
      Book b = (Book) it.next();
      if (Integer.parseInt(b.getQuantity()) == 0) {
         System.out.print("No books held for ");
         System.out.println("title " + b.getTitle() + " !!");
      }
    }
  }
}
```

Output

Now, compile `JAXBPrint.java` and run it:

```
> java JAXBPrint
No books held for title <<title name=Persuasion>> !!
No books held for title <<title name=Pride and Prejudice>> !!
```

This does seem to be a very promising way to tackle XML-Object mapping, but it is still early days. It remains to be seen whether JAXB does eventually take on more XML Schema support, which may well affect its uptake in the long run

Resources

❑ A description of this initiative and a link to the specification is available at:
http://java.sun.com/xml/jaxb/

❑ A link to the downloadable JAXB Early Access edition is available at:
http://developer.java.sun.com/developer/earlyAccess/xml/jaxb/.

Now, let's look at WebRowSet, a mechanism that allows thin clients to read and possibly update a set of rows using XML.

The WebRowSet

WebRowSet is an implementation of the RowSet interface that can read and write data in XML format. It is designed to be used by thin clients who do not need access to the whole of the JDBC API, but would benefit from being able to receive and send rowset data as XML (for instance between components of a distributed application).

WebRowSet inherits from the CachedRowSet class. Both of these implementations fall under the category of 'disconnected rowsets', whereas JdbcRowSet is an example of a connected rowset. 'Disconnected' means that a RowSet object caches its data outside of a data source. For example, once the RowSet is populated it will not maintain a connection to the underlying data source that produced the initial ResultSet.

WebRowSet API

The WebRowSet class uses various other classes and interfaces behind the scenes to read and write itself as an XML document. These are:

❑ XmlReader – an instance is registered with a WebRowSet object, and its readXML() method is called to read the rowset as an XML document

❑ XmlReaderImpl – the specific implementation of XmlReader, whose readXML() method does the actual work. This method sets up the parser and the source from which it will get the rowset as an XML document. It also sets up an instance of XmlReaderDocHandler as the document handler that will receive the parser's output.

❑ XmlReaderDocHandler – the default facility implemented to receive the output of the parser and use it to reassemble the rowset as an XML document

❑ XmlWriter – an instance is registered with a WebRowSet object, and its writeXML() method is called to write the rowset as an XML document

❑ XmlWriterImpl – the specific implementation of XmlWriter, whose writeXML() method does the actual work of writing the rowset as an XML document

Operations such as cursor movement and updating are performed using methods inherited from the ResultSet interface. We will have a formal look at the API since it may be useful also for the case study material in Chapter 12. We'll then develop an example.

Class WebRowSet

sun.jdbc.rowset

```
public class WebRowSet
extends CachedRowSet
```

This class extends the CachedRowSet class so that a rowset can read and write in XML format. Note that CachedRowset implements javax.sql.Rowset, which extends java.sql.ResultSet. So WebRowSet inherits the functionality of the ResultSet.

Fields

Field	Type	Description
PUBLIC_DTD_ID	String	The public identifier for the DTD
SYSTEM_ID	String	The URL for the DTD

Constructors

The WebRowSet() method constructs a new WebRowSet object that is initialized with the default values for a CachedRowSet plus default XmlReaderImpl and XmlWriterImpl object.

```
public WebRowSet()
```

Methods

```
public XmlReader getXmlReader()
```

```
public XmlWriter getXmlWriter()
```

```
public void setXmlReader(XmlReader xmlreader)
```

```
public void setXmlWriter(XmlWriter xmlwriter)
```

```
public void readXml(java.io.Reader reader)
```

```
public void writeXml(java.io.Writer writer)
```

```
public static void writeXml(java.sql.ResultSet rs,
                            java.io.Writer writer)
```

Parameters

Parameter	Type	Description
writer	java.io.Writer	The character stream to be used to serialize the rowset
reader	java.io.Reader	The character stream for reading and deserializing the rowset

Parameter	Type	Description
xmlwriter	sun.jdbc.rowset. XmlWriter	A custom implementation of the XmlWriter interface to handle serialization
xmlreader	sun.jdbc.rowset. XmlReader	A custom implementation of the XmlReader interface to handle deserialization
rs	java.sql. ResultSet	The result set used to populate a newly created WebRowSet object

Returned Values

Method	Return	Description
getXmlReader()	XmlReader	The XmlReader object for this rowset. A default implementation is assigned when the rowset is created.
getXmlWriter()	XmlWriter	The XmlWriter object for this rowset. A default implementation is assigned when the rowset is created.

We will look at the features of WebRowSet and how to use them by building an example and analyzing its code. We will create a database table that will contain students' social security numbers, names, and scores; we will then fetch the rows in a WebRowSet object, insert another row, and then update the table in the database. In this example, we have an Oracle database, but it will run from a different database without problems. The details of setting up this database are in the *Compile and Run the Program* section below.

Example: WebRowSet

This example illustrates using a WebRowSet in three stages, with the set of database rows persisted to the file system between the stages. The sample populates itself with data, adds a row, and then commits changes back to the database.

Source WebRowSetSample.java

```java
import java.io.FileReader;
import java.io.FileWriter;
import sun.jdbc.rowset.WebRowSet;
import sun.jdbc.rowset.WebRowReader;
import java.sql.*;

public class WebRowSetSample {

  public static void main(String args[])
        throws java.io.IOException,
```

```
java.lang.ClassNotFoundException {

    try {
      Class.forName("oracle.jdbc.driver.OracleDriver");
```

This creates a new `WebRowSet`, and populates it with all student records:

```
WebRowSet wrs1 = new WebRowSet();
wrs1.setUrl("jdbc:oracle:thin:@dbserver:1521:database");
wrs1.setUsername("test");
wrs1.setPassword("wrox");
wrs1.setCommand("SELECT * FROM record");
wrs1.setTableName("record");
wrs1.setTransactionIsolation
    (Connection.TRANSACTION_READ_COMMITTED);
wrs1.execute();
```

Now it writes the rowset to the specified file:

```
wrs1.writeXml(new FileWriter("before.xml"));
```

Here, it reads the file back into a new `WebRowSet` object and sets a reader:

```
WebRowSet wrs2 = new WebRowSet();
wrs2.setXmlReader(new WebRowReader());
wrs2.readXml(new FileReader("before.xml"));
```

The following code adds a row of data based upon command line input, and then serializes it to XML again:

```
wrs2.moveToInsertRow();
wrs2.updateString("ssn", args[0]);
wrs2.updateString("student", args[1]);
wrs2.updateString("score", args[2]);
wrs2.insertRow();
wrs2.moveToCurrentRow();
wrs2.writeXml(new FileWriter("after.xml"));
```

Now, it reads the file again and commits database changes made during the previous upload:

```
WebRowSet wrs3 = new WebRowSet();
wrs3.setXmlReader(new WebRowReader());
wrs3.readXml(new FileReader("after.xml"));
wrs3.setUsername("test");
wrs3.setPassword("wrox");
wrs3.acceptChanges();
System.out.println("The row has been inserted");
} catch (SQLException sqle) {
  sqle.printStackTrace();
  String except = sqle.getMessage();
```

```
        if (except == "acceptChanges Failed") {
            System.out.println("This is probably because " +
              "this SSN is" + " already in the database");
        }
      }
    }
  }
```

Source WebRowReader.java

Note that the following code is implemented in the WebRowSet's package in order to integrate with protected features of the package. It is essentially a workaround to the apparent dependence of WebRowSet on the old com.sun.xml.parser package. This will now allow the code to work with Xerces:

```java
package sun.jdbc.rowset;

import java.io.Reader;
import org.apache.xerces.parsers.SAXParser;
import org.xml.sax.InputSource;
import org.xml.sax.SAXException;

public class WebRowReader implements XmlReader {

  private SAXParser m_parser;

  public WebRowReader() {
    m_parser = new SAXParser();
  }

  public void readXML(WebRowSet caller,
    Reader reader) throws java.sql.SQLException {

    XmlReaderDocHandler docHandler = new
        XmlReaderDocHandler(caller);
    m_parser.setDocumentHandler(docHandler);
    m_parser.setErrorHandler(docHandler);

    try {
      m_parser.parse(new InputSource(reader));
    } catch (Exception e) {
      e.printStackTrace();
      throw new java.sql.SQLException(e.getMessage());
    }
  }
}
```

Compiling and Running the Code

In order to run the program you will need to download the required JAR files, create the database, compile the code and run the code.

We have provided a SQL script `src/wrs/createrecord.sql` that will create a RECORD table and insert some sample data.

This SQL script has been tested on an Oracle database, and it should work with most other RDBMS that support SQL.

Required JAR Files

You require the following files in your classpath:

❑   `rowset.jar` which is available as an Early Release at:
    http://developer.java.sun.com/developer/earlyAccess/crs/

❑   `jdbc2_0-stdext.jar` from the JDBC 2.0 Optional Package. This package is available at: http://java.sun.com/products/jdbc/download.html/

❑   Any files required by the database driver you use (for instance, the Oracle driver requires `classes12.zip`) which is available from Oracle Technet and with most Oracle installations in the `jdbc/lib` directory. Other implementations will require their own drivers: consult your documentation to find which ones you need.

❑   `xerces.jar` from the Xerces 1.4.0 release

Compiling the Program

Now that we have created our sample database table, populated it, and set the correct JAR files into our classpath, we can get on with compiling the code:

```
> javac WebRowSetSample.java
> javac sun/jdbc/rowset/WebRowReader.java
```

Running the Example

You can use the following command to run the program:

```
> java WebRowSetSample 335462187 Malcolm 85
```

The row has been inserted.

Once the message appears on the command line console, look in the working directory for the `before.xml` and `after.xml` files, which should describe the contents of the database changes.

If you are behind a firewall or proxy, the code may have trouble accessing the `RowSet.dtd` from its location at Sun. It uses this to validate the contents of the XML document when reading it in. You can either enter a workaround on the command line, such as:

```
> java -Dhttp.proxyHost=your_proxyhost
  -Dhttp.proxyPort=your_proxyport WebRowSetSample
    335462187 Malcolm 85
```

Alternatively, you could simply copy the DTD from the rowset distribution into your working directory – the DTD resolver should look there automatically.

Let's look at some of the code in our example in more detail.

First, we set the JDBC driver and create a new instance of the WebRowSet class. Although we have used an Oracle database here, it will work equally well for any database which has a compliant JDBC driver available:

```
Class.forName("oracle.jdbc.driver.OracleDriver")
WebRowSet wrs1 = new WebRowSet();
```

We define a number of parameters for our rowset to specify the database URL, user name, password, SQL query, and the Transaction Isolation Level. For the sake of simplicity, we have hard-coded the SQL query that this rowset will execute; in some cases you may want it to be passed as a parameter by the program:

```
wrs1.setUrl("jdbc:oracle:thin:@dbserver:1521:database");
wrs1.setUsername("test");
wrs1.setPassword("wrox");
wrs1.setCommand("SELECT * FROM record");
wrs1.setTableName("record");
wrs1.setTransactionIsolation
  (Connection.TRANSACTION_READ_COMMITTED);
```

The execute() method populates the rowset with data from the database, then the rowset is written to file as XML.

```
wrs1.execute();
wrs1.writeXml(new FileWriter("before.xml"));
```

The advantage of writing the XML to a file is that the data is persisted to a file space, so you can close down your application and read it in at some point in the future. Although we have written our data to file it could equally be transferred to another application running on this or another machine, if required.

Then, we create a new rowset and read in the XML from our file:

```
WebRowSet wrs2 = new WebRowSet();
wrs2.readXml(new FileReader("before.xml"));
```

The moveToInsertRow() method moves the cursor to the position after the last row (we could have traversed to a particular position if we needed to overwrite that row). To fill the new row with data we call the updateString() method.

```
wrs2.moveToInsertRow();
wrs2.updateString("ssn", args[0]);
wrs2.updateString("student", args[1]);
wrs2.updateString("score", args[2]);
```

The updated XML is written out to a new file. This is used to populate a further rowset, which is synchronized with the database using the acceptChanges() method. Note that it is necessary to set the user name and password twice during these operations, as this information is not stored in the XML file.

The WebRowSet is also employed in the case study in Chapter 14.

Java API for XML Messaging (JAXM)

One of the major efforts at Sun Microsystems, regarding XML, is the work in progress on the Java API for XML Messaging (JAXM). An implementation of the API code-named 'M project' is available as an 'Early Access API' from the Sun web site (for more details refer to the *Compile and Run the Program* instructions further along in this section).

JAXM aims to provide a high-level standard service for composing and sending messages, based on ebXML. A JAXM service provider maps the message to an appropriate physical messaging system (such as the JMS API). JAXM 1.0 will be available as an optional package for the Java 2 Platform, Standard Edition (J2SE). It may also be included in future releases of J2SE or the Java 2 Platform, Enterprise Edition (J2EE).

Currently there is no single standard way to exchange business documents securely and reliably. A number of industry standards are in progress to address this issue, however there is no standard Java API facilitating the exchange of XML messages over the web. JAXM is targeted to solve the latter, though the specification focuses exclusively on business applications written in the Java programming language and messages described using XML (as specified by open industry standards, such as ebXML). Such applications will be capable of interoperating with all other applications conforming to a common message exchange schema, as it would facilitate:

❑ Asynchronous messaging

❑ Routing of a message to more than one party

❑ Reliable messaging with features such as guaranteed delivery

JAXM is being developed through JSR-67 and is currently at the community review stage. JAXM 1.0 may be available as an optional package for J2SE in future releases though probably not in the near future.

Resources

❑ Download the M Project 1.0 Early Access version from here:
http://developer.java.sun.com/developer/earlyAccess/mproject/

❑ This page tracks updates on the JAXM API: http://java.sun.com/xml/xml_jaxm.html

The API in Action

We will look at a simple JAXM client example that illustrates the basic process of obtaining a connection object, creating a message, and sending it. The message is sent to the client-side router component of the M Project example installation. This will then transmit the message to the server and the acknowledgement will come back through the system.

The M Project is a prototype implementation of an XML-based messaging system. The M Project is available to members of the Java Developer Connection (JDC). At the time of writing, the current version is M Project Early Access 1.0.

To install and run the M Project server you need to follow these instructions. Note that the M Project comes with its own Tomcat web server that you need to configure.

- ❑ Unpack the archive
- ❑ Set the environment variable M_HOME to the absolute path of where you unpacked the M Project archive
- ❑ Quite likely you have a TOMCAT_HOME already set to your preferred server. Simply edit the M Project startup script to ensure that the variable is set as follows:

  SET TOMCAT_HOME=%M_HOME% (export TOMCAT_HOME=$M_HOME)

  This will just set the variable locally as needed.
- ❑ Run $M_HOME/bin/m.sh for Unix or %M_HOME%\bin\m.bat for Windows
- ❑ Point your browser at http://localhost:8080 to check if you have everything running. You should see a page titled "The M Project, Version 1.0 Alpha".

Let's now look at a program that connects with the M Project server and passes a string message using the JAXM API. We will then analyze the code.

Example: Sending a String Message

This code will send a String message, using the JAXM API. It uses the existing infrastructure of the M Project server. We have used the original client example code package name to implement this, because we need to access some protected features of classes of this package.

Source JAXMClient.java

```java
package com.sun.xml.messaging.client;

import javax.xml.messaging.*;
import java.net.*;

public class JAXMClient {

  Connection connection;
  URL client, server;
  ClientConnectionData ccd;

  public JAXMClient() throws MalformedURLException {
    client = new URL("http://localhost:8080/simple/client");
    server = new URL(
    "http://localhost:8080/messaging-server/client-handler");
    ccd = new ClientConnectionData("JAXMClient");
    ccd.setPartyId("sun.com/hardware");
    ccd.setProtocolServerURL(server);
    ccd.setClientURL(client);
    ccd.setListenerClassName(
      "com.sun.xml.messaging.tests.SimpleListener");
  }

  public Connection getConnection() throws JAXMException {
    if (connection != null) {
    return connection;
    }
```

Normally we would use a directory service, or perhaps the web application context (as in the M Project) to obtain a `Connection`, but here we simply use the implementation class so that we can run the example as a standalone client.

```
        connection = new ConnectionImpl
            (this.getClass().getClassLoader(), ccd);
    return connection;
}

public void send(String body) throws JAXMException {
    if (connection == null) {
      getConnection();
    }
    connection.start();
    ConnectionMetaData metaData = connection.getMetaData();
    System.out.println("Provider name: " +
        metaData.getProviderName());
    Destination destination =
       connection.createDestination("sun.com/hardware");
    MessageProducer producer =
        connection.createProducer(destination);
    Message message = producer.createMessage();
    BodyPart bodyPart = message.createBodyPart();
    bodyPart.setContent(body);
    message.addBodyPart(bodyPart);
    System.out.println("Dest: " + message.getDestination());
    producer.send(message);
}

public void close() {
    connection = null;
}

public static void main(String[] args) throws Exception {
    JAXMClient j = new JAXMClient();
    j.send("This is a JAXM message!");
  }
}
```

Compiling and Running the Program

The Ant target `tools.sun.jaxm` provided in Appendix A should extract the necessary client libraries from the M Project into your classpath and compile the sample.

Once you have Tomcat running and the M Project page displayed in your browser, go to http://localhost:8080/simple/index.jsp. The message, "This is a test of the Herald server." should appear on the screen. This needs to be run to initialize the server-side components, allowing our application to access it from within the code.

The demonstration server and client router code is well sprinkled with logger statements that allow us to see the progress of the message through the system:

```
> java com.sun.xml.messaging.client.JAXMClient
Client.Connection Start(JAXMClient)
Client.ProtocolServer Sending to http://localhost:8080/messaging-
server/client-handler
Client.ProtocolServer Receiving...
Listener.init(JAXMClient)
Provider name: Sun Messaging Server
Dest: sun.com/hardware
```

Meanwhile, on the Tomcat output window, you should see output similar to the following:

```
Server.ClientHandler doPost()
Server.ClientHandler doPost()
Server.ClientHandler doPost()
Server.MessageProcessor(toBeSent) Trying to send message to...
http://localhost:8080/messaging-server/ebxml-handler
Server.EbXML doPost()
Server.MessageProcessor(toBeSent) Message sent
Server.MessageProcessor(toBeDispatched) Trying to send message to
http://localhost:8080/simple/client
Client.Servlet Dispatching message
Lisnener.onMessage()
Server.MessageProcessor(toBeDispatched) Message dispatched
```

With the ebXML initiative finally getting underway, things are looking promising for a simple Java interface to the increasingly complex world of electronic web services and the XML messaging they depend upon. This is where JAXM should come in. No disapproval of the specification was registered in the Community Ballot of 16 participants on June 18, 2001.

Java API for XML Registry (JAXR)

JAXR is directed at sharing XML-related business information over the Internet.

There are two main uses for JAXR, to register a business or to search a registry. Typically, a registry so created would contain at least a name, description and some classifications to facilitate searching.

In addition to being used for the creation of a registry, JAXR can also be utilized to search for another business. JAXR also supports using a SQL query to search a registry. This is done using a SQLQueryManager object.

To ensure interoperable communication between a JAXR client and a registry implementation, the messaging is done using JAXM. This is done completely behind the scenes, so as a user of JAXR, you are not even aware of it. Because JAXM supports all the major registry standards, it can be used to access a variety of registries. The example shown here most naturally applies to an ebXML registry because it deals with generally public information.

JAXR is being developed through the JCP as JSR-93. Currently an expert group is developing the specification, and it is likely to be included in the J2SE, though not in the near future.

Resources

A description of this initiative and a link to the specification is available at:
http://java.sun.com/xml/xml_jaxr.html.

Java API for XML RPC (JAX RPC)

Two of the major standards for Remote Procedure Calls (RPC) are OMG's CORBA ORB and Sun's JRMP (RMI) API. Though these standards are good for solving a number of problems in this area, they were not really designed to work with XML-based RPC. Java API for XML RPC plans to provide a transport-independent API for standard XML-based RPC protocols.

The advantages associated with XML have made it a good candidate for usage in remote procedure calls. In XML-RPC, a procedure call is transmitted over the network as XML and is then delivered as a procedure call on another machine. JAX-RPC implements a remote procedure call as a request and a response SOAP message; however, a user of JAX-RPC is shielded from this level of detail. Currently there is a W3C Protocol Working Group developing a standard XML protocol "XP", which supports XML-based RPC.

The objective of JAX-RPC specification is to develop an API and a set of conventions for supporting XML-based RPC protocols in the Java platform. The main functions of this API would be to handle the marshaling/unmarshaling of arguments, transmitting and receiving calls and supporting portable stubs and skeletons.

It would also include the API and conventions for mapping XML based-RPC call definitions into Java interfaces, classes, and methods and vice versa. The purpose of the forward and reverse mapping (RPC call definitions into Java and Java interfaces, objects and methods into RPC calls) is to allow XML-based RPC interfaces that have been defined in other languages to be mapped into Java, and to allow programmers to define APIs in Java and then map them into XML-based RPC.

The executive committee of the Java Community Process (JCP) recently approved JAX RPC, and an expert group is being formed for carrying it forward (Java Specification Request-101). JAX-RPC 1.0 will be available as an optional package for the J2SE and maybe included later into the J2SE and J2EE.

Resources

A description of this initiative and a link to the specification is available at:
http://java.sun.com/xml/xml_jaxrpc.html

Summary

In this chapter we introduced some of the various Java-XML projects currently in progress through Sun's JCP. We also analyzed the early access implementations of three of those projects, JAXB, WebRowSet and JAXM, through some simple, but exciting examples.

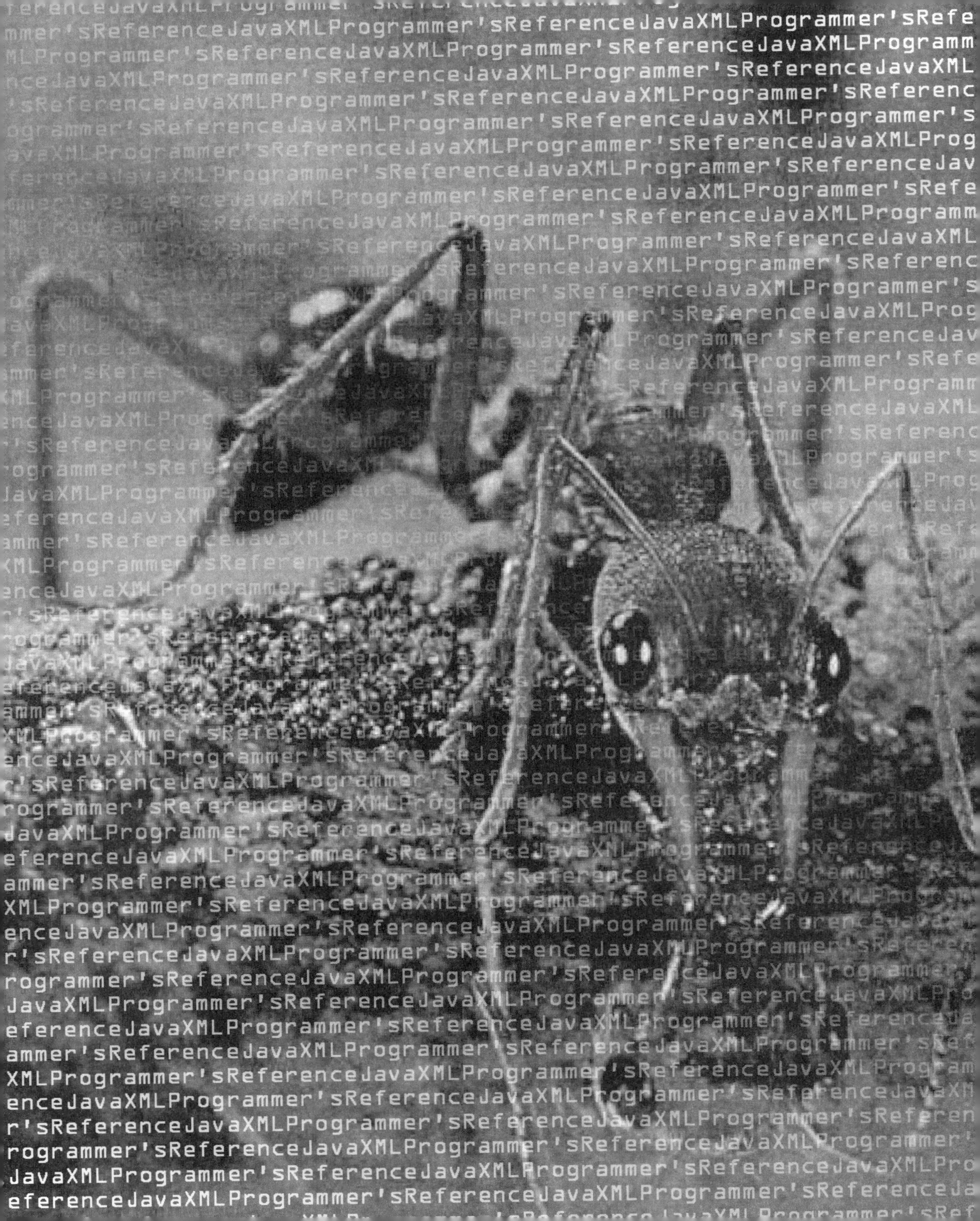

XML Tools for Information Appliances

This chapter focuses on Java, XML, and XSLT technologies for lightweight clients. **Lightweight clients** are defined as those with more limited resources than traditional clients. The term **information appliance** is used interchangeably with lightweight client. The obvious devices that fit within this category are personal digital assistants (PDAs), mobile phones, and pagers. However, many other embedded devices and consumer electronics may fit into this category: television set-top boxes, global positioning system (GPS) receivers, thermostats, watches, digital cameras, even Internet appliances such as kitchen stoves, refrigerators, and radios. Non-consumer-oriented devices also can fit in this category, such as industrial automation and control sensors.

However, this definition is not limited to non-PC devices. Any environment that requires the following should qualify:

❑   A small memory footprint

❑   Limited CPU overhead or availability

❑   Restricted network bandwidth

Applets, in a typical browser, also fit this lightweight category. As we shall see, XML generation, parsing and transformation are just as important for these types of clients as they are for thin clients (browsers) and servers.

In this chapter, we will address three key Java XML technologies for lightweight clients:

❑   **Lightweight parsers and document generators** – Reference material for three parsers and document generators. Through examples, we will demonstrate the usage of three lightweight XML parsers, two of which can also generate documents by enabling you to create a DOM-style node tree.

❑   **XSLT compiler** – a Java tool that creates fast and lightweight Java class files for transforming XML given an XSL stylesheet

❑   **CLDC (Connected Limited Device Configuration) and the Java KVM (Kilobyte Virtual Machine)** – a Java specification for limited devices, which includes a reference implementation written by Sun. The Java KVM, a virtual machine redesigned for the constraints of limited devices, is part of that implementation.

We can do the same essential processing, parsing, and transforming tasks with these tools that we have used elsewhere in the book. Examples in the chapter will show how to work around some of the limitations of these tools, and how we can leverage their small size to get them to run on devices that would not support their heavyweight counterparts.

There are a number of acronyms and terms you'll encounter in the following sections, so let's briefly cover some terminology before we continue:

Term	Definition
CDC	Connected Device Configuration – defines a base set of I/O, connectivity, and other classes for "heavy" lightweight clients such as set-top boxes and audio/visual equipment
CLDC	Connected Limited Device Configuration – defines a base set of I/O, connectivity, and other classes for lightweight clients such as pagers
J2ME	Java2 Platform, Micro Edition – the Java2 platform for information appliances (lightweight clients)
Java KVM	Java Kilobyte Virtual Machine – a Java virtual machine designed to minimize its memory footprint instead of maximizing its speed. Currently ported and compiled for Linux, Solaris, Windows, and Palm OS
PDA	Personal Digital Assistant – a digital organizer, consisting of applications such as an address book, date book, and notepad

This chapter starts by discussing why we should consider using XML on lightweight clients. We introduce the Java 2 Platform, Micro Edition (J2ME) and its architecture. Then, we cover three lightweight XML parsers and the XSLT Compiler. Finally, we conclude with a Palm OS application that beams address book entries in XML format from one Palm device to another using the Java KVM.

Any discussion of using XML on lightweight clients typically leads to solutions that do not adhere well to standards. W3C XML-related recommendations and standards usually don't have lightweight clients in mind, as they are written independently of any platform or operating system. The implementation of these recommendations often involves resource-intensive processing not possible on lightweight clients. Therefore, many W3C recommendations, for instance namespaces and DOM, are not supported, in order to keep library sizes down.

Instead of looking at the XML components covered in this chapter as non-standard, I encourage you to view them as you might have viewed tools of the early World Wide Web: useful, but non-standard and non-standardized. This will change with time, as we can see by the recent conglomeration of multiple lightweight Java initiatives into the far-reaching J2ME.

Lightweight Client Support for XML

Lightweight client support for XML has largely been ignored in the XML revolution. This may be a reflection of the role of the client-side developer. Traditional client-side developers have all but disappeared from many contemporary web application developments, ever since n-tier architecture has displaced the client-server paradigm in the enterprise.

Therefore, if the developers themselves have slimmed down in numbers, the tools they use are bound to become less common. The lack of these tools is also perhaps a construct of what today seems a predominantly server-dominated industry. Perhaps they are lacking because of the ease with which web applications enable developers to forget about them.

Prevailing attitudes can be summed up this way: "Anyone who understands my DTD or XML Schema, can display this document class as they please." Even server-side developers churning out WML today are probably still treating WML as yet another document class that their server application needs to support.

But the number of document classes being published by enterprises grows every day. Servers that produce one or more of these myriad of XML formats (WML being one of them) suddenly complicate things on the lightweight client where slick heavyweight browsers with ActiveX controls don't exist. Lightweight clients simply don't have the capabilities and resources available to browser environments.

The role of the lightweight client-side developer has now been boosted to that of browser developer or "XML processor" developer. More generally, the client-side developer now has a rejuvenated role as a Java XML developer in the world of lightweights, especially with the success of the Java 2 Platform, Micro Edition (see *J2ME*, page 567). In the future, if the modular and lightweight XHTML Basic (see *Too Many Client Formats*, page 565) becomes popular and natively supported by vendors, client-side development may be relegated back to that of scripting with most work done on the server-side. However, we have not yet reached that point.

Most contemporary discussions about XML technologies focus around server-side issues, such as document generation from a relational database, document parsing and persistence to a data store, document transmission, or document transformation for an anticipated client (such as a Compact HTML browser). When client-side issues *are* addressed, they are often limited to Microsoft Internet Explorer or Netscape Communicator.

Case in point: Microsoft has substantive support for XML with MSXML in Internet Explorer. The latest release of MSXML, 3.0, supports:

❏ XSL Transformations (XSLT)

❏ XML Path Language (XPath)

❏ XML Namespaces 1.0

❏ DOM

❏ SAX 2.0

❏ Organization for the Advancement of Structural Information Standards (OASIS) XML 1.0 test suite

❏ Secure server-to-server XML with HTTPS

This is impressive, but these services are implemented as ActiveX components intended for use within Internet Explorer on the client, or as ASP pages on the server. There are plenty of clients that don't support ActiveX components. I doubt that Microsoft's own UltimateTV and Xbox, two "heavy" lightweight clients, can make use of MSXML. UltimateTV is essentially a digital VCR that can record two channels simultaneously (similar to Tivo in the United States), and Xbox is their Sony Playstation-style games unit. Other consumer-oriented and embedded devices would have similar problems with MSXML. As a side note, Sony has announced that they will integrate Java technologies into the Playstation by the end of 2001 (see http://www.javasoft.com/features/2001/06/sony.html)

So, what do we do if we need to parse, generate, or transform XML on a lightweight client? Do we even need to do this at all?

The Need for XML On Lightweights

The future will show that, as Java and XML developers, we must pay more attention to XML technologies on lightweight clients. Even server-side-only developers, who today often just transform their XML into a subset of (X)HTML supported by the most common browser, will have to change their approach.

There are at least five reasons why you need or will need to parse, process, generate, and transform XML on lightweight clients. We will go into detail on each one of these:

❑ **Lightweight client-side development**. If you're a lightweight client-side developer that will be receiving content from providers who publish XML, you will need a way to parse and process XML documents of their document class. You may also need to generate XML documents to send back to the provider

❑ **Too many client formats.** If you're a lightweight client-side developer and your client is going to receive content from multiple providers, each of whom publish XML using different schemas (very likely given today's state of affairs!), you may want to transform those documents into a generic document class before processing them. As a server-side developer, you may want to publish your content in one form, instead of trying to keep up with all the latest standards and recommendations, and push the burden of transformation to the client

❑ **Peer-to-Peer networking**. If your lightweight client application is part of a peer-to-peer network or you are designing a peer-to-peer network, you may want to communicate with the other clients in the network through XML

❑ **Information appliance interoperability**. Embedded devices, smart consumer electronics, PDAs, mobile phones, and Internet appliances can all interoperate with each other and the Internet using technologies such as Bluetooth, Jini, Ricochet, CDPD, GSM and GPRS, WiFi (802.11b), and HomeRF. The need for common data exchange formats grows as the interoperability of these devices grows. Even if the underlying communications mechanisms are black boxes, the application developer is presented with new opportunities and challenges, as he now has a multitude of information appliances connected that previously weren't

❑ **Powerful lightweights**. If you extrapolate Moore's Law, we'll all eventually have turbo-charged mobile phones and PDAs at a cost too cheap to ignore. We could use some of that power for XML-related and XSLT tasks

Lightweight Client-Side Development

With the Java 2 Platform Micro Edition now a reality on PDAs, embedded devices, and actually shipping on some mobile phones, the possibility for rich Java applications with network connectivity on lightweight-clients is here.

All the lessons learned from the client/server days before XML are not forgotten simply because we're on a constrained device. If we want to leverage the benefits afforded by XML (which have been addressed by many other books and articles but is outside the scope of this chapter) on modern lightweight clients, we'll need a way to parse and process XML documents delivered to us by servers. From there, we can display the data to the user and/or store it locally.

We might then wait for user input, or gather system information, and package it up into an XML document for transfer to a server. For example, we might query the current price of an item on our auction web site.

Too Many Client Formats

Today there are numerous lightweight-client document classes. Here is a partial list:

❑ **Compact HTML (cHTML)** is used in the Japanese NTT-DoCoMo i-mode network (http://www.w3.org/TR/1998/NOTE-compactHTML-19980209)

❑ **Wireless Markup Language** and **WMLScript** for WAP networks

❑ **Web clipping applications** for Palm.Net and OmniSky networks

❑ **HTML**, and even though most agree it is inappropriate for information appliances, most web sites are still publishing their content only in this format. There's even the **HTML 4.0 Guidelines for Mobile Access** (http://www.w3.org/TR/1999/NOTE-html40-mobile-19990315), which describes what parts of HTML should be avoided for information appliances

❑ **Handheld Device Markup Language (HDML)**, originally created by Unwired Planet (Phone.com /Openwave – http://www.openwave.com) in 1995 and submitted to the W3C in 1997. It is not XML-compliant, nor does it have scripting capabilities as with WML's WMLScript (however, the Openwave WAP Edition browser does display WML/WMLScript as well as HDML, while its Universal Edition browser displays WML/WMLScript, xHTML, and cHTML)

❑ **Proprietary formats**, which may not even be XML, such as those for the Xircom Rex

❑ **XHTML Basic**, a W3C recommendation for a common (yet modular) information appliance document type. The recommendation can be found at http://www.w3.org/TR/2000/REC-xhtml-basic-20001219

This list isn't intended to be complete. It demonstrates the alphabet soup of lightweight client document classes. XHTML Basic is an attempt to rein in this rabble. It defines a common base that includes images, forms, basic tables, and object support. It is intended for web clients that cannot or do not support full XHTML or HTML 4.0, and can be extended through *modules* (see Modularization of XHTML at http://www.w3.org/TR/2000/CR-xhtml-modularization-20001020).

However, the verdict is out on whether or not XHTML Basic will be widely adopted: it was only officially made a recommendation in December of 2000. Even if it does become widely adopted, the recommendation seems inherently "user-interface-centric". The introduction states, "Because there are many ways *to subset HTML...*" By "user-interface-centric" I mean that data-driven applications, such as some of those found in industrial control, probably care nothing about subsetting HTML. They may not benefit as much by using XHTML Basic as, for example, mobile phone applications. However, even if XHTML Basic takes off and solves the multiple document class problem for user-interface-driven applications, there will still be browser developers on lightweight clients who will need to parse, process, and generate XHTML Basic.

In the meantime, we can make a generic J2ME client that understands all of these formats, or as many of our custom formats as we like. By transforming each of these formats into our own document class before processing, we could reduce the size of lightweight client code significantly. You can use a tool like XSLTC (see *XSLT Compiler*, page 604) to do this. Then, you can parse and process the transformed XML with one of the parsers reviewed in this chapter or the parser that comes with XSLTC. You might also need to use XSL on the client-side if you are displaying to the user a single, integrated service which is actually comprised of multiple smaller services from different servers, each publishing content in a different document class.

But ultimately, why should the document provider care about what kind of client he talks? He should publish his XML with a DTD or schema, and leave the rest to the client. This follows the lessons of encapsulation and distributed object-oriented design that we've learned as a development community over the years, even if it goes against the popular notion of "thin clients".

Use XML Document Servers

Imagine trying to publish content and data in HTML, cHTML, WML and WMLScript, HDML, and in the Web Clipping Application format. No problem, you say: we store all our data natively as XML. All we have to do is write XSL transformations for each format and expose addresses where each content type can be reached.

That could be a lot of work to reach all the new devices or networks, especially as new document classes are popping up all the time and old ones are dying out so we'll have to keep on writing new XSL transforms. Here is a case in point: if WML/WMLScript overtakes the older HDML format in the US, it might spell doom for thousands of existing HDML applications. Fortunately, WAP gateways transform HDML into WML – but relying on infrastructure providers for upgrade paths is dangerous.

Instead of publishing content data in one of the formats we talked about above (such as WML), we should consider publishing it to the client in XML with an associated DTD or XML Schema. As discussed previously, the transformation process rightfully belongs to the client.

Peer-to-Peer Networks

Client-to-client networks, like Napster and Jabber (which have centralized directory services) or GnuTella (with no centralized directory service), have yet to explode in the information appliance world. **Jini** technology and **Project JXTA** (http://www.jxta.org) are addressing them. Jini is a mechanism for connecting distributed services in a network using a directory service. Project JXTA is a mechanism for connecting distributed services in a peer-to-peer (P2P) network where no directory server exists. Additionally, data (called *codat*, to indicate anything from code, data, or applications, to text, images, serialized Java objects, or SOAP packets) is sent across JXTA pipes as XML.

JXTA is quite new, so there aren't many applications out there using it yet. However, it does come with a graphical application called InstantP2P. InstantP2P implements:

❑   Instant messaging within "peer groups"

❑   P2P file sharing

Peer groups are collections of peers that publish, limit, and control access to codat among other peers in the group. In addition, each peer group defines its own membership requirements to secure peer group membership.

The lack of widespread use of P2P networks might be partially due to the single-threaded operating systems that many information appliances employ. If you want to share applications or MP3s on your Palm OS device over a P2P network, for example, you won't be able to look up your wife's phone number at the same time.

Whatever the reason for the lack of their widespread use, P2P networks for lightweight clients have enormous potential. If we're to leverage the openness afforded by XML, we must give clients in P2P networks the ability to natively generate, parse, process, and transform XML. Then, the data (or codat) they exchange can be specified as XML documents.

Information Appliance Interoperability

What if you want your Java 2 Platform, Micro Edition mobile phone application to dial a phone number stored in your PDA?

If both devices are Bluetooth-enabled, and your mobile phone application uses the Java API for Bluetooth (JSR-000082, http://java.sun.com/aboutJava/communityprocess/jsr/jsr_082_bluetooth.html), we're almost able to dial that number. First, the address book application on your PDA must expose directory services in a standard way so that your mobile phone application can look up contact information. Then, the mobile phone application can request a telephone number, or an address book entry, and the address book application on the PDA can send a reply containing the telephone number.

The messaging format between the two applications needs to be understandable by both. It should also be generic enough so that other applications on the same or different devices could understand it.

If ever there was a cry for XML, this is one of them. The PDA application, as the document provider, needs to generate XML. The mobile phone application, as the document receiver, needs to parse and process XML. Only then can our applications take advantage of all the benefits of XML on a device-to-device level.

Powerful Lightweights

As of the time of writing, powerful lightweights are already available. For example, the Compaq iPaq 3670 comes with 64MB RAM and can be expanded to 128MB with an optional CompactFlash card. Instead of the extra RAM, we could choose an IBM Microdrive and we'll have 1GB of storage. With the Dual-Slot PC Card Expansion Pack, you can plug in two Type-II PCMCIA cards. Fill one of them with the Novatel Wireless Merlin for Richocet and you'd have 128 kbps wireless Internet access. In the other slot you could add yet another 16MB of RAM or perhaps a GPS receiver.

Consider all this, and that the unit has a built-in microphone, speaker, and even a light sensor, and I think you'll agree with me that this device can do more than some desktops.

Yet you don't see many people carrying these high-end configurations around, the most obvious reason for that being their high cost. A device like the one above, so outfitted, at present costs thousands of dollars.

If the past is any indicator, devices like this will come down in price and shrink in size. They may even become "wearable" (Sanyo has already announced a line of raincoats for sale in Japan that have a pocket custom-fit for your Palm). If all this happens we'll wonder how we ever survived without one.

So as prices come down and Internet appliances become more powerful and widespread, some of the burden of XML processing and transformation should be pushed onto the client. Complex XSL transforms and larger DOM trees won't pose problems, and the document provider can remain purely in its XML world. With powerful clients, client-side processing can become a reality.

J2ME

The Java 2 Platform, Micro Edition (or J2ME Platform) is one of the three Java 2 editions published by Sun Microsystems. You are probably more familiar with Standard (J2SE) and Enterprise (J2EE), but Micro is rapidly gaining popularity with vendors and developers.

Just as J2SE and J2EE comprise a set of tools and libraries, so too does J2ME. However, J2ME's tools and libraries are targeted at a different set of devices than its larger siblings. Everything from smart cards and pagers to mobile phones, PDAs, and set-top television boxes are potential targets. These information appliances span a wide range of functionality, features, and capabilities.

To address this range of functions, J2ME has a layered architecture that allows vendors and developers to maximize the capabilities of the target device while still retaining some interoperability and platform independence. Consider the differences between a set-top television box and one-line pager:

Set-Top Box	Pager
Virtually unlimited power supply	Battery powered
Lots of memory	Very little memory
Relatively speedy performance	Slow performance
Big monitor for user interface (TV)	Single line of LCD
Always – on high bandwidth network	Low bandwidth network
Persistent storage	Little persistent storage

We wouldn't want the libraries on the one-line pager to have to include the `class javax.swing.tree.DefaultMutableTreeNode`, but maybe we would want it on the set-top box. To maximize the capabilities of both devices while still using the same Java 2 edition, the following layered architecture was designed:

❑ **Operating System** – the unit's OS, for example Palm OS, Symbian/EPOC, or Windows Pocket PC

❑ **JVM layer**: the Java virtual machine and its services (such as the garbage collector) compiled for this OS. This layer is an implementation and compilation of the Java Virtual Machine for a particular operating system. It translates bytecode into native operating system calls. Sun has made available the Kilobyte Virtual Machine (page 571). We will be using the KVM in the sample application later in this chapter, but here is a list of some VMs currently available for information appliances

  ❑ IBM J9 (http://www.embedded.oti.com/)

  ❑ Kada Mobile http://www.kadasystems.com/)

  ❑ Esmertec Jbed (http://www.esmertec.com/)

  ❑ SuperWaba (http://www.superwaba.org/)

  ❑ Waba (http://www.wabasoft.com/)

  ❑ Symbian (http://www.symbian.com/) includes both an operating system and VM

  ❑ Sun KVM (http://java.sun.com/products/cldc/)

Some of these VMs may not fit into the J2ME-specified framework.

❑ **Configuration layer**: base classes that must be available to any profile (and application) compliant with a particular configuration. For example, I/O classes, data types and structures, and network connections are typically specified in this layer

❑ **Device profile layer**: classes built upon ones specified in the configuration layer. GUI classes are specified here. Choosing a profile dictates a configuration, as profiles are typically only available for one configuration. Applications written for a particular profile are guaranteed to work on any device that implements that profile

❑ **Application layer:** this is your application code. Before writing an application, you must decide upon what profile it will depend. Choosing a profile is an important step because it breaks interoperability; your application is not guaranteed to work on another profile. Just like any Java application, J2ME applications define their own classes and have `main()` entry points. Applications make use of classes published by the profile and configuration layers

It's worth mentioning that there are a number of products that allow applications written in Java to run on information appliance operating systems without virtual machines. They work by compiling Java bytecode into native operating system-dependent machine code. Some of these products are compilers that are intended to compile during an off-line build process, before application deployment. Others are complete VMs containing a compiler that compile during or just before runtime (similar to just-in-time and HotSpot).

Configurations

A configuration is a *device class*. If we remember our set-top box and pager comparison (see *J2ME*, page 567), these are clearly two different *classes* of devices. As such, they represent very different target platforms. The J2ME engineers knew the Write-Once, Run-Anywhere model that made J2SE and J2EE so successful wouldn't work for all classes of information appliances, so they made a decision to break application interoperability when they defined *configurations*.

> **A configuration is a *class* of information appliance.**

There are currently two configurations within J2ME: "connected devices" (like set-top boxes) and "limited connected devices" (like PDAs or pagers). Each focus has different qualities, so they have their own definition of classes, which must be available to the VM.

These two focuses, or configurations, are named:

❑ **Connected Device Configuration (CDC)**
http://java.sun.com/aboutJava/communityprocess/jsr/jsr_036_j2mecd.html

❑ **Connected Limited Device Configuration (CLDC)**
http://java.sun.com/aboutJava/communityprocess/jsr/jsr_030_j2melc.html

Sun provides reference implementations of these two configurations, but other vendors have also implemented them along with their own VMs.

In this chapter, we will concern ourselves primarily with the CLDC.

CLDC

As stated before, each configuration defines and implements a set of classes that must be available to the VM. The CLDC both inherits classes from the J2SE and defines its own classes. Here is a partial list of those classes inherited from the J2SE, many of which are subsets of their original, reducing them only to their essentials:

```
java.lang.Object, java.lang.Runtime, java.lang.System,
java.lang.Throwable, java.lang.Exception, java.lang.RuntimeException (and
all its subclasses) java.lang.Boolean, java.lang.Byte, java.lang.Character,
java.lang.Integer, java.lang.Short, java.lang.Void, java.lang.String,
java.lang.StringBuffer, java.lang.Math, java.util.BitSet,
java.util.Dictionary,  java.util.Enumeration, java.util.Hashtable,
java.util.Vector
```

Sun provides a reference implementation of the CLDC, which includes the Java KVM. Other vendors are working on CLDC implementations that hold great promise, such as IBM's VisualAge Micro Edition with the J9 virtual machine.

Profiles

Profiles specify another set of Java classes that must exist along with the classes made available by the configuration to which the profile belongs. They are targeted at specific industry segments. Together, a profile and its configuration specify a full set of Java classes for a particular type of device. Applications written for a particular profile are guaranteed to work on any device that implements that profile.

An important point to note is that user interface components are specified in profiles, not configurations. This is because the configuration encompasses too broad a spectrum. For instance, a PDA and a pager are both CLDC devices, but of what need is the CheckBox class on a one-line pager?

User Interface components are specified in profiles, whereas I/O, network connectivity, and data types are defined in configurations.

There are hundreds of proposed profiles. Here are four examples. Note that a profile defines the configuration on which it depends.

❑ **PDA Profile for CLDC** – defines user interface and data storage APIs for small, resource-limited handheld devices (this profile is not currently available). http://jcp.org/jsr/detail/075.jsp

❑ **Mobile Information Device Profile for CLDC** – defines user interface, data storage, messaging, networking, security, and wireless telephony for mobile devices. http://jcp.org/jsr/detail/037.jsp

❑ **Foundation Profile for CDC** – defines a base profile for devices that have 1MB ROM, 512KB RAM, rich network connectivity, but no user interface. User interfaces can be layered on top of this profile by defining another profile. http://jcp.org/jsr/detail/046.jsp

❑ **Personal Profile for CDC** – this profile/configuration combination actually defines the successor to PersonalJava (http://java.sun.com/products/personaljava/). Applications written to versions 1.1.x and 1.2 of the PersonalJava API specification will work with this combination. It appears that PersonalJava will be absorbed into the J2ME framework under this profile/configuration.

Java KVM

Part of Sun's reference implementation of the CLDC, the Java Kilobyte Virtual Machine (KVM) was designed to operate with as little as 160 to 512KB of total memory on 25MHz 16 or 32 bit RISC or CISC processors. It was written in C and is freely available for four operating systems:

❑ Win32 (Windows 2000/NT/ME/98)

❑ Solaris

❑ Linux

❑ Palm OS

It's interesting to note that Java Native Interface (JNI) calls cannot be made from Java code unless the native call was linked into the KVM when it was compiled. The KVM source code is provided so you can do this. The reason JNI calls cannot be made without this step is so that the size of the KVM is kept to a minimum. Opening up native access to a device allows for the execution of potentially hostile code unless security mechanisms are put into place, such as exist in the Java 2 Standard Edition. This would increase the footprint and complexity of the KVM. Its implementers apparently weighed the tradeoffs and chose size over secure JNI capabilities. Other VMs, such as the Kada VM (http://www.kadasystems.com/kada_vm.html), do allow JNI calls.

We'll be focusing on the Palm OS build of the KVM for this chapter since it's a good demonstration of the usability of the VM in a constrained device.

Package com.sun.kjava: A KVM User Interface

Remember that in the J2ME architecture, user interface and device-specific network classes are defined at the profile level. However, the KVM for the Palm was released at Sun's JavaOne conference in 1999 – before the CLDC was released and a PDA profile was defined. Actually, to date, there still isn't an implementation of the PDA Profile for the CLDC, just a Java Specification Request.

As the 1999 KVM release for the Palm wouldn't have been very interesting without including user interface classes, the `package com.sun.kjava.*` was born. It includes:

❑ A set of simple user interface classes, such as `com.sun.kjava.Button`

❑ An event callback mechanism so events like `penUp`, `beamReceive`, and `keyDown` can be handled by application code

❑ PDB (Palm database) access classes for file input/output

❑ Data structure classes, such as `com.sun.kjava.List` and `com.sun.kjava.IntVector`

The `package com.sun.kjava` is unsupported and quite limited. Additionally, with the newer J2ME architecture, it doesn't belong as part of the CLDC distribution (it is currently provided as an "overlay" to the CLDC files – see *Setting Up the Environment, CLDC/Java KVM*, page 618). It is generally accepted that the package will be renamed (for example, `com.palm.kjava`), rolled into the PDA profile, or incorporated into a Palm OS-specific profile.

kAWT

We won't be using **kAWT** (http://www.trantor.de/kawt/) in this chapter, but it's worth mentioning briefly. It is a simplified, lightweight version of the AWT API for the KVM. If you are going to do any serious GUI development with the KVM, this is the best package currently available. It also optionally includes some very useful I/O and networking classes.

One benefit of using the kAWT is that applications developed with it will run under the AWT with J2SE (although the converse isn't true). Currently, there are ports for Palm OS, IBM's J9, Blackberry RIM, and the MID Profile (See *Profiles*, page 570). The disadvantages to using the kAWT are:

- ❑ Higher storage capacity is required (the Palm OS port is a 178KB PQA, including UI, I/O, and all networking classes)
- ❑ Loading kAWT applications takes longer
- ❑ It's non-standard (although there currently *is* no standard CLDC GUI implementation for PDAs)

Parsers

In this section, we will concentrate on two XML parsers for lightweight clients:

- ❑ **NanoXML** (http://nanoxml.sourceforge.net/) – a slower parser with a DOM-style interface that offers document generation and optional SAX 1.0 support
- ❑ **MinML** (http://www.wilson.co.uk/xml/minml.htm) – a lean, fast SAX 1.0 parser without support for document generation

In addition to these, you might also want to check out kXML (http://kxml.enhydra.org/), TinyXML (http://www.gibaradunn.srac.org/tiny/index.shtml), and XPP (http://www.extreme.indiana.edu/soap/xpp/). They won't be used in this chapter, but we'll talk about a few of their features briefly in *Push, Pull, and Object Model Parsing*, below.

Each of these five parsers has advantages and disadvantages with varying support for W3C recommendations and standards. We will examine some of these issues in this section. For the two parsers we review in detail, there is a table of features included in corresponding sections.

We'll also discuss the three different types of parsers: **push**, **pull**, and **object model**, and the advantages and disadvantages of each in regard to lightweight clients.

After we've reviewed XML parsers for lightweight clients, we'll use some of the technologies discussed in the *J2ME* section (page 567), along with an XML parser, to create a peer-to-peer sample address book application.

Push, Pull and Object Model Parsing

There are currently three types of XML parser:

- ❑ Push parsers
- ❑ Object model parsers
- ❑ Pull parsers

Although push and object model parsers are the most popular and well known, they are not always the best type of parser for lightweight clients. We'll discuss this further in the next section. This chart outlines lightweight XML parsers and the models they implement. Note that some parsers give the option of parsing documents using different models. For comparison, a heavyweight parser, Xerces-J, has been included:

Parser	Type	Description	URL
NanoXML	Push and Object Model	Versions 1.x of this lightweight DOM-style parser offer optional SAX 1.0 support.	http://nanoxml.sourceforge.net/
MinML	Push	An incredibly small parser offering SAX 1.0 support.	http://www.wilson.co.uk/xml/minml.htm
TinyXML	Push and Object Model	Very small parser that offers both DOM- and SAX-style interfaces. No support for generating documents, just reading them.	http://www.gibaradunn.srac.org/tiny/index.shtml (CLDC/KVM port for the Palm OS available at http://www.microjava.com/news/techtalk/tinyxml/
XMLtp	Push	Offers a DOM-style tree interface. For non-lightweight clients, it has the optional feature of an element-style class that implements `javax.swing.tree.MutableTreeNode` and `javax.swing.tree.TreeNode`. This enables elements to be visualized directly by a `javax.swing.JTree`.	http://mitglied.tripod.de/xmltp/intro.html
XParse-J	Object Model	Tiny parser that "aspires to be the smallest Java XML parser on the planet", XParse-J offers custom DOM-style parsing interface. Also a JavaScript version.	http://www.webreference.com/xml/tools/xparse-j.html

Table continued on following page

Parser	Type	Description	URL
kXML	Pull	Works "out-of-the-box" with J2ME. Includes an XML writer and WAP Binary XML support (WBXML), a binary encoding optimized for the mobile phone Wireless Application Protocol standard.	http://www.kxml.org/
XPP	Pull	XPP is small (21KB JAR) and fast and has both Java and C++ implementations. Supports namespaces and mixed content. Uses very little memory during parsing.	http://www.extreme.indiana.edu/soap/xpp/
KVMJab XMLParser	Push	Works "out of the box" with J2ME and the Java KVM. Only 5629 bytes, quite limited.	http://www.alsutton.com/xmlparser/index.html
Xerces-J	Push, Object Model, and no pull but lazy parsing comes close.	A classic heavyweight XML parser intended for servers and desktops.	http://xml.apache.org/xerces-j/index.html

Now let's discuss the three XML parser models in more depth.

Push Parsers

Push parsers are the class of XML parsers that publish a set of interfaces, implemented by applications, through which the parser relays document information.

SAX is the most well known XML push parser. After your application tells the SAX parser to begin parsing, the parser calls back (or pushes) into the application code to notify the application of parse events. This model forces application code to maintain state within the callback class(es), and to evaluate that state at each event. That means many class variables in the callback class(es), as well as (possibly) getters and setters for those variables. This isn't very developer-friendly as it creates a lot of extra work.

Additionally, SAX and most push parsers parse an entire document at once. As soon as your code tells SAX to begin parsing a document, the document is parsed in its entirety. For very large documents, this means lots of state information must be maintained – causing a potentially large memory footprint, not to mention all the wasted processing and battery power that goes into parsing an entire document if not all of it is needed (though not nearly as much as a DOM parser would require).

We'll examine push parser issues in more detail in the *NanoXML* section (page 576).

Object Model Parsers

Object model parsers are that class of XML parsers that build in-memory representations of XML documents using tree-like data structures. The most popular are parsers conforming to DOM Level 1 and Level 2 specifications, but others exist (for example, NanoXML).

Object model parsers, unlike push parsers, don't usually require the developer to maintain document state during parsing, but they have their own drawbacks on lightweight clients. Most lightweight object model XML parsers keep an entire parsed document in memory all the time, until the parser and its resources are garbage collected. Parsing a large document with this kind of parser, even if only one node from the whole document is required, always means occupying large chunks of memory. This approach isn't desirable on lightweight clients since their memory is constrained.

Also, as with push parsers, all the object model parsers for lightweights that I know about parse an entire document at once. As soon as your code tells the parser to begin parsing, the entire document is parsed so an in-memory object model can be built. As with push parsers, this wastes a lot of processor and battery power if the entire document is not required.

Lazy Parsing

Some heavyweight object model parsers offer lazy parsing, for example Xerces-J. Parsing lazily means that the object model is built and stored in memory only as the calling application requests a node. However, usually the entire ancestor-or-self axis (with respect to the requested node) is stored in memory after the request. Certainly, the entire ancestor-or-self axis must be parsed when a node is requested. This isn't optimal for constrained devices, but it's better than the "parse-and-store-it-all-at-once" approach taken by present-day lightweight object model XML parsers.

At the time of writing, no object model XML parsers are available for lightweights that use lazy parsing. Hopefully, this will change in the near future.

Pull Parsers

A newer player in the world of XML parsing, pull parsers aren't nearly as prevalent as SAX and DOM parsers. kXML and XPP appear to be the only feasible contenders today.

Pull parsers are particularly useful for lightweight clients because they parse only the minimal chunk of a document necessary when an application requests the next piece of data. The application can process this data at its leisure and then ask for the next piece, spurring the parser to parse just another small chunk of the document. This is similar to the workings of a `java.io.Reader`. The benefits of this approach are:

❑ Processing and battery power are used when and only when the application needs the next piece of data; the application maintains control over its parsing needs

❑ Memory footprint is reduced; the parser only needs to maintain minimal state information and a pointer to the current element (although the document itself must remain in memory for as long as parsing might continue, so it's to the application's advantage to acquire what it needs quickly). An entire object model does not remain memory-resident.

Unfortunately, there is no standard interface yet for XML pull parsing, like SAX for XML push parsing or DOM for XML object model parsing. Therefore, although pull parsers sound great for lightweight clients, they may be too immature for use today in production applications. Applications would be stuck with the limitations of the parser selected by the development team without a clear upgrade path. It may be difficult or impossible (without rewriting the application) to change parsers in the future.

Let's briefly look at some code that demonstrates how pull parsers work. This code is based on sample kXML code from http://www.microjava.com/news/techtalk/kxml/. It outputs element names and document text. Note the use of recursion, something atypical in applications using push and object model XML parsers.

```java
public void traverse(Parser parser) throws Exception {
   boolean end = false;
   while (!end) {
     //request next document event
    Event event = parser.read();
    switch (event.getType()) {
      case START_TAG:
        System.out.println("start: " + event.getName());
        traverse(parser); //recursive call
        break;
      case END_TAG:
        System.out.println("end: " + event.getName());
        leave = true;
        break;
      case END_DOCUMENT:
        leave = true;
        break;
      case TEXT:
        System.out.println("text: " + event.getText());
        break;
    }
  }
}
```

NanoXML

A NanoXML document is a tree of `nanoxml.XMLElement` objects. These correspond to the `org.w3c.dom.Node` interface in the DOM specification.

> **NanoXML does not implement the DOM interfaces. You build and retrieve document contents through a proprietary API, but an optional SAX 1.0 component exists for document retrieval. This API is covered in this chapter.**

Originally written in April 2000, NanoXML has gone through a few iterations. The current release is 1.6.8. The next major release of NanoXML will be 2.0, and it is scheduled to be available in July 2001. The current beta release is promising, although it seems to have lost compatibility with 1.x releases. We will discuss both releases since they differ significantly in library size and features.

The web site for NanoXML is http://nanoxml.sourceforge.net/.

The source code is available under an open source license. The site is maintained by Marc De Scheemaecker, who is the author of the package. I have found him to be very responsive to support questions.

If your target platform is the Java KVM, the latest NanoXML won't do the job because it has dependencies on classes that are not included in the standard Java KVM. You'll have to get version 1.6.4 from the NanoXML web site and the kXMLElement class from http://www.ericgiguere com/microjava /cldc_xml.html.

Without a doubt, the greatest feature of NanoXML is also its smallest – its JAR file size. Its JAR file size is second only to MinML, but the size depends upon which version you use and whether or not you choose the optional SAX component. You can get away with XML parsing in as little as 6047 bytes!

Unfortunately, NanoXML suffers from some performance issues and memory usage problems, which we will discuss.

Current Release – Version 1.6.8

What's Supported, What's Not Supported, and What's Optional

Feature	Supported	Notes
Document validation	No	–
Well-formed XML only	Yes	`nanoxml.XMLParseException` thrown if malformed
Mixed content	No	Creates bugs in the internal document tree!
Entity expansion	Yes	Entities are specified in the `XMLElement` constructor as a hashtable of key-value pairs
SAX	Yes, SAX 1.0	–
DOM	No	–
Comments	Ignored	–
Processing Instructions	No	PI in the preamble `<?xml version="1.0" encoding="UTF-8"?>` is ignored; subsequent PIs throw `nanoxml.XMLParseException`
Namespaces	Indirectly	Prefixes aren't distinguished from local parts – `<prefix:name>` becomes an atomic element or attribute
JAR size	–	6047 bytes; 8618 with SAX support

Version 1.6.8 is a non-validating parser. Any reference to a DTD or XML Schema is ignored, although there is support for entity expansion.

Mixed content isn't supported, for example:

```
<Request>ItemDetail
  <ItemId>553</ItemId>
</Request>
```

will result in an incorrect internal document representation. XML namespaces aren't supported directly, although they won't cause any parsing difficulties. This SOAP envelope, for example, is parsed without problems:

```
<SOAP:Envelope xmlns:SOAP='http://schemas.xmlsoap.org/soap/envelope/'
   xmlns:xsi='http://www.w3.org/1999/XMLSchema-instance'
   xmlns:xsd='http://www.w3.org/1999/XMLSchema'
   xmlns:SOAP-ENC='http://schemas.xmlsoap.org/soap/encoding/'
   SOAP:encodingStyle='http://schemas.xmlsoap.org/soap/encoding/'>
</SOAP:Envelope>
```

The element `<Envelope>` is stored literally as `<SOAP:Envelope>` with no comprehension of the SOAP namespace prefix. It also contains five attributes: `xmlns:SOAP`, `xmlns:xsi`, `xmlns:xsd`, `xmlns:SOAP-ENC`, and `SOAP:encodingStyle`. Since document validation isn't supported, namespace URLs are not followed.

Comments are skipped by the parser and not stored internally. The first processing instruction in an XML document:

```
<?xml version="1.0" encoding="UTF-8"?>
```

is skipped and also not stored internally. Any subsequent processing instructions will throw a `nanoxml.XMLParseException`.

A SAX-compatible API can optionally be used with parsing (see *Package nanoxml*, page 578). If the SAX API is not used, retrieval of elements and attributes is through a completely proprietary API (see *public class XMLElement*, page 579).

Documents can also be built from scratch and written to any `Writer` object, or they can be modified using the `addChild()` and `removeChild()` methods.

The JAR file size of this release, excluding the optional SAX component, is 6047 bytes. Adding SAX functionality brings the library up to 8618 bytes. But this small size doesn't come without a price. As with most parsers reviewed in this chapter, NanoXML is not XML 1.0 compliant.

You have two choices for parsing: a DOM-style or SAX 1.0 interface. Both choices are multiple-pass parsers, iterating over the same document more than once in order to build an internal representation (this is true even of the SAX interface because it is built on top of the DOM-style interface). This negatively affects performance. Finally, even if the SAX parser is used, an entire document tree is built and kept in memory until the parser object is garbage collected. Not only does this lead to a large memory footprint when parsing large documents, but depending upon the garbage collection mechanism used by your VM, it may severely fragment the heap and prevent subsequent object creation. We discuss this issue in the Java KVM section (page 571).

Parsing large documents with this version of NanoXML may be inappropriate for lightweight clients. However, for relatively small documents, it could be just the thing.

Package nanoxml

This is the only package in the NanoXML library. This version has only two classes: `XMLElement` and `XMLParseException`. `XMLElement` represents an XML document and its content. `XMLParseException` is the exception that is thrown when a parse error occurs; for example, when a document that is not well-formed is encountered. Let's look at each of these classes in detail.

Class XMLElement

nanoxml

```
public class XMLElement
```

XMLElement is a representation of an XML document. In addition to being able to parse XML documents, this serializable class contains all the methods needed to get/set elements, subelements, attributes, and text in a document. It derives from `java.lang.Object`.

Constructors

```
public XMLElement()
```

```
public XMLElement(Properties conversionTable)
```

```
public XMLElement(boolean skipLeadingWhitespace)
```

```
public XMLElement(Properties conversionTable,
                  boolean skipLeadingWhitespace)
```

```
public XMLElement(Properties conversionTable,
                  boolean skipLeadingWhitespace,
                  boolean ignoreCase)
```

Arguments

The XMLElement constructor can only take a few different arguments. Each constructor makes use of a *conversion table*. A conversion table is simply a `Properties` object, which is used to map entities to their conversion values. When an entity is found in a parsed document, it is used as a key into the `Properties` object to find the replacement value.

The default constructor creates a new XMLElement object with a Properties map that converts the following predefined entities:

Entity	Maps To:
&	&
<	<
>	>
'	'
"	"

Here is a summary of the constructor arguments:

Arguments	Type	Effect
`conversionTable`	`java.util.` `Properties`	Entities are keys into the `Properties` map that provide a replacement value when the key is found in during parsing
`SkipLeadingWhitespace`	`boolean`	Directs the parser to ignore leading whitespace in `#PCDATA`
`ignoreCase`	`boolean`	Directs the parser to ignore element and attribute case. Useful for HTML parsing.

If a conversion table is specified, the base entities specified above (& < > ' ") are used in addition to that table. The default values for the other two arguments are `false` for `skipLeadingWhitespace` (whitespace won't be skipped), and notice that the default argument is `true` for `ignoreCase`.

Parse Methods

The `parse()` methods direct an `XMLElement` object to begin parsing an XML document.

```
public void parseString(String string)
      throws XMLParseException

public int parseString(String string, int offset)
      throws XMLParseException

public int parseString(String string, int offset, int end)
      throws XMLParseException

public int parseString(String string, int offset,
                        int end, int startingLineNr)
      throws XMLParseException

public void parseFromReader(java.io.Reader reader)
      throws IOException, XMLParseException

public void parseFromReader(java.io.Reader reader, int startingLineNr)
      throws IOException, XMLParseException
```

```
public int parseCharArray (char[]chrAry, int offset, int end)
        throws XMLParseException
```

```
public int parseCharArray(char[] chrAry, int offset, int end,
                              int startingLineNr)
        throws XMLParseException
```

The parseString() and parseFromReader() methods actually just resolve to one of the parseFromCharArray() method calls.

Arguments

Arguments	Type	Effect
string	String	XML source content is contained within a string
reader	java.io. Reader	XML source content is contained within a java.io.Reader
chrAry	char[]	XML source content is contained within a character array
offset	int	Marks where parsing should begin, counting from the first character
End	int	Marks where parsing should end
startingLineNr	int	Marks from which line the parser should begin parsing

Usage and Examples

To direct NanoXML to parse an XML file, we would write code like this:

```
BufferedReader br = null;
try {
  br = new BufferedReader(new
  FileReader("request.xml"));
}
catch (java.io.FileNotFoundException e) {
e.printStackTrace();
  System.exit(0);
}
XMLElement elem = new XMLElement();

try {
  elem.parseFromReader(br);
}
catch (java.io.IOException e) {
  e.printStackTrace();
}
```

Children Methods

These methods enable access to child elements. They are typically used after parsing a document. Remember that all elements in the document are represented as XMLElement objects.

> There is no way of accessing "sibling" elements in NanoXML as there is in DOM; each element is a child of the element directly above it.

```
public int countChildren()
```

```
public java.util.Enumeration enumerateChildren()
```

These methods take no arguments. Interestingly enough, countChildren() only returns the number of children one level deep in the tree. The other method returns the children *n*-levels deep.

Child Methods

These methods perform operations on elements in the document. It is helpful to think of the structure in memory as a Document Object Model (DOM), even though it is not. Remember that all elements in the document are represented as XMLElement objects; this is similar to the Node interface in the package org.w3c.Dom. Again, there are no siblings in NanoXML – only children.

```
public void addChild(nanoxml.XMLElement child)
```

```
public void removeChild(nanoxml.XMLElement child)
```

```
public void removeChild(String key)
```

```
public void setTagName(String tagName)
```

```
public String getTagName()
```

```
public void setContent(String content)
```

```
public String getContents()
```

```
public String toString()
```

```
public void write(java.io.Writer writer)
```

```
public void write(java.io.Writer writer, int indent)
```

Some of the quirks of this version of NanoXML are apparent here: we have a method called setContent(), but its accessor is called getContents().This is resolved in NanoXML 2.0 beta. setTagName() and getTagName() set the element name. setContent() and getContents() set the #PCDATA of the node. The write() methods output the node and its subnodes to a java.io.Writer.

Arguments

Arguments	Type	Effect
`child`	`nanoxml. XMLElement`	The element to be added or removed to or from the document
`key`	`String`	The name of the attribute to be removed from the `XMLElement`
`tagName`	`String`	The textual name given to the element
`content`	`String`	The `#PCDATA` content of the element
`writer`	`java.io. Writer`	The writer to which the element (or document) should be written
`indent`	`int`	The number of spaces to indent for each new nested element

Usage and Examples

Here is an example of how an XML document can be generated and written to a `java.io.Writer`.

Example: Generating and Writing an XML Document

The XML we generate is a request from our auction site, for the detail information on item numbers 553 and 554.

Sample Request.xml

```
<?xml version="1.0" encoding="UTF-8"?>
<Request name="ItemDetail">
  <Parameters/>
    <ItemId type="Integer">553</ItemId>
    <ItemId type="Integer">554</ItemId>
</Request>
```

NanoXML gives us no way to add processing instructions to a document, so we will output the prolog `<?xml version="1.0" encoding="UTF-8"?>` ourselves. The `addProperty()` methods haven't been introduced yet, but they will be in the next section.

Source Request.java

```
import nanoxml.XMLElement;
import java.io.*;

public class Request {
  public static void main(String args[]) throws IOException {

    //create the document and set the root
    XMLElement root = new XMLElement();
    root.setTagName("Request");
```

```
root.addProperty("name", "ItemDetail");

    //create and set the first child
    XMLElement child1 = new XMLElement();
    child1.setTagName("Parameters");
    root.addChild(child1);

    //create and set next child
    XMLElement child2 = new XMLElement();
    child2.setTagName("ItemId");
    child2.setContent("553");
    child2.addProperty("type", "Integer");
    root.addChild(child2);

    //create and set the last child
    XMLElement child3 = new XMLElement();
    child3.setTagName("ItemId");
    child3.setContent("554");
    child3.addProperty("type", "Integer");
    root.addChild(child3);
    //create a writer and output the prolog
    BufferedWriter bw = new BufferedWriter(new
      FileWriter("Request.xml"));
    bw.write(new String("<?xml version=\"1.0\"
      encoding=\"UTF-8\"?>"), 0, 38);

    //output the document and close the writer
    root.write(bw);
    bw.close();
  }
}
```

Compiling and Running

To compile `Request.java`, do the following from the directory in which `Request.java` is saved:

```
> javac -classpath \NanoXML\nanoxml.jar;. Request.java
```

To run `Request.class`, do the following:

```
> java -classpath \NanoXML\nano.xml.jar Request
```

The output is a file in the current directory called `Request.xml`. It should look like `Request.xml` in the beginning of this example.

Attribute Methods

These methods allow you to get and set attributes on an `XMLElement` object. Remember that NanoXML stores attributes for each element as a `java.util.Properties` object.

```
public void addProperty(String key, Object value)

public void addProperty(String key, int value)

public void addProperty(String key, double value)

public Enumeration enumeratePropertyNames()

public String getProperty(String key)

public String getProperty(String key, String default)

public int getProperty(String key, int default)

public double getProperty(String key, double default)

public boolean getProperty(String key, String
                     trueVal, String falseVal, boolean default)

public Object getProperty(String key, java.util.Hashtable
                     valueSet, String defaultValue)
```

Once again, we see some of the quirks of this release of NanoXML: the setter for `getProperty()` is called `addProperty()` instead of `setProperty()`, this is fixed for NanoXML 2.0 Beta.

The first three methods allow you to add or set different types of properties to an element. `enumeratePropertyNames()` allows you to enumerate through the set of attributes for an element, while `getProperty()` returns specific values for known named attributes. The `getProperty(String key)` method returns `null` if the property doesn't exist for the element.

Arguments

Arguments	Type	Effect
`key`	String	The name of the attribute to lookup
`value`	int, double, String	The value of the attribute
`default`	int, double, String	The value that is returned if the attribute doesn't exist
`trueVal`	String	The value of the attribute which should be interpreted as representing `true`; for example, `yes`, `true`, or `1`. This argument gives you the flexibility of specifying what value to use for Boolean `true` in the `getProperty()` methods that returns a `boolean`. *See Usage and Examples, below.*

Table continued on following page

Arguments	Type	Effect
falseVal	String	The value of the attribute that should be interpreted as representing false; for instance, no, false, or 0. This argument gives you the flexibility of specifying what value to use for Boolean false in the getProperty() method that returns a boolean. See *Usage and Examples*, below.
valueSet	Java.util. Hashtable	Stores the attributes of the element as key value pairs.

Usage and Examples

Let's first take a look at how to use this somewhat non-intuitive method, which was removed from Nano XML 2.0:

```
public boolean getProperty(String key, String trueVal,
                           String falseVal, boolean default)
```

This helper method makes it easier to determine values for Boolean attributes. A Boolean attribute is an attribute with only a Boolean value. Take, for instance, the <exec> element in Jakarta's Ant project:

```
<exec executable="runme.exe" dir="." failonerror="true"/>
```

The failonerror attribute is a Boolean attribute whose values are true and false. ColdFusion's <cfoutput> element also has a Boolean attribute:

```
<cfoutput query="MyQuery" group="id"
    groupcasesensitive="no"/>
```

However, its values are yes and no. getProperty() allows us to test the value of Boolean attributes generically. For example, to retrieve the value of groupcasesensitive, whose default value is yes if not specified, from <cfoutput>, we would write:

```
boolean b = elem.getProperty("groupcasesensitive", "yes",
                             "no", false);
```

If groupcasesensitive isn't specified, the last parameter, false in this case, marks its default value. Another example would be if we were parsing Ant's <exec> element. We could write:

```
boolean b = elem.getProperty("failonerror", "true",
                             "false", false);
```

Note, however, that we could also write:

```
boolean b = (elem.getProperty("failonerror",
    "false")).equalsIgnoreCase("false");
```

Now let's move to look at our previous XML document, `request.xml`. Here is an example that reads it and outputs the `#PCDATA` and `type` attribute value for each `<ItemId>` element. Recall the XML document looks like this:

```
<Request name="ItemDetail">
  <Parameters>
    <ItemId type="Integer">553</ItemId>
    <ItemId type="Integer">554</ItemId>
  </Parameters>
</Request>
```

First, we must read and parse the file:

```
BufferedReader br =
  new BufferedReader(new FileReader("request.xml"));
XMLElement elem = new XMLElement();
elem.parseFromReader(br); //elem is the root node
```

Then, we enumerate through each child node of the root. If any child element is named `<ItemId>`, we output its `type` attribute and its `#PCDATA` content. If the `type` attribute doesn't exist for some reason, the default value `unknown` is used.

```
Enumeration e = elem.enumerateChildren();
while (e.hasMoreElements()) {
  XMLElement child = (XMLElement)e.nextElement();
  //is the child named ItemId?
  if (child.getTagName().equals("ItemId"))  {
    System.out.print("Type = " +      child.getProperty("type", "unknown"));
    System.out.println(" and item id = " +
      child.getContents());
  }
}
```

Running our application against `request.xml`:

```
> java -classpath /usr/local/java/NanoXML/nanoxml.jar Request
Type = Integer and item id = 553
Type = Integer and item id = 554
```

Class XMLParseException
nanoxml

```
public class XMLParseException
        extends RuntimeException
```

> This class is usually thrown when a non-well-formed document is parsed or a processing instruction that isn't in the preamble is encountered.

This class represents a NanoXML parsing exception. It extends `java.lang.RuntimeException`. Even though processing instructions that aren't in a document's preamble can certainly be part of a well-formed XML document, NanoXML doesn't like it and will throw an exception.

Package nanoxml.sax

Adding the optional SAX 1.0 parser to NanoXML increases the library's size by another 2,571 bytes (for a total of 8,618 bytes). This is quite small, but it also increases your dependencies. For example, the package makes use of `java.net.URL`, `java.io.InputStream`, and `java.util.Locale` among others. Depending upon your particular virtual machine and device profile, some or all of these classes may not be available. You might be able to get creative and rewrite some of the package if you want to reduce its dependencies as was done for the Java KVM.

In addition to possibly not having all required classes, SAX is a push parser. After telling the parser to begin, the parser calls back (or pushes) into your application code to notify you of parse events. This model forces your code to maintain state within the callback class(es), and to evaluate that state at each event.

One of the nice things we've seen in the previous code examples is that there was no need for state information. This is much more programmer-friendly than the code we are about to see.

In SAX's defense, however, it will allow you to plug another parser underneath the hood without any code changes on your part. It's a standardized API. All you need to do is use different class files or a different JAR. If you're seeing performance or memory usage problems with NanoXML, this will allow you to plug another parser into your application without much work. However, you might be better off ignoring the SAX standard and using the pull model of parsing, such as that used by kXML and XPP.

Unfortunately, a standard pull API for XML parsing has yet to be decided upon, so if you choose a pull parser, your upgrade path is unclear.

Class SAXParser
nanoxml.sax

```
public class SAXParser
        implements org.xml.sax.Parser
```

This class implements the `org.xml.sax.Parser` interface published by David Megginson. It's built on top of the class `XMLElement` so it has all the features (or lack thereof) outlined in the **Features** table on page 577. Here is a list of other features applicable to this particular parser:

Feature	Support for org.xml.sax.Parser	Notes
Locales	English language only	`SAXException` thrown if another type of local is set with `setLocale()`
Whitespace	`ignorableWhiteSpace()` is never called	Leading whitespace in `#PCDATA` skipped
DTD validation	None	The objects implementing `interface org.xml.sax.DTDHandler` and `interface org.xml.sax.EntityResolver` in your application are never called back
Mixed content	None	XML such as `<Request>widgets<Item>553</Item></Request>` isn't permitted
Document locator	Support for line numbers and system identifiers	`org.xml.sax.Locator.getLineNumber()` and `org.xml.sax.Locator.getSystemId()` are supported
Processing instructions	`processingInstruction()` is never called	

Additionally, this parser only supports locales using the English language. It will throw a `SAXException` if another type of locale is set using the `setLocale()` method. Attribute data types are always reported as `CDATA`.

Since `SAXParser` makes use of the `nanoxml.XMLElement` class internally, it has to choose one of the `XMLElement()` constructors to use. These constructors dictate certain parsing behaviors (see the section *public class XMLElement*, page 579). The default parsing behavior is case insensitivity to element and attribute names, to skip leading whitespace in `PCDATA` elements, and to expand only the entities `&amp;`, `&lt;`, `&go;`, `&apos;`, and `&quot;`. However, this behavior can be overridden by deriving your own class from `SAXParser` and implementing its `createTopElement()` protected method to call a different `XMLElement()` constructor.

Error handlers and document locators are supported, as well as parsing from a URI.

Usage and Examples

Let's look at what it would take to implement one of our previous examples using the SAX interface. This will give you a good idea about what I mean by having to maintain state in your application for push parsers like SAX.

This example reads the XML document from the section *Attribute Methods* (page 596), `request.xml`, and outputs the `#PCDATA` and `type` attribute value for each `ItemId` element. Recall the XML document looks like this:

```
<Request name="ItemDetail">
  <Parameters>
    <ItemId type="Integer">553</ItemId>
    <ItemId type="Integer">554</ItemId>
  </Parameters>
</Request>
```

Remember, we want the same output that the previous code (which used NanoXML) produced. To refresh your memory, the output was:

```
Type = Integer and item id = 553
Type = Integer and item id = 554
```

Here is the code that uses SAX. You'll have to put David Megginson's sax.jar for SAX 1.0 (http://www.megginson.com/SAX/SAX1/index.html) in your CLASSPATH, as well as nanoxml-sax.jar.

```java
import nanoxml.sax.SAXParser;
import org.xml.sax.*;

public class RequestHandler extends HandlerBase {

  private String _type;

  public RequestHandler () throws Exception {
    SAXParser parser = new SAXParser();
    parser.setDocumentHandler(this);
    parser.setErrorHandler(this);
    parser.parse("request.xml");
  }

  public void startElement(String name,
      AttributeList attrs) throws SAXException {
    if (name.equals("ItemId")) {
      if (attrs.getValue("TYPE") == null)
        _type = "???";
      else
        _type = attrs.getValue("TYPE");
    }
  }

  public void characters(char ch[], int start,
      int length) throws SAXException {
    System.out.print("Type = " +_type + " and item id = ");
    System.out.println(ch);
  }

  public static void main(String args[]) throws Exception {
    RequestHandler t = new RequestHandler ();
  }
}
```

Notice the private member variable `type` that saves the value of the type attribute for the element currently being parsed. There is no other way to implement this in SAX. This is a small example, too. For more complex parsing, the amount of state needing to be saved increases.

This code is also quite a bit larger than the code that used `nanoxml.XMLElement`. SAX just isn't as programmer-friendly.

NanoXML Version 2.0 Beta

The second major release of NanoXML isn't due to be released until July 2001. A beta release is available now, however. It lacks SAX 1.0 support and there is still no direct support for XML namespaces, but the author assures me that a 2.1 release will support both SAX 2.0 and namespaces. NanoXML 2.0 is quite different from 1.x, so the 1.x port for the Java KVM won't work with 2.0 yet. Hopefully, a KVM port will be made available.

The beta release increases the JAR size from version 1.6.8 from 6,047 bytes to over 20,000 bytes, a significant increase. So what do we gain with that extra size?

For a start, the classes are in a different package this time, `net.n3.nanoxml`, instead of `nanoxml`. We lose backwards compatibility with version 1.x due to this and also interface and class changes within the packages. If you use 2.x., your code will not be usable with 1.x, although there is planned support for a "lite" version of 2.0 that is almost compatible with version 1.6. There are some advantages to using 2.0, however.

Probably the most significant enhancement is that the parser is now a single-pass parser. Version 1.x releases were multiple-pass and their performance suffered because of it. Performance in 2.0 has significantly improved upon this aspect.

Version 2.0 Beta occupies less memory while parsing than version 1.6.7, but the memory requirements still scale linearly with the size of the document. All elements are saved internally as a tree of `XMLElement` objects, with each `XMLElement` object containing a `java.util.Properties` object to store element attributes. This are kept in memory until garbage collected. As we shall see in another section, this can lead to memory fragmentation depending upon the garbage collector in the virtual machine you are using.

Mixed content is now supported, for example:

```
<Request>ItemDetail
  <ItemId>553</ItemId>
</Request>
```

but `class XMLWriter` has some peculiarities around it (see the *Child Methods* section, page 594). Although the parser is still non-validating, the DTD isn't completely ignored as it was in version 1.x. Except for the `<!ATTLIST>` declaration, other DTD declarations appear to work. Predefined, general, and parameter entities are all supported.

Predefined entities are still supported. Additionally, any character can be referred to by its numeric reference (for example, `&#64;` for @). Predefined entities need not be declared in a DTD.

General entities are macros for an XML document. They associate parsed text with a symbol and must be declared in the DTD. For example:

```
<!ENTITY copyright "© FishHeads, Inc. 2001">
```

Referencing this general entity in an XML document that uses the DTD in which `copyright` is declared can be done like so:

```
<rights>&copyright;</rights>
```

A parser that recognizes general entities should expand the parsed text to:

```
<rights>© FishHeads, Inc. 2001</rights>
```

Just like general entities, parameter entities act as macros and are declared in the DTD. However, unlike general entities, their use is limited to the DTD – they cannot be referenced in XML. Since NanoXML isn't a validating parser, parameter entities aren't very useful. Perhaps this is provided as an intermediary step towards making NanoXML a validating parser. In any case, parameter entities are declared with the ENTITY keyword, a percent sign, a name, and the replacement value.

For example:

```
<!ENTITY % requestParameters "name CDATA #REQUIRED">
```

Whenever the parser encounters `requestParameters` in the DTD, it will substitute the quoted string. Here's a usage example:

```
<!ATTLIST Request %requestParameters date CDATA #IMPLIED >
```

A parser that recognizes parameter entities should expand the above to:

```
<!ATTLIST Request name CDATA #REQUIRED date CDATA #IMPLIED>
```

Note that all parameter entities must be declared before they are referred to in a DTD. Interestingly enough, using parameter entities results in an `XMLParseException`, although they can be declared without any problems. Perhaps this will be fixed before a production release of NanoXML 2.0, but it's worth remembering in future.

Package net.n3.nanoxml

This package consists of four interfaces and nine classes. The interfaces, IXMLBuilder, IXMLParser, IXMLReader, and IXMLValidator, are all intended to allow you to plug your own code into NanoXML. You could write your own reader, for example, and by extending IXMLReader, it would then plug into the NanoXML framework. You might choose to do this if your data comes from an unconventional source, a Palm OS database for example.

We won't cover the interfaces in too much detail, as there are concrete classes that implement them. We'll cover those classes, StdXMLBuilder, StdXMLParser, StdXMLReader, and NonValidator instead.

Class XMLElement

net.n3.nanoxml

```
public class XMLElement
        implements java.io.Serializable
```

This class, even though it existed in version 1.x, has changed significantly. Some methods have been removed, and some new ones have been added.

Constructors

You no longer have to construct an XMLElement object unless you are building documents. When parsing documents, the object implementing IXMLBuilder (usually StdXMLBuilder) will provide the root element through its getResult() method (covered below). So you really only need to concern yourself with the following methods if you need to build documents with NanoXML.

```
public XMLElement()
```

```
public XMLElement(String name)
```

The default constructor is provided for #PCDATA text. To support mixed content in the XMLElement() class, #PCDATA is treated as an XMLElement object with no element name. We'll go into this in more detail in the *Child Methods* section (page 594), but this point is very important.

> Use the default constructor **XMLElement()** for **#PCDATA**. Use the other constructors for element nodes.

The name argument represents the name of the new element.

Children Methods

These methods enable access to child elements. They are typically used after parsing a document. Note that all elements in a document, including #PCDATA text, are represented as XMLElement objects. There is no concept of siblings in NanoXML as there is in the Document Object Model (DOM). Each element is a child of the element directly above it.

```
public int getChildrenCount()
```

```
public boolean isLeaf()
```

```
public boolean hasChildren()
```

```
public Enumeration enumerateChildren()
```

```
public Vector getChildren()
```

```
public XMLElement getChildAtIndex(int index)
```

```
public XMLElement getFirstChildNamed(String name)
```

```
public Vector getChildrenNamed(String name)
```

```
public Vector getChildren()
```

Again we see the quirkiness of NanoXML: `getChildrenCount()` was called `countChildren()` in version 1.6.7. There is no apparent reason for the name change except perhaps to further the incompatibility between the two releases! Also, `isLeaf()` and `hasChildren()` are redundant methods, providing the same information.

The arguments `name` and `index` are the name or index of the desired child(ren). `enumerateChildren()` and `getChildren()` existed in version 1.6.7 and return an `Enumeration` or `Vector` of child `XMLElements`.

`getChildAtIndex()` will throw an `ArrayIndexOutOfBoundsException` if its `index` argument isn't valid. Likewise, `getFirstChildNamed()` will return `null` if no such child with element name `name` exists.

Usage and Examples

Here's an example that gets all elements named `ItemId` in an XML document fragment and outputs each element's `#PCDATA` content. We'll cover the `getContent()` method in the next section.

```
Enumeration enum =root.getChildrenNamed("ItemId").elements();
while (enum.hasMoreElements()) {
  XMLElement elem = (XMLElement)enum.nextElement();
  System.out.println("content is " + elem.getContent());
}
```

Now let's go over the methods for adding, removing, and accessing individual child elements.

Child Methods

```
public void addChild(XMLElement child)
```

```
public void removeChild(XMLElement child)
```

```
public void public void removeChildAtIndex(int index)
```

```
public void setContent(String content)
```

```
public String getContent()
```

Arguments

Arguments	Type	Effect
child	net.n3.nanoxml. XMLElement	The element to add or remove to or from the document
index	int	The index into the document where the first element is 0
name	java.lang.String	The name of the element

`addChild()` adds an `XMLElement` to the document as a child of another element, while `removeChild()` and `removeChildAtIndex()` remove an element from a document. The latter provides a very simple XPath-style way of removing children.

setContent() and getContent() allow you to set the #PCDATA content between an element. It is important to know how these methods behave with regards to setName() and getName(), the functions used to get/set the name of an XMLElement. Using setContent() and getContent() incorrectly will break the XMLWriter class, which is used for outputting documents (see *Class XMLWriter*, page 600). If you create an XMLElement object with the constructor:

```
public XMLElement(String name)
```

this creates an element with name name. The correct way to add #PCDATA to this element is to create another XMLElement object using the default constructor:

```
public XMLElement()
```

then calling setContent() on the returned object, and adding that object to the first one using addChild(). If you instead call setContent() on the object returned by the named constructor, XMLWriter won't display subelements of that object.

To summarize, here is a code snippet that works just fine:

```
root = new XMLElement("Request");
XMLElement rootPCDATA = new XMLElement();
rootPCDATA.setContent("An Auction Request");
root.addChild(rootPCDATA);
XMLElement child1 = new XMLElement("Parameters");
root.addChild(child1);
XMLWriter writer = new XMLWriter(System.out); //output the
                                                  document
writer.write(root);
```

The output of this snippet is:

```
<Request>
  An Auction Request
  <Parameters/>
</Request>
```

and here is a code snippet that does *not* work fine (even though it looks like it should):

```
root = new XMLElement("Request");
root.setContent("An Auction Request");
child1 = new XMLElement("Parameters");
root.addChild(child1);
writer = new XMLWriter(System.out); //output the document
writer.write(root);
```

The output of this snippet is:

```
<Request>An Auction Request</Request>
```

You can see that the <Parameters> element is missing.

Attribute Methods

These methods allow you to get, set, and remove attributes on an XMLElement object. Remember that NanoXML stores attributes as a hashtable in memory (actually it's a java.util.Properties object, but that's derived from Hashtable). This interface is much more intuitive than the version 1.6.7 interface.

```
public void getAttribute(String name)

public void getAttribute(String name, String default)

public void setAttribute(String name, String value)

public void removeAttribute(String name)

public Enumeration enumerateAttributeNames()

public boolean hasAttribute(String name)

public Properties getAttributes()
```

The removeAttribute() method is new for this release. If you're familiar with version 1.6.7, you'll notice that all of the extraneous getAttribute() methods that take different data types (int, double, String) are now gone. All attributes are now treated as Strings, a much simpler approach. All the method names also now use the *xxx*Attribute() convention instead of the *xxx*Property() convention used in version 1.6.7. Again, this is more intuitive as the standard XML terminology for these items is *attribute*, not property.

The first two methods allow you to retrieve attributes of an element. The first method returns null if the attribute doesn't exist, while the second method returns default. enumeratePropertyNames() allows you to iterate through the set of attributes for an element, while getAttributes() returns the internal Properties structure to you directly.

Arguments

Arguments	Type	Effect
name	String	The name of the attribute to look up
value	String	The value of the attribute
default	String	The value that is returned if the attribute doesn't exist

Class XMLParserFactory

net.n3.nanoxml

```
public class XMLParserFactory
extends java.lang.Object
```

This class provides convenient static methods for instantiating a parser, reader, builder, and validator all at once. These four objects interact with each other to parse a document. The parser object is the "glue" which contains the reader, builder, and validator. It is represented by the `IXMLParser` interface (see section *Class StdXMLParser*, page 599).

This class, `XMLParserFactory`, is not essential and could actually be removed from the library. It would save almost one kilobyte. The *Usage and Examples* section below shows how to do this. However, typical NanoXML 2.0 code that parses XML will start by calling one of these methods:

```
public static IXMLParser createDefaultXMLParser()
        throws ClassNotFoundException, InstantiationException,
        IllegalAccessException

public static IXMLParser createDefaultXMLParser(
        IXMLBuilder builder, IXMLReader reader,
        IXMLValidator validator)
        throws ClassNotFoundException,
        InstantiationException,
        IllegalAccessException

public static IXMLParser createXMLParser(
        String className, IXMLBuilder builder,
        IXMLReader reader, IXMLValidator validator)
        throws ClassNotFoundException,
        InstantiationException,
        IllegalAccessException
```

Note that all the creation methods are static, typical of a factory class. Usually you'll want to call the second method, `createDefaultXMLParser()`, to obtain an instance of `StdXMLParser` and call `parse()` to begin parsing. `parse()` returns the top-most `XMLElement` in the document, and you can now access the document data. You'll have to create an `StdXMLBuilder` with the `Reader` or `String` to be parsed before you call `createDefaultXMLParser()`.

The first `createDefaultXMLParser()` method, although useful looking at first since it takes no parameters, actually isn't usable. The reason is because it creates a default `StdXMLBuilder` underneath the covers, and you have no way of telling that builder where your data source is! Hopefully, this will be resolved before the 2.0 Beta is finalized.

To summarize, here are the steps to parse a document using NanoXML 2.0 Beta:

❑ Create an `StdXMLBuilder` object, informing it of the `Reader` or `String` to be parsed.

❑ Call the static method `createDefaultXMLParser()`, passing it the builder created above, to obtain an `IXMLParser` instance.

❑ Call `parse()` on the `IXMLParser` instance.

❑ Iterate through the elements and attributes on the returned `XMLElement` to obtain your data (see *Class XMLElement*, page 593).

Arguments

Arguments	Type	Effect
builder	net.n3.nanoxml. IXMLBuilder	The object that builds a tree of XMLElement nodes from a data source
reader	net.n3.nanoxml. IXMLReader	The objects that reads the data to be parsed
validator	net.n3.nanoxml. IXMLValidator	The object that processes the DTD and resolves entity references. No document validation is performed!
className	String	The name of the class that implements IXMLParser

Usage and Examples

Here is an example that creates a parser, reader, builder, and validator using the `XMLParserFactory` class.

```
StdXMLBuilder builder = new StdXMLBuilder();
IXMLParser parser = XMLParserFactory.createDefaultXMLParser(builder, new
  StdXMLReader(new BufferedReader(new
  FileReader("request.xml"))), new
  NonValidator());
```

We could do the same thing without the `XMLParserFactory` class and remove it from our JAR, reducing its size from 19,692 bytes to 18,727 bytes (a savings of 965 bytes on our precious lightweight clients):

```
StdXMLBuilder builder = new StdXMLBuilder();
StdXMLParser parser = new StdXMLParser();
parser.setBuilder(builder);
parser.setValidator(new NonValidator());
parser.setReader(new StdXMLReader(new BufferedReader(new
  FileReader("request.xml"))));
```

An important point if you choose to use the latter method and ignore `XMLParserFactory` is to make sure you call `setBuilder()`, `setValidator()`, and `setReader()` with some non-null object. Otherwise, a `NullPointerException` will be thrown.

Class StdXMLReader

net.n3.nanoxml

```
public class StdXMLReader
        extends java.lang.Object
        implements net.n3.nanoxml.IXMLReader
```

The `StdXMLReader` class implements `IXMLReader`, an interface called by `StdXMLParser` to read XML data from a data source. It is the default implementation of `IXMLReader` used by `XMLParserFactory`.

Since you probably won't be implementing your own reader or parser, we'll only discuss two methods in this class. They allow you to choose one of two different data sources: `java.io.Reader` or `java.lang.String`.

```
public StdXMLReader(Reader reader)
```

```
public static IXMLReader stringReader(String str)
```

The first method, the constructor, is the one to use to read from a `Reader`. The second, static method, `stringReader()`, is the method to use to read from a `String`.

Class StdXMLParser

net.n3.nanoxml

```
public class StdXMLParser
        extends java.lang.Object
        implements net.n3.nanoxml.IXMLParser
```

The `StdXMLParser` class implements the `IXMLParser` interface. This interface is provided so that you can write your own parser and plug it into your application, if needed. `StdXMLParser` is a default implementation and is used by `XMLParserFactory`.

Unless you plan on implementing your own parser that meets the `IXMLParser` contract, you should use instances of `StdXMLParser`. Here are its methods:

```
public StdXMLParser()
```

```
public void setBuilder(IXMLBuilder builder)
```

```
public void setReader(IXMLReader reader)
```

```
public void setValidator(IXMLValidator validator)
```

```
public Object parse()
        throws IOException
```

You really will not need to call any of these methods unless you:

❑ Do not want to use the default parser class (StdXMLParser) when calling XMLParserFactory for parser instances

❑ Want to avoid using XMLParserFactory altogether (as discussed in the section *Class XMLParserFactory,* page 596)

The parse() method returns the top-most XMLElement after parsing completes. You can safely narrow the object returned by parse() to an XMLElement. Here are the arguments.

Arguments

Arguments	Type	Effect
builder	net.n3.nanoxml. IXMLBuilder	The object that builds a tree of XMLElement nodes from a data source
reader	net.n3.nanoxml. IXMLReader	The objects that reads the data to be parsed
validator	net.n3.nanoxml. IXMLValidator	The object that processes the DTD and resolves entity references. No document validation is performed!

Usage and Examples

Here is an example that parses a document using the XMLParserFactory and StdXMLParser classes.

```
StdXMLBuilder builder = new StdXMLBuilder();
IXMLParser parser = XMLParserFactory.createDefaultXMLParser(builder,
  new StdXMLReader(new BufferedReader(
  new FileReader("request.xml"))), new NonValidator());
XMLElement root = (XMLElement)parser.parse();
```

Class XMLWriter

net.n3.nanoxml

```
public class XMLWriter
        extends java.lang.Object
```

The XMLWriter class is used to output an XML document. In version 1.6.7, this functionality was included in the XMLElement class as write() methods. In version 2.0, however, a new class has been created to handle output, making the library more object-oriented.

```
public XMLWriter(Writer writer)
```

```
public XMLWriter(OutputStream st)
```

```
public void write(XMLElement elem)
```

```
public void write(XMLElement elem, int indent)
```

The entire document, or a document fragment, can be written to any class extending java.io.Writer or java.io.OutputStream. There are no output options; all attributes and #PCDATA are always output for each element.

Arguments

Arguments	Type	Effect
writer	java.io. Writer	The writer object to which output is written
st	java.io. OutputStream	The stream to which output is written
elem	net.n3.nanoxml. XMLElement	The element to output. Its children are also output.
indent	int	Number of spaces to indent for each new child of element

Usage and Examples

We'll use the example we've been building upon to write a full application that parses an XML document called request.xml and echoes its contents to System.out:

```java
import net.n3.nanoxml.*;
import java.io.*;

public class Echo {
  public Echo() throws Exception {
    StdXMLBuilder builder = new StdXMLBuilder();

    IXMLParser parser =
      XMLParserFactory.createDefaultXMLParser(builder,
      new StdXMLReader(new BufferedReader(new
      FileReader("request.xml"))), new NonValidator());
    XMLElement root = (XMLElement)parser.parse();

    //create a writer and output the document to System.out
    XMLWriter writer = new XMLWriter(System.out);
    writer.write(root);
  }
  public static void main(String[] args) throws Exception {
    Echo e = new Echo();
  }
}
```

MinML

MinML, presumably standing for minimal XML, can be downloaded from
http://www.wilson.co.uk/xml/minml.htm. It is the smallest parser reviewed in this book, and the fastest
one mentioned in this chapter. It is also SAX 1.0 compliant, and consumes less memory than NanoXML.

However, it does not offer a pull parsing mechanism. Parsing is only available through the SAX 1.0
interface, which "pushes" events into your application code (see *Push, Pull, and Object Model Parsing*,
page 572).

After telling the parser to begin, the MinML calls back (or pushes) into your application code to notify
you of parse events. This model forces your code to maintain state information within the callback
class(es), and to evaluate that state at each event. This is less programmer-friendly than pull parsers like
kXML and XPP, but it's hard to argue with MinML's raw speed.
For benchmarks see http://www.extreme.indiana.edu/~aslom/exxp/. Perhaps MinML wouldn't be as fast
if we account for the state information which application code must maintain that is maintained for us
automatically by pull parsers.

What's Supported, What's Not Supported

Feature	Supported	Notes
Document validation	No	DTDs are read but ignored
Well-formed XML only	Yes	Throws `org.xml.sax.SAXException` if not well-formed
Mixed content	No	Throws `org.xml.sax.SAXException`
Entity expansion	No	Throws `org.xml.sax.SAXException` if predefined or general entities are used in an XML document. Parameter entities in the DTD are OK.
SAX	Yes, SAX 1.0	
DOM	No	
Comments	Ignored	
Processing Instructions	Ignored	
Namespaces	Indirectly	Prefixes aren't distinguished from local parts – `<prefix:name>` becomes an atomic element or attribute
Document Locator	No	Provides document line and column information
JAR size		15.3KB

As stated above, SAX 1.0 is implemented in its bare-bones state. Locales aren't supported. Warnings and errors aren't supported; all errors and warnings are reported as `fatalerrors`. Public and system identifiers aren't supported.

Document locators, however, are supported. Document locators allow your application to locate the line and column number that triggered the SAX callback.

There is no support for entities, but parameter entities in a DTD are okay. Although this is a non-validating parser, DTDs are allowed (they are simply ignored). Processing instructions, although also ignored, don't throw exceptions like they do in NanoXML. Finally, ignorable whitespace is not reported to the application.

There is no pull-parsing mechanism, even as an add-on. This is a strict no-nonsense SAX 1.0 push parser, which will require you to track all state while documents are parsed.

Finally, and perhaps most significantly, there is no way to *build* a document. There is no interface that can build and output a document tree. If you require more than just parsing in your application, MinML won't be enough for you.

> MinML provides no way to natively build and output documents: there is no object model, or element/node class from which to build documents

Package uk.co.wilson.xml

In true minimalist fashion, this package contains only one class – `MinML`. However, let's briefly look at it.

Class MinML

uk.co.wilson.xml

```
public class MinML

        extends java.lang.Object

        implements

        uk.org.xml.sax.Parser,

        uk.org.xml.sax.DocumentHandler,

        org.xml.sax.Locator,

        org.xml.sax.ErrorHandler
```

Although this is the only class in its package, it implements and uses many of the SAX 1.0 interfaces and classes. Those interfaces and classes must be distributed with MinML and should be in the CLASSPATH variable.

This class can be used in one of two ways:

- ❏ Extending it with your own class and overriding the SAX methods in which you are interested

- ❏ Creating an instance of the class, calling setDocumentHandler() on the instance, and calling its parse() method with an org.xml.sax.InputSource object or a java.io.Reader object

You will notice that class MinML implements uk.org.xml.sax.Parser and uk.org.xml.sax.DocumentHandler instead of the org.xml.sax.Parser and org.xml.sax.DocumentHandler. These two interfaces actually just extend their SAX counterparts and override only three methods. It is by overriding these methods that MinML implements one of its unique features: sending output to a java.io.Writer object.

SAX's DocumentHandler interface has two methods, startElement() and startDocument(), both of which return void. The versions in uk.org.xml.sax.DocumentHandler, however, return a java.io.Writer. By overriding these methods in your application and returning a Writer, MinML will write character data to the Writer object instead of calling back the application's characters() method.

XSLT Compiler (XSLTC)

The XSLT Compiler, originally produced by Sun Microsystems, but now donated to the Apache XML Project, is a tool for compiling extensible stylesheets into lightweight Java code. The compiled XSL sheets consist of standard Java bytecode and are called *translets*. During runtime, whenever your code wants to transform some XML, only three steps need be taken:

- ❏ Ask the XSLTC runtime to parse an XML document

- ❏ Pass the object representing the parsed XML to the translet, along with an object implementing interface org.xml.sax.DocumentHandler or org.apache.xalan.xsltc.DOM

- ❏ Tell the translet to transform() the parsed XML

The translet calls back into the object implementing the org.xml.sax.DocumentHandler interface using the standard SAX 1.0 callback mechanism, or builds a DOM-style tree with the object implementing org.apache.xalan.xsltc.DOM.

In this way, the XSLTC runtime and translets can be used to repeatedly generate any type of output based upon original stylesheets and any input XML.

Compiled stylesheets are called translets.

The XSLT Compiler is itself written in Java, so translet creation can be done on any operating system with a Java 2 VM. Translets are merely Java classes, but are designed to run on any Java VM, not just Java 2 VMs. Since they are class files, their compilation is usually done with build scripts along with the rest of your project code.

The XSLT Compiler can be downloaded from http://xml.apache.org/xalan-j

It has two important dependencies:

❏ The Constructor of Useful Parsers (CUP) Parser Generator

❏ The Byte Code Engineering Library (BCEL)

The CUP Parser Generator is used to generate a Java parser and scanner from a stylesheet (the grammar). BCEL is used by XSLTC to convert the parser and scanner from Java source code to bytecode. Both are included as JARs in the Xalan distribution.

In this section, we will:

❏ Examine what is supported and not supported by XSLTC

❏ Discuss the benefits of translets over traditional transformation engines, specifically in regard to lightweight clients

❏ Make a translet using a real example

❏ Review the major classes and steps involved in using the XSLTC

What's Supported, What's Not Supported

Sun and Apache have done an excellent job covering the XSLT 1.0 recommendation. It will be easier to list the features of XSLT that *aren't* supported by XSLTC, rather than the ones that are.

Feature	Supported	Notes
SAX 2.0 callbacks (org.xml.sax.ContentHandler) for transformed documents	No	SAX 1.0's `org.xml.sax.DocumentHandler` is supported

Simplified stylesheets	No	The simplified syntax for stylesheets that consist of only a single template for the root node isn't permitted. The syntax is a literal result element that can represent the whole document. For example:
		
		`<total xsl:version="1.0" xmlns:xsl=`
		`http://www.w3.org/1999/XSL/Transform>`
		
		`<xsl:value-of select="cart/total"/>`
		
		`</total>`
		
		Notice the `<xsl:stylesheet>` prolog is missing, along with some other things.
		
		For more information, see
		
		http://www.w3.org/TR/xslt.html#result-element-stylesheet

Table continued on following page

605

Feature	Supported	Notes
Match patterns with id attribute	No	The ability to match elements by their unique id attribute is unsupported
Match patterns using <xsl:key>	No	The ability to match elements using implicit cross-referencing (keys) is unsupported. For more information, see http://www.w3.org/TR/xslt.html#key
Namespace axis	No	The namespace axis isn't supported. It is defined this way: if the starting node in the axis is an element, the axis selects all the namespace nodes that are in scope for that element; otherwise, the axis selects nothing. For instance: <<namespace::*>>
Document validatation	Yes	DTD validation of XML source
DOM parser included	Yes	If you're using XSLTC on a lightweight client, you can make use of the DOM Level 1 parser independent of XSLTC that comes with xml.jar. No need to include the JAR files for NanoXML or other parsers.
SAX parser included	Yes	A SAX 1.0 parser comes with the xml.jar library. The parser can actually be removed and replaced with another SAX library, but the current documentation on how to do this is non-existent.

Translets vs. Traditional Transformation Engines

There are at least four reasons why information appliances needing to do XSL transformations should consider translets over traditional transformation engines:

❑ **Smaller memory footprint** – translet and runtime classes are minimized by including only those XSLTC features required for that particular transformation

❑ **Performance** – Sun claims performance gains between 30-270% over Saxon, Xalan, and XT processors, depending upon stylesheet and XML input sizes – performance is even more of a key issue on limited devices

❑ **Freedom** – runtime and translet classes are Java 1.1 bytecode

❑ **Reduced network traffic** – XSL stylesheets need not be downloaded as they are already distributed with an application

Let's discuss each of these in a little more detail.

Smaller Memory Footprint

Traditional transformation engines have large memory footprints. For example, Apache's Xalan-Java 2.0.1 requires xalan.jar and xerces.jar (the Apache Xerces XML parser). This represents over 2.2 MB of bytecode! Not many would argue that this is an unreasonable demand for most of today's lightweight clients.

Translets, on the other hand, require three things:

- ❑ The XSLTC runtime JAR `xsltcrt.jar` (119 KB, 117 KB reduced)
- ❑ The `xml.jar` file (126 KB)
- ❑ Any translet class files your application needs to use (typically 2–10KB each, depending upon the size and complexity of the original XSL stylesheet)

XSL functionality used in most stylesheets is included in `xsltcrt.jar`, while functionality specific to certain stylesheets (and not already included in `xsltcrt.jar`) is compiled into those stylesheets' translets. This approach minimizes the size of the runtime library without sacrificing XSLT compatibility.

`xml.jar` was Sun Project X, the precursor to Apache Crimson. It contains the SAX 1.0 and DOM Level 1 interfaces, as well as SAX and DOM implementations. It's important to note that since this JAR file is required at runtime, you are given SAX and DOM parsers for free; there's no need to include another parser such as NanoXML.

> Since translets require Sun Project X (`xml.jar`), which contains both SAX 1.0 and DOM Level 1 parsers, there's no need to include another parser in your lightweight client. The parsers in `xml.jar` can be used independently and separately from translets, if needed.

Finally, the compiled XSL stylesheets themselves must be available on the target lightweight platform. These vary in size depending upon the original XSL stylesheet, but are usually 2–10KB. Of course, multiple translets can be deployed for a given application, allowing the application to transform different document classes in a variety of different ways.

Performance

The following performance graph was generated from data gathered by XSLTMark (http://www.datapower.com/XSLTMark/).

Processor Performance

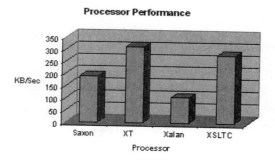

Kilobytes per second are the total number of bytes in the input and output XML documents divided by twice the elapsed time. See http://www.xml.com/pub/a/2001/03/28/xsltmark/results.html for more information. Although we have compared two different sets of data in the same graph (something the XSLTMark authors warn against), we have still used the graph for general comparisons. With an older version of XSLTC, we see it is second only to XT. Newer versions of XSLTC claim even better performance gains. Since the release notes for release Alpha 5 specifically state, "performance has been greatly improved" over Alpha 4, we'll have to perform more benchmarks to get the clearest performance picture.

Michael Kay, the creator of Saxon, stated in *XSLT Programmer's Reference, 2nd Edition ISBN 1861005067*, that he has found translet performance to be roughly comparable to Saxon and XT.

Clearly, XSLTC is a contender in regards to performance with the large, conventional XSLT processors. However, this only serves to draw attention to XSLTC's supreme advantage over these processors – the small size of the generated stylesheet bytecode compared to running a transformation in a large, powerful interpreter.

This is one factor which clearly points towards a big future for translets within information appliances.

Freedom

Although the XSLT compiler requires Java 2, the class files it generates can be used with any Java VM. This is an important point because even though we may not be able to compile XSL stylesheets on lightweight clients, we should always be able to use translets on lightweight clients with J2ME.

Reduced Network Traffic

Since translets can be distributed with an application, XSL stylesheets no longer need to be downloaded from a server. This is good news for devices using constrained wireless networks, such as the 9.6 kpbs Cellular Digital Packet Data (CDPD) connection. The flexibility of downloading new stylesheets as needed is not always lost, however. Translets, if used in applets, can be downloaded from the server on which the applet was downloaded just like any other Java class.

Package org.apache.xalan.xsltc

There are no Javadocs for this package, but let's hope Apache changes this soon. The package contains the interfaces and classes used and implemented by translets. Remember that translets are compiled XSL stylesheets. The primary interfaces and classes in this package are:

- ❑   `Translet`
- ❑   `TransletOutputHandler`
- ❑   `TransletException`

We will discuss each of these in this section.

Interface Translet

org.apache.xalan.xsltc

> **public interface** `Translet`

A class that implements interface `Translet` must be able to transform XML input into the output specified by the mapping in the original XSL stylesheet. The XSLTC library creates classes that implement this interface; you shouldn't ever need to write code that implements interface `Translet`. You will, however, need to call the `transform()` method to tell the implementing class when to begin the transformation process.

The transform() Method

```
public void transform(DOM Document,
                      TransletOutputHandler handler)
      throws TransletException
```

A transformation requires two items: a `org.apache.xalan.xsltc.dom.DOMImpl` object (which unfortunately carries no documentation!) and an object implementing the `org.apache.xalan.xsltc.TransletOutputHandler` interface. DOMImpl implements interface `org.apache.xalan.xsltc.DOM`. These two items are created in your application code and given to the translet.

Arguments

Arguments	Type	Effect
Document	`org.apache.xalan.xsltc.DOM`	The parsed XML input document to be transformed. It is a DOM tree implementing the DOM interface, and so is usually an instance of the DOM implementation class `org.apache.xalan.xsltc.dom.DOMImpl`
handler	`org.apache.xalan.xsltc.TransletOutputHandler`	The callback handler, which the translet uses to notify your application of transformed elements, attributes, and data. Conceptually very similar to SAX's `org.xml.sax.DocumentHandler`.

Usage and Examples

To create an instance of a class which implements `org.apache.xalan.xsltc.Translet`, we use the Java reflection API:

```
Class cls = Class.forName("MyClass");
Translet xlet = (Translet)cls.newInstance();
xlet.tranform(dom, handler);
```

"`MyClass`" is the name of the class generated by XSLTC during compilation (we go over how to compile an XSL stylesheet in the section *Example: Compiling and Using a Translet*, page 612). `xlet.transform()` method can now be called to perform the transformation.

Interface TransletOutputHandler
org.apache.xalan.xsltc

```
public interface TransletOutputHandler
```

This interface contains the callback methods which a translet calls as it transforms XML input to some output. Conceptually, a translet behaves just like a SAX parsing engine, calling back into interface `org.apache.xalan.xsltc.TransletOutputHandler` instead of interface `org.xml.sax.DocumentHandler` or `org.xml.sax.ContentHandler`. However, the designers of XSLTC have chosen natively to support `TransletOutputHandler` rather than SAX 1.0's `DocumentHandler` and SAX 2.0's `ContentHandler`.

> Conceptually, a translet behaves just like a SAX parsing engine, calling back into interface `org.apache.xalan.xsltc.TransletOutputHandler` instead of interface `org.xml.sax.DocumentHandler` or `org.xml.sax.ContentHandler`.

SAX 1.0 is supported by wrapping a `org.apache.xalan.xsltc.runtime.TextOutput` object around an object implementing `TransletOutputHandler`. Since SAX is the de facto push parser standard, we'll focus on how to use it with translets rather than the proprietary `TransletOutputHandler`. However, let's briefly examine some of `TransletOutputHandler` to further understand how translets work.

Callback Methods

```
public void startDocument()
      throws TransletException

public void endDocument()
      throws TransletException

public void characters(char[] characters, int offset, int length)
      throws TransletException

public void startElement(String elementName)
      throws TransletException

public void endElement(String elementName)
      throws TransletException

public void attribute(String attributeName, String attributeValue)
      throws TransletException

public void comment(String comment)
      throws TransletException

public void processingInstruction(String target, String data)
      throws TransletException
```

Although this isn't complete, you should immediately see the similarities between this interface and SAX 1.0's org.xml.sax.DocumentHandler and SAX 2.0's org.xml.sax.ContentHandler.

A helper class is given to us to enable SAX 1.0 support. org.apache.xalan.xsltc.runtime TextOutput not only implements interface TransletOutputHandler, but it also maps TransletOutputHandler methods to corresponding org.xml.sax.DocumentHandler methods.

Usage and Examples

So now let's look at some code, which transforms XML and notifies us of the new (transformed) document via SAX.

First, recall the signature of Translet.transform():

```
public void transform(DOM Document,
         transletOutputHandler handler)
      throws TransletException
```

And here's our code:

```
//load and create the translet
Class cls = Class.forName("MyClass");
Translet xlet = (Translet)cls.newInstance();
DOMImpl dom = new DOMImpl(); //will contain the parsed
                            //source XML

//build DOM tree from source XML into the dom object (not
//   shown)

Handler saxHandler; //implements sax.DocumentHandler
TextOutput textOutput; //implements TransletOutputHandler
try {
  saxHandler= new Handler();
  textOutput = new TextOutput(saxHandler);
  //pass the translet the source XML and a handler
  xlet.transform(dom, textOutput);
}
catch (Exception  e) {
  e.printStackTrace();
}
```

This code performs the following steps:

❑   Loads the translet with Java reflection

❑   Creates a DOM tree from source XML (this part has been removed, but we will demonstrate how to do this in the section *Example: Compiling and Using A Translet*, page 612)

❑   Creates an object which implements interface org.xml.sax.DocumentHandler (saxHandler)

❑   Creates a TextOutput object and passes it the saxHandler

❑   Starts the transformation by calling transform()

We can clearly see in the bolded line how `TextOutput` maps its implementation of `TransletOutputHandler` to `DocumentHandler`.

Class TransletException

org.apache.xalan.xsltc

```
public class TransletException
        extends java.lang.Exception
```

This is the exception class thrown by `Translet.transform()` and all of the methods in interface `TransletOutputHandler`. Since you probably will use the SAX interface via the `TextOutput` wrapper (never directly implementing `TransletOutputHandler`), you won't need to catch `TransletExceptions` except when calling `Translet.transform()`.

There aren't any special methods in this class. You should handle `TransletException` objects in the same manner that you treat other `Throwable` classes extending `java.lang.Exception`.

Now let's take a look at a creating a translet and an application which uses it.

Example: Compiling and Using a Translet

In this example, we have a trouble ticket system to which our client connects. The client can add, update, and view trouble tickets. For this example, however, we'll concern ourselves only with viewing trouble tickets already in the system. Here are the steps our client application will take:

❑   Read an XML document, representing a single existing trouble ticket. To simplify matters, we'll read the document from persistent storage instead of from a network

❑   Invoke a translet to convert the TroubleTicket document into Wireless Markup Language (WML). You don't need to know WML to understand this example, but if you do, we'll translate the single trouble ticket into a single card in one WML deck. A more advanced system might be able to query and collate multiple trouble tickets into multiple cards within the same deck to save network trips

❑   If we passed the WML to a browser at this point, or wrote our own browser within the application, we could view the WML. However, for simplicity, we'll just write the WML to `stdout`

Before we write the application, we will need to compile a translet from a "TroubleTicket to WML" XSL stylesheet. So, here's how we'll present this example:

❏ Examine a document instance of a trouble ticket document class

❏ Present an XSL stylesheet that transforms `<TroubleTicket/>` documents into WML

❏ Compile a translet from the XSL stylesheet

❏ Write the client application that uses the translet and a trouble ticket document instance to produce an instance of a WML document

Sample TroubleTicket.xml

So let's begin by taking a look at `TroubleTicket.xml`, a `TroubleTicket` document instance:

```xml
<?xml version="1.0" encoding="UTF-8"?>
<TroubleTicket ID="T746284" Importance="High"
  Status="Open" PrimaryHelpAgent="Melissa">
  <Description>Installation failed</Description>
  <Customer Name="Int'l Steel" ID="1573">
    <Contact Status="Primary" Name="Ann McKinsey"
      Phone="303-781-7777" Fax="303-781-7778"
      Email="AMcKinsey@IntSteel.com"/>
  </Customer>
  <Product Name="SteelPlant2001" Rev="2.0"
    Code="537010502"/>
  <Incident>
    <Call Type="Inbound" StartTime="02/17/2001 10:35"
      Duration="17" HelpAgent="Johnson">Customer received
      network errors during installation. Disconnection
      from network caused reboot msg. He will reboot and
      call back.
    </Call>
  </Incident>
</TroubleTicket>
```

This is pretty straightforward so we won't go into it much. This, and documents of this class, will be the source XML to our translet. For brevity's sake, the DTD for this document class has been omitted.

Sample TroubleTicket.xsl

Now let's take a look at the guts of the application: the XSL stylesheet that converts `TroubleTicket` document instances into WML. We'll call this `TroubleTicket.xsl`:

```xml
<?xml version="1.0" encoding="UTF-8"?>
<xsl:stylesheet version="1.0"
xmlns:xsl="http://www.w3.org/1999/XSL/Transform">
  <xsl:template match="/">
    <wml>
      <xsl:apply-templates select="TroubleTicket"/>
    </wml>
  </xsl:template>
  <xsl:template match="TroubleTicket">
    <card>
      <xsl:attribute name="id"><xsl:value-of select="@ID"/></xsl:attribute>
      <xsl:attribute name="title">Ticket:          <xsl:value-of
```

```
      select="@ID"/></xsl:attribute>
        <p>
          <b>
            <xsl:value-of select="Description"/>
          </b>
          <br/>
          <br/>
          <xsl:value-of select="Customer/@Name"/>
          <br/>
          <xsl:value-of select="Customer/Contact/@Name"/>
          <br/>
          <xsl:value-of select="Customer/Contact/@Phone"/>
          <br/>
          <xsl:value-of select="Product/@Name"/>
        </p>
      </card>
    </xsl:template>
  </xsl:stylesheet>
```

An XSLT processor, using the stylesheet above, will produce the following WML from the
`TroubleTicket` document instance in *The TroubleTicket Document* (page 613):

```
<wml>
  <card id="T746284" title="Ticket:T746284">
    <p>
      <b>Installation failed</b>
      <br/>
      <br/>
      Int'l Steel<br/>
      Ann McKinsey<br/>
      303-781-7777<br/>
      SteelPlant2001
    </p>
  </card>
</wml>
```

Compiling a Translet

Now let's compile the XSL stylesheet from the previous section into a translet (Java class file).
The compiler is class `org.apache.xalan.xsltc.compiler.XSLTC`, and you will need to
set your classpath to include the following JAR files:

```
/jaxp-1.1/jaxp.jar
/xalan-j_2_1_0/bin/xsltc.jar
/xalan-j_2_1_0/bin/runtime.jar
/xalan-j_2_1_0/bin/BCEL.jar
/xerces-1_4_0/xerces.jar
```

```
> java org.apache.xalan.xsltc.compiler.XSLTC TroubleTicket.xsl
```

Make sure that `TroubleTicket.xsl` is in the current directory, or provide its full path on the
command-line.

You should now have a class file called `TroubleTicket.class`. It resides in the directory from which you ran XSLTC, unless the `-d <directory>` argument is used. Note that a build script to build this with Apache's ant tool is available from http://www.wrox.com/. See Appendix A.

WML TroubleTicketViewer Application

Our last step is to build an application that uses the translet and source XML to generate WML.

You should be able to compile this code with the ant `build.xml` file available at the Wrox Press web site along with all source code (see Appendix A). Some of this code we've already seen.

```java
import org.apache.xalan.xsltc.*;
import org.apache.xalan.xsltc.dom.DOMImpl;
import org.apache.xalan.xsltc.runtime.TextOutput;

import javax.xml.parsers.SAXParser;
import javax.xml.parsers.SAXParserFactory;
import org.xml.sax.XMLReader;
import org.xml.sax.InputSource;
import java.io.FileReader;

public class TroubleTicketViewer {

  public TroubleTicketViewer(String inputfile) throws Exception {
    //load and create the translet
    Class cls = Class.forName("TroubleTicket");
    Translet xlet = (Translet)cls.newInstance();
    DOMImpl dom = new DOMImpl(); //will contain the
      parsed source XML

    //create SAX 2.0 parser & get the XMLReader object it
      uses
    SAXParserFactory factory =
      SAXParserFactory.newInstance();
    SAXParser parser = factory.newSAXParser();
    XMLReader reader = parser.getXMLReader();

    //Set the DOM's builder as the XMLReader's SAX 2.0 content handler
    reader.setContentHandler(dom.getBuilder());
    //parse
    reader.parse(new InputSource(new
      FileReader(inputfile)));
```

Now that we've parsed the source XML and have it in DOM, let's tell the translet to do the translation. We'll have the translet put the translated document into another DOMImpl object, wmlDOM, although we could have passed it a SAX 1.0 handler to receive callbacks instead.

```java
    DOMImpl wmlDOM = new DOMImpl(); //implements
      sax.DocumentHandler
```

```
TextOutput txtOutput; //implements
    TransletOutputHandler
txtOutput = new TextOutput(wmlDOM.getBuilder());
//pass the translet the source XML and a handler
xlet.transform(dom, txtOutput);
```

Finally, let's output the WML to `stdout`:

```
wmlDOM.print(1, 1); //print the root and its children
}

public static void main(String[] args) throws Exception
  {
  TroubleTicketViewer ttv = new
    TroubleTicketViewer(args[0]);
  }
}
```

Run the application:

```
> java TroubleTicketViewer TroubleTicket.xml
```

You should get this WML output. It's not pretty, but it's what we expect:

```
<wml><card
title="Ticket:T746284"
id="T746284"><p><b>Installation failed</b>
<br></br>
<br></br>
Int'l Steel<br></br>
Ann McKinsey<br></br>
303-781-7777<br></br>
SteelPlant2001</p>
</card>
</wml>
```

The Future

As XSLTC begins to benefit from the open source development cycle at Apache, expect new initiatives for transformation in the information appliance arena. Translets are ideally placed to foster a viable peer-to-peer environment on small devices, bringing with them the power of universal transformation to the growing support for XML on these appliances. Keep an eye on the `xalan-dev@xml.apache.org` mailing list!

SOAP On Lightweight Clients

The potential for SOAP on lightweight clients is big. SOAP is notoriously slow and resource-intensive compared to RPC, CORBA, and JNI calls, but with more powerful information appliances becoming available each day, this hopefully won't be an issue soon. Simple and relatively infrequent calls, such as requests for weather or stock data from HTTP SOAP servers, are certainly feasible with today's information appliances.

There are currently two lightweight Java SOAP libraries that are worth mentioning:

- ❏ **KVM kSOAP** (http://ksoap.enhydra.org/)

- ❏ **nanoSOAP** (http://www.extreme.indiana.edu/soap/), implementing only SOAP 1.0 and, unfortunately, no longer supported

Sample Application: Contact Infrared Beamer

In this section, we'll show you how to install the Java KVM and Palm OS Emulator on your machine. Then we'll bring together some of the different technologies we've talked about in this chapter – Java and XML on a Palm OS device. We'll create a complete lightweight Java XML application using these tools:

- ❏ **Java KVM for J2ME** – the Java Kilobyte Virtual Machine (KVM) is designed to operate with as little as 160 to 512 KB of total memory. See *Java KVM* (page 571).

- ❏ **NanoXML** – a lightweight DOM-style XML parser and document generator. See *NanoXML*. (page 576)

- ❏ **Palm OS Emulator (POSE)** – software that emulates the hardware of different Palm devices (Palm III, Vx, VII, etc.). This will be our unit testing platform. See *Palm OS Emulator* (page 618).

The application allows data entry of contact information into a **custom** Palm database we'll call the contact book. The term *database* in Palm OS lingo is rather deceiving as there is no way to create and drop tables on the database. It's better to think of a Palm OS database as permanent data residing in a section of non-volatile memory. The section is comprised of variable-length records. Each record is a variable-length array of bytes. There aren't tables, columns, or rows in a Palm OS database at all. Nevertheless, *database* is standard terminology.

> **A Palm OS "database" is not a database in the traditional sense. Rather, it is a persistent store comprised of any number of variable-length records. Each record is a variable-length array of bytes up to 64KB.**

Our application will beam contact information from a custom Palm database (called the "contact book") to the same database on another Palm OS device. Data will be packaged as an XML document on the sender's side, and received and parsed on the receiver's side. The user will then be prompted to accept the data into his contact book or not. If accepted, XML will be stored natively as a new record in the contact book database. The application also provides a mechanism to enter, search, view, and edit contact entries in the contact book database.

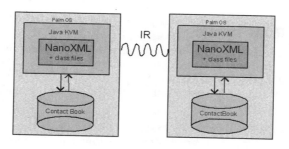

Setting Up the Environment

In this section, we'll walk through the setup and installation of the Java KVM and POSE.

CLDC and Java KVM

First, download the J2ME CLDC v1.0.2 (see *CLDC*, page 570) and the **kjava overlay** from:

http://www.sun.com/software/communitysource/j2me/cldc/download.html

Unzip `j2me_cldc-1_0_2-fcs-winunix.zip` first. Then unzip `j2me_cldc-1_0_2-fcs-kjava_overlay.zip` using the same directory base in which you unzipped the first file. Overwrite any existing files.

The first archive contains the CLDC reference implementation for Win32, Solaris, and Linux. It includes source code, runtimes, tools, and documentation for porting the CLDC to other platforms. This archive is designed to be used with a profile (see *Profiles*, page 570).

Since there is no PDA Profile implementation yet (see *PDA Profile*, page 570), we'll use the CLDC-compatible port for the Palm contained in the overlay archive. This is the second archive you downloaded, the kjava overlay. The overlay installs Palm-specific tools, samples, the all-important package `com.sun.kjava` (see *Package com.sun.kjava,* page 571), and `KVM.prc` – the Java KVM packaged as a Palm application.

> **The overlay is not intended to be used alone; it *must* be installed after and on top of the first archive, overwriting any existing files.**

Palm OS Emulator (POSE)

We'll use the POSE as our testing platform as we write our code. The POSE runs on Win32, Solaris, or Linux (although you could compile it for another platform as the source code is available). Remember our application will beam addresses from one Palm OS device to another. Obviously, the POSE doesn't have an infrared port since it's just software. So to test the application fully you must have two Palm OS devices (Handspring Visors, Sony Cliés, or IBM Workpads are fine).

Step 1 – Install the Emulator

First, download the emulator from http://www.palmos.com/dev/tech/tools/emulator/. It is available for Windows (as a ZIP file), Macintosh (as a SIT file), and for UNIX (source code in a TAR that you must compile). Extract the file.

Step 2 – Obtain a ROM Image

Before the emulator will operate, it needs a binary image of the environment to be emulated. The base installation doesn't come with any ROM images. If you own a Palm OS device, you can download an image of that device's ROM using the emulator. Simply run `emulator.exe`, which was installed in Step 1, and select "Download a ROM image from a Palm OS device." Detailed instructions are then given; it's really quite a simple process.

If you don't own a Palm OS device, you can download a ROM image from the Palm web site (http://www.palmos.com/dev/tech/tools/emulator/#roms). You'll need to join the Palm Alliance Program, which simply requires you to fill out an online form.

Step 3 – Run the Emulator for the First Time

Now you should run `emulator.exe`, which was installed in Step 1. Click the new button, Start a new emulator session. Under ROM file, select Other and navigate to the `.ROM` file you obtained in Step 2. The device field should automatically populate, but if it doesn't, select the correct Palm device type. Leave skin as generic. Finally, select the RAM size that corresponds to the actual RAM of the device you are emulating (for example, if emulating a Palm Vx, you should set this value to 8192KB, click OK. The emulator will then start.

Step 4 – Install the Java KVM On the Emulator

Now we must load the virtual machine onto the emulator. Right-click anywhere on the emulator. From the pop-up menu, select Install Application/Database and Other. Navigate to `j2me_cldc/bin/kjava/palm` and select `KVM.prc`. The virtual machine will be installed. Now do the same for `j2me_cldc/bin/kjava/palm/KVMutil.prc`. KVMutil is a debugging utility that allows you to set the maximum heap size and screen output (`System.out`) options.

Contact Classes

The contact beamer application is really four applications in one. We have a "sender" application which is invoked to list and beam contact book entries. We also have a "receiver" application, which is invoked to listen for documents sent by the sender. A search tool allows the user to view and edit entries. Finally, a contact adder allows the user to insert new contact entries into the contact book. The deletion of individual contact entries in the database is left as an exercise to the reader! However, the entire contact book database can be deleted using the standard means to delete a `.PDB`/`.PRC` from the unit.

The application is comprised of five major classes:

- ❑   Class **ContactBook**
  - ❑   The "main menu" of the application, this class simply displays four buttons to the user: add contacts, beam contacts, receive contacts, and quit.
  - ❑   One of the next three classes are instantiated when a button is selected

- ❑   Class **AddContact**
  - ❑   Displays a form into which the user enters information for a single contact: first name, last name, address, city, state/province, zip/postal code, country, phone number.
  - ❑   Allows the user to save the information as a new entry (or *record*) in the contact book database.

- ❑   The ability to quickly enter multiple records is provided by Class **BeamContact**
  - ❑   Displays contact book entries (or *records*) to the user
  - ❑   Prompts the user to select an entry to beam
  - ❑   Builds a `Contact` XML document instance from the selected entry using NanoXML
  - ❑   Beams the document to another device

- ❏ Class **ReceiveContact**
  - ❏ Displays a Waiting for beamed data message to the user
  - ❏ Blocks until a contact XML document is received
  - ❏ Prompts the user to import the contact entry into the local contact book database
  - ❏ Creates a new record in the contact book database if user chooses to keep the information

- ❏ Class **SearchContact**
  - ❏ Displays a text field, asking for the user to display the search criteria
  - ❏ Searches all eight fields of each record in the database for the specified criteria
  - ❏ Displays matching records as buttons whose text is the first and last name of each matching contact
  - ❏ Waits for the user to press one of the buttons, then displays that contact entry and allows the user to modify it in the database

Other classes are used by these five classes, but those classes are from the NanoXML library discussed in a previous section of this chapter. We'll discuss the first four classes in the chapter; for brevity's sake we'll leave examination of class SearchContact to the reader. So now let's take a look at the only class with a main() method, ContactBook.

ContactBook

```
public class ContactBook
        extends com.sun.kjava.Spotlet
```

ContactBook is the "main menu" of the application. It must extend com.sun.kjava.Spotlet to fit into the package com.sun.kjava application paradigm.

Spotlet is conceptually similar to java.applet.Applet in that it is a class for handling event callbacks. Overriding one of the event handlers, such as penMove(), keyDown(), or keyUp(), will enable the extended class (BeamAddress, in this case) to receive notification of these events.

ContactBook is quite simple. It displays five buttons to the user, then waits for user input. When one of the buttons is pressed, the flow of execution is handed off to class AddContact, class BeamContact, class ReceiveContact, class SearchContact, or it is terminated (if quit is selected). Here is a screenshot so you get a feel for how it looks:

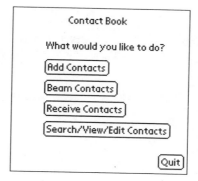

We'll examine three parts of class `ContactBook`:

❑   The constructor

❑   Painting the screen

❑   Handling `penDown()` events

Constructor

The constructor allocates objects for the `com.sun.kjava.Button` variables declared with private class scope:

```
public class ContactBook extends Spotlet {

  private Button exitBtn, addBtn, beamBtn, receiveBtn;

  public ContactBook() {
    exitBtn = new Button("Quit", 135, 140);
    addBtn = new Button("Add Contacts", 30, 50);
    beamBtn = new Button("Beam Contacts", 30, 70);
    receiveBtn = new Button("Receive Contacts", 30, 90);
    searchBtn = new Button("Search/View/Edit Contacts", 30,
        90);
    paint(); //paint the screen
  }
```

The `Button` constructor's three arguments are the button's text, and x and y screen coordinates in pixels. Most Palm OS devices have screens with 160x160 pixels, although Sony's new PEG-N710C doubles this to 320x320. We are assuming a 160x160 screen.

The last instruction in the constructor calls the `paint()` method, which brings us to our next topic.

Painting the Screen

Let's take a look at the `paint()` method, which is called to clear and paint the screen:

```
protected void paint()  {
  Graphics g = Graphics.getGraphics();
  g.clearScreen(); //clear the screen
```

Unlike other GUI environments you might be used to, which may have multiple graphics objects and device contexts, there is only one and it's `com.sun.kjava.Graphics` object available to all `Spotlets`. It is a static singleton object in `class Graphics`. with this object that all screen painting is done. The above code cleared the screen; now let's draw a title and buttons:

```
    //draw the title
    g.drawString("What would you like to do?", 30, 10);
    //draw the buttons
    exitBtn.paint();
    addBtn.paint();
    beamBtn.paint();
    receiveBtn.paint();
    searchBtn.paint();
}
```

`Graphics.drawString()` is pretty self-explanatory. The first argument is the string to paint, while the next arguments are the x and y screen coordinates, respectively, in pixels. The `Button.paint()` method simply paints the button on the screen with its defined button text and screen coordinates.

Handling penDown() Events

By extending `com.sun.kjava.Spotlet`, `ContactBook` is able to receive a variety of user interface events by overriding `Spotlet` event handlers. In this case, we are only interested in knowing when the user has clicked one of our buttons. We'll override `Spotlet.penDown()` to determine this.

```
public void penDown(int x, int y) {
  //exit btn pressed?
  if (exitBtn.pressed(x,y))
    System.exit(1);
  //add btn pressed?
  else if (addBtn.pressed(x,y)) {
    AddContact ac = new AddContact(this);
  }
  //beam btn pressed?
  else if (beamBtn.pressed(x,y)) {
    BeamContact ba = new BeamContact(this);
  }
  //receive btn pressed?
  else if (receiveBtn.pressed(x,y)) {
    ReceiveContact ra = new ReceiveContact(this);
  }
  //search btn pressed?
  else if (searchBtn.pressed(x,y)) {
    SearchContact sc = new SearchContact(this);
  }
}
```

`Spotlet.penDown()` receives the x and y screen coordinates, in pixels, where the stylus was pressed. The rest of the code calls `com.sun.kjava.Button.pressed()`, which returns Boolean `true` if (x,y) are within the `Button` boundaries, to determine if a `Button` was pressed. If a `Button` was pressed, one of the other user interface classes is called. We will discuss each of these in detail. The only exception is the quit `Button`, which terminates the program.

Let's take a look at the class, `AddContact`, that gets instantiated if the top-most `Button` is pressed.

AddContact

```
public class AddContact

    extends com.sun.kjava.Spotlet
```

AddContact is the class that enables the user to add contact entries into the custom Palm database, JavaXMLProgRef. A custom Palm database, also called a user-defined database, is a database that is not one of the system-defined databases: the address, date book, memo pad, and to do list databases. We have chosen not to use the address database because it defines its own record format for contacts; we would not be able to natively store XML if we used it. Creating our own user-defined database allows us to store bytes in any format we choose, and we choose XML, of course!

AddContact displays a data entry form to the user for the following fields:

- ❑ First name
- ❑ Last name
- ❑ Address
- ❑ City
- ❑ State/province
- ❑ Zip/postal code
- ❑ Country
- ❑ Phone number

Three buttons are also displayed:

- ❑ **quit** – return control to class ContactBook without saving the data entered (if any) in the form
- ❑ **save & quit** – creates a new record in the JavaXMLProgRef database using current form values, then returns control to ContactBook and its screen
- ❑ **save & continue** – creates a new record in the JavaXMLProgRef database using current form values, then erases all form field values so another contact can be entered.

Let's look at a screenshot:

We'll examine three parts of class AddContact:

❏ The constructor

❏ Saving the generated XML as a new record in the JavaXMLProgRef database

❏ Generating XML from the form's eight com.sun.kjava.TextField objects

Constructor

The constructor allocates objects for the com.sun.kjava.Button and com.sun.kjava.TextField variables declared with private class scope. It also registers as a listener for user interface events via the com.sun.kjava.Spotlet event handlers.

```
public class AddContact        extends Spotlet {

    private Button quitBtn, saveQuitBtn, saveAddMoreBtn;
    private ContactBookSpotlet _owner;
    private TextField fname, lname, address, city, state, zip,
        country, phone;

    public AddContact(ContactBookSpotlet owner) {
        //register for events
        register(NO_EVENT_OPTIONS);
        _owner = owner;
        quitBtn = new Button("Quit", 1, 140);
        saveQuitBtn = new Button("Save&Quit", 33, 140);
        saveAddMoreBtn = new Button("Save&Continue", 92, 140);
        fname = new TextField("First Name", 5, 10, 150, 10);
        lname = new TextField("Last Name", 5, 25, 150, 10);
        address = new TextField("Address", 5, 40, 150, 10);
        city = new TextField("City", 5, 55, 150, 10);
        state = new TextField("State", 5, 70, 150, 10);
        zip = new TextField("Zip", 5, 85, 150, 10);
        country = new TextField("Country", 5, 100, 150, 10);
        phone = new TextField("Phone", 5, 115, 150, 10);
        paint();  //paint the screen
    }
```

The TextField constructor's five arguments are similar. The first is the text or title that gets put in front of the text field (a colon is automatically appended to the supplied java.lang.String by the TextField class). The next four elements are measured in screen pixels and are, respectively, the upper (x,y) coordinates of the TextField, and the width (length) and height of the TextField. It's interesting to note that this simple UI element does not scroll if characters are entered after the full width of the element is occupied. Therefore, the maximum number of characters held by a TextField is determined by its width. Another oddity is that the Palm OS's use of a non-fixed-width font makes this maximum character length vary based upon the width of the characters entered (for example, less m's can be entered than l's)!

The last instruction in the constructor calls the paint() method, which we will skip since it is very similar to ContactBook.paint() (see *Painting the Screen*, page 621).

Saving the Form as XML

If **Save & Quit** or **Save & Continue** are clicked, the penDown() event handler (see *Handling penDown() Events*, page 622) routes processing to the save() method. This method has the responsibility for:

- ❑ Opening the `JavaXMLProgRef` database
- ❑ Creating the `JavaXMLProgRef` database if it doesn't already exist
- ❑ Writing a new record at the end of the `JavaXMLProgRef` database
- ❑ Closing the `JavaXMLProgRef` database

The name "database" is really a misnomer, as the Palm OS provides no way to create and drop tables on a "database." It's better to think of a Palm OS database as a section of permanent data resident in non-volatile memory. The section is comprised of variable-length records. Each record is a variable-length array of bytes. Since we're using a user-defined database, not a system-defined database like the address book, that means the possibility exists that `JavaXMLProgRef` doesn't exist on the system yet. In that case, we'll create a new, empty database. If it does exist, we'll open the existing one. Then we'll write a record at the end of the database and close it. Let's look at the code.

```
private void save() {
   Database db = new Database(ContactBook.creatorId,
      ContactBook.type, Database.WRITEONLY);
   if (!db.isOpen()) {
      //the database doesn't exist yet. create it.
      Database.create(0, ContactBook.dbName,
         ContactBook.creatorId, ContactBook.type, false);
      db = new Database(ContactBook.creatorId,
         ContactBook.type, Database.WRITEONLY);
   }
   if (db.isOpen())
      db.addRecord(getContactAsXML().getBytes());
      db.close();
   }
}
```

`ContactBook.creatorId` is an `int` (actually, the JNI call to the Palm OS requires the C/C++ `unsigned long` datatype, but that's handled for you). It identifies the application, company, or individual who created this database. When the user deletes an application in his Palm, all Palm databases (PDBs) with the same `creatorId` as the application get deleted also. To register your own `creatorId`, go to http://www.palmos.com/dev/tech/palmos/creatorid/. I've registered 0x4455434B for this application, so we'll use that throughout.

`ContactBook.creatorType` is also an `int` (actually, the JNI call to the Palm OS requires the C/C++ `unsigned long` datatype, but that's handled for you). It is used to distinguish between multiple databases with different types of information in them. I've chosen to use 0x32132132.

`ContactBook.dbName` is a `java.lang.String` that names our database. It must be unique for all database names on the device. In this case, we have named it `JavaXMLProgRef`. To truly ensure uniqueness, though, Palm Developer Support recommends using a name, followed by a hyphen, followed by your unique `creatorId`.

`com.sun.kjava.Database.addRecord()` creates a new record at the end of the database. Its content is set to the XML document, as bytes. All records must be passed as bytes to `com.sun.kjava.Database.addRecord()`.

Part of adding a record in the database is a call to `AddContact.getContactAsXML()`. Let's look at that method now.

Generating XML from the Form

Since we store XML natively in our `JavaXMLProgRef` database, we need to generate an XML document from the form fields as filled out by the user. The method which does this is `AddContact.getContactAsXML()`. Let's take a look at it:

```
private String getContactAsXML() {
    //construct an XML document from the form fields.
    //return it as a string
    kXMLElement root = new kXMLElement();
    root.setTagName("contact");
    root.addProperty("fname", fname.getText());
    root.addProperty("lname", lname.getText());
    root.addProperty("address", address.getText());
    root.addProperty("city", city.getText());
    root.addProperty("state", state.getText());
    root.addProperty("zip", zip.getText());
    root.addProperty("country", country.getText());
    root.addProperty("phone", phone.getText());
    return root.toString();
}
```

Here we use `class nanoxml.kXMLElement` from the NanoXML CLDC/KVM port to build a document. `kXMLElement` has the same methods as `nanoxml.XMLElement`. This method builds a simple XML document instance using `com.sun.kjava.TextField.getText().getText()` returns the text the user entered into a `TextField` object. Finally, `getContactAsXML()` returns the built document as a string. Here is a document instance:

```
<contact   fname="Frantic" lname="Neumann"
           address="123 Fake Street" city="Denver"
           state="Colorado" zip="80202" country="USA"
             phone="303-303-3000"/>
```

BeamContact

```
public class BeamContact
        extends com.sun.kjava.Spotlet
        implements com.sun.kjava.DialogOwner
```

`BeamContact` is the core class for sending a contact to the `ReceiveContact` class. It must extend `com.sun.kjava.Spotlet` to fit into the package `com.sun.kjava` application paradigm.

`Spotlet` is conceptually similar to `java.applet.Applet` in that it is a class for handling event callbacks. Overriding one of the event handlers, such as `penMove()`, `keyDown()`, or `keyUp()`, will enable the extended class (`BeamContact`, in this case) to receive notification of these events.

`BeamContact` behaves similarly to a web search engine result page. When you search for "apples" in a search engine, the result set matching "apples" is typically much larger than what you want displayed in your browser. So search engines usually include **Next** and **Previous** hyperlinks, allowing you to scroll through the result set corresponding to a search for "apples." Similarly, `BeamContact` displays six contact book records per page, with means to scroll through the result set.

`BeamContact` displays a preset number of buttons on a "page." Each button has text corresponding to the first and last name of a record. Clicking one of these buttons begins the document building and beaming process. Note that in this simple application; only one contact can be beamed at a time.

Here's a screenshot of the application so you get a feel for how it works:

We'll examine three parts of class `BeamContact`:

- ❏ Painting the screen
- ❏ Reading from the contact book database, `JavaXMLProgRef`
- ❏ Beaming the document

Painting the Screen and Reading the Contact Book

Let's take a look at the `paint()` method, which is called to clear and paint the screen:

```
private void paint() {
   Graphics g = Graphics.getGraphics();
```

Unlike other GUI environments you might be used to, which may have multiple graphics objects and device contexts, there is one and only `com.sun.kjava.Graphics` object available to all `Spotlets`. It's with this object that all screen painting is done.

```
g.clearScreen(); //clear the screen
//draw exit button and title
exitBtn.paint();
g.drawString("Select Contact to Beam", 35, 0);
```

Now we open the contact book database:

```
int numRecords = 0;
try     {
  Database db = new Database(0x44415441, 0x61646472,
    com.sun.kjava.Database.READONLY);
  if (db == null)
    System.out.println("Error opening contact book");
```

With the database open for read access, we're ready to read contact book records and display a page of buttons.

The first step is to determine, based on the current record being viewed, how many buttons we'll need for this page. When the user is viewing the 10th-15th records with 17 records in the database, and the user selects the Next button, we only need two buttons for the new page. We'll save this value in numEntryBtns, defined with class scope:

```
private int numEntryBtns = 0;
```

We need this value to have class scope so that when a penDown() event is handled, we know how buttons are being displayed on the current page.

To calculate numEntryBtns, we also need to store the number of records in the database. We'll call this numRecords. We also use this value to determine whether a Next button should be drawn at the bottom of a page. numRecords only needs method scope:

```
int numRecords = 0;
```

ENTRIES_PER_PAGE is the constant that determines how many records are displayed per page. It is also defined with class scope. You can change this value to easily vary how many buttons (contact entries) are displayed per page:

```
private final static int ENTRIES_PER_PAGE = 6;
```

We chose six because six fit nicely on a 160x160 pixel screen without looking cramped. If you have a 320x320 pixel Palm OS device, such as the Sony PEG-N710C, you should be able to double this value.

Each record's first and last name are displayed in a button. These buttons are defined with class scope so they are accessible in both penDown() and paint(). In penDown(), we ask each button individually if it was pressed() (see *Handling penDown() Events*, page 622). The buttons are stored in entryBtns

```
private Button[] entryBtns;
```

Here's the code to allocate the number of buttons we'll need for this page:

```
    //get at most ENTRIES_PER_PAGE records, but less if
      there aren't that many records left
    numRecords = db.getNumberOfRecords();
    numEntryBtns = Math.min(ENTRIES_PER_PAGE, numRecords -
      currentRecord);
    entryBtns = new Button[numEntryBtns+1];
```

Now we can read first and last names in each record, and display the allocated buttons with those names. First, let's look at the currentRecord variable, defined with class scope:

```
private int currentRecord = 0;
```

This integer represents which record in the database is currently being displayed at the top of the page. It's used in the penDown() method to determine which, if any, of the contact buttons were pressed. In our paint() method, however, we use currentRecord to draw the next or previous page of buttons:

```
for (int j=currentRecord; j<currentRecord + numEntryBtns;
  j++) {
  byte[] buf = db.getRecord(j);
  kXMLElement elem = new kXMLElement();
  elem.parseString(new String(buf));
  String lname = elem.getProperty("lname"), //last name
  fname = elem.getProperty("fname"); //first name

  entryBtns[j-currentRecord] = new Button(fname+" " +lname,
    5, (j-currentRecord)*20+15);
  entryBtns[j-currentRecord].paint();}
```

Here we make use of NanoXML to parse the first and last name in the record. The first and last name become the button text. `nanoxml.kXMLElement` is the CLDC/KVM port of `nanoxml.XMLElement` and has the same public methods. Records are written by `class AddRecord` (see *Generating XML from the Form*, page 626). A typical document instance might look like this:

```
<contact fname="Frantic" lname="Neumann"
         address="123 Fake Street" city="Denver"
         state="Colorado" zip="80202" country="USA"
         phone="303-303-3000"/>
```

Since we're through with the database, we can close it. The only thing that's left is to draw Next and Prev buttons.

```
db.close(); //close the database
```

We don't want to draw the Next button if there aren't any more records to be displayed, so this logic accounts for that:

```
//draw the "Next " button, if appropriate
if (currentRecord + numEntryBtns + 1 <= numRecords){
  nextBtn = new Button("Next", 100, 140);
  nextBtn.paint();
}
else
  nextBtn = null;
```

Likewise, we don't want to draw the Prev button if we're displaying the first page of records.

```
//draw the "Previous" button, if appropriate
if (currentRecord >= ENTRIES_PER_PAGE)       {
  prevBtn = new Button("Prev", 65, 140);
  prevBtn.paint();
}
else
  prevBtn = null;
```

Beaming the XML Document

When the user clicks one of the `entryBtns`, `BeamContact` receives a `penDown()` event. It's in this event handler that we determine which, if any, of the `entryBtns` were pressed. If one was pressed, `BeamContact.beamRecord()` is called with the record number to beam.

Infrared beaming itself is quite simple. The XML document must be beamed as a byte array, since `com.sun.kjava.Spotlet` requires all beamed content to be an array of bytes. `com.sun.kjava.Spotlet` provides a method called `beamSend()` that we will use for the physical data transfer:

```
public static boolean beamSend(byte[] data)
```

So let's look at our last method for this class, `beamRecord()`. It is called by `penDown()` when a button other than Quit, Next, or Prev is clicked. `recordNum` is the record in the contact book that the user wants to beam.

```
private void beamRecord(int recordNum) {
   Database db = new Database(ContactBook.dbType,
     ContactBook.creatorId, Database.READONLY);
   if (db == null)
     System.err.println("Error opening contact book");
   else {
     //read and beam it!
     if (beamSend(db.getRecord(recordNum)))
       new Dialog(this, "Success", "Beamed contact!",
         "Ok").showDialog();
   else
       new Dialog(this, "Failure", "Could not beam contact!",
         "Ok").showDialog();
   }
```

`com.sun.kjava.Database.getRecord()` makes a native Palm OS call and returns a byte array with the raw content of the desired record:

```
public native byte[] getRecord(int recordNumber);
```

ReceiveContact

```
public class ReceiveContact

       extends com.sun.kjava.Spotlet
```

`ReceiveContact` is the core class for receiving a contact from the `BeamContact` application. It must extend `com.sun.kjava.Spotlet` to fit into the package `com.sun.kjava` application paradigm.

`Spotlet` is conceptually similar to `java.applet.Applet` in that it is a class for handling event callbacks. Overriding one of the event handlers, such as `penMove()`, `keyDown()`, or `keyUp()`, will enable the extended class (`ReceiveContact`, in this case) to receive notification of these events.

Upon running `ReceiveContact`, the application blocks until it receives beamed data. Although this is hardly adequate for a commercial environment, the application nevertheless demonstrates the technologies in this chapter quite well.

> **ReceiveContact** blocks until it receives beamed data. If the data received is an XML document of the document class we've defined implicitly, the user is prompted to import the data into the contact book. If answered affirmatively, a new record is created in the database with that data. If the received data isn't XML or is not of the expected document class, it is ignored and **ReceiveContact** continues to block.

Here's a screenshot of the application before it receives a contact so you get a feel for how it works. There is only one other screen besides this one – the screen that prompts the user to import the contact.

We'll examine two parts of `class ReceiveContact`:

❏ Receiving beamed data and parsing it with NanoXML

❏ Writing the beamed data to the database

Receiving the XML Document

The process to receive beamed infrared data is quite simple. `com.sun.kjava.Spotlet` provides an event handler called `beamReceive()` that we override:

```
public static void beamReceive(byte[] data)
```

So let's look at our `ReceiveContact.beamReceive()`. It is called when the class `Spotlet` dispatches infrared data to our handler.

```
public void beamReceive(byte[] buf) {
  //parse the received xml using NanoXML
  contact = new String(buf);
  kXMLElement elem = new kXMLElement();
  try     {
    elem.parseString(contact);
  }
  catch (XMLParseException e)     {
    //can't parse received data--the sender probably
    //wasn't BeamContact!! ignore it and return.
    paint();
    return;
  }
```

All we're doing here is converting the byte array to a `java.lang.String` and passing it to NanoXML to parse. `nanoxml.kXMLElement` is the CLDC/KVM port of `nanoxml.XMLElement` and has the same public methods. See *NanoXML* (page 576) for more information. A typical document instance, after converted from a byte array to a `String`, might look like this:

```
<contact fname="Frantic" lname="Neumann"
         address="123 Fake Street" city="Denver"
         state="Colorado" zip="80202" country="USA"
         phone="303-303-3000"/>
```

The most common cause of an exception being thrown here is receiving data that isn't XML. The Palm OS routes received infrared data to the same application on the receiving unit that sent the data from the sending unit. This sandbox restriction pretty much guarantees that Palm's Memo Pad won't beam the contact book data, but it is restrictive; in our case, the sending and receiving applications, from the Palm OS's perspective, in the KVM. However, the Palm OS has no idea what application is running inside the KVM. It is therefore possible that another Java application running inside the KVM could beam data to `ReceiveContact`. If this occurs, `beamReceive()` calls `paint()`, which clears the screen and redraws the message, "Waiting for contact information…", and then returns.

Here's the rest of the `beamReceive()`:

```
String fname = elem.getProperty("fname"), lname =
    elem.getProperty("lname");
if (fname != null && lname != null) {
    g.clearScreen();
    g.drawString("Contact info was received for:", 0, 20);
    g.drawString(fname + " " + lname, 0, 40);
    g.drawString("Import into contact book?", 0, 60);
    yesBtn = new Button("Yes", 40, 80);
    noBtn = new Button("No", 60, 80);
    yesBtn.paint();
    noBtn.paint();
}
else paint();
}
```

`kXMLElement.getProperty()` returns `null` if a property doesn't exist in the element in which we are manipulating (in this case, the root element). If either the `fname` or `lname` properties don't exist, we ignore the received data, `paint()` the screen with the message "Waiting for contact information…" and then return. We could do further document checking by ensuring that the root element is named `contact`.

Writing the XML Document

The final step is to ask handle the **yes/no** button click. If **yes** is pressed, we must open the database and write the contact (received XML) as a new record. If **no** is pressed, we repaint the screen with the "Waiting for contact information…" message. As we've already seen, button clicks are handled by overriding the `com.sun.kjava.Spotlet.penDown()` event handler. If the **exit** button has been pressed, we register our "owner" – the `ContactBook` object – as the current `Spotlet` event listener (remember, there is only one `Spotlet` listening for events at a time), and tell `ContactBook` to paint itself. This effectively hands control back to the main menu. The owner is set in the `ReceiveContact` constructor:

```
import com.sun.kjava.*;
import nanoxml.kXMLElement;
import nanoxml.XMLParseException;

public class ReceiveContact extends Spotlet {

  private Button exitBtn = new Button("Quit", 135, 140),
    yesBtn, noBtn;
  private Graphics g = Graphics.getGraphics();
  private ContactBook owner;
  private String contact;

  public ReceiveContact(ContactBook owner) {
    register(NO_EVENT_OPTIONS);
    this.owner = owner;
    paint(); //paint the "Waiting for..." message
}

  public void penDown(int x, int y) {
    //did the user press the exit btn?
    if (exitBtn.pressed(x,y)) {
      owner.register(NO_EVENT_OPTIONS);
      owner.paint();
    }
    //did the user press the yes btn, telling us to
    //write the received contact into the database?
    else if (yesBtn.pressed(x,y))      {
      Database db = new Database(ContactBook.dbType,
        ContactBook.creatorId, Database.WRITEONLY);
      if (!db.isOpen()){
        //the database doesn't exist yet. create it.
        Database.create(0, ContactBook.dbName,
          ContactBook.creatorId, ContactBook.dbType, false);
        db = new Database(ContactBook.dbType,
          ContactBook.creatorId, Database.WRITEONLY);
      }
      db.addRecord(contact.getBytes());
      db.close();
      paint(); //repaint the "Waiting for..." message
    }
    else if (noBtn.pressed(x,y))
      paint();
  }

  public void beamReceive(byte[] buf) {
    //parse the received xml using NanoXML

    contact = new String(buf);
    kXMLElement elem = new kXMLElement();
    try      {
      elem.parseString(contact);
    }
    catch (XMLParseException e)      {
      //can't parse received data--the sender probably
      //wasn't BeamContact!! ignore it and return.
      paint();
```

```
      return;
   }
   String fname = elem.getProperty("fname"),
      lname = elem.getProperty("lname");
   if (fname != null && lname != null)      {
      g.clearScreen();
      g.drawString("Contact info was received for:", 0, 20);
      g.drawString(fname + " " + lname, 0, 40);
      g.drawString("Import into contact book?", 0, 60);
      yesBtn = new Button("Yes", 40, 80);
      noBtn = new Button("No", 60, 80);
      yesBtn.paint();
      noBtn.paint();
   }
   else
      paint();
}
```

```
public void paint() {
   g.clearScreen();
   yesBtn = noBtn = null;
   exitBtn.paint();
   g.drawString("Waiting for contact information...", 10,
      70);
   }
}
```

Summary

In this chapter, we examined Java and XML on lightweight clients, also known as information appliances. We talked about where XML on lightweight clients stands today, and why we need XML on lightweights.

Then we discussed the architecture of Java 2 Micro Edition: the application layer, the device profile layer, the configuration layer, and finally the operating system layer. Focusing more on the Connected Limited Device Configuration, as it is more "lightweight" than the Connected Device Configuration, we discussed the Java Kilobyte Virtual Machine, kjava, and kAWT.

Next we reviewed parsers for lightweights. Pull parsers such as kXML and XPP hold a lot of potential for information appliances, but since there is no industry-accepted standard interface, we focused on DOM-style and SAX parsers. We covered two very different versions of NanoXML in-depth, as well as NanoXML's SAX interface. We also discussed MinML with its SAX interface.

XSLT Compiler, by Sun Microsystems, was covered in detail. We wrote an XSL stylesheet, compiled a translet, and executed a small TroubleTicket application that used the translet with an input XML document. XSLTC's speedy execution and small size make it ideal for performing XSL transformations on information appliances.

SOAP on information appliances is very appealing, but library support is limited currently. It might be best to write your own library if you can't wait until kSOAP or another small library matures.

Finally, we built a peer-to-peer contact book application for the Palm OS using NanoXML, Java KVM, the Palm OS Emulator, and some GUI classes made available by Sun. This infrared beaming application prompted the user with a list of contact book entries to beam, while a receiving application waited for an XML document to insert into its contact book database.

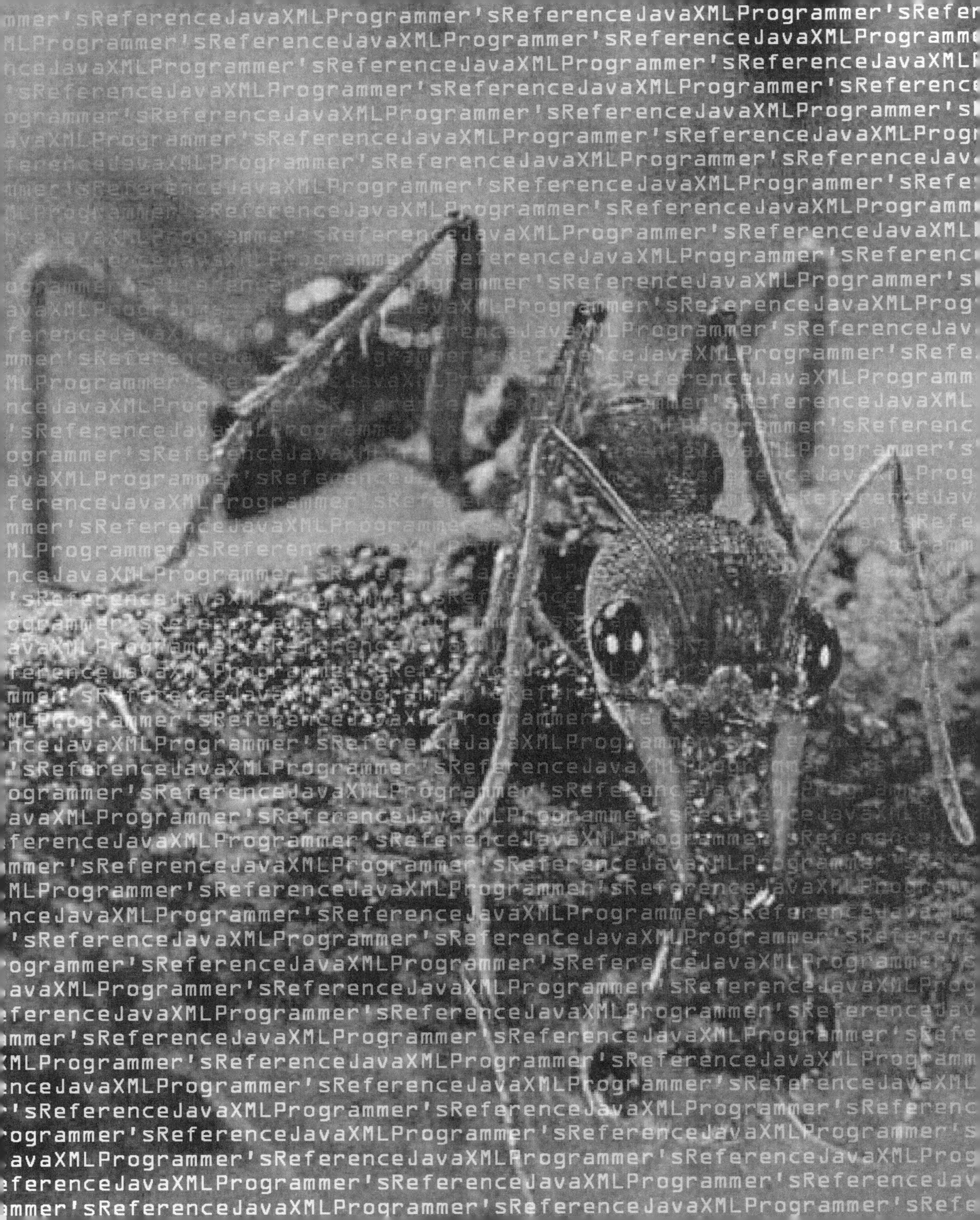

JavaXMLProgrammer'sReference

Configuring with XML

In the next five chapters we will develop an XML based business application. The aim of the case study is to highlight Java XML tools and APIs that work in various ways. In certain areas, we use object-oriented techniques to develop a hierarchy of implementations of the same functionality, with each solution using an alternate XML approach or tool. As such, the application is not a streamlined, finished product, but it makes up for that by packing in a lot of Java XML.

Overview

We'll develop an Auction and Appraisal Management System (AAMS). In addition to accepting bids for items registered in its database, the AAMS provides a professional appraisal (valuation) service for auction items to guide customers wishing to place a bid on them.

The company wishes to expose its item database and bid acceptance mechanism as web services. As well as providing these as general services, the plan includes the implementation of a client-side API to encapsulate remote access to the AAMS. This is because the AAMS has made deals with various portal sites who wish to incorporate the AAMS product into their own services. To do that, the client portals need a simple interface to the system that hides the web service layer, so that they can easily code the AAMS into JSP pages. We'll develop a presentation tier based on this scenario.

In summary, the complete system involves four distributed components:

o   An XML repository for storing system XML, schemas, and DTDs. The documents are available at fixed URLs.

o   The AAMS Server system. The main server receives SOAP requests over HTTP and dispatches the embedded XML requests to internal services, which in turn interact with the system's database. The server is deployed as a self-contained Web Application Archive (WAR) file. Responses are returned in XML.

o   Enterprise JavaBean components exposing third party services for internal AAMS use.

o   A sample AAMS Client system. The client system includes the client-side AAMS interface application, and an output and rendering system for delivering HTML and PDF documents based upon the service responses from the AAMS system. The client is deployed as a self-contained WAR file.

The diagram below shows the modular structure of the AAMS system:

How the Case Study is Organized

The following table provides a guide to where the components are discussed:

Project	Chapter	Target
Configuring with XML	12	Create a system configuration file, DTD, and schema, and a Java package to deliver the data to applications. Explore parsing and validation techniques.
Querying XML	13	Build on the previous project, using XPath alternatives to basic traversal techniques. Use several different XPath implementations, and other querying options.
Storing and Retrieving XML	14	Develop XML document types for representing the business requests, and design execution paths for turning XML business requests into XML responses populated with data. Explore several basic XML/Data toolkits approaches.
Transmitting XML	15	Build a client API for interacting remotely with the system using SOAP over HTTP. Develop both the server and client, and explore possibilities for XML transmission using the SOAP protocol. Integrate a third party web service exposed as an EJB.
Transforming XML	16	Build the client portal site, using various transformation techniques to deliver the content of the system's response tickets as HTML and PDF.

We've decided to use two presentation devices to make the case study as accessible as possible. Each chapter has a "project deployment sheet" which clearly states the requirements of the chapter, describes the flow of information in the project using a detailed diagram, and lists all files required (which are provided with the download bundle for this book). The second approach is that we use Jakarta Ant as the build tool for the project. Appendix A explains how to configure your system to use Ant with the case study.

In each deployment sheet, we indicate which Ant "targets" can be invoked to build and deploy the relevant parts of the project. Ant takes care of ensuring that all dependent components are constructed first.

Once you have configured your system, it is possible to undeploy and rebuild all four components automatically in less than a minute. This gives you the ability to try out your own approaches and improvements to the system – without spending too much time on repeated manual tasks.

Configuration

A global XML configuration file is used to define how the services provided by the Auction and Appraisal Management System (AAMS) should be initialized.

In this project we will do the following:

- o   Define the configuration data through use of a DTD or schema

- o   Design a Java component to read in the data from a remote XML repository and make the information available to the local system

We'll cover various approaches to this, showing how to populate the configuration object using DOM, SAX, JAXP, and JDOM, using parsing and traversal techniques.

Project Deployment Sheet

The objective is to create a configuration package `serviceconfig.jar` that will provide a Java interface to an XML file that configures the AAMS system. The package is designed to be a dropin package for the main AAMS server application, but could also be used by remote portal sites using client components of the AAMS system.

Information Flow

The `ServiceConfiguration` object is used throughout the application to define the runtime characteristics of the application. The contents are read in from a URL and should be validated against a DTD or schema.

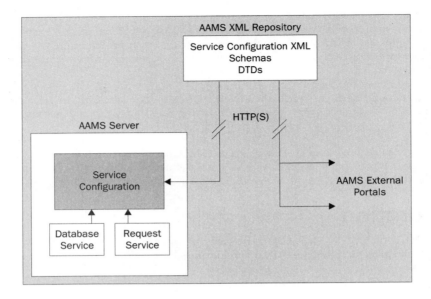

Requirements

The required tools for this chapter are:

o   Xerces-J

o   JDOM

o   JAXP 1.1 (Note that Xerces currently provides an implementation of the
     `javax.xml.parsers` component).

Details for obtaining these packages and configuring your system to use the Ant build tool with this part of the AAMS project are given in Appendix A.

The Files

The source files required for this chapter are listed below:

Example XML Files

These are located in the `src/storingxml/xmlrepository` directory:

```
serviceconfiguration.dtd
serviceconfiguration.xml
serviceconfiguration.xsd
```

Java

Package `configuringxml` is stored in `src/configuringxml`:

```
ServiceConfiguration.java
ServiceConfigurationContentHandler.java
ServiceConfigurationDOM.java
ServiceConfigurationDOMJAXP.java
ServiceConfigurationErrorHandler.java
ServiceConfigurationJDOM.java
ServiceConfigurationSAX.java
ServiceConfigurationSAXJAXP.java
```

The Java Code

We take the approach of implementing several subclasses of the abstract `ServiceConfiguration` class that will take the XML file defined by our DTD or schema and use it to populate the object with configuration information. These implementation classes will demonstrate parsing techniques using SAX, DOM, JAXP, and JDOM to perform essentially the same tasks.

Ant Targets

The Ant targets for this project are given in full in Appendix A:

```
techniques.configuringxml.classpath
```

Call this target and then run the **setcp** script to set the classpath for command-line testing for this project.

```
techniques.configuringxml.compile
```

Compiles the code and creates the `serviceconfig.jar` archive in the `apps` directory. This will later be deployed as a unit within the AAMS server.

```
techniques.configuringxml.deploy
```

Creates the XML repository as a WAR file and deploys it to the web server application root `webapps`. This repository also contains other XML resources such as DTDs for the various business process tickets. These will be covered in following chapters.

The Result

We create the Service Configuration package `serviceconfig.jar` to provide dynamic configuration information to the AAMS. This information can be edited within an XML file and placed on a web server. It is then retrieved over the net and validated by configuration objects servicing various distributed components of the system

The configuration framework provides an outline implementation that can be extended to more sophisticated configuration requirements without impacting other components.

Service Configuration

Although the configuration file would eventually contain information regarding many aspects of the system, for simplicity we will limit our discussion to those components associated with the database service. The database service is responsible for maintaining connections to the database and satisfying queries submitted by the business process service.

We need the following types of information for database access configuration:

Info	Meaning
Database	Database type – the type of database that is being accessed. This can be any database that has a JDBC driver available for it. However, for the sake of simplicity, we will look at PostgreSQL and Oracle.
ConnectionURL	JDBC ConnectionString – this is a URL string that is used to establish a connection to the database, such as jdbc:oracle:thin: @localhost:1521:test for Oracles.
Driver	JDBC Driver class – this is the Java class that will be loaded as the JDBC driver (for instance, org.postgresql.Driver or oracle.jdbc.driver.OracleDriver).
ResultSetType	The result set format that the XML will be generated in. The possible choices include Oracle's XSU, JDOM's ResultSetBuilder, Sun's WebRowSet and custom JDBC.
User	User ID – the identifier to use when making the connection to the database.
Password	Password – for making the connection to the database

Document Type Definition

In order to ensure that the configuration file is maintained in the correct format, we construct a **Document Type Definition (DTD)**. First we must consider how the services will be run. It is safe to assume that the services will require various settings based on whether they are in production, test, or other mode. It thus makes sense to have separate configuration sections based on the run mode we are using. Therefore, the service configuration consists of a <RunMode> element, followed by one or more <Configuration> elements:

```
<!ELEMENT ServiceConfiguration (RunMode, Configuration+)>
<!ELEMENT RunMode (#PCDATA)>
```

In order to ensure that each set of database parameters is enclosed in its own <Configuration> element, the following line is added to our DTD:

```
<!ELEMENT Configuration (Database)>
```

Note that a configuration would have more than just a database subcomponent in a full implementation, for example:

```
<!ELEMENT Configuration (Database,Logging,ErrorHandling,...)>
```

The `<RunMode>` element is used to configure the actual configuration parameter set within the document to be used. For instance, by just changing the run mode from `test` to `prod`, we can switch between different configurations for all the services.

> *These configuration document elements use the default namespace URI*
> `http://www.wrox.com/javaxmlref`. *DTDs have no support at all for namespaces.*
> *When covering the XML Schema approach later, we'll see that namespaces can be accommodated.*

Next, we will use an attribute for each `<Configuration>` element to define what run mode it relates to. Additionally, we want to make sure that only valid run modes are selected. Inserting the following line will add an attribute list to our DTD to enforce this:

```
<!ATTLIST Configuration runmode NMTOKEN #REQUIRED>
```

This will make sure that every configuration entry contains a `runmode` attribute. The global run mode of the system indicates which particular set of configuration data to choose (for example, test or production).

Specifying the Database Configuration

Next we will add a connection-specific element to each database section. This will store the parameters needed to connect to the specified database.

```
<!ELEMENT Database (Connection)+>
<!ATTLIST Database type CDATA #IMPLIED>
```

The lines above will make sure that at least one connection element is included in the database element. Additionally, the database type is defined as an attribute. Currently, we only support Oracle and PostgreSQL. Like the `runmode`, we will enforce the supported databases by including an attribute list for the `<Database>` element.

Finally, we will add the definitions for each of the connection-specific parameters.

```
<!ELEMENT Connection(Driver,ConnectionURL,User,Password,ResultSetType)>
<!ELEMENT ConnectionURL (#PCDATA)>
<!ELEMENT Driver (#PCDATA)>
<!ELEMENT Password (#PCDATA)>
<!ELEMENT ResultSetType (#PCDATA)>
<!ELEMENT User (#PCDATA)>
```

The Service Configuration DTD

After adding an element to describe the current run mode, and grouping all of the configuration information under the `<ServiceConfiguration>` element, we have the `serviceconfiguration.dtd` file overleaf:

```
<!ELEMENT ServiceConfiguration (RunMode, Configuration+)>
<!ELEMENT RunMode (#PCDATA)>
<!ELEMENT Configuration (Database)>
<!ATTLIST Configuration runmode NMTOKEN #REQUIRED>
<!ELEMENT Database (Connection)+>
<!ATTLIST Database type CDATA #IMPLIED>
<!ELEMENT Connection(Driver, ConnectionURL, User, Password, ResultSetType)>
<!ELEMENT ConnectionURL (#PCDATA)>
<!ELEMENT Driver (#PCDATA)>
<!ELEMENT Password (#PCDATA)>
<!ELEMENT ResultSetType (#PCDATA)>
<!ELEMENT User (#PCDATA)>
```

Sample Service Configuration

The following sample service configuration file is valid with respect to the above DTD. By adding the DOCTYPE declaration to the document, we can ensure that modifications to the file will be validated against the DTD located on our web server alongside the configuration file.

```xml
<?xml version="1.0" encoding="UTF-8"?>
<!DOCTYPE ServiceConfiguration SYSTEM "serviceconfiguration.dtd">
<ServiceConfiguration xmlns="http://www.wrox.com/javaxmlref">
  <RunMode>prod</RunMode>
  <Configuration runmode="test">
    <Database type="PostgreSQL">
      <Connection>
        <Driver>org.postgresql.Driver</Driver>
        <ConnectionURL>
          jdbc:postgresql://192.168.1.51:5432/test
        </ConnectionURL>
        <User>test</User>
        <Password>test</Password>
        <ResultSetType>4</ResultSetType>
      </Connection>
    </Database>
  </Configuration>
  <Configuration runmode="prod">
    <Database type="Oracle">
      <Connection>
        <Driver>oracle.jdbc.driver.OracleDriver</Driver>
        <ConnectionURL>
          jdbc:oracle:thin:@dbserver:1521:database
        </ConnectionURL>
        <User>test</User>
        <Password>wrox</Password>
        <ResultSetType>3</ResultSetType>
      </Connection>
    </Database>
  </Configuration>
</ServiceConfiguration>
```

The Abstract ServiceConfiguration Class

Now that we have a well-formed and valid configuration file, we need to get it into a format that is accessible to our Java application. In order to makes the configuration information easy for developers to use, we will define a common interface to accessing the configuration properties. The configuration class reads in the XML data, and stores it using an internal `java.util.Properties` object. `Properties` extends `java.util.Hashtable` and allows for fast random access of data via property keys. Speed of access is one factor to consider when thinking of the alternative of storing XML data as a DOM tree.

In this project, we'll look at various ways of reading in the data. We'll do this by extending the abstract `ServiceConfiguration` class as shown in the diagram below:

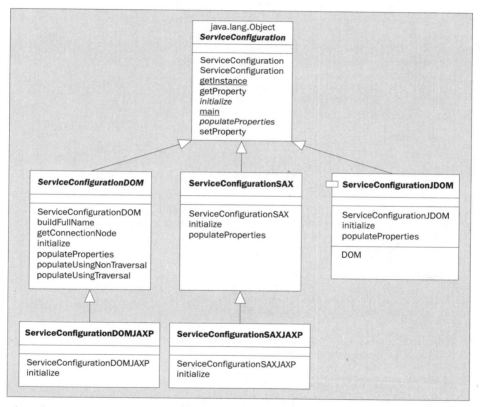

As the class diagram illustrates, there is a common `ServiceConfiguration` class that implements the tasks of getting and setting the properties. The details of that class are below.

```
package configuringxml;
import java.util.Properties;

public abstract class ServiceConfiguration {

  private Properties properties;
  private static ServiceConfiguration instance;
```

```
public static final int RB_RESULT_TYPE = 1;
public static final int STRING_RESULT_TYPE = 2;
public static final int XSU_RESULT_TYPE = 3;
public static final int WRS_RESULT_TYPE = 4;
public static final StringNAMESPACE = "http://www.wrox.com/javaxmlref";

protected ServiceConfiguration(String configFile) {
  properties = new Properties();
  initialize(configFile);
  populateProperties();
}
```

The following methods are needed to enforce the Singleton pattern and to force the use of the
getInstance() method:

```
private ServiceConfiguration() {}

public static ServiceConfiguration getInstance() {
  if (instance == null) {
    System.out.println("Getting config file");
    instance = new ServiceConfigurationJDOM(
      "http://localhost:5202/xml/serviceconfiguration.xml");
  }
  return instance;
}

public String getProperty(String property) {
  return properties.getProperty(property);
}

protected void setProperty(String name, String value) {
  if (value != null && value.length() > 0) {
    properties.put(name, value);
  }
}

public abstract void initialize(String configFile);
public abstract void populateProperties();
```

A small test method harness is added. Note that you should have deployed the XML repository
xml.war and have the webserver running for this to work:

```
public static void main(String args[]) {
  ServiceConfiguration sc = ServiceConfiguration.getInstance();
  System.out.println("Class: " + sc.getClass().getName());
  System.out.println("Server: " +
    sc.getProperty("ConnectionURL"));
  }
}
```

If you have installed the system according to Appendix A, then you should be able to test the setup
using:

```
> ant techniques.configuringxml.classpath
> setcp
CLASSPATH set to: .\build;.\lib\jdom.jar;.\lib\xerces.jar
> ant techniques.configuringxml.deploy
> java configuringxml.ServiceConfiguration
Getting config file
Class: configuringxml.ServiceConfigurationJDOM
Server: jdbc:oracle:thin:@dbserver:1521:database
```

The ServiceConfiguration class is an abstract class that wraps the functionality of the Properties object. It implements the Singleton design pattern and will create a new instance of the class using the configuration file located on the web server. Since the ServiceConfiguration class is abstract, it is up to the concrete implementation classes to provide the details of accessing the properties stored inside the XML configuration file. Each concrete class must implement two methods that actually perform the work. We will now take a closer look at those methods.

First, each implementation must include an initialize(String configFile) method. This method is responsible for setting up any variables that the class will need to populate the Properties object. As you will see later, this method will set up the needed DOM and SAX environments that will be used to read the configuration file. Next, the populateProperties() method must be implemented. This method is responsible for taking the information from the XML document and populating the local Properties object.

ServiceConfiguration with SAX

Now that we have an understanding of the interface that will be provided to the users of the application, let's look at an example implementation using the Simple API for XML (SAX). For this example we will use Xerces, although we could use any SAX-compliant parser. In creating the ServiceConfigurationSAX class we will focus only on the two methods we need to implement to extend the ServiceConfiguration class.

Initialization

First, we need to implement the initialize(String configFile) method, which is responsible for setting up the environment for the class. In our SAX example, this is where we will instantiate the parser, set any features, set the appropriate handlers, and finally parse the configuration file passed in.

```
public void initialize(String configFile) {
  try {
    XMLReader xr =
      XMLReaderFactory
        .createXMLReader("org.apache.xerces.parsers.SAXParser");
    xr.setFeature("http://xml.org/sax/features/validation", true);
    xr.setFeature("http://xml.org/sax/features/namespaces", true);
    requestHandler = new ServiceConfigurationContentHandler();
    xr.setContentHandler(requestHandler);
    xr.setErrorHandler(new ServiceConfigurationErrorHandler());
    System.out.println("Parsing: " + configFile);
    xr.parse(configFile);
```

```
    } catch (Exception ex) {
      System.out.println("Exception parsing file: " + ex);
    }
  }
```

The first thing that the `initialize()` method does is create the parser. The `XMLReaderFactory` class, which is part of the SAX package, is used to do this. It takes in the name of the specific parser to instantiate as a parameter and returns an object that implements the `XMLReader` interface. Once the XML reader is instantiated, the validation and namespace features can be enabled.

SAX is an event-driven API, which relies on the definition of handlers that process event callbacks. In order to process the content callbacks for the service configuration file, we have created and set the `ServiceConfigurationContentHandler` class as the document content handler. The code for this handler is listed below:

```
package configuringxml;

import org.xml.sax.*;
import org.xml.sax.helpers.*;
import java.io.*;
import java.util.*;

public class ServiceConfigurationContentHandler extends DefaultHandler {
```

A buffer for collecting data from the "characters" SAX event:

```
  private CharArrayWriter contents = new CharArrayWriter();
  private String runMode;
  private boolean configNode = false;
  private Hashtable properties = new Hashtable();

  public void startElement(String namespaceURI,
  String localName, String qName,
    Attributes attr) throws SAXException {
    contents.reset();
    if (localName.equals("Configuration")) {
      System.out.println(
        "\tAttribute: " +
        attr.getLocalName(0) +
        "=" +
        attr.getValue(0));
      if (attr.getValue(0).equals(runMode)) {
        configNode = true;
      }
    }
  }

  public void endElement(String namespaceURI,
      String localName, String qName) throws SAXException {
    if (localName.equals("RunMode")) {
      runMode = contents.toString().trim();
```

Since we are validating the document using namespace awareness, we can assume that the `<Configuration>` element belongs to the correct namespace. Therefore, we can extract the value without checking the namespace:

```
    } else if (localName.equals("Configuration")) {
      configNode = false;
    } else if (configNode) {
      properties.put(localName, contents.toString().trim());
      System.out.println(
        localName + ":" +
        contents.toString().trim());
    }
    contents.reset();
  }

  public void characters(char[] ch, int start,
      int length) throws SAXException {
    contents.write(ch, start, length);
  }

  public Hashtable getProperties() {
    return properties;
  }
}
```

The first thing to notice about the content handler is that it is derived from the `DefaultHandler` class. This class is a helper class that provides "do nothing" methods for all the methods needed to satisfy the SAX `ContentHandler` interface. By starting with this base class, we are able to override just the specific methods that we need to, consequently leaving our code fairly clean.

The first method we override is `characters()`: this method is responsible for collecting the contents of an element and storing it in a local variable. There is no requirement that all of the data for an element be returned in one call to the `characters()` method. To support this possibility, the contents of each call are appended to a local character array that will be used to populate a local variable.

The next method overridden is `startElement()`; if you recall from Chapter 2 this method is called every time a new element is encountered in the XML document. Since the name of the element and any of its attributes are passed into the method, we are able to determine if we have encountered the correct configuration element using the code below:

```
if (localName.equals("Configuration" )){
  if (attr.getValue(0).equals(runMode)){
    configNode = true;
  }
}
```

If we are at the correct `<Configuration>` element, then we will set a local variable that will be used to collect the element's configuration parameters.

The last method that is overridden is `endElement()`. This method is called when the end of an element is encountered. For our configuration example, we use this method to capture the desired run mode (for instance, `test` or `prod`) and store it in the local variable `runMode`. This variable was used in the `startElement()` method to check if we were processing the correct configuration element.

Finally, the following endElement() code segment uses the configNode attribute to determine if it should collect the parameter and store it in the local hashtable.

```
else if(configNode) {
  properties.put(localName, contents.toString().trim());
}
```

Error Handling

After the content handler for the SAX parser has been set up, an error handler must be assigned as well. As you might recall from Chapter 2, the error handler is responsible for processing any errors or warnings.

The ErrorHandler interface provides three methods to catch problems during processing:

o   error

o   fatalError

o   warning

Since failure to register an error handler will result in errors being ignored, the following handler code is included in our ServiceConfigurationErrorHandler example:

```
package configuringxml;

import org.xml.sax.ErrorHandler;
import org.xml.sax.SAXException;

public class ServiceConfigurationErrorHandler implements ErrorHandler {
   public void warning(org.xml.sax.SAXParseException exception)
       throws org.xml.sax.SAXException {
     System.out.println("SAX Warning " +
       exception.getMessage() +
       " in " +
        exception.getSystemId() +
       " at line " +
       exception.getLineNumber());
     throw new SAXException("SAX Warning");
   }

   public void error(org.xml.sax.SAXParseException exception)
       throws org.xml.sax.SAXException {
     System.out.println("SAX Error " +
       exception.getMessage() +
       " in " +
       exception.getSystemId() +
       " at line " +
        exception.getLineNumber());
     throw new SAXException("SAX Error");
   }

   public void fatalError(org.xml.sax.SAXParseException exception)
       throws org.xml.sax.SAXException {
     System.out.println("SAX Fatal Error " +
```

```
            exception.getMessage() +
            " in " +
            exception.getSystemId() +
            " at line " +
            exception.getLineNumber());
       throw new SAXException("SAX Fatal Error ");
    }
 }
```

As our parsing code relies on a well-formed and valid document, we want to stop processing in the event of any error or warning condition. This is accomplished by rethrowing the SAXException in each of the handler methods.

After the handlers are set up, the XML configuration file is parsed using the code:

```
    xr.parse(configFile);
```

Population

The next method that ServiceConfigurationSAX must implement is populateProperties(). This method is responsible for storing the actual property values in the Properties object.

Using the accessor method getProperties() on the ServiceConfigurationContentHandler, we are able to get access to the hashtable containing the property values that was created during the parse of the XML file. As the code below illustrates, it is now just a matter of looping through all the parameters and setting them into the Properties object:

```
    public void populateProperties() {
       Hashtable properties = requestHandler.getProperties();
       Enumeration keys = properties.keys();
       while (keys.hasMoreElements()) {
          String key = (String) keys.nextElement();
          setProperty(key, (String) properties.get(key));
       }
    }
```

We are now able to access any of the configuration properties by instantiating our ServiceConfigurationSAX class and calling the getProperty() method on it.

Altering the main() method and running the commands as shown on page 644 is all that is necessary to test the various ServiceConfiguration implementations in this chapter.

ServiceConfiguration with DOM

Although SAX is extremely fast for processing, it is often difficult for Java developers to work with because it uses an event-based paradigm, rather than an object-oriented one. For instance, it does not provide an easy way to traverse the XML document. To alleviate this, the Document Object Model (DOM) approach was created. We are now going to populate the ServiceConfiguration object using the DOM.

Let's focus on the two methods we need to implement to extend the `ServiceConfiguration` class. First we need to implement the `initialize(String configFile)` method. As you saw in the SAX example, this method is responsible for setting up the environment for the class.

Initialization for ServiceConfigurationDOM

For our DOM example, this is where we will instantiate the parser, set any features, and finally parse the configuration file passed in.

```
public void initialize(String configFile) {
    System.out.println("Getting " + configFile);

    DOMParser parser = new DOMParser();
    parser.setErrorHandler(new ServiceConfigurationErrorHandler());
    try {

        // Set the parser features and parse the config file
        parser.setFeature("http://xml.org/sax/features/validation", true);
        parser.setFeature("http://xml.org/sax/features/namespaces", true);
        parser.parse(configFile);
    } catch (SAXException se) {
        se.printStackTrace();
    } catch (IOException ioe) {
        ioe.printStackTrace();
    }
    document = parser.getDocument();
}
```

From the code above we can see the `initialize()` method creates the DOM parser first. After the parser is created, the error handler is set. Since DOM uses SAX to parse the input source, we can use the same error handler as we did in our SAX example. Next, the validation and namespace features are enabled. Finally, the document is parsed and stored in the `Document` local variable for use by the `populateProperties()` method.

Population

The `ServiceConfigurationDOM` class must also implement the `populateProperties()` method. Unlike SAX, the DOM allows you to go to a position within the document tree and traverse through it. DOM provides helper functions such as `getChildren()` and `getFirstChild()` to assist with this traversal. The DOM2 specification introduces a new Traversal and Range specification (http://www.w3.org/TR/DOM-Level-2-Traversal-Range/) which is discussed in more detail in Chapter 4. In our DOM example we will illustrate both of them. Also, the DOM3 requirements document (see http://www.w3.org/DOM/ for the latest version) includes support for XPath expressions, which will provide yet another method to navigate document trees.

As you can see below, our `populateProperties()` method checks to see if the parser being used supports the new Traversal specification. If it does, it will use traversal to populate the properties; otherwise, it will use the standard DOM method:

```
public void populateProperties() {

    // Use the DOM2 Traversal and Range if it is available.
    if (document.isSupported("Traversal", "2.0")) {
      populateUsingTraversal(getConnectionNode());
    } else {
      populateUsingNonTraversal(getConnectionNode());
    }
}
```

Regardless of whether the parser supports traversal, we must first find the connection element that corresponds to the requested run mode and then pass it into the corresponding population method. To facilitate this, a helper method called getConnectionNode() is added to our example. The code below illustrates how the correct starting node is found:

```
private Node getConnectionNode() {

    String runMode =
      document
        .getElementsByTagNameNS(NAMESPACE, "RunMode")
          .item(0)
            .getFirstChild()
              .getNodeValue().trim();
    Node connectionNode = null;
    if (runMode != null) {
```

Get the list of configuration settings:

```
    NodeList configurationList =
      document
        .getElementsByTagNameNS(NAMESPACE, "Configuration");
    for (int i = 0; i < configurationList.getLength(); i++) {
      Element currNode = (Element) configurationList.item(i);
```

The DTD requires that a run mode attribute be set for each <Configuration> element. We now need to find the matching configuration for the current run mode:

```
      if (currNode
        .getAttribute("runmode").trim()
          .equals(runMode)) {
        connectionNode =
          currNode
            .getElementsByTagNameNS(NAMESPACE, "Connection")
              .item(0);
      }
    }
  }
  return connectionNode;
}
```

In order to find the proper connection element, we must know the desired run mode. Since the document is valid, we know there is a single <RunMode> element, which contains the current <RunMode>. We can get the run mode element by calling the getElementsByTagNameNS() method on the document, that was parsed in the initialize() method.

```
String runMode = document.getElementsByTagNameNS(NAMESPACE,
"RunMode").item(0).getFirstChild().getNodeValue();
```

Since our DTD indicates that there must always be one <RunMode> element, we are able to get that element using the `item()` method. After that we get the value of the <RunMode> element using `getFirstChild().getNodeValue().trim()`;

Once the value of the desired <RunMode> is obtained, it can be used to find the <Configuration> element that contains the corresponding RunMode attribute. Like obtaining the <RunMode>, the `getElementsByNameNS()` method is called to return all of the <Configuration> elements. The code below illustrates how the resulting NodeList is searched for the first element that contains the requested runmode attribute.

```
for (int i=0; i < configurationList.getLength(); i ++){
  Element currNode = (Element) configurationList.item(i);

  if (currNode.getAttribute("runmode").trim().equals(runMode)) {
    connectionNode =
    currNode.getElementsByTagNameNS(NAMESPACE, "Connection").item(0);
  }
  break;
}
```

Populating Without Using Traversal

The first matching <Connection> element in the document is then returned and will be used as the starting point in populating the properties.

If you are using a parser that does not support Traversal (such as Crimson), once the proper <Connection> element is found the following code steps through it, populating the underlying Properties object:

```
private void populateUsingNonTraversal(Node node) {

  switch (node.getNodeType()) {

  case Node.ELEMENT_NODE:

    System.out.println("Element: " +
      " [" + name + "]." +
      node.getFirstChild().getNodeValue());
    String name = node.getLocalName();
    String value = node.getFirstChild().getNodeValue().trim();
    NodeList children = node.getChildNodes();
    if (children != null) {
      int len = children.getLength();
      for (int i = 0; i < len; i++) {
        populateUsingNonTraversal(children.item(i));
      }
    }
    setProperty(name, value);
    break;
  }
}
```

The first thing that needs to be done is to determine if the type of node being passed in is one that we are interested in. Since the DTD specifies all of the properties as elements, it is safe to assume that all we are interested in are elements. The code, however, has been written using a `switch()` statement – so if we are ever interested in any other node types they can easily be added. Assuming that the node is an element, the `populateUsingNonTraversal()` is called on all of the child nodes. This will get the value of the current property as well as any nested properties.

Populating Using Traversal

The traversal specification (Chapter 4) introduces the use of three new constructs:

Interface	Description
`NodeIterator`	Steps through a set of nodes defined by a `NodeList`
`NodeFilter`	Filters out nodes while navigating a document tree using `NodeList` or `TreeWalker`
`TreeWalker`	Used to navigate a document tree

Using the `<Connection>` element as its starting point, a `TreeWalker` that will only process elements is created. The individual properties are added by iterating through the elements.

```
private void populateUsingTraversal(Node startNode) {

  TreeWalker walker =
    ((DocumentTraversal) document)
      .createTreeWalker(startNode,
        NodeFilter.SHOW_ELEMENT, null, false);

  Node currentNode = walker.nextNode();
  while (currentNode != null) {
    String name = currentNode.getLocalName();
    String value = currentNode.getFirstChild().getNodeValue().trim();
    setProperty(name, value);
    currentNode = walker.nextNode();
  }
}
```

Adding JAXP Support

The way an XML parser object is obtained and the methods called for parsing the document, has been inconsistent among the different parser implementations. In order to avoid having to recode parts of the application when deciding to use a different product, project teams should create wrapper classes for individual parsers to provide a consistent interface to the rest of the application. Through the JSR process, Sun is attempting to standardize this through the Java API for XML Processing (JAXP).

As discussed in Chapter 5 there are three pluggable areas supported in JAXP 1.1; SAX, DOM and XSLT. In order to change the parser or processor that you are using without recompiling your application code, you can use the Services API or change the property specified in the `jaxp.properties` file.

Below is an example of a `jaxp.properties` file.

```
javax.xml.parsers.SAXParserFactory =
  org.apache.xerces.jaxp.SAXParserFactoryImpl

javax.xml.parsers.DocumentBuilderFactory =
  org.apache.crimson.jaxp.DocumentBuilderFactoryImpl

javax.xml.transform.TransformerFactory =
  com.icl.saxon.TransformerFactoryImpl
```

As you can see, any applications using the above `jaxp.properties` file will use Xerces for SAX parsing, Crimson for DOM parsing, and Saxon for XSL transformation. To switch any of these components is simple; just modify the `jaxp.properties` file and ensure that the new classes are accessible at run time.

> While it is technically possible to intermingle vendor offerings as we have done above, this will increase the complexity of the interdependencies between the versions of products, so should be done with caution.

JAXP with SAX

Now let's see what we would have to do to our earlier SAX example in order to have it take advantage of JAXP.

We have already separated our population logic from the parser initialization in our abstract `ServiceConfiguration` class. Therefore we can create a new class that extends the `ServiceConfigurationSAX` class, all we need do to provide JAXP support is to override the `initialize()` method.

```
public void initialize(String configFile) {

    SAXParserFactory spf = SAXParserFactory.newInstance();
    spf.setValidating(true);
    spf.setNamespaceAware(true);

    XMLReader xmlReader = null;
    try {
      SAXParser saxParser = spf.newSAXParser();
      xmlReader = saxParser.getXMLReader();
    } catch (Exception ex) {
      System.err.println(ex);
      System.exit(1);
    }
    requestHandler = new ServiceConfigurationContentHandler();
    xmlReader.setContentHandler(requestHandler);

    xmlReader.setErrorHandler(new ServiceConfigurationErrorHandler());

    try {
      xmlReader.parse(configFile);
```

```
    } catch (SAXException se) {
      System.err.println(se.getMessage());
      System.exit(1);
    } catch (IOException ioe) {
      System.err.println(ioe);
      System.exit(1);
    }
  }
```

This method gets a SAX parser from the factory class then a new instance can be created. Once the parser is created an XMLReader is obtained from it, the content and error handlers are then set, and the document is parsed.

JAXP with DOM

We can add JAXP support to the DOM example in the same way that we did for SAX by simply extending the ServiceConfigurationDOM class, and overriding the initialize() method. The code for the new initialize() method is shown below:

```
public void initialize(String configFile) {DocumentBuilderFactory dbf =
    DocumentBuilderFactory.newInstance();
  dbf.setValidating(true);
  dbf.setNamespaceAware(true);
  DocumentBuilder db = null;
  try {
    db = dbf.newDocumentBuilder();
  } catch (ParserConfigurationException pce) {
    System.err.println(pce);
    System.exit(1);
  }

  db.setErrorHandler(new ServiceConfigurationErrorHandler());

  try {
    document = db.parse(configFile);
  } catch (SAXException se) {
    System.err.println(se.getMessage());
    System.exit(1);
  } catch (IOException ioe) {
    System.err.println(ioe);
    System.exit(1);
  }
}
```

ServiceConfiguration with JDOM

JDOM was introduced to simplify the usage of XML in Java programs. By utilizing SAX and internal Java structures, it is intended to be faster and less memory-intensive than the DOM. At the time of this writing JDOM is currently at Beta 6, and consequently many of the memory and performance tuning issues remain to be completed. However, we can be optimistic that this will be done, and that JDOM will continue to be accepted in the JSR process.

Initialization

We are now going to take our `ServiceConfiguration` class and create a JDOM implementation. Again, we are able to inherit from the `ServiceConfiguration` abstract class and simply implement the `initialize()` and `populateParameters()` methods:

```
public void initialize(String configFile) {
  try {
    SAXBuilder builder = new SAXBuilder();
    document = builder.build(configFile);
  } catch (JDOMException je) {
    System.out.println("JDOMException creating documnent:" + je);
  }
}
```

The initialization of a JDOM object is quite straightforward. Like the earlier DOM example, a builder is needed to create the document. JDOM provides an input package that currently includes two builders, `DOMBuilder` and `SAXBuilder`. However, JDOM.org are working on additional builders – including one that will construct a document from a JDBC result set.

Using SAXBuilder

In general, the `SAXBuilder` is used to create new documents. In fact, at the time of this writing, the `DOMBuilder` delegated its build process to the `SAXBuilder` by calling it to perform the parsing. The `SAXBuilder` takes the name of the SAX parser to use as a parameter to the constructor. If no parameter is supplied, SAXBuilder will attempt to first locate a parser via JAXP, then will try to utilize a set of default SAX drivers. Like JAXP, JDOM provides parser -independence by wrapping parser-specific implementation details into a series of adaptors in the `org.jdom.adapters` package. As we discussed earlier, if support for your favorite parser is not included, you can create your own adaptor by simply extending the `AbstractDOMAdapter` class, implementing a few methods and making sure the classes are available at run time.

Once the builder is instantiated, calling the `build()` method easily creates the JDOM document. It is important to realize that at this point the document object contains an `org.jdom.Document` object, *not* an `org.w3c.dom.Document` object. If you need a pure DOM object this can be obtained by using the `DOMOutputter` class included in the handy `org.jdom.output` package.

Population

Once the `initialize()` method has been executed, the constructor will call the `populateProperties()` method. As the code below illustrates, accessing the JDOM object is as straightforward as accessing any Java object:

```
public void populateProperties() {

  // Get the Connection Node
  Element root = document.getRootElement();
  String runMode = root
    .getChildTextTrim("RunMode",
      Namespace.getNamespace(NAMESPACE));
  List propertyList = new ArrayList(0);

  // Get the connection Element
```

```
    List configList = root
      .getChildren("Configuration",
        Namespace.getNamespace(NAMESPACE));
    for (int configCount = 0;
      configCount < configList.size();
        configCount++) {
      Element currentConfig =
        (Element) configList.get(configCount);
      String configRunMode =
        currentConfig.getAttributeValue("runmode").trim();
      if (configRunMode != null && configRunMode.equals(runMode)) {

        // This is safe because the document is validated
        propertyList =
          currentConfig
            .getChild("Database",
              Namespace.getNamespace(NAMESPACE))
            .getChild("Connection",
                Namespace.getNamespace(NAMESPACE))
              .getChildren();
      break;
    }
  }
```

The JDOM code is similar to the DOM example in structure. First, we must get the value of the current run mode using the `getChildTextTrim()` method. This will return the trimmed text value of the element <RunMode> that was requested. The code below shows how all of the configuration elements are returned, and how they are searched to find the first element with the `runmode` attribute equal to that of the current <RunMode> element.

It is important to notice that the list returned from the `getChildren()` method is an actual Java `List` object, *not* a `NodeList` like that returned in the DOM example. This allows the full use of the List API, and the inclusion of the resulting list in other APIs that provide integration with the Java Collection API.

Converting JDOM Output

Once the JDOM document is created, it is possible to use the classes provided in the output package to convert the document type. Currently, there is support for outputting the document as a series of SAX events, a DOM `Document`, or a `String` object. The code below will convert our JDOM object into a DOM object that can be used interchangeably with other DOM-based systems:

```
public org.w3c.dom.Document getDOM() {
  DOMOutputter domOutputter = new DOMOutputter();
  org.w3c.dom.Document domDocument = null;
  try {
    domDocument = domOutputter.output(document);
  } catch (JDOMException je) {
    System.out.println("JDOMException in getDOM() " + je);
  }
  return domDocument;
}
}
```

Adding Schema Support

A new term called **schema valid** is applied to those documents that satisfy an XML schema. Since the specification is still in the early stages of adoption, there is only limited support among parser vendors – Oracle XML Parser v2 and Apache Xerces are two parsers that do provide support for schemas. However, the ebXML project (http://www.ebxml.org/) has integrated SOAP into its messaging layer. As SOAP is entirely schema based this could lead to a rapid expansion in schema support if ebXML takes off.

Let's take a look at how we can visualize the `ServiceConfiguration` document type:

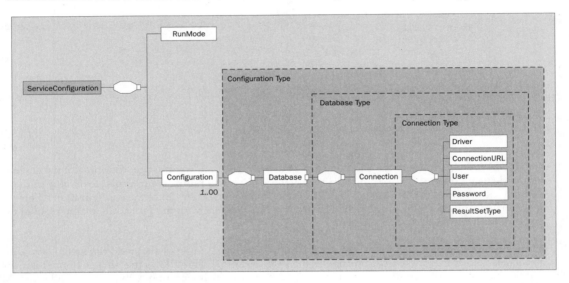

We define **types** to represent internal structures within the document. This powerful feature of schemas enables us to reuse the same type definitions elsewhere in the document by simply referring to their name, rather than having to paste in a cloned set of DTD declarations (for example we might want to use the same connection type for a different resource such as an `<LDAPConnection>`). The diagram shows the nested `ConfigurationType`, `DatabaseType`, and `ConnectionType` types.

Below is an XML schema representation of the `ServiceConfiguration` document type:

```
<?xml version="1.0" encoding="UTF-8"?>
<xsd:schema targetNamespace="http://www.wrox.com/javaxmlref"
    xmlns="http://www.wrox.com/javaxmlref"
    xmlns:xsd="http://www.w3.org/2000/10/XMLSchema"
    elementFormDefault="qualified">
```

Our top-level declaration defines the service configuration to consist of a `<RunMode>` element, and an unbounded sequence of `<Configuration>` elements, with a minimum of one. Note that when the number of occurrences is not specified in an element type definition, then the default specification is that exactly one element should occur. Similarly, when the `minOccurs` element is omitted, then at least one must occur:

```
<xsd:element name="ServiceConfiguration">
  <xsd:complexType>
    <xsd:sequence>
      <xsd:element name="RunMode" type="xsd:string"/>
      <xsd:element
        name="Configuration"
        type="ConfigurationType" maxOccurs="unbounded"
      />
    </xsd:sequence>
  </xsd:complexType>
</xsd:element>
```

Create the definition for `ConfigurationType` which includes making the `runmode` attribute compulsory:

```
<xsd:complexType name="ConfigurationType">
  <xsd:sequence>
    <xsd:element name="Database" type="DatabaseType"/>
  </xsd:sequence>
  <xsd:attribute name="runmode" type="xsd:NMTOKEN"
      use="required"/>
</xsd:complexType>
```

Define the `ConnectionType` type as a collection of required elements in the specified order, each occurring exactly once:

```
<xsd:complexType name="ConnectionType">
  <xsd:sequence>
    <xsd:element name="Driver" type="xsd:string"/>
    <xsd:element name="ConnectionURL" type="xsd:string"/>
    <xsd:element name="User" type="xsd:string"/>
    <xsd:element name="Password" type="xsd:string"/>
```

The nested simple type `ResultSetType` specifies a code number that will determine which tool will be used to generate XML data from the database in Chapter 14.

```
<xsd:element name="ResultSetType">
  <xsd:simpleType>
    <xsd:restriction base="xsd:byte">
      <xsd:minInclusive value="1"/>
      <xsd:maxInclusive value="4"/>
    </xsd:restriction>
  </xsd:simpleType>
</xsd:element>
</xsd:sequence>
</xsd:complexType>
```

The `DatabaseType` specifies a `<Connection>` element of type `ConnectionType` with a mandatory `type` attribute flagging the type of database connection specified:

```
<xsd:complexType name="DatabaseType">
  <xsd:sequence>
    <xsd:element name="Connection" type="ConnectionType"/>
  </xsd:sequence>
```

```
        <xsd:attribute name="type" use="required"/>
    </xsd:complexType>
</xsd:schema>
```

Unlike a DTD, a schema is an XML document itself that is constrained by a schema called `XMLSchema.xsd` (http://www.w3.org/2000/10/XMLSchema.xsd), which, to confuse matters, is itself constrained by an embedded XML 1.0 DTD. Because they are XML compliant, this allows schemas themselves to be processed using XML tools including XPath and XSL transformers.

Using schemas should future-proof our system, particularly in respect of the inadequacy of DTDs in handling namespaces. Namespaces play an important role in the ever-increasing complexity of XML data interchange.

In order to support the schema, we must modify the `serviceconfiguration.xml` to look for the schema file. We do this by removing the `DOCTYPE` and modifying the root element as follows to include a reference to the schema:

```
<ServiceConfiguration
  xmlns:xsi="http://www.w3.org/2000/10/XMLSchema-instance"
  xsi:schemaLocation="http://www.wrox.com/javaxmlref
    ServiceConfiguration.xsd"
  xmlns="http://www.wrox.com/javaxmlref"
 >
```

Note the whitespace between the default namespace declaration for the schema document and the schema URL itself.

Parsers will look for the schema file at the same document root at which the declaring XML file is located. We could specify a fully qualified URL if we wanted:

```
xsi:schemaLocation="http://www.wrox.com/javaxmlref
    http://localhost:5202/xml/ServiceConfiguration.xsd"
```

Using a parser that supports schemas, such as Apache Xerces-J, we can run any of our earlier examples unchanged (apart from modifying the reference to the schema in the sample configuration file).

If the XML `ResultSetType` parameter is changed in the XML file to 7, the error handler will be invoked by the schema verifier and a message similar to the one below is shown:

```
SAX Error Datatype error: In element 'ResultSetType' : 7 is out of bounds:[ 1 <= X
<= 4 ].
```

> It is important to note that the level of support and implementation for schemas varies significantly among vendors. Care should be taken when implementing them until the specification is widely accepted.

Summary

There are many ways to access XML data available to the Java programmer. The mature offerings, such as the DOM Java bindings and the SAX call-back mechanism, continue to evolve and provide new features. Meanwhile new players in the area such as JDOM add a competitive edge to encourage further enhancements of the API and tools. The Java standard JAXP, which is a new component of JDK 1.4, makes it possible to work with alternative parsers without reprogramming.

We continue to develop the AAMS project in the following chapters.

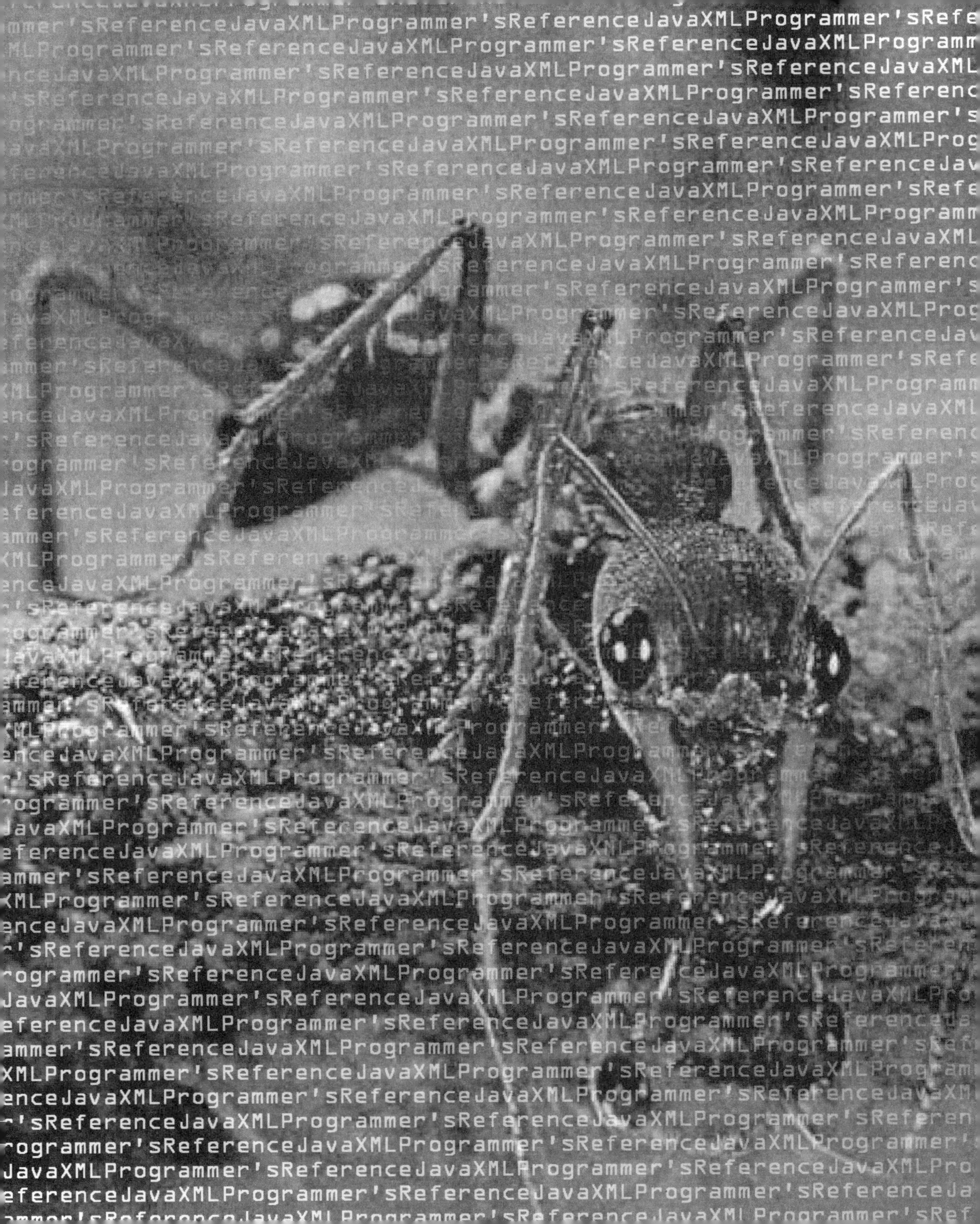
JavaXMLProgrammer'sReference

Querying XML

XPath is a language that describes a way to locate and process items in Extensible Markup Language (XML) documents by using an addressing syntax based on a path through the document's logical structure or hierarchy. This makes writing programming expressions easier than if each expression had to understand typical XML markup and its sequence in a document. XPath also allows the programmer to deal with the document at a higher level of abstraction. XPath is a language that is used by and specified as part of both the Extensible Stylesheet Language Transformations (XSLT) and by XPointer (SML Pointer Language). It uses the information abstraction defined in the XML Information Set (Infoset). Since XPath does not use XML syntax itself, it could be used in contexts other than those of XML.

XPath uses a syntax that is something like an informal set of directions for finding a particular geographic location. When telling someone how to find the Minneapolis campus of the University of Minnesota within the United States, for example, you might write:

```
US/MN/Mpls/SE/WashingtonAve/bridge
```

which would put the user in the middle of the campus.

The key difference between XPath and earlier languages (such as XPointer) is that XPath specifies a route, rather than pointing to a specific set or sequence of characters, words, or other elements.

XPath uses the concepts of:

❑ The context node (the point from which the path address begins)

❑ The logical tree that is inherent in any XML document

The logical relationships between nodes are defined in the XML Information Set; these include ancestor, attribute, child, parent, and self.

XPath also includes a small set of expressions for specifying mathematical functions and the ability to extend these with other functions.

The serviceconfiguration.xml File

In this chapter, the service configuration file from Chapter 12 will be used for all XPath examples:

```xml
<?xml version="1.0" encoding="UTF-8"?>
<!DOCTYPE ServiceConfiguration SYSTEM "serviceconfiguration.dtd">
<ServiceConfiguration xmlns="http://www.wrox.com/javaxmlref">
  <RunMode>prod</RunMode>
  <Configuration runmode="test">
    <Database type="PostgreSQL">
      <Connection>
        <Driver>org.postgresql.Driver</Driver>
        <ConnectionURL>
          jdbc:postgresql://192.168.1.51:5432/test
        </ConnectionURL>
        <User>test</User>
        <Password>test</Password>
        <ResultSetType>4</ResultSetType>
      </Connection>
    </Database>
  </Configuration>
  <Configuration runmode="prod">
    <Database type="Oracle">
      <Connection>
        <Driver>oracle.jdbc.driver.OracleDriver</Driver>
        <ConnectionURL>
          jdbc:oracle:thin:@dbserver:1521:database
        </ConnectionURL>
        <User>test</User>
        <Password>wrox</Password>
        <ResultSetType>3</ResultSetType>
      </Connection>
    </Database>
  </Configuration>
</ServiceConfiguration>
```

Two of the three XPath evaluators used in this chapter failed to correctly handle the original document's default namespace declaration:

```
xmlns="http://www.wrox.com/javaxmlref"
```

The presence of the default namespace declaration caused the XDK to return an empty node-set for all XPath expressions that were tested. The Werken XPath JDOM Extension library beta does not provide operational namespace support. Note:that future versions of these may not have these limitations. Therefore that declaration was dropped from this example.

Namespace support by existing XPath evaluators, across the board, has been erratic and inconsistent. Partly this is due to ambiguities in the original XPath specification. The specification says that the **expression context** is used to determine the in-scope namespaces, but it is not explained where that context comes from. In fact, both the Xalan and XDK API's ask you, the programmer, to supply the needed context. On top of that, how the expression context changes in conjunction with namespace scoping during evaluation of the XPath expression is not specified.

Building unit tests to verify program correctness is extremely important if XPath is used in conjunction with namespaces. The bulk of XPath evaluation examples in this chapter can effectively test the evaluator's conformance to the XPath standard.

Project Deployment Sheet

The objective is to explore alternatives to the standard methods used in Chapter 12 for extracting information from the service configuration file.

Requirements

The required resources for testing the code in this chapter are:

- ❑ JAXP 1.1
- ❑ JDOM
- ❑ Xerces-J
- ❑ Werken XPath JDOM Extension library (version 0.9.4)
- ❑ Oracle XML Parser version 2.1.0
- ❑ Xalan 2.1.0

Details for obtaining these packages and configuring your system to use the Ant build tool with this part of the book are given in Appendix A.

The Files

The source files required for this chapter (and provided with the code for this book) are listed below:

Example Files

The following XML file is from `src/queryingxml`:

```
serviceconfiguration.xml
```

Java

Java source is also stored in `src/queryingxml`:

```
DOMquery.java
JDOMXPath.java
NodePrinter.java
RelXPathListTester.java
```

```
SAXquery.java
URLutil.java
XPathListTester.java
XPathQuery.java
XPathTester.java
```

and in `src/queryingxml/creatingxml`:

```
ServiceConfigurationXPath.java
ServiceConfigurationXPathDOM.java
```

The Java Code

We illustrate different ways of querying XML through a variety of example programs.

Ant Targets

`techniques.queryingxml.compile`
Compiles all the code for the chapter to the `build` directory.

`techniques.queryingxml.test`
This target can be used to run a check through all the example programs.

Why Query XML?

XML documents contain structured information that is ordered in a hierarchical way. These documents can hold associated metadata, contained in a DTD or XSchema declaration. (Currently no API's exist that make queries about a document's DTD metadata. Since an XSchema is just another XML document, the techniques introduced in this chapter can all be used to explore a document's XSchema metadata.)

XML documents can have extremely complex schemas. For example, a typical B2B purchase order document contains everything needed to describe a purchase transaction. It has information on the customer and the vendor, on how they are paying (or billing) for the items, and what items (and quantities) are to be purchased. Hundreds of items can be purchased with a single purchase order document.

In an automated order fulfillment system, Java programs will be processing the incoming purchase order. Those programs will have to easily find each important piece of the document. A query facility makes it possible to target both individual fields as well as major document sections.

How To Query XML

Good object-oriented systems try and break the complexities of a big system into simpler logical sub-groups. A good design would separate the mechanics of querying an XML document from the application business rules implementation. Intermingling complicated query processing in with the rest of an application is a bad idea. (As an analogy, remember the Model View Controller programming paradigm – always divide and conquer.)

There are several different approaches that can be used for a Java program to perform complex document queries. SAX, DOM, and XPath are alternative frameworks to perform XML queries from inside Java programs. The examples later in this chapter will show the pros and cons of these various approaches to querying XML.

SAX

As we saw in Chapter 2, SAX event processing can be used to look for specific fields in an XML document. As Chapter 12 showed, the programmer must know in advance the document structure to some extent. They must maintain, in Java objects, a certain amount of document state information received from the actual events being fired. For instance, assume the document has a property named `cost`. Here is one example of how this information might be transmitted in an XML fragment:

```
<cost>5.00</cost>
```

With SAX three different event callbacks are fired for this XML fragment:

- ❏ `startElement()`
- ❏ `characters()`
- ❏ `endElement()`

The name of the property must be remembered by the event handler object so that it can match up the property value to the correct property during the later `characters()` callback. The `characters()` method does not provide any contextual information about how that text fragment relates to the rest of the document. At the very least, all of this error-prone manual programming is a bother.

Another disadvantage to this approach is that all information regarding the document's hierarchical structure is lost. It is possible to programmatically create a stack to hold the path from the root of the document to the last seen element, but for many applications this is insufficient. SAX gives a flat view of the document, and provides no explicit element hierarchy information.

One significant advantage that SAX provides over a parser such as DOM, for instance, is that huge XML documents do not have to be stored in memory. So, SAX can be safely used to parse monstrous XML documents. One example where these can be generated is from a database query, which might produce millions of output XML document fragments.

> DOM's overhead comes from the need to allocate memory for the entire document's contents, a node at a time. Garbage collection runtime overhead can be a problem when many documents have to be processed. (Which means that nodes are being frequently allocated and deallocated as each document, in turn, is processed.)
>
> Look closely at the EJB architecture, and you will see that it was optimized for the worst-case frequent memory allocation/deallocation scenario. Preallocation of bean pools and reusing bean instances is motivated strictly by performance gains. You can see this overhead just by comparing the time needed for a SAX parse versus a DOM creation parse on the same document!

Another example is the stream of XML data that a stock trade monitoring system could produce. There might literally be millions of trade occurrences in a single day. Only a SAX-style parser can handle that amount of data, or, alternatively, the trades could be transmitted as millions of small XML documents. The disadvantage here is that none of the query tools are capable of inter-document queries. They can only perform intra-document queries related to a single document.

669

Example: SAX Query Example

A simple example is in order. Let's query the <ConnectionURL> element from the *test* configuration (from `serviceconfiguration.xml`). The test <Configuration> element has a `runmode` attribute with a value of `"test"`.

The SAX event handler class has some tricky bookkeeping to do. First it has to remember when the *test* <Configuration> element is being processed (and ignore all of the other configurations). Otherwise the <ConnectionURL> property for *all* configurations will be reported. Second, it has to remember when a <ConnectionURL> element is being processed, so that the subsequent `characters()` event handler will report the event. (The `characters()` method provides no information about the text fragments location in the document.)

Here is the SAX event handler implementation for this example. The event handler is the point of Java customization with SAX. In this case, the custom SAX event handler class is called `EventHandler`. The XML parser is here invoked using JAXP.

Source SAXquery.java

```java
import java.io.IOException;
import org.xml.sax.*;
import javax.xml.parsers.*;
import org.xml.sax.helpers.DefaultHandler;

public class SAXquery {
  static public void main(String[] argv) {
    if (argv.length != 1) {
      System.err.println("Usage: SAXquery URL ");
      System.exit(1);
    }
    SAXParserFactory factory = SAXParserFactory.newInstance();
    factory.setNamespaceAware(true);

    try {
      SAXParser parser = factory.newSAXParser();
      parser.parse(argv[0], new EventHandler());

    } catch (Exception e) {
      System.out.println(e.getMessage());
    }
  }
}

class EventHandler extends DefaultHandler {

  private boolean inTestConfig = false;
  private boolean inConnectionURL = false;
```

```java
public void startElement(String namespaceURI,
  String localName, String qName, Attributes attrs)
  throws SAXException {

  // Remember that we are in 'test' configuration
  if (localName.equals("Configuration")
      && attrs.getValue("runmode").equals("test")) {
    inTestConfig = true;
  } else if (localName.equals("ConnectionURL") &&
    inTestConfig) {
    inConnectionURL = true;
  }
}

public void endElement(String namespaceURI,
  String localName, String qName)
  throws SAXException {
  if (localName.equals("Configuration") && inTestConfig) {
    inTestConfig = false;
  }
  if (localName.equals("ConnectionURL")) {
    inConnectionURL = false;
  }
}

public void characters(char[] ch, int start,
  int length) throws SAXException {
  if (inConnectionURL) {
    System.out
      .println("ConnectionURL property for test " +
        "configuration is: \"" +
          new String(ch, start, length) + "\"");
  }
}
}
}
```

Output

```
> java SAXquery serviceconfiguration.xml
ConnectionURL property for test configuration is:
"jdbc:postgresql://192.168.1.51:5432/test"
```

As we can see, SAX is a relatively difficult way to implement simple queries. It requires lots of coding for a simple query. SAX does have the very important advantage of a small memory footprint. For large documents or data streaming, this becomes critical.

671

DOM

When an XML document is parsed using a DOM-compliant parser, a complete copy of the document is stored in memory as hierarchical tree-based data structure. Each piece of the document is assigned to a specific node in the tree. This tree preserves all of the node interrelationships. Programs can *walk* the tree in the process of satisfying a query.

One significant disadvantage of DOM is both the runtime memory allocation overhead and the space consumed when parsing larger XML documents.

Example: DOM Query Example

This is the same example as before, but this time it uses DOM to evaluate the same query.

First, `doc.getElementsByTagName()` is called to find all `<Configuration>` elements in the document. These are iterated over until the `<Configuration>` that has the attribute runmode equal to `"test"` is found. Next `config.getElementsByTagName()` searches the descendants of the `config` `<Configuration>` node to find all `<ConnectionURL>` elements. Since we know that there is only one `<ConnectionURL>` node per `<Configuration>`, the desired `<ConnectionURL>` property value is found by getting its child text node.

Source DOMquery.java

```java
import java.io.IOException;
import javax.xml.parsers.*;
import org.w3c.dom.*;
import org.xml.sax.*;

public class DOMquery {
   static public void main(String[] argv) {
      if (argv.length != 1) {
         System.err.println("Usage: DOMquery URL ");
         System.exit(1);
      }
      DocumentBuilderFactory factory =
         DocumentBuilderFactory.newInstance();
      factory.setNamespaceAware(true);

      try {
         DocumentBuilder builder = factory.newDocumentBuilder();
         Document doc = builder.parse(argv[0]);
```

Let's do the DOM equivalent of this XPath query (note this is all one line):

```
/ServiceConfiguration/Configuration[@runmode='test']/
   Database/Connection/ConnectionURL/text()
```

```
            NodeList configs =
              doc.getElementsByTagName("Configuration");
            for (int i = 0; i < configs.getLength(); i++) {
              Element config = (Element) configs.item(i);
              String runMode =
                config.getAttribute("runmode").trim();
              if (runMode.equals("test")) {
                NodeList connectionURLs =
                  config.getElementsByTagName("ConnectionURL");
            System.out.println(connectionURLs.item(0)
             .getNodeName() + "=" +  connectionURLs.item(0)
               .getFirstChild().getNodeValue());
                return;
              }
            }
          } catch (Exception e) {
            System.out.println(e.getMessage());
          }
        }
      }
```

Output

```
> java DOMquery serviceconfiguration.xml
ConnectionURL=jdbc:postgresql://192.168.1.51:5432/test
```

As can be seen, it takes quite a bit of hand coding to evaluate this query. As a rule of thumb, querying a document using the DOM API is substantially easier than using SAX (though not in this example). So there exists a tradeoff between runtime performance efficiency and development effort.

A further disadvantage is that the DOM method calls anticipate a certain document layout. If the XML document DTD change in the future, this code would have to be modified.

The side-effect impact of changing document (or database) schemas (over time) cannot be underestimated. The author has been involved with some applications where the underlying schemas were changing frequently – sometimes daily. In a large application, literally thousands of lines of code might have to be checked, modified, and unit tested.

> *This assertion is true for all the approaches. The question is really one of how large a maintenance effort is required in the future.*

XPath Evaluators

XPath provides a good alternative to custom DOM or SAX-based coding. An XPath evaluator takes as its input an XPath expression. Typically, it returns a node-set containing all of the nodes that match the query. There are other expression datatypes but this is the predominant case in practice. (The XDK API does not support these other data types.)

An XPath evaluator plays a similar role to JDBC's handling of SQL queries. JDBC returns a resultset and the XPath evaluator returns a node-set.

Invoking an XPath evaluator takes just one method call, as we shall see. Contrast that simplicity to using either DOM or SAX, which take a lot of custom coding to achieve the same result.

Most XML parser implementations have an associated XPath evaluator. The Apache organization packages the XPath evaluator as part of its Xalan 2.1.0 Java 2 XSLT processor implementation, and more information on this, as well as the download, is available from http://xml.apache.org/xalan-j/index.html.

XPath Versus DOM Document Model

XPath 1.0 and DOM Level 2 do not share the same Document Model. A number of differences exist between them. For example, a number of DOM node types are not part of the XPath Document Model and vice versa.

The most important difference, in practice, is that XPath always works with expanded and merged text nodes. Character references, entity references, and CDATA sections are all expanded into a text node and adjacent text nodes are then merged together. (The individual nodes' text contents are concatenated together.)

For instance, the following XML fragment is represented by two DOM text nodes and two DOM entity reference nodes:

```
This is a &quot;quoted string&quot;
```

With the XPath document model, these four different nodes would be expanded and merged into this equivalent single text node:

```
This is a "quoted string"
```

CDATA sections are similarly converted to text nodes. (Adjacent text nodes are always merged together.)

As of this writing, efforts are being made to converge the different object model standards for XPath, XSLT, and DOM.

Feature	DOM Level 2 Core	XPath 1.0
Document node	Yes	No (uses root node instead)
Root node	No (uses document node instead)	Yes
Namespace node	No, but namespace accessor methods provided	Yes

Feature	DOM Level 2 Core	XPath 1.0
XML declaration	Yes	No, omitted
Document Type Declaration	Yes	No, omitted
CDATA Sections	Yes	No, fully expanded into text node
Entity References	Yes	No, fully expanded into text node
Character References	Yes	No, fully expanded into text node

It should be noted that the standards do not force particular implementation architectures on the XML parser creators. The Document Models are *logical* models and may be quite different from the implementation's internal object model. For instance, the XPath Document Model incorporates namespace nodes. For an actual evaluator implementation, these could be actually be *virtual* and not be actually stored in the document tree. Other implementations might create a separate XPath document model copy of the original DOM tree for doing XPath queries against.

XPath Evaluator's Dependence on DOM

Parser designers integrate these two different object models within a single XPath DOM extension API. Today, the implementation hides these document model details from Java programmers. The Java programmer works at the DOM document level. Any document model conversion is done implicitly.

The context node input to the XPath evaluator is a DOM node. The XPath evaluator then returns a DOM node-set, which can be further manipulated using DOM methods. There is an implicit conversion between the XPath document model and the DOM document model and vice versa.

Usually, the difference between the document models never becomes an issue. But what happens with text nodes that have embedded entity references? As shown before, the XPath document model is quite different from the DOM document model.

How should the vendor deal with the expression:

```
anElement[.='This is a "quoted string"']/text()
```

when matching this XML fragment?

```
<anElement>This is a &quot;quoted string&quot;</anElement>
```

With the XPath document model, the output node-set has a single text node. But back in the DOM document model, this single text node is stored as two text nodes and two entity references. This type of implicit document model conversion issue is left to the interpretation, of each parser designer. The upcoming DOM Level 3 specification has XPath evaluator support methods and should mandate how these types of ambiguous cases should be implemented.

From a performance perspective, it is important to remember that XPath evaluation API is actually an extension of a DOM framework. So to use XPath, a complete DOM document must be parsed into memory. Though XPath makes it easier to do a query from Java, there are no performance benefits over normal DOM. In practice, the XPath interpreter and evaluator adds a negligible runtime penalty.

Example: XPath Query Example

Here is the same query again, but this time, we use the Xalan XPath evaluator to get the answer.

> *Query the* `<ConnectionURL>` *property inside the test configuration* (`from` `serviceconfiguration.xml`). *The test configuration has a* `<Configuration>` *attribute runmode setting of* `"test"`.

As we have seen previously, XPath is a mini-language, so the input to the XPath evaluator is always an XPath expression string. The following XPath expression performs the query stated above:

```
/ServiceConfiguration/Configuration[@runmode='test']/
    Database/Connection/ConnectionURL/text()
```

The first part finds the `<Configuration>` element, which is the child of the `<ServiceConfiguration>` root element, whose `runmode` attribute is equal to `"test"`. (Note: XPath strings constants are delimited by either a single or double quote.)

```
/ServiceConfiguration/Configuration[@runmode='test']
```

The second part then finds the text child node of the `<ConnectionURL>` element descended from the correct `<Configuration>` element node.

> Note: if the text() node ending is removed, then the XPath expression evaluates to the `<ConnectionURL>` element node (but the desired property value is found in its child text nodes).

```
Database/Connection/ConnectionURL/text()
```

This example source demonstrates how easy it is to get the results for a given XPath expression. With Xalan, the static method `XPathAPI.selectNodeList()` returns a `NodeList`, which contains all matching nodes. In this case, we are expecting a single `ConnectionURL` text node (whose parent is the `<ConnectionURL>` element node).

Source XPathQuery.java

```java
import java.io.*;
import java.net.*;
import org.w3c.dom.*;
import org.apache.xpath.XPathAPI;
import javax.xml.parsers.*;
```

```
public class XPathQuery {

  static public void main(String[] argv) {
    try {
      if (argv.length != 1) {
        System.out.println("Usage: java XPathQuery " +
          "filename");
        System.exit(1);
      }

      // Generate a URL from the filename.
      URL url = URLutil.makeURL(argv[0]);

      // Parse the document.
      DocumentBuilderFactory factory =
        DocumentBuilderFactory.newInstance();
      Document doc =
        factory.newDocumentBuilder().parse(url.toString());
      String expr =
        "/ServiceConfiguration/Configuration" +
        "[@runmode='test']/" +
        "Database/Connection/ConnectionURL/text()";

      NodeList list = XPathAPI
        .selectNodeList(doc, expr, doc);
      System.out.println(list.item(0)
        .getParentNode().getNodeName() + "=" +
        list.item(0).getNodeValue());
    } catch (Exception e) {
      System.out.println(e.getMessage());
    }
  }
}
```

Output

```
> java XPathQuery serviceconfiguration.xml
ConnectionURL=jdbc:postgresql://192.168.1.51:5432/test
```

XPath 1.0 Primer

XPath is a mini-language for searching parts of XML documents. It is a core component inside XSLT and XPointer implementations. Similarly, it can be invoked directly from a Java program. Rather than walk a convoluted path through a DOM tree using DOM method calls, it is frequently much simpler to use an XPath evaluator to select the nodes that are desired.

As we have already seen, XPath works on a tree document data model, which is almost identical to a DOM document tree. Some parts of the DOM tree are omitted, such as the XML declaration and document type declaration, and all CDATA sections, entity references and character references are fully expanded.

XPath location expressions select sets of nodes from this tree, when that XPath expression is evaluated. This set of nodes is typically called a **node-set**. Finding nodes in a document tree is the most common usage of XPath. However XPath expressions can represent booleans, numbers, string values, as well as node-sets. (Some additional datatypes are defined for XSLT and XPointer.)

In a Java framework, a node-set is a collection of object references to nodes in the actual document tree. It is very important to remember that XPath evaluators return a set of nodes, not just a single node. For existing DOM-based XPath evaluators, the returned node-set is an instance of a DOM `NodeList` class.

XPath's motivation was to emulate the simple Unix pathname syntax used to traverse file directories. In Unix the command line processor, or shell, understands this syntax. Like XML, virtually all file systems represent hierarchical tree structures – file systems are composed of directories that contain individual files or even other directories. Relative to XML, you can think of directories as being analogous to XML elements and files correspond to text nodes in an XML tree.

Like file paths, XPaths can be both absolute and relative to some specific location. In a Unix file system, that specific location is called the working directory. With XPath, the specific location in the Document tree is called the **context node**.

An absolute XPath expression always begins with a forward slash, for instance this is an absolute expression:

```
/ServiceConfiguration
```

and this one is relative:

```
./Configuration
```

RunMode Element Query Example

Let's digress briefly to show a simple example that finds the `<RunMode>` element in a document. At this point, without a formal introduction to the XPath syntax, you can see how similar these are to file pathnames. This expression is:

```
/ServiceConfiguration/RunMode
```

When evaluated against the file `serviceconfiguration.xml`, this expression returns a node-set containing a single node. That node points to an `Element` node with the tag `<RunMode>`. If you are looking for the text enclosed by the `<RunMode>` element, you will be disappointed. You can either use DOM Java method calls to find the text, or use a slightly different XPath expression.

To get the text enclosed by that element, you have two alternative XPath expressions which return related but different information. The first returns a node-set containing a single text node.

```
/ServiceConfiguration/RunMode/text()
```

The second returns a string. (Note, only one of the Java XPath evaluators can handle string datatyped XPath expressions. This style of expression would be useful in XSL `<xsl:value-of select="..."` /> expressions.)

```
string(/ServiceConfiguration/RunMode)
```

Location Paths

Let's look at the XPath syntax more closely. This discussion is intended to be a primer, not a rewritten specification, so be sure to consult the XPath specification at http://www.w3.org/TR/xpath/ for more details.

As stated before, XPath expressions can evaluate to `Booleans`, `Numbers`, `Strings`, or `nodesets`. Most of the time only those expressions that evaluate to node-sets are used in practice. So these `LocationPath` expressions will be discussed here. A `LocationPath` expression evaluates to a node-set.

Queries with absolute location paths always start from the tree root of the current context (the '/' represents the root node), which is conceptually similar to the document node in a DOM tree. Relative location paths start the match evaluation from the context node. This initial context node can be anywhere in the node tree. The initial context node is always supplied to the evaluator, either explicitly through the Java XPath invocation method, or implicitly from XSL.

Location Steps

A `LocationPath` is comprised of one or more location steps that are separated by a '/'. Each step represents a node-set match evaluation. The individual step evaluations are logically concatenated, as the output of one step becomes the input to the next. The node-set evaluation progresses from left to right. Each evaluation step results implicitly in an intermediate node-set. This node-set is the input to the next matching step to the right.

Let's look at the `serviceconfiguration.xml` example file once again. The expression `/ServiceConfiguration` matches any `<ServiceConfiguration>` element nodes, which are direct children of the root node. Here the evaluated node-set has a single `<ServiceConfiguration>` element node. The expression `/ServiceConfiguration/Configuration` evaluates to a node-set having two `<Configuration>` element nodes in it. Similarly the expression `/ServiceConfiguration/Configuration/Database` evaluates to a node-set having two `<Database>` element nodes in it.

The examples so far have actually shown abbreviated location steps. For example, the abbreviated expression `/ServiceConfiguration` is fully described as `/child::ServiceConfiguration`. (See the section on XPath abbreviations on page 684.)

LocationSteps – Axes and Node Tests

Syntactically, a `location step` is comprised of up to three components:

❑ An **axis** – determines the "direction to" (or choice of) the candidate nodes, upon which the following node test will be applied

❑ A **node test** – the actual name or type test match

❑ Optionally, there is also one or more **predicates** – further Boolean qualifications

This example location step has an axis [`child::`], a node test [`database`], and a single predicate [`@name='Oracle'`].

```
child::database[@name='Oracle']
```

This example location step will succeed, if the context node has one or more child database elements, each having a name attribute equal to `'Oracle'`.

Axes

An axis is the instruction for determining which nodes become candidate nodes. In a sense, the axis signifies the direction to search for candidate nodes. The directions are always relative to the current node (from the intermediate resulting node-set generated by a prior location step). Candidate nodes are then given the node test, to see if they become part of this step's resultant node-set.

Axis	Description
`ancestor`	Selects all ancestor nodes of the context node, such as parents and grandparents. Always includes the root node.
`ancestor-or-self`	Selects all ancestor nodes of the context node, such as parents and grandparents as well as the context node itself. Always includes the root node.
`attribute`	Selects all attribute nodes of the context node, if the context node is an element node. Selects nothing otherwise.
`child`	Selects all the child nodes of the context node
`descendant`	Selects all the descendant element nodes of the context node, such as children and grandchildren. If the context node is not an element node, nothing is selected.
`descendant-or-self`	Selects all the descendant element nodes of the context node such as children and grandchildren, as well as the context node itself
`following`	Selects all element nodes that are after the context node in document order, excepting the descendant element nodes
`following-sibling`	Selects all element sibling nodes that are after the context node in document order
`namespace`	Selects all namespace nodes belonging to the context node. A namespace node represents a namespace that is in scope on either an element or an attribute. (There are no corresponding namespace nodes in DOM.)
`parent`	Selects the parent node of the context node. If the context node is the root node, nothing is selected.
`preceding`	Selects all element nodes that are before the context node in document order, excepting the ancestor element nodes
`preceding-sibling`	Selects all element sibling nodes that are before the context node in document order
`self`	Selects the context node itself

> Note: the nodes selected by the ancestor, descendant, following, preceding, and self axes should never intersect (a node cannot be selected by more than one of these 5 axes). Also, the union of nodes selected by these 5 axes is the same as the union of all the element nodes in the document.

In the following diagrams, the shaded node is the context node to which the axis is being applied. The heavy dark bordered nodes are the nodes placed in the resulting node-set:

Axis	Description
ancestor	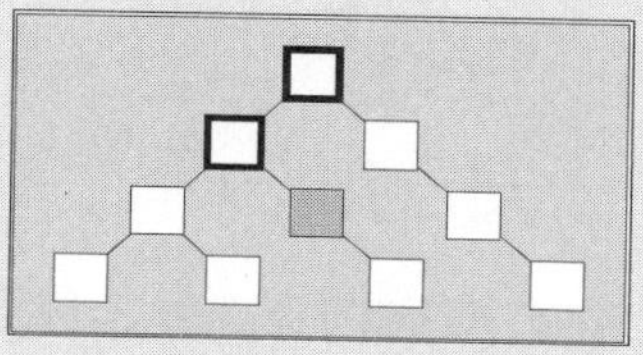
ancestor-or-self	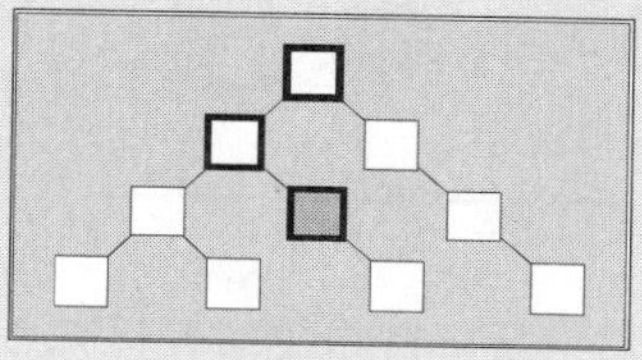
child	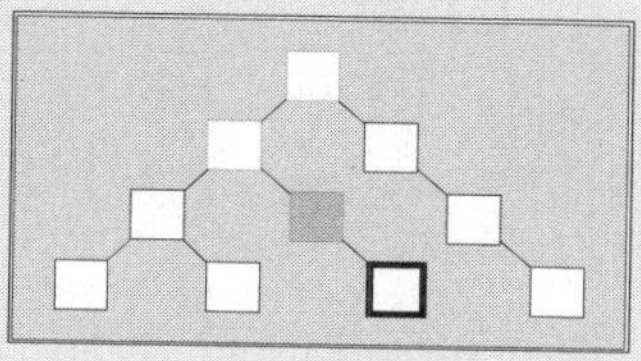
descendant	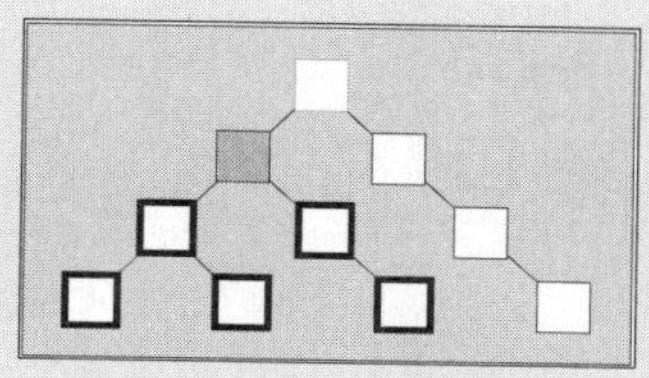

descendant-or-
self

following

following-
sibling

parent

preceding

preceding-
sibling

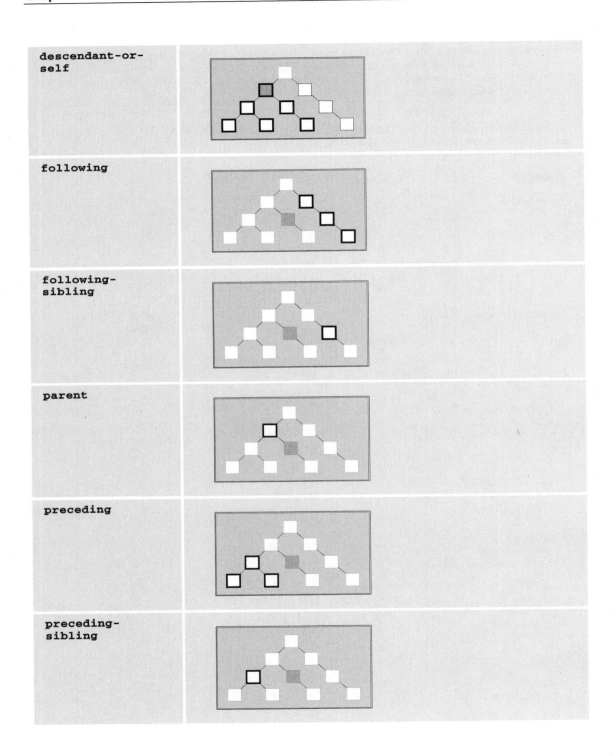

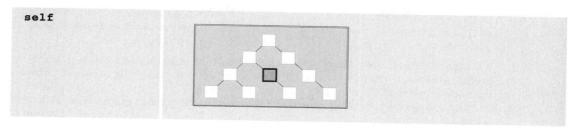

self

Node Test

Conceptually, the axis determines which nodes will be given the node test. The node test then determines which of these candidate nodes are eliminated from further consideration.

These are the node test rules:

❑ If the candidate node is an element node, the node test succeeds if the node test string is identical to the element's name. If the node test string is `'*'`, then any candidate element node is matched.

Note: if the axis is `attribute::` or `namespace::`, then the node test string `'*'` can be used to match all attributes and namespaces, respectively.

❑ If the candidate node is an attribute node and the axis is `attribute::`, the node test succeeds if the node test string is identical to the attribute's name. If the node test string is `'*'`, then any candidate attribute node is matched.

❑ If the candidate node is an attribute node, the node test succeeds if the node test string is `attribute()`

❑ If the candidate node is an namespace node, the node test succeeds if the node test string is `namespace()`

❑ If the candidate node is a text node, the node test succeeds if the node test string is `text()`.

❑ If the candidate node is a comment node, the node test succeeds if the node test string is `comment()`.

❑ If the candidate node is a processing instruction node, the node test succeeds if the node test string is `processing-instruction()`

Note: the next rule allows you to further refine the test to only match specific named processing instructions.

❑ If the candidate node is a processing instruction node, the node test succeeds if the node test string is `processing-instruction("name")` and the instruction's name is the same as the `"name"` argument

❑ If the node test string is `node()`, then the node test succeeds for any node

Predicates

Predicates are XPath sub-expressions, which are appended to the node test of a location step. A predicate is always a sub-expression enclosed in brackets.

A predicate takes the candidate node-set, which results from the preceding node test, and applies one of several tests on each node in the set:

- ❑ If the predicate evaluates to a number, then the predicate is considered an abbreviation of: `[position()=number]`. That predicate is then applied to the node-set, that is, `./Configuration[2]` picks the 2nd child `<Configuration>` element.

- ❑ For each node in the candidate node-set, the predicate is evaluated against it. If the predicate evaluates to false, that node is removed from the resulting node-set. Otherwise, the node remains in the resulting node-set. For example, `./Configuration[type='Oracle']` selects only the `<Configuration>` element that is has a type attribute equal to the string "Oracle". The `[type='Oracle']` portion of the expression is a predicate.

Zero, one, or more predicates can be appended as part of a location step. The predicates are evaluated from left to right. The output node-set from the left predicate then becomes the input node-set to the predicate on the right. The current context for the predicate is the node that the predicate is being applied to (the context node for the node test).

XPath Abbreviations

XPath provides some abbreviations that are commonly used.

Abbreviation	Full Expression	Usage
.	`self::node()`	`./alpha` Selects all child elements named `<alpha>`
..	`parent::node()`	`..` Selects the parent node of the context node
*	`child::*`	`./*` Selects all child elements of the context node
abc	`child::abc`	`/abc` Selects all child elements (of the root node) named `<abc>`
//*	`descendant-or-self::*`	`thisOne//*` Selects all elements descendant from element `<thisOne>` as well as the `<thisOne>` element itself

Abbreviation	Full Expression	Usage

`//abc`	`descendant-or-self::abc`	`//thisOne`
		
		Selects all elements in the document having the name `<thisOne>`
		
		`.//thisOne`
		
		Selects all `<thisOne>` elements that are either descended from the context node or the context node (if it's a `<thisOne>` element itself)

`@xyz`	`attribute::xyz`	`@xyz` Selects the xyz attribute of the context node
`@*`	`attribute::*`	`@*` Selects all attributes of the context node
`[1]`	`[position()=1]`	`./[2]` Matches only the 2nd child (in document order) of the context node

Some Common XPath Terms

A couple of terms that are commonly found in XPath documentation need some explanation:

String-Value

The string-value of a node depends on the type of node.

Node Type	String-Value
`Root`	Concatenation of all descendant text nodes' string-values in document order
`Element`	Concatenation of all descendant text nodes' string-values in document order
`Attribute`	The normalized attribute value
`Namespace`	The namespace URI for this node's prefix
`Processing Instruction`	The part of the instruction following the target (and any whitespace). It does not include the closing "?>".
`Comment`	The text after the leading <!-- and before the closing -->
`Text`	The character data inside the text node

Example XML Fragment

Let's look at a small XML fragment to see the resulting string values:

```
<example>
  An Example
  <outer name="alpha">
    <inner name="beta">Inner's contents</inner>
    Some more outer text.
  </outer>
</example>
```

The table below shows the string-value for portions of this XML fragment. The quotation marks have been added here to make it easier to see the leading and trailing whitespace in the calculated string-values. The surrounding quotation marks themselves are not part of the string-values.

Which node	Quoted String-Value (shown with explicit quotes)
`<inner>`'s `"name"` attribute	`"inner"`
`<inner>` element	`"Inner's contents"`

`<outer>` element	`"`
	
	`                    Inner's contents`
	`Some more outer text.`
	`"`

`<example>` element	`"`
	
	`    An Example                 Inner's contents`
	`                Some more outer text.`
	
	`"`

Document Order

The process of parsing an XML document scans the nodes from the top of the document down to the bottom (and in a left-to-right order on each line). This parser-generated sequence is called the **document order**.

An element node always precedes its child elements' nodes. An element's namespace and attribute nodes always follow it and precede any of its child element nodes. The namespace nodes precede the attribute nodes. The arrangement of the individual namespace nodes and the individual attribute nodes is implementation-dependent.

XPath Built-in Functions

XPath provides a variety of built-in functions that are primarily used inside of predicates.

Node-set Functions

These are the node-set related functions:

Function	Description
number **last**()	Returns the highest index for the context position, the context size, for this expression evaluation context For example: `./*` with 5 child elements, `last()` will return 5
number **position**()	Returns the current context position for this expression evaluation context. Counts from 1, not 0. It returns the iterator position when traversing the node-set.
number **count**(node-set)	Returns the number of nodes in the node-set
node-set **id**(object)	Selects all element nodes, having an attribute named id, and whose id attribute is equal to the input parameter's string value
string **local-name**(node-set ?)	Returns the local part of the `<prefix:localName>` element name – only for the first node in the document order, or the context node if no node is specified For example: `local-name(dd:name)` returns the string `"name"`
string **namespace-uri**(node-set ?)	Returns the namespace URI for namespace prefix, which is part of the `<prefix:localName>` element name – only for first node in node-set, or context node is no node-set is specified For example: `Namespace-uri (dd:name)` returns the namespace URI defined for prefix dd
string **name**(node-set ?)	Returns the `<prefix:localName>` combination for an element node For example: `name(dd:name)` returns the string `"dd:name"`

String Functions

These are the string manipulation related functions:

Function	Description
string **string**(object ?)	Converts the input argument to string form: If the in-out object is a node-set, this returns the string-value of the first node in the node-set If Boolean false, returns the string "false". If Boolean true, returns the string "true" If the argument is a number, the number is converted to string. Integer values have no decimal point. See the spec for more details. For example: string(7) returns the string "7"
string **concat** (string, string, string*)	Concatenates two or more strings together For example: concat("fat", "cat") returns "fatcat"
boolean **starts-with**(string, string)	Returns true if first argument begins with the second argument For example: starts-with("testString", "test") returns true
boolean **contains**(string, string)	Returns true if first argument contains the second argument For example: contains ("testString", "BAD") returns false
string **substring-before** (string, string)	Returns the substring from the first argument that occurs just before the substring second argument does. Returns an empty string if substring does not exist. For example: substring-before("testString", "String") returns "test"

string **substring-after** (string, string)	Returns the substring from the first argument that occurs just after the substring second argument does. Returns an empty string if substring does not exist. For example: substring-after("testString", "test") returns "String"
string **substring** (string, number, number?)	Returns the substring from the first argument that starts from the second argument position. The substring's length is provided by the optional third parameter. If the third argument is not provided, the substring continues to the end of the string. Returns an empty string if substring does not exist. For example: substring("testString", 5) returns "String" substring("testString", 1, 4) returns "test"
number **string-length**(string?)	If a string argument is provided, returns the number of characters in the string. Otherwise, returns the length of the string-value of the context node. For example: string-length("aString") returns 7
string **normalize-space** (string?)	Each whitespace sequence is stripped from the string argument and replaced by a single blank character. All leading and trailing whitespace is stripped. If no string argument is provided, it returns the normalized string-value of the context node. For example: normalize-space(" this is a test") returns "this is a test"
string **translate**(string, string, string)	Returns the first string after all characters occurring in the second string are replaced by the corresponding character in the third string. For example: translate("CAT", "ABC", "abc") returns "caT" If the corresponding character position in the third string is missing, then the corresponding character in the second string will be removed. For example: translate("cow", "abc", "AB") returns "ow"

Boolean Functions

These are the Boolean-related functions:

Function	Description

`boolean` **`boolean`** `(object)`	Converts the input argument to a `Boolean` value. If numeric – returns `false` if = 0, `true` otherwise
	
	For example:
	
	`boolean(45)` returns `true` whereas `boolean(0)` returns `false`
	
	If node set – returns `false` if empty, `true` otherwise. If string – returns `false` if length = 0, `true` otherwise
	
	For example:
	
	`boolean("aString")` returns `true`
	`boolean ("")` returns `false`

`boolean` **`not`** `(boolean)`	Returns `true` if argument is `false`, and `false` if the argument is `true`
`boolean` **`true`** `()`	Returns boolean `true`
`boolean` **`false`** `()`	Returns boolean `false`

Number Functions

These are the number related functions:

Function	Description
number **number** (object?)	Converts input object to a number. Conversion depends on the input argument type:
	If a string, translates the string into the equivalent number. If no translation is possible, returns NaN.
	For example:
	number("5") returns the number 5
	If boolean true, return 1, otherwise return 0
	For example:
	number(true) returns the number 1
	If node-set, the first item in node-set is first converted to a string, then that string value is converted to a number.
number **sum** (node-set)	Sums the numeric equivalent of the individual string-values of the nodes in the set
number **floor** (number)	Returns the largest integer number (closest to positive infinity) that is not greater than the argument's value
	For example:
	floor(3.14) returns the number 3
number **ceiling** (number)	Returns the smallest integer number (closest to negative infinity) that is not less than the argument's value
	For example:
	ceiling(3.14) returns the number 4
number **round** (number)	Returns the closest integer number to the input argument
	For example:
	round(3.14) returns the number 3

XPath Operators

Here is a table of XPath operators.

Note that the division operator is not '/', but instead is the keyword div.

Operator	XPath 1.0
-	Unary minus, for example: -10
+	Addition, for example: 1+1 returns 2
-	Subtraction, for example: 5-3 returns 2
*	Multiplication, for example: 5*4 returns 20
div	Division, for example: 6 div 2 returns 3
mod	Modulus, for example: 6 mod 4 returns 2
and	Boolean and, for example: ($a > 5 and $a <10)
or	Boolean or, for example: ($b = 4 or $b =12)
|	Node-set union, for example: /chars/a | /chars/b
<	Less than
<=	Less than or equal
>	Greater than
>=	Greater than or equal
=	Equal
!=	Not equal
$	XSLT Variable reference, for example: $aVariable
()	Expression grouping

Note: Boolean negation is done using the not() function Boolean true is obtained from the true() function and Boolean false is obtained from the false() function

The rules for the operators =, !=, <, <=, >, and >= operators are complex. There are a lot of special cases when node-sets are compared against text strings or numbers. See the XPath specification for details.

One common predicate pattern is:

```
[.='a String']
```

This predicate is true when the string-value of the current node is equal to the string "a String".

Operator Precedence Chart

The operators are here grouped from the highest priority at the top to the lowest priority at the bottom. Parenthetical groupings, `(expr)`, can be used to override these priorities.

Operator
`$`
`- (Unary minus)`
`*, div, mod`
`+, -`
`<, <=, >, >=`
`=, !=`
`and`
`or`
`|`
`()`

Freehand XPath Examples

Let's use the following simple document hierarchy structure for these XPath example expressions:

```
book
    chapter
        section
            picture
```

In other words, a book has chapters. A chapter has sections. A section has pictures.

```
/book//picture
```

This expression finds all `<picture>` elements descended from the `<book>` element.

```
/book/chapter
```

This expression finds all `<chapter>` child elements in the topmost `<book>` element.

```
/book/chapter[@title='Querying XML']
```

This expression finds all `<chapter>` child elements, having a title attribute equal to "Querying XML", in the topmost `<book>` element.

```
/book/chapter[@title='Querying XML' or @title='Storing XML']
```

This expression finds all <chapter> child elements, having a title attribute equal to either "Querying XML" or "Storing XML", in the topmost <book> element.

```
/book/chapter[count(./section)=2]
```

Finds all <chapter> elements that have two <section> child elements.

```
/book/chapter[count(./section)=2]/section[2]
```

Finds the second <section> element from the chapters having two <section> child elements.

```
//chapter[count(./section)=2][1]/section[position()=2]
```

Finds the second <section> element from the first chapter, which has two <section> child elements.

Configuration Examples

XPath can be used to easily query quite complex XML configuration files. We will once again look at serviceconfiguration.xml, which holds multiple configuration settings for the AAMS Server. Each complete configuration is enclosed in a <Configuration> element. These are distinguished, from each other, by a unique runmode attribute.

Contained inside the <Configuration> element is a <Database> element. This element describes the type of database that is being connected to (with the product's name in the type attribute). For each database, unique JDBC connection information is contained inside the <Connection> element. Each JDBC connection-related property has its own element.

These are organized as follows:

```
<PropertyName>property value</PropertyName>
```

This is an extract of the first part of the configuration file:

```
<ServiceConfiguration >
  <RunMode>prod</RunMode>
  <Configuration runmode="test">
    <Database type="PostgreSQL">
      <Connection>
        <Driver>org.postgresql.Driver</Driver>
        <ConnectionURL>jdbc:postgresql://192.168.1.51:5432/test
        </ConnectionURL>
        <User>test</User>
        <Password>test</Password>
        <ResultSetType>4</ResultSetType>
      </Connection>
    </Database>
  </Configuration>
  <Configuration runmode="prod">
```

Let's say we don't know which properties are required by the JDBC connection. We would like to query serviceconfiguration.xml to find which properties have to be set.

One initial strategy is to query the names for all the different properties directly from the configuration file.

First, let's try this initial XPath query. It queries all of the children for every `<Connection>` element:

```
/ServiceConfiguration/Configuration/Database/Connection/*
```

This should return the following:

```
<Driver>
<ConnectionURL>
<User>
<Password>
<ResultSetType>
<Driver>
<ConnectionURL>
<User>
<Password>
<ResultSetType>
```

This duplication of property names is a result of the way XPath functions. XPath returns a node-set that points to *all* of the nodes that match the query. This is what XPath is doing in this example. But upon inspection, we can see that the file has two different configurations, one for testing and one for production. (They have different `runmode` attribute values). Hence, we see the duplication of element names, referring to different nodes.

Let's narrow this query down to look at just the `test` configuration. It is important that only the `test` configuration (the `<Configuration>` element having a `runmode` of `"test"`) be selected. For `serviceconfiguration.xml`, XPath will report the extra property names unless a predicate is added to the `<Connection>` location step.

Here `[@runmode='test']` is a predicate attached to the `<Configuration>` location step. It will toss out any nodes that do not satisfy the predicate when the node-set is being evaluated:

```
/ServiceConfiguration/Configuration[@runmode='test']/Database/Connection/*
```

This should produce the following result:

```
<Driver>
<ConnectionURL>
<User>
<Password>
<ResultSetType>
```

Now we have narrowed the output down to just the properties that are needed. Next, let's find the enclosed properties' values using XPath. (In practice as an alternative, DOM method calls might be combined with XPath evaluation to find these value strings.)

A location step consisting of `text()` finds all of the children text nodes for the property elements:

```
/ServiceConfiguration/Configuration[@runmode='test']/Database/Connection/*/text()
```

This should produce the following result:

```
org.postgresql.Driver
jdbc:postgresql://192.168.1.51:5432/test
test
test
4
```

Our next example shows how to do an inverse query. Here we want to work backwards from a specific property value, to find which configuration specifies that property setting. In this case, the goal is to find the correct `runmode` value.

With this XPath expression we are trying to find the `runmode` attribute for the `Configuration` element, whose `ResultSetType` is equal to 4.

```
/ServiceConfiguration/Configuration
    [Database/Connection/ResultSetType/text()=4]/@runmode
```

This should produce the following result:

```
runmode="test"
```

The key to this inverted type of query lies with the predicate. Without the predicate, the query is: `/ServiceConfiguration/Configuration/@runmode`. But, this simpler query returns the `runmode` settings for all configurations.

A predicate can be used to narrow the returned node-set to just the specific `runmode`. Remember, if the predicate is `false` for a candidate node, then that node is removed from the resultant node-set.

The predicate `[Database/Connection/ResultSetType/text()=4]` is `true`, only when the `ResultSetType` property has a value of 4. Thus all `Configuration` elements that have a `ResultSetType` property not equal to 4 will be eliminated from further consideration. (That is because this predicate applies to the `Configuration` node test.)

XPath Evaluation Utility

This section demonstrates a simple, but very useful utility for evaluating XPath expressions against an XML document. The example is longer than many, but the usefulness of the utility is undeniable. We will show the full source code for the Xerces and Xalan version on page 702. Later, on page 707, excerpts from the XDK version will be shown.

The XPathListTester Class

The signature for this class is:

```
public class XPathListTester
```

The code listing for `XPathListTester` can be found on page 702.

Not only is this an excellent example of how to use the XPath evaluator, but also the resulting utility program can be used to help troubleshoot XPath expressions that may be failing in an XSL stylesheet. (XSL stylesheets tend to have no output when there is an XPath problem. They can be extremely frustrating to troubleshoot.)

Description of the Utility (Absolute Expressions)

This utility takes both an input XML file (against which the XPath expressions will be evaluated) and an XPath expression list file. The list file is expected to have one or more XPath expressions, one expression per line.

The optional deep printing mode setting makes it possible to print out the complete subtrees, below any element nodes that are returned in the node-set.

The XPathListTester class only handles absolute XPath expressions (those whose first character starts with a slash, "/".) We will use a utility that handles relative XPath expressions. This is further explained below.

The usage for this utility is:

```
> java XPathListTester xmlFile XPathListFile [shallow | deep]
```

Parameter	Description
xmlFile	Input XML file to process XPath expressions against
XPathList file	A collection of XPath expressions to try. One expression per line of input.
[shallow | deep] (Default is shallow)	Shallow prints out just the nodes returned by the XPath evaluator. Deep prints out not only the nodes on the nodelist, but the entire sub-tree below any element nodes on the nodelist as well.

Example Usage

In this example, our XML input file is serviceconfiguration.xml, and our XPath list input file is xpaths:

```
/ServiceConfiguration/Configuration[@runmode='test']/@runmode
/ServiceConfiguration/Configuration[@runmode='prod']/Database
/ServiceConfiguration/RunMode
/Service
```

The first example below shows the output when using shallow mode printing. Note how just the <Database> element node is printed. The last entry in the XPath list input file is /Service, which matches nothing, since there is no <Service> element in serviceconfiguration.xml.

```
> java XPathListTester serviceconfiguration.xml xpaths
```

This should produce the following result:

```
Shallow XPath Evaluator Printing mode.
==== XPath Expr=
    /ServiceConfiguration/Configuration[@runmode='test']/@runmode
runmode="test"

==== XPath Expr=
    /ServiceConfiguration/Configuration[@runmode='prod']/Database
<Database type="Oracle">

==== XPath Expr=/ServiceConfiguration/RunMode
<RunMode>

==== XPath Expr=/Service
====== Xpath returns nothing ======
```

In deep printing mode, the entire subtrees below the <Database> and the <RunMode> elements are
printed out:

> **java XPathListTester serviceconfiguration.xml xpaths deep**

This should produce the following result:

```
Deep XPath Evaluator Printing mode.
==== XPath Expr=
    /ServiceConfiguration/Configuration[@runmode='test']/@runmode
test

==== XPath Expr=
    /ServiceConfiguration/Configuration[@runmode='prod']/Database
<Database type="Oracle">
    <Connection>
        <Driver>oracle.jdbc.driver.OracleDriver</Driver>
        <ConnectionURL>
            jdbc:oracle:thin:@localhost:1521:test
        </ConnectionURL>
        <User>test</User>
        <Password>test</Password>
        <ResultSetType>3</ResultSetType>
    </Connection>
</Database>

==== XPath Expr=/ServiceConfiguration/RunMode
<RunMode>prod</RunMode>

==== XPath Expr=/Service
====== Xpath returns nothing ======


Successful XPATH evaluation
```

Description of the Utility (Relative Expressions)

The absolute XPath expression list utility can be easily modified to support relative XPath expressions.

For relative expressions, one difference is that this utility requires an expression pair for each evaluation. The first expression is an absolute expression that creates an intermediate set of context nodes. The second relative expression is then evaluated using those context nodes. (Remember that the context node is always the root node for an absolute XPath expression.)

The usage is:

```
> java RelXPathListTester xmlFile XPathListFile [shallow | deep]
```

Function	Description
`xmlFile`	Input XML file to process XPath expressions against
`XPathListfile`	A collection of XPath expressions to try. Each relative expression evaluation requires two expressions. The first is an absolute expression to determine the context node for the second relative expression. One XPath expression per line of input.
`[shallow	deep]` (Default is shallow)	Shallow prints out just the nodes returned by the XPath evaluator. Deep prints out not only the nodes on the nodelist, but the entire subtree below any element nodes on the nodelist as well.

Example Usage

In this example, our XML input file is `serviceconfiguration.xml`, and our XPath list input file is `RelXPathList`:

```
/ServiceConfiguration/Configuration
```

```
./Database/@type
```

```
/ServiceConfiguration/Configuration[@runmode='test']/Database/Connection/*
```

```
../../@type
```

```
/ServiceConfiguration/Configuration[@runmode='test']/Database/Connection/Driver
```

```
../../@type
```

```
/ServiceConfiguration/Configuration[@runmode='test']//Driver
```

```
../../@type
```

This is the output of evaluating four different relative XPath expressions in the list file.

```
> java RelXPathListTester serviceconfiguration.xml RelXPathList
```

This should produce the following result:

```
Shallow XPath Evaluator Printing mode.
==== Absolute XPath Expr=/ServiceConfiguration/Configuration
====    Relative XPath Expr=./Database/@type
type="PostgreSQL"
type="Oracle"

==== Absolute XPath Expr=
    /ServiceConfiguration/Configuration[@runmode='test']
        /Database/Connection/*
====    Relative XPath Expr=../../@type
type="PostgreSQL"
type="PostgreSQL"
type="PostgreSQL"
type="PostgreSQL"
type="PostgreSQL"

==== Absolute XPath Expr=
    /ServiceConfiguration/Configuration[@runmode='test']
        /Database/Connection/Driver
====    Relative XPath Expr=../../@type
type="PostgreSQL"

==== Absolute XPath Expr=
    /ServiceConfiguration/Configuration[@runmode='test']//Driver
====    Relative XPath Expr=../../@type
type="PostgreSQL"

Successful XPATH evaluation
```

Xalan/Xerces XPath API

Xalan XPath support comes from the XPathAPI class. This class has a variety of alternative methods for evaluating XPath expressions. Namespace support is provided through overloading the methods.

xalan.jar contains the Xalan XPath API. This JAR file is required in addition to the core Xerces parser Jar file, xerces.jar.

Class XPathAPI

org.apache.xpath

```
public class XPathAPI
```

XPathAPI provides a number of static convenience methods for evaluating XPath expressions against an input DOM document or XML fragment. For the API sections of this chapter, we have only listed those methods relevant to the examples. A full listing is provided in the JavaDocs distributed with the packages.

The selectNodeList() Methods

```
public static NodeList selectNodeList(Node contextNode, String str)
        throws TransformerException
```

```
public static NodeList selectNodeList(Node contextNode, String str,
            Node namespaceNode)
        throws TransformerException
```

The first selectNodeList() evaluates the XPath expression relative to the supplied context node. This evaluator method returns a DOM NodeList object containing the output node-set. In the second method, the namespaceNode is the node that namespace prefixes will be resolved against.

The selectSingleNode() Methods

```
public static Node selectSingleNode(Node contextNode,
            java.lang.String str)
        throws TransformerException
```

```
public static Node selectSingleNode(Node contextNode, String str,
            Node namespaceNode)
        throws TransformerException
```

These methods are analogous except that they return a single Node instead of a NodeList.

The eval() Methods

Unlike the selectNodeList() and selectSingleNode() methods, the eval() methods all return an XObject object instance. XObject is a base class for Xboolean, XnodeSet, Xnumber, Xstring, XRTreeFrag, and Xnull. The net effect of this is that the eval() methods can handle all XPath expression types, not just node-set typed ones.

In practice, the actual XObject will be an instance of one of its derived sub-classes. The Java instanceof operator can be used to determine which it is.

The selectNodeList() and selectSingleNode() methods, on the other hand, are restricted to XPath expressions that evaluate to node-sets.

```
public static XObject eval(Node contextNode, String str)
        throws TransformerException
```

```
public static XObject eval(Node contextNode, String str,
        Node namespaceNode)
    throws TransformerException
```

```
public static XObject eval(Node contextNode, String str,
        PrefixResolver resolver)
    throws TransformerException
```

The `eval()` methods evaluate the XPath expression relative to the supplied context node. The `namespaceNode` is the node that namespace prefixes will be resolved against. The `resolver` object will be used to resolve the namespace prefixes that are encountered.

Xalan XPath List Utility Implementation

In the source code below, the Xalan/Xerces specific code is bolded. To use a different XML parser implementation, the bolded sections of code must be replaced with the equivalent methods from the other implementation.

The main method creates the DOM document instance by parsing the input XML file. Next, it reads the `XPathList` file and starts reading it line-by-line. For each XPath expression read from the list file, the method calls `evalXPath()` to do the XPath evaluation.

```
import java.io.*;
import java.net.*;
import org.w3c.dom.*;
import org.apache.xpath.XPathAPI;
import javax.xml.parsers.*;
import javax.xml.transform.*;
import javax.xml.transform.dom.*;
import javax.xml.transform.stream.*;

public class XPathListTester {

    static public void main(String[] argv) {
        try {
            if (argv.length != 2 && argv.length != 3) {
                System.out
                    .println("Usage: java XPathListTester filename
                            xpathListFile [shallow|deep]");
                System.out.println("        Shallow printing by default");
                System.exit(1);
            }

            URL url = URLutil.makeURL(argv[0]);

            DocumentBuilderFactory factory =
```

```
    DocumentBuilderFactory.newInstance();
    Document doc = factory.newDocumentBuilder()
      .parse(url.toString());

    Transformer serializer =
      TransformerFactory.newInstance().newTransformer();
    serializer
      .setOutputProperty(OutputKeys.OMIT_XML_DECLARATION,"yes");

    boolean shallow = (argv.length == 2) ? true
                        : argv[2].equalsIgnoreCase("shallow");
    System.out.println((shallow ? "Shallow" : "Deep")
                        + " XPath Evaluator Printing mode.");

    BufferedReader is =
      new BufferedReader(new FileReader(argv[1]));
    String line = null;

    while ((line = is.readLine()) != null) {
      evalXPath(doc, serializer, line, shallow);
      System.out.println();
    }

    System.out.println("Successful XPATH evaluation");
  } catch (Exception e) {
    System.out.println(e.getMessage());
  }
}
```

The evalXPath() method does the actual XPath expression evaluation. A NodeList object is returned from the evaluator. Then, using the desired printing style, the items in the resultant node-set are printed to standard output.

With Xalan, the XPathAPI class is the Java XPath evaluator. This statement does the actual XPath evaluation for this example. Here, list holds the output node-set that matched the XPath expression.

```
NodeList list = XPathAPI.selectNodeList (doc, match, doc);
```

Further on, the serializer Transformer object handles the deep recursive printing style. This type of serialization transformer prints out the entire XML fragment below an element node. The serializer takes an XML document fragment (pointed at by a node in the output node-set) and prints it to the output stream. Here that stream has been set to System.out.

Since Xalan does not provide built-in methods for the shallow printing style, this NodePrinter class is provided (see below):

```
static void evalXPath(Document doc,
  Transformer serializer, String match,
  boolean shallow) throws Exception {
  System.out.println("==== XPath Expr=" + match);

  NodeList list = XPathAPI.selectNodeList(doc, match, doc);
```

```
    if (list.getLength() == 0) {
      System.out.println("====== Xpath returns nothing ======");
    }
  Node node = null;
  if (shallow) {    // shallow or deep print
    // Shallow print of node list
    for (int i = 0; (node = list.item(i)) != null; i++) {
      NodePrinter.print(node, System.out);
    }
  } else {
    // deep print of node list
    for (int i = 0; (node = list.item(i)) != null; i++) {
      serializer.transform(new DOMSource(node),
                           new StreamResult(System.out));
      System.out.println();
    }
  }
 }
}
```

The `NodePrinter` class implements shallow printing support. Based on the type of DOM node, type-dependent printing code is activated:

```java
import java.io.OutputStream;
import java.io.PrintStream;
import org.w3c.dom.*;

public class NodePrinter {
  public static void print(Node node, OutputStream os) {
    PrintStream ps = new PrintStream(os);
    switch (node.getNodeType()) {
    case Node.ELEMENT_NODE:
      ps.print("<" + node.getNodeName());

      NamedNodeMap map = node.getAttributes();
      for (int i = 0; i < map.getLength(); i++) {
        ps.print(" " + map.item(i).getNodeName() + "=\""
                 + map.item(i).getNodeValue() + "\"");
      }
      ps.println(">");
      return;
    case Node.ATTRIBUTE_NODE:
      ps.println(node.getNodeName() +
        "=\"" + node.getNodeValue() + "\"");
      return;
    case Node.TEXT_NODE:
      ps.println(node.getNodeValue());
      return;
    case Node.CDATA_SECTION_NODE:
      ps.println(node.getNodeValue());
      return;
    case Node.PROCESSING_INSTRUCTION_NODE:
      ps.println(node.getNodeValue());
```

```
            return;
        case Node.DOCUMENT_NODE:
        case Node.DOCUMENT_FRAGMENT_NODE:
            ps.println(node.getNodeName() +
                "=" + node.getNodeValue());
            return;
        }
    }
}
```

Xalan Relative XPath List Utility Implementation

The relative XPath expression list utility, `RelXPathListTester.java`, now takes two different expressions. The first is an absolute location path, which creates the context for evaluating the second expression.

To do this, the node-set returned from the evaluation of the absolute expression becomes the input for evaluating the relative expression. The relative expression is evaluated once for each node in the absolute expression's resultant node-set.

```
static void evalXPath(Document doc, Transformer serializer,
    String absolute, String relative,
    boolean shallow) throws Exception {
  System.out.println("==== Absolute XPath Expr=" + absolute);
  System.out.println("====    Relative XPath Expr=" + relative);

  NodeList list = XPathAPI.selectNodeList(doc, absolute, doc);

  // Print out the entire subtree starting at the selected nodes
  Node node = null;
  if (list.getLength() == 0) {
    System.out.println("====== Xpath returns nothing ======");

  }
  if (shallow) {

    // Shallow print of node list
    for (int i = 0;
        (node = list.item(i)) != null; i++) {
      NodeList innerList =
        XPathAPI.selectNodeList(node, relative, doc);
      Node innerNode = null;
      for (int j = 0;
          (innerNode = innerList.item(j)) != null; j++) {
        NodePrinter.print(innerNode, System.out);
      }
    }
  } else {

    // Deep print of node list
    for (int i = 0; (node = list.item(i)) != null; i++) {
      NodeList innerList =
```

```
        XPathAPI.selectNodeList(node, relative, doc);
    Node innerNode = null;
    for (int j = 0;
        (innerNode = innerList.item(j)) != null; j++) {
        serializer.transform(new DOMSource(node),
            new StreamResult(System.out));
        System.out.println();
    }
  }
 }
}
```

Oracle XDK's XPath Support

With Oracle's XDK, the XPath extensions methods are part of the XDK's XMLNode class that implements the abstract DOM Node class.

XPath API support is built into the standard XDK parser Jar file, xmlparserv2.jar.

Class XMLNode
oracle.xml.parserv2

```
public class XMLNode
implements org.wc3.dom.Node
```

As before only a few selected methods are listed here.

The selectNodes() Methods

```
public NodeList selectNodes(java.lang.String str)
        throws XSLException
```

```
public NodeList selectNodes(java.lang.String str,
                            NSResolver resolverNode)
        throws XSLException
```

The first selectNodes() method evaluates the XPath expression relative to this node (which is the context node). This evaluator method returns a DOM NodeList object containing the resultant node-set. The resolverNode in the second case can be any Document or Element node. It resolves any namespace prefixes.

The selectSingleNode() Methods

```
public Node selectSingleNode(java.lang.String str)
        throws XSLException
```

```
public Node selectSingleNode(java.lang.String str,
                                  NSResolver resolverNode)
        throws XSLException
```

The first `selectSingleNode()` method evaluates the XPath expression relative to this node (which is the context node). This evaluator method returns a single DOM `Node` object. This call only returns the first node from the node-set produced by the evaluator. The `resolverNode` in the second case can be any `Document` or `Element` node. It resolves any namespace prefixes.

The valueOf() Methods

```
public java.lang.String valueOf(java.lang.String str)
        throws XSLException
```

```
public java.lang.String valueOf(java.lang.String str,
                                   NSResolver resolverNode)
        throws XSLException
```

The first `valueOf()` method evaluates the XPath expression relative to this node (which is the context node). Again, the `resolverNode` can be any `Document` or `Element` node. It resolves any namespace prefixes.

Oracle XDK XPath List Utility Implementation

This code fragment shows the XDK specific modifications for the `evalXPath()` method.

With the XDK, the `XMLNode` class provides XPath evaluator methods. The following statement does the actual XPath evaluation in this example:

```
NodeList list = ((XMLNode)doc).selectNodes (match,
    (NSResolver)doc.getDocumentElement());
```

For deep-style XML fragment output, the `XMLNode` `print()` method is used. Once again for *shallow* style output, the `NodePrinter` class provides printing support:

```
static void evalXPath (Document doc, String match,
    boolean shallow)
    throws Exception {

  System.out.println ("==== XPath Expr=" + match);
  NodeList list = ((XMLNode)doc).selectNodes (match,
    (NSResolver)doc.getDocumentElement());

  Node node = null;
```

```
    if (shallow) {
        // Shallow print of node list
        for (int i = 0; (node = list.item(i)) != null; i++) {
        NodePrinter.print(node, System.out);
        }
    } else {
        // Deep print of node list
        for (int i = 0; (node = list.item(i)) != null; i++) {
        ((XMLNode)node).print (System.out);
        }
    }
    }
    }
    }
```

Werken XPath Extension for JDOM

The core JDOM facility, provided by `jdom.jar`, has no native support for XPath evaluation. An optional Extension package is available for XPath evaluation support.

The Werken XPath JDOM Extension library can be downloaded from http://code.werken.com/xpath/. The latest version was (0.9.4), at the time of writing. It is considered a beta release.

The most notable feature that the provided namespace context support is inoperative. (For all practical purposes, the namespace support methods are placeholder stubs reserved for future implementation.)

Two JAR files are supplied as part of the Werken XPath JDOM extension library: `werken.xpath.jar` and `antlr-runtime.jar`. Both are necessary.

Werken XPath Boilerplate

The following code snippet shows how to use the XPath evaluator.

The Werken evaluator does not support namespaces, functions, and variables by default. A separate `ContextSupport` object has to be created and initialized to provide that support. This helper object is supplied as one of the arguments to the `applyTo()` method.

The returned `nodeSet` `List` object can then be manipulated using standard JDOM methods.

```
        XPath xpath = new XPath(xpathExpr);

        // Add standard namespace, functions, and variable support
        // to the context support helper (needed by the evaluator)
        ContextSupport helper = new ContextSupport(
          new ElementNamespaceContext(doc.getRootElement()),
            XPathFunctionContext.getInstance(),
            new DefaultVariableContext());

        List nodeSet = xpath.applyTo(helper, contextNode);
```

Class XPath

com.werken.xpath

```
public class XPath
```

XPath is the Werken XPath evaluator class for JDOM. It provides a variety of methods to evaluate an XPath expression relative to a specific context node.

Constructors

```
public XPath(java.lang.String xpathExpr)
```

This constructor takes an XPath expression string as an argument. Note that this implies that a separate XPath object instance is needed for each XPath expression.

The applyTo() Methods

Usage of a ContextSupport helper object is optional. However, any XPath expressions that have either namespace prefixes or ordinary XPath functions, require a ContextSupport helper object.

```
public java.util.List applyTo(ContextSupport helper,
                              org.jdom.Document doc)
```

```
public java.util.List applyTo(ContextSupport helper,
                              org.jdom.Element ele)
```

```
public java.util.List applyTo(ContextSupport helper,
                              java.util.List nodes)
```

```
public java.util.List applyTo(org.jdom.Document doc)
```

```
public java.util.List applyTo(org.jdom.Element ele)
```

```
public java.util.List applyTo(java.util.List nodes)
```

These helper objects provide XPath evaluation support for the Werken XPath evaluator.

The applyTo() methods evaluate the XPath expression relative to this specific document, element or node list. This evaluator method returns a List object containing the resultant node-set. The additional ContextSupport object can be provided to hold information about the context node for the XPath processor.

```
public java.lang.String getString()
```

This method returns the XPath expression string used in constructing this object.

Class ContextSupport
com.werken.xpath

```
public class XPath
```

The Werken `ContextSupport` class assists the XPath evaluator in handling functions, variables, and namespaces.

Constructors

```
public ContextSupport()
```

This method creates a semantically empty context support object.

```
public ContextSupport(NamespaceContext nc, FunctionContext fc,
                      VariableContext vc)
```

`ContextSupport()` creates a fully initialized context support object.

Selected Methods

```
public void setFunctionContext(FunctionContext fc)
```

```
public void setNamespaceContext(NamespaceContext nc)
```

The first `setFunctionContext()` method sets the function context. For XPath, use this code fragment to get the function context:

```
FunctionContext fc = XPathFunctionContext.getInstance();
```

The second `setFunctionContext()` method sets the namespace context. For XPath, use this code fragment to get the context:

```
NamespaceContext nc = new
  ElementNamespaceContext(doc.getRootElement());
```

```
public void setVariableContext(VariableContext vc)
```

This method sets the variable context. For XPath, use this code fragment to get the variable context:

```
VariableContext vc = new DefaultVariableContext();
```

Werken JDOM XPath List Utility Implementation

The main method creates the JDOM document instance by parsing the input XML file. Next, it reads the XPathList file and starts reading it line-by-line. For each XPath expression read from the list file, the method calls evalXPath() to do the XPath evaluation.

For deep printing support, the JDOM XMLOutputter class provides the necessary functionality. However, shallow printing requires some extra code (which is part of the evalXPath() method).

```java
import java.io.*;
import java.util.List;
import java.util.Iterator;
import org.jdom.*;
import org.jdom.input.*;
import org.jdom.output.*;
import com.werken.xpath.*;

public class JDOMXPath {

    static public void main(String[] argv) {
        try {
            if (argv.length != 2 && argv.length != 3) {
                System.out
                    .println("Usage: java JDOMXPath filename " +
                        "xpathListFile [shallow|deep]");
                System.out.println("        Shallow printing by default");
                System.exit(1);
            }

            SAXBuilder builder =
                new SAXBuilder("org.apache.xerces.parsers.SAXParser");

            // Create the document by parsing an XML file
            Document doc = builder.build(new File(argv[0]));

            // create XML Outputter
            XMLOutputter outputter = new XMLOutputter();

            boolean shallow = (argv.length == 2) ? true
                            : argv[2].equalsIgnoreCase("shallow");
            System.out.println((shallow ? "Shallow" : "Deep")
                            + " JDOM XPath Evaluator Printing mode.");

            BufferedReader is =
                new BufferedReader(new FileReader(argv[1]));
            String line = null;

            while ((line = is.readLine()) != null) {
                evalXPath(doc, outputter, line, shallow);
                System.out.println();
            }
```

```
      System.out.println("Successful XPATH evaluation");
  } catch (Exception e) {
    System.out.println(e.getMessage());
  }
}
```

This version of the `evalXPath()` method is fairly complicated. The standard Werken pattern is easy to see and is straightforward. The complexity is in the formatting and printing code:

```
static void evalXPath(Document doc,
    XMLOutputter outputter, String match,
    boolean shallow) throws Exception {
  System.out.println("==== XPath Expr=" + match);

  XPath xpath = new XPath(match);

  ContextSupport helper = new ContextSupport();
  helper.setFunctionContext(XPathFunctionContext.getInstance());

  // Required if you have any namespace declarations.
  helper.setNamespaceContext(new ElementNamespaceContext(
    doc.getRootElement()));

  // Apply the XPath to the document
  List results = xpath.applyTo(helper, doc);
  if (results.size() == 0) {
    System.out.println("====== Xpath returns nothing ======");

  }
  Iterator iter = results.iterator();

  // Walk the returned nodeSet printing each item
  while (iter.hasNext()) {
    Object it = iter.next();

    if (it instanceof Element) {
      if (shallow) {
        StringBuffer result = new StringBuffer();

        Element ele = (Element) it;
        result.append("<").append(ele.getQualifiedName());

        List attrs = ele.getAttributes();
        for (int i = 0; i < attrs.size(); i++) {
          Attribute attr = (Attribute) attrs.get(i);

          result.append(" ").append(attr.getName())
            .append("=\"").append(attr.getValue()).append("\"");
        }
        result.append(">");

        System.out.print(result.toString());
```

```
          } else {
            outputter.output((Element) it, System.out);
          }

        } else if (it instanceof Attribute) {
          Attribute attr = (Attribute) it;
          System.out.print(attr.getName() + "=\"" +
            attr.getValue() + "\"");

        } else if (it instanceof String) {
          System.out.print((String) it);

        } else if (it instanceof Comment) {
          outputter.output((Comment) it, System.out);

        } else if (it instanceof Document) {
          if (shallow) {
            outputter.output("/", System.out);
          } else {
            outputter.output((Document) it, System.out);
          }

        } else if (it instanceof ProcessingInstruction) {
          outputter.output((ProcessingInstruction) it, System.out);

        } else {    // we have not handled it correctly
          System.out.println("*** it's class=" +
            it.getClass().getName() + " ***");
        }
        System.out.println();
    }
  }
}
```

Using XSLT to Test XPath

XSL can be used for testing individual XPath expressions. Surprisingly, figuring out how to do this was rather difficult.

The XSL stylesheet must select XML output mode and suppress the initial `<?xml?>` declaration. This is done by the `<xsl:output>` instruction.

There is a subtle trick that is needed. XSL provides several built-in `<xsl:template>` rules. These built-in rules may be explicitly overridden in the XSL stylesheet file. If not overridden, all text nodes and attribute values will be printed to the output – which is undesirable.

One further observation is that the `<xsl:copy-of>` does a deep copy of its selected node-set to its output. This is equivalent to the *deep* output printing style in the earlier Java utility examples. For *shallow* printing, an `<xsl:copy>` instruction should be substituted.

This stylesheet only works with absolute XPath expressions. Those expressions are hard coded into the stylesheet (however, you could pass in global parameters via most XSLT processors' parameter mechanisms).

```
<?xml version="1.0" ?>
<xsl:stylesheet version="1.0"
    xmlns:xsl="http://www.w3.org/1999/XSL/Transform">
<xsl:output method="xml" omit-xml-declaration="yes"/>

<xsl:template match="/">
    <xsl:copy-of select="/ServiceConfiguration/RunMode"/>
</xsl:template>

<!-- override the built-in templates for text nodes,
     attributes, and elements (make them do nothing)
-->
<xsl:template match="text() | @*"/>
<xsl:template match="*"/>

</xsl:stylesheet>
```

Summary

In this chapter we've seen some alternative, and in many ways preferable, solutions to the basic parsing techniques used in Chapter 12. There are a growing number of tools for using XPath, and it continues to be an essential component of XSL transformation. In fact, most of the more complex features of XSL are related to XPath expressions. So, in this chapter we've looked at both ways of extracting information from documents and in the underlying technology of how to apply powerful transformations.

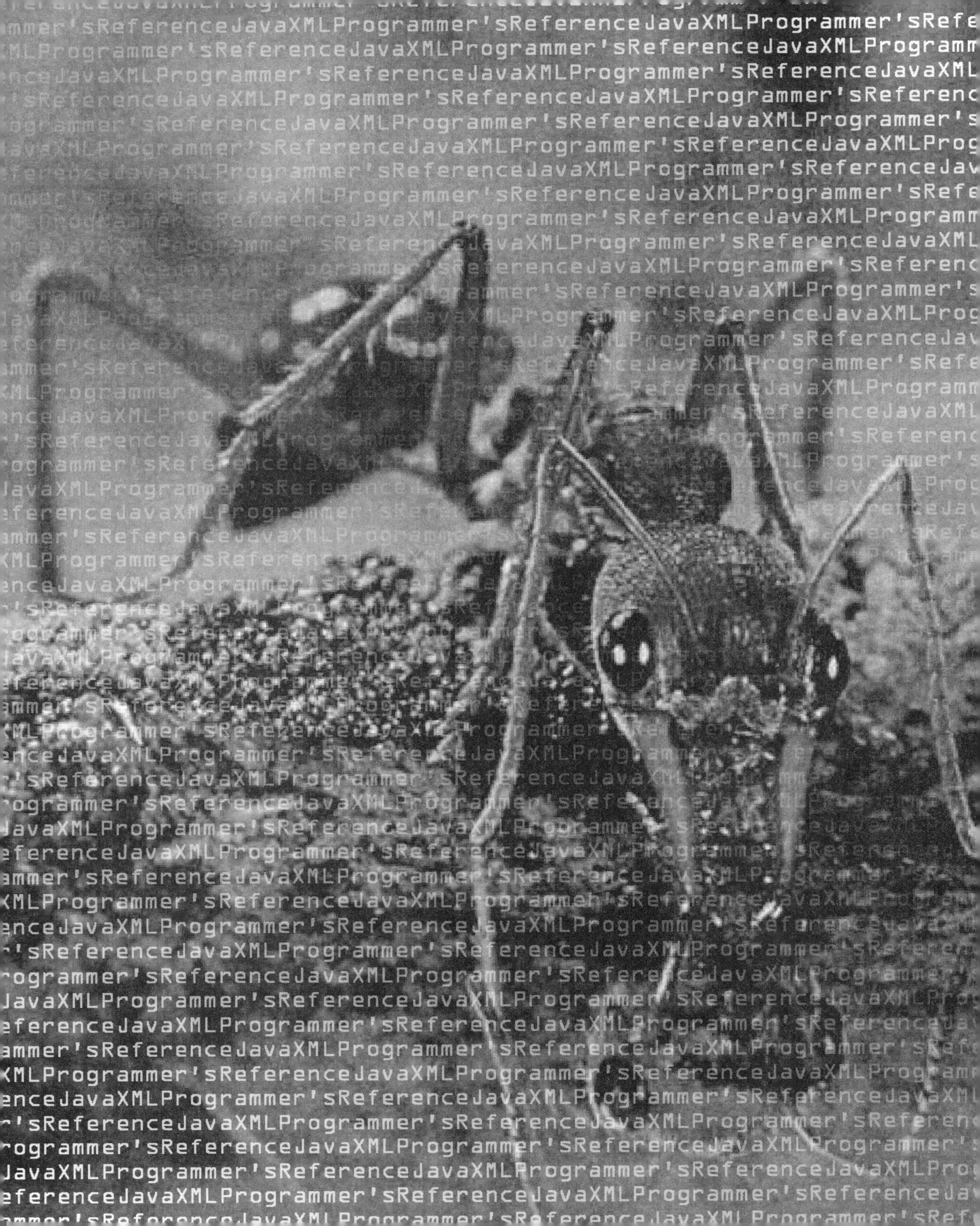

Storing and Retrieving XML

The Auction and Appraisal Management System (AAMS) stores its data in two relational database tables: item and bid. The item table stores details of items that have been submitted for auction, including a unique key for each item, and the bid table stores customer bids for those items referenced by their unique key.

In this project we will build a database service request infrastructure based upon the following requirements:

❑　Requests for data access, search, and update are received as well-defined XML service tickets

❑　Responses, including search results, are returned as well-defined response tickets

In Chapter 15 we add to this infrastructure by exposing the service as a Simple Object Access Protocol (SOAP) web service.

XML validation with respect to system document types stored in a separate XML repository (introduced in Chapter 12) will be required at each appropriate stage of processing since the AAMS does not wish to limit servicing of requests to those generated by its own client applications.

The chapter will focus primarily on illustrating development with XML database tools like Oracle XSU, Sun Microsystems WebRowSet implementation of disconnected rowsets, and JDOM ResultSetBuilder.

We will cover the following:

❑　Introduce the **Request Service** and how it dispatches incoming XML requests, such as item searches, to the appropriate handler classes

❑　Implement retrieving XML results from the database for the item search and item detail requests

❑　Explain how to get XML data into a database for the item update and item bid requests

Project Deployment Sheet

The objective is to develop a package `requestservice.jar` containing handler classes for each type of request. This package will form part of the AAMS server system that is deployed as a web application in Chapter 15. The task of the request service package is to interpret and validate incoming XML requests, execute the required database updates or retrievals, and generate the response XML.

Information Flow

An XML document is received by the AAMS server and dispatched to the appropriate handler class. The handler generates the required SQL code to service the request. The data is generated by the SQL code and the resultset is mapped to an XML representation that is stored in a JDOM document. The document is then serialized as the response ticket that is returned by the AAMS to the client. More detail is contained in the diagram below:

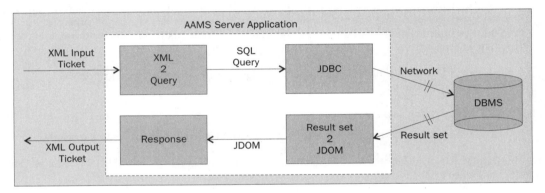

Requirements

The following toolkits are used:

- ❑ Oracle XML SQL Utility (covered in Chapter 7)
- ❑ JDBC Standard Extensions package
- ❑ The early-access release of the JDBC Rowset implementations
- ❑ Xerces-J for parsing/validation
- ❑ JDOM, including a non-standard contributed utility, `ResultSetBuilder`

Details for obtaining, installing, and configuring these for use with the case study are included in Appendix A.

The Files

The following files are in the `src/storingxml` directory of the code bundle:

Example XML Files

These DTD files are stored in `src/storingxml/xmlrepository`:

```
itemsearch.dtd
itemdetail.dtd
itemupdate.dtd
itembid.dtd
```

Java

Package `storingxml`:

```
Bid.java
BidWRS.java
BidXSU.java
BusinessObject.java
BusinessProcess.java
DatabaseService.java
Item.java
ItemBid.java
ItemDetail.java
ItemFactory.java
ItemSearch.java
ItemUpdate.java
ItemWRS.java
ItemXSU.java
RequestResponse.java
RequestResultSet.java
RequestService.java
ServiceRequest.
RequestStatus.java
ServiceRequest.java
```

SQL

A DDL script is contained in:

```
src/storingxml/createtables.sql
```

The Java Code

The coding approach uses object-oriented techniques to develop a hierarchy of examples. The examples use different techniques, but inherit common functionality where possible. Class diagrams are on pages 726 and 736.

Ant Targets

Ant carries out all necessary compilation and deployment for this chapter. See Appendix A for details of how to configure your system. These targets use the dependency structure of Ant to automatically detect and build any required components from other chapters:

```
techniques.storingxml.classpath
```
Call this target and then run the **setcp** script to set the classpath for command-line compilation or testing for this project.

```
techniques.storingxml.compile
```
This will compile the Java code to the `build` directory.

```
techniques.storingxml.deploy
```
Creates the `requestservice.jar` package and stores it in the `apps` folder. This will be incorporated into the main AAMS build in the following chapters.

The Result

We have created the main processing machinery of the AAMS and deployed it as a package `requestservice.jar`.

This project builds a framework that illustrates a variety of different techniques and Java XML toolkits.

The Request Service

The following diagram illustrates the request service machinery in more detail than the schematic flow diagram in the deployment sheet above. We also show how the service configuration utility (Chapter 12) works in conjunction with the request service:

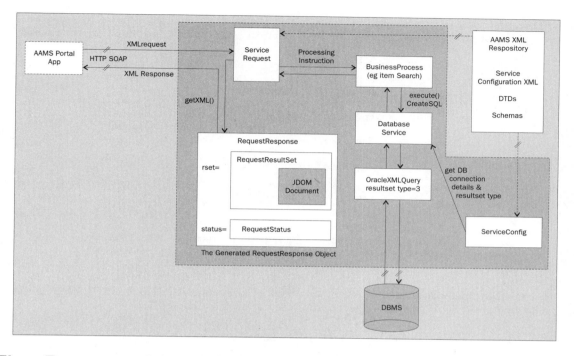

The RequestService Class

The "request service" itself is a deployed SOAP service which will be covered in detail in Chapter 15. The job of the `storingxml.RequestService` object is to expose the more specific services as one unified web service. The actual lower-level service to be invoked is derived from a **processing instruction** in the incoming ticket.

Here is the `RequestService` code:

```
package storingxml;

import org.w3c.dom.Element;
import java.io.StringReader;
import java.io.BufferedReader;
import java.io.ByteArrayOutputStream;
import java.io.ObjectOutputStream;
import java.io.IOException;

public class RequestService {
```

A no-argument constructor is required so we can create an application scope `RequestService` object (Chapter 15) in the AAMS server web application:

```
public RequestService() { }
```

The request service can be invoked using one of two `dispatch()` methods – one taking an `xmlRequest` string and one a `ServiceRequest` object – that return a `RequestResponse` object.

```
public RequestResponse dispatch(ServiceRequest request) {
  RequestResponse response = null;
  if (request != null && request.isValid()) {
    try {
      BusinessProcess bpObject = (BusinessProcess)Class.forName(
                          request.getRequest()).newInstance();
      response = bpObject.execute(request);
    } catch (Exception ex) {
      System.out.println("Error Dispatching Request: " + ex);
    }
  }
  return response;
}

public RequestResponse dispatch (String xmlRequest) {
  return dispatch(new ServiceRequest(xmlRequest));
}
```

The following methods illustrate the standard encoding methods available for building SOAP envelopes with the Apache SOAP toolkit, and will be discussed in detail in Chapter 15.

```
public RequestResponse dispatch(String xmlRequest) {
  return dispatch(new ServiceRequest(
    new BufferedReader(new StringReader(xmlRequest))));
}

public String dispatchSOAPRequest(String request) {
  return dispatch(request).getRequestResultSet().getXML();
}

public Element dispatchLiteralSOAPRequest(String request) {
  return dispatch(request).getRequestResultSet().getDOM()
    .getDocumentElement();
}

public RequestStatus dispatchApacheSOAPRequest(String request) {
  return dispatch(request).getStatus();
}

public byte[] dispatchSOAPBase64Request(String request) {
  RequestResponse resp = dispatch(request);
  ByteArrayOutputStream ba = new ByteArrayOutputStream();
  try {
    ObjectOutputStream p = new ObjectOutputStream(ba);
    p.writeObject(resp);
    p.flush();
    ba.close();
  } catch (IOException io) {
    System.out.println("Exception creating byte array: " + io);
  }
  return ba.toByteArray();
}
```

The ServiceRequest Class

The first dispatch method of `RequestService` takes a `ServiceRequest` object as a parameter. The `ServiceRequest` object is a wrapper, containing the incoming XML request stored in a JDOM object. The code below shows that by providing a wrapper class we are able to isolate the manipulation of the DOM object containing the request to one place. This approach allows us to easily swap out the JDOM implementation with little impact on the rest of the application:

```
package storingxml;

import java.io.BufferedReader;
import java.io.StringWriter;
import java.io.Writer;
import java.io.IOException;
import java.io.StringReader;
import org.jdom.Document;
import org.jdom.Element;
import org.jdom.Namespace;
import org.jdom.ProcessingInstruction;
import org.jdom.input.SAXBuilder;
import org.jdom.output.XMLOutputter;
import org.apache.xerces.parsers.DOMParser;
import org.xml.sax.InputSource;
import org.xml.sax.SAXException;
import configuringxml.ServiceConfiguration;

public class ServiceRequest {
```

The XML representation of the business process is stored in a JDOM document called `requestDocument`. In addition, we have defined constants that will be used to help traverse the XML request. For example, the PARAMETERS_ELEMENT constant defines the name of the `<Parameters>` element in the request that contains the business process parameters:

```
private Document requestDocument;
private boolean valid = false;
public static final String PARAMETERS_ELEMENT = "Parameters";
public static final String DISPATCH_PI = "DispatchInfo";
public static final String REQUEST_PI = "class";
public static final String PARAMETER_OPERATOR = "operator";
public static final String PARAMETER_TYPE = "type";
public static final String STRING_TYPE = "String";
public static final String INTEGER_TYPE = "Integer";
public static final String FLOAT_TYPE = "Float";
public static final String DOUBLE_TYPE = "Double";
```

There are two ways to create a `ServiceRequest` object from incoming XML, either directly from a reader or from a `String`:

```
public ServiceRequest(BufferedReader request) {
  try {
    SAXBuilder sb = new SAXBuilder();
    requestDocument = sb.build(request);
    sb.setValidation(true);
  } catch (Exception ex) {
    System.out.println("Exception creating ServiceRequest " +
      ex);
  }
  valid = true;
}
```

```
public ServiceRequest(String xmlRequest) {
  try {
    SAXBuilder sb = new SAXBuilder();
    requestDocument = sb.build(xmlRequest);
  } catch (Exception ex) {
    System.out.println("Exception creating ServiceRequest " +
      using string: " + ex);
  }
  valid = false;
}
```

In order to process the request, it is necessary to extract any parameters that were included in the XML request. This is done with the help of the getParameter() method:

```
public String getParameter(String parameter) {
  Element parmElement =
    requestDocument.getRootElement()
      .getChild(PARAMETERS_ELEMENT,
        Namespace.getNamespace(ServiceConfiguration.NAMESPACE));
  return parmElement
    .getChild(parameter, Namespace
      .getNamespace(ServiceConfiguration.NAMESPACE))
        .getTextTrim();
}
```

The following code could be replaced with Document.getSerializedForm(), planned to be included with JDOM in the near future:

```
public String toString() {
  Writer xmlOut = new StringWriter();
  XMLOutputter outputter = new XMLOutputter("  ", true);
  outputter.setTrimText(true);
  outputter.setExpandEmptyElements(true);
  try {
    outputter.output(requestDocument, xmlOut);
  } catch (IOException ioe) {
    System.out.println("IOException in toString():" + ioe);
  }
  return xmlOut.toString();
}
```

Once the ServiceRequest object is created and validated, the request service dispatches it by dynamically creating an instance of the BusinessProcess class and calling the execute() method on it whilst passing it the ServiceRequest object as a parameter. The name of the business process class to create and method to call is included, as part of the XML request, in a <DispatchInfo> processing instruction like the one below:

```
<?DispatchInfo class="storingxml.ItemSearch"?>
```

The helper method, getRequest(), is provided on the ServiceRequest object to provide assistance in extracting the class and method information.

```
public String getRequest() {
    String request = null;
    ProcessingInstruction pi =
      requestDocument.getProcessingInstruction(DISPATCH_PI);
    if (pi != null) {
      request = pi.getValue(REQUEST_PI);
    }
    return request;
  }
```

In order to make sure that only valid requests are processed, each request is validated. To facilitate this, the isValid() method is called by the request service on each ServiceRequest object prior to dispatching it.

```
public boolean isValid() {
    return valid;
  }
```

In order to allow the underlying JDOM document to be used by other processes, the getJDOM() accessor is provided.

```
public org.jdom.Document getJDOM() {
    return requestDocument;
  }
```

Finally, the getDOM() method will convert the JDOM document to a W3C Document that can easily be used to interchange with other DOM based systems.

```
public org.w3c.dom.Document getDOM() {
    org.w3c.dom.Document domDocument = null;
    DOMParser domParser = new DOMParser();
    try {
      domParser
        .setFeature("http://xml.org/sax/features/validation", true);
      domParser
        .setFeature("http://xml.org/sax/features/namespaces", true);
      domParser.parse(new InputSource(
        new StringReader(this.toString())));
    } catch (SAXException se) {
      System.out.println("SAXException " +
        "converting Request to DOM: " + se);
      se.printStackTrace();
    } catch (IOException ioe) {
      System.out.println("IOException " +
        "converting Request to DOM: " + ioe);
      ioe.printStackTrace();
    }
    return domParser.getDocument();
  }
}
```

The first constructor in the ServiceRequest class takes a BufferedReader as a parameter. In addition to providing flexibility of input, this constructor allows the ServiceReqest object to be created directly from XML sent in the input stream of the request parameter of the HttpServlet.doPost() method of a servlet as shown below:

725

```
    public void doPost(HttpServletRequest request,
        HttpServletResponse response)
        throws ServletException, IOException {

    ServiceRequest serviceRequest =
        new ServiceRequest(request.getReader());
}
```

The second `ServiceRequest` constructor uses the first constructor to create the `ServiceRequest`.

Business Processes

Business process objects handle all of the business functionality of the application:

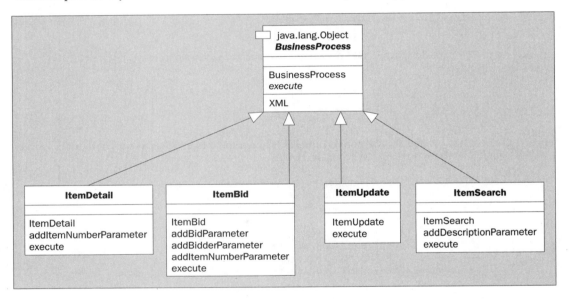

Each `BusinessProcess` object must implement an `execute()` method that is responsible for performing the business logic needed to satisfy the request. This method may employ whatever enterprise services – including database and LDAP access – which are necessary to accomplish the task. This allows the request service to use polymorphism to call the corresponding `BusinessProcess.execute()` method at run time.

The ItemSearch Request

The first business process we need to provide is the ability to return a list of items matching a particular set of criteria. This will be satisfied by the `ItemSearch` request.

In the following we illustrate how information required to execute a database request can be stored in a declarative manner that decouples us from the SQL itself.

Document Type Definition

Since the request service validates each request before dispatching it, the following DTD is needed for incoming `ItemSearch` requests:

```
<!ELEMENT Request (UserProfile, Parameters*)>
<!ATTLIST Request
      name (ItemSearch) #REQUIRED
>
<!ELEMENT Parameters ((Description | ItemId)*)>
<!ELEMENT Description (#PCDATA)>
```

The request is composed of the basic user profile and parameter information. The two possible parameters, `<Description>` and `<ItemId>`, must provide a type and operator that will be used to build the search criteria. Including the following `ATTLIST` in the DTD will enforce this:

```
<!ATTLIST Description
      type (String) #REQUIRED
......operator (1 | 4) #REQUIRED
>
<!ELEMENT ItemId (#PCDATA)>
<!ATTLIST ItemId
......type (Integer) #REQUIRED
......operator (1 | 2 | 3) #REQUIRED
>
<!ELEMENT UserProfile (#PCDATA)>
```

Since an enumerated attribute list can only contain values that are valid XML names, it is necessary to create lookup values for operation symbols (=, <, and >) that are not allowed in an XML name. We use the following associations:

- ❑ = is represented by a 1
- ❑ > is represented by a 2
- ❑ < is represented by a 3
- ❑ The LIKE operator is represented by a 4

ItemSearch Request Example

Using this DTD and our knowledge of the required `DispatchInfo` processing instruction it is possible to derive the following `ItemSearch` request example:

```
<?xml version="1.0" encoding="UTF-8"?>
<?DispatchInfo class="storingxml.ItemSearch"?>
<Request
    xmlns:jxpr="http://www.wrox.com/javaxmlref"
    name="ItemSearch">
  < UserProfile/>
  <Parameters>
    <Description type="String" operator="4">IBM%</Description>
  </Parameters>
</Request>
```

Note that the `<UserProfile>` element remains unimplemented and unused in this case study. We could employ here for instance data extracted from the web request to determine database access rights and to fine-tune the response.

The execute() Method of ItemSearch

The first thing that the `execute()` method does is build the SQL statement that will be used to satisfy the search. This is done by starting with a base SQL statement and dynamically building the WHERE clause to include all of the `<Parameter>` elements. Since we know that, in order for the request to be a valid `ItemSearch` request, it must include type and operator attribute with each parameter, we are able to build the entire SQL WHERE clause dynamically:

```
public RequestResponse execute(ServiceRequest req) {
   String sqlStmt = "SELECT * FROM item ";
   String whereClause = " ";
```

Iterate through adding the search parameters to the SQL WHERE clause:

```
Node parmNode =
   (Node) req.getDOM()
     .getElementsByTagNameNS(ServiceConfiguration.NAMESPACE,
        req.PARAMETERS_ELEMENT).item(0);
NodeList parmList = parmNode.getChildNodes();
int numberOfParms = parmList.getLength();
if (numberOfParms > 0) {
  whereClause = "";
```

The following code iterates through a conjunction of search criteria encoded in `<Parameter>`:

```
for (int parmCount = 0;
        parmCount < numberOfParms; parmCount++) {
  Node currentNode = (Node) parmList.item(parmCount);
  if (currentNode.getNodeType() == Node.ELEMENT_NODE) {
    if (whereClause.length() == 0) {
      whereClause = " where ";
    } else {
      whereClause = whereClause + " and ";
    }
    Element currentParm = (Element) currentNode;
    switch (Integer.parseInt(
      currentParm.getAttribute(
        req.PARAMETER_OPERATOR).trim())) {
    case EQUAL:
      whereClause = whereClause +
        currentParm.getLocalName() + " = ";
      break;
    case GREATER:
      whereClause = whereClause +
        currentParm.getLocalName() + " > ";
      break;
    case LESS:
      whereClause = whereClause +
        currentParm.getLocalName() + " < ";
```

```
        break;
      case LIKE:
        whereClause = whereClause +
          currentParm.getLocalName() + " like ";
        break;
    }
    if (currentParm.getAttribute(req.PARAMETER_TYPE).trim()
        .equals(req.STRING_TYPE)) {
      whereClause =
        whereClause + "'"
        + currentParm.getFirstChild()
          .getNodeValue()
            .trim() + "'";
    } else {
      whereClause =
        whereClause
        + currentParm.getFirstChild().getNodeValue().trim();
    }
  }
}
}
}
```

Now we extract the `RequestResponse` object (see the diagram on page 721) by executing the SQL on the database connection:

```
  RequestResponse resp =
    new RequestResponse(DatabaseService.getInstance()
      .executeQuery(sqlStmt + whereClause));
  resp.setStatus(new RequestStatus(true, "Search Completed"));
  return resp;
}
```

The RequestResultSet Object

Like the `ServiceRequest` object (see page 723), the `RequestResultSet` object below is a wrapper that represents the result set from the query. The underlying result set is stored in a JDOM document:

```
package storingxml;

import java.io.Writer;
import java.io.StringWriter;
import java.io.StringReader;
import java.io.IOException;
import java.sql.ResultSet;
import java.sql.Connection;
import java.sql.ResultSetMetaData;
import org.jdom.Document;
import org.jdom.JDOMException;
import org.jdom.output.XMLOutputter;
import org.jdom.output.DOMOutputter;
import org.jdom.input.SAXBuilder;
import org.jdom.contrib.input.ResultSetBuilder;
import org.apache.xerces.dom.DocumentImpl;
import oracle.xml.sql.query.OracleXMLQuery;
```

```
import sun.jdbc.rowset.WebRowSet;
import configuringxml.ServiceConfiguration;

public class RequestResultSet implements java.io.Serializable {
  Document resultSetDOM;
```

The constructor will create the `RequestResultSet` object using the `<ResultSet>` type defined in the `serviceconfiguration.xml` file (described in Chapter 12) and then `ResultSet` passed into it:

```
public RequestResultSet(ResultSet rset, Connection conn) {
  switch (Integer
          .parseInt(ServiceConfiguration.getInstance()
            .getProperty("ResultSetType"))) {
  case ServiceConfiguration.RB_RESULT_TYPE:
    System.out.println("Using JDOM ResultSetBuilder");
    buildResultBuilder(rset);
    break;

  case ServiceConfiguration.STRING_RESULT_TYPE:
    System.out.println("Using Manual ResultSet Builder");
    buildJDBCResultSetDOM(rset);
    break;

  case ServiceConfiguration.XSU_RESULT_TYPE:
    System.out.println("Using Oracle XSU");
    buildJDBCResultSetXSU(rset, conn);
    break;

  case ServiceConfiguration.WRS_RESULT_TYPE:
    System.out.println("Using RowSet implementation");
    buildWebRowSet(rset);
    break;
  default:
    System.out.println("Using manual JDBC by default");
    buildJDBCResultSetDOM(rset);
    break;
  }
}

public RequestResultSet(String resultSetXML) {
  setResultDOM(resultSetXML);
}

private void setResultDOM(String xml) {
  try {
    SAXBuilder sb = new SAXBuilder();
    resultSetDOM = sb.build(new StringReader(xml));
  } catch (Exception ex) {
    System.out.println("Exception setting XML " +
      "string into JDOM Result " + ex);
  }
}
```

The getXML() method will obtain a serialized version of the XML. Eventually, this functionality will be included in the Document.getSerializedForm(). However, this was not implemented at the time of writing:

```
public String getXML() {
  Writer xmlOut = new StringWriter();
  XMLOutputter outputter = new XMLOutputter("  ", true);
  outputter.setTrimText(true);
  outputter.setExpandEmptyElements(true);
  try {
    outputter.output(resultSetDOM, xmlOut);
  } catch (IOException ioe) {
    System.out.println("IOException in toString():" + ioe);
  }
  return xmlOut.toString();
}

public org.w3c.dom.Document getDOM() {
  org.w3c.dom.Document domDocument = null;

  // Create a DOM object from the JDOM Document
  DOMOutputter domOutputter =
    new DOMOutputter("org.jdom.adapters.XercesDOMAdapter");
  try {
    domDocument = domOutputter.output(resultSetDOM);
  } catch (JDOMException je) {
    System.out.println("JDOMException in getDOM() " + je);
  }
  return domDocument;
}
```

Using Hand-Coded XML

The buildJDBCResultSetDOM() method builds the RequestResultSet object by looping through the JDBC resultset and building the XML as a string.

```
private void buildJDBCResultSetDOM(ResultSet rset) {
  try {
    StringBuffer result =
      new StringBuffer(
        "<?xml version=\"1.0\" encoding=\"UTF-8\" ?> ");
    result.append("<result>");
    ResultSetMetaData metaData = rset.getMetaData();
    int numFields = metaData.getColumnCount();
    System.out.println("num field: " + numFields);
    int rowCount = 1;
    while (rset.next()) {
      result.append("<row rowNumber= \"");
      result.append(rowCount);
      result.append("\" >");
      for (int currField = 1;
          currField <= numFields; currField++) {
        result.append("<column name=\"");
        result.append(metaData.getColumnName(currField));
        result.append("\">");
```

This solution will not escape special characters:

```
        result.append(rset.getString(currField));
        result.append("</column>");
    }

    result.append("</row>");
    rowCount++;
  }
  result.append("</result>");
  setResultDOM(result.toString());
} catch (Exception ex) {
  System.out.println("Exception converting to JDOM:   " + ex);
}
}
```

Below is an example of the XML produced for a completed `ItemSearch` request:

```
<?xml version="1.0" encoding="UTF-8"?>
<result>
  <row rowNumber="1">
    <column name="ITEMID">2</column>
    <column name="DESCRIPTION">IBM Net Server</column>
    <column name="VALUE">6300.45</column>
  </row>
</result>
```

> Since the data from the database may contain special characters such as & and <, a more robust implementation of this approach would encode these values with their XML equivalent entity values, & and < respectively, before adding it to the String.

Using JDOM ResultSetBuilder

As part of the 1.0 version of JDOM, there are only two builders included in the core package, `SAXBuilder` and `DOMBuilder`. However, like most open source projects, there is constant development and continued improvement of the tool. To support this, an additional `org.jdom.contrib` package is provided and can currently be accessed via CVS from http://cvs.jdom.org/. One of the components in the `contrib` package is a ResultSetBuilder. As the name implies, the `ResultSetBuilder` builder will create a JDOM `Document` from a JDBC `ResultSet`.

Like most of the JDOM API, the usage of the `ResultSetBuilder` class is straightforward as shown below in the `buildResultBuilder()` method of the `RequestResultSet` class:

```
private void buildResultBuilder(ResultSet rset) {
  try {
    ResultSetBuilder rsb = new ResultSetBuilder(rset);
    resultSetDOM = rsb.build();
  } catch (JDOMException je) {
    System.out.println("JDOMException: " + je);
  }
}
```

This will take the JDBC `resultset` from the `ItemSearch` query and generate the following XML output:

```
<?xml version="1.0" encoding="UTF-8"?>
<result>
  <entry>
    <ITEMID>2</ITEMID>
    <DESCRIPTION>IBM Net Server</DESCRIPTION>
    <VALUE>6300.45</VALUE>
  </entry>
</result>
```

Using Oracle XSU

The Oracle XML SQL Utility is intended to provide a simple way to transform relational data into XML for the purposes of communication. The `buildJDBCResultSetXSU()` method in the `RequestResultSet` object below will create an XML document from the `ItemSearch` result set:

```
public void buildJDBCResultSetXSU(ResultSet rset,
    Connection conn) {
  OracleXMLQuery query = new OracleXMLQuery(conn, rset);
  setResultDOM(query.getXMLString());
}
```

Like the JDOM `ResultSetBuilder` example, using XSU is very straightforward. Given a JDBC 2.0 compliant connection and the JDBC resultset, the following XML is generated by the `OracleXMLQuery` constructor:

```
<?xml version="1.0" encoding="UTF-8"?>
<ROWSET>
  <ROW num="1">
    <ITEMID>2</ITEMID>
    <DESCRIPTION>IBM Net Server</DESCRIPTION>
    <VALUE>6300.45</VALUE>
  </ROW>
  <ROW num="2">
    <ITEMID>6</ITEMID>
    <DESCRIPTION>Compaq Presario 5310</DESCRIPTION>
    <VALUE>800.53</VALUE>
  </ROW>
</ROWSET>
```

Unlike the JDOM `ResultSetBuilder` technique, XSU provides the ability to customize the XML that is output. For example, we can change the row and column elements to more meaningful names by adding the following method calls to the `buildJDBCResultSetXSU()` method:

```
query.setRowsetTag("Items");
query.setRowTag("Item");
```

This would result in the following XML to be stored in the underlying JDOM object in the `RequestResultSet`:

```
<?xml version="1.0" encoding="UTF-8"?>
<Items>
  <Item num="1">
    <ID>2</ID>
    <DESCRIPTION>IBM Net Server</DESCRIPTION>
    <VALUE>6300.45</VALUE>
  </Item>
</Items>
```

Using WebRowSet

Sun has produced several reference implementations of the JDBC standard extension
`javax.sql.RowSet` interface, including `CachedRowSet` and `WebRowSet` class. A `CachedRowSet`
provides a way to derive a data model from an original resultset that can be updated while
disconnected from the database. The rowset can then be intermittently synchronized with the original
data model. A `WebRowSet` object extends a `CachedRowSet` object and adds the ability to read in and
write out itself as XML.

The `ItemSearch` request is processed by `WebRowSet` by calling the
`buildJDBCResultSetRowSet()` method shown below:

```
public void buildWebRowSet(ResultSet rset) {
  Writer result = result = new StringWriter();
  try {
    WebRowSet.writeXml(rset, result);
    setResultDOM(result.toString());
  } catch (Exception ex) {
    System.out.println("Exception creating WebRowSet XML " +
      "from ResultSet " + ex);
  }
}
```

Like XSU and the JDOM `ResultSetBuilder` options, the JDBC resultset is used as a parameter to
generate the XML. In the case of the `WebRowSet` class, a static method is called that will store the
following XML in a `StringWriter` object:

```
<?xml version="1.0" encoding="UTF-8"?>
<!DOCTYPE RowSet PUBLIC "-//Sun Microsystems, Inc.//DTD RowSet//EN"
"http://java.sun.com/j2ee/dtds/RowSet.dtd">
<RowSet>
  <properties>
    <command>
      <null></null>
    </command>
    <concurrency>1007</concurrency>
    <datasource>
      <null></null>
    </datasource>
    <escape-processing>true</escape-processing>
    <fetch-direction>0</fetch-direction>
    <fetch-size>0</fetch-size>
    <isolation-level>2</isolation-level>
    <key-columns></key-columns>
```

```
        <map></map>
        <max-field-size>0</max-field-size>
        <max-rows>0</max-rows>
        <query-timeout>0</query-timeout>
        <read-only>true</read-only>
        <rowset-type>1004</rowset-type>
        <show-deleted>false</show-deleted>
        <table-name>
           <null></null>
        </table-name>
        <url>
           <null></null>
        </url>
      </properties>
      <metadata>
        <column-count>3</column-count>
        <column-definition>
           <column-index>1</column-index>
           <auto-increment>false</auto-increment>
           <case-sensitive>false</case-sensitive>
           <currency>true</currency>
           <nullable>0</nullable>
           <signed>true</signed>
           <searchable>true</searchable>
           <column-display-size>21</column-display-size>
           <column-label>ITEMID</column-label>
           <column-name>ITEMID</column-name>
           <schema-name></schema-name>
           <column-precision>10</column-precision>
           <column-scale>0</column-scale>
           <table-name></table-name>
           <catalog-name></catalog-name>
           <column-type>2</column-type>
           <column-type-name>NUMBER</column-type-name>
        </column-definition>
      </metadata>
```

Only one column definition (out of three) is shown here. The actual data is stored here:

```
      <data>
        <row>
           <col>2</col>
           <col>IBM Net Server</col>
           <col>6300.45</col>
        </row>
      </data>
   </RowSet>
```

Once the XML above is generated, it is placed into the JDOM object that is returned as part of the RequestResultSet. By creating the RequestResultSet class as a wrapper, it is possible for us to later replace the JDOM implementation with a different implementation.

The BusinessObject Class

The other business process classes (ItemDetail, ItemUpdate and ItemBid) use a BusinessObject to store data:

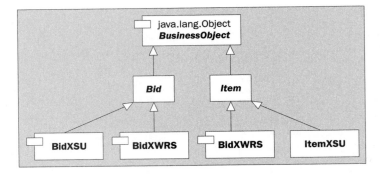

The code for the abstract BusinessObject class is given below:

```java
package storingxml;

import java.io.StringWriter;
import org.w3c.dom.Document;
import org.apache.xml.serialize.OutputFormat;
import org.apache.xml.serialize.XMLSerializer;

public abstract class BusinessObject {

  private boolean valid = false;
  protected Document objectDOM;

  public String getXML() {
    OutputFormat format = new OutputFormat(objectDOM);
    StringWriter stringOut = new StringWriter();
    XMLSerializer serial = new XMLSerializer(stringOut, format);
    try {
      serial.asDOMSerializer();
      serial.serialize(objectDOM.getDocumentElement());
    } catch (Exception ex) {
      System.out.println("Exception: " + ex);
    }
    return stringOut.toString();
  }

  public boolean isValid() {
    return valid;
  }

  protected void setValid(boolean value) {
    valid = value;
  }
}
```

The abstract `BusinessObject` stores the underlying data for the item in a DOM `Document` and provides several helper methods to display the XML and check the item's validity.

There are two further abstract classes that extend `BusinessObject`: `Item` and `Bid`.

The Item Class

The `Item` object represents an item that is made available by one of the customers of the appraisal company. It contains information such as the description and appraised value:

```java
package storingxml;

public abstract class Item extends BusinessObject {

  public static final String ITEM_TABLE = "item";
  public static final String ITEM_SELECT_SQL =
    "SELECT * FROM item, bid WHERE item.itemid = " +
      "bid.item_id AND item.itemid =";
  public static final String ITEM_ID_COLUMN = "ItemId";
  public static final String ITEM_DESCRIPTION_COLUMN =
    "Description";
  public static final String ITEM_VALUE_COLUMN = "Value";

  public abstract boolean setValue(double value);
  public abstract boolean setDescription(String description);
  public abstract boolean update();
}
```

Like the `ServiceConfiguration` object, the `Item` object is an abstract class that will defer to its descendants for the actual implementation. These concrete classes will implement the `Item` object via XSU and `WebRowSet` class.

Each of the concrete classes, `ItemXSU` and `ItemWRS`, must implement a pair of mutator methods that will set the values of the item's appraised value and its description. In addition, each descendant must implement an update method that will be responsible for persisting the item to the database.

The Bid Class

The other descendant of the `BusinessObject` abstract class is the `Bid` class:

```java
package storingxml;

import org.w3c.dom.Document;

public abstract class Bid extends BusinessObject {

  protected Document bidDOM;
  public static final String BID_SELECT_SQL =
    "SELECT * FROM bid WHERE id=";
  public static final String BID_TABLE = "bid";
  public static final String ITEM_ID_COLUMN = "item_id";
  public static final String BID_COLUMN = "bid";
  public static final String BIDDER_COLUMN = "bidder";
```

```
      public abstract int getItemId();
      public abstract double getBid();
      public abstract String getBidder();
  }
```

Like the Item object, we have created an abstract Bid object that will serve as our generic interface to creating bids. As the class diagram on page 736, illustrated, the Bid class is accompanied by two concrete implementations, BidXSU and BidWRS.

The BidWRS Class

This implementation of the Bid class uses the WebRowSet API to insert the bid into the database:

```
    package storingxml;

    import sun.jdbc.rowset.WebRowSet;
    import java.sql.SQLException;
    import java.io.StringWriter;

    public class BidWRS extends Bid {

      private WebRowSet wrs = null;
```

The bid is inserted into the database during execution of the object's constructor:

```
    public BidWRS(int itemId, double bid, String bidder) {
      try {
        wrs = DatabaseService.getWRS(BID_TABLE, "SELECT * FROM bid");
        wrs.moveToInsertRow();
        wrs.updateInt(ITEM_ID_COLUMN, itemId);
        wrs.updateDouble(BID_COLUMN, bid);
        wrs.updateString(BIDDER_COLUMN, bidder);
        wrs.insertRow();
        wrs.moveToCurrentRow();
        wrs.acceptChanges();
      } catch (Exception ex) {
        System.out.println("Error inserting bid: " + ex);
      }
    }

    public String getXML() {
      StringWriter xmlString = new StringWriter();
      try {
        wrs.writeXml(xmlString);
      } catch (SQLException se) {
        System.out.println("Exception getting XML from Item: " + se);
      }
      return xmlString.toString();
    }

    public int getItemId() {
      int returnValue = 0;
      try {
        wrs.moveToCurrentRow();
```

```
          returnValue = wrs.getInt(ITEM_ID_COLUMN);
        } catch (SQLException se) {
          System.out.println("Exception getting ItemId: " + se);
        }
        return returnValue;
    }

    public double getBid() {
        double returnValue = 0.0;
        try {
          wrs.moveToCurrentRow();
          returnValue = wrs.getDouble(BID_COLUMN);
        } catch (SQLException se) {
          System.out.println("Exception getting Bid: " + se);
        }
        return returnValue;
    }

    public String getBidder() {
        String returnValue = null;
        try {
          wrs.moveToCurrentRow();
          returnValue = wrs.getString(BIDDER_COLUMN);
        } catch (SQLException se) {
          System.out.println("Exception getting Bidder: " + se);
        }
        return returnValue;
    }
}
```

The BidXSU Class

Inserting a bid using XSU is also done in the constructor of the `BidXSU object`:

```
package storingxml;

import oracle.xml.sql.dml.OracleXMLSave;
import java.sql.Connection;
import org.apache.xerces.dom.DocumentImpl;
import org.w3c.dom.Element;
import org.w3c.dom.NodeList;

public class BidXSU extends Bid {
```

We build the DOM object using the parameters passed into the constructor and then pass it to Oracle's XSU for processing:

```java
public BidXSU(int itemId, double bid, String bidder) {
  try {
    objectDOM = new DocumentImpl();
    Element root = objectDOM.createElement("ROWSET");
    Element row = objectDOM.createElement("ROW");
    root.appendChild(row);
    Element item = objectDOM.createElement(ITEM_ID_COLUMN);
    item.appendChild(
      objectDOM
        .createTextNode(Integer.toString(itemId)));
    row.appendChild(item);
    item = objectDOM.createElement(BID_COLUMN);
    item.appendChild(
      objectDOM
        .createTextNode(Double.toString(bid)));
    row.appendChild(item);
    item = objectDOM.createElement(BIDDER_COLUMN);
    item.appendChild(objectDOM.createTextNode(bidder));
    row.appendChild(item);
    objectDOM.appendChild(root);
  } catch (Exception ex) {
    System.out.println("Exception creating DOM " +
      "for Bid insert" + ex);
  }

  Connection conn = DatabaseService.getConnection();
  OracleXMLSave sav = new OracleXMLSave(conn, Bid.BID_TABLE);
  try {
    int rowCount = sav.insertXML(objectDOM);
    System.out.println("successfully added bid");
    sav.close();
    conn.close();
    setValid(true);
  } catch (Exception se) {
    System.out.println("Exception writing item out to DB " +
      "via XSU: " + se);
  }
}

public int getItemId() {
  NodeList itemList =
    objectDOM
      .getElementsByTagName(ITEM_ID_COLUMN);
  int returnValue = 0;
  if (itemList != null) {
    returnValue =
      Integer.parseInt(
        itemList.item(0).getFirstChild().getNodeValue().trim());
  }
  return returnValue;
}

public double getBid() {
  NodeList itemList = objectDOM.getElementsByTagName(BID_COLUMN);
  double returnValue = 0.0;
  if (itemList != null) {
```

```
        returnValue =
          Double.parseDouble(
            itemList.item(0).getFirstChild().getNodeValue()
              .trim());
    }
    return returnValue;
  }

  public String getBidder() {
    NodeList itemList =
      objectDOM
        .getElementsByTagName(BIDDER_COLUMN);
    String returnValue = null;
    if (itemList != null) {
      returnValue = itemList
        .item(0).getFirstChild().getNodeValue().trim();
    }
    return returnValue;
  }
}
```

Once the XML below is generated, the `OracleXMLSave` utility is used to insert the record into the database.

```
<?xml version="1.0" encoding="UTF-8"?>
<ROWSET>
  <ROW>
    <ID>1</ID>
    <ITEM_ID>1</ITEM_ID>
    <BID>1001.98</BID>
    <BIDDER>dave</BIDDER>
  </ROW>
</ROWSET>
```

Using the Item Object

The first place that the `Item` object is used is in the `ItemDetail` request. The `ItemDetail` request is responsible for retrieving all of the relevant information about an item. The request will take an `ItemId` and retrieve the values for the item from the database.

```
<!ELEMENT Request (UserProfile, Parameters)>
<!ATTLIST Request name (ItemDetail) #REQUIRED>
<!ELEMENT Parameters (ItemId)>
<!ELEMENT ItemId (#PCDATA)>
<!ATTLIST ItemId type (Integer) #REQUIRED>
<!ELEMENT UserProfile (#PCDATA)>
```

The following is a sample `ItemDetail` request:

```
<?xml version="1.0" encoding="UTF-8"?>
<!DOCTYPE Request SYSTEM
    "http://localhost:5202/xml/itemdetail.dtd">
```

```
<?DispatchInfo class="storingxml.ItemDetail""?>
<Request xmlns="http://www.wrox.com/javaxmlref" name="ItemDetail">
..<UserProfile/>
..<Parameters>
    <ItemId type="1">3</ItemId>
  </Parameters>
</Request>
```

In the `ItemDetail` class below, an `ItemFactory` helper class is used to get an instance of the concrete implementation (`ItemWRS` or `ItemXSU`) of the `Item` class. Once the object is obtained using the `<ItemId>` parameter included in the XML request, the XML resultset is returned via a `RequestResultSet` object:

```
package storingxml;

import configuringxml.ServiceConfiguration;

public class ItemDetail extends BusinessProcess {

  public RequestResponse execute(ServiceRequest req) {
    Item currentItem =
      ItemFactory
        .getInstance(Integer
          .parseInt(req.getParameter(Item.ITEM_ID_COLUMN)));
    return new RequestResponse(
      new RequestResultSet(currentItem.getXML()));
  }
}
```

The ItemFactory Class

We use the `ItemFactory` to find the appropriate item and return it back to the `RequestService`.

```
package storingxml;

import configuringxml.ServiceConfiguration;

public class ItemFactory {

  public static Item getInstance(int itemId) {
    Item currentItem = null;
    switch (
      Integer.parseInt(
        configuringxml.ServiceConfiguration
          .getInstance()
            .getProperty("ResultSetType"))) {

    case ServiceConfiguration.RB_RESULT_TYPE:
    case ServiceConfiguration.STRING_RESULT_TYPE:
    case ServiceConfiguration.XSU_RESULT_TYPE:
      currentItem = new ItemXSU(itemId);
      break;
    case ServiceConfiguration.WRS_RESULT_TYPE:
      currentItem = new ItemWRS(itemId);
```

```
      break;
    default:
      currentItem = new ItemXSU(itemId);
      break;
    }
    return currentItem;
  }

}
```

Once the item is found, the XML below is returned back to the request service so it can be returned back to the client application if we are using the XSU ResultType.

```
<?xml version="1.0" encoding="UTF-8"?>
<ROWSET>
  <ROW num="1">
    <ITEMID>1</ITEMID>
    <DESCRIPTION>Gateway PIII 866</DESCRIPTION>
    <VALUE>900.75</VALUE>
  </ROW>
</ROWSET>
```

Since we were using the XSU ResultType, the ItemFactory used the ItemXSU class below to create the XML.

The ItemXSU Class

```
package storingxml;

import java.io.StringReader;
import java.io.IOException;
import java.sql.Connection;
import org.w3c.dom.Node;
import org.xml.sax.SAXException;
import org.xml.sax.InputSource;
import org.apache.xerces.parsers.DOMParser;
import oracle.xml.sql.dml.OracleXMLSave;

public class ItemXSU extends Item {

  public ItemXSU(int itemId) {

    DatabaseService dbs = DatabaseService.getInstance();
    String sqlStmt = Item.ITEM_SELECT_SQL + itemId;
    DOMParser parser = new DOMParser();
    try {
      parser.setFeature(
        "http://xml.org/sax/features/namespaces", true);
      parser
        .parse(new InputSource(
          new StringReader(dbs.executeQuery(sqlStmt).getXML())));
    } catch (SAXException se) {
      se.printStackTrace();
    } catch (IOException ioe) {
```

```
      ioe.printStackTrace();
   }
   objectDOM = parser.getDocument();
}
```

In the `update()` method, after getting a connection from the database service, a new `OracleXMLSave` object is created. This object takes in the connection and the relevant table name in its constructor. Next, the key fields to use for updating the table are set. Finally the updated DOM document is written to the database via the `updateXML()` method:

```java
public boolean update() {
   Connection conn = DatabaseService.getConnection();
   OracleXMLSave sav = new OracleXMLSave(conn, ITEM_TABLE);
   String[] keyColumns = {
      ITEM_ID_COLUMN.toUpperCase()
   };
   boolean returnValue = true;
   sav.setKeyColumnList(keyColumns);
   int rowCount = sav.updateXML(objectDOM);
   System.out.println(" successfully updated " +
      rowCount + " rows in item table");
   sav.close();
   try {
      conn.close();
   } catch (java.sql.SQLException se) {
      returnValue = false;
      System.out.println("Exception writing item out to DB "+
         "via XSU: " + se);
   }
   return returnValue;
}

public boolean setDescription(String desc) {
   setElementValue(ITEM_DESCRIPTION_COLUMN.toUpperCase(), desc);
   return false;
}

public boolean setValue(double value) {
   setElementValue(ITEM_VALUE_COLUMN.toUpperCase(),
                   Double.toString(value));
   return false;
}
```

The `setElementValue()` method updates the underlying DOM object that contains the data for the item object. This updated XML document will be used by the update method to persist the updates to the database:

```java
private void setElementValue(String elementName, String elementValue) {
   try {
      Node xmlElement =
         (Node) objectDOM.getElementsByTagName(elementName).item(0)
            .getFirstChild();
      xmlElement.setNodeValue(elementValue);
```

```
        } catch (Exception ex) {
          System.out.println("Exception setting " +
            elementName + "='" + elementValue + "'" + ex);
        }
      }
    }
```

The ItemUpdate Request

The appraisal company used in our example provides to its customers a certified fair market value for each item. In order to do that, an `ItemUpdate` request must be developed. As the DTD below illustrates, the `ItemUpdate` request follows a similar layout to that of the `ItemDetail` and `ItemSearch`.

```
<!ELEMENT Request (UserProfile, Parameters)>
<!ATTLIST Request name (ItemUpdate) #REQUIRED>
<!ELEMENT Parameters (ItemId, Description, Value)>
<!ELEMENT ItemId (#PCDATA)>
<!ATTLIST ItemId type (Integer) #REQUIRED>
<!ELEMENT Description (#PCDATA)>
<!ATTLIST Description type (String) #REQUIRED>
<!ELEMENT Value (#PCDATA)>
<!ATTLIST Value type (Double) #REQUIRED>
<!ELEMENT UserProfile (#PCDATA)>
```

When submitting an update for an item the `<ItemId>`, `<Description>` and `<Value>` may be provided as a parameter in the XML request. The update request below will update the description and the value of the item with the ID of 1:

```
<?DispatchInfo class="storingxml.ItemUpdate"?>
<Request xmlns:jxpr="http://www.wrox.com/javaxmlref"
    name="ItemUpdate">
  <UserProfile/>
  <Parameters>
    <ItemId type="Integer">1</jxpr:ItemId>
    <Description type="String">Compaq Presario 5410</Description>
    <Value type="Double">789.33</Value>
  </Parameters>
</Request>
```

The request service reads the PI and calls the `execute()` method below on the `ItemUpdate` object:

```
    public RequestResponse execute(ServiceRequest req) {
      Item currentItem =
        ItemFactory
          .getInstance(Integer
            .parseInt(req.getParameter(Item.ITEM_ID_COLUMN)));
      currentItem
        .setDescription(req.getParameter(
          Item.ITEM_DESCRIPTION_COLUMN));
      currentItem
        .setValue(Double
```

```
          .parseDouble(req.getParameter(Item.ITEM_VALUE_COLUMN)));
    currentItem.update();
    return new RequestResponse(
      new RequestResultSet(currentItem.getXML()));
}
```

As with the `ItemDetail` request, the `ItemFactory class` is used to get an instance of the item given the `ItemId` and the `ResultSetType`. Once an instance is obtained, the mutator methods are called to set the values into the object. Finally, the `update()` method is called to persist the item to the database and the resulting XML is returned to the `RequestResponse` object.

The ItemWRS Class

If we are using `WebRowSet` as our `<ResultSetType>` as specified in the service configuration, the `ItemFactory object` will return an instance of the `ItemWRS` object below:

```
package storingxml;

import sun.jdbc.rowset.WebRowSet;
import java.sql.SQLException;
import java.io.StringWriter;

public class ItemWRS extends Item {

  private WebRowSet wrs = null;

  public ItemWRS(int itemId) {
    wrs = DatabaseService.getWRS(
      ITEM_TABLE, ITEM_SELECT_SQL + itemId);
    if (wrs.size() == 1) {
      setValid(true);
    } else {
      setValid(false);
    }
  }
}
```

The `update()` method will set the changes made into the rowset by calling the `updateRow()` method. Next, the changes are written to the database using the `acceptChanges()` method:

```
public boolean update() {
  boolean success = false;
  try {
    wrs.updateRow();
    wrs.acceptChanges();
    success = true;
  } catch (SQLException se) {
    System.out.println("Error updating item " + se);
    success = false;
  }
  return success;
}
```

The `setDescription()` and `setValue()` methods will update the underlying `WebRowSet` object with the values passed into them:

```java
public boolean setDescription(String desc) {
  boolean success = false;
  try {
    if (!wrs.getString(ITEM_DESCRIPTION_COLUMN).equals(desc)) {
      wrs.updateString(ITEM_DESCRIPTION_COLUMN, desc);
      success = true;
    }
  } catch (Exception se) {
    System.out.println("Error setting description " + se);
    success = false;
  }
  return success;
}

public boolean setValue(double value) {
  boolean success = false;
  try {
    if (wrs.getDouble(ITEM_VALUE_COLUMN) != value) {
      wrs.updateDouble(ITEM_VALUE_COLUMN, value);
      success = true;
    }
  } catch (Exception se) {
    System.out.println("Error setting value " + se);
    success = false;
  }
  return success;
}

public String getXML() {
  StringWriter xmlString = new StringWriter();
  try {
    wrs.writeXml(xmlString);
  } catch (SQLException se) {
    System.out.println("Exception getting XML from Item: " + se);
  }
  return xmlString.toString();
}
}
```

As you can see from the `ItemWRS` class above, the `setDescription()` and `setValue()` methods perform their update operations against the `WebRowSet` object. For example, the `setDescription()` method uses the `updateString()` method below to set the value of the `<DESCRIPTION>` column equal to the passed-in value:

```java
wrs.updateString(ITEM_DESCRIPTION_COLUMN, desc);
```

Once the changes have been stored into the underlying `WebRowSet` object by using the mutator methods, the `update()` method writes the object to the database. Calling the `updateRow()` method on the `WebRowSet` object marks the row as modified. Finally the `acceptChanges()` method generates and sends the update SQL request to the database.

> Although this example does not manipulate the XML directly, it is possible to do so using the **WebRowSet** API. This can be accomplished by using the **readXml()** and **writeXml()** methods (see page 734).

The ItemBid Request

The final business process that needs to be fulfilled is to give the users the ability to submit bids on items. This essentially will insert a record into the bid table.

Only the execute() method of the class is described, as the other methods are similar to those described for other business processes. The execute() method creates the appropriate Bid object based on the ResultSetType set in the ServiceConfiguration object.

```java
public RequestResponse execute(ServiceRequest req) {
  Bid bid = null;
  switch (Integer.parseInt(
    configuringxml.ServiceConfiguration
      .getInstance()
      .getProperty("ResultSetType"))) {
  case 1:  // Handler not implemented
  case 2:  // Handler not implemented
  case 3:  // Oracle XSU
    bid =
      new BidXSU(Integer.parseInt(req.getParameter("ItemId")),
        Double.parseDouble(req.getParameter("Bid")),
          req.getParameter("Bidder"));
    break;

  case 4:  // WebRowSet
    bid =
      new BidWRS(Integer.parseInt(req.getParameter("ItemId")),
        Double.parseDouble(req.getParameter("Bid")),
          req.getParameter("Bidder"));
    break;

  default:  // Oracle XSU
    bid =
      new BidXSU(Integer.parseInt(req.getParameter("ItemId")),
        Double.parseDouble(req.getParameter("Bid")),
          req.getParameter("Bidder"));
    break;
  }

  RequestResponse resp =
    new RequestResponse(new RequestResultSet(bid.getXML()));
  if (bid.isValid()) {
    resp.setStatus(new RequestStatus(true, "Bid Accepted"));
  } else {
    resp.setStatus(new RequestStatus(false, "Bid NOT Accepted"));
  }
  return resp;
}
```

The appropriate `Bid` object (`BidWRS` or `BidXSU`) is populated with the bid information, which is then inserted into the database. Note that the processing of the bid occurs in the constructor so that creating the bid object executes the appropriate database logic.

Summary

We've examined a number of low-level approaches to moving data to and from a database in the form of XML, covering Oracle, Sun and JDOM tools. Despite following a number of different trajectories and developing some object-oriented models for the data along the way to illustrate the different tools, we have nevertheless succeeded in our objective of providing a database request service implementation for the AAMS, which we will now proceed to deploy as part of the AAMS server implementation.

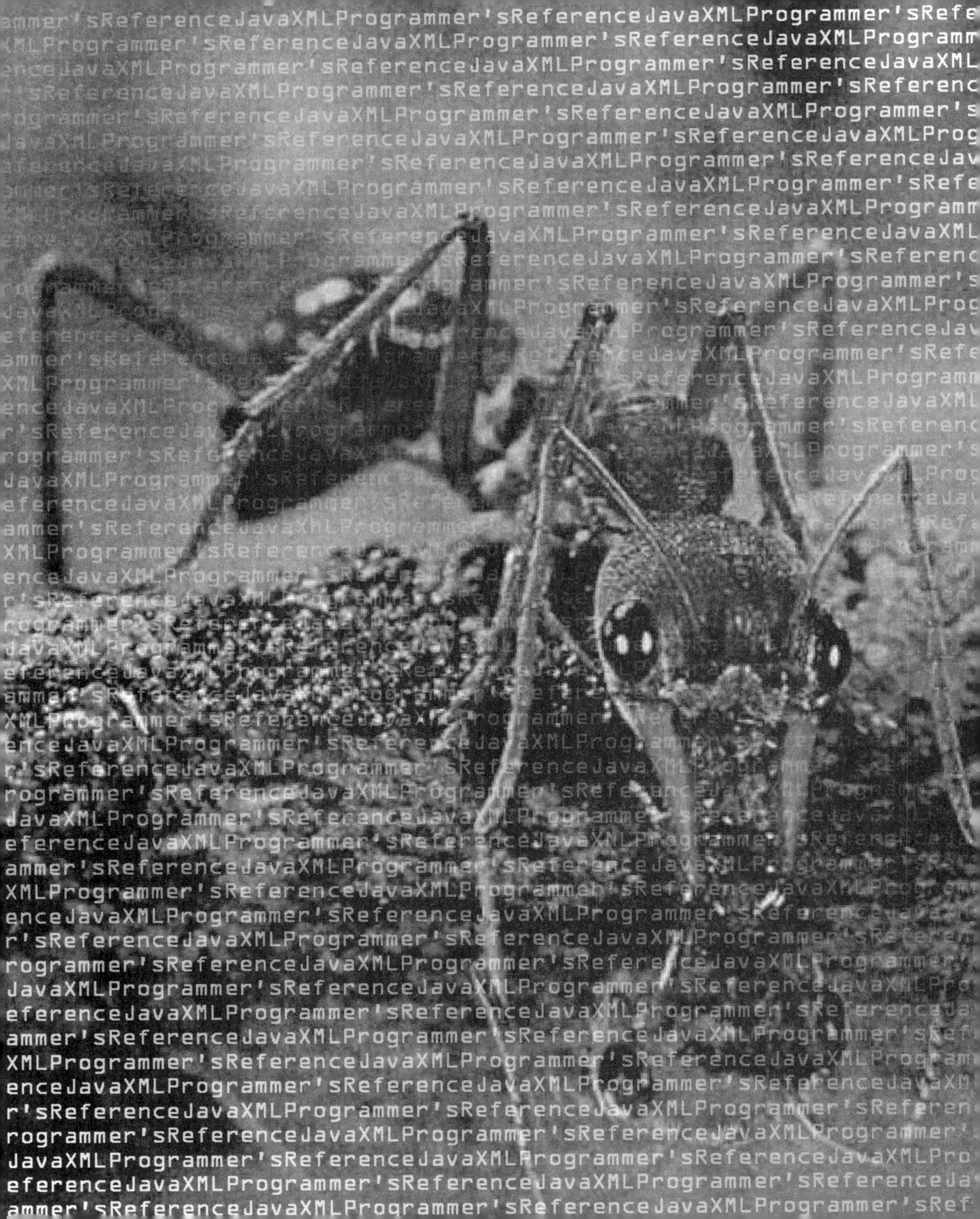
JavaXMLProgrammer'sReference

15

Transmitting XML

The Auction and Appraisal Management System (AAMS) provides an appraisal service (professional valuation) for items, and the ability for customers to bid on those items. The Request Service is an internal service of the AAMS that accepts XML information request tickets and data update tickets, and sends back XML response tickets incorporating data from the system's databases. The request service was covered in Chapter 14. In this project, we cover the part of the system connecting the request service with remote applications.

One of the goals of the AAMS system is to provide a suite of JavaBeans that will allow commercial customers of the AAMS to integrate the request service into their own portals, providing access for the general public to search for, and bid on auction items that have been professionally appraised.

In this chapter we will:

- ❏ Provide web access to the internal request service via the Simple Object Access Protocol (SOAP)
- ❏ Build a JavaBean with a simple API that provides the functionality of the request service directly to the commercial customers' web applications

By deploying the process as a web service via SOAP, we maximize the possibilities for resale of the service, and for reuse of the service within AAMS projects.

These are the tasks:

- ❏ Deploy the request service as a SOAP 1.1 compatible web service
- ❏ Implement a client-side JavaBean to hide the SOAP transport layer from the client
- ❏ Provide a scalable architecture by employing Enterprise JavaBeans to service the requests
- ❏ Integrate a third party web service into the EJBs that will provide currency conversion for international bidders

In doing this, we will illustrate the following techniques:

- ❏ Creating a service descriptor for a SOAP service
- ❏ Creating a JavaBean that can be used in JSP to make SOAP calls to the request service defined in Chapter 14

❑   Creating SOAP versions of the item search, item detail, and item bid requests

❑   Creating a stateless session bean that will provide access to a third party SOAP service that provides currency conversion

Project Deployment Sheet

This project will implement the transport layer between the AAMS client and the internal request service introduced in Chapter 14. In addition, we will implement the integration of a live currency conversion service for normalizing all customer bids to dollars before insertion in the database. This will involve building a remote EJB SOAP client and registering it as a service within Apache SOAP.

Information Flow

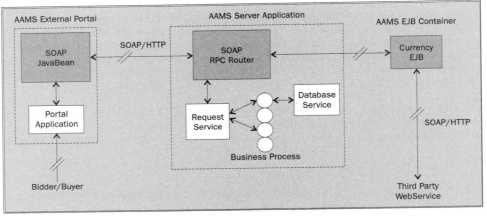

Requirements

There are quite a few requirements for this project. We will need all the toolkits for Chapters 12 and 14. In addition, a Java Servlets 2.3 web server and EJB container are needed to deploy the services. We recommend:

❑   Version 2.2.1 of the open-source JBoss application server; the necessary client libraries are included within its distribution tree

❑   Version 4.0 of Jakarta Tomcat web server. A server configuration file is provided in the code bundle.

❑   The extra toolkits used are:

❑   Apache SOAP 2.2, which needs Xerces-J

❑ JavaMail 1.2

❑ Java Activation Framework 1.0.1

Details for obtaining and configuring the servers and toolkits for use with the automated Ant build script for the case study are included in Appendix A.

The Files

The following files are in the `src/transmittingxml` directory of the code bundle:

XML Configuration

Apache SOAP descriptors for the Request Service and EJB currency service:

```
DeploymentDescriptor-javaxmlref.xml
DeploymentDescriptor-soapejb.xml
```

EJB descriptor files:

```
META-INF/ejb-jar.xml
META-INF/jboss.xml
```

The Java Code

Package `transmittingxml`:

```
SOAPClient.java
SOAPRequestBean.java
EJBRequestService.java
EJBRequestServiceHome.java
EJBRequestServiceBean.java
EJBRequestServiceClient.java
```

A server configuration file for Tomcat 4.0 is in `config/server.xml`.

Ant Targets

Precise details of the resources you need for this chapter are given in Appendix A. All necessary compilation and deployment for this chapter is carried out automatically by Ant.

`techniques.transmittingxml.classpath`
Call this target and then call **setcp** in the prompt window to set the classpath for the chapter on the command line.

`techniques.transmittingxml.compile`
Compiles the code for this chapter and creates `soapjavabean.jar` and `soapejb.jar` in the `apps` directory. These are the client SOAP access bean and the EJB JAR file for the currency service respectively.

`techniques.transmittingxml.deploy`
Bundles Apache SOAP 2.2 and our custom service implementations as a single WAR to Tomcat 4 (or other Servlets 2.3 compatible container). All required libraries are installed in `WEB-INF/lib` of the `aamsserver.war` application.

`techniques.transmittingxml.descriptors`
Remotely configures and deploys the request service and the EJB currency service using `org.apache.soap.server.ServerManagerClient`.

`techniques.transmittingxml.monitor`
Launches a tunnel monitor between ports 8080 and 5202 of the local machine so that you can watch traffic between client and server.

The Result

We have now created the client and server applications for remote execution of `ItemSearch`, `ItemBid`, `ItemUpdate`, and `ItemDetail` via the SOAP protocol. The server is deployed as a single web application with the Apache SOAP `rpcrouter` servlet acting as the front-end. The router servlet dispatches requests to the request service according to the details specified in the XML deployment descriptor, `DeploymentDescriptor-javaxmlref.xml`, for this service.

We have bundled the EJB currency converter service into `soapejb.jar` and deployed it to JBoss. (The server application also contains `soapejb.jar` so that it can obtain a remote reference to the EJB application deployed on JBoss).

We have also created the `soapjavabean.jar` application. This is for use on the remote machine and we will be incorporating it into the client in the project in Chapter 16.

The Service

We will use the Apache SOAP 2.2 implementation to transmit messages from the client to the AAMS server.

This is the descriptor for deploying the AAMS Request Service. For each service, a unique identifier must be provided. This ID will be used to look up the service when a SOAP request is received:

```
<isd:service
    xmlns:isd="http://xml.apache.org/xml-soap/deployment"
    id="urn:javaxmlref-RequestService">
```

After the identifier for the service has been defined, the provider that will process the request must be set. By specifying `java` as the provider type, when the request is received, the specified class will be dynamically created and the method called on it using the Java reflection API. Only the methods defined in the `methods` attribute will be published as part of the service.

```
<isd:provider type="java"
    scope="Application"
    methods="dispatchSOAPRequest dispatchLiteralSOAPRequest
    dispatchApacheSOAPRequest dispatchSOAPBase64Request">
  <isd:java class="storingxml.RequestService"/>
</isd:provider>
```

There are three general types of errors that can occur in a SOAP application: transport errors, SOAP errors, and application errors. A transport error happens when there is a problem with the underlying communication protocol. For example, if the URL specified as the endpoint is not valid, an HTTP error will be reported back to the calling program.

A SOAP error, such as an encoding problem and application errors are processed using fault listeners. We will use the fault listener that comes with Apache to handle any such errors.

```
<isd:faultListener>
    org.apache.soap.server.DOMFaultListener
</isd:faultListener>
```

The SOAP specification is intended to support cross-platform and language-independent development. Consequently, the specification itself can only provide support for low-level datatypes that are available in most languages.

But in addition to providing the functionality defined in the SOAP 1.1 specification, the Apache implementation also provides a way to customize the encoding of objects as they are passed in SOAP calls. The `<xsd:mapping>` portion of the service descriptor defines a custom serializer for a parameter called `status` that is a `storingxml.RequestStatus` object (recall this is a wrapper for a success status information that is created as part of the final response object of any request).

```
<isd:mappings>
  <isd:map
    encodingStyle="http://schemas.xmlsoap.org/soap/encoding/"
    xmlns:x="urn:javaxmlref-RequestService-mapping"
    qname="x:status" javaType="storingxml.RequestStatus"
    java2XMLClassName=
      "org.apache.soap.encoding.soapenc.BeanSerializer"
    xml2JavaClassName=
      "org.apache.soap.encoding.soapenc.BeanSerializer"
  />
</isd:mappings>
</isd:service>
```

The Ant `techniques.transmittingxml.descriptors` target will deploy this descriptor (and one for the EJB service) to the running SOAP server. You'll need to check with Appendix A that you've got the full system configured correctly.

The JavaBean

The client-side JavaBean provides a simple API for accessing the AAMS Request Service. The bean provides the ability for customers to easily integrate the web service client code into their web applications. The bean will be a session bean that will be created for each user.

Specifically, the bean will provide the following methods:

❑ itemSearch() – takes an item description in and returns all the items that will contain the text specified in the description

❑ itemDetail() – will return the detail for an item, given its unique item ID

❑ getCurrencyConversion() – given an amount and the base country it will return the amount converted to US dollars

❑ itemBid() – will place a bid on an item

Normally all of the methods would be developed using a similar approach, however, we are going to use different encoding styles to illustrate their uses.

```
package transmittingxml;

import configuringxml.ServiceConfiguration;
import storingxml.RequestService;
import storingxml.RequestResponse;
import storingxml.RequestStatus;
import storingxml.ItemSearch;
import storingxml.ItemDetail;
import storingxml.ItemBid;
import java.net.URL;
import java.util.Vector;
import org.w3c.dom.Element;
import org.apache.soap.util.xml.QName;
import org.apache.soap.Fault;
import org.apache.soap.Constants;
import org.apache.soap.rpc.Call;
import org.apache.soap.rpc.Parameter;
import org.apache.soap.rpc.Response;
import org.apache.soap.encoding.SOAPMappingRegistry;
import org.apache.soap.encoding.soapenc.BeanSerializer;
import java.io.ByteArrayInputStream;
import java.io.ObjectInputStream;
import java.io.IOException;

public class SOAPRequestBean {
   private RequestService reqService = null;
   private Parameter result = null;
   private URL url;
   private Call call;
```

Note that although our web server is listening on port 5202, we will talk to it on port 8080 and use a tunnel monitor to link between client and server:

```
public static final String SOAP_ENDPOINT =
   "http://localhost:8080/aamsserver/servlet/rpcrouter";
```

The bean constructor will initialize the RequestService and Call objects. Since the bean will be used within a user's session, each bean instance will be unique to each user. Consequently, it is possible to use only one Call object, which will be used to submit all of the requests. The service ID, urn:javaxmlref-RequestService, that we saw in the service descriptor, is used as the target URI. As we will see later, before each method is called, the Call object's state will be modified to reflect the appropriate method and encoding style to use for the call:

```
public SOAPRequestBean() {
  reqService = new RequestService();
  try {
    url = new URL(SOAP_ENDPOINT);
  } catch (Exception ex) {
    System.out.println("Exception creating soaprequestbean");
  }
  call = new Call();
}
```

The invokeMethod() method will be used by the business process methods to dispatch the SOAP request:

```
private Parameter invokeMethod() {
  Parameter result = null;
  try {
    Response resp = call.invoke(url,
      call.getTargetObjectURI() +
      ":" + call.getMethodName());
    if (resp == null || resp.generatedFault()) {
      Fault fault = resp.getFault();
      System.out.println("SOAP call failed: ");
      System.out.println("Fault Code = " + fault.getFaultCode());
      System.out.println("Fault String = " +
        fault.getFaultString());
    } else {
      result = resp.getReturnValue();
    }
  } catch (Exception ex) {
    System.out.println("Exception calling " +
      "SOAP encoded method " + ex);
  }
  return result;
}
```

The itemSearch() method will take in a String description and use it to call the request service.

```
public String itemSearch(String description) {
  ItemSearch request = new ItemSearch();
  String xmlResult = null;
  request.addDescriptionParameter(description);
  call.setTargetObjectURI("urn:javaxmlref-RequestService");
  call.setMethodName("dispatchSOAPRequest");
  call.setEncodingStyleURI(Constants.NS_URI_SOAP_ENC);
  Vector params = new Vector();
  params.addElement(new Parameter(
    "xmlRequest", String.class,
    request.getXML(),Constants.NS_URI_SOAP_ENC));
  call.setParams(params);
  Parameter resultParameter = invokeMethod();
  if (resultParameter != null) {
    xmlResult = resultParameter.getValue().toString();
  }
  return xmlResult;
}
```

The `itemSearchBase64()` method will use the Base 64 encoding supported in SOAP to pass objects via serialized streams:

```
public RequestResponse itemSearchBase64(String description) {
  ItemSearch request = new ItemSearch();
  request.addDescriptionParameter(description);
  call.setTargetObjectURI("urn:javaxmlref-RequestService");
  call.setMethodName("dispatchSOAPBase64Request");
  call.setEncodingStyleURI(Constants.NS_URI_SOAP_ENC);
  Vector params = new Vector();
  params.addElement(new Parameter(
    "xmlRequest", String.class,
    request.getXML(), Constants.NS_URI_SOAP_ENC));
  call.setParams(params);
  byte[] ba = (byte[]) invokeMethod().getValue();
  ByteArrayInputStream istream = new ByteArrayInputStream(ba);
  RequestResponse reqResp = null;
  try {
    ObjectInputStream p = new ObjectInputStream(istream);
    reqResp = (RequestResponse) p.readObject();
    istream.close();
  } catch (IOException io) {
    System.out.println("Exception reading object:  " + io);
  } catch (ClassNotFoundException cnf) {
    System.out.println("Exception reading object:  " + cnf);
  }
  return reqResp;
}
```

The `itemDetail()` method will return the details for an item, using the unique item number that is passed in:

```
public Element itemDetail(int itemNumber) {
  ItemDetail request = new ItemDetail();
  request.addItemNumberParameter(itemNumber);
  call.setTargetObjectURI("urn:javaxmlref-RequestService");
  call.setMethodName("dispatchLiteralSOAPRequest");
  call.setEncodingStyleURI(Constants.NS_URI_LITERAL_XML);
  Vector params = new Vector();
  params.addElement(new Parameter(
    "xmlRequest", String.class, request.getXML(),
    Constants.NS_URI_SOAP_ENC));
  call.setParams(params);
  return (Element) invokeMethod().getValue();
}
```

The `itemBid()` method will place a bid on the item using the item ID, amount, and bidder passed:

```
public RequestStatus itemBid(int itemNumber, double bidAmount,
    String bidder) {
  ItemBid request = new ItemBid();
  request.addItemNumberParameter(itemNumber);
  request.addBidParameter(bidAmount);
  request.addBidderParameter(bidder);
```

```
    try {
        SOAPMappingRegistry smr = new SOAPMappingRegistry();
        BeanSerializer beanSer = new BeanSerializer();
        smr
            .mapTypes(Constants.NS_URI_SOAP_ENC,
              new QName("urn:javaxmlref-RequestService-mapping",
                "status"),
              storingxml.RequestStatus.class, beanSer, beanSer);
        call.setSOAPMappingRegistry(smr);
        call.setTargetObjectURI("urn:javaxmlref-RequestService");
        call.setMethodName("dispatchApacheSOAPRequest");
        Vector params = new Vector();
        params.addElement(new Parameter(
          "xmlRequest", String.class,
          request.getXML(),Constants.NS_URI_SOAP_ENC));
        call.setParams(params);
        call.setEncodingStyleURI(Constants.NS_URI_SOAP_ENC);
    } catch (Exception ex) {
        System.out.println("Error setting up method: " + ex);
    }
    return (RequestStatus) invokeMethod().getValue();
}
```

The `getCurrencyConversion()` method will take an amount in and convert it to United States dollars:

```
public double getCurrencyConversion(double amount,
    String fromCurrency) {
  call.setTargetObjectURI("urn:ejbprovider");
  call.setMethodName("getCurrencyConversion");
  call.setEncodingStyleURI(Constants.NS_URI_SOAP_ENC);
  Vector params = new Vector();
  params.addElement(new Parameter("amount", Double.class,
    Double.toString(amount), Constants.NS_URI_SOAP_ENC));
  params.addElement(new Parameter("toCurrency", String.class,
    fromCurrency, Constants.NS_URI_SOAP_ENC));
  call.setParams(params);
  Double convertedAmt = (Double) invokeMethod().getValue();
  return convertedAmt.doubleValue();
  }
}
```

Example Client

The client code below illustrates how a `SOAPRequestBean` can be used to submit business process requests:

```
public class SOAPClient {
  public static void main(String[] args) throws Exception {
```

Create an instance of the `SOAPRequestBean` and use it to submit business process requests. In practice, the parameters passed to each business process will be variables passed in via a user interface.

```
      SOAPRequestBean client = new SOAPRequestBean();
      System.out.println("SOAP Value:\n" + client.itemSearch("%"));
      System.out.println("Base64 value:\n" +
        client.itemSearchBase64("Compaq%")
          .getRequestResultSet().getXML());
      System.out.println("Literal Value: " +
        client.itemDetail(2).getLocalName());
      System.out.println("Apache Serializer Value:  " +
        client.itemBid(2, 27.02, "pete").getMessage());
      System.out.println("Converted Value:" +
        client.getCurrencyConversion(1000000, "Japan"));
    }
}
```

Here is the output for the code above. Note you will need to have run the deploy target first, and started your web server and EJB container:

```
> ant techniques.transmittingxml.classpath
> setcp
CLASSPATH set to: .\build;.\lib\activation.jar;.\lib\jdom-
contrib.jar;.\lib\jdom.jar;.\lib\mail.jar;.\lib\soap.jar;
.\lib\xerces.jar
> java transmittingxml.SOAPClient
SOAP Value:
<?xml version="1.0" encoding="UTF-8"?>
<ROWSET>
   <ROW num="1">
     <ITEMID>1</ITEMID>
     <DESCRIPTION>Compaq Monitor ER-2343</DESCRIPTION>
     <VALUE>1245</VALUE>
   </ROW>
   <ROW num="2">
     <ITEMID>2</ITEMID>
     <DESCRIPTION>IBM A-Y6 Mainframe</DESCRIPTION>
     <VALUE>10999</VALUE>
   </ROW>
   <ROW num="3">
     <ITEMID>3</ITEMID>
     <DESCRIPTION>Presario Midi Tower with DVD-RAM</DESCRIPTION>
     <VALUE>1925</VALUE>
   </ROW>
</ROWSET>

Base64 value:
<?xml version="1.0" encoding="UTF-8"?>
<ROWSET>
   <ROW num="1">
     <ITEMID>1</ITEMID>
     <DESCRIPTION>Compaq Monitor ER-2343</DESCRIPTION>
     <VALUE>1245</VALUE>
   </ROW>
</ROWSET>

Literal Value: ROWSET
Apache Serializer Value: Bid Accepted
Converted Value: 8357.710000000001
```

The Requests

Each method in the SOAPRequestBean generates an XML request and passes it to a method in the Request Service. To accomplish this, the appropriate business process class is instantiated. Next, any applicable parameters are added to the request. As we saw earlier, the request service then calls the appropriate business process to satisfy the request. The result is then returned as a JDOM document in the RequestResult object.

Item Search

The SOAP 1.1 specification relies heavily on the W3C Schema recommendation. Part of this recommendation is the definition for language-independent datatypes, such as string, float, and integer. For a complete definition of the available datatypes, please see http://www.w3c.org/TR/xmlschema-2/. Apache SOAP 2.2 supports a subset of the primitives defined. This subset includes string, boolean, double, float, long, int, short, byte datatypes.

We will implement the item search request that will use the standard SOAP 1.1 encoding provided in the SOAP 1.1 Specification. In addition, we will illustrate how to take advantage of having the same language on both the client and server to implement a language-specific encoding mechanism.

In the itemSearch() method of the SOAPRequestBean, the description parameter that is obtained from an HTML form, is passed to the ItemSearch request class. Each BusinessProcess contains a base XML request and supporting methods to assist in the addition of parameters to the XML request.

Once the complete XML request has been built, the ItemSearch business process is added to the parameter vector as a string and passed into the dispatchSOAPRequest() method defined on the SOAP service.

Item Search SOAP Request

In Chapter 8, we discussed that the SOAP specification is protocol independent. Support for HTTP and SMTP are provided in Apache's implementation. The AAMS has chosen to implement our services via a HTTP. Consequently, the SOAP request is packaged as part of an HTTP request. The request below contains an example of the item search request that is generated when the itemSearch() method is called on the SOAPRequestBean.

```
POST /aamsserver/servlet/rpcrouter HTTP/1.0
Host: localhost
Content-Type: text/xml; charset=utf-8
Content-Length: 1107
SOAPAction: "urn:javaxmlref-RequestService:dispatchSOAPRequest"

<?xml version='1.0' encoding='UTF-8'?>
<SOAP-ENV:Envelope xmlns:SOAP-ENV =
  "http://schemas.xmlsoap.org/soap/envelope/"
  xmlns:xsi="http://www.w3.org/1999/XMLSchema-instance"
  xmlns:xsd="http://www.w3.org/1999/XMLSchema">
<SOAP-ENV:Body>
<ns1:dispatchSOAPRequest xmlns:ns1="urn:javaxmlref-RequestService" SOAP-
ENV:encodingStyle="http://schemas.xmlsoap.org/soap/encoding/">
```

```
<xmlRequest xsi:type="xsd:string">

&lt;?xml version=&quot;1.0&quot; encoding=&quot;UTF-8&quot;?&gt;
&lt;!DOCTYPE Request SYSTEM
&quot;http://localhost:5202/xml/itemsearch.dtd&quot;&gt;
&lt;?DispatchInfo class=&quot;storingxml.ItemSearch&quot;?&gt;
&lt;Request xmlns=&quot;http://www.wrox.com/javaxmlref&quot;
name=&quot;ItemSearch&quot;&gt;
  &lt;UserProfile&gt;&lt;/UserProfile&gt;
  &lt;Parameters&gt;
    &lt;Description type=&quot;String&quot;
operator=&quot;4&quot;&gt;%&lt;/Description&gt;
  &lt;/Parameters&gt;
&lt;/Request&gt;

</xmlRequest>
</ns1:dispatchSOAPRequest>
</SOAP-ENV:Body>
</SOAP-ENV:Envelope>
```

The first part of the request contains the HTTP headers. This is like any other HTTP POST request in that it contains the method type (POST), the URL of the destination server, and the content of the HTTP request. In addition, there is a SOAPAction variable included. This optional variable is included in the HTTP to provide a means for the web server to redirect the request to the appropriate destination.

The XML part of the SOAP request follows the headers. If you recall from the SOAPRequestBean code, much of the XML is created for us by using the org.apache.soap.rpc.Call class.

By reviewing the XML created on the previous page, you can see that the business process Java String request was represented using an xsd:string type. Again, for more information regarding the SOAP 1.1 encoding and the XML Schema Part 2: Datatypes, see http://www.w3.org/TR/SOAP/ and http://www.w3.org/TR/xmlschema-2/.

Item Search SOAP Response

The response back from the web service is wrapped in an HTTP response:

```
HTTP/1.0 200 OK
Content-Type: text/xml; charset=utf-8
Content-Length: 1174
Date: Mon, 04 Jun 2001 13:04:00 GMT
Server: Apache Tomcat/4.0-b5 (HTTP/1.1 Connector)
Set-Cookie: JSESSIONID=0197C4E993B6B09291F2A4D697281603;Path=/aamsserver

<?xml version='1.0' encoding='UTF-8'?>
<SOAP-ENV:Envelope xmlns:SOAP-ENV=
   "http://schemas.xmlsoap.org/soap/envelope/"
   xmlns:xsi="http://www.w3.org/1999/XMLSchema-instance"
   xmlns:xsd="http://www.w3.org/1999/XMLSchema">
<SOAP-ENV:Body>
<ns1:dispatchSOAPRequestResponse
   xmlns:ns1="urn:javaxmlref-RequestService"
```

```
        SOAP-ENV:encodingStyle=
        "http://schemas.xmlsoap.org/soap/encoding/">

    <return xsi:type="xsd:string">

    &lt;?xml version=&quot;1.0&quot; encoding=&quot;UTF-8&quot;?&gt;
    &lt;ROWSET&gt;
      &lt;ROW num=&quot;1&quot;&gt;
        &lt;ITEMID&gt;1&lt;/ITEMID&gt;
        &lt;DESCRIPTION&gt;Compaq Monitor ER-2343&lt;/DESCRIPTION&gt;
        &lt;VALUE&gt;1245&lt;/VALUE&gt;
      &lt;/ROW&gt;
      &lt;ROW num=&quot;2&quot;&gt;
        &lt;ITEMID&gt;2&lt;/ITEMID&gt;
        &lt;DESCRIPTION&gt;IBM A-Y6 Mainframe&lt;/DESCRIPTION&gt;
        &lt;VALUE&gt;10999&lt;/VALUE&gt;
      &lt;/ROW&gt;
      &lt;ROW num=&quot;3&quot;&gt;
        &lt;ITEMID&gt;3&lt;/ITEMID&gt;
        &lt;DESCRIPTION&gt;Presario Midi Tower with DVD-RAM&lt;/DESCRIPTION&gt;
        &lt;VALUE&gt;1925&lt;/VALUE&gt;
      &lt;/ROW&gt;
    &lt;/ROWSET&gt;

    </return>
    </ns1:dispatchSOAPRequestResponse>
    </SOAP-ENV:Body>
    </SOAP-ENV:Envelope>
```

The first part of the response includes HTTP-specific information including the HTTP response status information regarding the specific server and any settings it has. Next, like the request input parameter, the resulting string response is encoded as an `xsd:string` object and returned back to the requesting client where it can be manipulated as needed.

Passing Objects Using Java Serialization

In addition to supporting the data types defined in the XML Schema Part 2: Datatypes Recommendation, it is possible to use a language-specific encoding mechanism. For example, since both our client and server are written in Java, it is possible for us to use Java serialization to transmit Java objects over a network.

This approach utilizes standard serialization where the objects were written to `ObjectOutputStreams` and then serialized in byte arrays and read back in using `ObjectInputStreams`.

As we saw on page 758, in the `itemSearchBase64()` method, the submission of the item search request is the same as the earlier item search request. The XML SOAP request will encode the request as an `xsd:string` datatype.

After the request service finishes executing the method on the request service below, the result will be returned as a serialized object in a byte array.

Once again the SOAP response is wrapped in an HTTP response. However, unlike the earlier example, the response is encoded as a Base 64 encoded object.

```
<ns1:dispatchSOAPBase64RequestResponse
   xmlns:ns1="urn:javaxmlref-RequestService"
   SOAP-ENV:encodingStyle=
     "http://schemas.xmlsoap.org/soap/encoding/">
<return xmlns:ns2="http://schemas.xmlsoap.org/soap/encoding/"
xsi:type="ns2:base64">
rO0ABXNyABpzdG9yaW5neG1sLlJlcXVlc3RSZXNwb25zZXt7ZSpelxifAgACTAAEcnNldHQAHUxzdG9yaW
5neG1sLlJlcXVlc3RSZXN1bHRTZXQ7TAAGc3RhdHVzdAAaTHN0b3Jpbmd4bWwvUmVxdWVzdFN0YXR1czt4
cHNyABtzdG9yaW5neG1sLlJlcXVlc3RSZXN1bHRTZXTMxYW55943gIAAUwADHJlc3VsdFN1dERPTXQAE0
xvcmcvamRvbS9Eb2N1bWVudDt4cHNyABFvcmcuamRvbS5Eb2N1bWVudDgLkIKz2JPiAgADTAAHY29udGVu
dHQAEExqYXZhL3V0aWwvTGlzdDtMAAdkb2NUeXBldAASTG9yZy9qZG9tL0RvY1R5cGU7TAALcm9vdEVssZW
11bnR0ABJMb3JnL2pkb20vRWxlbWVudDt4cHNyABRqYXZhLnV0aWwuTGlua2VkTGlzdAwpU11KYIgiAwAA
eHB3BAAAAAFzcgAQb3JnLmpkb20uRWxlbWVudKAUGoU3GCMWAwAFTAAKYXR0cmlidXRlc3EAfgAITAAHY2
9udGVudHQAFkxqYXZhL3V0aWwvTGlua2VkTGlzdDtMAAhkb2N1bWVudHEAfgAFTAAEbmFtZXEXQAEkxqYXZh
L2xhbmcvU3RyaW5nNO0wABnBhcmVudHEAfgAKeHBwc3EEAfgAMdwQAAAADdAAECiAgIHNxAH4ADnNxAH4ADH
cEAAAAAXNyABJvcmcuamRvbS5BdHRyaWJ1dGVuYGCD/nIvVgMAA0wABG5hbWVxAH4AEEwABnBhcmVudHEA
fgAKTAAFdmFsdWVxAH4AEHhwdAADbnVtcQB+ABR0AAExdAAACQB+ABp4eHNxAH4ADHcEAAAAB3QABwogIC
AgICBzcQB+AA5wc3EEAfgAMdwQAAAABdAABMXhwdAAGSVRFTU1EcQB+ABRxAH4AGnEAfgAAaeHQABwogICAg
ICBzcQB+AA5wc3EEAfgAMdwQAAAABdAAWQ29tcGFxIE1vbml0b3IgRVItMjM3M3hwdAALREVTQ1JJJUFRJT0
5xAH4AFHEAfgAAcQB+ABp4dAAHCiAgICAgIHNxAH4ADnBzcQB+AAx3BAAAAAF0AAQxMjQ1eHB0AAVWQUxV
RXEAfgAUcQB+ABpxAH4AGnh0AAQKICAgeHB0AANST1dxAH4AEXEAfgAAcQB+ABp4dAABCnhxAH4AC3QABl
JPV1NFVHBxAH4AGnEAfgAaeHhwcQB+ABFzcgAYc3RvcmluZ3htbC5SZXF1ZXN0U3RhdHVzQ23Y0q1905gC
AAJaAADzdWNjZXNzTAAHbWVzc2FnZXEAfgAQeHABdAAQU2VhcmNoIENvbXBsZXR1ZA==</return>
</ns1:dispatchSOAPBase64RequestResponse>
```

> **Note –** This approach will only work when your client and server can interpret the same serialization protocol.

Item Detail

In addition to providing support for a subset of the primitive datatypes defined in the SOAP 1.1 specification, the Apache SOAP distribution also supports literal XML encoding. Literal XML encoding sends `org.w3c.dom.Element` objects as parameters by embedding the literal XML serialization of the DOM tree. The code from the `itemDetail()` method below will enable support for literal XML encoding for the method call.

```
call.setEncodingStyleURI(Constants.NS_URI_LITERAL_XML);
call.setMethodName("dispatchLiteralSOAPRequest");
```

With the exception of the lines above that change the method to call and the encoding style to use, the SOAP invocation is identical to the `itemSearch()` method.

Item Detail SOAP Response

Once the method is called, the following `RequestReponse` portion of the XML response is returned to the `SOAPRequestBean`.

```
<ns1:dispatchLiteralSOAPRequestResponse
   xmlns:ns1="urn:javaxmlref-RequestService"
   SOAP-ENV:encodingStyle=
     "http://xml.apache.org/xml-soap/literalxml">
```

```
<return>
<ROWSET><ROW num="1"><ITEMID>2</ITEMID><DESCRIPTION>IBM A-Y6
Mainframe</DESCRIPTION><VALUE>10999</VALUE></ROW></ROWSET>
</return>
</ns1:dispatchLiteralSOAPRequestResponse>
```

Initially, the response looks very similar to the SOAP 1.1 encoded string result we obtained through the `itemSearch()` method. However, you will notice that unlike the string result, where the return type was set as `xsd:string`, the literal encoded DOM object is embedded directly into the SOAP XML response.

Client Output

By calling the item detail method below, the result from `itemDetail()` method is an `org.w3c.dom.Element` object. As you can see, this object can now be manipulated like any other DOM element we have worked with in the past. We extract the root element to check:

```
Literal Value: ROWSET
```

Item Bid

As we saw earlier, the service descriptor allows for the definition of custom mappings for parameters and their datatypes. Apache provides several custom serializers including `BeanSerializer` and `VectorSerializer`.

> In addition to the included serializers, it is possible to create your own serializer for your objects that implement the `org.apache.soap.util.xml.Serializer` and `org.apache.soap.util.xml.Deserializer` interfaces. By creating an object that implements these interfaces, the custom serializer will write the object out in a manner that will allow it to be transmitted and deserialized by the recipient.

The code segment from the service descriptor below illustrates using a serializer to encode the `RequestStatus` bean in the SOAP response for the item bid request.

```
<isd:mappings>
  <isd:map
    encodingStyle="http://schemas.xmlsoap.org/soap/encoding/"
    xmlns:x="urn:javaxmlref-RequestService-mapping"
    qname="x:status" javaType="storingxml.RequestStatus"
    java2XMLClassName=
      "org.apache.soap.encoding.soapenc.BeanSerializer"
    xml2JavaClassName=
      "org.apache.soap.encoding.soapenc.BeanSerializer"/>
</isd:mappings>
```

As you can see from the XML above, the `java2XMLClassName` and the `xml2JavaClassName` attributes are used to identify the serializer/deserializer that must be available at run time to process the `RequestStatus` object.

The XML request for the item bid is similar to the earlier requests we looked at. The request is encoded as an `xsd:string` object. That request is then sent to the `RequestService` for processing.

Item Bid SOAP Response

Like the other SOAP responses, the item bid response is wrapped in an HTTP response. Since we are using custom serializers, the response will return a serialized version of the `RequestStatus` object below.

```java
package storingxml;

import java.io.Serializable;

public class RequestStatus implements Serializable {
  private boolean success = false;
  private String message;

  public RequestStatus() { }

  public RequestStatus (boolean status, String message) {
    setSuccess(status);
    setMessage(message);
  }

  public boolean isSuccess() {
    return success;
  }

  public void setSuccess(boolean status) {
    this.success = status;
  }

  public String getMessage() {
    return message;
  }

  public void setMessage(String message) {
    this.message = message;
  }
}
```

If you look closely at the `dispatchApacheSOAPRequestResponse` element, you will notice that each attribute of the `RequestStatus` object is converted to its corresponding datatype. For example, the `boolean status` attribute is encoded as an `xsd:boolean` type. This is done automatically by specifying the `BeanSerializer` as the handler for the `RequestStatus` object in the service descriptor.

```xml
<ns1:dispatchApacheSOAPRequestResponse
  xmlns:ns1="urn:javaxmlref-RequestService"
  SOAP-ENV:encodingStyle=
    "http://schemas.xmlsoap.org/soap/encoding/">
<return
  xmlns:ns2="urn:javaxmlref-RequestService-mapping"
  xsi:type="ns2:status">
<message xsi:type="xsd:string">Bid Accepted</message>
<success xsi:type="xsd:boolean">true</success>
</return>
</ns1:dispatchApacheSOAPRequestResponse>
```

Client Output

Once the `itemBid()` method is called on the `SOAPRequestBean`, the `RequestStatus` object returned could be accessed like any other Java object. For example, the code will print out the message text contained in the status object:

```
Apache Serializer Value: Bid Accepted
```

Debugging the Request

As part of the SOAP distribution offered by the Apache group, they include a Java based monitoring tool that allows Transmission Control Protocol (TCP) messages to be inspected. The screenshot of the TCP Tunnel/Monitor below shows an example of how the HTTP request and response are processed. In essence, the program serves as a proxy for HTTP requests to the server. As you will see later, the service endpoint is specified as the port of the monitoring tool. Once the tool receives a request, it displays the requests in the left pane. Next, it will dispatch the request to the server and display the response in the right pane:

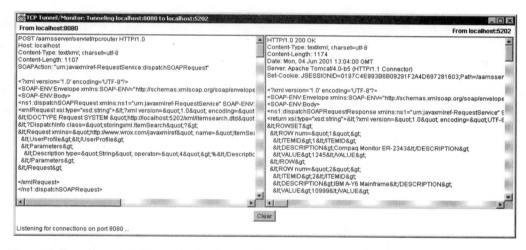

To start the monitoring tool you need to make sure that the SOAP JAR file is in your classpath and then issue the following command:

```
> java org.apache.soap.util.net.TcpTunnelGui 8080 localhost 5202
```

This will start the `TcpTunnelGui` application to listen on port 8080 for a request. Additionally, it will forward all incoming requests to the localhost server on port 5202.

This tool is helpful in debugging SOAP applications, particularly when working with different vendors' implementations of SOAP, or remote services with which you are unfamiliar.

EJB Support

According to the Apache documentation a **provider** is the bridge between the SOAP engine and the service being invoked. The provider is responsible for:

- ❑ Locating the service
- ❑ Loading the service
- ❑ Invoking the service
- ❑ Converting the result from the service into a SOAP envelope

In addition to the RPC Java provider that we used earlier, the Apache SOAP distribution also provides additional providers including support for EJB and message based services. It is also possible to create custom providers that will allow support for other services such as CORBA and COM.

In order to create a provider you must implement the `org.apache.soap.util.Provider` interface below:

```
public interface Provider {

    public void locate(DeploymentDescriptor dd,
        Envelope env, Call call,
        String methodName,
        String targetObjectURI,
        SOAPContext reqContext)
        throws SOAPException;

    public void invoke(SOAPContext req, SOAPContext res)
        throws SOAPException;
}
```

The `locate()` method is called to verify that the service exists and is available to process the request. The `invoke()` method then executes the requested method on the EJB using the Java reflection API and return the result.

Since many users of the AAMS are international companies, we need to provide support for multiple currencies. We choose to normalize the value of items in a base currency and convert requests to and from that currency. For the AAMS, we store values in US dollars. We provide the method below in the `SOAPRequestBean` to assist with the currency conversion:

```
public double getCurrencyConversion(double amount,
    String fromCurrency) {
    call.setTargetObjectURI("urn:ejbprovider");
    call.setMethodName("getCurrencyConversion");
    call.setEncodingStyleURI(Constants.NS_URI_SOAP_ENC);
    Vector params = new Vector();
    params.addElement(new Parameter("amount", Double.class,
        Double.toString(amount), Constants.NS_URI_SOAP_ENC));
    params.addElement(new Parameter("toCurrency", String.class,
        fromCurrency, Constants.NS_URI_SOAP_ENC));
    call.setParams(params);
    Double convertedAmt = (Double) invokeMethod().getValue();
    return convertedAmt.doubleValue();
}
```

This method will submit a request to the `urn:ejbprovider` service passing it two parameters. The first parameter is the value that needs to be converted to US dollars. The second parameter is the currency that the amount is being converted from.

The `urn:ejbprovider` service is deployed to Apache SOAP using the following service descriptor:

```xml
<?xml version="1.0"?>
<isd:service
   xmlns:isd="http://xml.apache.org/xml-soap/deployment"
   id="urn:ejbprovider">
  <isd:provider
    type="org.apache.soap.providers.StatelessEJBProvider"
    scope="Application" methods="create">
    <isd:java class="javaxmlref/EJBRequestService"/>
    <isd:option
      key="FullHomeInterfaceName"
      value="transmittingxml.EJBRequestServiceHome"/>
    <isd:option key="ContextProviderURL" value="localhost:1099"/>
    <isd:option
      key="FullContextFactoryName"
      value="org.jnp.interfaces.NamingContextFactory"/>
  </isd:provider>
  <isd:faultListener>
    org.apache.soap.server.DOMFaultListener
  </isd:faultListener>
</isd:service>
```

As you can see in the descriptor above the provider is specified as `org.apache.soap.providers StatelessEJBProvider`. This provider takes in parameters including the JNDI name in the Java class name attribute. In addition, the home class and naming context parameters are also provided.

The `StatelessEJBProvider` takes the name provided as the Java class, looks it up in the naming services, and calls the `create()` method on the bean's home interface. Once a reference to the remote bean is obtained, the `getCurrencyConversion()` method is called on it, using reflection.

Instead of keeping track of our own currency tables and values, the AAMS will take advantage of an already published web service. We will create a stateless session bean that will convert the currency using the SOAP service available at http://www.xmethods.com/detail.html?id=5 (see the web site itself for more details).

Since the discussion of the creation of EJBs is out of the scope of this book, we will simply list the required files for our stateless session bean. If you need additional information regarding programming Enterprise JavaBeans, please refer to *Professional Java Server Programming*, ISBN 1861004656, or *Professional EJB*, ISBN 1861005803, from Wrox Press.

The Remote Interface

```java
package transmittingxml;

import java.rmi.RemoteException;
import javax.ejb.CreateException;
import javax.ejb.EJBHome;
```

```
public interface EJBRequestServiceHome extends EJBHome {

  EJBRequestService create()
    throws RemoteException, CreateException;
}
```

The Home Interface

```
package transmittingxml;

import storingxml.RequestResponse;
import javax.ejb.EJBObject;
import java.rmi.RemoteException;

public interface EJBRequestService extends EJBObject {
  public Double getCurrencyConversion(double amount,
    String toCurrency) throws RemoteException;
}
```

The Bean

```
package transmittingxml;

import storingxml.*;
import java.rmi.RemoteException;
import javax.ejb.SessionBean;
import javax.ejb.SessionContext;
import org.apache.soap.transport.http.*;
import org.apache.soap.rpc.*;
import org.apache.soap.*;
import java.net.URL;
import java.util.Vector;

public class EJBRequestServiceBean implements SessionBean {
```

Note that if you are behind a firewall, you will need to ensure that the following system properties are appropriately set in your EJB container. You can usually do this by adding lines to the container startup script:

```
set PROXYHOST=-Dhttp.proxyHost=proxyhostname
set PROXYPORT=-Dhttp.proxyPort=proxyhostport
```

Then ensure that the java command which launches the container includes these two variables in its option list:

```
java %PROXYHOST% %PROXYPORT% <other options> <class> <arguments>
```

```
  private static String tunnelhost =
    System.getProperty("http.proxyHost");
  private static String tunnelport =
    System.getProperty("http.proxyPort");
```

Convert the amount in the `fromCurrency` to US dollars:

```
public Double getCurrencyConversion(double amount,
  String fromCurrency) throws RemoteException {
  Call call = new Call();
  System.out.println("Created call");
  call.setTargetObjectURI("urn:xmethods-CurrencyExchange");
  call.setMethodName("getRate");
  call.setEncodingStyleURI(Constants.NS_URI_SOAP_ENC);
  Vector params = new Vector();
  System.out.println("Adding params");
  params.addElement(new Parameter("country1",
    String.class, fromCurrency, null)); // From Country
  params.addElement(new Parameter("country2",
    String.class, "US", null)); // To Country
  call.setParams(params);
  Double rate = new Double(0.0);
  try {
    URL url = new URL("http://services.xmethods.net/soap");
    SOAPHTTPConnection sht = new SOAPHTTPConnection();
```

This is the bit where we tunnel through the proxy if necessary:

```
    if (tunnelhost != null) {
      sht.setProxyHost(tunnelhost);
      sht.setProxyPort(Integer.parseInt(tunnelport));
    }
    call.setSOAPTransport(sht);
    System.out.println("Calling web service...");
    Response response = call.invoke(url, "");
    if (!response.generatedFault()) {
      Parameter result = response.getReturnValue();
      System.out.println("Result = " + result.getValue());
      rate = new Double(result.getValue().toString());
    } else {
      Fault f = response.getFault();   // an error occurred
      System.err.println("Fault= " + f.getFaultCode() + ", "
                         + f.getFaultString());
    }
  } catch (Exception e) {
    System.out.println("Exception during xmethods call: "
                       + e.getMessage());
  }
  return new Double(amount * rate.doubleValue());
}
```

Lifecycle methods:

```
public void ejbCreate() {}
public void ejbRemove(){}
public void ejbActivate(){}
public void ejbPassivate(){}
public void setSessionContext(javax.ejb.SessionContext p1) {}
}
```

Like the SOAP calls in the `SOAPRequestBean`, the `EJBRequestService` bean's `getCurrencyConversion()` method will make a SOAP call to a web service. The call will take in the amount to be converted as well as the currency the amount is in. The resulting conversion rate is then used to calculate the converted value that is returned back to the calling program. This flow is illustrated in the sequence diagram below:

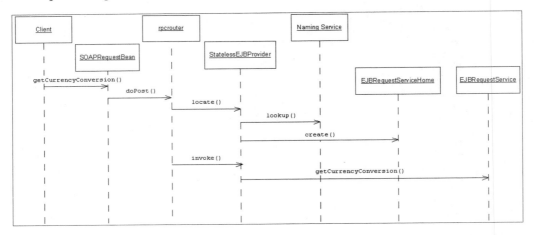

Client Output

Below we call the method on the `SOAPRequestBean`, passing it 1 million Yen. As you can see by the result below, this value is converted to 8,166 dollars using our EJBs and the third party web service.

```
System.out.println("Converted Value: "
  + client.getCurrencyConversion(1000000, "Japan"));

Converted Value: 8166.59
```

Summary

Web services are the next step in distributed programming. They provide a high-level service-oriented architecture that complements the technology that drives the Internet. Through the use of pervasive stateless protocols such as HTTP, FTP, and SMTP, web services are able to be widely deployed using SOAP.

We have seen how easy it is to integrate third party services into an enterprise application. There are currently numerous approaches evolving including Universal Description, Discovery, and Integration (UDDI) and Web Services Description Language (WSDL) to standardize the publishing and identification of these distributed web services (see Chapter 9). In this chapter, we've covered some low-level approaches to illustrate the mechanics of XML communication between distributed processes.

There are products becoming available that will simplify the integration of EJB servers and web services. For example, Cape Clear (http://www.capeclear.com/) is currently offering a product that will create a SOAP interface for your EJB and CORBA services.

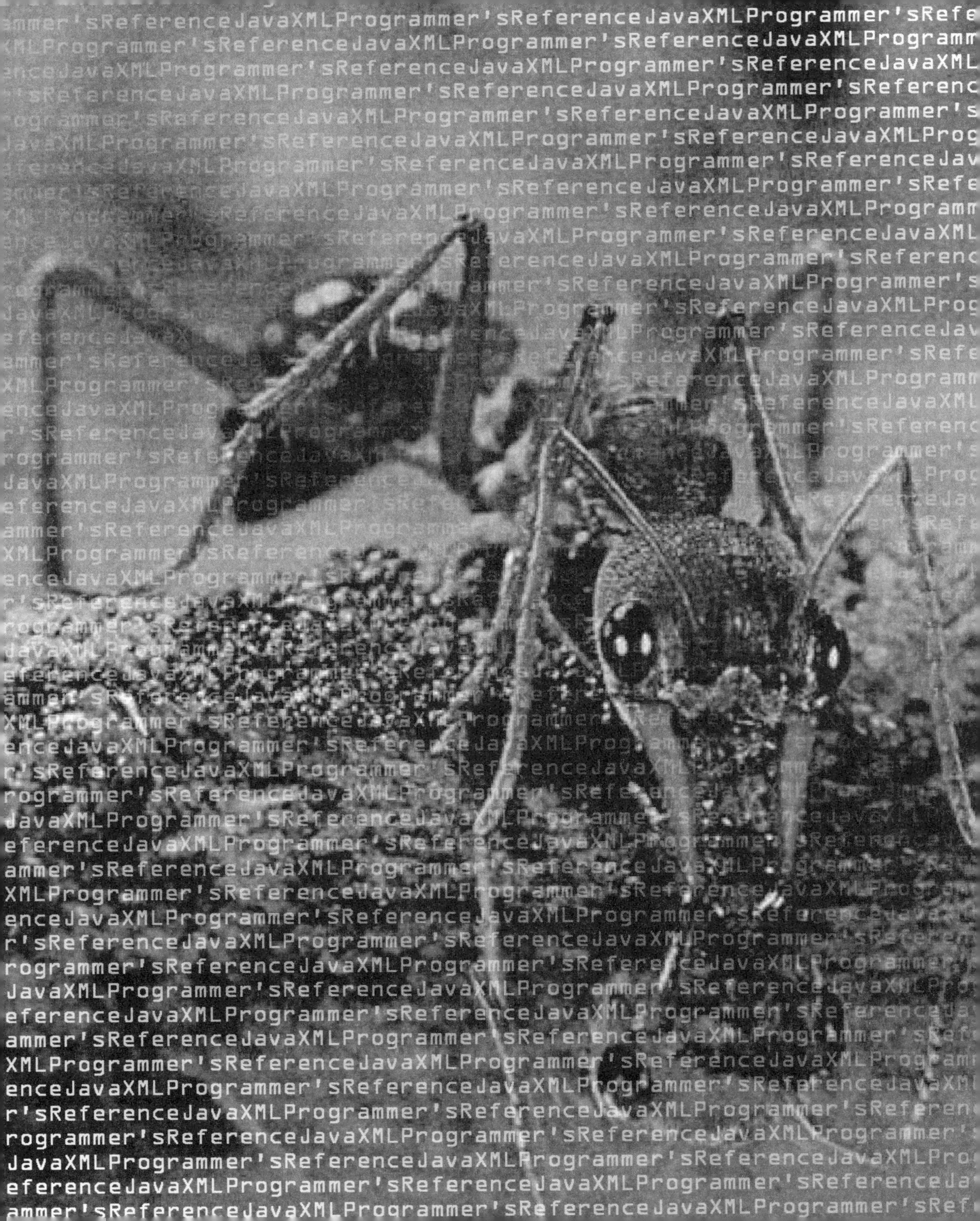
JavaXMLProgrammer'sReference

16

Transforming and Presenting XML

Following the service-oriented approach we have been employing in the Auction and Appraisal Management System (AAMS), we will create an output service that will be responsible for taking the output from the various business requests and formatting them. This processing occurs on the client portal application and the choice of format for presentation is left open to the client implementation. Recall that the AAMS simply provides the `soapjavabean.jar` package along with some supporting packages. It is up to the clients to integrate the service as they like within their own portals.

In this chapter we will accomplish the following:

❑ Create Java ServerPages (JSP) that will submit the business processes and transform the responses using the defined stylesheets

❑ Illustrate the use of custom tag libraries to simplify the integration of XML and XSLT into JSP output

❑ Create a rendered PDF bid report using XSL Format Objects and the XML output of a bid search request

Project Deployment Sheet

We illustrate a user interface to the Appraisal and Auction Management System (AAMS). This user interface will give the users the ability to search for, and bid on, items they want to buy.

Information Flow

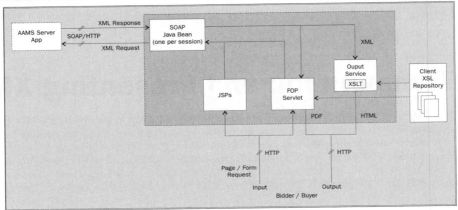

Requirements

The required Java resources for the chapter are indicated in the `prepare` Ant target below. Details for downloading and installing each JAR file (referred to here by their property name) and any necessary build setup can be found in `Build.xml` see Appendix A.

In addition, a JSP and servlet engine is needed to host the user interface of the AAMS.

The Files

These files are used in the project:

XSLT Files

Stylesheets are in `src/transformingxml`:

```
itemDetail.xslt
itemsearch.xslt
itemsearch.xsl
```

JSP

The following JSP pages are in `src/transformingxml`:

```
itemsearch.jsp
itemdetail.jsp
itembid.jsp
itemsearchTL.jsp
itemdetailTL.jsp
itemdetailreport.jsp
```

Java

The following files are in the `transformingxml` package:

```
OutputService.java
AppraisalReportServlet.java
```

The Java Code

In this project we will utilize the `SOAPRequestBean` (see page 780) to submit business process requests. Once the XML output is obtained, it will be transformed into HTML using the `OutputService` class (see page 781).

Ant Targets

Ant carries out all necessary compilation and deployment for this chapter automatically. See Appendix A for details of configuring the build system. The following targets perform the work:

`techniques.transformingxml.compile`
Compiles all the code for the chapter to the `build` directory.

`techniques.transformingxml.deploy`
Creates the AAMS client web application and deploys it to the `webapps` directory.

The Result

After completing this phase, we will have created a JSP-based user interface that will allow customers the ability to search for and bid on items. We will also be able to generate PDF documentation for the current bid status of an item.

Item Search

As you recall from our earlier discussion about the item search business process, the process allows a user to enter a description for an item and the business process will find all of the items that contain a description matching the search criteria.

To facilitate the use of the business processes, the `SOAPRequestBean` is provided. This bean provides a simple API that will submit the appropriate SOAP requests to the request service. One of the methods provided on the `SOAPRequestBean` is the `itemSearch()` method. The method call below will search for all items in the database starting with the word Compaq:

```
SOAPRequestBean client = new SOAPRequestBean();
System.out.println(client.itemSearch("Compaq%"));
```

Assuming that the request service is configured to use Oracle's XML SQL Utility, the following XML is returned from the call:

```xml
<?xml version="1.0" encoding="UTF-8"?>
<ROWSET>
  <ROW num="1">
    <ITEMID>1</ITEMID>
    <DESCRIPTION>Compaq Presario</DESCRIPTION>
    <VALUE>1099.03</VALUE>
  </ROW>
  <ROW num="2">
    <ITEMID>2</ITEMID>
    <DESCRIPTION>Compaq Laptop</DESCRIPTION>
    <VALUE>900.44</VALUE>
  </ROW>
</ROWSET>
```

Once the XML is returned, we need to convert it into HTML that can be rendered by a browser. This transformation process will be accomplished using XSLT.

The first thing to do is to create a stylesheet that will be used to transform the given XML into a new XML result tree consisting of HTML elements. This new result tree will be then be returned to the browser for presentation to the user. It is important to remember that we could have chosen any variant or ancestor of XML, including HTML, WML, or our own proprietary XML format to present the information in.

XSLT Stylesheet

The following stylesheet (`itemsearch.xslt`) will transform our earlier XML into HTML:

```xml
<?xml version="1.0" encoding="UTF-8"?>
<xsl:stylesheet xmlns:xsl="http://www.w3.org/1999/XSL/Transform" version="1.0">
  <xsl:output method="html"/>
  <xsl:template match="/">
    <xsl:apply-templates/>
  </xsl:template>
```

Now we apply the following template to each `<ROWSET>` element of the document root:

```xml
<xsl:template match="ROWSET|/ROWSET">
  <center>
    <B>Below is a list of items matching your search: </B>
    <table width="60%">
      <th align="center">Description</th>
      <th align="center">Value</th>
```

The next step is to create a hyperlink element for each item row in the XML document:

```xml
<xsl:for-each select="ROW">
  <tr>
    <td>
      <xsl:element name="a">
```

```
                <xsl:attribute name="href">
                  itemdetail.jsp?itemId=
                     <xsl:value-of select="ITEMID"/>
                </xsl:attribute>
                <xsl:value-of select="DESCRIPTION"/>
              </xsl:element>
            </td>
            <td align="right">
              <xsl:value-of select="VALUE"/>
            </td>
            <td align="right">
              <xsl:element name="a">
                <xsl:attribute name="href">
                    servlet/appraisalReport?itemId=<xsl:value-of
                    select="ITEMID"/>
                </xsl:attribute>
                Get Appraisal Report
              </xsl:element>
            </td>
          </tr>
       </xsl:for-each>
     </table>
   </center>
 </xsl:template>
</xsl:stylesheet>
```

In order to apply the stylesheet to the XML document, some code similar to the following should be implemented (we will see a longer example of this in full later).

```
transformer = tFactory.newTransformer(new
          StreamSource(stylesheet));
transformer.transform(new StreamSource(new
          StringReader(inputXML)), new StreamResult(out));
```

As part of the JAXP 1.1 specification, the **Transformation API for XML (TrAX)** is defined. **TrAX** essentially is a layer of abstraction on top of the transformation process, providing an implementation-neutral interface. Although TrAX is currently used with XSLT, it is not dependent on it.

The first thing to do is get a reference to the TrAX `TransformerFactory`. Once the factory is created, it is used to create a transformer for the `itemsearch.xslt` we defined earlier. Next, the actual transformation occurs by invoking the `transform()` method. Assuming the transformation was successful, the following HTML is generated:

Output

```
<center>
<B>Below is a list of items matching your search: </B>
<table width="60%">
<th align="center">Description</th><th align="center">Value</th>
<tr>
<td><a href="itemdetail.jsp?itemId=1">Compaq Presario</a></td><td
align="right">1099.03</td>
</tr>
```

```
<tr>
<td><a href="itemdetail.jsp?itemId=2">Compaq Laptop</a></td><td
align="right">900.44</td>
</tr>
</table>
</center>
```

Now that we have our stylesheet and can apply it to our XML, we can generate dynamic output using Java ServerPages (JSP). The first step is to create a screen that will allow the user to enter their search criteria.

Below is a sample HTML page that can do just that:

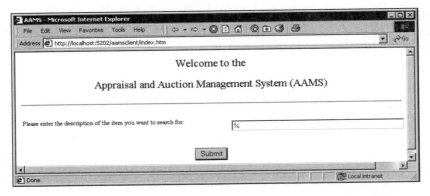

This form will take in user data and submit a request to the server. To process such a request, an `itemsearch.jsp` must be created. This JSP is then attached to the action attribute of the form on the page.

```
<form method="POST" action="itemsearch.jsp">
```

JSP

When the user clicks the Submit button, the contents of the form will be sent to the `itemSearch.jsp` below for processing.

Here is the header:

```
<!DOCTYPE html PUBLIC "-//W3C//DTD HTML 4.0 Transitional//EN">
<html>
<head>
<title>AAMS</title>
</head>
<body>
```

Next, we define the beans to be used on the page. This includes the `SOAPRequestBean` (which we covered in Chapter 15) to submit the SOAP requests, and the `OutputService` that we will be covering shortly.

```
    <jsp:useBean id="requestBean" scope="session"
             class="transmittingxml.SOAPRequestBean" />
    <jsp:useBean id="transformationBean" scope="application"
             class="transformingxml.OutputService" />
  <center>
```

If a description is filled in, we then obtain the XML result by using the `SOAPRequestBean` to execute the appropriate business process. Next, the resulting XML is transformed using the `Output Service` bean.

```
<%
  String description = request.getParameter("description");
  if ( description != null ) {
    String xsl = pageContext.getServletContext().getResource
           ("/itemSearch.xslt").toString();
    out.println(transformationBean.transform
           (requestBean.itemSearch (description), xsl));
  }
%>
</center>
</body>
</html>
```

The Output Service

Once the search result is obtained, the `OutputService` bean below is used to transform the output into HTML:

```
package transformingxml;

import javax.xml.transform.TransformerFactory;
import javax.xml.transform.Transformer;
import javax.xml.transform.stream.StreamSource;
import javax.xml.transform.stream.StreamResult;
import javax.xml.transform.dom.DOMSource;
import org.apache.xerces.parsers.DOMParser;
import org.xml.sax.InputSource;
import org.w3c.dom.Element;
import org.apache.fop.apps.Driver;
import org.apache.fop.apps.Version;
import java.io.ByteArrayOutputStream;
import java.io.StringReader;
import java.io.StringWriter;

public class OutputService {
  private TransformerFactory tFactory;
  private Transformer transformer;

  public OutputService() {
    tFactory = TransformerFactory.newInstance();
  }
```

Here we take an XML string as input, and transform it using the provided stylesheet:

```
   public String transform(String inputXML, String stylesheet) {
   StringWriter out = new StringWriter();
   try {
     transformer = tFactory.newTransformer(new
                 StreamSource(stylesheet));
     transformer.transform(new StreamSource(new
                 StringReader(inputXML)), new StreamResult(out));
   } catch (Exception ex) {
     System.out.println("Transformation Exception: " + ex);
   }
   return out.toString();
   }
```

And here again, we take a DOM element as input and transform it using the provided stylesheet:

```
   public String transform(Element inputDOM, String stylesheet) {
     StringWriter out = new StringWriter();
     try {
       transformer = tFactory.newTransformer(new
                 StreamSource(stylesheet));
```

The DOMSource provides the ability to use the DOM as input to our transformation:

```
   public String transform(Element inputDOM, String stylesheet) {
     StringWriter out = new StringWriter();
     try {
       transformer = tFactory.newTransformer(new
                 StreamSource(stylesheet));
       transformer.transform(new DOMSource(inputDOM), new
                 StreamResult(out));
     } catch (Exception ex) {
       System.out.println("Transformation Exception: " + ex);
     }
     return out.toString();
   }
   }
```

This is how the page should appear in the browser, after it has been generated:

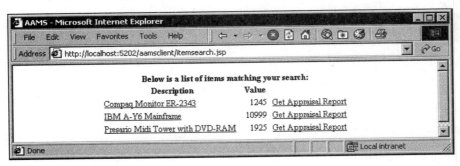

Item Detail

As you can see, our search result consists of a list that includes hyperlinks to click on to get additional information about each item. We will again utilize XSLT to transform the XML result from the `itemDetail()` method into HTML.

As you recall from Chapter 14, the following XML is generated from the item detail business process:

```
<?xml version="1.0" encoding="UTF-8"?>
<ROWSET>
  <ROW num="1">
    <ITEMID>1</ITEMID>
    <DESCRIPTION>Compaq Presario</DESCRIPTION>
    <VALUE>1099.03</VALUE>
  </ROW>
</ROWSET>
```

XSLT Stylesheet

Given the details for an item, we will apply the following XSLT stylesheet, `itemDetail.xslt`, to generate our HTML user interface:

```
<?xml version="1.0" encoding="UTF-8"?>
<xsl:stylesheet xmlns:xsl="http://www.w3.org/1999/XSL/Transform" version="1.0">
<xsl:output method="html"/>
<xsl:template match="*|/">
<xsl:apply-templates/>
</xsl:template>
```

We now apply the following template to the ROWSET returned from the item detail business process:

```
<xsl:template match="ROWSET">
<center>
<form method="POST" action="itembid.jsp">
```

Next, we extract the `item ID`, description, and value from the XML document and include it in the HTML output:

```
<table>
   <tr>
       <td align="left" width="132"><b>Item Id:</b></td>
       <td width="300"> <xsl:value-of select="ROW/ITEMID" />
       </td>
       </tr>
       <tr>
       <td align="left" width="132"><b>Description:</b></td>
       <td width="300"> <xsl:value-of
                select="ROW/DESCRIPTION" /></td>
       <tr>
       <td align="left"><b>Value:</b></td>
```

```
              <td align="left"><xsl:value-of select="ROW/VALUE" />
              </td>
              </tr>
         </tr>
       </table>
<hr/>
<h4>To place a bid, please enter the user ID, amount, and the country you are
in:</h4>
<table>
<tr>
```

Here, we include the item ID as a hidden field in the HTML form, so that it is included in the data that is posted to the itembid.jsp.

```
<input type="hidden" name="itemId" value= "{ROW/ITEMID}" />
<td align="right">Bidder Name:</td>
<td><input type="text" name="bidder" size="10"/></td>
</tr>
<tr>
<td align="right">Bid Amount:</td>
<td><input type="text" name="bidAmount" size="10"/></td>
</tr>
<tr>
<td align="right">Country:</td>
<td><select size="1" name="country">
    <option value="England">England</option>
    <option value="Taiwan">Taiwan</option>
    <option value="Japan">Japan</option>
    </select>
</td>
</tr>
</table>
<input type="submit" value="Place Bid" name="bid"/>
</form>
</center>
</xsl:template>
</xsl:stylesheet>
```

As you can see from the stylesheet above, the detail page of the item includes the same information from the search page, plus the ability to place a bid on the item.

As in the item search business process, we will perform the transformation in a JSP page using the OutputService as a bean. The itemdetail.jsp is listed below:

```
<!DOCTYPE html PUBLIC "-//W3C//DTD HTML 4.0 Transitional//EN">
<html>
<head>
<title>AAMS</title>
</head>
<body>
<p align="center"><font size="6">Item Detail</font></p>
<hr>
```

JSP

Here we include the `SOAPRequestBean` and `OutputService` for use in the JSP:

```
<jsp:useBean id="requestBean" scope="session"
        class="transmittingxml.SOAPRequestBean" />
<jsp:useBean id="transformationBean" scope="application"
        class="transformingxml.OutputService" />
<%
  String itemId = request.getParameter("itemId");
  if ( itemId != null ) {
    String xsl = pageContext.getServletContext().getResource
        ("/itemDetail.xslt").toString();
    out.println(transformationBean.transform(requestBean.itemDetail
        (Integer.parseInt(itemId)), xsl));
  }
%>
</body>
</html>
```

You will notice in the JSP code above that, unlike the `itemSearch` that manipulated the resulting XML as a `String`, the `itemdetail.jsp` processes the XML as a DOM element. After the element is returned from the `ItemDetail()` method on the `SOAPRequestBean`, it is used to create a `DOMSource`.

Once the transformation is complete, the following page is displayed to the user:

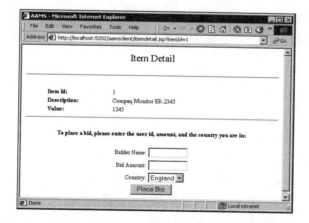

Item Bid

Assuming the user likes the item, they need to be able to place a bid on it. As we saw on the item detail page, there are fields where the user can enter the relevant bid information and a button to submit the bid.

Similarly to the other business processes, the item bid process utilizes the `SOAPRequestBean`.

JSP

This bid process is handled in the `itembid.jsp` below:

```
<!DOCTYPE html PUBLIC "-//W3C//DTD HTML 4.0 Transitional//EN">
<html>
<head>
<title>AAMS</title>
</head>
<body>
<center><font size="6">Item Bid Status</font>
<hr>
```

This defines the `SOAPRequestBean` for use in the page:

```
<jsp:useBean id="requestBean" scope="session"
class="transmittingxml.SOAPRequestBean" />
<%
  String itemId = request.getParameter("itemId");
  String bidder = request.getParameter("bidder");
  String bidAmount = request.getParameter("bidAmount");
  String country = request.getParameter("country");
```

Now we convert the entered bid amount to US dollars, and submit the bid:

```
  if ( itemId != null && bidder != null && bidAmount != null
            && country != null) {
      double convertedBid = requestBean.getCurrencyConversion
            (Double.parseDouble(bidAmount), country);
      storingxml.RequestStatus status = requestBean.itemBid
            (Integer.parseInt(itemId), convertedBid, bidder);
      out.println(status.getMessage() + " for " + convertedBid
            + " by " + bidder);
  }
%>
</center>
</body>
</html>
```

Unlike the other business processes, no transformation occurs as part of the item bid process. The JSP page above simply calls the `itemBid()` method and includes the status into the HTML result. This is illustrated in the item bid result page below:

Custom Tag Libraries

As part of the JSP specification it is possible to utilize custom tag libraries to help simplify your JSP scripting. These tag libraries can be customized to your application and business domain, or be used in the form of general-purpose libraries that are available commercially or via the open source community.

We will be using the XSL Taglib that is part of the Jakarta Taglibs project sponsored by the Apache Group (see http://jakarta.apache.org/taglibs/index.html). The tag library allows the processing of an XML document with a defined stylesheet in place.

Setting Up the Tag Library

Like all custom tag libraries, the Jakarta XSL Taglib must be set up before it can be used. To use this XSL library within the AAMS project:

- ❑ Copy the tag library descriptor file (`xsl/xsl.tld`) to the `/WEB-INF` subdirectory of your web application

- ❑ Copy the tag library JAR file (`xsl/xsl.jar`) to the `/WEB-INF/lib` subdirectory of your web application

- ❑ Copy `xerces.jar` and `xalan.jar` to the `/WEB-INF/lib` directory of your web application

- ❑ Add a `<taglib>` element to your web application deployment descriptor in `/WEB-INF/web.xml`:

```
<taglib>
    <taglib-uri>http://jakarta.apache.org/taglibs/xsl-1.0</taglib-uri>
    <taglib-location>/WEB-INF/xsl.tld</taglib-location>
</taglib>
```

Using the Tag Library

To use the tags from this library in your JSP pages, add the following directive to the top of each page:

```
<%@ taglib uri="http://jakarta.apache.org/taglibs/xsl-1.0" prefix="xsl" %>
```

Here `xsl` is the tag name prefix you wish to use for tags from this library. You can change this value to any prefix you like.

The XSL taglib provides the following tags:

- ❑ `<xsl:apply>` will apply the specified stylesheet to the XML provided

- ❑ `<xsl:export>` will export the contents of the specified bean to the output stream

- ❑ `<xsl:import>` will import the contents of the specified page, and stores them as a string in the specified bean

- ❑ `<xsl:include>` includes the contents of the specified page

In our example, we will utilize the `<xsl:apply>` tag extensively to transform the XML generated by our business processes into user-readable output.

Item Search

We will now recreate the user interface that was built earlier using the Jakarta XSL tag library. The first request that we must implement is the item search business process. We will be able to reuse the index.htm page that enabled the user to enter an item description and perform an item search. In order to do this, using custom tag libraries, we will modify the form action to point to the itemsearchTL.jsp below.

```
<!DOCTYPE html PUBLIC "-//W3C//DTD HTML 4.0 Transitional//EN">
<html>
<head>
<title>Appraisal and Auction Management System (AAMS)</title>
</head>
<body>
<jsp:useBean id="requestBean" scope="session"
class="transmittingxml.SOAPRequestBean" />
```

We define the XSL tag library for the use on the page as below:

```
<%@ taglib uri="http://jakarta.apache.org/taglibs/xsl-1.0"
    prefix="xsl" %>
<center>
<%
```

Assuming a description look-up value is provided, we transform the XML returned from the call to the itemSearch() method on the SOAPRequestBean, using the itemsearch.xslt file located in the root of the application context.

```
    String resultString = null;
    if ( request.getParameter("description") != null ) {
        resultString = requestBean.itemSearch(request.getParameter
        ("description"));
    }
%>
<xsl:apply xsl="itemSearch.xslt" >
<%= resultString.toString() %>
</xsl:apply>
</center>
</body>
</html>
```

In the item search example above, resultString obtained from the SOAPRequestBean is used to provide the XML as the body of the apply tag. The apply tag will take the XML input and use the itemsearch.xslt stylesheet to generate the resulting HTML.

Item Detail

Once the item is found, the item detail business process is called to present the detailed information for the selected item. Unlike the item search request, the SOAPRequestBean uses Literal XML encoding to return the result as a DOM element. The itemdetailTL.jsp below illustrates how the <xsl:apply> tag can employ beans, like the itemDOM, to process the results as input parameters.

```
<!DOCTYPE html PUBLIC "-//W3C//DTD HTML 4.0 Transitional//EN">
<html>
<head>
<title>AAMS</title>
</head>
<body>
<p align="center"><font size="6">Item Detail</font></p>
<hr>
```

This defines the SOAPRequestBean for use within the user's session:

```
<jsp:useBean id="requestBean" scope="session"
        class="transmittingxml.SOAPRequestBean" />
```

Now we create a DOMSource bean that will be used as input to the <xsl:apply> tag

```
<jsp:useBean id="resultDOM" scope="session"
        class="javax.xml.transform.dom.DOMSource" />
<%@ taglib uri="http://jakarta.apache.org/taglibs/xsl-1.0"
        prefix="xsl" %>
<center>
<%
```

If an item ID is passed in, we then use the SOAPRequestBean to generate the XML. The resulting XML is then set into the resultDOM bean defined earlier:

```
    String itemId = request.getParameter("itemId");
    if ( itemId != null ) {
        resultDOM.setNode(requestBean.itemDetail(Integer.parseInt
            (itemId)));
    }
%>
```

Now we transform the item detail business process XML, using the itemdetail.xslt stylesheet located in the root of the application's context. The resultDOM bean's node property is passed in as the name of the bean to use as input into the transformation process.

The <xsl:apply> tag will take the input bean and call the getNode() method on it. This gets the input to use in the transformation process.

```
<xsl:apply nameXml="resultDOM" propertyXml= "node" xsl="itemDetail.xslt" >
</xsl:apply>
</body>
</html>
```

Generating Appraisal Report

One of the products that the appraisal company provides to its customers is a formal appraisal report. Included in this report is detailed information about the appraised item, as well as information about recent bids on the item. Our code will utilize the item detail business process to generate a PDF document.

PDF Output

Since the product that the AAMS produces is the final appraisal report, it is necessary for this to be a high-quality printed product. In addition, however, the reports also need to be electronically transferable. The Portable Document Format (PDF) from Adobe meets both of those requirements.

The FO specification (http://www.w3.org/TR/xsl/slice6.html#fo-section) provides fine-grained control over how a document will be presented. This control includes precise positioning, font and style layout.

The XSL Formatting Objects process is outlined in the diagram below:

Like our earlier HTML transformation example, the input to the PDF generation process is an XML resultset from the item detail business process. After this, the XML is transformed into an FO XML document using a XSL stylesheet. Once the FO document is created, it is passed onto an FO rendering agent, such as FOP from Apache (http://xml.apache.org/fop/index.html) or XEP from RenderX (http://www.renderx.com/), to generate the PDF output.

Creating the PDF

We will utilize the item detail business process to create the XML data that is needed to produce the appraisal report. Since one of the requirements of the appraisal report is to include a fair market view of the item, we will modify the item search request to bring back all outstanding bids for the item. To do this, the SQL used to bring back an ITEM will include a JOIN to the bid table.

The resulting XML is shown below:

```
<ROWSET>
  <ROW num="1">
    <ITEMID>1</ITEMID>
    <DESCRIPTION>Compaq Presario</DESCRIPTION>
    <VALUE>1099.03</VALUE>
    <ID>24</ID>
    <ITEM_ID>1</ITEM_ID>
    <BID>1010</BID>
    <BIDDER>XSU</BIDDER>
    <BIDTIME>5/16/2001 23:25:36</BIDTIME>
  </ROW>
  <ROW num="2">
    <ITEMID>1</ITEMID>
```

```
      <DESCRIPTION>Compaq Presario</DESCRIPTION>
      <VALUE>1099.03</VALUE>
      <ID>25</ID>
      <ITEM_ID>1</ITEM_ID>
      <BID>1211</BID>
      <BIDDER>XSU</BIDDER>
      <BIDTIME>5/16/2001 23:31:34</BIDTIME>
   </ROW>
   <ROW num="3">
      <ITEMID>1</ITEMID>
      <DESCRIPTION>Compaq Presario</DESCRIPTION>
      <VALUE>1099.03</VALUE>
      <ID>41</ID>
      <ITEM_ID>1</ITEM_ID>
      <BID>1252.388</BID>
      <BIDDER>XSU</BIDDER>
      <BIDTIME>5/17/2001 20:44:51</BIDTIME>
   </ROW>
</ROWSET>
```

As you can see, the Oracle XSU result set will return a row element for each matching record in the database. This XML document will then be used to feed the PDF transformation process.

To assist in the creation of the PDF document, the `createPDF()` method below is added to the `OutputService` described earlier:

```
      System.out.println("Transformation Exception: " + ex);
   }
   return out.toString();
}
```

```
public ByteArrayOutputStream createPDF(Element inputDOM,
                                       String stylesheet) {
   String fo = this.transform(inputDOM, stylesheet);

   // Create a DOM Document from the resulting string
   DOMParser parser = new DOMParser();
   try {

     // Set the parser features and parse the config file
     parser.setFeature("http://xml.org/sax/features/namespaces",
           true);
     parser.parse(new InputSource(new StringReader(fo)));
   } catch (Exception ex) {
     System.out.println("Exception duing parse: " + ex);
     ex.printStackTrace();
   }
   org.w3c.dom.Document foDocument = parser.getDocument();
```

The PDF is created using the FOP XSL-driven print formatter from the Apache Group. The resulting PDF is stored in a `ByteArrayOutputStream` that is ultimately returned back to the browser via the servlet output stream:

```
    // Create the PDF
    ByteArrayOutputStream out = new ByteArrayOutputStream();
    try {
       Driver driver = new Driver();
       driver.setRenderer(Driver.RENDER_PDF);
       driver.setOutputStream(out);
```

This code creates the FO tree, formats it and writes it to the output stream:

```
       driver.buildFOTree(foDocument);
       driver.format();
       driver.render();
    } catch (Exception ex) {
       System.out.println("Exception: " + ex);
       ex.printStackTrace();
    }
    return out;
  }
}
```

Creating the FO Tree

The PDF is not created directly from the XML input. Rather, it is created from an FO result tree by taking the XML input and transforming it using a XSL stylesheet.

The stylesheet, `itemdetail.xsl`, used to create the appraisal report is listed below:

```
<xsl:stylesheet
     xmlns:xsl="http://www.w3.org/1999/XSL/Transform" version="1.0"
xmlns:fo="http://www.w3.org/1999/XSL/Format">
```

For each rowset element in the document, the following template is applied. This starts by defining the page layout to be used, including the page size and its margins:

```
<xsl:template match ="ROWSET">
  <fo:root xmlns:fo="http://www.w3.org/1999/XSL/Format">
    <!-- defines page layout -->
    <fo:layout-master-set>
      <fo:simple-page-master master-name="simple"
        page-height="11in"
        page-width="8.5in"
        margin-top="1.5cm"
        margin-bottom="1.5cm"
        margin-left="2.5cm"
        margin-right="2.5cm">
        <fo:region-body margin-top="1.5cm"/>
        <fo:region-before extent="1.5cm"/>
        <fo:region-after extent="1.5cm"/>
        </fo:simple-page-master>
    </fo:layout-master-set>
    <fo:page-sequence master-name="simple">
```

Here we create a header for each page that will contain the `item` ID of the item being reported on:

```
    <fo:static-content flow-name="xsl-region-before">
      <fo:block text-align="end"
        font-size="12pt"
        font-family="serif"
        line-height="14pt"
        font-style="italic">
          Apprasial Report for item#
        <xsl:value-of select="ROW/ITEMID"/>
      </fo:block>
      <fo:block text-align="end" font-size="10pt"
        font-family="serif" line-height="14pt" >
          page: <fo:page-number/>
      </fo:block>
    </fo:static-content>
    <fo:flow flow-name="xsl-region-body">
      <fo:block font-size="18pt"
        font-family="sans-serif"
        line-height="24pt"
        space-after.optimum="15pt"
        background-color="blue"
        color="white"
        text-align="center">
          Appraisal Report for
        <xsl:value-of select="ROW/DESCRIPTION"/>
      </fo:block>
```

Next, we create a table that will contain the item information, including the description and appraised value:

```
    <!-- create a table for the item information -->
    <fo:table space-after.optimum="15pt">
    <fo:table-column column-width="4cm"/>
    <fo:table-column column-width="1cm"/>
    <fo:table-column column-width="6cm"/>
    <fo:table-body font-size="10pt"
      font-family="sans-serif">
    <fo:table-row line-height="12pt">
      <fo:table-cell>
        <fo:block  font-weight="bold"
          text-align="end" >
          <xsl:text>Description:</xsl:text>
        </fo:block>
      </fo:table-cell>
      <fo:table-cell/>
      <fo:table-cell>
        <fo:block text-align="start" >
          <xsl:value-of select="ROW/DESCRIPTION"/>
        </fo:block>
      </fo:table-cell>
    </fo:table-row>
    <fo:table-row line-height="12pt">
      <fo:table-cell>
        <fo:block font-weight="bold"
```

```
                text-align="end" >
                  <xsl:text>Value:</xsl:text>
              </fo:block>
          </fo:table-cell>
          <fo:table-cell/>
          <fo:table-cell>
            <fo:block text-align="start" >
            $<xsl:value-of select="ROW/VALUE"/>
            </fo:block>
          </fo:table-cell>
        </fo:table-row>
      </fo:table-body>
    </fo:table>
```

Next, we generate a table containing the recent bids on the item. This is done by iterating through each row in the XML document:

```
    <!-- generates table of recent bids -->
    <fo:block font-size="12pt"
        font-family="sans-serif"
        line-height="18pt"
        space-after.optimum="15pt"
        text-align="start">
        Below is a list of current bids for the item
    </fo:block>
      <fo:table space-after.optimum="15pt">
        <fo:table-column column-width="2cm"/>
        <fo:table-column column-width="4cm"/>
        <fo:table-column column-width="3cm"/>
        <fo:table-column column-width="3cm"/>
        <fo:table-body font-size="10pt"
            font-family="sans-serif">
          <fo:table-row line-height="12pt">
            <fo:table-cell/>
            <fo:table-cell>
              <fo:block  font-weight="bold"
                  text-align="center" >Bid Time
              </fo:block>
            </fo:table-cell>
            <fo:table-cell>
              <fo:block  font-weight="bold"
                  text-align="center" >Bidder
              </fo:block>
            </fo:table-cell>
            <fo:table-cell>
              <fo:block  font-weight="bold"
                  text-align="center" >Bid Amount
              </fo:block>
            </fo:table-cell>
          </fo:table-row>
          <fo:table-row>
            <fo:table-cell/>
            <fo:table-cell/>
            <fo:table-cell/>
```

```
            <fo:table-cell/>
        </fo:table-row>
          <xsl:for-each select="ROW">
    <fo:table-row line-height="12pt">
        <fo:table-cell>
            <fo:block text-align="end" >
```

This creates a row count in the first column of the bid table:

```
                  <xsl:number value="position()"
                        format="1"/>)
              </fo:block>
          </fo:table-cell>
          <fo:table-cell>
              <fo:block  text-align="start" >
                  <xsl:value-of select="BIDTIME"/>
              </fo:block>
          </fo:table-cell>
          <fo:table-cell>
              <fo:block  text-align="start" >
                  <xsl:value-of select="BIDDER"/>
              </fo:block>
          </fo:table-cell>
          <fo:table-cell>
              <fo:block  text-align="end" >
                  $<xsl:value-of select="BID"/>
              </fo:block>
          </fo:table-cell>
        </fo:table-row>
      </xsl:for-each>
      </fo:table-body>
    </fo:table>
    </fo:flow>
  </fo:page-sequence>
</fo:root>
</xsl:template>
</xsl:stylesheet>
```

After the item detail XML document is processed, the FO result tree can then be used by an FO rendering agent to create the paginated output. For this example, we will be utilizing FOP from Apache to create our output.

Transmitting the PDF

After we have created the FO tree using XSL and generated the PDF byte array using the `OutputService`, the document must be returned to the user.

The current JSP specification template creates a `JSPWriter` at the beginning of each page. Since the creation of this writer obtains exclusive access to the output stream, it is not possible for us to return binary data using JSP. Consequently, the servlet below will be used to return the PDF to the user's browser.

```
package transformingxml;

import javax.xml.transform.TransformerFactory;
import javax.xml.transform.Transformer;
import javax.servlet.ServletConfig;
import javax.servlet.ServletException;
import javax.servlet.http.HttpServlet;
import javax.servlet.http.HttpServletRequest;
import javax.servlet.http.HttpServletResponse;
import java.io.IOException;
import java.io.ByteArrayOutputStream;
import java.io.OutputStream;

import configuringxml.*;
import storingxml.*;
import transmittingxml.*;

public class AppraisalReportServlet extends HttpServlet {
  private SOAPRequestBean requestBean;
  private OutputService transformationBean;
  private String xslURL;

  public void init(ServletConfig config) throws ServletException {
    super.init(config);
    try {
      xslURL =
        config.getServletContext().getResource("/itemDetail.xsl")
          .toString();
    } catch (java.net.MalformedURLException m) {}
    requestBean = new SOAPRequestBean();
    transformationBean = new OutputService();
  }

  public void doGet(HttpServletRequest request,
        HttpServletResponse response) throws ServletException,
        IOException {
    doPost(request, response);
  }

  public void doPost(HttpServletRequest request,
        HttpServletResponse response) throws ServletException,
        IOException {
    int itemId = Integer.parseInt(request.getParameter("itemId"));
    if (itemId > 0) {
      try {
        response.setContentType("application/pdf");

        // Transform the XML result into PDF.
        ByteArrayOutputStream content =
            transformationBean.createPDF(requestBean.itemDetail
            (itemId), xslURL);

        // Write the PDF to the output stream
        byte[] out = content.toByteArray();
        OutputStream output = response.getOutputStream();
```

```
            response.setContentLength(out.length);
            output.write(out);
            output.flush();
            output.close();
        } catch (Exception ex) {
            System.out.println("Exception: " + ex);
        }
    }
}

    public String getServletInfo() {
        return "Servlet creates a PDF apprasial report";
    }
}
```

Assuming the user has Adobe Acrobat installed on their machine, the appraisal report will be returned to the user in the format illustrated below:

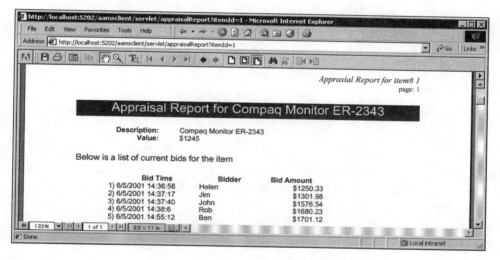

Summary

As you can see, much of the true power of XML is not in XML itself, but rather in the tools surrounding it. We have seen that through using XSL and XSLT we have been able to create a very flexible output in both HTML and PDF, and it is also possible to extend this to other formats, such as WML for example.

We utilized these tools to provide a user interface to the AAMS. This interface provides the ability to search for items, place bids, and view a detailed PDF appraisal report.

In addition, we have seen how JSPs can be augmented using custom libraries that provide inline transformation services.

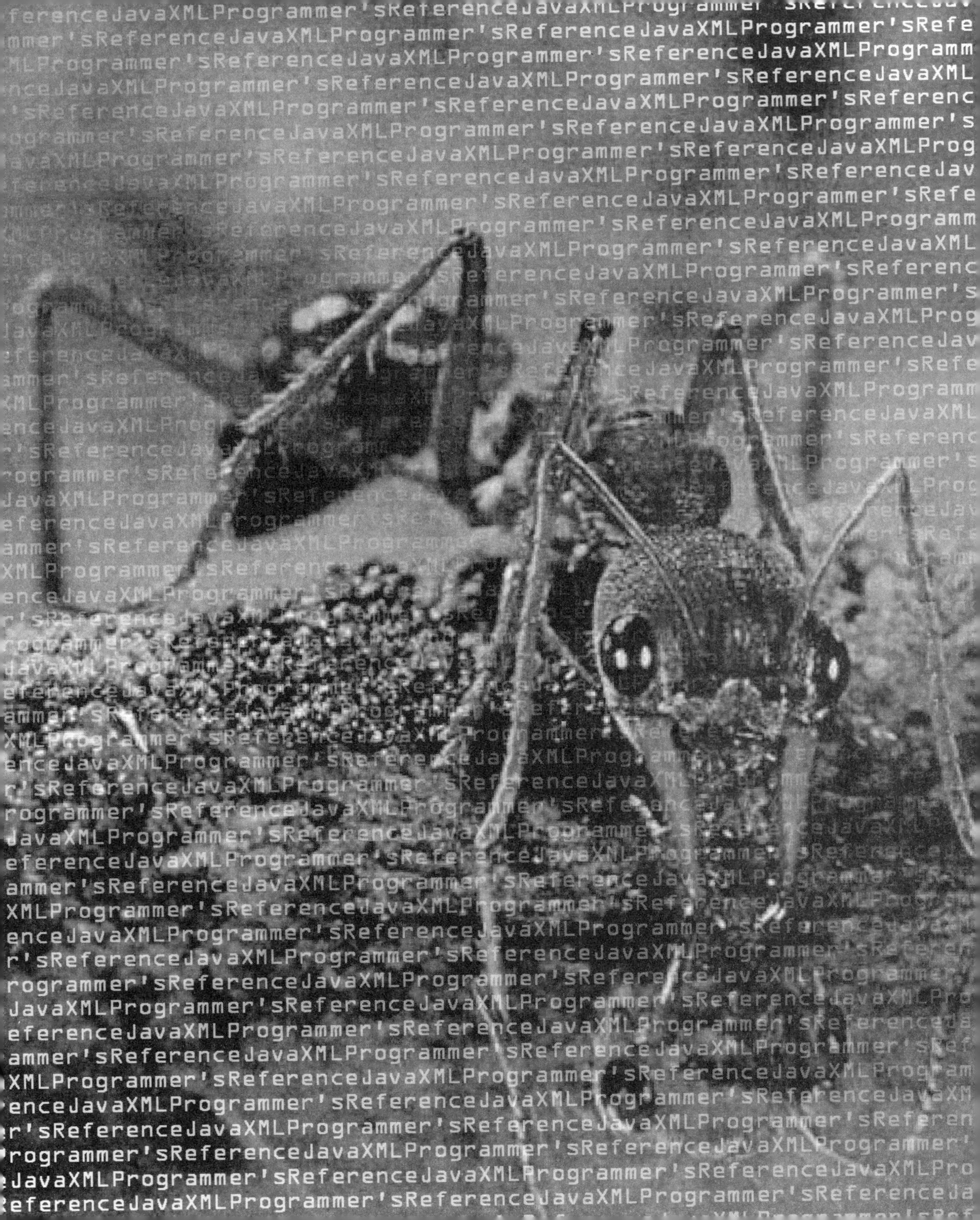
JavaXMLProgrammer'sReference

Using the Code

This appendix provides details for using the code in this book. The smaller examples can easily be run with the guidelines given in the book and the summaries later in this appendix. However, for the more complex examples that require a number of different stages of compilation and deployment, we have provided some scripts in the Ant language. The aim of this is primarily:

❑ To abstract detailed deployment instructions from the body of the book

❑ To provide deployment instructions in a "machine-checked" form that should work on any Java platform

This appendix will look at using Ant to run the code samples, and then we go through each chapter, adding summaries of the code where this is not given in full in the chapter.

There is a table at the end of the chapter giving a full listing of all the packages used in the book.

We also include the licences relating to the Java documentation from which the basis of the API Chapters 2-6 was generated.

Using Ant

Ant is part of Jakarta, a sub-project of the Apache Software Foundation. It is an open source tool, written in Java, and used for Java code building, deployment, and project maintenance. It was built specifically to handle the increasing complexity of compiling and rebuilding the Tomcat web server. It is now widely used for all kinds of Java projects, and even some .NET ones.

With Ant, you specify `<target>` elements in an XML `<project>` document using a range of built-in `<task>` elements. Running Ant on this document executes the build instructions.

There are about 50 or so built-in `<task>` commands, ranging from compilation with `<javac>`, to creating a WAR file with `<war>` There is a make-like dependency mechanism that uses an attribute `depends="target1, target2, . . . "` within a `<target>` definition. This causes the referenced targets to be executed recursively in reverse order, starting from the leaf targets that have no dependents. There is also the ability to perform tasks conditionally. Here is a simple example build file called `test.xml`:

```
<?xml version="1.0" encoding="UTF-8"?>
<project name="test" default="run">
  <target name="compile">
    <echo message="This will be done first"/>
    <javac srcdir="./src" destdir="./build"
        includes="HelloWorld.java"/>
  </target>
  <target name="run" depends="compile">
      <java classname="HelloWorld" classpath="./build" />
  </target>
</project>
```

We would get the following output, assuming that we have a Java test class HelloWorld.java, which prints a suitable message, in the src directory:

```
> ant -buildfile test.xml
Buildfile: test.xml
compile:
     [echo] This will be done first

run:
Hello World!

BUILD SUCCESSFUL
Total time: 0 seconds
```

The download bundle for this book is available from http://www.wrox.com. It contains a build file called build.xml that will set up, compile, and deploy all the non-trivial examples and applications in this book.

Once you have installed the required packages and toolkits, you would need to edit a simple text properties file that the build program reads in, and which specifies the location of all the resources on your particular machine. The build.xml script itself should not need to be edited.

Installing Ant

To install Ant, download the latest version from the Apache XML Project at http://jakarta.apache.org/ant. You'll find a range of .zip or tar.gz files called jakarta-ant-1.3-bin.zip or similar, depending on the current release and compression type. The bin indicates the compiled version – that is ready-to-run out of the box. Unless you want to build a new version of Ant with a previous version of Ant, you need the bin version. You should use the .zip files for Windows machines, or the .tar.gz version for Unix. But it doesn't really matter. It's just that you're more likely to have only a ZIP decompression tool on a Windows machine.

Extract the archive to your root drive C:\ or /usr/lib so that you have now a directory called C:\jakarta-ant-1.3 or /usr/lib/jakarta-ant-1.3. From now on, we'll assume that you're using one of these directories. On a multiuser system, it is recommended that you install Ant in /usr/lib. If this is not possible, you may need to install it in your home directory /home/myhome/jakarta-ant-1.3, where myhome is your user name.

Now you need to ensure that the ant script which is used to call Ant is visible on your command path. In **Windows 95/98**, you should add the path C:\jakarta-ant-1.3\bin to the PATH environment variable at the end of your system's autoexec.bat file:

```
set ANT_HOME=C:\jakarta-ant-1.3
set PATH=%PATH%;%ANT_HOME%\bin
```

You will now need to restart your machine to ensure that the new variables propagate to all new command windows. As a temporary measure, you can call the following to reset the environment in a command window:

```
> C:\autoexec
```

In **Windows 2000**, select Start | Settings | Control Panel. Then open Administrative Tools and System. Select the Advanced tab. Click on Environment Variables.... In the System variables grouping, scroll to the Path variable and double click on it. Add C:\jakarta-ant-1.3\bin to the end of the path, remembering to put a semicolon between the last character of the existing path and the drive-letter of the Ant path. Click Ok to get out of the System dialog. Now open up a new command prompt and type:

```
> echo %ANT_HOME%, %Path%
```

You should see the correct version of the Ant home directory, and updated path variable. Now you can test the system by typing ant -help, or if you have already installed the code download, change directory to javaxmlref and run the example at the beginning of the chapter.

In **Unix** or **Linux**, you will need to edit your shell start-up script, usually called .cshrc or .bashrc, or something similar, depending on your chosen shell program. This script is found in your home directory. Add the lines:

```
export ANT_HOME=/usr/lib/jakarta-ant-1.3
export PATH=$PATH:$ANT_HOME/bin
```

Test the set-up by typing:

```
> bash            #or csh or whichever shell you use
> ant -help
```

You should see a table of options, of which the most useful to get going with are:

Option	Description
-help	Print these and many other options
-verbose	Trace what Ant is doing
-buildfile <file>	Use a specific buildfile. The default is to use build.xml in the directory from which Ant was invoked

Installing the Code Bundle

The code bundle comes as a ZIP file from http://www.wrox.com. The structure of the directories is as follows:

```
javaxmlref/
    bin/
    build/
    config/
    lib/
    src/
    webapps/
```

Once you've extracted this to your disk, you can jump to the next section to just get going. Each directory is explained in the following paragraph, but we have used the standard directory-naming conventions recommended by Ant, and this system is mostly self explanatory.

src – All Java source code is in this directory. Subdirectories are used to contain code for project units relating to chapters in the book. These directories may contain their own package structure. The project unit contains XML files and configuration files for the project. So the Java package structure for the `configuringxml` project looks like:

```
src/configuringxml/packagename/Code.java
```

bin – This can be used to contain any administrative scripts that you need to run. But preferably all build-type instructions should be coded into Ant targets in the `build.xml` file. There is a special script **setcp** in the toplevel directory, which can be used to set the environment variable CLASSPATH to all the JAR files in the `lib` directory. This is useful for command-line testing of applications built using Ant.

lib – This is a temporary library build directory where all libraries needed for compilation or packing into WAR files etc. should be copied. Use Ant to do this. The reason for doing this, instead of referring to JARs all over the filesystem, is that it makes it easier to write the `setcp` utility above, but also it is a technique that makes Ant tasks much easier to define, and is a method recommended by Ant. When building WARs, you have to copy libraries anyway.

build – This is a temporary working directory for building projects. Use `javac` from within Ant to output bytecode to this directory in its correct package structure, as per the example. Code can be left here for intermediate command-line testing. The `setcp` utility includes `build` in its classpath.

config – This is where we store the properties and configuration files for Ant, and other configuration files.

webapps – We deploy all webapps to this folder and point the web server context root to it. We would recommend that you use Tomcat 4.0 for running the web applications. With Tomcat 4.0, you can specify a new `<Service>` element in the `server.xml` file and point `appBase` at `C:\javaxmlref\webapps` (or wherever you place the code root). A sample `server.xml` is provided in the `config` directory. You should back up your Tomcat `conf/server.xml` and copy `config/server.xml` file to Tomcat. You will need to adjust the pointer to the `webapps` folder in the relevant `<Service>` element before starting the server.

Some Hints On Installing Packages

When you install a new package (like Xerces, etc.) then use the default directory structure, including the version number in the toplevel directory, for example `C:\xerces-1_3_1`. Also, install them in the simplest possible place, like `C:\` or `/usr/lib/`. Avoid installing things in paths like `Program Files` which are particularly platform-specific, and which contain problematic characters like spaces.

> If you install everything in the default way suggested, then you will not have much to do in configuring the build process, because the locations for all the resources should be similar if not identical to those already configured in the supplied code.

Also, we suggest not using the JRE extension directory for development work. It's tempting to put JAR files in there, but particularly with XML parsers, this will lead to problems.

> *You need to be sure of where your application is getting its SAX, DOM, and JAXP classes, for instance, because of the tendency for SAX and JAXP versions that are subtly different being included in many parser JAR files.*

These strategies will lead to clarity in what works with what version, and will also simplify the classpath issue.

The following sections summarize the resources needed for each chapter, and list the example files for reference where these have not been detailed elsewhere.

Chapter 1 – XML by Example

The required resources for this chapter are:

❑   JAXP 1.1 (includes the appropriate DOM and SAX classes)

❑   JAXP 1.1 compatible parser and transformer (Xerces-J and Xalan-J are ideal)

❑   JDOM and Oracle XML Parser v2 (optional for one example).

Sample XML and DTD

These are located in the `src/examples`

```
anotherbook.xml
anotherdtd.dtd
comment.xml
entities.xml
identity.xsl
mailpi.xml
mixedbooks.dtd
mixedbooks.xml
namespace.xml
supportticket.dtd
supportticket.xml
supportticket.xsd
supportticket.xsl
```

Java Classes

These are located in the `src/examples` directory:

```
DTDEntity.java
Encoding.java
MailPI.java
Namespace.java
SaxTest.java
TrAXUtil.java
SchemaParser.java
```

Chapters 2 To 6 – The APIs

The required resources for these chapters are the same as for Chapter 1, with a parser supporting DOM Extensions (Views, Events, Traversal, Ranges) such as Xerces-J needed for Chapter 6. The example files for each of these chapters are summarized at the beginning of the chapter. Scripts are provided in each of the following directories to run the code.

❑ Chapter 2: `src/sax`

❑ Chapter 3: `src/domcore`

❑ Chapter 4: `src/domext`

❑ Chapter 5: `src/jaxp`

❑ Chapter 6: `src/jdom`

Chapter 7 – Oracle XDK

The required resources for testing the code in this chapter are:

❑ Oracle XDK v9.0.0.0.0 (or v8.1.7.0.0)

❑ JDOM

❑ Xerces-J (for SAX 2.0)

❑ Oracle JDBC drivers and an Oracle database instance (only for the XSU and XSQL related examples)

❑ JDeveloper or Tomcat 4.0 for testing XSQL Servlet code

The Files

Sample XML

These are located in the `src/oracle` directory:

```
classifiedAds.xml
example_dtd.dtd
example_xml.xml
example_schema.xsd
```

```
findAds.xsl
listEmployeesText.xsql
listEmployees.xsl
listEmployeesHTML.xsl
listEmployeesPad.xsl
listEmployeesText.xsl
listemployees.xsql
listEmployeesHTML.xsql
listEmployeesPad.xsql
listEmployeesXML.xsql
troubleticket.xml
```

Java Classes

Java source is also stored in `src/oracle`:

```
JavaXSQL.java
JaxpDOM.java
JaxpSAX.java
ListEmployeesHTML.java
ListEmployeesText.java
ListEmployeesXML.java
ListEmployeesXSL.java
StrUtil.java
TraxXSL.java
URLutil.java
XdkDOM.java
XdkJDOM.java
XdkSAX.java
XdkXSchema.java
XdkXSL.java
XpathDemo.java
```

Ant Targets

`techniques.oracle.compile`
Compiles all the code for the chapter to the `build` directory.

`tools.oracle.test`
This target can be used to run a check through all the example programs.

Chapter 10 – Apache XML Project

The required resources for testing the code in this chapter are:

❑   Apache SOAP

❑   Xerces-J

❑   JavaMail 1.2

❑   Java Activation Framework 1.0.1

❑   Xalan-J 2.1.0

The Files

The source files required for this chapter and provided with the code for this book are listed below:

Example Files

These are located in the `src/apache` directory:

```
result.dtd
DC_DeploymentDescriptor.xml
recordbook.xml
result1.xml
result2.xml
scoreStyleSheet.xsl
```

Java

Java source is also stored in `src/apache`

```
DParser.java
SearchRecords.java
SParser.java
TransformStudentSSN.java
```

Ant Targets

`tools.apache.compile`
Compiles all the code for the chapter to the `build` directory.

`tools.apache.[soapserver, deployservice, deployjar]`
Rebuild and redeploy the Apache SOAP web application, add services as classes or JARs, together with the appropriate descriptor.

Chapter 9 IBM Web Services Toolkit

The required resources for testing the code in this chapter are:

- ❑ The IBM Web Services Toolkit (currently version 2.3)
- ❑ Apache SOAP
- ❑ Jakarta Tomcat 4.0 (currently beta 5)

The Files

The source files required for this chapter and provided with the code for this book are listed below:

Sample WSDL

These are located in the `src/ibm/wsdl` directory:

```
BookLookup.wsdl
Simple.wsdl
```

Java Classes

Java source is stored in `src/ibm`:

```
uddi/ContactsBuilder.java
uddi/UDDIFind.java
uddi/WSDLTModel.java
wsdl/BookLookupClient.java
wsdl/BookLookupService.java
wsdl/DynamicClient.java
wsdl/SimpleService.java
```

Configuration

For configuring the book-lookup servlet:

```
wsdl/web.xml
```

Ant Targets

The following are useful high-level Ant targets to build and deploy the code for this chapter.

`tools.apache.[soapserver, deployservice, deployjar]`
Rebundles and redeploys Apache SOAP as a web application. Two further targets deploy a class or JAR file with a specified name.

`techniques.transmittingxml.monitor`
Runs the Apache tunnel monitor GUI between ports 8080 and 5202 on `localhost`. (We usually use 5202 as the server listening port and 8080 as the client port so that we can see the traffic between them on
the monitor).

`tools.ibm.wsdl.[generateproxy, ..., all]`
A sequence of targets to generate, compile, and deploy the book lookup service examples. May be done from start to finish by calling the `all` target.

`tools.ibm.uddi.[tmodel, find, contacts]`
Used to compile and set classpath for three automated UDDI examples.

Chapter 10

The required resources for testing the code in this chapter are:

- ❑ JAXB1.0 Early Access edition
- ❑ JDBC Rowset Early Access release
- ❑ JDBC 2.0 Optional Package
- ❑ M Project Early Access 1.0

The Files

The source files required for this chapter, and provided with the code for this book, are listed below:

JAXB1.0 Early Access Example Files

The code for running this example can be found in `src/jaxb`.

```
library.dtd
library.xjs
library.xml
JAXBPrint.java
```

JDBC RowSet Example Files

The code for running this example can be found in `src/wrs`.

```
WebRowSetSample.java
WebRowSetReader.java
```

M Project Early Access Example Files

The code for running this example can be found in `src/`

```
JAXMClient.java
```

Ant Targets

`tools.sun.jaxm`
Compile the program and copy needed JAR files for testing to the `lib` folder.

Chapter 11 – Information Appliances

The required resources for testing the code in this chapter are:

- ❑ NanoXML version 1.6.8
- ❑ NanoXML version 2.0 Beta
- ❑ SAX 1.0
- ❑ JAXP 1.1
- ❑ Xalan 2.1.0 (includes XSLTC)
- ❑ J2ME CLDC
- ❑ Java KVM for J2ME
- ❑ Palm OS Emulator

The Files

The source files required for this chapter provided with the code for this book are listed overleaf:

NanoXML 1.6.8

The NanoXML 1.6.8 code snippets are in `src/nanoxml_1.6.8`:

```
request.xml
Fragments1.java
```

SAX Example Files

The files required for the SAX example are also found in `src/nanoxml_1.6.8`:

```
request.xml
RequestHandler.java
```

NanoXML 2.0 Beta

The files used for the NanoXML version 2.0 Beta examples are located in the `src/nanoxml_2.0.beta` directory:

```
request.xml
Fragments2.java
echo.java
```

Compiling and Using a Translet

The files for the translet example are stored in `src/xsltc`:

```
TroubleTicket.wml
TroubleTicket.xml
TroubleTicket.xsl
TroubleTicketViewer.java
```

Palm Contact Book

The Java source for the Palm Contact Book example is stored in `src/contactbook`:

```
AddContact.java
BeamContact.java
ButtonRecord.java
ContactBook.java
ContactBookSpotlet.java
ReceiveContact.java
SearchContact.java
```

Ant Targets

```
tools.infoapp.compile
```
Compile all the classes.

```
tools.infoapp.preverify
```
Run the preverifier for porting the addressbook application to Palm

```
tools.infoapp.buildprc
```
Make the PRC file for the Contact Book application.

809

Chapters 12 to 16

Summaries and requirements for these chapters are given at the beginning of each chapter as an integral part of the chapter.

Where To Obtain Software

The file `config/windows.properties` (or `linux.properties`, etc.) contains a listing of the keys used by the build tool to refer to resources on your system. Where the software was obtained from is added as a comment. For instance the following snippet specifies the location of the Xerces JAR file, the Xerces home directory, and as a special case, the Xerces 1.2.3 JAR file as well. (This might be specifically required by an application, rather than `xerces` "the most current, or default, version of Xerces".)

```
#Xerces
#
#Xerces 1.x.x can be obtained from http://xml.apache.org/xerces-j
#1.2.3 and 1.4.0 work with Apache SOAP okay
#
xerces=C:/xerces-1_4_0/xerces.jar
xerces.home=C:/xerces-1_4_0
xerces123=C:/xerces-1_2_3/xerces.jar
```

All the information you need to obtain the appropriate packages and configure them for use with the book is essentially in the file described above. We will provide a summary here as well:

Software	Location
ANTLR runtime support for parsing	http://code.werken.com/xpath
Apache Formatting Objects	http://xml.apache.org/fop
Apache SOAP	http://xml.apache.org/soap
Crimson	http://xml.apache.org/crimson
IBM Web Services toolkit	http://alphaworks.ibm.com/tech/webservicestoolkit
J2ME CLDC	http://java.sun.com/products/cldc
Java Activation Framework	http://java.sun.com/products/javabeans/glasgow/jaf.html
JavaMail	http://java.sun.com/products/javamail/
JAXB	http://java.sun.com/xml/jaxb.html

Software	Location
JAXM	http://java.sun.com/xml/xml_jaxm.html
JAXP	http://java.sun.com/xml
JBoss	http://www.jboss.org
JDBC Extensions classes	http://java.sun.com/jdbc
JDOM	http://www.jdom.org
JDOM ResultSetBuilder	http://cvs.jdom.org
JTA	http://java.sun.com/products/jta/
NanoXML	http://nanoxml.sourceforge.net
Oracle JDBC Driver **	http://otn.oracle.com/software/tech/java/sqlj_jdbc/software_index.htm (You may need to register)
Oracle XDK, Parser, XSU, XSQL Servlet	http://technet.oracle.com/tech/xml/xdk_java (You may need to register)
Saxon	http://users.iclway.co.uk/mhkay/saxon
Tomcat 4.0	http://jakarta.apache.org
WebRowSet	http://developer.java.sun.com/developer/earlyAccess/crs/ (You may need to register)
Werken XPath for JDom	http://code.werken.com/xpath
Xalan	http:// xml.apache.org/xalan-j
Xerces	http://xml.apache.org/xerces-j
XSL Tag Library	http://jakarta.apache.org/builds/jakarta-taglibs

** Note that we have used the pure Java Oracle 'Thin' JDBC driver in the book. Other drivers use native code, which is platform specific.

Software Licences

In order to ensure that the statements made about the functionality of certain APIs documented in this book are as accurate as possible, and follow the canonical information available from the source, we made use of JavaDoc comments in the source code of the DOM and SAX APIs to provide some of the descriptive text in chapters 2, 3 and 4 of the book.

SAX was originally written by David Megginson, and is now in the public domain. We reproduce elements of the SAX documentation with our thanks to David for his contribution of SAX to the XML community.

The DOM bindings were published by the World Wide Web Consortium. This material is reproduced in accordance with, and here published under, the following terms and conditions:

W3C IPR SOFTWARE NOTICE

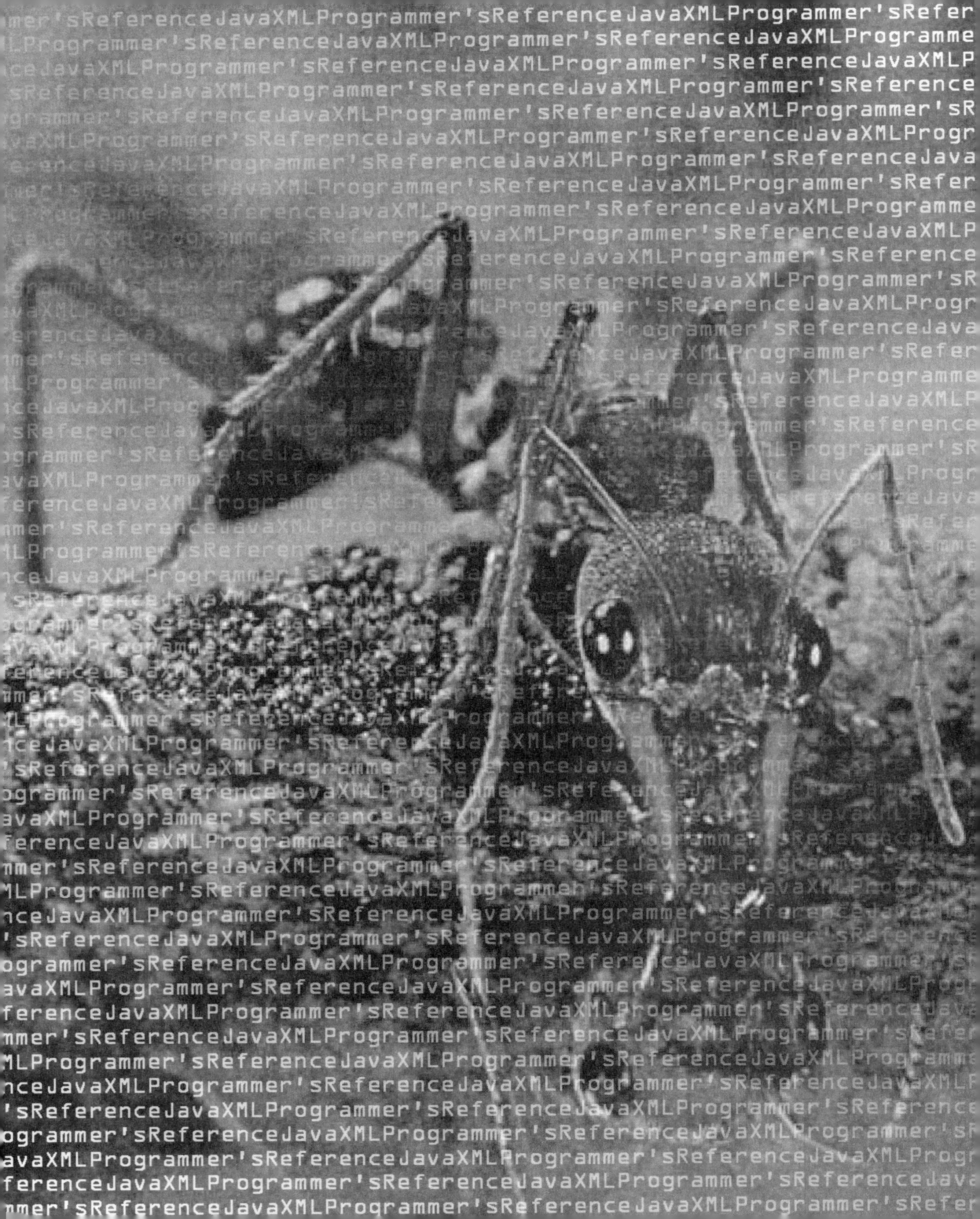
JavaXMLProgrammer'sReference

Index

A Guide to the Index

The index is arranged hierarchically, in alphabetical order, with symbols preceding the letter A. Most second-level entries and many third-level entries also occur as first-level entries. This is to ensure that users will find the information they require however they choose to search for it.

H

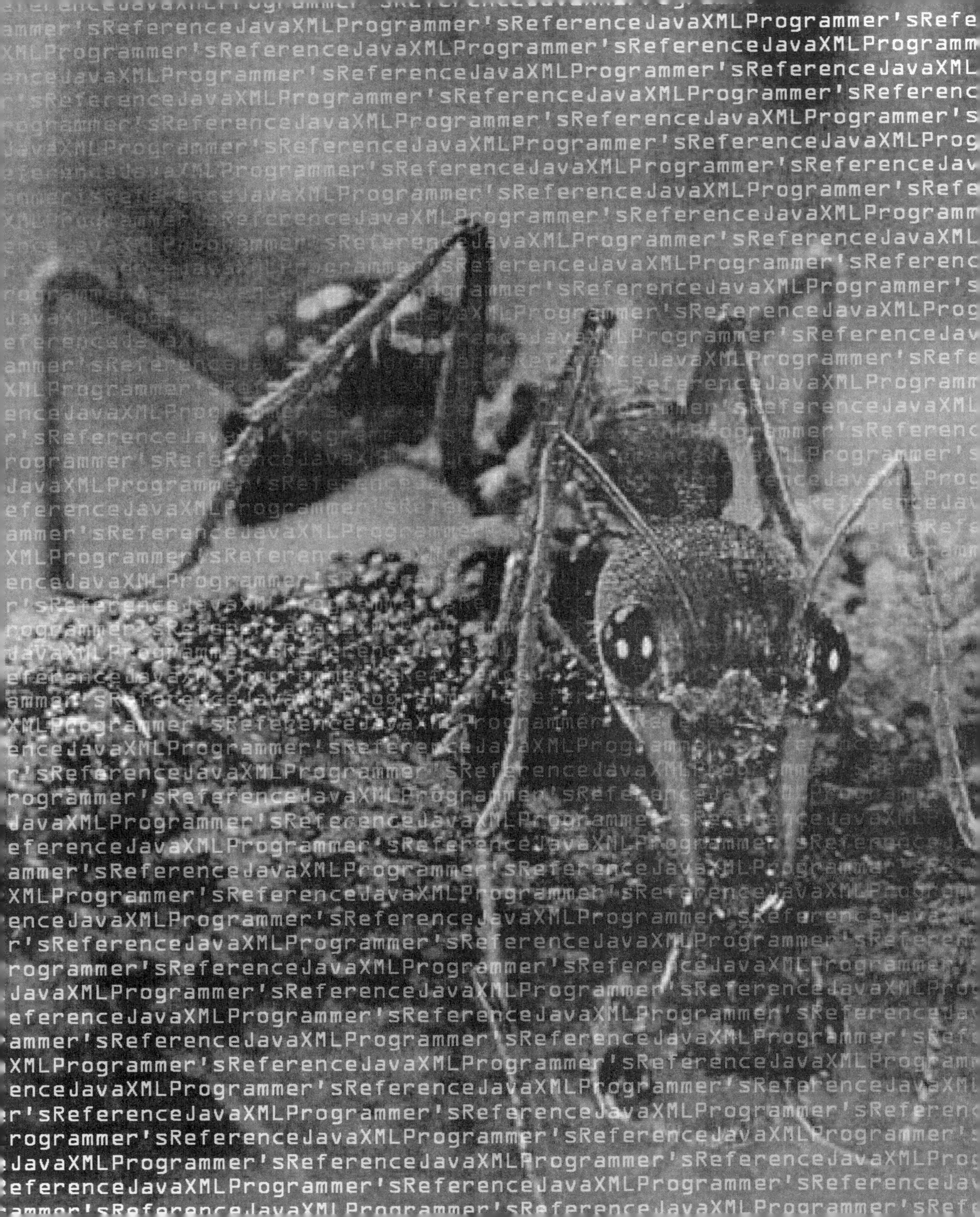
JavaXMLProgrammer'sReference

p2p.wrox.com
The programmer's resource centre

A unique free service from Wrox Press
with the aim of helping programmers to help each other

Wrox Press aims to provide timely and practical information to today's programmer. P2P is a list server offering a host of targeted mailing lists where you can share knowledge with your fellow programmers and find solutions to your problems. Whatever the level of your programming knowledge, and whatever technology you use, P2P can provide you with the information you need.

ASP
Support for beginners and professionals, including a resource page with hundreds of links, and a popular ASP+ mailing list.

DATABASES
For database programmers, offering support on SQL Server, mySQL, and Oracle.

MOBILE
Software development for the mobile market is growing rapidly. We provide lists for the several current standards, including WAP, WindowsCE, and Symbian.

JAVA
A complete set of Java lists, covering beginners, professionals,and server-side programmers (including JSP, servlets and EJBs)

.NET
Microsoft's new OS platform, covering topics such as ASP+, C#, and general .Net discussion.

VISUAL BASIC
Covers all aspects of VB programming, from programming Office macros to creating components for the .Net platform.

WEB DESIGN
As web page requirements become more complex, programmer sare taking a more important role in creating web sites. For these programmers, we offer lists covering technologies such as Flash, Coldfusion, and JavaScript.

XML
Covering all aspects of XML, including XSLT and schemas.

OPEN SOURCE
Many Open Source topics covered including PHP, Apache, Perl, Linux, Python and more.

FOREIGN LANGUAGE
Several lists dedicated to Spanish and German speaking programmers, categories include .Net, Java, XML, PHP and XML.

How To Subscribe

Simply visit the P2P site, at **http://p2p.wrox.com/**

Select the 'FAQ' option on the side menu bar for more information about the subscription process and our service.

wrox

Programmer to Programmer™

Wrox writes books for you. Any suggestions, or ideas about how you want information given in your ideal book will be studied by our team.
Your comments are always valued at Wrox.

Free phone in USA 800-USE-WROX
Fax (312) 893 8001

UK Tel.: (0121) 687 4100   Fax: (0121) 687 4101

Java XML Programmer's Reference – Registration Card

Name _____

Address _____

_____

_____

City _____ State/Region _____

Country _____ Postcode/Zip _____

E-Mail _____

Occupation _____

How did you hear about this book?

☐ Book review (name) _____

☐ Advertisement (name) _____

☐ Recommendation _____

☐ Catalog _____

☐ Other _____

Where did you buy this book?

☐ Bookstore (name) _____ City_____

☐ Computer store (name) _____

☐ Mail order _____

☐ Other _____

What influenced you in the purchase of this book?

☐ Cover Design   ☐ Contents   ☐ Other (please specify):

_____

How did you rate the overall content of this book?

☐ Excellent   ☐ Good   ☐ Average   ☐ Poor

What did you find most useful about this book? _____

_____

What did you find least useful about this book? _____

_____

Please add any additional comments. _____

_____

What other subjects will you buy a computer book on soon?

_____

What is the best computer book you have used this year?

_____

Note: This information will only be used to keep you updated about new Wrox Press titles and will not be used for any other purpose or passed to any other third party.

wrox

Programmer to Programmer™

Note: If you post the bounce back card below in the UK, please send it to:

Wrox Press Limited, Arden House, 1102 Warwick Road,
Acocks Green, Birmingham B27 6HB. UK.

Computer Book Publishers